THE PATH AHEAD
Readings in Death and Dying

Readings in Death and Dying

THE PATH AHEAD

Lynne Ann DeSpelder
Cabrillo College

Albert Lee Strickland

Mayfield Publishing Company
Mountain View, California
London • Toronto

163115

Library of Congress Cataloging-in-Publication Data

The path ahead : readings in death and dying / [edited by] Lynne Ann
    DeSpelder, Albert Lee Strickland.
        p.   cm.
    Includes bibliographical references and index.
    ISBN 1-55934-256-0
    1. Death.   I. DeSpelder, Lynne Ann.   II. Strickland,
    Albert Lee.
    BD444.P37   1994   94-30529
    306.9--dc20   CIP

Manufactured in the United States of America
10   9   8   7   6   5   4   3   2   1

Mayfield Publishing Company
1280 Villa Street
Mountain View, California 94041

Sponsoring editor, Franklin C. Graham; *production editor,* Merlyn Holmes; *copyeditor,* Dale Anderson; *text and cover designer,* Margery Cantor; *manufacturing manager,* Aimee Rutter. The text was set in 10/12 Sabon by TBH/Typecast, Inc. and printed on 50# Ecolocote by Malloy Lithographing, Inc.

Cover photo © 1994 Albert Lee Strickland.

Interior photography by Boris Levitsky and James Bryant © 1994 Mayfield Publishing Company. The art on pages 1, 95, and 317 is from the Mexican Día de los Muertos folk art collection of Lynne Ann DeSpelder and Albert Lee Strickland; the art on page 225 is by Irene Aguilar, Ocotlán, Oaxaca, Mexico from the collection of Faye Augustine.

Text credits are integrated into the notes and references section, beginning on page 357.

 This book is printed on acid-free, recycled paper.

contents

The study of death is based on a wealth of research and insightful writings from the social and behavioral sciences, humanities, and medicine. Reviewing this literature for successive editions of our text, *The Last Dance: Encountering Death and Dying*, we frequently discover well-written and thought-provoking pieces about death, dying, and bereavement. Since the format of *The Last Dance* requires distilling the main points from these publications rather than sharing them in their entirety, we regret that readers do not enjoy a firsthand encounter with each author's style and special contribution to our understanding.

Now, through the pages of this anthology, we can share some of the best selections from the recent literature on death and dying. Over 80 percent of the readings collected here are from the 1990s. *The Path Ahead: Readings in Death and Dying* focuses on the impact of death on individuals and society, with special emphasis on multicultural and transcultural perspectives. Authoritative voices in the field of death studies are augmented by insightful commentators from intersecting disciplines and pathways, bringing depth and range to converging issues involving death, dying, and bereavement.

The authors you will encounter in these pages are indeed pathfinders. Some are new to the field of death studies; others have spent decades pointing out useful landmarks and cautioning against pitfalls. In conversations with the authors, we asked about the events that inspired each of them to set out on his or her particular path. Individuals encounter death and its meaning in different ways. In the biographical sketches that introduce each selection, you will read about the author's journey as it relates to the study and experience of death, dying, and bereavement.

The readings in this book are organized into four main parts: cultural contexts, social issues, personal dimensions of loss, and death in life. Each part includes an introduction which provides a context for reading the individual selections. An annotated listing of further readings concludes each part of the book. The writings in this volume can serve as landmarks, helping us gain our bearings on the journey through life to death.

As you read each selection, consider how it expands upon or challenges contemporary theory, research, and practice. Death studies, or thanatology, is a comparatively young discipline. Theories evolve, research broadens to include populations previously unstudied, and practices related to care of the dying, funerals, and mourning change over time. Notice how the insights expressed in a particular selection provoke an evolution in your own understanding about death and dying.

This book owes its genesis to Franklin C. Graham, our editor at Mayfield Publishing Company. It was his vision to create a contemporary collection of readings that would delineate the path ahead in death studies and related policy issues in the last decade of the twentieth century. A number of reviewers provided helpful comments at various stages in the project's development. We thank professors John B. Bond, Jr. of the University of Manitoba, Winnipeg; Charles A. Corr of Southern Illinois University, Edwardsville; Robert Kastenbaum of Arizona State University; Rita S. Santanello of Belleville Area College, Illinois; Marcia A. Schroeder of Indiana University/Southeast, New Albany; and Mark A. Shatz of Ohio University, Zanesville.

We are grateful to Linda Toy and Jeannie Schreiber of Mayfield's production and art department for taking time from their busy schedules to help select pieces from our collection of artwork related to the Mexican celebration of El Día de los Muertos. Examples of that culture's unique encounter with death are included in this book for your enjoyment and appreciation. Also at Mayfield, Merlyn Holmes shepherded the project through production and Jon Silvers lent his expertise in promoting and marketing. We are especially grateful to the authors whose work appears in these pages. Their enthusiastic participation made the vision for this book a reality.

L.A.D.
A.L.S.

THE PATH AHEAD
Readings in Death and Dying

Cultural Contexts

*D*eath is a universal human experience, yet the response it elicits is shaped by the attitudes and beliefs present in a particular culture. During the course of the twentieth century, the characteristic American mode of dealing with death has been dramatically altered by a variety of social and cultural changes. At the beginning of the century, medicine had not yet become a technological marvel; it focused more on comfort than cure. Death typically occurred at home, with the dying person cared for by relatives. The body of the deceased was laid out in the family parlor, and a wake was held with friends and family members—including children—in attendance. People experienced the deaths of loved ones firsthand.

By mid-century, such experiences were rare. Dying and death were increasingly removed from public view. Death touched people's lives, but care of the dying and the death was given over to professionals. Whereas mourners once *joined together to construct the coffin and dig the grave, these tasks were now handled by specialists. The greater familiarity with death and dying that once prevailed did not necessarily make the death of a loved one easier to accept than it is today, but it was surely harder to avoid or deny the reality of death.*

Increased social and geographical mobility, longer life expectancy, and the pressures of modern life all played roles in lessening Americans' familiarity with death, as has the transformation of the extended family into the nuclear family and then again into the single-parent family. The combined effect of these social changes is to remove death from view, radically altering the conventional means of learning about death.

Many commentators, both scholarly and popular, have labeled the predominant attitude toward death in modern society as "death avoiding" or "death denying." The basis for such labeling is apparent when we take a look at contemporary funeral practices and methods of care for the dying. Within the span of a few decades early in this century, a revolution in funeral service took death out of the home and brought it into the mortuary. Professional care of the dead is now the norm. Participation in funeral rites may be limited to the symbolic gesture of sending flowers. In care for the dying, too, we find a nearly complete reversal of practices that were common as recently as a century ago. Most deaths now occur in institutional settings such as hospitals and nursing homes. Friends and relatives may be left out of the dying process as the patient conforms to the demands of formal institutional procedures.

If a culture is characterized by the attitudes, values, goals, and practices that prevail within it, then surely the attitudes, values, goals, and practices that relate to the central human experiences of dying and death ought to be examined consciously, not merely left to chance. As Robert Kastenbaum points out in "Reconstructing Death in Postmodern Society," in setting out on this investigation we should be wary of a tendency to be attracted to simple answers and certitude rather than to the more arduous path of complexity and doubt. This latter path can take us beyond safe images of death that implicitly deny its meaning. In taking up Kastenbaum's more challenging but ultimately more rewarding route, consider the extent to which your own exploration of death and dying is motivated by a desire for greater comfort, perhaps a wish to learn about death, not necessarily of it.

If social forces during the first half of this century lessened Americans' familiarity with death and gave rise to avoidance or denial, the pendulum has now begun to swing in the other direction. Far from remaining in the closet, death has been forcibly brought to our attention. In his address to the American Psychological Association entitled "Psychology and Death: Meaningful Rediscovery," Herman Feifel calls attention to some of the key reasons for this reversal and the obstacles encountered in changing course. Special attention should be paid to his discussion of empirical findings and clinical perceptions as well as to the perspectives advanced within the "death movement." If, as Feifel suggests, such social issues as abortion, AIDS, euthanasia, and capital punishment and such behaviors as alcoholism, drug abuse, and violence are linked with the meanings that death holds for us, it could be useful to reflect on how your own views about these issues relate to your perception and understanding of death.

Although death has been a perennial topic for philosophical and religious speculation, only as recently as the mid-1950s was there a deliberate and sustained effort to understand the place of death in society and gain sensitivity to the needs of the dying and grieving. The pioneers in the death awareness movement were hardy souls who persevered through many professional battles to gain a foothold for bringing death out of the closet. The fruit of their labors is evident in a burgeoning professional literature as well as in the growing public awareness that dying and death do affect all of us and, ultimately, cannot be avoided.

The AIDS epidemic, beginning with the first reported cases in the early 1980s and continuing to the present, has been a dramatic wake-up call. The reality of AIDS has given rise to a renewed recognition of death, as Charles Rosenberg points out in the excerpt from "What Is an Epidemic? AIDS in Historical Perspective." In reading this selection, ask yourself how AIDS and the social response to it have altered your own views about the threat of disease and the inevitability of death.

The way we think about death is shaped to a great extent by what we hear, read, and see in the mass media, which tend to report or depict only deaths linked with violence or catastrophe. These images do not create an impression of death as something natural to human beings, nor do they match the reality of how most people die. Without firsthand experiences with death and dying, we are prone to accept what is reported or portrayed at face value. This may not be in our best interests, however, as we find in contemplating Jack Lule's account of "News Strategies and the Death of Huey Newton." It seems that the newspapers that Lule analyzed were more interested in placing Newton's death in a questionable political context than in sticking to the facts about his life and death. In the process, Huey Newton's death became a cliché, and opportunities to assess its meaning were largely ignored.

Understanding how people in other cultures approach death can shed light on our own attitudes. The ideas and practices of cultures different from our own are often viewed either as exotic curiosities or as deviations from an assumed standard about what is right and proper. It is one of humankind's less admirable traits to view one's own social group as "the people" and everyone else as uncivilized aliens. This perspective not only leads to conflict and war, it gives rise to generalizations about human behavior and emotions that are less than exact. Then we are surprised, if not shocked, when it turns out that people in other cultures do not necessarily share our sense of what constitutes appropriate action and feeling.

The social context described by Nancy Scheper-Hughes in "Death Without Weeping," for example, involves a degree of indifference to the deaths of young children that most North Americans would find abhorrent. How can mothers seemingly shrug off the deaths of their children and go on as if an extraordinarily devastating event has not taken place? Such apparent complacency does not square with our understanding of grief. Yet these women are not devoid of "normal" human emotions in other situations. It is useful to go beyond the cultural veils of our experience and make the effort to understand the character of life in other social settings.

Increasingly, modern communication and transportation systems blur geographic and cultural boundaries, creating a milieu in which people of varying ethnic traditions are our neighbors. Consequently, social patterns of knowledge, belief, and behavior are in flux, as are individual beliefs, values, and practices. The account of Native Canadians' experiences in urban hospitals, as reported by Joseph Kaufert and John O'Neil, illustrates how conflict between competing sets of cultural values and practices can heighten feelings of being left out and ignored. Perhaps you can think of similar situations in your own community.

The beliefs, social forms, and material traits that define a culture exert a powerful influence on how individuals in that culture deal with dying and death. When two differing sets of cultural values and practices meet, the result may be conflict or competition over the "proper" way of doing things. This is the situation facing Hmong refugees from

Laos, as described by Christopher Hayes and Richard Kalish. Consider the plight of the Hmong seeking to carry out their traditional death and bereavement practices in a new cultural setting and notice how your own reaction to such practices leads to judgments about what is appropriate. We develop a more complete understanding of death by learning about the beliefs and practices of others as well as by submitting our own beliefs and practices to objective examination.

Despite the pervasive influence of modern communications and commerce, individuals and societies nevertheless display attitudes and behaviors that remain culturally distinct. This is evident when we look at major cultural traditions as well as when we examine racial, religious, and social groups that form unique subcultures within larger populations. In his discussion of "Contemporary African-American Funeral Rites and Traditions," Ronald Barrett describes how various ecological and subcultural factors—primarily religion, ethnicity, and social class—interact to influence how people in one group confront death and dying.

An evolving sensitivity to the needs of the dying and grieving in the last four decades has contributed to more flexible ways of dealing with death and dying. Individuals across the country and around the world are actively involved in putting this new understanding into practice. Increasingly, terminally ill patients and their families are able to choose from among several options for obtaining appropriate care at the end of life. These options include palliative care units situated within hospitals, freestanding hospices providing residential care, and hospice and home care service organizations that supplement conventional forms of care. Similarly, funeral service personnel are becoming more attuned to offering a range of choices and meeting the particular needs of bereaved families. There are signs of movement away from a "one-size-fits-all" orientation to an understanding that different approaches provide flexibility.

Given the central place of death in human life, it should come as no surprise to find that feelings run high when strongly held attitudes and behaviors are taken lightly or ignored by others, unwittingly or not. Attention is increasingly being paid to efforts that allow individuals and families to experience the powerful events of death and dying in personally meaningful ways. Such efforts can be difficult to implement and may require substantial reworking of institutional rules and standard operating practices. Yet such flexibility is needed if the mission of care providers is to be accomplished. Stemming from the recognition by visionaries four decades ago that death and dying ought to be discussed openly, people in all walks of life are discovering that it is not only possible but desirable to shape our social institutions in ways that meet diverse human needs in today's multicultural environment.

Confronting Death

Reconstructing Death in Postmodern Society

ROBERT KASTENBAUM

ROBERT KASTENBAUM, PH.D. is a professor in the Department of Communication at Arizona State University in Tempe. He has been involved with death-related challenges as a clinician, researcher, program director, and educator since the late 1950s. Dr. Kastenbaum has reflected on his entrance into death studies: "Perhaps it goes back to meeting Babe Ruth. Here was this living legend, a powerfully built man who seemed to be imprisoned in the business suit he wore on this occasion. As editor of our high school newspaper, I had the unexpected opportunity to conduct a brief interview with him. In those days, however, I did not know how to interview a dead man or, rather, a man who was all but dead. Close up, 'The Babe' was fragile and bearing up under what must have been terrible suffering. When his hoarse voice sounded, even a kid like me knew that he had cancer of the throat (at least) and was not long for this world. At the same time there was a warmth and kindness about him, a sense of wisdom earned through a rough and enterprising life. 'This death is real,' I thought to myself, 'and we all have to deal with it.' But nobody seemed to be dealing with it. Not in journalism and newspaper work, where I made my start. Not in psychology courses. Not even in philosophy (other than Socrates' exit scene and some oddments found here and there). I did not understand much about life and death, and I especially did not understand how people could understand one without at least trying to understand the other. Well, it was not just the day I met Babe Ruth, of course. I could mention many other little episodes, each in its own way reminding us of the mortality we share with all living creatures."

Finding little in academia or professional studies to guide his learning about life and death, Dr. Kastenbaum started his own studies. He contributed a chapter on adolescents' thoughts about death to Herman Feifel's pioneering book *The Meaning of Death* (1959) and has since authored and edited many other works. Dr. Kastenbaum directed the first major study of dying and death in a geriatric hospital—and later introduced a tavern to the same facility to make a statement for the importance of conviviality. He contributed to the planning and analysis of the National Hospice Study, the findings of which persuaded the federal government to provide financial support to hospice organizations.

Dr. Kastenbaum is a past president of the American Association of Suicidology and recipient of awards from the Association for Death Education and Counseling and the National Center for Death Education. His current studies include the analysis of deathbed scenes in reality and in imagination, elderly suicide, and changing concepts of death. He is editor of *Omega: Journal of Death and Dying* and of the *International Journal of Aging and Human Develop-* *ment*. His recent books include *The Psychology of Death* (rev. ed., 1992); *Death, Society, and Human Experience* (4th ed., 1991); and two works he edited, *Encyclopedia of Death* (1989) and *The Encyclopedia of Adult Development* (1993). Dr. Kastenbaum is also a dramatist. *Defining Acts: Aging as Drama* (1994) includes eight of his original one-act plays, and he has provided the libretto for *Dorian, the Opera* (scheduled to premiere in 1995). "If there is a next life," he muses, "I would like to bat just ahead of Babe Ruth so I would get some good pitches."

DEATH TRANSLATES INTO loss or fear of loss. Distress is the natural consequence of loss. Solidarity is the response that human society offers itself as protection or comfort when confronted with mortal distress.

This formulaic approach to death, distress, and solidarity has the usual charms of its genre: simplicity, categoricality, and certitude. Not surprisingly, the usual flaws also apply: simplicity, categoricality, and certitude. In this article the equally flawed and rather less charming attributes of complexity, dialectics, and doubt will be introduced. The objectives are to offer an assessment of the thanatology movement up to this point in time and identify some of the issues that could become of increasing significance in the future. The emphasis will be upon our changing relationship to death as the modern becomes the postmodern.

A Few Definitions

Thanatology is usually defined as the study of death. I have come to think of it a little differently and propose an alternative definition: *thanatology* is the study of life, with death left in.

The *death system* is society's multi-faceted, multi-level attempt to mediate our relationship with mortality. Components of a society's death system include people with particular death-related roles and involvements (e.g., funeral directors), places (e.g., cemeteries, massacre sites), times (e.g., memorial anniversaries), objects (e.g., hearses, guns), and symbols (e.g, black borders enclosing an announcement, skull-and-crossbone labels).[1] Functions of a death system include warnings and predictions, preventive efforts, caring for the dying, disposing of the dead, social consolidation after death, making sense of death, and killing. The relationships among these components and functions are dynamic, frequently contradictory or oppositional, and utilize many of the same channels of communication and influence that carry the main burden of socio-physical interaction.

Postmodernity is a condition of society that represents a shift from the emphasis on control of land, exploitation of property, and production of hard goods to the manipulation of rapidly disseminated signals, images, and other forms of information. Power, fortune, and success are achieved through the management of information/images rather than through ownership of static and finite resources. As a society becomes "postmodern" it also becomes vulnerable to the attenuation or loss of the beliefs, values, and communication patterns that had provided its sense of identity and continuity. Such dominant images of "modern times" as smoke puffing out of towering factory chimneys and iron locomotives thundering across the plains have given way to the incoming fax message that mocks distance and the VCR that rescues electronic images from the relentless stream of time.

Those scholars who have attuned themselves to the challenges of postmodernity need never be without crises that require viewing-with-alarm. Foucault did more than his share by undermining both the modernistic faith in objectivism as well as the traditional inclination toward categorical thinking.[2] Even the very possibility of "scientific truth" has been reviewed as a snare and a delusion.[3] Art has been proposed as more truly truth, and a nasty-sounding academic concoction—"critical theory"—has been advanced by some as the (dis)solution for our creaky post-industrial societies.[4] Horkheimer's analysis of the brutal and even lethal consequences of fascist language-and-power games is a compelling example of postmodernistic thinking applied to a substantial issue.[5]

Through a heightened appreciation of the interconnectivity of truth, language, and power, postmodernism offers the opportunity to extricate ourselves from the compounded follies of the past. But postmodernity itself generates new problems for both society and its scholars, including a reconsideration of the assumptions that underlie the very idea of scholarship.

Deconstruction is a term that was first applied to a hypercritical critique of metaphysical theories. In effect, Derrida and other early practitioners rounded up all the usual suspects (realism, idealism, logical positivism, etc.) and found them guilty as charged.[6] These familiar theories were found guilty not just of wrong answers to the wrong questions: they were also charged with falsifying the primary relationship between mind and world. Even this guilt, however, is contingent upon context, frame of analysis, and the state of the observer/analyzer.

All the world is a text, and each reading is also part of the world and interacts with the text in an unique way. One can no more avoid interpretive bias in reading human affairs than can the post-Heisenberg physicist claim to make measurements that are independent of the act of measuring.

Dismantling its own nest, deconstructivism has also been turned on Marxist theory.[7] The dissection of existing intellectual traditions has spread from philosophy, science, and architecture to other realms of symbolic activity, including fiction, biography, and all the creative arts. The entire intellectual heritage of humankind is being subjected to deconstructive criticism.

Meanwhile, life and death go on, whether or not one has ever heard of thanatology, the death system, postmodernity, and deconstruction. Here we will make a very small beginning to the imposing challenge of understanding *how* life and death go on as political structures, as well as ideological systems, crumble into dust.

Thanatology: A Late Modern Construction Project

Despite its Greek classical etymology, thanatology is a term that came in with the twentieth century. Elie Metchnikoff, a protege of Louis Pasteur, urged his fellow scientists to establish two new branches of investigation with aging and death as the foci.[8] Let's call the one "gerontology," he suggested, and the other "thanatology." Despite the significance of these topics and the prestige of the author, few heeded the call. A decade later, Rosswell Park, an American physician, made his own "plea for a neglected study."[9] Also ignored.

After a number of other scattered calls and contributions also fell into the void, something resembling a thanatological movement patched itself together in the wake of World War II. Why then, and not before? And how did the sociohistorical context influence the shape of the nascent movement? Future historians will discover or invent the whole story. Here is a provisional account:

- *Power Lust (Kraftlust).* Emerging technologies and increased industrial power offered the opportunity to pursue establishment goals more vigorously while also providing encouragement for alternative perspectives.

  In a word, there was more power up for grabs. In the early going, the new industrial muscle generally served the interests of the existing political and ideological systems. There was a harmonious relationship between belief in the superiority of one's own race, religion, and nationality and such compelling rhetorical devices as the Gatling gun that would persuade those living in ignorance on the other side of the world to become grateful dependents. Gradually, however, other hands with other intentions reached for the tools of power. Why continue to endure social and financial inequities, now that a remedy might be available for those willing to take a chance? Both the establishment and its critics saw "progress" as the road to success.

- *Death Is for Losers.* Aging and death became assimilated with the other detritus of a fast-moving society. A wise and respected old age and a life fulfilled at death were ideals that became increasingly alienated from the expansionistic and materialistic spirit of the times. Meanwhile, the religious establishment was experiencing its own doubts and stress in a world that now sought immediate material success rather than remote spiritual bliss. Death was for losers. Thanatology could not find a secure foundation in the besieged religious

establishment, the superheated commercial sector, or the scientific enterprise that was stepping into harness as modernity's new docile beast of burden.

- *A Haunting Episode.* A spectral kind of thanatology did arise during the difficult period when long-held assumptions were rocked first by Darwin's "ape theory," and Freud's "devil theory." I refer to the sometimes touching, sometimes amusing, sometimes brilliant, but mostly pitiful phenomena of spiritism. Physical mediums produced ectoplasmic evidence of ghostly presences, and mentalistic mediums proved their virtuosity by transmitting messages not only from the beloved dead, but also from fictitious characters requested by skeptical investigators. Contemporary thanatology is haunted to some extent by the imperfectly laid ghosts that flourished around the turn-of-the-century. When tough-minded scientists scoff at thanatology they may be influenced by residual emanations from the glory days of spiritism.

- *Demonics.* It also remained difficult to think of thanatology as a serious research enterprise because Death had become an entertainer who could be enjoyed from time to time as a specialty act, and then dismissed. Two roles were especially appealing to the populace. Horrific mergings of life and death at the shifting borders of reality and imagination were spectacularly represented by Frankenstein's monster and Dracula, as well as a variety of others. Drawing some of its emotional power both from science's newly emboldened tampering with life and death and the throbbing vein of suppressed sexuality, the demonic representation of death exercised an appeal that has not entirely withered in our own day.

Meanwhile, Sherlock Holmes was only the most celebrated among a diversified battalion of sleuths who "solved" deaths, although not death. E. T. A. Hoffman and Edgar Allan Poe succeeded in combining the creepy-crawly demons at the edge of the mind with Death's unexpected invasions of domestic snuggery. Later, radio and Hollywood would dole out generous servings of monstrous terror and beguiling murder mysteries. Together, these incarnations of death offered safety valves for anxieties that neither society nor its scholars were ready to face directly. That everybody dies even without a crazed scientist or master criminal lurking about the premises was a fact that faded between one blink and the next.

♦ *Enter Social Science, Exit Death.* The growing strength and influence of psychiatry and the behavioral and social sciences offered a new potential for thanatology. Here were skilled observers of the human condition, equipped with new concepts and methods. Surely they would recognize the pervasive workings of mortality upon our thoughts, feelings, actions, and relationships. But this new breed seemed all but oblivious. Early psychoanalysis, so enterprising in other realms, virtually bypassed death. The apparent fear of death was but a neurotic symptom (thanatophobia) that disguised a "deeper" cause.

Robust American behaviorism and functionalism was virtually a death free zone. For example, an impressive textbook that I read as a graduate student had more than a million words to offer on experimental psychology.[10] Of this total, only 166 words were spared for death: divided between the *death-faking* behavior of opossums and the revelation that old people sometimes die. This was a typical example of the behavioral sciences' ability to go about their business without taking death as either an applied challenge or a conceptual issue. Even the philosophically astute Piaget laboriously constructed a view of human development in which permanence, constancy, and invariance were given pride of place, while awareness of transience and loss were but missteps on the road to maturity.[11] Basically, one could have subtracted dying, death, and grief from human experience and it would have made little difference to the studies, texts, and courses promulgated by the social and behavioral sciences until the past few years—and even today, it is possible for future scholars and practitioners to complete their formal education with only the wispiest of thanatological encounters.

♦ *Finally—A Thanatology, Of Sorts.* This is not the place for a compilation of who did what when. Pine has brought together a number of the specific developments that occurred in the expansionistic decade, 1976–1985.[12] Prior to that time, protothanatological outcroppings could be seen in the postwar existential literature, the nascent hospice movement, and pioneering work in research, counseling, and education by a number of individuals in what had yet to be recognized as a legitimate field of activity.

The towering memory of World War II overcame, at least for the moment, our powers of denial. Nazi genocide and the nuclear inferno ignited by a people who considered themselves humane and peace-loving were paramount among the many war-generated trauma. Almost simultaneously, the United States, Canada, and much of Europe realized that we were growing elders on an unprecedented scale.

Although this obviously meant a victory for life, it also intensified the symbolic association between aging and death. Our current thanatology, then, found its origins in the wake of massive death, destruction, and loss and in the dawning realization that we had entered upon a new era in which the invisible threat of nuclear megadeath vied with the palpable graying of society. During these same years there was also a sustained upsurge in youth suicide throughout much of the Euro-American world, but this phenomenon did not make much of an impression in the thanatology movement as such then and even today has been taken as a concern mainly by specialists in suicide.

That larger social forces have influenced the shaping of thanatology can be inferred from such other contemporaneous phenomena as the renewed interest in the "retribalization" of entry as well as exit, i.e., the emergence of birth education, birthing centers, and a more prominent role for the father-to-be. The new humanism devoted to prenatal care and the ritual of entry into society itself developed against a background of effective birth control practices. It is not likely that the birth control and death control movements influenced each other directly to any significant extent (although there were connections), but both grew out of the same post World War II attitudinal and technological matrix.

The Social Integration of a Well-Behaved Thanatology

Up to this point in time, thanatology has been well behaved, almost astonishingly so. The rule-governed behavior demonstrated by so many thanatological activists has probably contributed to the modest success that has been achieved in the acceptance of the death awareness movement. True, the occasional death educator has popped out of a casket in a dubious pedagogical stunt, and ultra-conservatives have been irked by attempts to introduce "death ed" into schoolrooms where "sex ed" remains a touchy subject. By and large, though, thanatology has been content to utilize existing modalities and procedures, endorse traditional values, and look the part of the responsible citizen. This tack is perhaps not surprising, because so many participants in the death awareness movement have themselves been responsible and well-integrated contributors to society, i.e., clergy, nurses, physicians, social workers, and volunteers from various walks of life.

"Deathniks" who have stepped out of line seem to have been excluded from the thanatological mainstream. Cryonics provide an instructive example. There has been a decidedly hands-off response of thanatology to the proposal that corpses be maintained under hypothermic conditions until technological advances make it possible to reanimate them. The topic is seldom discussed, even more rarely in depth. I am convinced that this neglect of the cryonic movement is not based solely on the perceived improbability of high tech necromancy. Rather, thanatologists, along with the societal mainstream, feel distinctly uncomfortable with the challenging moral issues associated with suspension and reanimation as well as with the physicalistic aspects of the procedure. The nineteenth century's horror of being buried alive has perhaps a thread of continuity with the contemporary recoil from both the prospect of prolonged hypothermic internment and prolonged vegetative existence on a life support system.

Thanatology—for all its focus on a dreaded subject—is operating primarily in the service of established social values and practices. Far-out and destabilizing ideas need not apply.

Hospice programs at their best represent the thanatology movement at its best. And the hospice accomplishment not only takes the form of a well-integrated innovation, but also contributes to the improved integration of societal values and resources in general. In a model hospice program, technical expertise, managerial skill, and community interest are devoted to the needs and preferences of individuals and their family caregivers. Claims for specialized knowledge, social feeling, and the uniqueness of the individual are not at war with each other as is so often the case in our society. When hospice care achieves its objectives, all the participants can sense a common purpose and togetherness. Although successful hospice programs require the coordinated responses of an integrated society, these programs themselves contribute significantly to society's rediscovery of its potential for actualizing its own values.

The most profound social value actualized by successful hospice programs is perhaps the simplest: the community has not retreated from death and loss. Instead, social solidarity has been affirmed and strengthened at the very edge of existence. "We accompany you to the border, as far as we can go, and we stay with you as long as you are a member of our community." Hospice programs, then, along with their support in death education, grief counseling, and research, provide society with many opportunities to demonstrate the forces that bind person to person when faced with the prospect of loss, dissolution, and lack of control.

Reconstructing Death: A Progress Report

We have looked briefly at a few of the background factors and dynamics. Now we can explore, also briefly, several trends that can be discerned in reconstructing our concept of death. This is a "progress" report only in the sense that thanatology is attempting to cope

with a series of complex and continuing changes in the sociotechnical context of life and death; I do not mean to imply that our concepts are becoming "better and better every day," but simply that many individuals and working groups are trying to develop ways of thinking that take emerging situations into account.

There have been a few surprising turns already—

Habeas Corpus?

The dead body was once central to society's construction of death. To put it another way: the inanimate remains of what was once a living being was itself an obvious (de)construction that all societies were obliged to acknowledge. Premodern societies and those contemporary societies that have maintained the core of their traditions continue to take the corpse seriously. The particular concepts and practices that are considered appropriate vary widely, as anthropologists have often noted. However, there is a common if not quite universal belief that how we behave with respect to the corpse is a matter of some consequence.

Furthermore, there are still influential religious belief systems within modern/postmodern society that specify proper treatment of the human corpse. The specifics of these systems also differ markedly, but all involve rules and obligations that are intended to govern the behavior of survivors. Long-standing religious/ethnic beliefs often are involved when next of kin will not consent to a request for a postmortem exam or when a bitter intrafamily dispute arises over the propriety of cremation. The conflicts can expand to the political arena, as, for example, in the demands of Native-Americans for return of physical remains as well as sacred artifacts that have fallen into the hands of government archives, museums, or scientists. An entire issue of *Death Studies* (guest editors, Davidson and Zimmerman) has been devoted to this challenge.[13] It is clear that, as a society, we still have strong emotional connections to the human corpse as a construction that bridges our understandings of life and death.

Nevertheless, thanatology—in general—has been distancing itself from the dead body. Those who teach death education in schools of nursing and medicine are the most apt to keep the body in focus. But the trend, as I have seen it, is to move discourse away from both the dead body and the physical realities associated with terminal illness. The body is replaced with words and other symbols. Instructors and authors as well as students and readers often seem more comfortable when in a tacit agreement to "cover death" without having to face up to the implacable reality of the dead body. In *The Death of Ivan Ilych,* Tolstoy made sure that the already-emerging recoil from confrontations with the dead body would not go unchallenged.[14] Peter Ivanovich is assailed by "the faint odor of a decomposing body" even as he attempts to glide smoothly through the discomforting obligation of paying his respects to Ivan's newly-widowed wife. He also could not help but observe that "The dead may lay, as dead men always lie, in a specially heavy way, his rigid limbs sunk in the soft cushions of the coffin. . . ." The olfactory and tactile images introduced by Tolstoy have a nasty knack of slipping past our verbal defenses. Like Peter Ivanovich, we are often prompted to restore the customary sense of invincibility through some sort of symbolic maneuvers, even if these take place entirely within our own minds.

The staying power of the "famous five stages" owes much to this same need.[15] The stages not only provided a guide for the anxious visitor or caregiver, but have also been pressed into service as a consensually certified distractor. It was easier for the observer to "deny" the physical side of dying when one could focus instead on movement from one stage to the next. Whatever these were stages of, they were not stages of physical deterioration. Even highly self-selected students with backgrounds and career interests in such fields as nursing and social work prefer to avoid the recognition of negative physical changes during the dying process.[16]

It would appear that, by and large, thanatology is making itself agreeable to society's increasing disposition to think of death without being encumbered by confrontations with the dead body. As already mentioned, there is still a set of strong residual traditions in which the corpse is salient, but postmoderning society appears headed in the other direction.

Death Education Without Death?

It seems preposterous, of course. Death education is about death, isn't it? And any reconstruction of the concept of death must certainly focus on death!

Not necessarily. Thanatologists have their clever moments, and many of these appear to be devoted to establishing an image of death comparable to those food products which advertise themselves as sans cholesterol, sans caffeine, sans fat, sans calories, sans, sans, sans. An era that can market foodless food perhaps can be forgiven its assumption that deathless death must be just around the corner.

There are incentives. Careers, for example. Bioethics has become a thriving field. There are lectures to be given, books to be written, and consultations to be offered. People may enter this field through various doors, such as medicine, history, law, and philosophy. The essential stuff of bioethics is decision-making. The practitioner analyzes many types of decision-making situations and frequently offers advice. As we all know, some of the most difficult decisions are about death. What are the rules about terminating life support for a person who cannot express his or her own wishes? What are the rules about assisting the self-willed death of a dying person? Should these rules apply also to a person who is not dying but is alarmed and depressed by what the future might bring? What are the rules for deciding who should decide about prolonged life-sustaining care for a newborn who is born without a cerebral cortex or is otherwise incapable of becoming a sentient and competent adult? The abortion controversy is another major area in which the rules for making the rules are themselves in doubt and require the most searching thought.

But all of this is *about* death. It is not *of* death. All these decisions relate to judgments and actions that can result in an earlier or a later cessation of life. And all these decisions are significant not only to the people most directly involved, but also to society at large. The bioethicist movement, however, has found little to say about what happens after the cessation of life. What is this death that "begins" when life ends?

There are careers to be made—valuable and legitimate careers—in bioethical decision-making. But in this postmodernistic career track, one is not called upon to meditate upon the heart of the matter. What is this death toward which the desperately suicidal yearn? Is it the same death that is shunned by stricken people who are passionate lovers of life? Why don't the bioethicists and other career thanatologists devote systematic attention to death itself? Because they don't have to. Because they don't have much to say. Because it's not really helpful to their (our) careers in a pluralistic society that has trouble agreeing upon its own basic story about death.

Near-death experience (NDE) is the near exception to postmodern thanatology's curious disinterest in death.[17] The state of altered awareness reported by survivors has been interpreted in a variety of ways. The most spectacular interpretation is that the person was actually "temporarily dead" or "in death," but somehow returned to life. The primary reports themselves and a number of the commentaries do touch upon death as the state

(or non-state) that follows life. And yet there has been little in-depth examination of the "deathy" aspects of the NDE, and the research focus has shifted away from the experience itself to its consequences and corollaries. The opportunity provided by NDE's for a searching re-examination of death per se seems to have been squandered. The NDE has become a fascinating special case, and thanatology moves along without contributing much and apparently without thinking much about what this death stuff is really all about.

Death Is How People Die

Thinking *of* death is not so easy. Humankind has had abundant difficulty in just thinking *about* death (which usually translates into thinking about dying, loss, suicide, war, and murder). Our strained imaginations have often seized upon certain modes of dying and borrowed their characteristics to create an image of death itself. This is not the place to offer a history of death imagery as a consequence of experiences with dying. I have suggested elsewhere that both "safe" and "unsafe" images of death have been crafted by society in various historical periods on the basis (in part) of their practical experiences with particular modes of dying that were dominant at the time.[18]

Let us just consider a few catastrophic modes of dying and their power to influence the death-constructing imagination (see Table 1).

Each of the older forms of catastrophic dying contributed to images of death. To take but one example, the lingering idea of a "romantic death" (as in the movies *Love Story* and *Dying Young*) is part of our heritage from the dismal nineteenth century experience with epidemic tuberculosis.

In our own times, hospice care, along with a more enlightened public attitude, has reduced the terror formerly associated with cancer. Today cancer does not always mean death, nor do cancer-related deaths necessarily mean severe pain, anxiety, social isolation, and even

Table 1

Modes of Dying and Their Symbolism

Disease	Markers and Signifiers
The Black Death	Agony, disfiguration, partial decomposition (necrosis) while still alive, putrefaction: *human vanity and pride, punished and abandoned by God.*
Syphilis	Facial disfiguration, dementia, degradation: *wages of sin.*
Tuberculosis	Death steals our breath; blood flows from our bodies which increasingly become skeletonized: *curse of the cities and factories, but also romantic exit for the brilliant and beautiful doomed youth.*
Live burial	Supposed fate of some who fainted, seized, or otherwise lost consciousness: *terror of life in death.*
Cancer	Pain, anxiety, body damage and distortion: *insidious attack by an enemy from within.*
Persistent vegetative state	Profound helplessness, inability to think, act, or act on one's own behalf: *despair of death in life.*
AIDS	Symptoms and stigma of many of the earlier forms of catastrophic dying—blood and body fluid related; disfiguration, dementia, skeletonization, respiratory distress, plus linkage with prohibited sexuality: *death embraces all of the meanings associated with the signifiers listed with the foregoing conditions.*

shame. Progress in reducing the fearsome aspects of cancer was important from a symbolic as well as a practical standpoint. Cancer had become the emblem of death in our society, and when thanatologists discussed the dying process the probabilities were high that it was a cancer-related death that they had in mind. If it had now become safer to live and, if necessary, die with cancer, then death itself had been revised a little closer to the heart's desire.

And then came AIDS.

The old catastrophic images of death associated with the old catastrophic modes of dying seem to have returned from their shallow graves in our collective psyche. This is not to say that society has responded only in a passive and unreflective way to the new threat. There have been thoughtful, resourceful, and courageous responses on the part of some persons afflicted with AIDS as well as some caregivers and members of the public. Nevertheless, AIDS

is making death itself "unsafe" again in the minds of many people. The emerging image of a long-lived and well-lived person drifting off gratefully to a comfortable sleep once seemed a strong candidate to represent death in our changing society. But if death seems welcome or at least "no big deal," if it is the destination of a sleepy old head, then death is also apt to seem nightmarish when it follows a ravaging and stigmatized disease that has separated a vital young person from his or her life.

The images of death that arise in postmodern society will surely have some relationship to the modalities of dying that meet our eyes and seize our imagination.

Solidarity Against Distress

It would be naive to expect that our ideas of death and our behaviors about death would somehow remain constant while so much else is being transformed. Thanatology, itself a new force on the scene, has had some success in sensitizing people to the human plight of the dying and the grieving, and also in modifying social institutions to be more responsive to these needs. A creature of its own society, however, thanatology has pretty much accepted such mainstream preferences as the de-emphasis on both the physical evidences of mortality and the fundamental nature of death. Our images of death, wavering as they are, seem likely to be influenced by alterations in the pattern of modes of death as well as by such further legislative and regulatory actions that may come to pass.

I cannot help but think of what several students of mortuary science once told me during a group session. At the first few funerals in which they served in a professional capacity, they would sneak looks at the mourners to see "how they expected us to act." Later, the young funeralists judged that "They were really looking at us, to see how *they* should act!" We are engaged in a tentative and insecure reconstruction of death and all its attendant values and practices. There will continue to be a reciprocal flow of influence between our symbolic groupings with mortality and the large-scale challenge of attempting to develop solidarity in our globalizing society.

Two recent examples hint at the broad range of alternatives from which we might choose. Sociologists Debra Umberson and Kristin Henderson have examined the social construction of death in the Gulf War, drawing upon war-related stories that appeared in *The New York Times* during the hostilities.[19] "Perhaps the most striking finding . . . is the absence of direct references to death or killing and the patterned use of indirect references. Although the words 'death,' 'die,' and 'kill' rarely appeared in media reports, a number of euphemisms for death were used repeatedly. The most common euphemisms for dead and death include 'casualty' and 'loss' [which] . . . may refer to injury or to death and both terms

were applied to the destruction of equipment as well as people. The equation of humans with equipment occurred often and in various ways."

"Smash," "bring down," "take out," "grind down," and "soften" were frequent euphemisms for "kill." The killing of Iraqi civilians was presented as "collateral damage." As the authors note, "None of these terms explicitly indicate human injury or destruction; they could be used in reference to any inanimate object. The psychological consequence is to dehumanize the human victims of war."

These and other findings will not come as a surprise to those who have followed coverage of other wars in which the news was censored or managed. But as media power expands, so does the ability of those who control the media to place death-related events and even death itself in a frame of their own choosing. What would happen if the symbolic representations that characterized coverage of the Gulf War were to become the standard line on death? Note that medical and legal rhetoric also tends to replace direct "die" and "death" words with jargon and circumlocutions. In fact, thanatology has very nearly accepted the quiet substitution of "terminal patient" for "dying person."

It is possible, then—not certain, but possible—that death will be assimilated into other, more remote and affect-neutral concepts and nearly disappear as a potent, primary expression. If this development does occur, then I would also expect death to be refurbished and redistributed for use only with its connotative meanings. Actual death might be disguised as "collateral damage," for example, while the term *death* would be restricted to figurative use, as in a "sudden death playoff game."

A far different approach has been observed in a different kind of war. Anthropologist David Lee Kozak reports that violent death among the young has been decimating the Tohono O'odham, a Native-American people with a reservation in Arizona.[20] While teen-agers and young adult males in the general population also are at relatively high risk for fatal accidents, homicide, and suicide, the Tohono O'odham rates have even more alarm-ingly elevated in the past few years. The increased mortality, especially among males between the ages of twenty to twenty-four, is closely related to the reduction of employment opportunities and a generally depressed local economy. Many young men reluctantly move away in search of employment and suffer stress and deprivation while doing so; those who stay on the reservation have few prospects to make a living for themselves and continue with their normal adult development and responsibilities.

As Kozak observes, the O'odham have responded to this challenge with changes in their ritual and religious belief systems. They suffer not only the individual grief of each loss, but, as a society, face a threat to their contin-ued survival as so many in the youth genera-tion perish. Furthermore, there is a threat that is specific to the O'odham belief system: vio-lent deaths are bad deaths, and these leave the souls of the dead "unrestful, unfulfilled, and desirous of returning to the living out of a longing for what has been taken away."[21] This adds greatly to the population of "dangerous ghosts." The O'odham society therefore has been engaged in a process of behavioral and ideological change that is intended to reduce the menace posed by dangerous young ghosts.

In this war, the social solidarity of a dis-tressed society is being strengthened by com-munal responses that focus on death and the dead. An outsider might not know how suc-cessful the O'odhams have been in placating dangerous ghosts, but the people themselves will have their own enhanced sense of determi-nation and unity as a gauge of their efforts. Confronting this double peril—a high death rate and the perceived menace from the dan-gerous dead—the O'odham may well succeed in solidifying their stressed society.

And we cannot for a moment forget that the O'odham comprise a small traditional society that is a speck in the desert. The larger soci-ety—enormously larger—is lurching rapidly if unevenly from modern to postmodern status, while the O'odham are still attempting to gain a foothold in the industrial era. And yet their ongoing transformations of ideology and ritual to cope with the undeclared war on their young has a postmodernistic flair: reconstruct the symbolic patterns and the reality itself might come under control (not that the symbolic and the real can be so neatly distinguished).

The government and media attempts to por-tray the action in the Persian Gulf as a war without death represent one type of significant pressure on the whole concept of death; the O'odham's resolve to face up to both the phys-ical and the symbolic forms of death represents a very different approach in which traditional beliefs demonstrate a strength and flexibility to deal with emerging challenges. These are but two of the many choices that we will be con-fronting in the years ahead as death, as well as life, steps into the postmodern world.

Psychology and Death: Meaningful Rediscovery

HERMAN FEIFEL, PH.D., is acknowledged internationally as the founder of modern death psychology. His book *The Meaning of Death*, published in 1959, defined the emerging field of death studies and quickly attained the status of a classic in the literature. It resulted from his awareness of psychology's neglect of the existential richness of life, its slighting of the role of the future in shaping present behavior, and its inattention to studying stress as it actually occurs in life. Researchers in death studies often date the beginning of the modern death awareness movement to a symposium titled "The Concept of Death and Its Relation to Behavior" that Dr. Feifel organized and presented at the 1956 annual meeting of the American Psychological Association in Chicago. The core of Dr. Feifel's work has been characterized by the *American Scientist* as "basic and foundational on the psychological and philosophical meaning of death in contemporary society."

In a recent interview with Inge Corless published in the book *Dying, Death, and Bereavement: Theoretical Perspectives and Other Ways of Knowing* (1994), Dr. Feifel observes that the social forces stimulating the modern death awareness movement include "a revival of consumerist, populist, and ethnic dispositions during the 1960s and 1970s that attempted to recapture greater governance over one's life—including the sectors of dying, death, and grief." The events of World War II and the advent of the atomic bomb also contributed to a renewed concern with death. Dr. Feifel says: "A personal note in this regard—and one that may be of some psychobiographical pertinence. In 1945, I was stationed on the island of Tinian in the Marianas, in readiness for the anticipated invasion of the Japanese mainland. This was the island from which the *Enola Gay* took off in August, 1945, to bomb Hiroshima and usher in the age of mega-death. In the Feifel family album, there is a picture of me in shorts snapped two days after the bombing standing next to the *Enola Gay*."

Now retired, although still active as a writer and speaker, Dr. Feifel continues to challenge the status quo and focus attention where it is most needed. He has the rare gift of making the scholarly findings of psychology relevant to individuals and to society as a whole. Dr. Feifel's former positions include clinical professor of psychiatry and the behavioral sciences in the School of Medicine at the University of Southern California and chief psychologist at the Veterans Administration Outpatient Clinic in Los Angeles. His work has been recognized by numerous honors and awards, including the California State Psychological Association's Distinguished Scientific Achievement Award (1974), the American Psychological Association's Distinguished Professional Contributions to Knowledge Award (1988), and the Association for Death Education and Counseling's Outstanding Death Educator Award (1990).

To DIE IS the human condition, and reflection concerning death exists practically among all peoples. From the beginnings of recorded history, realization of finitude has been a powerful concern and shaping force. Indeed, many feel that one of humanity's most distinguishing characteristics, in contrast to other species, is its capacity to grasp the concept of a future—and inevitable—death. Yet, except for a few sporadic forays, the place of death in psychology was practically *terra incognita* and an off-limits enterprise until the mid-20th century.[1]

There were a number of influential reasons for psychology's inordinate delay in coming to grips with such a universal matter. One was 17th-century Western individuals' transfer of their intellectual inquisitiveness and libido from theology to science.[2] We witnessed a shift from spiritual mastery over self to physical conquest of nature. A major consequence was that we became impoverished in possessing religious or philosophic conceptual creeds, except nominally, with which to transcend death. Death became a "wall" rather than a "doorway." A taboo of considerable measure was placed on death and bereaved persons. Death and its concomitants were sundered off, isolated, and permitted into society only after being properly decontaminated. In this context, further circumstances making the area uncomfortable to deal with were (a) an expanding industrial, impersonal technology that steadily increased fragmentation of the family and dismantled rooted neighborhoods and kinship groups with more or less homogeneous values—what sociologists call a change from *gemeinschaft* to *gessellschaft*—thus depriving us of emotional and social supports with which to cushion the impact of death when it intruded into our lives; (b) a spreading deritualization of grief, related to criticism of funerary practices as being overly expansive, baroque, and exploitive of the mourner's emotions; (c) a gradual expulsion of death from everyday common experience; death has developed into a mystery for many people, increasingly representing a fear of the unknown, and has become the province of the "professional," whose mastery, unfortunately, is more technical than human these days; and (d) in a modern society that has emphasized achievement, productivity, and the future, the prospect of no future at all, and loss of identity, has become an abomination. Hence, death and mourning have invited our hostility and repudiation.[3]

A second powerful reason was psychology's natal need to raise its flag independently of mental philosophy and metaphysics. Steered by the burgeoning fields of experimental psychophysiology and psychophysics evolving in Europe, American psychologists moved to declare the independence of their new science. Scientific respectability meant occupying oneself with measurable stimuli and responses that were repeatable and public. Experimental and objective study of behavior became psychology's commanding posture, and logical positivism became its dominant notion of the scientific undertaking. Areas such as love, will, values, and death, elusive to operational definition and measurement, were slighted in favor of such spheres as memory, reaction time, size constancy, and perception of form and color. This, it was felt, would bring psychology in line with physics and mathematics.[4]

The sway of logical positivism on psychology was unquestionably wholesome, in part. It was responsible for producing imposing diagnostic instruments, discrediting anecdotal data, and stimulating the demand for more exacting standards of evidence. Additionally, it was responsible for more intelligible communication because of its emphasis on operational clarity. But it also brought stultifying effects, for example, tending to exclude explanation in terms of inner traits, purposes, or interests. Explanatory efforts were mainly confined to events lying outside the organism. Interest in the existential richness of life was muted.[5] Even the emerging role of psychoanalysis on the American scene, with its attention to processes of mind, undervalued the import of death in the psychic economy by interpreting death attitudes and fears as being essentially derivative and symbolic of other mainsprings such as castration fear and separation anxiety.[6]

Death Reconsidered

This was the regnant state of affairs until World War II. Events of that war, with its defense of democratic values, the Holocaust, challenge of racism, and ensuing press of urgent social problems, forced psychology to look beyond its traditional positivism. A wax-ing humanism, the growing prominence of existential psychology in Europe with its accentuation of death as a philosophical theme, and Piaget's work in cognitive develop-ment all contributed to fostering the view that a vital psychology must be rooted in human beings not in a mathematical physics model.

Most compelling, perhaps, was the legacy of the A-bomb with its potential for providing us all with a common epitaph. Not only the individuality of death, but posterity and social immortality, were now at risk. Physical science had made it possible for us to destroy not only society but history as well. Issues of meaning, purpose, and temporality started to move cen-ter stage. In this juncture of psychology's expanding interest in the pulse of human life and intensified awareness of life's transience, attention to and research in the area of dying and death began to emerge as an authentic and fertile undertaking.[7]

Early Years of the Death Movement

Although a few empirical articles by psycholo-gists had been published in the mid-1950s relating mental illness and old age to death and measuring affective responses to death-related words,[8] psychology's first organized approach to death was a symposium titled *The Concept of Death and Its Relation to Behavior* which I initiated and chaired and which was presented at the 1956 annual meeting of the American Psychological Association (APA) in Chicago. Other participants were Irving E. Alexander, Jacob Taubes, Arnold A. Hutschnecker, and Gardner Murphy. The symposium served as the basis for the 1959 book, *The Meaning of Death*, which I edited. Authorities agree that the book was seminal in galvanizing regard for the field and in familiarizing the scholarly com-munity with the issues and concerns of dying, death, and grief. The same year I received what was probably the first research grant awarded to an individual by the National Institute of

Mental Health (NIMH) to study attitudes toward death. Despite these initial signs of recognition of the legitimacy of investigating the thanatological domain, numerous scientific Grundys still felt that the topic of death was not appropriate for psychology. *Contemporary Psychology*, for instance, rejected considering *The Meaning of Death* because the book had just received a review by *Time* magazine and, hence, had attained its allotted morbid fascina-tion exposure. More significant was the com-munication that the subject was not germane to genuine scientific inquiry.

The attempt to implement my NIMH re-search mandate relating attitudes toward death and behavior was also beset with mani-fold tribulations and frustrations. Some of the professional personnel with whom I was work-ing told me that at no time did they ever inform patients that they had a serious illness from which they could die. "The one thing you never do," it was emphasized, "is to discuss death with a patient." Along this same line, after a three-month delay in responding to my request for permission to gather data from some of his patients, the chief physician-in-charge of a leading metropolitan hospital finally replied, "Excuse my immoderate delay in answering, but you have to be a staff mem-ber," a lack known to him at the inception of our discussion about obtaining patients. The commissioner of hospitals of a major city responded to my request for subjects by say-ing, "It is not consonant with our policy to set aside patients for this purpose." Then there was the chief research psychiatrist of a promi-nent medical center who "knew" that the research project would induce what he termed "test toxicity" in the patients, despite already demonstrated results to the contrary.[9]

The realization soon began to sink in that what I was up against were not idiosyncratic personal quirks, the usual administrative vicis-situdes, pique, or nonacceptance of an inade-quate research design. Rather, it was personal position, bolstered by cultural structuring, that death is a dark symbol not to be stirred—not even touched—an obscenity to be avoided. I must admit to more than passing vagaries about chucking the whole thing. Two things, though, held me to the task. One was my ego. I had made a dent or two, *mirabile dictu,* here and there, using "gamesmanship" of an order that would have warmed Stephen Potter.[10] Second was my sentiment, albeit occasionally dampened by repeated rejections, that study of the area was important and, come hell or high water, should be implemented. Fortunately, as I have noted, there were exceptions to the situation I have been describing. I did find congenial colleagues and professional personnel who perceived what I was striving to do, acknowledged its importance, and helped me get my work off the ground.[11]

Succeeding years saw a burst of activity in the field. The 1960s and 1970s were characterized by the introduction of workshops and courses on dying, death, and mourning in various universities and professional schools. There were also noteworthy pioneering books by Kastenbaum and Aisenberg, the psychiatrists Eissler, Hinton, Kübler-Ross, Parkes, and Weisman, sociologists Fulton, and Glaser and Strauss, the nurse-sociologist Quint-Benoliel, the philosopher Choron, and cultural anthropologist Gorer, among others.[12] Journals such as *Omega* (1969: Robert Kastenbaum, editor), *Death Education* (1977: now called *Death Studies,* Hannelore Wass, editor), and the *Journal of Thanatology* (1973: Austin H. Kutscher, editor) came into being. Additionally, a number of scientific and professional associations devoted specifically to thanatological matters were founded. Among the more prominent were the International Work Group on Death, Dying, and Bereavement, the Forum for Death Education and Counseling, and Foundation for Thanatology. Bolstering these groups were several self-help and lay groups, for example, Make Today Count (1973), The Society of Compassionate Friends (1969), and widow-to-widow programs sparked by Phyllis Silverman (1969).

Empirical Findings and Clinical Perceptions

What are some empirical findings and clinical perceptions issuing from work already carried out in the field?

- ◆ Death is for all seasons. Its directive force is present from the very beginning in all of us, young and old, healthy and sick. It is not just for the combat soldier, dying person, elderly individual, or suicidal person. It is an ingredient of import throughout the entire life span. In this frame, we do not serve children well by shielding them from the experience of death. We only hinder their emotional growth. We are learning that children are more capable of withstanding the stress brought on by their limited understanding of death than by its mystery and implied abandonment.[13]

- ◆ Death fear can be a secondary phenomenon reflecting, for example, clinical displacement of separation anxiety. Incoming findings, however, increasingly suggest that the reverse may be more to the point. Apprehensiveness and concern about dying and death can themselves assume dissembling guises and gain expression in such symptoms as insomnia, depression, above-average fears of loss, and sundry psychosomatic and even psychotic manifestations.[14]

- ◆ Fear of death is not a unitary or monolithic variable. Various subcomponents are evident, for example, fear of going to hell, loss of identity, loneliness. For a good number of persons, negative connotations of death are associated substantially with feelings of rootlessness and having to face the "unknown" with minimal mastery. These features appear to be more prominent than even such aspects as "I may not have lived completely" or "My family may suffer." For many, death no longer signals the possibility of atonement and salvation, or a point in time on the road to eternity, but isolation and loss of self.[15]

- Significant discrepancies exist in many people between their conscious and nonconscious fear of death. Fear of death evidences itself as a lockstitching phenomenon with little reported fear of death on a verbal conscious level, coupled with one of ambivalence at a fantasy or imagery level, and outright negativity at the nonconscious level. This apparent counterbalance of coexisting avoidance–acceptance of personal death appears to serve powerful adaptational needs. In the face of personal death, the human mind ostensibly operates simultaneously on various levels of reality, or finite provinces of meaning, each of which can be somewhat autonomous. We, therefore, need to be circumspect in accepting at face value the degree of fear of death affirmed at a conscious level.[16]

- Coping with a life-threatening illness or death threat varies in significant fashion not only among differing groups but among situations. Meaningful disparities seem to exist in how cancer patients, heart patients, and elderly individuals contend with their serious illness and old age compared to the way they deal with nonlife-threatening stresses such as competition, marital discord, decision making, or loss of a job. Differences noted in these situations suggest not so much the employment of new coping strategies as modifications in the patterning or configuration of an individual's more usual coping modes. This is in contrast to much of the clinical literature, which reports that coping efforts used in the face of severe threat and impending death reflect but an intensified or more pervasive employment of an individual's coping deportment previously applied to generally aversive situations in personal life.[17]

- Most dying patients do not expect "miracles" concerning their biological condition. Their essential communication is the need for confirmation of care and concern. When emotional and psychosocial needs of dying patients are attended to, we discover competence in many of them for responsible and effective behavior. Moreover, when appreciation of their integrity and recognition of their input in decision making are major features in the treatment process, there is reduced depression, less projection of blame onto others, and diminished feelings of guilt and inadequacy not only in the patient but also in the helping care professionals and family members involved with that patient. The patient, in this type of context, moves toward the death of a person rather than of an illness. And, as professionals, we end up not merely as voyeurs of another's pain and tribulations but are prodded by the process to probe our own values and aspirations.[18]

One of the superb responses to this understanding has been the hospice movement. Its alertness to the problem of chronic pain, involvement of the family and friends as part of the caring team, and value of the meaningfulness of life are resulting in a prolonging of *living* rather than dying for many terminally ill persons. Being in a dying state does not veto respect for the sanctity and affirmation of life.[19]

- Grief is not a sign of weakness or self-indulgence. Rather, it demonstrates a necessary and deep human need most of us have in reacting to the loss of a significant person in our lives, and it recognizes no age boundaries. Furthermore, it is multifaceted, arises from differing types of loss, and manifests itself in numerous representations: anticipatory grief, high–low grief, self-grief, survival grief, or anniversary grief.[20]

Increasing privatization of death and grief needs to be undercut. There is a traditional Jewish proverb that "to grieve alone is to suffer most." The community needs to expand its current institutional networks and communal resources in responding to grief. Suppressing or minimizing it and failure to acknowledge the healing process of grief are maladaptive not just for the individual and immediate family but for the larger community. Indeed, there is growing comprehension that community sharing of grief decreases feelings of guilt and depression in survivors and minimizes the break in the societal fabric.[21]

Bereavement lacks precise criteria as a clinical entity, and the line between healthy and unhealthy grief, at times, can become blurry and difficult to distinguish. An instructive criterion in this circumstance seems to be that unhealthy grief may reveal itself in deviant behavior that violates conventional expectations or imperils the health and safety of self and others.[22]

We need to be cautious in encouraging survivors to abandon grief prematurely, or to wallow in it for that matter, because of our own painful and uncomfortable feelings. We are learning that if mourning is neglected or short-circuited, or does not take place close in time to a serious loss, its expression may occur later on in a more inappropriate and regressive manner. We are now aware that grief can gain expression in such masked appearances as school absenteeism and bed-wetting in children; drug abuse and delinquency in adolescents; and promiscuity, suicide, and diverse physical and mental illnesses in adults. We are also now more keenly informed about the "high-risk" group status of the bereaved in the area of somatic and emotional illness, particularly during the

first year or two after a loved one's death; the well-being of one who mourns is itself in a kind of jeopardy. Additionally, we increasingly realize that the grieving person not only can experience deprivation of sex, companionship, and economic support but is further vulnerable to a loss of social role, autonomy, and power. Moreover, it is being reestablished that the funeral ceremony and mourning rituals can be liberating as well as enslaving for survivors in their grief.[23]

- We are discovering that just as there are multitudinous ways of living, there are numerous ways of dying and grieving. Despite the equanimity of sorts that it offers, and a prevailing chic, the hard data do not support the existence of any procrustean stages or schedules that characterize terminal illness or mourning. This does not mean that, for example, Kübler-Ross's "stages of dying" and Bowlby's "phases of mourning" cannot provide us with implications and insights into the dynamics and process of dying and grief, but they are very far from being inexorable hoops through which most terminally ill individuals and mourners inevitably pass.[24] We should beware of promulgating a coercive orthodoxy of how to die or mourn. In the last analysis, applying Weisman's wise admonition, an "appropriate" dying or mourning is one acceptable to or tolerated by the dying person or mourner, not one so designated by either the helping professions, significant others, or the community.[25] Individual differences and esteem for personhood must be our principal guides.

- It is important for members of the health care team working with severely ill and terminally ill patients, and mourners, to be alert to signs of personal denial, avoidance, or antipathy in themselves concerning the reality of death. The more nonaccepting and unresolved helping care personnel tend to be about their own fears concerning personal death, the less likely they are to provide the optimal assistance of which they are capable. Ministry to the dying and bereaved is extremely difficult if we ourselves are not comfortable with the idea of personal death. Even if the professional's anxieties in the field are not completely resolved they, at least, have to be looked at and contended with. Grappling with our own somber feelings about death and grief will tend to moderate our disposition to seek refuge in the technical functions of disease, skulk behind theological dogmas, and equivocate with intellectual words in order to evade open encounter with the dying patient or grief of the mourner.[26]

♦ Redefinition is called for concerning the function of the helping professional, particularly that of the physician. When cure is definitely not in the cards, the provision of comfort and care is just as valid and authentic a contribution in meeting the real needs of the dying patient. In a significant sense, the growing hospice movement is a reaction to this prevailing lack in much of cure-oriented modern medicine.[27]

Perspectives From the Death Movement

What are some of the perspectives advanced by the death movement?

♦ Dying is not only a biological affair but a human one. The movement has underscored the importance of healing the humanity of the person wounded by illness and oncoming death. It has indicated that technology and competence have to be infused with compassion and benevolence and that life is not just a matter of length but of depth and quality as well. In this regard, the movement has emphasized the importance of controlling chronic pain in the dying so that terminal patients can use their full potential and has also stressed the moral, spiritual, and ethical dimensions inherent in health-care giving.

♦ It has refocused attention on the role of the future in steering conduct. Just as the past, the future abides dynamically in the present. How we anticipate future events—and death—governs our "now" in substantive fashion and provides an important organizing principle in determining how we behave in life. This is providing us with a needed corrective to a widespread vogue of being mesmerized by the moment.[28]

♦ It is forwarding the realization that we must be at home with fear of death and with the enigma of death if we are not to become alienated from our nature and destiny and lose basic contact with who we are and what we are about. Acceptance of personal mortality is one of the foremost entryways to self-knowledge. Human maturity brings along with it a recognition of limit. In truth, we have a legitimate need to face away from death. Unfortunately, too many of us resort to unhealthy expulsion and camouflage of the actuality of death, resulting in self-estrangement and social pathology. If we accepted death as a necessity and did not try to demote it to the level of mischance or fortuity, if we accepted death as lodged in our bowels from the very beginning, energies now bound up in continuing strivings to shelve and subdue the idea of death could be available to us for the more constructive and positive aspects of living, perhaps even fortifying our gift for creative splendor against our genius for destruction.[29]

As time-ridden beings, we are faced with the task of identifying ourselves with history and eternity. I think our most viable response will issue from basic philosophic, religious, or psychological deliberations about death already in our possession. This is difficult for a generation that finds itself dislodged from time-honored anchors. But we must establish bearings with the idea of death. Whether we do so via faith, love, art, or intelligence is a matter of *de gustibus*. In pondering death, the agony of selfhood is not endurable for most of us without resources, be they transcendental, inspirational, or existential. The evolution of an *ars moriendi* prior to the advent of death is needed.[30]

- Clearly, life can be menaced and compromised in many ways short of death and on varying levels of experience. In this context, such notions as "partial death," "symbolic death," and mourning over deprivation other than life such as a limb, sense, marriage, or old neighborhood will also profit from a more comprehensive theory of death and grief.[31]

- It is evident that death and grief are too multisplendored and complex to be trussed up in the conceptual straitjacket of any one discipline. We must be more cognizant of the positive synergistic effect of a transdisciplinary rather than unilateral approach in dealing with the dying and survivors.

- The time is overdue for death education to assume a rightful role in our cultural upbringing as a preparation for *living*. We have disabused ourselves of the fancy that sex first comes to life at puberty, as a kind of full-bodied Minerva emerging from Jupiter's head. In a similar vein, it is fitting that we now concede the psychological presence of death in ourselves from childhood on and attend to it at all stages of life development, not merely at its beginning and end. Naturally, its qualitative

form of expression will embody such variables as individual differences, values and belief systems, social context, and differing developmental periods. But, just as it is belated to start reading sex manuals on the marriage bed, it is rather tardy to begin developing a philosophy of life and death when one is terminally ill or newly bereaved. The pertinence of death education is not only for those of us in the health care professions who deal with dying, death, and bereavement but for all—in the home, school, religious institution, and general culture. The mandate is to alter cultural perspective, not just achieve a palliative concern.[32]

Implications for Psychologists

We must expand our information base so that application does not outrun knowledge. William James once stated that he was no lover of disorder but feared to lose the truth by pretensions to wholly possessing it. Knowledge of the specified links and interactive bonds of widespread variables to the meaning of death, for example, "will to live," life-style, coping strategies, need for achievement, and ethnic background, among others, is still not available to us in an organized fashion because of methodological complexities. Inconsistent findings reported in the death literature mirror the use of differing populations, ages, assessment devices, "conditions under which," and failure to fully appreciate the untidy nature of attitudes toward death. Some pitfalls, already alluded to, are nonconsideration of the multi-meanings that death acquires for people and perception of fear of death as a homogeneous variable. Another shortcoming has been neglect of the discrepancies that exist in individuals between conscious and nonconscious levels of death anxiety. Analysis of these incongruities may prove more instructive than merely noting the presence or degree of death concern.[33]

Experimental manipulation of variables has also been sparse. Case-based offerings continue to be informative in identifying phenomena and in suggesting leads for theory and practice. Nevertheless, although the medley of human responses to death-related situations is often noted by the clinician, these discernments do not, per se, provide a robust foundation for empirical generalizations.

At this stage of development, major desiderata for the field are more generative theory-based formulations, conversion of major assumptions into operationalized empirical inquiry, longitudinal studies, cross-validation and reliability analyses of prevailing procedures, more astute incorporation of multilevel aspects, and extended examination of functional and behavioral correlates of attitudes toward death. Psychotherapeutic functioning and models of personality and psychopathology require amplified representation of the future and death in their horizons. There is a definite need to integrate the clinician's admiration for individuality and complexity with the researcher's demand for precise and vigorous documentation.[34] We require comprehension and images that are more applicable to contemporary death and grief.

Refinement in the pursuit of our craft, however, will not be sufficient unless it is carried on in the context of healing the humanity of the dying patient and wounded mourner. Our model of understanding and treatment must be the humanity of the person. The requisite is not just to succor the body but also to speak to the soul. The humanities, ethics, and the spiritual dimension must be in our ken along with biology and the behavioral sciences. Death and grief bring with them a preoccupation with a vision of life.

Our field of regard should focus on the individual as purposive and striving: one whose scope is not made parochial by a limiting philosophy of science, and whose concepts are not derived essentially from methods of study but rather from the functioning of human life. Too often have we worked with portions of the human individual and tried to make a virtue of this. The challenge is to enlarge horizons without sacrificing our gains. Humanity cannot be grasped in its totality by a view that exempts personhood, meaning, and redemption from its purview, by a perspective whose criterion is the machine rather than man.[35]

Leaving the mountain top for more earthly ground, it is becoming plain that power is needed along with scholarship and learning. It is not enough to offer advice, instructive as it may be. The call is to integrate existing knowledge concerning death and grief into our communal and public institutions. There is no way in a dynamic society that a strict line can be drawn between scholarship and *wissenschaft* and the tides of social change. The glorious Apollo program in the United States to put an American on the moon, for example, for all its benefits, was more the child of politics than of the craving for exploration. Like it or not, political motives have been telling in driving science and technology these past decades. In other words, we must be valid participants in helping formulate public policy or else be its victims. Power can be enabling as well as corrupting.

Conclusion

A discipline is defined by the questions it asks as well as the validity of its measuring instruments. Recognition of death and knowledge of finiteness has contributed to psychology's progression into adulthood. It betokens a certain loss of innocence and youth and has probably introduced a repressive element into relationships. At the same time, however, it can serve positively as a galvanizing force—an Aristotelian *vis-a-tergo*—pushing us toward creativity and accomplishment. No less a person than Michelangelo said, "No thought is born in me that has not 'Death' engraved upon it."[36]

In final consideration, the death movement and social engineering will obviously never exorcize death of its demonic power. Still, the movement has been a major force in broadening our grasp of the phenomenology of illness, in helping humanize medical relationships and health care, and in advancing the rights of the dying. It is highpointing values that undergird the vitality of human response to catastrophe and loss. Furthermore, it is contributing to reconstituting the integrity of our splintered wholeness. More important, perhaps, it is sensitizing us to our common humanity, which is all too eroded in the present world.[37] It may be somewhat hyperbolic, but I believe that how we regard death and how we treat the dying and survivors are prime indications of a civilization's intention and target.

Concern with death is not the fixation of a cult indifferent to life. Conversely, in emphasizing awareness of death, we sharpen and intensify our appreciation of the uniqueness and preciousness of life. In responding to our temporality, we shall find it easier to define values, priorities, and life goals.

Because of advances in medical technology and an expanding aging population, the years ahead will behold increasing numbers of people wrestling with chronic and life-threatening illness and prolonged dying. Furthermore, such urgent social issues as abortion, AIDS, euthanasia, and capital punishment, and such behaviors as alcoholism, drug abuse, and certain acts of violence, may well have links to overt and latent meanings that death holds for us. After all, life-threatening behaviors involve confrontation, in one way or another, with the threat of possible injury or ultimate death to self and others.

Death possesses many faces and meanings, and perceptions of it vary in divergent cultures and in differing epochs. It is obviously too intricate to be the special province of any one discipline. Nevertheless, psychology's contributions in the past to thanatology have succeeded in increasing understanding of and coping with dying, death, and bereavement. Our future mandate is to extend our grasp of how death can serve life.

What Is an Epidemic? AIDS in Historical Perspective

CHARLES E. ROSENBERG

CHARLES ROSENBERG, PH.D., is Janice and Julian Bers Professor of the History of Science at the University of Pennsylvania. In describing how he began working in this area, Dr. Rosenberg says, "I started out as a bored pre-med student at the University of Wisconsin searching for a more challenging discipline. One semester, I found more or less by accident a course in the school of medicine open to undergrads entitled 'The History and Geography of Disease.' It seemed a lot more interesting than organic chemistry. That was in 1954, and the subject was so intriguing that I spent the next four decades studying the historical interrelationships among medicine, science, and society. Disease and the doctor-patient relationship have been central concerns for me. How doctors think about medicine and how doctors and patients think about each other are compelling and fascinating topics and central areas of my research as a professional historian. From my first book on cholera to the most recent book explaining epidemics, I have been working at different pieces of this puzzle."

Dr. Rosenberg's published work includes *The Cholera Years: The United States in 1932, 1849,* *and 1866* (rev. ed., 1987), *The Trial of the Assassin Guiteau: Psychiatry and Law in the Gilded Age* (1968), *No Other Gods: On Science and American Social Thought* (1976), *The Care of Strangers: The Rise of America's Hospital System* (1987), and *Explaining Epidemics and Other Studies in the History of Medicine* (1992). He is also the editor or co-editor of four other books and author of some sixty articles about the history of medicine and science.

Dr. Rosenberg has received research awards from the Guggenheim and Rockefeller Foundations, the National Endowment for the Humanities, and the National Institutes of Health, and he has been a visiting fellow at the Institute for Advanced Study in Princeton and the Center for Advanced Studies in the Behavioral Sciences at Stanford. He is a member of the Institute of Medicine of the National Academy of Sciences and of the American Academy of Arts and Sciences. Dr. Rosenberg was awarded the Welch Medal by the American Association for the History of Medicine, and *The Care of Strangers* was one of three books nominated for the Pulitzer Prize in history in 1987.

AIDS in Historical Perspective: Remembering to Remember

Our experience with AIDS during the past decade has reminded us of some very traditional truths. Most strikingly, we seem not to have conquered infectious disease. Death is not associated exclusively with a particular—and advanced—age. AIDS has reminded us as well that managing death has been traditionally a central responsibility of the physician (though by no means of the physician alone). We have not, it seems, freed ourselves from the constraints and indeterminacy of living in a web of biological relationships—not all of which we can control or predict. Viruses, like bacteria, have for countless millennia shared our planet and our bodies. In some ways AIDS is a very traditional phenomenon indeed.

Nor have we revolutionized the framework within which we respond as a community to epidemic disease. In a good many ways the AIDS experience has reenacted the traditional dramaturgic structure of earlier epidemics. One, of course, is the gradual and grudging acceptance of the epidemic as reality—and the resentment expressed toward bringers of bad tidings, the physicians and activists who demand a response to this new threat.[1] Equally obvious is the way in which coping with randomness provides an occasion for reaffirming the social values of the majority, for blaming victims. Framing and blaming are inextricably mingled; the details vary, but the end is similar. The peculiar mixture of biological mechanism invested with moral meaning is equally traditional.

Most Americans prefer to deal with a threat that they do not see as "meant" for them. The search for a reassuring connection of volition, behavior, and pathological consequence is as much alive today as it was during earlier epidemics. Transgression implies punishment; affliction implies prior transgression. The historic circumstances and epidemiological peculiarities of AIDS have made such connections unavoidable in the public mind—and in their seemingly empirical character have obscured the social and psychological functions implicit in the underlining of that connection.

AIDS has reminded us as well of the apparently inevitable juxtaposition of suffering and death with a search for meaning that has always characterized epidemics. Meanings vary, but the need to impose them does not. Most Americans find reassurance in their accustomed faith in the laboratory and its products; they see AIDS as a time-bound artifact of that unfortunate but essentially transitional period between the discovery of this new ill and the announcement of its cure. Others, of course, see its primary meaning in the realm of morality and traditional piety. Many of us, of course, impose multiple frames of meaning on these biological events. The majority of Americans retain their faith in the laboratory but at the same time believe that AIDS points variously to truths about government, the political process, and personal morality.[2] The linked sequence of biological event and its moral management seems unavoidable.

But there is another aspect of public-health history that AIDS also recalls. For the sake of convenience diseases can be divided into two categories: diseases whose prevention demands individual behavioral change—like syphilis, AIDS, and lung cancer—and diseases that can be prevented by collective policy commitments—like typhoid fever, where the aggregated knowledge and decisions of bacteriologists, civil engineers, administrators, and elected officials have protected individuals whose habits need not have changed at all.[3] AIDS reminds us of the difficulty of inducing changes in behavior and thus of the intrinsic complexity of the decisions facing local governments and public-health authorities.[4]

Contemporary sensitivity to individual rights only underlines the centrality of this dilemma, as does our novel public willingness to publicly discuss sexual behavior. Despite these characteristic aspects of today's social scene, parallels with earlier health campaigns are obvious. During the first decades of this century, for example, public-health workers who urged the use of condoms and prophylactic kits to prevent syphilis met some of the same kind of opposition their successors in the 1980s faced when they advocated distributing sterile needles to intravenous drug users. In both cases ultimate values came into conflict. In both cases debate turned on distinctions between "deserving" and "innocent" victims—in the case of syphilis, the presumed innocents being the wives of erring husbands and their infants; in the case of AIDS, the recipients of contaminated blood or the offspring of infected mothers.[5]

These cases remind us as well of the need for ritual, even in a fragmented modern society. It is a need that is recognized in the AIDS memorial patchwork quilt that has recently circulated throughout the United States; it is recognized, I suggest, even in the whimsically self-conscious and public distribution of condoms on college campuses and in other public spaces; it is recognized in the calling of conferences graced by individuals representing various agencies of social authority—scientists, administrators, even the odd historian. Each ritual implies collective responsibility and communal identity. Each invokes a differentially nuanced frame of meaning—in the case of the quilt, a commitment to egalitarian compassion; in the distribution of condoms, a commitment to the potential of applied science. If science and technology allow us to control and predict, it is a realm of value worth invoking collectively.

AIDS, a Modern Epidemic

In a number of obvious ways, however, AIDS does not fit easily into the traditional pattern I have outlined. One, for example, is the rapidity of its geographic spread and the parallel rapidity of its identification as a unified clinical entity.[6] It might well be described as modern, and even postmodern, in its relationship to scientific medicine and institutional structures. AIDS is postmodern in the self-conscious, reflexive, and bureaucratically structured detachment with which we regard it. Countless social scientists and journalists watch us watch ourselves; that reflexive process has become a characteristic aspect of America's experience with AIDS.

More generally the epidemic has existed at several levels simultaneously, mediated by the at first uninterested, then erratically attentive media. For most Americans—insofar as this epidemic can be construed as a national phenomenon—it is a media reality, both exaggerated and diminished as it is articulated in forms suitable for mass consumption. The great majority of Americans have been spectators, *in* but not *of* the epidemic.

Another significant difference between this and earlier epidemics grows out of the novel capacities of late twentieth-century medicine. Without its intellectual tools, the epidemic would not have been understood as an epidemic; we could not easily have determined that it is a clinical entity with protean manifestations. Providing substantive cognitive change during the course of an ongoing epidemic, the laboratory and its intellectual products have played a novel role in the narrative structure of our encounter with AIDS. Without the option of serological screening, for example, the intense and multifaceted debate over the impo-

sition of such tests could hardly have been framed. Without knowledge of an infectious agent, the options for public policy would necessarily have been defined differently.

Another modern characteristic of America's experience with AIDS mirrors the institutional complexity of our society. That structured complexity has in scores of ways shaped responses to this crisis. (Response to epidemics has, of course, always been constrained by pre-existing institutional forms and prevailing values, but twentieth-century institutional structures seem categorically different—if only in scale.)

Institutional complexity implies institutional interest—and thus conflict. Certainly we have seen this in the case of AIDS. Blood banks, hospitals, the National Institutes of Health and its several components, and state and municipal departments of public health have all played particular yet necessarily linked and interactive parts. Similarly, the not always consistent interests of local and national government, and of political parties, have also helped shape the nature and pace of our society's response to AIDS. Even patients and their advocates have become public activists in a generation newly conscious of individual and group rights. Perhaps least surprising is the way in which our courts have provided a mechanism for resolving the difficult policy choices posed by AIDS. As we are aware, American courts have become the residuary legatee of a variety of intractable social problems. Recently, a judge in Florida, for instance, decided that a child with AIDS should not be excluded from the classroom—but would have to remain within a glass-enclosed cubicle while in attendance.[7] As in many other instances in our society, conflicting attitudes and interests find their way into courts where judges and juries must of necessity make *ad hoc* decisions.

Finally, Americans have created a complex and not always consistent health-care system, and AIDS has been refracted through the needs, assumptions, and procedures of that system. The epidemic might be seen as a socio-assay of that system. Just as costs have been problematic in the system, so have they in the case of AIDS. AIDS has, in particular, force-fully reminded us of the difficulty of providing adequate care for the chronically ill in a system oriented disproportionately toward acute intervention—and of the complex linkages between disease categories, hospital policies, and reimbursement formulas. In this sense, AIDS might be seen as an exacerbation of a chronic pathology.[8]

The gap between isolating an infectious agent in a laboratory in Paris or Bethesda and the imposition of a preventive program alter-ing the behavior of particular people in partic-ular places is difficult and problematic. But this is no more than characteristic; clinical applica-tion does not follow inevitably from technical consensus. AIDS provides a powerful *de facto* argument for an integrated system-oriented approach to public health and health care; nei-ther the laboratory's contributions nor the social contexts in which that knowledge is employed can be seen in isolation.[9]

AIDS as a Postmodern Epidemic

The role of the media and social scientists in our contemplating ourselves is obvious enough, but AIDS can be seen as postmodern in several other ways as well. Perhaps most strikingly, it is a postrelativist phenomenon.[10] After a generation of epistemological—and political—questioning of the legitimacy of many disease categories, AIDS has underlined the inadequacy of any one-dimensional ap-proach to disease, either the social construc-tionist or the more conventional mechanisti-cally oriented perspective. AIDS is socially constructed (as society perceives and frames the phenomenon, blames victims, and labori-ously negotiates response) yet at the same time fits nicely into a one-dimensionally reduction-ist and biologically based model of disease. AIDS can hardly be dismissed as an exercise in victim blaming, even if it is an occasion for it. It is no mere text, words arranged to mirror and legitimate particular social relationships and perceptions. On the other hand, we can no longer remain unaware that biopathological phenomena are framed and filtered through such agreed-on texts.

Of course, a good many Americans never succumbed to the relativist mood of the late 1960s and 1970s, while others have always regarded the social claims of medicine with skepticism, even if they did not question the legitimacy of its disease categories. Others of us have tried to steer a more tentative course. We live in a fragmented society, and not even the most myopic cultural anthropologist would find it easy to impose a neatly coherent and unified cultural vision on the diverse group of individuals who inhabit the continental United States.

Yet AIDS has reminded us that we all share at least some common fears and ways of responding to social crisis. "They fancied themselves free," as Camus wrote of the citi-zens of the soon-to-be plague-stricken Oran, "and no one will ever be free so long as there are pestilences." At the end of his narrative, Camus's physician-narrator reflects, even as he listens to the cries of joy that greet the opening of the city and the official conclusion of the epidemic, ". . . that perhaps the day would come when, for the bane and the enlightening of men, it would rouse up its rats again and send them forth to die in a happy city."[11] Plague reminds us that human beings will not so easily escape the immanence of evil and the anxiety of indeterminacy. Mortality is built into our bodies, into our modes of behavior, and into our place in the planet's ecology. Like other epidemics, AIDS has served well to remind us, finally, of these ultimate realities.

News Strategies and the Death of Huey Newton

JACK LULE

JACK LULE, PH.D., is an associate professor in the Department of Journalism and Communication at Lehigh University in Bethlehem, Pennsylvania. A former reporter, he now specializes in media studies and ethics. His involvement in issues of death and dying began with his analyses of media coverage of victims. In this coverage Dr. Lule found that the media present complex and compelling interpretations of life and death—interpretations that help shape and are shaped by social and cultural life. Some of Dr. Lule's early research looked at how the news media transformed victims of terrorism into national heroes whose portrayals affirmed the significance of life in the face of seemingly random death. Conversely, his research into media coverage of the death of Huey Newton revealed how news stories demonized and degraded Newton's life and work with the Black Panthers.

Dr. Lule has received several research awards and grants for his work in media criticism published in the *Journal of Mass Media Ethics*, *Journalism Quarterly*, *Critical Studies in Mass Communication*, *Political Communication and Persuasion*, and other journals, as well as in newspapers such as the *Atlanta Constitution*, *Baltimore Sun*, *Chicago Tribune*, *Philadelphia Inquirer*, and *San Francisco Chronicle*. He is a recipient of the Lehigh University Award for Distinguished Teaching.

COVERAGE OF RADICAL black politics raises numerous concerns for U.S. news media. The issues often are provocative and difficult: resistance of—and aggression toward—legal and judicial authority; threats of violence; critiques of the white establishment, including the press; and other direct opposition to social order.

From Malcolm X to the Black Panthers to Louis Farrakhan to Al Sharpton, black leaders who espouse radical views confront the ambivalent and troubled relationship between the media and racial politics as well as between the media and radical politics.

How do the media handle radical, racial politics? Writers long have argued that the media simply miss or ignore such politics because of the overwhelming white face of the nation's newsrooms.[1] Others say that the media take a more active role, degrading black activists and situating moderate black leaders on more "legitimate" middle ground.[2]

Other writers take a more critical stance. They argue that press coverage of radical politics, especially black politics, seeks to delegitimize and disarm the perceived threats to social order. The news media are seen as a significant ideological force, serving as "agents of social control" and preserving "the status quo by providing unsympathetic coverage to those whose behavior threatens it."[3]

An excellent opportunity for exploring press coverage of radical black politics from this more critical perspective was afforded by the 1989 death of Huey Newton, co-founder of the Black Panther Party. Newton's public career spanned two tumultuous decades. He was a complex figure with an international reputation forged as much from his passionate defense of black power as from his notorious confrontations with police. His death provided an occasion for the press to summarize and assess his life and work.[4]

The purpose of this research is to study news coverage of the death of Huey Newton. It employs interpretive analysis to isolate and organize predominant portrayals and determine to what extent news reports did debase and disavow the threat to social order embodied by Huey Newton.

Background:
Huey Newton and the News

Revolutionary, Mercedes owner, killer, protector, illiterate, doctor of philosophy—Huey Newton had a host of public roles. Born in Louisiana in 1942, named after Huey Long, populist governor of the state, Newton was the youngest of seven children. Within a year, the family moved to Oakland, California. By his own testimony, Newton was a student of the street and graduated illiterate from high school.[5]

Soon after, however, he taught himself to read and enrolled in Oakland's Merritt College during the ferment of the mid-1960s. His interest was radical black politics, specifically those of Malcolm X.[6] Through coursework, Newton met Bobby Seale. Concerned with police treatment of blacks in Oakland, Newton and Seale formed the Black Panther Party for Self Defense in 1966.[7] They patrolled behind police, photographing arrests of blacks. They published a newspaper; the first issue explored the killing of an Oakland black man by a police officer.

The Panthers first reached the national stage in May 1967 when well-armed members marched in Sacramento to protest restrictions on carrying arms. In the charged context of violence between blacks and police, the message of the armed Panthers was electrifying. Newton's blistering critique of police oppression was given nationwide play.

Trouble kept Newton in the national spotlight. In 1967, he and a friend were stopped by Oakland police. In a struggle, an officer was killed; Newton, critically wounded, was charged with his murder. His impassioned defense won him admirers in ghettoes, on college campuses and in select social circles.[8] "Free Huey" became an anthem.[9]

Newton and the Panthers resisted easy categorization. They were committed to the black community; they organized voting drives, free health clinics, breakfast programs for children, an accredited elementary school, a clothing outlet and a bus service for relatives visiting prison inmates. Panther chapters were opened nationwide.

Yet violence followed the Panthers. At least fifteen were killed in confrontations with police. It was later revealed that J. Edgar Hoover personally had overseen COINTELPRO, a program of FBI harassment of the Panthers and other groups.[10] Newton, too, was shadowed by violence. In 1974 he was accused of murdering a seventeen-year-old prostitute. He took asylum in Cuba. After three years, he returned to stand trial; the jury deadlocked and charges were dropped. Soon after, in the early 1980s, torn by the deaths, trials and dissension, the Panthers disbanded.

Newton pressed on. In 1980, he earned a doctorate in an interdisciplinary program, the history of consciousness, at the University of California at Santa Cruz.[11] In his last years, he fought drug and weapons charges. He worked on a book and movie proposals.

In the early morning of August 22, 1989, Newton was shot and killed on a West Oakland street known for drug deals. He was forty-seven.[12] Newton's death was front-page news, an opportunity for the press to look back on twenty years of black politics, an occasion for analysis and assessment. Assessing Newton would be no easy task. He was radical, violent, charismatic, revolutionary. He gave civil rights a compelling urgency and served a pivotal role on the American scene in the 1960s and 1970s. The central question: How did the press portray Newton and his work?

Method: News Strategies

This study analyzed coverage of Newton's death in a dozen U.S. newspapers, selected for geographical diversity as well as elite quality and influence.[13] The study employed a qualitative, interpretive analysis based on the work of the literary and social critic Kenneth Burke.[14]

Burke argues that all language is symbolic action that offers *strategies for situations*.[15] He says these strategies "size up the situations, name their structure and outstanding ingredients, and name them in a way that contains an attitude toward them."[16] He suggests a critic can categorize various strategies, assembling them in groups, "made on the basis of some strategic element common to the group."[17]

James Carey has long been an advocate of applying Burke's notions to news.[18] Citing Burke, Carey calls journalism "a creative and imaginative work, a symbolic strategy."[19] Like Burke, Carey notes the notion of *strategies* must be conceived broadly. Press reports are indeed complex texts. Products not only of a reporter, news accounts are also influenced by sources, news conventions, editorial policy, and other forces that make interpretations intricate and rich.[20]

Following Carey and Burke, a textual analysis tracked and grouped "strategic elements" in news reports of Newton's death. Briefly, the analysis first examined within each report the selection and portrayal of actors and acts. Of particular significance were the choice of titles, verbs, adverbs, qualifiers. For example, one report stated that Newton was a "self-proclaimed" revolutionary. The phrase cast doubt on his status. Similarly, another report said that Newton at times "portrayed himself to be an intelligent academician."

The study then examined symbols and metaphors. For example, many accounts reported in the lead that Newton was shot in the "same troubled neighborhood where he began his work." Why note the neighborhood? Analysis suggested the reports used the neighborhood as an ironic symbol for the failure of Newton's work.

Assumptions and beliefs that grounded each report then were considered. For example, many reports followed convention and gave over much space to the official record, a recitation of Newton's criminal charges. In the context of the reports, the record was used to foster the belief that Newton's life was spent largely on violence and crime.

With this approach, the study analyzed strategies employed in news coverage of Newton's death. As the following sections show, analysis found that news reports overwhelmingly degraded and demeaned Newton and his work. Specifically, the study identified three strategies: irony, incongruity and citation.[21] The following sections isolate and discuss each strategy and show how each diminished Newton's life and death.

But it first should be noted that many strategies could have been employed by the press. Newton could have been depicted with strategies that emphasized his heroic, almost cult-like status among many blacks or that highlighted his battles against poverty, racism and other social ills that continue to confront the black community. This study will argue, however, that as an integral member of the established order, the press rejected Newton's life-long questioning of that order. Faced with assessing the radical politics of the Panther leader, news reports disabused those politics and affirmed the authority of the status quo.

Disavowal Through Irony

The first strategy encountered in news reports on Newton's death employed irony that disavowed the importance of his life. The irony, prominent in leads and headlines, was derived from an emphasis on the fact that Newton was shot dead in the same neighborhood where he co-founded the Panthers. Why the emphasis on the site? Certainly irony and paradox are employed as journalistic conventions. But why this particular irony? A preliminary suggestion can be made. By linking Newton's work and death, the irony may have implied that nothing was changed by Newton's work. He could not even better his home neighborhood, the reports suggested. In Burke's terms, the strategy was to disavow through irony the importance of Newton's life.[22]

For example, a *Kansas City Times* headline said, "Black Panthers Leader Dies on Turf Where Work Began."[23] Likewise, a *New York*

Times jumphead said, "Huey Newton Found Shot to Death In Part of City Where He Began."[24] Leads also stressed the killing site. The *New York Times* said Newton was shot to death "in the neighborhood were he began his organizing."[25] *USA Today* reported he died "violently Tuesday morning on the mean streets of Oakland, Calif., two blocks from the one-time headquarters of the Black Panthers movement he co-founded."[26] The *Atlanta Constitution* reported he was "shot to death in the same troubled neighborhood where 23 years ago he co-founded the militant Black Panther Party to protect blacks from police violence."[27]

Local papers added more irony. *The Tribune* of Oakland said, "Black Panther Party co-founder Huey P. Newton, who at one time preached power through guns, was found shot to death early yesterday on a West Oakland sidewalk not far from the birthplace of the radical group."[28] The *San Francisco Chronicle* added another perspective and said he was shot "in the West Oakland neighborhood where he was accused of gunning down a police officer 22 years ago."[29]

The irony seems to imply that Newton could not even save his own neighborhood. A second possible implication is more troubling. Some reports may also have suggested that Newton received a just reward, a kind of ironic justice. Newton "at one time preached power through guns." He was killed in the same neighborhood "where he was accused of gunning down a police officer." The irony has the feel of consummation. One report quoted a source who voiced, in a deadening cliche, the very sentiment: "He who lives by the sword dies by the sword."[30]

Invalidation by Incongruity

A second and complementary strategy, which also emphasized the murder scene, could be identified in news reports on Newton's death. This strategy devalued and invalidated Newton's work by employing descriptive contrasts

between the once-genteel neighborhood and the ugliness of Newton's demise. Supporting this strategy were detailed and gory descriptions of Newton's body—descriptions often employed in mob slayings—that made clear the demeaning circumstances of his death.

What was the possible role of references to the neighborhood and Newton's body? The descriptions effected a journalistic convention of contrast. The contrast suggested the intolerable incongruity of Newton's death: How could a man find such a sordid end on a street once so grand? And further: What kind of man finds such an end?

Reports prominently included neighborhood descriptions. The *San Francisco Chronicle* and *St. Louis Post-Dispatch* noted in their second paragraphs that Newton was found in front of "two Victorian style houses."[31] The *Washington Post* went further, stating that Newton was found in front of "a small, faded blue-and-white Victorian house in West Oakland. Large trees line the street, and a rose bush is in bloom."[32]

The description implicated Newton, complementing the strategy of the leads: Newton's work was in vain, the reports implied; he could not make even this tranquil setting safe. The *Washington Post* article stated this strategy explicitly, charging Newton with failure. Newton was found, the *Post* said, "in a neighborhood as depressed and beaten down by violence as the Oakland streets that he and his Panther colleagues once promised to make safer for young black children."[33]

The strategy was enhanced by other neighborhood descriptions. Many reports used the wire service line that "the echo of gunfire regularly disturbs the night." The *Houston Post* called the neighborhood a "rundown section of Oakland where residents fear they are losing the war against drug dealing and poverty."[34] The *Wall Street Journal* called it a "drug-infested neighborhood."[35] The *Los Angeles Times* termed it a "drug-plagued area."[36] Combined with the leads' irony, the words made plain: The streets where Newton began his work—once a stately, urban site—were a deadly place; Newton's work had little effect.

Newton's ineffectuality was also suggested by descriptions of his death. His murder was granted gore and detail reserved for especially noteworthy murders. The *New York Times* noted he was "shot several times, including at least once in the head."[37] The *Los Angeles Times* said he was "shot three times in the head."[38] *The Tribune* said he was "shot at least twice at point-blank range in the head and face."[39] The *St. Louis Post-Dispatch* noted he was "sprawled on his back."[40] The *Washington Post* reported that he was found "face up and fully clothed."[41] Many newspapers reported—probably unnecessarily, since they had noted he was shot three times in the head—that Newton was found in the archetypal "pool of blood." *The Tribune* called it "a spreading pool of blood,"[42] while the *San Francisco Chronicle* increased the fluid description to a "river of blood."[43]

The bloody details are not rare in news accounts. But by news conventions, the details usually are included for particularly notorious slayings, especially the murder of mobsters. Too, in the context of the articles, the details complemented the portrayal of Newton as ineffectual. Shot three times in the face and head, face-up and fully clothed, in a pool of blood, he is the picture of dissolution.

Repudiation Through Citation

A third strategy repudiated Newton's work by dismissing his accomplishments and portraying his life through a one-dimensional focus on violence. This was accomplished in large part by disparaging comments of government sources and by use of another journalistic convention— citation of the criminal record. There was some justification for this strategy. Newton's life was violent and his police record was long. But Newton's struggles with police took place in a rich and troubled context that included urban strife, police oppression, government harassment, and an intense debate over civil rights tactics. Stripped of context and interpretation, the violence of Newton's life was leveled into an emphatic indictment of him.

The newspapers followed convention by including positive and negative comments about Newton. However, many reports gave over much more space to authorities who were quite critical. Accounts gave four to six paragraphs to the negative comments of Tom Orloff, the district attorney who had failed on a number of occasions to get convictions of Newton. Orloff called Newton "a thug," "a man who lived by violence and outside the law," and "nothing but a gangster."[44] The *San Francisco Chronicle* placed Orloff's comments prominently in the third paragraph of its lead story: "I must say I am not surprised he ended up meeting a violent death because violence was so much a part of his life. As they say: 'He who lives by the sword dies by the sword.'"[45] Likewise, in *The Tribune* of Oakland, an unidentified Oakland police sergeant said Newton "finally got what he deserved. It's really a shame they made a martyr out of him. He died like the thug he was."[46]

The papers themselves disparaged Newton. *USA Today* suggested Newton deceived his followers. The paper said, "in the early '70s, Newton and the Panthers pulled in donations from the 'radical chic,' but one, at least, felt he had been 'suckered' by 'the black hero of the left.'"[47] The *Washington Post,* too, suggested Newton was a fraud; the paper offered this description of Newton's court appearances: "Newton, working toward a doctorate in the History of Consciousness program at the University of California at Santa Cruz, tried to portray himself as an intelligent academician being persecuted for political reasons."[48]

Complementing these portrayals of Newton were long recitations of Newton's criminal record. One fourth to a third of many reports was devoted to past charges, with little distinction made between charges and convictions.

No attempt was made to place the arrests in the context of political confrontation between Panthers and police. The *Houston Post* began this section: "Newton, like other Panther leaders, accumulated a long criminal record, and was tried five times in two slayings."[49] The *Atlanta Constitution* changed this last statistic to "five counts of murder."[50] A *New York Times* sidebar gave over most of its space to 10 paragraphs of criminal charges.[51] A *San Francisco Chronicle* report headlined, "Troubled Life of Huey Newton," was a chronology of court dates from Oct. 22, 1966, to Aug. 22, 1989.[52]

Critical commentary and criminal records are standard news fare. But in Newton's case, the sources of criticism, the amount of space given to charges and the context of overall coverage supported the portrayal of a man of violence who accomplished little and got the end he deserved. The strategy was a repudiation of Newton's accomplishments, a reduction of his life to court dates and a criminal record.

Exception and Convention

Exceptions to this overwhelmingly negative portrayal were found. As might be expected, the three California newspapers reported, although in quite varied degrees, the grief and mourning of people in Oakland at word of Newton's death, a grief incomprehensible if Newton was indeed merely a thug. In the hours after the killing, the site—used so ironically against Newton in newspaper leads—became a kind of shrine. Flowers were placed along the sidewalk. Notes of thanks to Newton were attached to some bouquets. One note said, "Huey, thanks for all you tried to do. We won't let the children forget." Banners were draped on a fence. Candles and incense were burned. Videotapes of Newton's speeches were played. People remained into the night.[53]

No newspaper outside of California reported the events. Even the Bay Area newspapers, with their saturation coverage, found little room for the mourning in Oakland. For example, the *San Francisco Chronicle* included only an Associated Press photograph that showed a long-haired black man crouched in front of flowers placed at the spot where Newton was shot.[54] *The Tribune* of Oakland provided numerous interviews with local people whose lives had been touched by Newton. But a report dismissed those who gathered in devotion, saying they were on "a somewhat ghoulish pilgrimage."[55]

Only the *Los Angeles Times* departed from the antagonistic portrait of Newton to report the devotion on the street and allow a more complex picture of Newton to emerge.[56] The paper included the Associated Press photo of the man crouched in front of flowers.[57] In the middle of its lead account, the paper reported the clusters of people visiting the scene, the flowers, the banners, the videotapes. And in this account, the paper recorded an eerie, memorable image from the aftermath of the killing, an image that appeared in no other paper:

> One elderly man who declined to give his name spent several minutes using a white plastic-foam coffee cup to scoop up blood that had pooled in a gutter. When he had filled a plastic juice container, he left.
>
> "Huey was very special, very special," he said while walking off to catch a bus back to his East Oakland home. "You don't find too many black men like Huey."
>
> "That blood is highly symbolic," said Ojo Pede, 38, a Nigerian exchange student who had watched the old man. Pede, who said he had come down from Berkeley for a personal vigil, did not elaborate.[58]

But even this signal scene was given no context, no elaboration. The depth of feeling suggested, the meanings of Huey Newton for people of color in Oakland, was touched upon but then dropped. Yet, for a few paragraphs, a hint of a different strategy had been raised.

Deadline pressures did not explain the omissions of these scenes by other newspapers. Newton was shot in the early morning of August 22. Stories would not run until the following day. Reporters were filing their accounts as the devotions were taking place. Nor can it be said the memorial—dramatic and spontaneous—lacked news value. Rather, the conclusion of this study will suggest that homage and devotion simply did not fit with larger news strategies that degraded and demeaned Newton and his work while upholding the order he challenged.

Conclusion

Textual analysis has shown that three strategies dominated news reports about the death of Huey Newton. The reports depicted Newton's death in terms that degraded and devalued his life and work. Through irony, the reports disavowed the importance of his life. Through incongruity, the reports built descriptive contrasts that emphasized the sordidness of his demise. Through citation of his criminal record, the reports portrayed him as a cheap thug, a gangster. They omitted sources and events that might refute or balance the portrayal. They marginalized and trivialized his goals and accomplishments.

Burke and Carey suggest that all reporting, indeed all symbolic works, rely upon strategies that offer "ways to size up situations."[59] Many strategies might have been employed to depict Newton's death. One strategy already has been suggested. News reports could have focused on Newton's stature and role in black neighborhoods of Oakland. Too, the news could have retained its focus on Newton's trouble with the law but placed these troubles within a drama of a rogue outlaw confronting the system. Yet

another strategy might have been to see Newton as an embodiment of the struggle against racism, poverty, and drugs. These strategies could have been employed—without violating news values or sacrificing dramatic interest.

For Burke and Carey, a primary question of criticism must be: Why are certain strategies employed and not others? That is, why did twelve U.S. newspapers all choose to demean and diminish Newton? The analysis offers support to those who argue that the news media act as proponents of social order, defending the status quo by marginalizing opposition. News reports put forth the view that Newton's demise was the logical, just result of a life lived outside of and opposed to the social order. The irony of the leads, the neighborhood descriptions, the emphasis on his criminal record, the choice of sources—all combined to structure a portrayal that found in Newton's death justice and retribution. His radical ways brought to Newton, the reports suggested, a deserved fate.

Todd Gitlin has stated that an important task of a dominant ideology is to define—but also define away—radical opposition. The news media, Gitlin argues, often take on this task of "defining away" the opposition.[60] In these terms, the life and work of Huey Newton were "defined away" by devalued assessments offered at his death.

It is difficult to judge if the devaluations in the news were reactions to politics or race. Certainly, white activists, as Gitlin has shown, also have met with derogation.[61] Yet the secondary literature on the Panthers asserts the early and persistent racial antagonism of the media for Newton and the Panthers. "The distortions about the Panthers to which white America has been subjected have appeared everywhere in the media," wrote Gene Marine of *Ramparts,* "not merely in the 'good' and conscientious newspapers." The news, he added, "can hardly be expected to seek out subtleties about black men with guns."[62] Gilbert Moore, a black reporter for *Life,* wrote that the "myth" of the fearsome black man "was picked up and perpetuated by a near-sighted press which could not see past Huey's bandoliers. White readers could readily believe the mass circulation of half-truths."[63]

Questions of intentionality remain. Can reporters be held responsible for consciously degrading Newton and his work? Answers to the question certainly lie outside the limits of a case study of content. Burke, however, offers suggestions. Though his term strategy implies that writers intentionally and consciously shape their works, Burke is clear that the strategy of a work is really the result of writer, text and interpreter working in personal, political, and cultural contexts both conscious and unconscious.[64] The intent of reporters is not really at issue in this case study; the possible interpretations of news language is at issue.

There was no need for news strategies that portrayed Newton as a hero. There was no question that Newton lived a life strung taut by violence. But that violence and its meaning were not to be captured in some dry recitation of court appearances and quotes from a frustrated district attorney. Newton and violence were part of a context of racism, police perse-cution, civil rights strategy and revolution, and the tension between law and authority, books and streets, words and guns. Newton was a worthy, compelling subject for the news. But because he strained against societal preconceptions and journalistic conventions of political protest, he was strategically and emphatically placed outside of the social order.

In the news, the rich, troubled life of Huey Newton was presented as a desultory cliche: "He who lives by the sword dies by the sword." The meaning of his life and its tremendous and troubling connections to persistent plagues of poverty, drugs, racial barriers, and oppression were crushed beneath the dead weight of the cliche and its iron-clad irony. The news proved the words of James Baldwin:

> Huey Newton is one of the most important people to have been produced by the American chaos. His fate is very important. And not one person in white America, if they read the mass media, knows anything about Huey, what produced him or what produced the Black Panther Party.[65]

Multicultural Perspectives on Dying and Death

Death Without Weeping:
The Violence of Everyday Life in Brazil

NANCY SCHEPER-HUGHES, PH.D. is a professor in the Department of Anthropology at the University of California, Berkeley, and in the Department of Social Anthropology at the University of Cape Town, South Africa. She was drawn into a ten-year (1982–1992) study of mother love and child death in rural northeast Brazil after she witnessed, nearly fifteen years earlier, a veritable die-out of Brazilian "angel babies" in the absence of parental or community grief. As a community health worker with the Peace Corps in hillside shantytowns, or *favelas,* during the mid-1960s, she was called on to deliver babies, give shots, treat parasitic infections, and prepare very small and emaciated bodies for burial. When she expressed her grief over these deaths, bemused older women would sometimes ask, "Why are you crying? It's only a baby!" To explain "death without weeping" in these shantytown women—who were otherwise emotionally vibrant and caring—required deep analysis of the political and cultural shaping of emotions, desires, and needs.

Dr. Scheper-Hughes's study of the "acceptable death" of angel babies in Brazil led to her current research on the routinization and normalization of death in South African townships, where thousands of marginalized people, many of them very young, die each year from burnings ("necklacings") in the absence of a legitimate police force and judiciary. "These necklacings," says Dr. Scheper-Hughes, "are the direct heritage of nearly half a century of *apartheid,* continuing the dirty work of African genocide now in the name of 'popular justice.'"

Dr. Scheper-Hughes's writings on death concern the terrifying ability of hungry and oppressed people to adjust to miserable social conditions, to the point of sometimes playing the role of their own executioners. She says, "I see my role—whether as university professor, writer, or 'barefoot anthropologist'—as that of an alarmist, reminding people of the utter abnormality of the normal and of the chronic state of emergency in which we are living."

In addition to an edited volume, *Child Survival* (1987), Dr. Scheper-Hughes is author of *Saints, Scholars, and Schizophrenics: Mental Illness in Rural Ireland* (1982), which was honored with the Margaret Mead Award; and *Death Without Weeping: The Violence of Everyday Life in Brazil* (1992), from which the following selection is excerpted.

Two Feet Under and a Cardboard Coffin:
The Social Production of Indifference to Child Death

A child died today in the favela. He was two months old. If he had lived he would have gone hungry anyway.
—Carolina Maria de Jesus[1]

The opposite of love is not hate, but indifference.
—Elie Wiesel[2]

Forebodings

"Why do the church bells ring so often?" I asked Nailza de Arruda soon after I had moved into a corner of her tiny mud-walled hut near the top of the Alto do Cruzeiro. It was the dry and blazingly hot summer of 1964, the months following the military coup, and save for the rusty, clanging bells of Nossa Senhora das Dores Church, an eerie quiet had settled over the town. Beneath the quiet, however, were chaos and panic.

"It's nothing," replied Nailza, "just another little angel gone to heaven." Nailza had sent more than her share of little angels to heaven, and sometimes at night I could hear her engaged in a muffled, yet passionate, discourse with one of them: two-year-old Joana. Joana's photograph, taken as she lay eyes opened and propped up in her tiny cardboard coffin, hung on a wall next to the photo of Nailza and Zé Antônio taken on the day the couple had eloped a few years before. Zé Antônio, uncomfortable in his one good, starched, white shirt, looked into the camera every bit as startled as the uncanny wide-eyed toddler in her white dress.

Nailza could barely remember the names of the other infants and babies who came and went in close succession. Some had died unnamed and had been hastily baptized in their coffins. Few lived more than a month or two. Only Joana, properly baptized in church at the close of her first year and placed under the protection of a powerful saint, Joan of Arc, had been expected to live. And Nailza had dangerously allowed herself to love the little girl. In addressing the dead child, Nailza's voice would range from tearful imploring to angry recrimination: "Why did you leave me? Was your patron saint so greedy that she could not allow me one child on this earth?" Zé Antônio advised me to ignore Nailza's odd behavior, which he understood as a kind of madness that, like the birth and death of children, came and went.

It was not long after that Nailza was again noticeably pregnant, and the nightly prayers to Joana ceased, momentarily replaced by the furtive noises of stolen marital intimacies. By day, Nailza's appetite and her normally high spirits returned, much to my relief. The peacefulness was, however, soon rent by the premature birth of a stillborn son. I helped Nailza dig a shallow grave in our *quintal,* the trash-littered excuse for a backyard where pigs and stray goats foraged and where we hoped to dig a pit latrine before the start of the winter rains. No bells would ring for this tiny fellow, nor would there be any procession of the angels accompanying his body to the graveyard. Still-births remained (in those days prior to hospital delivery for Alto women) outside the net of public and medical surveillance. And when curious neighbors commented the next day on Nailza's flat stomach, she tossed off their questions with a flippant "Yes, free and unburdened, thanks be to God!" Or with a sharp laugh, she would deny having been pregnant at all. Even living with Nailza in our close quarters, I had a hard time knowing what she was experiencing in the weeks and months that followed, except that Joana's photo disappeared from the wall, and her name was never again mentioned as long as I lived in that house. The stillborn son returned Nailza to her senses and to an acceptance of the reality in which she lived. Neighbors would say approvingly that Nailza had learned to *se conformar* to the unalterable conditions of her existence. But at what price I wondered, at what physical, psychic, and social cost to Nailza and other women like her and at what risk to their seemingly unbroken succession of "replacement" babies and subsequent angel-children? . . .

The Overproduction of Angels: Keeping Track, Losing Count

The child shall be registered immediately after birth and shall have the right from birth to a name.
—Article 7, United Nations Convention on the Rights of the Child[3]

Throughout Northeast Brazil, whenever one asks a poor woman how many children she has in her family, she invariably replies with the formula, "*X* children, *y* living." Sometimes she may say, "*Y* living, *z* angels." Women

themselves, unlike the local and state bureaucracies, keep close track of their reproductive issue, counting the living along with the dead, stillborn, and miscarried. Each little angel is proudly tabulated, a flower in the mother's crown of thorns, each the sign of special graces and indulgences accumulating in the afterlife. There are a great many angels to keep track of. It is just as well that so many women are doing the counting. . . .

When I returned to the state of Pernambuco in northeastern Brazil in 1982 and had begun, through various and sometimes creative means, to assess the extent of child mortality in the town of Bom Jesus, I made a visit to the first and newly appointed secretary of health for Bom Jesus. Responding to inquiries about the greatest health risks to the population of the *município,* the debonair and energetic Dr. Ricardo offered without a moment's hesitation, "Stress." And he began to outline his proposals for a stress-reduction education program that would target the substantial business and professional class of the community. Heart problems and cancer were, the secretary of health continued, the two greatest causes of death in the bustling little metropolis. When confronted with the data painstakingly culled from the civil registry office in Bom Jesus indicating that almost a half of all deaths in the *município* each year were of children under the age of five and that diarrhea, not heart disease, and hunger, not stress, were the main pathogens, Dr. Ricardo sighed and raised his eyes to the heavens: "Oh, child mortality! If we were to talk child mortality . . . an absurdity, surely. And unknowable as well."

"What do you mean?"

"When I took over this office last August, the municipal administration had no figures on child mortality, none whatsoever. I had to send for them from the state, and they were unusable: an infant mortality of 120 percent!"

"How can that be?"

"And why not? It's quite straightforward. The official figures said that of every 100 infants born in Bom Jesus, 120 of them died before they reached the age of one year! What a disaster! No wonder we are so underdeveloped in Brazil—more of us die than are even born!"

"Surely there are other ways of counting the dead," I suggested. "For example, how many charity baby coffins does the mayor's office distribute each month?"

"Oh, there's no limit there, no limit at all. We give the people as many as they want. In fact, the more they want, the better! It's one of the things we take care of very efficiently and well."

The doctor was pulling my leg, of course, but his remarks captured both the social embarrassment and the bureaucratic indifference toward child mortality as a premodern plague in a self-consciously modernizing interior town.

Later that day I stopped in again to visit Seu Moacir, the municipal "carpenter," although what he "carpenters" for the city are poor people's coffins, mostly baby coffins. Nonetheless, Moacir strongly objected to being called the municipal coffin maker or having his crowded annex to the back of the municipal chambers referred to as a coffin workshop or a *casa funerária*. And so the discreet sign over his door read, "Municipal Woodworks." But even here there was some deception at play, for the media in which Moacir worked were as much cardboard and papier-mâché as plywood and pine. His "product," he told me, cost the city between two and eight dollars apiece, depending on size.

Yes, he was quite busy, Moacir said, but he could answer a few questions. He has been the municipal carpenter since 1965, when Seu Félix decided that every citizen had the right to a decent burial. There were more than twice as many baby coffins requested as adult ones. February and March were the "busiest" months for his work. Why? Perhaps it was, he hazarded a guess, because people liked to marry in June after the *festas juninas* were over

and boys and girls on the Alto had begun to "pair up." Moacir was a man of few words, and his own curiosity in the matters I was raising was limited. But the craftsman in him readily agreed to pose for pictures, and he held up both an adult coffin and a baby one, pointing out that the style was similar for both—a cardboard top and a plywood bottom.

All adult coffins, regardless of sex, were painted a muddy brown ("Earth tone," said Moacir), and all children's coffins, males and females, to the age of seven were painted "sky blue, the favorite color of the Virgin." Moacir noted a detail: there were no fasteners on the children's coffins because parents preferred to put their angels into the ground as unencumbered as possible so that the children's spirits were free to escape their premature graves. Moacir found it difficult to estimate how many coffins "left" the workshop each week: "Some days as many as five or six will leave the shop. And then there are days when there are no requests at all." But, he added, "this doesn't affect my productivity. I just keep on working steadily so that coffins are never lacking in the *município*. I don't like to fall behind in my work; even on a holiday a comrade can find me, and I will have a coffin in stock that will serve his needs."

I asked Moacir if he would be willing to go over his requisitions for the previous few weeks, and, somewhat reluctantly, he agreed. We moved over to a cluttered desk with slips of paper in small, untidy piles. "Here," he said picking up one pile, "I'll read them out to you. But I warn you, things are a little chaotic. Here's one: baby, female, three months, June 22, 1987." And he continued, "Newborn, male, June 17, 1987. Female, about six months, June 11, 1987. Male, four months, June 17, 1987."

Then something had him stumped, and he had a hard time reading the slip of paper. As I approached him to look at it myself, he put it down abruptly: "This has nothing to do with anything. It's an order for seventeen sacks of cement! I warned you that everything was all mixed up here."

When I learned that all the requisition orders were referred back to Seu João in the town hall, I approached João himself for access to the records on all materials furnished by the *prefeitura*. Grumbling, Seu João got down the ledger books, but he warned me not to trust any of them: "If you want numbers," he suggested, "just double everything that's put down here—our inventory is incomplete." In the books that documented in neat columns the "movement" of all supplies in and out of the *prefeitura,* the data on baby coffins were there, interspersed with data on Brillo pads, light bulbs, chlorine bleach, kerosene, toilet paper, cement, alcohol, and soap. In a six-month period in 1988 the *prefeitura* had distributed 131 free infant and child coffins. . . .

Our Lady of Sorrows:
A Political Economy of the Emotions

They do not grieve the way we do.
—General William Westmoreland,
Vietnam

(1) Sir, their light hearts turned to stone.
It is not remembered whether in gardens
stone lanterns illumined peasant ways.
(2) Perhaps they gathered once to delight in blossom,
but after the children were killed
there were no more buds.
(3) Sir, laughter is bitter to the burned mouth.
—Denise Levertov [4]

WHAT FINALLY CAN be said of these Alto women? How do they make sense of their lives and of their babies' foreshortened lives? What, after all, does mother love look like in this inhospitable context? Are grief, remorse, and anger present, although deeply repressed? If so, where shall we look for them? Or if we take Alto women at their word, are these feelings absent? And if so, what does this tell us about the nature of emotions and affects? Moreover, how are the mothers able to do what they feel they must do? What is the human cost to those who are forced into moral dilemmas and into choices that no woman should have to make? What are the moral visions that guide their actions? How do they protect themselves from being overwhelmed at times (as we might) by ambivalence and doubt?

I have been chastised for presenting an "unflattering" portrait of poor women, women who are themselves the victims of severe social and institutional neglect. True, I have described these women as allowing, even helping, some of their children to die. But I do not see these practices as unnatural, inhuman, or unwomanly but rather as reasonable responses to unreasonable constraints and contingencies. . . .

The Muted Moral Voices of Women

Don't pity the infants who died here on the Alto do
Cruzeiro. Don't waste your tears on them. Pity us
instead. Weep for their mothers who are con-
demned to live.

—Black Irene, *Moradora*, Alto do Cruzeiro

On the Alto do Cruzeiro the survival of any one child is generally subordinated to the well-being of the entire domestic group, especially to that household core made up of adult women and their older, and therefore more dependable, children. In a world of great uncertainty about life and death it makes no sense at all to put any *one* person—not a parent, not a husband or lover, and certainly not a sickly toddler or fragile infant—at the center of anything.

In the desperate context of shantytown life mothers do sometimes favor the survival of older and healthier children, and sometimes of their own selves, over that of younger and weaker family members. One does encounter often enough the unsettling image of relatively well-fed adults and older children side by side with famished toddlers and marasmic infants. Such were the cases in the household of Terezinha, Manoel, and Edilson and in the household of Dalina, Prazeres, and Gil-Anderson. Gil was the one-year-old skeletal toddler I encountered on the Rua dos Magos whose stocky seventeen-year-old mother, Prazeres, had been feeding him various patent medicines (including sedatives) while simultaneously, and largely unconsciously, denying him food.

When Prazeres refused to have Gil hospitalized in Recife, where I was sure he could be saved, I resorted to bringing fresh milk, mashed vegetables, and a hearty meat broth for the famished little boy every other day. But I discovered that the food that I brought for the little boy was being distributed among the bigger and healthier household members, including Gil's great-grandmother, Dalina, my oldest *comadre* on the Alto do Cruzeiro.

Meanwhile, the antibiotic skin cream that my field assistant, Cecilia de Mello, brought to heal the badly infected diaper rash of Gil's newborn infant cousin, the youngest member of the household, was being passed around among the teenage women of the household to use for their skin "blemishes." But Cecilia's and my immediate and self-righteous indignation passed as we had to confront the inappropriateness of our "humanitarian" gestures. Our too frequent visits and, if I may be excused, our "half-assed" interventions on behalf of this altogether miserable and threatened household only provoked jealousy and conflict.

"Why were you *wasting* so much money on Gil?" old Dalina asked, when there were older children and working adults who were also sick and "hungry." Gil's mother, Prazeres, had a painful toothache, and the side of her face was dangerously swollen. Her aunt had a stomachache resulting from some spoiled fish she had eaten the night before. She was doubled over with pain and could not therefore get the laundry back to her *patroa* on time, which might cost her the coming week's market money. A twelve-year-old nephew lay on the tattered straw mattress in the front room, his face turned to the wall hiding his unmanly tears; his stubbed toe was badly infected, and the pain (when I thought to inquire) was, the boy admitted, "unbearable." Dalina's youngest son, a twenty-four-year-old alcoholic, had begun to show signs of madness. Was he now sniffing glue as well? He was sleeping on the floor in the back room. "Be careful you don't trip over him," warned Dalina, as I went out back to use the latrine. "He's *brabo*." Old Dalina's legs were edemic, but she still went out twice a day to the public *chafariz* to collect a dozen large cans of water, which she would resell at a few cents a can to the neighbors along her hillside path. Dalina must have been ancient; she was already an "old woman" in the 1960s when she carried water to my little Alto house. Dalina complained of a nervous attack that had left her shaky and unable to balance the heavy cans of water on her head. She said she had fallen down on the descent from the *chafariz* earlier that day, and now her bones were sore. When I walked shamefacedly across the tiny room to comfort her, she began to cry, "You used to be a mother to me. When I was hungry, you brought me good things to eat. When I was sick you took me to the hospital. Don't you care about me anymore?"

The fact is that life on the Alto do Cruzeiro resembles nothing so much as a battlefield or an emergency room in a crowded inner-city hospital. Consequently, moral thinking is not guided by the blind justice and commitment to abstract universal principles that Lawrence Kohlberg[5] equated with highly developed ethical reasoning and that Carol Gilligan[6] later attacked for its unconscious male bias. The moral thinking of women of the Alto conforms in a very general sort of way to Gilligan's notion of a womanly nurturance that is fundamentally relativist, concrete, and context specific. But the premises on which the womanly ethic of "care" and "responsibility" are based on the rocky hillside of the Alto do Cruzeiro are quite different from those described by Gilligan.

In the shantytown, day-to-day moral thinking is guided by a "lifeboat ethics."[7] The central ethical dilemma of the lifeboat concerns the decisions as to who among the shipwrecked is to be saved when it would spell certain disaster to try saving all. Infants and toddlers first? Women and children? The young and the strong? The hardworking? The brave and the beautiful? The wise old men? The sick and the vulnerable? In emergency situations the morality of triage—the rudimentary pragmatics of saving the salvageable—often supersedes other, more aesthetic or more egalitarian ethical principles. In the specific instance just cited, Gil-Anderson was not viewed as salvageable. He could not walk, he did not speak, and he was, as everyone in the family agreed, an unattractive child. His aunt noted with pity

that he looked like the movie character E. T. (the extraterrestrial), which she had seen on a poster displayed in downtown Bom Jesus. And he did, poor little hungry fellow.

It is unfair to ask these women to defend their moral thinking under what can only be described as cruel and unusual circumstances. Do we ask the survivors of prison and refugee camps or released prisoners of war to describe the moral visions and moral reasoning that obtain in those inhuman contexts? It would be unseemly to do so. Moreover, what of the "moral voices" and visions of Alto men, who are decidedly absent here? The burden of child survival and the responsibility for governing the moral economy and distributive justice within the Alto household fall unfairly on the shoulders of Alto women, those who are single and those who are not. Perhaps the most exploitative relationship of all is that which demands of poor women not only that they give birth again and again and again, as these women do, but that they must display "appropriate" maternal sentiments. . . .

Angel-Babies: The *Velório de Anjinhos*

If he died at this angelic age, the small child became an object of adoration. The mother rejoiced over the death of the angel . . . weeping with delight because the Lord had carried away her fifth child.

—Gilberto Freyre[8]

From colonial Brazil to the present the death of an infant or a very young child was treated as a blessing among the popular classes, an event "to be accepted almost joyfully, at any rate without horror."[9] The dead baby was an *anjinho*, a "little cherub," or an *innocente*, a "blameless creature" who died unregretted because his or her future happiness was assured. The bodies of the little angels were washed, their curls were prettily arranged, and they were dressed in sky blue or white shirts, with the cord of the Virgin tied around their waists. Their little hands folded in prayerful repose, their eyes left open and expectantly awaiting the Beatific Vision, angel-babies were covered with wild flowers, including floral wreaths on their heads. Little petition prayers and messages to the saints were tucked into their hands to be delivered to the Virgin on arrival. Even the poorest were arranged on wooden planks laden with flowers or in large, decorated cardboard boxes "of the kind used for men's shirts."[10] The *velório de anjinho* was immortalized in Euclides da Cunha's classic, *Rebellion in the Backlands*: "The death of a child is a holiday. In the hut the poor parents' guitars twang joyfully amid the tears; the noisy, passionate samba is danced again and the quatrains of the poetic challengers loudly resound; while at one side, between two tallow candles, wreathed in flowers, the dead infant is laid out, reflecting in its last smile, fixed in death, the supreme contentment of one who is going back to heaven and eternal bliss."[11]

The festive celebration of angel wakes, derived from the Iberian Peninsula, has been noted throughout Latin America from the Andes of Peru to the pampas of Argentina to the tropical coastal regions of Brazil and Colombia.[12] It is found among Amerindians, blacks, whites, and *criollos* and among the wealthy as well as the poor. Roger Bastide attributed the angel wake customs to the introduction of the "baroque" in Brazil,[13] whereas Freyre suggested that the Jesuits introduced *anjinho* beliefs to console native women for the alarming death rate of Indian children resulting from colonization.[14]

All-night drinking, feasting, party games, courting rituals, special musical performances, and dances cross many culture areas in South America, where the infant wake may last for three or four consecutive days.[15] Weeping is proscribed at the infant wake because a mother's tears make the angel-baby's path slippery and dampen its delicate wings.[16] Rather, the mother is expected to express her joy, as

did the plantation mistress from Rio de Janeiro who exclaimed, "Oh, how happy I am! Oh, how happy I am! When I die and go to the gates of Heaven I shall not fail of admittance, for there will be five little children pressing toward me, pulling at my skirts, and saying, 'Oh, mother, do come in, do come in.'"[17] In rural Venezuela, the mother of the dead baby generally opens the dancing at her child's wake so that her angel may rise happily to the kingdom of heaven.[18]

The body of the dead infant was fetishized during traditional angel wakes in rural Latin America. The little corpse was sometimes taken out of the tiny coffin and handled like a doll or live baby. The corpse could be displayed like a saint, propped up on a home altar in between candlesticks and vases of sweet-smelling flowers. Or the dead child might be seated in a little chair, elevated on a small platform, set up inside an open box, tied to a ladder placed on top of the casket (to suggest the angel's ascent into heaven), or even tied to a swing suspended on ropes from the house beam. The infant's flight on the swing was said to symbolize the baby's transformation into an angel. The custom of leasing out angel-corpses to enliven local fiestas was described for the late nineteenth through the twentieth centuries in the Argentine pampas as well as in Venezuela, Chile, and Ecuador.[19] In all, the traditional infant wake was a grand pretext for "unbridled merry-making," perhaps (some suggested) as a culturally institutionalized "defense" against grief and mourning in a context in which infant death was all too common.

But what of a situation where neither festive joy nor deep grief is present? My own startlingly different ethnographic observations of angel-babies and the *velório de anjinho* in Bom Jesus today lead me to another set of conclusions, which I must touch on as a prelude to my final discussion of mother love, attachment, grief, and moral thinking. In Bom Jesus today, where an angel-baby is sent to heaven on the average of one every other day, infant wakes are brief, rarely lasting more than a couple hours, and dispensed with a minimum of ceremony. The *velório* of an infant younger than one is at best perfunctory. There are no musical accompaniments, no songs, no prayers, no ritual performances of any kind. Neither food nor drink is offered the casual visitor, most of them curious neighborhood children. Household life simply goes on as usual around the infant in her or his little casket, which may be placed on the kitchen table or across one or two straight-backed kitchen chairs. The infant's grandmother or god-mother is in charge, in addition to the older woman who specializes in preparing the body for burial. There is neither great joy nor grief expressed, and the infant is rarely the focus of conversation.

I recall one particularly poignant infant wake that took place in an Alto household in 1987 on the day following the celebration of the one-year-old birthday party and formal christening of another child of the household. Mariana, the middle-aged mother of the one-year-old *caçula*, had purchased christening clothes, a large decorative birthday cake with candles, soft drinks, a wine punch for the adults, balloons, and party favors. The frosted cake was the centerpiece, and Mariana was quite protective of it, frequently brushing away flies that gathered near it and more than once dusting away a persistent procession of little ants. A borrowed record player was turned up loud; samba and lambada music blasted into the main street of the Alto, and the dancing spilled outside of the tiny house. The fiesta lasted for the better part of that Sunday afternoon and early evening. The little birthday girl in her ruffled dress was the center of a great deal of praise and attention. Meanwhile, Mariana's oldest, sixteen-year-old daughter, herself the single mother of a four-month-old infant, sat out the festivities very much on the margins. Her boyfriend was nowhere in evidence. To engage and entertain the girl a bit, I asked if

I might take a peek at her baby. She brought me into the back room where her infant, in an advanced stage of marasmic malnutrition, had been left to sleep through the party. She slept very deeply, indeed, for the next morning I was called back for her brief, understated wake and burial.

The young mother sat in the front room repairing a fishing net. The grandmother's only comment was the usual *moradora* words of consolation: "Man makes; God takes." The "snowball baby" in her white tunic, decoratively strewn with sweet forget-me-nots, took the place of the birthday cake as the center-piece on the table in the front room. A few crumbs of cake and frosting left over from the day before were still on the table, and a couple of deflated pink balloons lolled about on the mud floor. The crepe paper decorations were still in place. The previous day's little birthday girl seemed confused by the muted and ambivalent sentiments so soon after her own animated party, and she was fussy and demanding, insisting to be lifted up to see her infant niece. Finally, Mariana carried the child over to the table and let her peek inside the little casket. "Baby, baby," said the toddler. "Yes," repeated her tired mother, "baby is sleeping," and as Mariana leaned over to adjust the infant in her little cardboard pauper's coffin, I saw her hand once again, almost instinctively, brush away a line of ants, but this time from the infant's frosted, white face.

Men are rarely present at a *velório de anjinho*. Female relatives, neighbor women, and children often mill about. Meanwhile, however, the women and young girls of the household often go about their regular house-work. They wash clothes at the back of the house, sort beans in preparation for the main meal, and do piecework for the local hammock industry, while the children do homework, play checkers, cut out paper dolls, or read comic books on the floor.

The procession of the angels to the cemetery is formed on the spur of the moment from the children who happen to be present. No special clothes are worn. There may or may not be a small floral wreath carried in front of the rag-tag little parade. Some adults, but never the infant's own mother, may follow the procession to the graveyard. On one occasion the father, godfather, and paternal grandfather attended the funeral of a firstborn child, and all were deeply and visibly affected. On another occasion the godfather (and uncle to the dead child) followed the children's procession at some distance while walking his bicycle. Although he came as far as the graveyard, before the baby was put into the grave, the godfather left to attend a previously scheduled soccer game.

The procession of the angels takes the main, and only paved, street of the Alto, but once at the foot of the hill it veers away from the main *praça* of town and bypasses the church of Nossa Senhora das Dores. The procession does not stop (as it once did) for the priest's blessing; consequently, the bells of Our Lady of Sorrows no longer toll for the death of each child of Bom Jesus da Mata. That way of counting the dead has gone the way of many other folk Catholic pieties, swept away by the reformist spirit of the Vatican Council and by the socialist philosophy of the new regime of liberation theology. And no priest accompanies the procession to the cemetery, where the body is disposed of casually and unceremoniously. Children bury children in Bom Jesus da Mata today. Where once clergymen and religious sisters taught patience and resignation to child death and other domestic tragedies, which were said to reveal the imponderable workings of God's will, the new church participates in the public indifference and social embarrassment toward infant death, which exists only as a bloody breech, a rupture with, and a glaring contradiction to the hierarchy's prolife and pronatalist teachings. So instead of the church *praça* in the dead center of Bom Jesus, the procession of the angels discreetly passes through the back streets of town, under the trestles of the railroad or across the tracks, through the

open-air yam market, past the rural sugar workers syndicate building, just under the barred windows of the municipal jail, close to the edge of the new reform school for abandoned street children run by the FEBEM, and up the muddy trail to the municipal cemetery at the farthest edge of town. The children know the route by heart; most have been part of other processions to bury dead siblings or playmates' siblings. The procession shares the street with cars, trucks, donkeys, wagons, and carts. Most cars and trucks hurriedly whiz by, and the children have to run to the side of the road with their little charge.

At the cemetery Seu Valdimar, the disabled and often ill-tempered municipal gravedigger, and an assistant lead the children to the common space where pauper children are buried. The temporary space is normally already waiting, and in a few minutes the coffin is placed in the grave and covered over, thereby leaving a small, fresh mound to mark the space. No prayers are recited, and no sign of the cross is made as the coffin goes into its shallow grave. Valdimar often chides the children for one reason or another. It may be that the coffin is larger than expected, and he will have to enlarge the grave. Or he may scold the children for not tacking closed the top of the coffin, although he surely knows well the customs of the region. "Didn't you have any nails, any tacks?" he asked the brother of one deceased child. "Soon the bugs will get to your little sister," he said unnecessarily. Other times Valdimar can be gentle with the children, in his own gruff way.

"Have you any flowers?" Valdimar once asked the older sister of a little toddler who had just been buried. "No," she shook her head sadly. "Well, hurry up and get some, then. . . . I haven't all day." Permission granted, the children scampered off in opposite directions to pull up flowers from other fresh graves. "Not *that* many; be careful," yelled Valdimar. And the children returned to scatter the picked flowers on top of the little one's grave. That is normally the extent of the ceremony, except the washing off of muddy hands and feet in the public spigot on the way out.

If an adult is present, the children in the procession have the right to expect a treat on the way home. *"Picolé* [ices] *Picolé!"* the cry may go up, and the responsible adult will be pulled toward a little storefront shack. I have seen a grandfather gather the children into a small shop and carefully count out his few, wrinkled cruzados and negotiate quietly with the shopkeeper so that every child in the procession could have two pieces of hard candy. He himself carefully distributed the sweets, two by two to each child, a sad, gentle smile on his face.

I have tried to imagine, working slowly, intuitively, and unobtrusively with the people of the Alto and with women and children in particular, what meaning the angel-baby and the *velório de anjinho* has for them. At times it seems as if the dead infant were a "transitional object" for the women of the Alto, not only in the ritual, anthropological sense of a liminal being in between social statuses ("Neither here nor there," as one mother said of her dying infant) but in the psychoanalytic sense of a liminal, transitional "attachment" (as to a teddy bear or a "rubby" blanket), which, created out of the imagination, has a self-soothing quality.[20] *Anjinhos* allow Alto mothers to "let go" of so many of their young children by allowing them to "hold on" to an idealized image of spirit-children populating the heavens, as close, really, as the stars can seem on a still night. All transitional objects ultimately foster autonomy and independence through the breaking or the breaking out of "impossible" attachments (as in infancy the "rubby blanket" or teddy bear substitutes for the "impossible" desire to have mother's breast available at will). Just so, for Alto women, *anjinhos* in heaven substitute for the impossible attachment to half-live babies in the hammock.

The shaping of the emotions and responses at child death is formed in early childhood as Alto children, mere babies themselves, are schooled in the normalization of child death as they are sooner or later delegated the role of their dead siblings' and playmates' pallbearers and undertakers. The average Alto girl between the ages of five and thirteen participates in two or more angel processions each year. The average boy participates in at least one a year. One notes, in the reactions and fantasy play of Alto children, the awesome power of these early "primal scenes" in shaping, routinizing, and muting later adult responses to child death.

Many little girls on the Alto do Cruzeiro have no baby dolls to play with. Nor do they tend to fashion them out of available scrap materials, such as torn socks or the corn husks discarded on the main streets after *feira* in the harvest months of June and July. Nor do they fashion dolls and play furniture from the red clay that is commonly found not far from the banks of the local river. Alto girls prefer active games, circle dances, and pretend "talent shows" in which they can imitate the beautiful and seductive children's television star, Xuxa. Girls covet the cheap, plastic soccer balls that any of their older brothers are lucky enough to own. Playing with dolls and playing house are of little interest to Alto girls. I soon learned to bring costume jewelry, hair ribbons, play cosmetics, and small, battery-run video games as gifts for Alto girls and to leave at home the pretty little baby dolls, which elicited so little interest or curiosity. In a half dozen of the more prosperous Alto homes where the children have an abundance of toys, girls are given dolls as presents, but these are treated as display, rather than play, objects and are often kept in the original cellophane-covered boxes standing up on a shelf and are taken down for visitors to admire and are then carefully replaced.

I am tempted to suggest why Alto children are so uninterested in a form of play that is so common among little girls the world over. This lack of interest is born, perhaps, of an early and negative association between lifeless dolls in pretty cardboard boxes and lifeless siblings in decorated cardboard coffins. This possibility was brought home to me during a conversation with Xiquinha, the elderly praying woman of the Alto, who had been washing and dressing dead children for their angel wakes since she was seven and a half. In the following conversation, Xiquinha explained how she became a specialist in angel wakes at so tender an age.

"Whenever a baby died on the Rua dos Sapos, where I had been raised since I was a tiny child, a neighbor would call for me because I always enjoyed dressing the baby for its wake. The other little girls would run away; some didn't even like being in the procession of the angels. But not me; I adored it all. I would take the baby on my lap across my knees, and it was *just like a little doll for me to play with.* Little angel-bodies are different from [dead] big bodies. Angel-bodies stay soft and flexible, so you can handle them easily. I would wash it and put on its blue or white clothes and a veil for the little girls and, if their mother had one, a blue ribbon around their waist. All little angel-girls are dressed like little brides. White is the color of virgins, which all of them are. When an infant is stillborn, people call it an angel-*carobim* [i.e., possibly derived from cherubim] because it is untouched by this world. Blue is the color that the Virgin Mary loves best. So you want to have the little angels dressed that way when they arrive to greet the Virgin at the gates of heaven."

When my Brazilian informants tell me that they do not weep, that they are pleased to have a little *coração santa* in heaven looking after them, I am inclined to believe them and to take them at face value. In most cases the socialization experience has been adequate. Angel-baby beliefs not only "console" *moradores,* they shape and determine the way that death is experienced.

Once as my then-fifteen-year-old daughter, Jennifer, and I were on our way up the Alto to an angel wake near the very top of the hill, Jennifer burst into angry tears. She was to have been the "official" photographer at the wake because the mother of the baby was unable to pay for a professional photographer from the town. I had quite insensitively offered Jennifer's services without asking her permission. "I don't want to photograph a dead baby," she yelled at me, quite reasonably. I apologized and brought her inside Terezinha's house along the way to compose herself. Terezinha and her teenage daughter Rosália were quite concerned. Why was Jennifer so upset? Did she have "boyfriend troubles"? Rosália wanted to know. When I explained that she was upset about having to attend an infant wake, they stared at her unbelievingly. "Why?" they asked. "It's only a baby!"

On only one occasion out of the dozens of angel wakes and burials that I have witnessed over the years did a child express a subdued, yet nonetheless ravaged, grief. It was just as little Mercea's body was going into the dirt that her seven-year-old cousin, Leonardo, turned to me to say in an anxious aside: "Nancí, I don't want any more of mine to die." Ashamed, I put aside my camera and my dog-eared, rain-soaked notebook and allowed myself, too, to sit down on a low marble stone and rediscover and feel pain and grief for a moment: "I don't either, Leonardo. I don't either."

Grief Work: A Political Economy of the Emotions

Sorrow concealed, like an oven stopp'd,
Doth burn the heart to cinders where it is.
—William Shakespeare, *Titus Andronicus*

And so when an infant dies on the Alto do Cruzeiro, few tears are shed, and women are likely to say that the death came as a blessing or a great relief. "I feel free" or "I feel unburdened" is what many say. This is not to suggest, however, that the women are "cold" and unfeeling, for very often the mother expresses pity (*pena*) for the dead child, saying, "*Faz pena* [what a shame], *menina,* to see them suffer and die." But pity is distinctly different from the sentiments of grief (*desgosto, nojo, luto*), sadness (*tristeza*), depression (*depressão, deprimida*), or bittersweet longing or yearning for a lost or dead loved one (*saudade*). And just as there is no immediate display of grief or mourning in many Alto mothers, I have found no evidence of "delayed" or "displaced" grief in the days, weeks, and months following the death of an infant, unless, perhaps, a new pregnancy can be seen as a symptom of displaced grief.

I made a point of visiting the homes of women who had recently lost an infant, both to offer support and observe their responses to death. What I found did not conform to the conventional biomedical wisdom concerning "normal" grieving following child death, a model of "human" behavior that is, in part, the creation of a few influential psychologists, among them John Bowlby, Elisabeth Kübler-Ross, and Robert Jay Lifton.[21]

Several days following the death and burial of her first baby, a three-month-old daughter named Daniella, I visited the young mother, Anita, to see how she was getting along. She had been calm, composed, and dry-eyed during the wake and had gone back to work on the next day.

"Are you *triste* [sad]?" I asked.

"No, ma'am, not much; Mario says I'll soon have another."

"Did you cry?"

"Oh, no! It's not good to cry, for it will keep the baby from rising up to heaven."

"Did you sleep all right?"

"Oh, yes, I was very tired yesterday."

"Did you eat well?"

"No, I didn't," she said sadly. But then the resilient girl added, "There was nothing in the house to eat but *fubá* [cornmeal], and I *hate* fubá!" Then Anita went outside, humming along with a popular tune on the radio, to wash clothes. I stayed behind to chat with a few of her neighbors, who confirmed that one does not really miss a very young baby.

Sometimes, it is more obvious why grief at the death of an innocent "angel" is not forthcoming. When Dona Amor received word that her first and only grandson was born puny and weak to her adopted and mentally disabled teenage daughter, who had been seduced and raped by a pimp, the old woman hurriedly lit a candle to São Antônio, her patron saint. She begged the saint to carry off the day-old infant, born, she said, of a "race of beasts." Amor's prayers were answered later that same day. Laughing and clapping her hands, Amor told how she went to the local *casa funerária* to pick out the little coffin. She carried it to the hospital, where she washed and dressed the infant in his baptismal/burial clothes. Then jauntily, as if "it were a basket of fruit," Amor put the little casket on her head and started off across town to the municipal cemetery. When street children laughed to see Dona Amor balancing the little coffin on her head in a solitary procession, the old woman shooed them off, saying, "There is no shame in burying the dead." There was certainly no sorrow either.

Against these altogether normative responses to infant death on the Alto do Cruzeiro are the modern psychiatric theories of "healthy" versus "disordered" mourning, which constitute a hegemonic theory of the emotions. The psychologists and psychiatrists of mourning consider child death, and infant death in particular, to be among the most wrenching of all experiences of loss, especially for the mother who may not yet feel herself to be separate from the newborn.[22] "Infant death is," Marshall Klaus remarked, "a kind of death to the self not dissimilar to the loss of a limb."[23] Bowlby described the phases of *normal* mourning after the death of a young child as follows: numbing and shock, disbelief, anger, depression, disorganization, and reorganization.[24]

Every major hospital today has clinical social workers and nurses who specialize in helping women (and men) to grieve the premature death of an infant. They distribute helpful booklets, such as "Newborn Death," to the bereaved parents.[25] The advice offered is succinct and *very* direct. It counsels the parents to "see, hold, touch, and name your [dead] newborn" and stresses the importance of the mother's presence at a graveside service and burial.[26] Weeping over the death is cast as a human right and a necessity: "We have finally come to realize that crying is a strength. . . . Remember, you have a right to cry when your baby dies. Allowing your tears to come, while talking to others, can help you move through your grief."[27] But the booklet cautions against taking to heart the "insensitive" comments of relatives and friends who may not know the "right" things to say. Those around may offer just the kind of advice and comfort that "you *don't* need": "Every parent will hear some well-meaning person say that you can have another baby. You'll get the 'don't cry' messages, and 'just forget about it' statements. Some people will act as if your baby never existed. Others will act as if you can be a *little* sad, but not as much as if your baby were older. It's as if they think the amount of sadness is somehow connected to the size of the dead person."[28]

If the inherent psychological conflicts produced by the loss of an infant or a very young child are not resolved, various pathologies are believed likely to occur, of which chronic mourning (similar to Freud's notion of melancholia) or its opposite, a "prolonged absence of conscious grieving,"[29] is common. The absence of grief or the "inability to mourn" was first identified by Helene Deutsch in her clinical practice with women, some of whom were evidently rather "merry" widows.[30] The "denial" of an "appropriate" grief may last, Bowlby wrote, for years, decades, and even in some cases "for the rest of a person's life."[31] The "disordered mourner" may feel relief and may be quite cheerful and seem well adjusted. Some may even report feelings of relief and euphoria following the death of a loved one. But such feelings are disallowed and pathologized. Lifton was direct: "To be unable to

mourn is to be unable to enter into the great human cycle of death and rebirth; it is to be unable to 'live again.'"[32] Those who cannot grieve are scarcely human. This is a weighty moralism, indeed.

It strikes me as no coincidence that so much of the psychological literature on disordered mourning concerns *female* patients who appear to be at a "high risk" of producing, according to the canons of psychotherapy, the wrong emotions in response to death, either too much or too little sadness. In the grief and mourning literature, as in the attachment and bonding literature, we are faced with a biomedical prescription concerning the womanly duty not only to marry and procreate but to *love* offspring and mourn the family's dead. Emotion work is frequently gendered work. And we may want to consider whether the psychological theories on maternal love, attachment, grief, and mourning are not a "rhetoric of control" and a discourse on power "by other means."[33]

Catherine Lutz recently pointed out in this regard that conventional biomedical theories of emotion represent an American "ethnopsychology" based on Western notions of mind and body, feeling and reason, nature and culture, self and other, male and female, and individual and society.[34] Psychotherapy is concerned with fostering emotional expression; with "speaking truth" to the deeply repressed, hidden spaces of individual emotional life; and with overcoming the "cultural" constraints that produce distortions and defenses against knowing what one is *really* thinking and feeling.[35] There is a presumed binary split between public sentiments and private feelings, between what is cultural and what is "natural." Culture emerges as an artificial facade concealing the dangerous intensity of hidden or unconscious human passions and desires. What is "real" and "authentic" is just what is most concealed from view.

Along this same binary divide, women and the female are associated with nature, body, and feeling, just as men and the male are associated with culture, mind, and reason. It is expected that women will be more emotionally responsive than men; consequently, society relegates more emotion work, including love work and grief work, to them. In the extensive psychological literature on grief and bereavement,[36] it is assumed that the sexes differ in emotionality. Men are said to cry less than women following the death of a family member and are less often depressed. Often they do not appear to be deeply moved or touched by death. But this is treated as appropriate gender behavior. There is no respected body of psychological research on the "inability of men to cry" comparable to the research on the "inability of mothers to love." And the clinical portraits of "failure to grieve" are almost exclusively concerned with the absence of "appropriate" emotionality in women following the death of a spouse or a child.

Bereavement customs worldwide commonly assign women to prolonged and ritualized grieving, both during the funeral services and long after they are over.[37] It is widows who commonly cut their hair, cover themselves with ashes, mutilate their bodies, or shroud themselves in black for the remainder of their lives, while widowers walk freely, indistinguishable from "ordinary" men. This cross-cultural "specialization" of women in the division of emotional labor may be related to the generally lower status of women in the societies observed. Just as women may be coerced into feeding males before they themselves eat or into carrying the heaviest loads, they may be coerced into assuming the emotional burden for grief work. Just as plebeians were expected to weep openly on the death of their king, women are expected to show proper "deference" by weeping publicly for the death of kin.

Alternatively, the expectation that women will grieve for the dead may be an extension of the division of labor found in many traditional rural and peasant societies that delegates to older women specialists the task of washing and dressing the bodies of the dead, as they do, for example, in the two ethnographic instances that I know best: western Ireland and rural Northeast Brazil. In "Ballybran," Ireland, the old women who dress the dead are also expected to recite long and sorrowful ritualized laments; on the Alto do Cruzeiro the old women who dress the dead are expected to recite special mortuary prayers, but they do so only for dead adults. "Why pray for angel-babies who have no need of our prayers?" asked Xiquinha. "It's *their* job to pray for us!" Given the often "coerced" nature of pregnancy on the Alto do Cruzeiro . . . —it is also possible that the refusal to grieve for the death of their infants is at times a gesture of defiance. It could be a way of saying, "You can make me pregnant, but you cannot make me love all of them . . . or *keep* all of them either."

Death Without Weeping

And so I maintain that Alto women generally face child death stoically, even with a kind of *belle indifférence* that is a culturally appropriate response. No one on the Alto do Cruzeiro criticizes a mother for not grieving for the death of a baby. No psychiatrist, pediatrician, or social worker visits the mother at home or tells her in the clinic what she is "supposed" to be feeling at a particular "phase" in her mourning. She is not told that crying is a healthy (and womanly) response to child death or that it is "natural" to feel bitter and resentful (which reduces anger to a manageable medical "symptom") or that she must "confront" her loss and get over her unhealthy emotional "numbness."

Poor Brazilians "work" on the self and emotions in a very different fashion. Instead of the mandate to mourn, the Alto mother is coached by those around her, men as well as women, in the art of resignation (*conformação*) and "holy indifference" to the vagaries of one's fate on earth and a hopefulness of a better life beyond. In this cultural milieu a deficit of emotion is not viewed as unhealthy or problematic (as in the overly repressed Anglo-Saxon culture of the United States);

rather, an excess is. To experience strong emotions and passions—of love and lust, envy and anger, ecstasy and joy, grief and longing—is for most Brazilians, rich as well as poor, urban as well as rural, the most "natural" and expected occurrence. It is what being human is all about. But if allowed to run riot, these emotions are understood as the harbingers of much misery and suffering. Excessive emotions can bring down large and powerful households as well as small and humble ones. They can ruin lives and livelihoods. They can destroy relationships. They can cause physical as well as mental sickness. The Brazilian folk ethnopsychology of emotion is based on a very different construction of the body, self, personhood, and society. One can, for example, contrast the once popular belief in American society that cancers were caused by the repressions of the inner self, by passion turned inward and feeding on itself,[38] with the popular belief in Brazilian culture that emotional outbursts can dissipate the individual, poison the blood, and cause tuberculosis or cancer.

The strong mandate *not* to express grief at the death of a baby, and most especially not to shed tears at the wake, is strongly reinforced by a *Nordestino* folk piety, a belief that for the brief hours that the infant is in the coffin, she is neither human child nor blessed little angel. She is something other: a spirit-child struggling to leave this world and find its way into the next. It must climb. The path is dark. A mother's tears can impede the way, make the road slippery so that the spirit-child will lose her footing, or the tears will fall on her wings and dampen them so that she cannot fly. Dona Amor told of a "silly" neighbor who was weeping freely for the death of her toddler when she was interrupted by the voice of her child calling to her from his coffin: "Mama, don't cry for me because my *mortália* is very heavy and wet with your tears." "You see," Amor said, "the child had to struggle even after death, and his mother was making it worse for him. The little one wasn't an angel yet because angels never speak. They are mute.

But he was no longer a human child either. He was an *alma penanda* [wretched, wandering soul]."

"What is the fate of such a child?"

"Sometimes they are trapped in their graves. Sometimes when you pass by the cemetery, you can see little bubbles and foam pushing up from the ground where such infants are buried. And late at night you can even hear the sound of the lost souls of the child-spirits wailing."

In all, what is being created is an environment that teaches women to contain their affections and hold back their grief during the precarious first year of the child's life. The question remains, however, whether these cultural "conventions" actually succeed in producing the desired effects or whether the dry-eyed stoicism and nonchalant air of Alto mothers are merely "superficial" and skin-deep, covering up a "depth of sorrow," loss, and longing. Nations and Rebhun, for example, maintained that the lack of grief is mere facade: "The inner experience of grief may be hidden by the flat affect of impoverished Brazilians. This behavior is part of a culturally mandated norm of mourning behavior; rather than signify the *absence* of strong emotion at child and infant death, it reveals the *presence* of grief."[39]

What they wish to suggest, drawing inspiration from the writings of Robert J. Lifton and other psychologists of mourning, is that the "blankness" and "flat affect" that they observed in certain poor women of Northeastern Brazil "is the blankness of the shell-shocked."[40] They continued, "The loss is too great to bear, too great to speak of, too great to experience fully. . . . Their seeming indifference is a mask, a wall against the unbearable. . . . While flamboyantly open about such emotions as happiness and sexual jealousy, they adopt a generally flat affect when discussing painful topics."[41]

Although I have no doubt (and have gone to great lengths to show) that the local culture is organized to defend women against the psychological ravagings of grief, I assume that the culture is quite successful in doing so and that we may take the women at their word when they say, "No, I felt no grief. The baby's death was a blessing." One need not speak of "masks" or "disguises" or engage in second-guessing on the basis of alien and imported psychological concepts of the self. Nations and Rebhun assumed a "divided self" that conforms to our Western ethnopsychiatry: a split between a public and a private self and between a "true" and a "false" self-expression. Moreover, when they suggested that the "mothers' flat affect in response to infant deaths is due more to folk Catholic beliefs than to a lack of emotional attachment to infants,"[42] they projected a very secular view of religious belief as a superficial feature of the interior life, rather than as a powerful force that penetrates and constitutes the person.

Until recently, most cultural and symbolic anthropologists tended to restrict their interest in emotions to occasions when they were contained within formal, public, collective, highly stylized, and "distanced" rites and rituals, such as in healing, spirit possession, initiation, and other life cycle events. They left the discussion of the more private, idiosyncratic feelings of individual, suffering subjects to psychoanalytic and biomedical anthropologists, who generally reduced them to a discourse on universal drives and instincts.[43] This division of labor, based on a false dichotomy between collective, "cultural" sentiments and individual, "natural" passions, leads to a stratigraphic model of human nature in which biology emerges as the base and culture as the mere veneer or patina, as the series of carnival masks and disguises alluded to previously.

But the view taken here is that emotions do not precede or stand outside of culture; they are part of culture and of strategic importance to our understanding of the ways in which people shape and are shaped by their world. Emotions are not reified things in and of themselves, subject to an internal, hydraulic mechanism regulating their buildup, control, and release. Catherine Lutz and Lila Abu-Lughod,

among others, understand emotions as "historical inventions" and as "rhetorical strategies" used by individuals to express themselves, to make claims on others, to promote or elicit certain kinds of behaviors, and so on.[44] In other words, emotions are discourse; they are constructed and produced in language and in human interaction. They cannot be understood outside of the cultures that produce them. The most radical statement of this position is that without our cultures, we *simply would not know how to feel.*

In fieldwork, as in daily life, we often encounter radical difference, and we come up against things we do not like or with which we cannot immediately identify or empathize. These "discoveries" can make us supremely uncomfortable. As anthropologists with a commitment to cross-cultural understanding, we worry—as well we should—how our written materials will be read and received by those who have not experienced the pleasures (as well as the pains) of living with the complex people whose lives we are trying to describe. Consciously or unconsciously we may "screen out" or simply refuse to accept at face value what we see or what we are being told, as, for example, when Renato Rosaldo at first refused to believe that his Ilongot friends were capable of headhunting, as they insisted, for the simple expressive "joy" of it as well as to "kill" the sadness and anger they felt.[45] Rosaldo preferred to believe that there was a more "rational" and "instrumental" purpose behind Ilongot headhunting, such as avenging the death of a loved one. But his informants, after listening attentively to Rosaldo's explanation of the anthropologists' model of exchange theory, replied that "Ilongots simply did not think any such thing" at all.[46]

The temptation to second-guess our informants is particularly keen when their own explanations of their lives are "experience-distant" or counter-intuitive to our own sociological or psychological understandings of human behavior. Sometimes, as in Rosaldo's case, it is because people's explanations may appear, as they did to him, "too simple, thin, opaque, implausible, stereotypic, or otherwise unsatisfying."[47] Similarly, Thomas Gregor, who investigated the "psychological impact" of infanticide among the Brazilian Amazonian Mehinaku Indians, found that he could not accept the villagers' claims that infanticide was easily accomplished and left no residue of guilt or blame: "We profoundly reject interring healthy children and therefore we assume that deep down the Mehinaku must feel the same way. Yet they claim otherwise. They institutionalize infanticide and assume that it is nearly painless: 'The white man really feels for his infant. We do not. Infants are not precious to us.'"[48]

These statements produced cognitive dissonance for Gregor, who began from the premise of a "universal human imperative requiring that children be protected and nurtured."[49] While aware of the danger of projecting his own moral repugnance toward infanticide on the Amerindian villagers, Gregor found himself ultimately unable to "take Mehinaku opinion at face value."[50] The oft-repeated phrase "Infants are not precious to us," while emblematic of the "official" culture of Mehinaku infanticide, was covering a large reservoir of personal ambivalence and doubt. The Mehinaku mother, Gregor wrote, who brought an infant to term simply could not "be emotionally neutral about infanticide" because she was subject to the same psychobiological feelings as the Western mother.[51] And so Mehinaku cultural practices were interpreted as psychological "defenses" and "distancing devices": the rejected neonate was not referred to as a "baby" but rather as a *kanupa,* a "tabooed" or "forbidden" thing; the infanticidal act was accomplished very rapidly; and so forth. These led Gregor to conclude that, despite what the Indians told him, "Mehinaku infants are, in fact, precious to the villagers and infanticide is edged with moral and emotional ambivalence."[52] The burden of proof was, however, very thin, overinterpreted, and extremely cir-

cumstantial. It would not hold up in court. And it strikes me as indefensible to argue in a post hoc fashion that Mehinaku villagers *must* consider all their newborns precious because Western psychobiological theories tell us that all humans *are* this way.

Gregor's detailed descriptions of Mehinaku beliefs and practices toward their *kanupa* lead me to think that these women view and treat some of their neonates as prehumans, just as many women in the United States view and treat their fetuses. If we want to draw comparisons and analogies, it may be more appropriate to consider Mehinaku neonaticide as a form of "postpartum abortion." It seems to be practiced with similar intent and with a similar range of sentiments, explanations, and emotions. And just as Gregor would second-guess his informants' *real* feelings on the matter, some psychologists similarly dismiss the apparent psychological relief and the "indifference" of middle-class women who have had to abort a fetus as "denial" of their loss, grief, and deep moral ambivalence. With theories such as these, what is being "denied" are the disparate voices and moral sensibilities of women.

Renato Rosaldo, while later recovering from a profound personal loss in his own life, was moved to reflect on his initial refusal to "hear" what his Ilongot informants told him about "grief and the headhunter's rage."[53] In rethinking Ilongot emotions in light of his own recent experience, Rosaldo came to accept that one could indeed feel a passionate, murderous, yet almost joyously self-affirming, rage in response to the death of a loved one. Or perhaps his own experience of grief was shaped by his Ilongot teachers, for fieldwork *is* transformative of the self. And so Rosaldo returned from his own mourning to challenge his anthropological colleagues to pay more attention to what their informants were telling them and to make room in their highly abstract theorizing for the often unanticipated "force" and intensity of emotions in human life. . . .

Cultural Mediation of Dying and Grieving Among Native Canadian Patients in Urban Hospitals

JOSEPH M. KAUFERT AND JOHN D. O'NEIL

JOSEPH M. KAUFERT, PH.D., is a professor in the Departments of Community Health Sciences and Anthropology at the University of Manitoba. He previously worked in the cultural dimensions of community health in the Department of Psychiatry, School of Medicine, at the University of Texas in San Antonio. Between 1972 and 1976, Dr. Kaufert headed the Social Science Section at St. Thomas Medical School of the University of London. He was cofounder of the British Medical Anthropology Society. His research in the United Kingdom focused on community living among elderly residents of the inner city and the long-term experience of people receiving home treatment for hemophilia. Dr. Kaufert has authored and edited books on medical sociology, African ethnicity, and biomedical ethics. Dr. Kaufert is currently involved in research examining the cultural context of decision making relative to living wills and organ donation among Native Canadians. He continues to work in cultural advocacy activities within both Native Canadian health programs and the disabled consumers' movement in Canada.

JOHN D. O'NEIL, PH.D., is an associate professor in the Department of Community Health Sciences at the University of Manitoba. He received his doctorate in medical anthropology, from the University of California in San Francisco and Berkeley. For the past eighteen years he has been investigating cultural factors affecting the delivery of health services to Canadian Inuit communities. These interests have led him to investigate comparative issues among native peoples in Australia and Siberia as well as other parts of Canada. He is currently a consultant to the Royal Commission on Aboriginal People, which he advises on health policy, and is directing a multisite research project investigating environmental health-risk perception and communication in Native Canadian communities.

Dr. O'Neil has published widely on a variety of Native Canadian health issues, including perceptions of environmental health risks, birthing options in remote communities, and health communication. His paper in *Medical Anthropology Quarterly* on medical interpreters and patient satisfaction won the 1990 Rudolf Virchow Award from the Society for Medical Anthropology, an award given for excellence in applying critical theory to medical anthropological research.

For several years, Drs. Kaufert and O'Neil have been conducting research on the problems that Canadian Native people face when they interact with the biomedical systems in urban hospitals. They have also focused on the role conflicts experienced by Native Canadian medical interpreters who serve as culture brokers between indigenous people and health professionals.

This research has addressed problems of translating biomedical concepts into the frameworks of the Native peoples. Translation and cultural mediation become particularly critical in situations where there is conflict between Native Canadians and hospital personnel over the nature of death, the appropriate expression of grief, and the proper treatment of dying and dead persons.

THIS ARTICLE FOCUSES on the process of interpreting culturally based understandings of dying, grieving and postmortem care for Native patients in urban hospitals. Case examples will be used to illustrate conflicts between Native patients' and Euro-Canadian health professionals' interpretations of appropriate care for the dying and grieving processes. We emphasize the role of Native interpreter/advocates who mediate between conflicting interpretations of dying and grieving among patients, family members and clinical staff in urban hospitals.

We draw our case studies describing the work of medical interpreters in terminal care settings from a continuing program of research on interpreter roles in health communication in Winnipeg hospitals and Inuit communities in the Northwest Territories. The case studies are used to illustrate the following: (a) contrasts between biomedical and Native cultural understandings of viability, death, and grieving behavior; (b) problems of interpreting the organizational structure of the hospital for Native patients receiving palliative care; (c) impact of conflicting cultural values related to autopsies and postmortem disposition of the body; (d) conflicts between biomedical beliefs emphasizing rational causation and technological intervention and Native beliefs emphasizing spiritual causation and non-interference; and (e) problems of integrating traditional healing practices into terminal care in urban hospitals.

Palgi and Abramovitch have suggested that experience with death in Western societies is characterized by extreme mortality anxiety reflected in the definition of death and dying as a "private affair."[1] The dying person is likely to be referred to a hospital when the family and wider support group can no longer cope with the range and intensity of caring functions. For Native Canadians this recourse to care of elderly, chronically ill and dying patients in institutional settings evokes fundamental conflicts with cultural values emphasizing the kin group and community's obligation to take care of its own. Cultural ideologies emphasizing family care contrast with the reality of managing long-term care of chronically ill and terminally ill patients in northern communities with minimal home care resources or in urban migrant households without community support. Although Native people recognize the need for the technical and personal care services provided by the hospital, the problems of maintaining communal support in the hospital environment are profound.

In urban hospitals, the organizational structure of the ward and professional control of terminal care further isolates the patient from family and community support networks. It also interferes with rituals that integrate the family's experience of dying and grieving into community life. Sociological studies of terminal care management by Glaser and Strauss emphasize that hospital-based management of terminal care shifts the responsibility for support of the dying person from the kin group and community-based support networks to specialized care provided by professional staff.[2]

In both Euro-Canadian and Native Canadian cultures, dying and grieving are defined as pivotal events of transition and passage within the life of the community. However, when terminal illness occurs in the specialized and technologically oriented environment of hospital wards, the work of caring and providing psychosocial support is performed by health professionals who may not share the patients' framework for interpreting their experience.[3] The fundamental differences between the interpretive perspective of patients and the outlook of health professionals may be amplified by differences in the culturally based explanatory models used to interpret illness and healing. In addition to the overlay of biomedical cultural values, health professionals also come from a wide range of ethnic backgrounds. This diversity introduces another dimension of variation. Although health professionals generally subscribe to biomedical and dominant Euro-Canadian values, their own ethnic identities may introduce a second set of cultural values that influence their response to dying patients and grieving families.

Contemporary Native Experience of Death and Dying

Technological and organizational approaches to caring adopted by health professionals may conflict with traditional cultural ideologies emphasizing kin support and spiritual intervention. Among Indian and Inuit patients treated in urban centers, cultural and linguistic barriers compound the feeling of alienation and depersonalization experienced by all hospitalized patients. Native Canadians are unfamiliar with the institutional and professional culture of the hospital. They are also geographically and culturally isolated from their families and community support systems.

In most parts of Canada, the federally supported medical services program and provincial health insurance plans provide tertiary care for Indian and Inuit clients through a highly centralized system of treatment and referral. Health services on reserves and in other Native communities are generally provided by nurse practitioners in local primary care clinics or nursing stations. This care has usually been oriented towards management of minor health problems and disease prevention. The capability of northern community-based health facilities to treat and provide personal care services for a growing proportion of the Native population who require care for chronic conditions is limited. Native people with chronic illnesses and acute life threatening health problems are, therefore, referred for specialized diagnostic studies, surgery, and long-term care to urban tertiary care hospitals. The current system of triage and referral means that Native people with acute illnesses and long-term chronic conditions are increasingly likely to die in hospitals distant from their home communities. Physical relocation of the patient, often without accompanying members of the family, means that death occurs in the alien cultural environment of the urban hospital.

Within this organizational and institutional context it is not surprising that Native perceptions are dominated by images of hospitalization as an experience isolating the person from the cultural context of kin group and community support. Perceptions of hospital-based management of terminal care are also influenced by Inuit and Indian historical experience in which acutely ill patients were evacuated from northern communities to southern hospitals for treatment of infectious diseases. Polio, tuberculosis, and measles epidemics devastated Inuit and boreal Indian communities during the lifetimes of older members of some communities. Many people were evacuated without systematic records of their family and community of origin. Few interpretive services were available, and systematic information about the patient's death or recovery was seldom returned to home communities. Present day evacuation of acutely or terminally ill patients to southern hospitals is frequently interpreted in the context of older peoples' experiences as long-term inpatients in isolated sanitoriums and city hospitals during the tuberculosis epidemics of the 1940s, 1950s and 1960s. Evacuation to a sanitorium was described by older patients as "being taken out of the community to die in southern hospitals."

In response to the problems of alienation associated with urban hospitalization, many Native communities are trying to develop community-based services for managing chronic care and terminally ill patients. For example, the Baker Lake Health Committee recently expressed interest in converting their old nursing station into a hospice facility. The hospitals in which our own research was conducted also had an informal policy of working with the Native Services Program and reserve nursing stations to discharge terminally ill patients to enable them to return to their home communities. Unfortunately, northern community-based health services cannot provide the supportive pain management and palliative services which are available to terminally ill patients receiving home care in urban centers. Despite these initiatives, most Native Canadians with acute and degenerative conditions will die in urban hospitals.

The Role of Hospital-Based Interpreter/Advocates in Care of Dying Patients

In this article our primary objective is to examine the process of mediation between Cree, Ojibway, and Inuit patients' views of death, grief, and post-mortem care, and the views held by health professionals. The basis of our study of mediation processes was observation of the work of medical interpreters who act as culture brokers and patient advocates in urban hospitals.[4] Our study of Native interpreters working in Winnipeg hospitals found that they performed a primary role in mediating between the cultural models of death, dying and grieving of Native clients and those held by health professionals. Opportunities for cultural mediation of terminal care experience were also expanded as work by language interpreters in patient advocacy, counselling, and health education became recognized and legitimated.[5] We found that Native interpreters played multiple roles as (a) language translators; (b) cultural informants describing Native health practices and community health issues; (c) interpreters of biomedical concepts; and (d) patient and community advocates.[6] In each of these roles interpreter/advocates mediated between biomedical and Native approaches to care of dying persons.

The narrowest definition of the medical interpreter role emphasizes technical translation of biomedical concepts into linguistically appropriate terms in Cree, Ojibway, or Inuktitut. The policy of involving interpreters in clinical interaction with Native patients who had little or no English gave dying patients access to a person with both language competence and knowledge of their culture and community. In the confusing surroundings of the hospital ward, the interpreter was able to clarify complicated and impersonal procedures. They explained biomedical intervention in aid of life support and pain control using parallel terminology from the Native language where possible. In many cases, however, interpreters had

to develop appropriate metaphors or examples which had personal meaning for the client. Interpreters also played a pivotal role in communicating the dying person's choices about alternative treatment, intervention, and palliative care proposed by clinicians. In several cases, interpreters played a critical role in informing patients that they had rights and could choose between, or reject, proposed treatment plans.

In caring for dying patients, interpreters also performed a pivotal brokerage function by explaining Cree, Ojibway and Inuit cultural perspectives on terminal illness and post-mortem rituals to clinical staff. Interpreters were also able to act as "informants" for clinicians by explaining environmental factors in Native communities and the constraints of local and regional medical services which limited treatment options for palliative care on reserves. Interpreters worked with patients to develop culturally meaningful translations of terminal prognosis, relative risks associated with alternative treatment measures, and options for palliative care.

The expanded role of the Native language interpreters in patient advocacy and counselling involves mediation between strategies of patient management based on biomedical approaches to causation and treatment and traditional beliefs maintained by the client and family. Until recently, interpreters had no systematic training for involvement in advocacy and counselling for terminal care patients. However, in 1985–86, four of the hospital-based interpreters in Winnipeg graduated from a two-year para-professional training program which included instructional modules on counselling, care of dying patients and integration of traditional healing practices. Several parts of the curriculum emphasized client-centered counselling skills based on standard social work and family therapy interventions.

However, training modules also included an emphasis on utilizing Native elders and traditional healers as resource teachers. In contrasting biomedical and traditional knowledge components of their training, several interpreters felt the overall training had enabled them to more effectively deal with death and other family crises. Some of the graduates also reported feelings of dissonance related to their experience in attempting to combine more directive social work counselling strategies with "traditional" approaches to supporting dying patients and their families. Other informants described their personal problems in reconciling traditional beliefs emphasizing family and community responsibility for care of the dying with the increasing inability and unwillingness of relatives to provide terminal care on reserve communities. [One] interpreter described her difficulties in reconciling the models of a patient's acceptance of dying (emphasizing the framework developed by Elisabeth Kübler-Ross[7]) with the framework of traditional Ojibway beliefs about the process of dying. She emphasized that themes of denial, anger and reconciliation in the palliative care literature could not be reconciled with the themes of self-control and noninterference idealized in Cree and Ojibway beliefs.

In response to the general aversion of Native people to hospital-based care, interpreters often played pivotal roles in making arrangements for Native patients to return to spend their final days with their families. Over the past seven years we observed that the role of interpreters in Winnipeg hospitals evolved to include a wider range of caring and mediation activities. These activities have particular significance for dying patients and grieving family members. The expanded role played by medical interpreters in cultural mediation and advocacy for Native patients contained the potential for conflicts of loyalty. Although interpreters were hospital employees and thus indirectly controlled by administrative and clinical managers, most maintained their primary loyalty to the client and the family. Consequently, they had to represent the dying patient's individual interests, and in some cases

the perspective of family and community groups, in situations in which clinicians and administrators favored alternative courses of action.

Although the role of medical interpreters was legitimated and professionalized through training establishing their credentials, their main source of power in clinical communication continued to be based upon linguistic and cultural access to the patient and family. While co-workers value the interpreters' capacity to interpret the patient's concept of illness, these same co-workers sometimes resent advocacy activities which counter organization rules or standards of clinical practice. For example, the involvement of interpreters in integrating traditional healers and healing practices into the care of dying patients is met with resistance from some clinicians and pastoral care workers. Several interpreters emphasized that this sort of situation involved loyalty conflicts and personal dissonance resulting in stress and "job burnout."[8] Divided loyalties were also present in situations in which the interpreters' identity as kin group or community members conflicted with their role as professionals and hospital employees. In these situations, cross-pressures were reduced by referral to other interpreters and through intervention by supportive clinical supervisors and administrators who defended the interpreter's role as advocate for kin or members of the home community.

Mediating the Organizational Structure of the Hospital

A critical function of interpreter/advocates in their work with Native patients in terminal care was to explain and mediate the effects of the organizational structure of the hospital. The social science literature on institutionalization[9] and medicalization[10] emphasized that the organizational structure of hospitals reinforces institutional and professional control over all clinical situations, including terminal care.[11] For all patients, the organizational structure and function of large hospitals is difficult to understand. Like inmates in archetypical "total institutions," patients must be socialized to fit into the hospital's basic organizational structure. From the provider's perspective, organizational rules and care regimens are justified on the basis of rationales emphasizing the "good of the institution" or the need to "consider the rights of all patients and staff." For Indian and Inuit people, the problems of understanding how specialized diagnostic and treatment wards function and how they effect the person's own care are compounded by cultural and linguistic barriers.

Our wider research program examining the expansion of interpreter roles suggested that Native patients felt "powerless" because of their lack of familiarity with the organizational structure of the hospital. Hospital rules and sanctions imposed by clinicians were therefore often perceived by Native patients and their families as oppressive as well as confusing.

Our observation of medical interpreters' work provided several examples of situations in which the organizational rules of the hospital conflicted with Native concepts about family involvement in terminal care. In one case, an elderly Cree woman with terminal gastric cancer was assigned to a double room on the post-surgical ward. Her extended family assembled at the hospital to attend the patient. The kin group included recent urban migrants and other family members who had travelled two hundred miles from the women's home community. As the patient lapsed into unconsciousness, eight members of the family arrived at the ward to attend the patient. The hospital-based interpreter who was translating for the family described the initial encounter between the family and the nursing staff:

> The head nurse called the assistant head nurse for an emergency meeting, and asked why there were so many people there. The head nurse then said there was no need for all these people to be here, so the assistant

was to remove all these people from the hallway. The charge nurse went over to the patient and adjusted her I.V. She looked at the people there and said "I'm sorry, but you'll have to leave! At least some of you, anyway. She is only allowed two visitors at a time!" Everyone just got up immediately and started leaving.

The interpreter later commented that her presence may have influenced the nurse's response. As the interpreter became involved in translating, the nurse emphasized that the restriction of the number of visitors was necessary to protect the patient from unnecessary disturbances. The interpreter described her interaction with the nurse.

> The nurse commented to the patient's daughter, "The thing is, she was doing so well yesterday when she was not being bothered by anyone. She was so active in the morning, and after she had so many visitors all day, she's not doing so well today." I [the interpreter] just stood and looked at her after everyone had left the room, appalled at the tone of voice and the implications of her words, as if reproaching the family for visiting their mother.

Despite this encounter, the support group of family members on the ward continued to grow as more members in the group learned of the patient's condition. Family members slept in the lounge and hallways and rotated to maintain a twenty-four hour vigil in the patient's room. Until the interpreters intervened, no attempt was made to accommodate the needs of the patient and/or the family by providing either a single room or placing the patient in a ward with other Cree-speaking patients.

The head nurse had asked the interpreter to explain the rules governing visiting hours and limitations on the number of visitors. The head of the interpreter program talked to the family and explained that hospitals had their own rules which sometimes were hard to understand and respect. The nurses explained that rules limiting visiting privileges were enforced to prevent infringement on the rights of other patients and to avoid tiring the patient. The head nurse later complained to the interpreter that she had observed that Native visitors did not seem to "do" anything for the patients during visits. She commented that Native visitors "just sat in their chairs and knitted." When the Director of Native Services was asked about this perception, she explained that Native people feel it is important just to "be with" someone who is acutely or terminally ill and that it was not necessary for visitors to interact. She emphasized that Native people found it inappropriate when clinicians and non-Native visitors expected patients to converse throughout a visit because this seemed very tiring for the patient. East Cree people emphasize the importance of visiting terminally ill friends and allowing kin to "say goodbye." In urban hospitals, paradoxically, both clinicians and the family members perceived each other's approach to attending terminal care patients as culturally inappropriate and "tiring" for the patient. Other values defining appropriate dying and grieving behavior also were difficult to realize in the setting of the medical ward. Traditional emphasis upon the need for the dying person to maintain autonomy and personal control were overridden by organizational rules and ward schedules that minimized the ability of the dying patient and his/her family to control time or personal space. The related values of self knowledge and personal competence were also difficult to achieve in the unfamiliar institutional setting of the ward. The notion of a "good death" in which continuity and balance is maintained in human and environmental relationships, contrasts sharply with "decontextualized death" of persons on the ward.

Faced with a situation of conflict between two value systems, the Director for Native Ser-

vices also asked the head nurse whether it was necessary to be inflexible in applying rules limiting the number of visitors in terminal care situations. The Director explained that rules defining the level and duration of family visits conflicted with the belief that several family members should be present continuously to protect the patient from spiritual malevolence. The Director asked whether the regulations governing the life of the ward should be applied inflexibly in the care of dying patients. She pointed out that limitations in visiting hours and number of visitors meant that the patient could not go through the process of "leave taking" with members of her community who had travelled from the home community. The nursing supervisor incorporated a more transcultural perspective into the patient's care plan and allowed the extended family group to attend the patient on a twenty-four hour basis. The interpreter organized a schedule in which several members of the family could visit the patient on a rotating basis.

The case was one of several examples of terminal care situations involving Native clients characterized by conflict between the formal organizational rules of the hospital and patient and family assertions of their right to follow traditional practices for attending the dying. Although such incidents were discussed widely by the clinical staff, few Native patients were referred to specialized hospice units.

Hospice units are designed and staffed to provide for flexible involvement of the family and more psychosocial support of the patient than could otherwise be provided. When a physician working with the hospice program was asked about the underutilization of the program by Native clients, he responded that the system of referral seldom transferred Native clients to the unit. One barrier to native participation in the hospice program was felt by interpreters to be the cultural model of terminal care emphasized by the unit. This is because the psychosocial orientation to patient management in the hospice was partially based upon the model of staged acceptance of dying developed by Elisabeth Kübler-Ross,[12] a framework incompatible with Cree and Ojibway values defining a "good death." While problems of reconciling the values of Native clients and hospice staff are significant, members of the unit are currently examining ways to accommodate Native beliefs in their care programs. In the future, hospice units may adopt pluralistic models for terminal care, thereby accommodating the culturally based interpretive frameworks of Native people. Interpreters also are currently working with clinicians and administrators to develop more flexible policy guidelines to govern ward organization and nursing practice.

Integration of Traditional Healing Practices

The broader context of health care for Native Canadians is increasingly recognized as a "pluralistic" system in which patients may consult both biomedical practitioners and practitioners of traditional Cree and Ojibway medicine. One critical role of Native interpreter/advocates working with terminal care patients and family groups involves ensuring that hospital patients have access to traditional healers.[13]

Native Services workers estimate that one-third of the Cree and Ojibway patients entering Winnipeg tertiary hospitals continue to value traditional ideas about illness and medicine. The general perception among physicians and nurses was that adherence to traditional belief systems was more prevalent among older Native patients. However, the interpreter/advocates observed that a significant proportion of middle-aged and young adult patients also believed in traditional medicine. They further observed that a growing number of patients of all ages wanted to participate in traditional healing rituals while in hospital. This growing interest was particularly apparent in terminal care situations.

Although some hospitals adjoining Native communities have developed policies which incorporate healers as members of the consultant staffs, the two teaching hospitals in Winnipeg had no formal provision for involving traditional healers. Despite this lack of official legitimacy, Native language interpreters frequently became involved in helping hospital patients to contact elders and healers. They also assisted terminal care patients and members of their families to contact traditional practitioners, and participated in rituals surrounding death and the post-mortem care of the body.

The integration of healers and traditional care practices into palliative care was observed in the cases of several older patients in oncology wards. For example, a seventy-year old Ojibway patient was referred for palliative care on a specialized medical ward of a teaching hospital. Although the man was diagnosed as having advanced gastric cancer, the attending physicians initially prescribed a chemotherapy regimen to sustain minimal digestive function. During his initial interview with the interpreter the man indicated that he knew he was dying, and the interpreter asked whether he would like to involve an elder or traditional healer in his care. At the patient's request, the interpreter consulted with several healers living in the city. None was willing to perform rituals on the ward because they felt that the hospital environment was alien to their approach to healing. Several days later the interpreter was able to contact an elder in a neighboring reserve community who was willing to perform a healing ceremony in the hospital.

Once the informal arrangement was made, the interpreter had to get official permission and financial support to facilitate the healer's travel and his access to the hospital ward. The oncologist initially rejected the interpreter's proposal to involve the healer, because he was concerned that traditional interventions might conflict with the prescribed biomedical regimen. The physician emphasized that the patient was still actively receiving treatment and he was afraid that the healer's botanical medication might interact with chemotherapy. Transportation expenses for the healer were available from the federal government through the Medical Services Branch, but the attending physician was asked to approve the request for consultation with the healer. After extensive negotiation with the interpreters, assurances were given that no plant medication would be administered. The oncologist finally consented to the involvement of the healer. The healer ultimately agreed to perform a healing ceremony within the cancer center, but requested that some of the more invasive monitoring equipment be turned off while he worked with the patient.

In a similar case, a female patient with advanced renal cancer was being treated by an oncologist who was also initially reluctant to involve a healer in the patient's care. In this case the interpreters' roles as patient advocates involved them in circumventing hospital rules. The interpreters brought the elder to visit the patient during a slack period on a Sunday. The healer performed a healing ritual which required burning ceremonial offerings of sweet grass and tobacco. The interpreters recognized that burning sweet grass might set off the ward smoke detector system so they helped the family cover the smoke detector with plastic and participated in the ceremony themselves. These cases illustrate the expansion of unofficial interpreter roles to include brokering relationships between traditional healers and clinicians.

In both teaching hospitals, health professionals and administrators were sometimes reluctant to accommodate or recognize the role of Native elders and healers in terminal care. This is true even though interpreters from one hospital were themselves active in traditional cultural activities and used community elders and medicine people as their spiritual advisors and as a personal support group. Nevertheless, their efforts to facilitate consul-

tation with spiritual advisors and healers were often limited to unofficial interventions or subterfuge.

Biomedical and Spiritual Understandings of Causality: The Tragedy of Co-terminus Symbols

Several incidents illustrate the potential for culture conflict that can arise when biomedical and traditional interpretations of terminal prognosis and cause of mortality do not coincide. One case involved a female infant born to an Ojibway family living on a reserve 100 kilometers from an urban tertiary care hospital. The child was diagnosed as suffering from a genetically-based degenerative condition with a survival prognosis of a few weeks.

Biomedical explanations of the child's illness emphasized the genetic origins of the problem. The pediatrician and a genetic counselor attempted to explain to the parents that positive and negative traits are passed from one generation to another. When the genetic explanation was translated for the parents, the mother became distraught. Her interpretation of the genetic cause was that the medical diagnosis confirmed her responsibility for the child's condition. In talking with the interpreter the mother stressed that the child's problems were the result of a personal transgression of traditional rules. The Native interpreter explained to the attending physician that the mother understood the child's condition in terms of the concept of *ondjine*. The Ojibway belief system explaining courses of illness or misfortune is based on the belief that individuals may receive retribution for previous transgressions.[14] Transgressions may include harming animals, ridiculing the physical characteristics of another person, or desecrating grave sites or the physical remains of the deceased.[15] Retribution may miss the guilty person and strike his or her family members. The root meaning of the word *ondjine* implies "earning" or "receiving in return." In traditional interpretations, the concept had both positive and negative connotations, stressing that individuals might be positively rewarded for acts of kindness or respect to elders or kind acts to animals. However, in contemporary usage the concept of *ondjine* is primarily related to behavior which has resulted in illness or misfortune befalling a family member. Although the genetic explanation was congruent with the mother's belief that she was responsible for her child's condition, she refused to accept the idea that the condition was degenerative and irreversible. She requested assistance from the Department of Native Services to bring a traditional healer into the hospital to see the baby. The Director contacted an elder who was recognized for her success in working with Native children suffering from convulsions. The elder, who lived on a reserve in a neighboring province approximately 400 miles from the hospital, talked on the telephone with the mother and indicated that, while she could not travel to treat the child directly, she would pray for spiritual intervention.

The interpreter's explanation of the mother's spiritual beliefs and request for a healer were recorded in the case notes by the medical staff. However, no formal accommodation was made to involve healers or work with the parents to reconcile discrepancies and conflicts in their interpretation of the child's illness. In the days that followed, the mother became increasingly depressed and began to distance herself from her child. The mother's withdrawal was particularly distressing to the nursing staff because of their own cultural expectations regarding parental involvement in the care of terminally ill children. Pediatric intensive care nursing staff placed great value on the self-sacrificing parent who spends twenty-four hours a day at the child's bedside. Nurses evaluated the level of the parent's concern in terms of their commitment to be with the child on a round-the-clock basis. As the mother began to withdraw from interaction with the infant, her behavior was described as "uncaring" by the ward staff.

The woman's behavior did not fit the staff's previous experience with other Native families who attended patients day and night. Constant attendance is based on the belief that a dying person must have family present in order to ensure the spirit or ghost of the deceased is not angered. The mother's belief in her own responsibility for the child's illness meant that she had to withdraw from the child in order to protect it from further spiritual malevolence associated with her presence. Her behavior was considered callous by the attending clinicians, and the nursing staff committed extra time to the child's care.

The attempt by the nursing staff to compensate for the mother's withdrawal was perceived by the family as a further assertion of the hospital's control of the process of dying. One of the interpreters compared the terminal care experience on the ward with the alternate scenario of the child dying at home:

> Now if the child had died at birth the parents would have just gone ahead and buried the child and accepted it as something that just had happened. However, when the medical profession became involved they took the child away from the parents and maintained the child in hospital to try and find out what was wrong. From the parents' perspective it looks like experimentation. They felt disconnected from the child . . . as though it wasn't their child anymore. From the parents' perspective they were prohibited from taking their child out of hospital and from their own cultural standpoint were seen to be deficient parents.

The intensive medical and social management of the child extended to the ward staff's management of the parents' involvement with the child. One of the interpreters described the feeling of alienation that the parents experienced as they were forced to take part in token caring activities for the child.

> When the parents came to Winnipeg the nurses would get the mother to bathe the baby, to hold the baby and nurture the baby. I'm not sure how she felt, but she must have felt anguish in looking after a little child with all those machines around her. I asked the parents how they felt about it at first and they didn't respond. I asked them whether they felt their baby was continuing to grow and thrive, they hesitated and then he [the father] said, "Yes, she's growing," but there was no facial expression. He said in Ojibway "she is not part of us anymore." This is very difficult to translate into English without sounding callous; it doesn't mean she's dead or gone, but more like there's no hope or what's the point? We're here; you've got our child—it's yours—you took our child away from us.

As the interpreters sensed the growing level of alienation in the parents, they enlisted the aid of a consultant pediatrician with extensive experience in Native health, asking him to assume the role of advocate for the family. In conveying the family's wish for withdrawal of life support equipment, one interpreter described her perception of the circumstances surrounding the child's impending death:

> If the child had died in her arms shortly after birth that would have been more acceptable than the way the child is today with all those machines. That is what we believe in—that part of us—we have to accept it. We've lost other children and that was the way it was meant to be. They feel badly because they've lost other children and the chances are that this child will die as well. For me it's the medical staff who can't accept this approach to dying and they see the parents as being fatalistic.

The interpreter also attempted to convey the perspective of the medical profession to the parents. She described physicians' and nurses' commitment to sustain life.

> From the perspective of the medical profession the loss of three other children is enough to go to extraordinary lengths to try to save this baby. Medical ethics demand that they always try to preserve life. They live by that, they eat it, they administer drugs that way; it's their primary goal to save life.

As the child's condition worsened, the clinical staff continued to provide intensive care, and openly expressed their frustration with the parents' apparent callousness. During an informal clinical consultation, the interpreter overheard one of the residents describing the child's case history. The physician commented on the apparent lack of parental concern over the child's terminal condition. Speaking with a colleague, the doctor mentioned that the parents had lost three other children and suggested in a demeaning tone that these children were probably "buried in the bush." When the physician's statement was repeated in a case conference, the interpreter challenged the physician's interpretation of the family's parenting experience and current reaction to their child's impending death. The interpreter described her reaction.

> The second time I heard that I thought "What's happening here?" Can you imagine the sort of image that creates for an intern? "Indian people just throw their dead out in the bush." I went to see one of the doctors who had been involved in the conversation; he was quite surprised at my reaction. He said, "Perhaps you are being too sensitive." However, I've been here long enough to try to be open-minded and understand, but those kinds of statements don't sit well with me, particularly when I'm trying to make people aware of the differences and values and

customs. Maybe twenty-five years ago those statements would have been okay. We were ignorant of how the hospitals worked and doctors and nurses were ignorant of our values. However, they must understand that we value life. So do these parents value life. It's a gift to them. However, if there's a sickness or something that happens, it's seen as being meant to happen because of something that had happened to them before and therefore it's acceptable. This explanation just isn't accepted by the medical profession. The medical staff seem to be willing to dismiss them as callous parents rather than to try and find out the way they feel about the situation.

During the final hours of the child's life, the interpreters remained with the parents. The mother wanted to know how the child was doing. The physician apparently answered with a reference to the clinical condition which did not directly acknowledge that the child's death was imminent. The interpreter described the mother's response.

They never say, "your child is dying," they use a lot of words sometimes you don't understand what they mean. Sometimes I wish they would just come out and say things directly—they don't, it's not the way they do things.

Immediately after the death of the child, the interpreter attempted to organize a series of in-service training sessions in which physicians and nurses could be sensitized to the cultural values governing Native definitions of viability, quality of life, and rituals appropriate for caring for dying patients. She described her experience in these in-service sessions.

It's very hard to convince medical staff that these things are important, that it's important to know that Native people don't simply bury their dead in the bush. There are ceremonies that are to be performed because life

is sacred to these parents and they value life much the same way as a doctor values life.

This case illustrates the problems of interpreting Native and biomedical understandings of terminal prognosis, cause of death, and grief response by members of the family group. The misinterpretation of causal explanations and appropriate approaches to caring and grieving illustrates the tragedy of co-terminus symbols among clients and care providers. The mother's interpretation of the child's illness as punishment for her own transgression (harming an animal) led her to distance herself to prevent further retribution. The clinical staff's interpretation of the mother's behavior caused them to stereotype the family as uncaring. Reciprocally the family interpreted the imposition of a more medicalized regimen on the final hours of the child's life as inappropriate. Finally, Native interpreters regarded the clinical staff's characterization of the family as stereotypic and discriminatory.

Mediation of Cultural Explanations of Autopsy

Cultural differences in understandings were also apparent in situations where there was conflict between biomedical and traditional understandings of postmortem care of the body. One case involved a ten-month old female Ojibway child from a reserve community. The child had a wide range of neurological problems and was eventually referred for diagnostic evaluation to an urban pediatric hospital. The child's illness was finally diagnosed as lucodystrophy, and the attending physicians attempted to communicate the child's diagnosis to the parents. They told the parents that lucodystrophy involved progressive degeneration of the brain tissue and that it was genetically transmitted. The physicians also stressed that the condition was inevitably fatal, and that they would primarily be providing life support and palliative care.

During the final stages of the child's illness the medical staff of the pediatric intensive care unit were heavily involved in the clinical management of the child's condition. As the level of medical intervention was increased and respiratory support equipment was used, the grandparents and parents became concerned that the medical staff were providing "experimental care" that would prolong the child's suffering. The next day the parents decided to take the child from hospital and return to the reserve to seek the intervention of a traditional healer. As they were driving back to the reserve community, the child stopped breathing and was admitted to a community hospital, where she was pronounced dead on arrival.

The body of the child was then returned to the pediatric hospital, and the parents and grandparents were contacted by the attending physician for their consent to perform an autopsy. In speaking with the relatives, the medical staff emphasized that autopsies were required in cases where the cause of death was undetermined. The parents refused to consent to the procedure, saying that it conflicted with their spiritual beliefs about the care of the body of the deceased. When it became evident that an autopsy was going to be performed by the hospital, the grandfather, who was a community elder and band council member, called on the band chief to try to intervene to prevent the autopsy. Even the pediatricians who had cared for the child supported the need for postmortem examination, despite the fact that death was almost certainly related to the degenerative effects of lucodystrophy. Ultimately, the provincial medical examiner ordered the autopsy, despite the protests of the parents. Interpreters were finally called in when the child's grandparents returned to the hospital and were informed that an autopsy had been performed as ordered by the provincial medical examiner. The parents and grandparents reacted emotionally and requested assistance from the community leaders from their reserve. When the band chief and council

asked the provincial medical examiner and attending pediatricians for a detailed explanation of why the autopsy was performed without parental consent, a spokesperson for the hospital explained that autopsies were often performed to determine the cause of death, particularly when there was the possibility of it being associated with infectious diseases posing wider community threats. The interpreters and family reacted angrily because they felt the spokesperson had rationalized the decision by introducing considerations of potential threats of infectious disease to the community. They pointed out that there was nothing in the medical history of the case which suggested the presence of communicable disease. Unfortunately, the damage had been done, and rumors spread throughout the Native community that the child had died from an unknown contagious disease. When the child's body was flown back to the reserve, family and community responses at the viewing of the body and burial continued to be influenced by the rumor that the child had died from an infectious disease. At the church, community members did not approach the open casket.

Under pressure from the hospital interpreters, the hospital spokesperson finally stated that, in fact, infectious disease had not been suspected in this particular case. The band chief then contacted the medical examiner and demanded that existing guidelines for performing autopsies be re-examined. Pediatricians involved with northern health care and Native interpreters proposed that the subject be discussed in a wider forum in which clinicians, representatives of the medical examiner's office and representatives of the Native community could discuss the cultural and medical basis for post-mortem examinations.

The case of the infant with lucodystrophy was one of three incidents in which the biomedical criteria for performing autopsies came into conflict with cultural ideologies about post-mortem care. The medical staff of the pediatric hospital, therefore, decided to convene an in-service training workshop dealing with the general issue of the cultural interpretation of autopsies among Native people. The provincial medical examiner, attending medical and nursing staff, and Native Services workers were invited. The interpreters also invited a woman who was identified as an elder who had special knowledge of Ojibway spiritual beliefs and healing practices.

The meeting opened with a general discussion of conflicting interpretations of the function of an autopsy. The biomedical perspective of the physicians emphasized the importance of an autopsy for improving the general level of medical knowledge. Native speakers argued that a paramount value in Native culture was the corporal integrity of the body after death and explained that this value was linked to spiritual understandings about the length of time required for the transition of a person's soul to the afterworld. The deputy medical examiner stated that he felt that there had been an exaggerated response by the Native community. He attempted to dispel what he described as a "popular myth" that autopsies were automatically performed on all patients who died in hospitals. He explained that there was a legal requirement that autopsies be performed in cases of unexplained deaths, accidents, violent deaths, suicides, maternal and infant deaths, suspected clinical malpractice, poisoning and people who died while in prison or legal custody. He emphasized that requirements that autopsies be performed had grown out of traditions in forensic medicine and biomedical research which emphasized that postmortem investigations were the key to understanding all disease processes.

Another pathologist stressed that a physician's involvement with a patient extended beyond terminal illness to post-mortem examination. He emphasized that physicians who were heavily involved in trying to save a patient's life often requested an autopsy in order to more fully understand why they had "lost the struggle to save the person." The deputy medical examiner emphasized that autopsies in the case of unexplained deaths, violent crimes and suspected clinical mismanagement provided protection for the individual and the community. He stated that he felt Native clients' objections to autopsies must be balanced against the wider community interest in assuring deaths do not occur without determination of negligence or malevolent cause. The deputy medical examiner also stressed that post-mortem examination was also sometimes necessary to control contagious or environmentally caused diseases. Finally he emphasized that autopsies were one of the main ways that scientific medicine learned about disease processes.

Following the deputy medical examiner's remarks, the Director of the Native Services program was asked to provide an overview of the concerns of Native clients about the current policies governing autopsies. She described her personal experience with health professionals who had misinterpreted the approach of Native clients and communities to dying, grieving and care of the body. In her remarks, the interpreter/advocate contrasted the analytical approach, used in medical and legal determination of the cause of mortality, with Ojibway beliefs about dying and postmortem care of the deceased. She emphasized that traditional beliefs focused on the importance of understanding the reasons for a person's death in terms of violation of traditional beliefs or moral transgressions. She pointed out that, like autopsies, traditional approaches to understanding the cause of death also involved identifying events or acts performed by the deceased or members of their family which might have contributed to the person's death. She emphasized that, like doctors, traditional believers were also concerned with identification of cause of death and stressed that Cree or Ojibway traditions also emphasized environmental influences—influences such as the relationship of the deceased to animals or spirits. The interpreter stated that in contrast to the narrower understanding of causation in biomedical culture, Ojibway beliefs fostered an integrative approach. Funeral rituals provided mechanisms which transformed death into an integrative event for the community. Determination of causation also allowed offending individuals to understand and ritually remedy their offenses.

The interpreter followed her remarks by introducing an elder from the community and asked the woman to describe Ojibway perspectives on the post-mortem care of the body as it influenced Native beliefs about autopsies. The elder began by relating the family's refusal of consent for autopsy to traditional beliefs: "Autopsy is a sensitive issue for traditional people and is very difficult to talk about because it is linked with spiritual concepts such as *ondjine*."

The elder stressed that post-mortem examination conflicted with traditional Ojibway beliefs about the process of dying and movement of the spirit after physical death. She emphasized that traditional believers would be opposed to any procedure which disturbed corporal integrity, including amputation or tissue removal in biopsies. The elder explained that Ojibway people believed the spirit resided in the body for a defined period after death. Procedures which involved opening the body cavity or removal of tissue disrupted the departure of the spirit and thereby engendered the possibility of retribution via *ondjine*.

Following the elder's statement, a pathologist asked whether autopsy procedures could be modified to accommodate traditional beliefs stressing the maintenance of corporal integrity. He suggested that it was very often possible to determine the cause of death from the medical history, blood samples and external physical examination. He asked whether this kind of approach to determining the cause

of death might overcome objections raised by traditional believers. The elder replied that prohibitions would apply to any procedure which disturbed the body and therefore that there could be no such thing as a "non-invasive autopsy."

Discussion then shifted the question of whether traditional beliefs should be respected in situations in which there was potential wrong-doing or risk to the community. A pediatrician asked whether the function of autopsies to protect the individual and the community could be balanced against considerations of respect for client beliefs or community values. The physician described a hypothetical case of a pediatric patient who had died from apparent insecticide poisoning. The physician asked the elder whether, in a case where an autopsy might be able to detect a threat to the entire community, traditional prohibitions against autopsies might be set aside. The elder demurred, saying that spiritual beliefs governing the disposition of the body after death were absolute. Concepts of the wider security of the community or protection from unknown diseases were not part of the traditional framework of knowledge.

Following the elder's explanation, an oncologist observed that there were important parallels in the ways that Orthodox Jewish families were able to restrict autopsies. The physician stated that as both a scientist and a member of an Orthodox Jewish congregation, he often questioned whether autopsies either contributed to research or individual clinical understanding of causality. He emphasized that in his own experience in pediatrics, autopsies of juvenile cancer patients frequently had minimal value in terms of extending general medical knowledge or benefit in terms of protecting the individual family or wider community. He suggested that, in his own experience, determining the need for an autopsy was influenced more by statutory requirements and payment for pathologists. He emphasized that the success of the Orthodox Jewish community in restricting autopsies had been related to their retention of legal council. In pursuing his comparison of Native and Orthodox Jewish teachings about post-mortem dispositions of the body, he emphasized the common belief about the need to preserve the corporal integrity of the body after death. He concluded his statement by expressing his surprise that his medical colleagues would dismiss Native beliefs about post-mortem disposition of the body as mere "customs" which could be strategically accommodated or circumvented. He asked whether the deputy medical examiner would have considered attempting to persuade an Orthodox Jewish family or their representatives to reverse their refusal to consent to the autopsy. The deputy examiner replied that, with the understanding of the prohibitions related to Cree and Ojibway traditional beliefs, he felt that Native clients and community groups could successfully challenge orders for autopsies using the provisions of the Canadian Charter of Rights.

The conference was followed up with continuing informal consultations between interpreter/advocates, clinicians and the medical examiner in later instances in which autopsies were contemplated for Native patients. In some cases the consultation and mediation by the interpreters resulted in family acceptance of the autopsy. In other situations the pathological examination was limited to minimally invasive procedures. However, in several instances families and community groups pursued their opposition to autopsy through legal channels or through going to the media.

Discussion

These case studies demonstrate the very real problem of mediation between Native and biomedical explanations of death, dying and grieving. Examination of work of interpreters in advocacy for Native patients and their families illustrates the problem of reconciling Native beliefs about appropriate care of the dying with the organizational constraints of the hospital and the biomedical culture of the health professional. Case studies of attempts to integrate traditional healers and to develop more sensitive post-mortem care illustrate the profound problems of reconciling alternative approaches to causality and remediation. They bring approaches to care of the dying emphasizing professional and technological control of terminal care into sharp contrast with tradiional approaches which stress the need to maintain autonomy, spirituality and continuity.

In the final analysis, the emphasis upon mediation, interpretation and accommodation of alternate systems of understanding may place interpreter/advocates in a vulnerable position of brokering fundamentally irreconcilable values. Culturally sensitive support for dying and grieving Native patients and families may require that individuals and communities assert their prerogative to die in their homes and local communities.

Death-Related Experiences and Funerary Practices of the Hmong Refugee in the United States

CHRISTOPHER L. HAYES AND RICHARD A. KALISH

CHRISTOPHER L. HAYES, PH.D., is an associate professor of gerontology at Long Island University, Southampton, New York. He is the director and founder of the graduate program in gerontology, a three-campus multidisciplinary program with over 140 graduate students. Dr. Hayes is also director and founder of the National Center for Women and Retirement Research, a research entity addressing the pre-retirement planning needs of middle-aged women. His major areas of concern include aging among members of ethnic and minority groups and clinical practice issues in working with the elderly.

His interests in the field of death and dying evolved from setting up a peer counseling program for older adults in Orange County, California, entitled PACE (Psychological Alternative Counseling for Elders). Through this experience, he developed a keen appreciation of minority aging concerns. At the time PACE was established, Southern California was experiencing a large influx of refugees from Southeast Asia. Many agencies aimed at providing services to older adults were ill-prepared to deal with the cultural barriers that existed. Dr. Hayes spent the next three years researching and studying the death-related needs of Southeast Asian refugees.

Dr. Hayes is the author of many articles and books in the field of gerontology, including *European-American Elderly: A Guide to Practice* (1986). His real appreciation of the field of death and dying came from his relationship with the late Dr. Richard Kalish, his doctoral faculty advisor and mentor.

RICHARD A. KALISH, PH.D., was active in the field of death studies as a writer, researcher, teacher, and consultant. At his death from cancer in 1988, he was dean for external graduate programs at Antioch University in Ohio. Previously, he had taught at the California School of Professional Psychology, the Graduate Theological Union in Berkeley, the University of California at Los Angeles, the University of Hawaii, the University of New Mexico, and the College of Santa Fe. He was a charter member of the Association for Death Education and Counseling and a prime mover in initiating the journal *Omega: Journal of Death and Dying*. Dr. Kalish was the recipient of grants to research death and bereavement from the National Institute of Mental Health and the Center for Studies of Suicide Prevention.

Among Dr. Kalish's publications are more than 130 articles and chapters and fourteen books, including *Psychology of Human Behavior*, first published in 1966; *Death and Ethnicity: A Psychocultural Study* (1976); *Death and Dying: Views from Many Cultures* (1977); *Exploring Human Values* (1980); *Late Adulthood* (2d ed., 1982); and *Death, Grief, and Caring Relationships* (2d ed., 1984).

In a memorial to Dr. Kalish published in the *Forum*, the newsletter of the Association for Death Education and Counseling, his friend and colleague Robert Kastenbaum recalled: "Keenly aware of our common mortality, at times touched, depressed, and angered by the failings his observations so often revealed, Dick nevertheless retained his zeal and wholeheartedness. The literature of thanatology and quite a few thanatologists will continue to benefit from the knowledge he acquired and shared."

DEATH EDUCATORS AND counselors have always been aware of the need to understand ethnic and subcultural differences in values, attitudes, expectations, rituals, and customs. During the last decade, two major studies involving death and ethnicity have both been conducted in southern California, along with funeral practices of the Amish; Hispanics; blacks; and Appalachian whites.[1]

In this article, we will review the death-related experiences and concerns of the Hmong refugees from Laos, a numerically small, recently arrived ethnic group in the United States. We will focus on recent encounters with death along with current funerary and burial practices. As we describe their practices and preferences, we shall comment briefly on the often obvious problems of maintaining cultural values and traditions in the United States.

Hmong Refugees in the United States

It is estimated that there are approximately 60,000 Hmong in this country. This number represents about 8.3 percent of all southeast Asian refugees who have settled here during the past decade.[2] For these Hmong, death has been very much a part of their history. In the early 1960s, fully 10 percent of their population were killed while fighting the invading Pathet Lao and North Vietnamese, and virtually every family lost at least one or two members.[3] When Laos fell under Communist domination in the summer of 1975, thousands of Hmong, fearing that they would be killed, fled to Thailand.

Their escape from Laos, however, required a long march through mountainous areas and rain forests, and an eventual crossing of the Mekong River. During their flight an estimated 35 percent died from illness, drowning, starvation, jungle accidents, or Pathet Lao forces.[4] The Hmong seldom had time to bury their dead, who were left to rot where they fell; often the ill and wounded were also left behind.[5] Even their arrival in refugee camps in Thailand did not necessarily provide adequate relief, and many more died in the camps. It is unlikely that any Hmong refugee arrived in the United States without having observed numerous deaths at first hand, including those of family and clan members, and without having

experienced the frustration of not being able to provide all of these individuals with proper funerals and burial.

The authors believe that Holocaust research may provide a lead for understanding the significance of what the Hmong have experienced emotionally. Lifton's work, for example, with the *hibakusha,* survivors of the initial nuclear blasts in Japan, describes the numbing effect on these individuals—their disbelief, incredulity, and confusion.[6] They suffered tremendous guilt, in part because so many others were calling for help and could not be helped; virtually any survivor had inevitably ignored at least one dying person; in addition, the well-known survivor guilt was evident. Studies of survivors of the Nazi Holocaust have also established the overwhelming, long-range effects on those who lived through concentration camps and comparable experiences.[7] Unfortunately, very little is known about the impact on an individual of viewing many deaths, including deaths of family members and close friends, in a brief span of time. However, the high level of depression and inactivity experienced by elderly Hmong, as reported by Hayes, can be at least partially explained through Kastenbaum's concept of bereavement overload.[8] The intensity of such bereavement might be expected to increase exponentially when the losses that follow each other in rapid succession include not only deaths, but also losses in status, possessions, familiar surroundings, and separation from loved ones.

Another more recent kind of encounter with death is also an inevitable cause for deep concern. Between 1983 and 1987, thirty-five Hmong died in their sleep. This has been termed "Sudden Death Syndrome," an obvious allusion to the Sudden Infant Death Syndrome, which up until very recently was assumed to occur among infants who showed no signs of ill health. Since the Hmong who were victims of Sudden Death had all presumably been in good health prior to their deaths, stress has been suggested as the cause.[9]

This phenomenon is reminiscent of a similar epidemic of deaths among the Filipino population of Hawaii in the 1950s, when it was termed "sleeping death" and was sometimes attributed to food eaten at the previous meal. To our knowledge, no definitive explanation of these deaths has ever been presented. Weisman and Hackett have written about post-operative deaths that occurred without known cause, other than perhaps stress or readiness to die, and Kalish has described what he terms "non-medical interventions in life and death," which appear to have some comparability to the Hmong experience.[10]

Funeral and Burial Practices: In Laos and in Transition

The Hmong have resided in the mountains of northern Laos for a relatively brief period of time. They arrived in Laos during the 1820s after having been forced out of southern China by the military forces of the Han emperor. Thus, their customs in Laos have been influenced by the Chinese. The following account is based on the works of Betts, Barney, Geddes, and Vang, as well as the interviews that Hayes conducted with numerous Hmong refugees in the Orange County and Long Beach areas of southern California.[11]

When a person dies, three mortars are fired to alert the village and relatives. Soon after, paper money is burned in the presence of the deceased, a custom also found among the Chinese. The paper money is not actual currency, but a symbolic form of money for the dead person to use in the next existence. The next step is for the children and grandchildren of the deceased to wash the body and clothe it. Special shoes for the body are made by men of a different clan (there are, altogether, about twenty Hmong clans), and the body is placed in the central room of the house on two benches that represent a seat of honor. The death now becomes the occasion for an elaborate ceremony that lasts several days until the burial.

During this period, a lamp is kept burning to guide the spirit, and incense is ignited next to a bowl of uncooked rice to ward off demons.

How are these customs expressed in southern California? Obviously, the mortars cannot be fired, although other methods of notifying family and clan members can certainly be used. The paper money can still be burned, since the laws against destroying real money are not involved. Washing and clothing the body at home are possibilities if the person has died at home or if arrangements are made in advance with the hospital, although it is likely that the washing and dressing might need to be done at the hospital prior to transporting the body home. Most certainly, men of other clans can still make shoes, and neither the light nor the incense violates western laws or southern California customs. In fact, both flame and "sweet odors" are familiar in western religious ceremonies.

Prominent elders and clan leaders from the village may remain in the house for as long as five days because more oxen and buffalo will need to be killed to provide food for those who come from far away for the ceremony.[12] It seems likely that housing the leaders can still be accomplished or can be done symbolically, and that substitutes for oxen and buffalo may be obtained (if money is available) at the grocery store. The major difficulty produced by the customs described above is that of keeping the body unembalmed for considerably longer than public health laws or health safety (as defined in this country) permit.

On the day of the burial, the *txi txhia tso* (funeral director) leads a procession of musicians; a sacrificial cow; a horse that has been owned by the deceased and has been kept, saddled and bridled, in the yard of his house since just after his death; and the mourners to the burial spot that had been selected previously by the dead person. A service is then conducted by the funeral director, who recites chants to the *tlan* (spirit) world on behalf of the deceased. After about an hour of chanting, an animal (normally a cow) is usually sacrificed to sustain the soul on its journey to the spirit realm. Following the burial, a giant feast is held for the entire village. The total process takes about two weeks. This is connected with the Hmong belief that for thirteen days after burial, the soul is transforming from a human state to a spiritual one that will return to the place of birth.

Most of the activities described in the previous paragraph are difficult or impossible to conduct in southern California, although a rural area might be more hospitable. Neither Long Beach nor Orange County permits horses to be maintained in the yard for any time interval; the kind of procession described would probably require a permit that might well be turned down; and walking to the graveyard is virtually impossible in southern California. Obviously, the sacrificial animal is completely contrary to both law and custom in the United States. On one occasion for another kind of ceremony, a Hmong family that sacrificed a chicken drew vociferous complaints from neighbors and a warning visit from the authorities.

In reviewing these last three paragraphs, it seems probable that most funeral customs can be maintained or adapted without significant violation of the Hmong value system. However, the use of animals and the funeral procession would require extensive change. The former might need to be conducted in some symbolic form, while the latter could be done with automobiles. The foot procession would be held only at the cemetery or, perhaps, at some other previously designated and approved location.

Major Concerns of the Elders

The elders interviewed by the senior author had a variety of concerns that involved funeral and burial practices in the United States, but three of them were primary. First, most of the Hmong complained about not being able to select their own burial spot. In Laos, an auspi-cious place for a burial had the same characteristics as a lucky site for a home or village: "The shoulder of a mountain sloping at 30–60 degrees, surrounded by other mountains."[13] The Hmong are accustomed to selecting their own burial spot that, given the relatively sparse population of their mountainous homeland, did not require official or legal approval. As one elder discussed in the interview: "It is difficult to accept that I cannot have freedom to decide where I am to be buried. In Laos the old found comfort knowing where they were to be placed." However, in the United States their options are obviously limited by laws and, because of their reduced finances, influenced by their ability to pay. The Hmong not only are unable to be buried in an appropriate site but also reject the act of placing graves side by side.[14] Obviously, when a Hmong contemplates his or her death or that of a family member, it can be only with apprehension that some important ceremonies will be missing or will be provided in symbolic form only.

The suspicions that the Hmong elders hold of local cemeteries are extensive. For example, several expressed the belief that the cemeteries do not keep the bodies in the designated grave but remove them to conserve space by placing them much closer to each other. One informant asked Hayes if the government decided whether or not a body was to be moved.

The second concern of the elders, expressed almost unanimously, was the introduction of embalming fluid into the body. Several explicated their position by explaining that this substance would prevent the soul from returning to its birthplace. Others objected on the grounds that the fluid would cause the body to be deformed when it was reincarnated in the next life. One Hmong elder expressed the feeling that "embalming could be accepted provided wiring is not used to secure the jaws and assurances made that no additional metals or plastics are in the body."

The third issue was equally perplexing for the Hmong. As indicated earlier, the Hmong are accustomed to keeping the body at home for several days so that relatives could come by for viewing. The elders find the familiar policy of funeral parlors that permit viewing only for limited hours to be unsatisfactory. Their bind, of course, resembled the classic "Catch-22." Without embalming the body, it cannot be maintained for any duration in the home; with the body embalmed, the soul could not return home and would presumably continue to wander.

There are some indications that funeral directors in Fresno, California, which has a large settlement of Hmong refugees, are attempting to address some of the elders' concerns. Space in the chapel is being reserved for the body to be displayed for three to five days. Certain directors are allowing the Hmong to bring food and beverages into the chapel without a cleaning deposit that could cost as much as $1,000. In addition, assurances are being given that during the embalming process no foreign objects such as eyecaps nor wire to secure the jaw will be used.

Some Final Thoughts

Although this article focuses on the death and bereavement practices of a very small ethnic community in the United States, the implications are considerable for professionals who provide death-related services. There is a strong tendency for service providers in general to develop personal treatment or intervention philosophies and policies based on their own background and experiences. These perspectives are then generalized to segments of the population that might not share the implicit values on which the philosophies and policies were developed. People who work with the dying and the grieving members of refugee groups frequently have little or no concept of the cultural expectations of these groups, and the time or ability to communicate across cultural and language barriers is often lacking.

The issues, however, do not begin when death is imminent or has occurred. Rather, as has been obvious with the Hmong, the potential violation of their deeply held values became obvious to them shortly after their arrival in this country. Thus, although death, funerals, and burial are the content of their concern, the process is constant and ongoing. In many instances, it is impossible to reconcile the Hmong culture with public health laws. In some instances, those Hmong who have relocated to areas more rural than Orange County have been able to follow their familiar rituals and ceremonies more closely. However, while there are many valid reasons to require the Hmong to forego some of their death-related practices, there is no valid reason for the health care professionals to maintain ignorance of and insensitivity to the nature and importance of these values to the Hmong. Perhaps if each of us were required to go through the ritual of sacrificing a cow, we would experience the visceral level reactions that the Hmong feel when they are forbidden to practice some of the most important ceremonies of their culture.

To generalize from the Hmong experience to that of other groups is not difficult. Basically, it would seem highly appropriate for those who work with the dying and the grieving, as well as service providers in general, to acquire some basic knowledge of the customs and values of the peoples with whom they have professional contact. In addition. they also need to be aware of the recent history and present circumstances of these ethnic communities. Policies, programs, and practice all need to be based on the solid ground of knowledge and understanding, not simply on good will and kind feelings. The Hmong have faced losses of unbelievable proportions and now confront constant violations of their cherished customs and values. To provide services in ignorance of their circumstances is, to put it in the most crass of terms, cost-inefficient, both in human and in dollar terms.

Contemporary African-American Funeral Rites and Traditions

RONALD K. BARRETT

RONALD K. BARRETT, PH.D., is an associate professor of psychology at Loyola Marymount University in Los Angeles. Dr. Barrett says, "I vividly recall my first experience at a traditional funeral as a young African-American child. It was replete in ritual and cultural symbolism, although much of it I did not understand at the time. Later, during my freshman year of college, I read Jessica Mitford's book, *The American Way of Death,* as an assignment for an English class. This book had a great impact on me, as did my participation in a provocative death and dying survey which was part of a special issue of *Psychology Today.* Other than these experiences, I had little occasion to think about or contemplate issues related to death and dying until nearly fifteen years later.

At Loyola Marymount University, my friend and colleague Dr. Howard Delaney had taught for years a course on the philosophy of death. He was about to retire and suggested that I teach it. I remember him saying, "It would be a natural for a psychologist." Reluctantly, I said that I'd think about it. Howard began sending me articles and books. Boxes of material would mysteriously show up on my doorstep. I subsequently proposed a new course on the psychology of death and dying and, with the blessing of the Department of Psychology and its dean, the new course was born. With an increased commitment of my resources, research focus, and volunteer time, the issues of death and dying evolved as my professional priority and specialty. The more I became involved with the literature of death and dying, the more disturbed I became at what seemed a conspicuous absence of published research on the African-American experience. So, I've made a commitment to study and document this experience in the death and dying literature."

In addition to teaching, Dr. Barrett is a researcher and the author of scholarly publications on topics related to mental health. He also conducts workshops and seminars, both in southern California and nationally, and is a consultant to public-service agencies and institutions. His presentations at the 1990 National Black Studies Convention and at the 1991 King's College International Conference on Death and Dying in London, Ontario, ultimately led to publication of the chapter "Psychocultural Influences on African-American Attitudes Towards Death, Dying, and Funeral Rites," in *Personal Care in an Impersonal World,* edited by John Morgan (1993). The following selection is from Dr. Barrett's forthcoming book, *Death, Dying, and Funeral Rites: The African-American Experience.*

CONTEMPORARY AFRICAN-AMERICAN funeral rites and practices are a fusion of traditional African and Western psychocultural influences. The way African Americans ritualize their dead is deeply rooted in the attitudes, beliefs, and values of their African ancestry—particularly those of West Africa.[1] The diaspora to the North American continent during the institution of slavery occurred largely through seaports in Western Africa. Thus, it is more than coincidental that influences on present practices among African Americans can be traced back to West Africa.[2]

Influenced by acculturation in the Americas during slavery and following emancipation, African Americans adopted many of the ways of their masters and became westernized. While many traditional notions regarding death and dying that derived from African religion, philosophy, and world view remained relatively intact, others were significantly modified during the adaptations and adjustments to the New World. Having left behind their homeland and traditional culture, the African slaves soon lost many of their traditional religious practices, adopting in their place the religious practices of their captors. In practicing this new religion, however, these African people still maintained aspects of their traditional past. As many observers have noted, the African-American expression of Christianity consistently reflects aspects of the African tradition, as is evident in the Black idiom and the legacy of the Black church. Although African Americans routinely do many of the same things in their religious services (preach, witness, pray, make music) as their European American counterparts, they do so with an element of traditional African influence commonly referred to as *soul*. The unique and colorful character of the Black church is a byproduct of the African-American interpretation of the Western church and, as with traditional West African funeral rites, the normative practice of African-American funeral rites is significantly related to religious beliefs.

Ecological and Subcultural Influences

The African-American experience is as varied as the many shades of skin tones observed in African Americans. It is more heterogeneous than homogeneous. It reflects a behavioral style affected by the ecological and subcultural influences of religious beliefs, ethnicity, and social class. Ethnicity or race alone is too broad a concept to articulate meaningful generalizations or rules that can be applied to all African Americans. In studying the social and psychological differences found among African Americans, scholars have come to appreciate the insight gained when the interactive influences of religion, ethnicity, and social class are considered together. An appreciation of these influences is important for understanding the unique and rich patterns by which African Americans confront dying and death.

Religion

The faith or belief system of an individual inevitably plays a significant role in influencing his or her attitudes, beliefs, and values. It is reasonable to assume that the influence of religion also depends on (a) the type of religious experience and denomination, (b) the age at which religious conversion occurs, (c) the extent of religious practice and internalization of belief, and (d) the degree of religious socialization within the family and supporting community. These aspects of religious experience mediate the influence of religion on world views, attitudes, beliefs, and values.[3]

A body of research findings in social psychology suggests that the earlier and greater the amount of developmental life experiences one has in a belief system and faith community, the more likely one is to internalize the prescribed religious attitudes, beliefs, and values of that belief system or faith community. Similarly, the earlier and greater one's socialization experiences related to a belief system or religion, the more influential the attitudes, beliefs, and values of that religion or faith community on the individual's subsequent behaviors—attitudes, beliefs, and values. For example, consider the following case illustration of contrasting reactions to death, dying, and funeral practices in the experiences of two African-American families.

Frank Smith and James Robinson participated in their employer's ride-share program. One evening, a drunk driver collided with the pickup truck driven by Robinson; Smith was a front-seat passenger. Neither man was wearing a seat belt, and both were thrown through the truck's windshield upon impact. Both men were in critical condition and remained in that condition in intensive care for several weeks. Given the extent of head trauma, neither was expected to live or fully recover.

Frank Smith was a fifty-four-year-old African-American man with a wife and two young teenage children. The Smiths belonged to the neighborhood Mt. Zion A.M.E. Church. They were a close-knit, lower-income African-American family. During the lengthy period of Smith's illness—as he lay in critical condition for some forty-five days—his family was approached by the hospital staff about donating his vital organs. During the last twenty-four hours of his life, they decided to give their consent for an autopsy and donation. The family choose to memorialize Smith in a private ceremony and to cremate his body. The arrangement for a simple cremation came to a total cost of about $1,500.

James Robinson was a fifty-three-year-old African-American man who was widowed with no children. His wife, Ella, had died of breast cancer seven years earlier. The Robinsons had been members of the Southern Baptist Community Church. His most immediate survivor was Anna Robinson, his eighty-three-year-old mother, who attended church and Bible study at the community's Jehovah's Witness temple. When approached by the hospital staff about tissue donations, Anna Robinson flatly refused, nor would she permit the attending physicians to conduct an autopsy to determine the exact cause of her son's death. Anna Robinson's religious views also influenced her decision not to authorize a critical life-saving blood transfusion upon James's admission to the emergency room. Upon his death, Anna decided to memorialize James's death with a traditional home-going ceremony. The cost included $4,500 for the funeral and $2,800 for a traditional cemetery burial with an upright grave marker near his deceased wife's plot.

Different religions and religious denominations shape spirituality in different ways. The more conservative the religious experience, the more conservative and traditional will be the attitudes, beliefs, and values that ultimately affect behavioral style (see Figure 1). The more conservative believers can be characterized as the "keepers of tradition." They hold to old ways of relating to death, dying, and funeral rites. Many conservative believers object to

Figure 1

Major African-American Spiritual and Religious Experiences

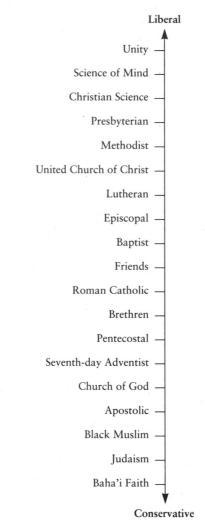

blood donations, the medical autopsy, and tissue or organ donations. More liberal believers typically take more liberties and risks, breaking with tradition and conventional practices, including those related to death, dying, and funeral rites (see Table 1). Of course, no set of believers is monolithic; each denomination has its conservative and liberal practitioners.

Table 1

Major Religious Views on Life, Death, and Dying

Religion	Baptism	Anointing	Postmortem Examination	Body Donation	Blood Transfusion	Organ Transplants	Burial or Cremation	Euthanasia
Anglican Church	Priority	Routine	No position	No position	No position	No position	B/C	Against
Roman Catholic	Priority	Routine	No position	No position	No position	No position	B/C	Against
Jehovah's Witness	Priority	Routine	No position	No position	Against	No position	B/C	Against
Mormon	Priority	Routine	No position	No position	No objection	No position	B	Against
Christian Science	Priority	Routine	Against	Against	Against	Against	C	Against
Afro-Caribbean	Rare	Rare	Against	Against	No objection	No objection	B	Against
Rastafarianism	Rare	Rare	Against	Against	Against	Against	B	Against
Buddhism	Rare	Rare	No objection	No objection	No objection	No objection	C	Against
Baha'i faith	Rare	Rare	No objection	No objection	No objection	No objection	B	Against
Judaism	Rare	Rare	Against	No objection	No objection	No objection	B	Against
Islam	Rare	Rare	Against	No objection	Against	Against	B	Against
Hinduism	Rare	Rare	Against	No objection	Against	No objection	C	Against
Sikhism	Routine	Routine	No objection	No objection	No objection	No objection	B	Against
Zoroastrianism	Rare	Rare	Against	Against	Against	Against	B/C	Against

SOURCE: Based on information in J. Green and M. Green, *Dealing with Death* (New York: Chapman and Hall, 1922), 147–230.

Ethnicity

The subcultural influence of ethnicity and race consciousness has been extensively studied, with the general agreement that African Americans differ in the degree of their identification and internalization of Black consciousness. Psychologist Jerome Taylor's pioneering work with a similar concept, termed *racialism,* enabled a number of notable research studies by the Pittsburgh Group in the 1970s.[4] Consistent with the findings and theory of race consciousness, these studies show that African Americans whose racialism scores reflected a negative set of internalized beliefs were more likely to respond negatively towards other African Americans and towards African-American culture while responding more favorably toward European Americans and European-American culture and values.

Cultural identification has been extensively studied relative to self-reference or identification preferences, friendship preferences, and marital patterns. Consistent with the theory of racial identification, African Americans who fostered a positive racial identity and consciousness were more likely to respond positively towards other African Americans and towards African-American culture and tradition. Therefore, although it is reasonable to assume that African Americans' experiences will generally produce certain characteristic attitudes, beliefs, values, and world view, there are differences among African Americans. Those who have a positive sense of African-American consciousness are more likely to behave in ways that reflect their subcultural racial consciousness. Consequently, the stronger the sense of cultural identification, the greater the tendency to adopt traditional attitudes, beliefs, and values regarding death and funeral rites.

Social Class

As studies by demographers and social scientists have shown, socioeconomic status is significantly linked to a number of correlates, suggesting that social class is an influential subcultural variable. Understandably, a person's experience with poverty or wealth may have a significant impact on his or her attitudes, beliefs, and values. The impact of this environmental and ecological variable depends upon the (a) degree to which one is near the extremes of socioeconomic status (poverty or wealth), (b) experience of socioeconomic status during one's childhood, and (c) extent to which the experiences resulting from one's socioeconomic status are internalized and identified with. An individual raised in a poor family will develop attitudes, beliefs, values, and a world view reflecting the limitations and constraints of poverty, whereas a child of more advantaged circumstances is likely to develop a world view affirming wealth. A person who was not raised in poverty but who in adult life falls below the poverty line typically maintains the values, attitudes, and world view nurtured during his or her formative years.

The assumption that early childhood and family experiences are more influential than experiences of the later years is held widely by psychodynamic clinicians (for example, the object relations school) as well as students of child development (as seen in studies of imprinting, primary effect, and modeling). In fact, there is a considerable body of theoretical and empirical data supporting the notion that an individual's attitudes, beliefs, and values— including those regarding death, dying, and funeral rites—are significantly influenced by the intimate environment of his or her formative years and are sensitive to considerations related to socioeconomic status.

An important environmental and ecological influence on African Americans is the extent to which traditional Southern subcultural values and life styles are internalized and identified with. Among African Americans, the Southern life style is typically traditional and Afro-centric with distinctive elements of *soul* observable in music, foods, family and relational styles, practice of religion and worship, and so forth.

Sociologists have noted that as African Americans have migrated throughout the country, leaving family members and community behind, they have also become less traditional, soon adopting a more Westernized life style and world view. This assertion is supported by the observation that the more traditional African approaches to funeral rites are still routinely practiced in some regions of the southeastern United States.[5] As Elaine Nichols documents in *The Last Miles of the Way*, many practices associated with African-American funeral rites can be traced to the southeastern seashores of South Carolina and from there to West African traditions.[6] An overview of those African-American rituals and practices regarding death and dying will be provided in the following sections.

Care of the Sick and Dying

In contrast to the Western emphasis on selfhood and individualism, African-American values have historically emphasized a genuine concern for community and for others. Traditional norms and expectations suggest that caring for the less fortunate, the ill, and the dying is the proper and socially acceptable thing to do. Even if this traditional African value of sacrificing for others had not been adopted and internalized, the institution of slavery, by involving African Americans in caregiver roles, promoted such attitudes. Throughout their early years on this continent as well as later, African Americans demonstrated compassion and the capacity to care for others, both family members and strangers.

With their adoption of Christian theological precepts, African Americans often became so good at being caregivers that they routinely became self-sacrificial martyrs. Care of the elderly, the sick, and the terminally ill was something quite natural. It was customary for people to be born at home and to die at home. Dying and death were regarded as part of the natural rhythms of life. Witnessing firsthand the processes of birth and death, children

as well as adults naturally became *death-accepting*. In the traditional African family setting, embraced by an atmosphere of openness, the process of dying was sustained with an attitude of acceptance. This provides stark contrast to the modern Western situation where care and regard for the elderly, ill, and dying is typified by institutional care in hospitals and nursing facilities. Consequently contemporary Western society has been characterized as *death-denying*. African Americans have tended not to adopt this modern western view. They have been shown to underutilize institutional health care and related services, they generally do not place their elderly in nursing homes, and hospice care is typically not chosen for the terminally ill.

In traditional African culture, illness is met with a community response, with many people present to offer spiritual support to the patient and his or her family.[7] Relatives and members of the community are encouraged to gather for visitation vigils when someone is ill. There is no sense of limits to the number of visitors or timed visits, as found in the institutional care routinely practiced throughout the Western world. As the literature on hospice and home care shows, however, patients benefit from being able to maintain a sense of connectedness, which is fostered when family members are involved in caregiving. Just as the arrival of a new baby represents an addition to the community, the death of an elderly or infirm citizen represents a loss to the community. According to the Western world view, life and death are opposites, as seen in the linear model shown in Figure 2, with birth and death appearing at opposite ends of the life line. In contrast, the traditional African world view sees birth and death as part of a cycle, in which life is portrayed as a circle or cosmogram.[8] Ancient African drawings of cosmograms symbolically represented the four moments of the sun in the four quadrants of the circle. Similar representations of the circle as a symbol of life and the wholeness of life are found in ancient Egyptian

Figure 2

Symbolized Meaning of Life and Death

African Cosmogram

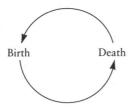

Western Linear Model

art, which is believed to have influenced traditional African art and belief systems. A holistic view of life and death minimizes the emotional trauma when death occurs.

Preparation for Death

When a death is anticipated, members of the family and community assemble. According to traditional African beliefs and folklore, assembling for prayer and meditation assists the dying person in making his or her transition to the afterlife and spirit world.[9] West African death and funeral rites reflect a belief in the reality of the unseen spiritual world and the thinness of the veil separating the living from the dead (see Figure 2).[10]

According to this belief, the dying pass beyond the veil; their happiness in the other world depends upon the due and effective performance of customary rites.[11] These rites may include preparation of food and clothing; chanting and singing; and prayerful appeals to God, deities, or ancestral spirits who assist and ensure the dying person's passage into the spirit world.[12] Physical death is simply a transition to the spirit world, which is regarded as a happy place. Consequently the dying are assuaged and reassured by this belief and do not resist death. References to the welcomed respite of the afterlife form the substance of

African-American spirituals, gospel, blues, and jazz.[13] Similar references are reflected in other dimensions of African-American art, including poetry, literature, drama, and visual arts.

The belief that death involves a transition from the material to the spirit world is not unique to Africans. Many cultures and groups share that view. Indeed, ancient Egyptian beliefs about the afterlife became a significant influence on West African beliefs.[14] Such beliefs are reinforced by modern accounts of the dying process and reports of near-death experiences. These accounts consistently report that dying and life transition involve out-of-the-body experiences, movement through a dark tunnel or corridor followed by visions of a bright light at the far end, feelings of serenity and calm, the presence of deceased loved ones who greet the dying person at the threshold of the afterlife, and the need to choose whether to proceed or turn back. Through countless accounts, such experiences bear a remarkable similarity to the ancient and traditional beliefs.

Other traditional African-American beliefs about death are that (a) "death comes in threes," claiming three members of a family or community in a relatively short period of time; (b) with every death there is a birth into the family or community; (c) it is important to acknowledge and honor the dead by naming babies after the dead; and (d) on the occasion of the funeral of a loved one, it brings good luck to newborn babies to pass them over the casket of the dead person.[15]

Funeral Guilds and Pre-Need Arrangements

Consistent with African tradition, African Americans expect that the higher the social status and esteem of the dead person, the greater should be the priority given to, the investment in, and the sacrifice made for disposing of the dead.[16] Most African Americans express the desire to have a decent funeral. A grand finale is also viewed as important for individuals whose lives have been characterized by modest living, delayed gratification, and self-sacrifice.[17] Because of the importance of ritual and the enactment of customary burial rites, the funeral and disposition of the dead is regarded as a "primary ritual" involving considerable investment of capital and sacrifice.

Membership in funeral guilds was common in ancient Egypt as well as West Africa. Such membership provided assurance that money would be available for burials and that customary and highly esteemed funeral rituals would be adhered to when death comes. The funeral societies among African Americans in the colonial southeastern United States were direct extensions of the ancient funeral guilds.[18] These African-American funeral societies became quite elaborate and often competitive, evolving into powerful political and social forces within a community. They were organized like social clubs, with officers, regular social functions, and uniforms. Members would dress up in their uniforms for "turnouts" and parades, as well as for funerals of the society's members. Visual presentation was impressive, significantly enhancing the sense of ritualized ceremony and thereby transforming an ordinary funeral into a grand event.

As insurance plans became affordable to African Americans in the early 1900s, traditional funeral societies began to fade away. Insurance policies offered the advantages of convenient affordable payments as well as of portable death-benefit options, a feature that was especially appealing to the growing number of African Americans migrating North in pursuit of jobs and a better way of life. The larger portion of the face value of these insurance policies often would be designated for burial purposes, with little consideration for survivor benefits or estate planning. Many insurance companies reaped sizable profits by marketing such burial policies to poor and poorly educated individuals. While many people could not afford term or whole-life insurance, most (even the poor) could afford the weekly premiums that would ensure their proper burial.

The process of aging and becoming an elder in the community involves most senior African Americans in some form of planning for death. The term *pre-need*, coined by morticians, refers to arrangements for funeral rites and body disposition made prior to death. (Where made at the time of death, they are termed *at-need* arrangements.) Financial planning is now viewed as a routine aspect of living responsibly as an adult and a parent. Although education and socioeconomic levels determine the extent of one's preparations, the National Funeral Directors and Morticians Association reports that about 60 percent of African Americans over age fifty make some kind of pre-need funeral arrangements. Kalish and Reynolds report that elderly African Americans were more likely to make pre-need funeral and burial arrangements than any other group.[19]

Grieving and the Care of the Dead

Distinctive African-American traditions are evident in the procedures and practices that take place once death has occurred. Beginning with the first call to the funeral establishment and throughout the period of mourning that culminates in disposition of the body, unique aspects of traditional funeral practice remain important to African Americans.

The First Call

The term *first call* is used by funeral homes to refer to the first formal contact with a family regarding funeral arrangements when a death has occurred. Calling the funeral home initializes plans for a funeral.[20] It establishes a formal business relationship with the funeral home, allowing the mortician to take possession of the body and to begin preparations for the funeral. The person making these at-need funeral arrangements, usually including the legal next of kin, then meets with the funeral director to discuss details of how the funeral will be conducted and payment made.[21]

Normally, the funeral director also assists families in making arrangements for the final disposition of the body. This may include contacting cemeteries, obtaining burial permits, and so forth. Within traditional African culture, it was customary for close family members to be involved in the physical preparation of the body and of the burial place. Turning these tasks over to funeral directors is a fairly recent development, one that has occurred within the last century.[22]

In the southeastern United States, once the body is removed from the home or hospital, it is customary for the funeral director to place a memorial wreath on the front door of the family dwelling. The front porch light is kept burning day and night until the burial is completed, symbolizing the family's loss and alerting friends and members of the community to the fact that a death has occurred. Although the traditional funeral wreath is commonly used in the southeast, it is rarely found in the North or West.

Choosing a funeral home is subject to a number of considerations, including cost, convenience, rapport with staff, and the level of community esteem for the establishment. For African Americans, an additional consideration has to do with the mortuary's professional reputation for making the deceased look natural. The art of embalming African Americans is quite challenging given the varieties of skin tones and shades. In comparison with funeral directors generally, African-American funeral directors typically demonstrate greater skill in this respect and therefore enjoy a more favorable professional reputation among African Americans. Historically, racism and segregation nurtured the growth of African-American funeral directors, and it is common in the African-America community for funeral directors to be highly esteemed and given much dignity and honor.

Notifications and Announcements

Following a death, family members and relatives are notified as soon as possible. The immediacy of notification is equated with importance and respect. To not be informed of the death in a timely manner is considered insensitive, lacking respect, and an insult.

Because it is important for family members to gather together and be present at the funeral, the funeral may be postponed for as long as a week to ten days to allow time for relatives and friends to gather from afar. Since the death of a loved one is regarded as a primary ritual, attendance and participation in the funeral rites are expected.

African Americans have traditionally used word-of-mouth for death notification and funeral announcements. The use of formal newspaper obituaries for notification has evolved fairly recently, but word-of-mouth remains the preferred and more common medium. In announcing a death, it is usual to say that the deceased has "passed," "slipped away," or "gone home." As with the wider society, avoiding the word *dead* reflects, in part, an attitude of death denial.

The Community Response

A death within the African-American community usually evokes a variety of strong emotional reactions that vary according to a number of factors: the age at which the person died, the circumstances of death, the social esteem or likability of the deceased, the timing of the death, and so on. With the death of a seriously ill or aged person, survivors may experience a sense of relief or joy. The death of a baby, child, or other young person, on the other hand, usually evokes considerable sorrow and sadness. African Americans are not alone in regarding the death of a young person as a contradiction of the order of nature.

Violent, tragic, and other such unnatural deaths that cut short a life also tend to evoke more sorrow and sadness. Homicide has become a leading cause of death among young African-American males.[23] Indeed, homicidal violence is having a significant impact on death rates and life expectancy among all African Americans. An eroded quality of life, illicit drug use, and gang activities have combined to cause the homicide rate to soar to an all-time high. The persistent trend of homicidal violence in the African-American community has been regarded as an emerging public health concern. As homicidal violence becomes chronic and persistent in many African-American communities, individuals become desensitized to a mode of death that is socially unacceptable yet a daily occurrence in some communities.

Suicide and other self-destructive behaviors are also evident within the African-American community. Although the suicide rate in the United States is highest among white males, self-destructive behavior is increasingly evident among African Americans as well, particularly among young males. A variety of life style choices—including smoking, substance abuse, and failing to take responsibility for one's own health—also contributes unnecessarily to the mortality rate of African Americans.[24]

HIV-related diseases and AIDS-related deaths have presented immense challenges for the African-American community as unprecedented numbers of young people are diagnosed with the virus, suffer the effects of illness, or face the prospect of dying. Parents and grandparents find it especially hard to face the prospect of burying sons and daughters. For African Americans of some sociopolitical and religious backgrounds, the stigma of HIV-related deaths raises further emotional conflicts around issues of moral behavior and sexuality. The deaths of persons with AIDS are often publicly explained as being caused by some other ailment—much as cancer has sometimes been stigmatized—with patients and their loved ones publicly denying the actual cause of death. Incurable diseases tend to produce fear, dread, and denial, all of which may increase the risk of complicated mourning.

Public awareness of the facts about HIV and AIDS can help mourners deal with their losses. Within the African-American community, the church is well situated to provide leadership that can help patients and their loved ones to cope successfully with the challenging issues of moral judgment, compassionate care, spiritual crisis, and the tendency to blame the victim.

Sit-ups and Wakes

Although not as common as they once were, "sit-ups" historically have been an important element of African-American mourning behavior. Following the announcement of a death, it is customary for close relatives and friends to gather for a vigil with the aim of assuaging the grief and sorrow of the mourners. This vigil, or sit-up, goes on day and night, with participants taking turns to relieve one another for rest or to attend to other responsibilities and commitments. Relatives and friends who come to the home of the immediate family take charge, serving as greeters and hosts for the other visitors who come calling to express their condolences. Food and beverages from friends and others in the community are donated to feed visitors and the family. During the early phase of mourning, family members are not expected to cook or prepare food; they are given the opportunity to simply rest and be with their grief. Monetary gifts are also made to assist the family in paying funeral expenses.

Although sit-ups are not common today, the wake is a widely practiced funeral tradition among African Americans. Wakes and sit-ups share many features; in the wake, however, the body of the deceased is present for viewing. Like sit-ups, wakes are usually held in the home. In the traditional wake, the mortuary brought the body to the family home for display in the parlor or living room, where it would remain until the funeral. Customarily, the wake is held the evening before the funeral. The assembled family, friends, and community members engage in a marathon of storytelling, recalling memorable experiences with the deceased, keeping the stories positive and light while avoiding excessive expressions of sorrow, weeping, or overt grief.[25]

Wakes may be held either at the family home or at the mortuary, in the early evening the day before the funeral. There is often an open casket to facilitate viewing by those who work during the day. Wakes held in the home rarely include the presence of the casket and the body for viewing; in these cases, visiting with the family is done in the home and viewing of the body takes place at the funeral parlor. In both types of wakes, however, family members and close friends of the deceased are expected to be present to greet and receive visitors. Funeral homes customarily provide a registry for visitors to sign to record their presence as a symbolic gesture of support.

In the African-American tradition, acknowledging the death and showing one's supportive presence is expected, especially of family, friends, and other close associates. Intentional absence or lack of acknowledgment is considered disrespectful. According to traditional African folklore, such untoward behavior could be interpreted as evidence of ill will or even as sorcery intended to undermine

Figure 3

Contemporary African-American Gestures of Condolence

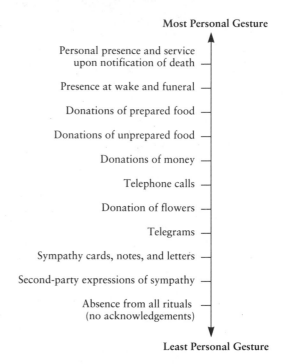

Most Personal Gesture

Personal presence and service upon notification of death

Presence at wake and funeral

Donations of prepared food

Donations of unprepared food

Donations of money

Telephone calls

Donation of flowers

Telegrams

Sympathy cards, notes, and letters

Second-party expressions of sympathy

Absence from all rituals (no acknowledgements)

Least Personal Gesture

the well-being of the dead.[26] It is not unusual for African Americans to travel great distances at considerable personal sacrifice to attend funerals. The more significant the relationship and the more esteemed the deceased, the greater the expectation for being present and acknowledging the loss (see Figure 3).

The Funeral as a Home-Going Ceremony

Consistent with the African belief that the dead pass beyond the veil into the spirit world to joyfully commune with ancestral spirits, African Americans customarily refer to funerals as "home-going" ceremonies.[27] Funeral ritual is regarded as a celebration of the life of the deceased. Thus, it usually takes an upbeat form, although the specific content and form varies depending upon the religious orientation and preference of the family. African-American funeral services are characteristically emotional and spirit-filled, as evidenced through music, symbols, testimonials, commentary, and the eulogy.[28]

Historically, African-American funerals were lengthy and unstructured, allowing for spontaneity. As the spirit might dictate, aspects of the ceremony could be drawn out, thereby lengthening the service. These services were especially characteristic of particular religious and socioeconomic groups within the African-American community, and they closely resembled traditional African funerals. During the 1950s, printed funeral programs came into vogue, giving more structure to the services and consequently decreasing their length. As the funeral became more structured, the degree of spontaneous and unpredictable emotionalism decreased. This development reflected Western influences, and it has suppressed much of the traditional African influence, but the underlying emotional thrust of the service still remains.

West African tradition encouraged emotionalism in funeral rituals.[29] Music and dance were means for evoking feelings. Mourners openly wept and grieved. It was expected that the closer and more significant the loss, the more intense the grief and sorrow, with immediate family expected to express their sorrow overtly. African Americans have similar beliefs. Among African Americans, funeral ceremonies are proving grounds where the intimacy of relationships is demonstrated. Overt emotional displays of grief serve to publicly acknowledge a relationship that may have gone unacknowledged during the lifetime of the deceased. The classic African-American movie, *Imitation of Life,* demonstrates this point well, as does the 1970s rhythm-and-blues single by the Supremes, "Love Child."

During the period of mourning, family members are expected to dress and behave in a manner that shows respect for the dead. In a cross-cultural study of attitudes and expectations towards widows and widowers, Kalish and Reynolds reported that African Americans tend to have specific expectations about how long the bereaved should wait before returning to work, beginning to date, or deciding to marry.[30] While these expectations are generally more liberal than conservative, African-American widows tend to be judged more harshly than widowers when these expectations are violated. (African Americans are not unique in having higher expectations of widows than widowers.)

Although viewing the body of the deceased is customary for African-American funerals, this practice varies, particularly with respect to differing religious beliefs. Typically, decisions about viewing are made in accordance with the preferences of the family and officiating clergy. Some clergy do not favor post-funeral viewing, claiming that it "opens wounds and evokes feelings that the funeral service should assuage." Concern about evoking excessive emotional displays of grief may also influence decisions about open-casket services.

To make peace with the dead in the spirit world—and also to honor an ancient African tradition—some African Americans follow the ritual of passing the youngest child among the relatives over the casket of the deceased. In traditional practice, it was not unusual for a newborn child to be named after the dead person as a way of showing honor to the deceased and maintaining the continuity of intergenerational family relations.[31] Underlying such practices is the belief that the dead continue to be spiritually present and remain an important part of the family and community. In many social gatherings, the dead continue to be honored and acknowledged, both formally and informally. An example of this is seen in the actions of brothers in the 'hood cracking a bottle of wine and spilling a portion of its contents on the ground to honor their comrades who have passed on.

The "Ring Shout" at the Grave Site

Traditionally, the "ring shout" at the grave site provided an emotional and buoyant send-off of the dead. Mourners gathered in a circle around the grave or burial site, waving and flailing their arms in the air as if in a trance as they walked in a processional around the grave. Although rarely practiced today, the ring shout was an essential part of traditional African-American graveside practice.

Consistent with traditional African practice, ground burials are the preferred choice for disposition of the dead among African Americans. Cremation, which is not traditional, is less common, although it is becoming more widely adopted in response to the rising cost of traditional funerals and burials.

A Merger of Tradition and Innovation

As this brief survey shows, contemporary African-American funeral rites and practices reflect a blending of traditional African practices and Western (or European American) psychocultural influences. From the days of their earlier experiences in the institution of slavery on the North American continent, African Americans have continued to adapt and adjust, often adopting the practices of their captors while managing to preserve elements of their traditional African culture. Contemporary practices among African Americans continue to reflect this fusion of tradition and innovation.

Confronting Death

Philippe Ariès. *Images of Man and Death,* translated by Janet Lloyd. Cambridge, Mass.: Harvard University Press, 1985. Conceived as an "imaginary film," this book is a visual presentation of how individuals and society have reshaped images of death to meet prevailing beliefs and social realities of dying. It provides a vivid demonstration that the attitudes and practices in Western culture have not been static over the last two thousand years, nor are they likely to be unchanging in the future.

John R. Elliott. "Funerary Artifacts in Contemporary America." *Death Studies* 14, no. 6 (1990): 601–12. As with people of other cultures and times, many Americans today bury "grave goods" of various kinds with their dead. In this survey of artifacts that are buried and the motives of the bereaved in burying them, Elliott discusses the function and value of such practices, especially their role in effecting closure in relationships. The work also helps us appreciate the concerns voiced by indigenous peoples when their ancestors' graves are disturbed.

Robert Fulton and Greg Owen. "Death and Society in Twentieth Century America." *Omega: Journal of Death and Dying* 18, no. 4 (1988): 379–95. An excellent overview of how attitudes and responses toward death of present generations, especially those born after the advent of the atomic age, differ from those of their predecessors. The images of death in popular culture exhibit a fascination with death despite competing tendencies to avoid or deny its reality.

George Gerbner. "Death in Prime Time: Notes on the Symbolic Functions of Dying in the Mass Media." *Annals of the American Academy of Political and Social Science* 447 (January 1980): 64–70. Gerbner examines how death and dying are portrayed in the mass media, both in news reports and entertainment programs, and suggests that such portrayals are embedded in a structure of violence that leads to a heightened and irrational sense of danger, insecurity, and mistrust that he calls "the mean world syndrome." Our images of death have political as well as psychological implications.

Paul E. Irion. "Changing Patterns of Ritual Response to Death." *Omega: Journal of Death and Dying* 22, no. 3 (1990–1991): 159–72. Changes in the understanding of death and grief produce changes in funeral and memorial rites. The author examines current practices in the context of a number of mainstream faiths whose practices reflect a new awareness of the mourning process. As a rite of passage marked by symbolic and mythic dimensions, the funeral is a medium for expressing feelings and meanings that might not be expressible otherwise.

Tony Walter. "Modern Death: Taboo or Not Taboo?" *Sociology* 25 (May 1991): 293–310. This article questions the conventional wisdom that death is the taboo of the twentieth century and offers explanations for why it is frequently perceived as such. If death is indeed taboo, why is it discussed so widely and often? Perhaps the situation is more complex than it first appears.

Multicultural Perspectives on Dying and Death

David R. Counts and Dorothy Counts, eds. *Coping with the Final Tragedy: Cultural Variation in Death and Dying.* Amityville, N.Y.: Baywood Publishing, 1991. This collection of cross-cultural studies of dying and grieving highlights both the different ways various social groups deal with loss and the common concerns and experiences shared by all people. The initial fascination with what seem to be "exotic" expressions of grief turns out to be only the first halting step toward a new appreciation of diversity that offers insights and tools for understanding.

Linda C. Garro. "Culture, Pain and Cancer." *Journal of Palliative Care* 6, no. 3 (1990): 34–44. Although pain and suffering are experiences known by all people, they are also subjective and ultimately unshareable. The experience of pain is communicated through language, and different languages provide different avenues for this discussion. How do these variations in the "language of pain" affect our perception of pain?

John Greenleigh and Rosalind Rosoff Beimler. *The Days of the Dead: Mexico's Festival of Communion with the Departed.* San Francisco: Collins, 1991. This evocative collaboration between photographer John Greenleigh and cultural scholar Rosalind Rosoff Beimler offers a glimpse into Mexico's traditional celebration honoring departed relatives and friends. Behind the colorful accoutrements of the *fiesta*—sugar-candy skulls and papier-mâché skeletons—lies a rich and mystical understanding of death and the meaning of loss.

Donald P. Irish, Kathleen F. Lundquist, and Vivian Jenkins Nelsen, eds. *Ethnic Variations in Dying, Death, and Grief: Diversity in Universality.* Washington: Taylor and Francis, 1993. This collection of articles focuses on beliefs and practices that differ from the dominant patterns in the United States and Canada. Included are chapters describing the perspectives and customs of Native Americans, Hispanics, African Americans, and the Hmong from Southeast Asia, as well as the orientation toward death and dying found in Judaism, Buddhism, and Islam and among Quakers and Unitarians. Embracing the idea that different cultures and religions are lenses through which reality is viewed, the writings assembled here provide a necessary corrective to the ethnocentric notion that all human beings experience reality the same way.

Pearl Katz and Faris R. Kirkland. "Traditional Thought and Modern Western Surgery." *Social Science and Medicine* 26, no. 12 (1988): 1175–81. With our culture's scientific world view, we are apt to categorize as "primitive" such practices as personalizing disease causes and cures or employing ritual behaviors to deal with illness. It may be surprising, then, to find concepts and practices associated with traditional societies coexisting with the thinking and practice of modern surgery. It turns out that traditional thought and practice may contain a considerable measure of the scientific while modern thought and practice manifest persistent aspects of the traditional.

Unni Wikan. "Bereavement and Loss in Two Muslim Communities: Egypt and Bali Compared." *Social Science and Medicine* 27, no. 5 (1988): 451–60. Presenting the view that culture—more than religion or even ethnic identity—shapes the response to loss, Wikan examines bereavement and grief in two Muslim societies, finding that the contrasts between them reveal different culturally constructed notions of self, body, and interpersonal obligation. Without minimizing the influence of religion and ethnic distinctions, we need to pay attention to the role of culture and social setting as influences on human behavior.

part two

Social Issues

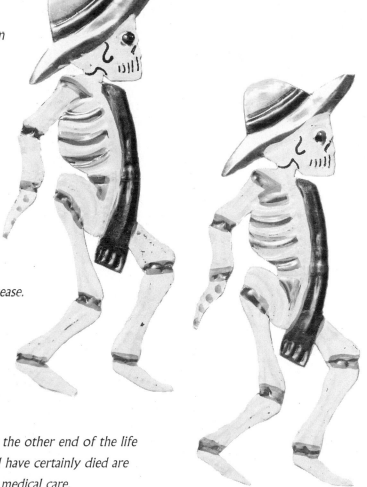

*I*n the previous section we examined broad cultural perspectives on dying and death. Here
we focus on social values and behaviors
related to death and dying in terms of the
health care system, medical ethics and decision
making, violence, and suicide.

Of the many sweeping social changes of
the twentieth century, perhaps none has
more far-reaching implications than the
revolution in medicine and health care.
Life expectancy has increased dramatically
while mortality rates have plummeted to
all-time lows. There has been a corresponding shift, too, in the patterns of
disease and death. The typical death at
the turn of the century was rapid and
sudden, resulting from an acute infectious disease.
Now most deaths follow a course of slow,
progressive deterioration due to such illnesses as heart disease, cancer, and stroke.
Whereas death at a relatively young age
was common before, now about two-thirds
of the deaths each year in the United States
occur among persons sixty-five and older. At the other end of the life
span, low-birthweight infants who once would have certainly died are
now able to survive, sustained by advances in medical care.

Yet the benefits of modern health care and medical technology entail costs that individuals and societies find increasingly hard to bear. In the United States, health care costs now comprise about 13 percent of the gross domestic product, over $750 billion each year. Some individuals cannot afford adequate care while others struggle to preserve hard-won savings that are rapidly depleted by the costs of health and medical care.

These financial costs are only one aspect of this dilemma, although assuredly an important one. In addition to financial hardship, burdensome moral and ethical issues result from modern medical technologies. These issues are addressed in the context of the balance between saving life and the quality of life in "The Limits of Medical Progress: A Principle of Symmetry" by Daniel Callahan. Can individuals and society afford a seemingly unlimited expansion of the development and use of medical technology? Should limits be placed on how technology is used in the service of medicine? These are the central questions in this brief piece.

The nature of the health care system is determined not only by patients and caregivers but also by a broader community of interests, both private and public. Insurance companies, government bureaucrats, elected officials, lawyers, ethicists, and philosophers all play a role in defining the agenda and mission of health care. Health care issues are also influenced by the actions of individual voters and taxpayers. Indeed, individuals play a major role in shaping the health care system by virtue of the choices they make in selecting a particular doctor, hospital, or form of treatment.

Although some patients are happy to let doctors make decisions regarding treatment, others want an active role. In discussing the "Era of the Patient," Stanley Joel Reiser traces some of the key developments leading to the present emphasis on informed consent and autonomy in medical care. Clearly, given the legal and ethical imperatives that a patient's autonomy or self-direction not be eclipsed, physicians are increasingly adopting the view that listening to patients is simply good doctoring. In considering Reiser's proposal that consumer consultants be part of defining the mission of health care and educating medical students, ask yourself whether you would be comfortable taking on this more active role. Do you already take an active role in determining your own medical care?

The advent of modern hospice care provides a good example of how patient choices are related to social values and practices. The capacity of modern medicine to forestall death even when it cannot cure is not universally viewed as a good thing by patients and their families. Dying is not always seen as the worst possible outcome, especially when the alternative involves unremitting pain and suffering. Instead of denying the inevitability of death, hospice care seeks to relieve the physical, social, and psychological suffering that typically accompanies incurable illness. As William Lamers points out in "Hospice: Enhancing the Quality of Life," the widespread acceptance of the hospice as a mode of caring for the terminally ill suggests that the approach meets significant needs in patients, families, and caregivers. In important ways, as we see both in Lamers's remarks and in "Keeping the Mission" by Balfour Mount, hospice care represents a departure from some of the assumptions of modern medical care. Yet hospice care can also be seen as a return to medicine's founding principles, particularly in the emphasis on easing pain and offering comfort.

Although hospice care has been heralded as humane and sensitive, as well as cost effective, both Lamers and Mount cite a number of obstacles that prevent hospice care from becoming more available. For various reasons, including the need to follow required guidelines for financial reimbursement, hospice programs are sometimes inflexible and narrow in their rules for accepting and treating patients. Often, however, hospice workers feel they have no choice but to follow requirements that have been shaped by political or institutional decisions. Who should decide what hospice care is and who qualifies for it? As you read these analyses by Mount and Lamers, identify the essentials of hospice care and think about how such qualities could be incorporated into other aspects of medical care.

While hospice care may comfort the terminally ill through the last stages of their lives, we should not lose sight of the fact that being told one has a terminal condition is a shocking, life-shattering experience. Legally and ethically, most physicians feel duty-bound to disclose to a patient all the pertinent facts about his or her illness so that he or she can exercise autonomy in making decisions about treatment and care. However, this emphasis on disclosure is a relatively recent development, having evolved out of the patients' rights movement and the legal-ethical imperative of obtaining a patient's informed consent to treatment. Not long ago, kindness and compassion meant keeping bad news from the patient so that some hopefulness could be maintained. Withholding the truth that an illness is terminal remains the practice among some cultural groups. In some situations, members of a patient's family are informed while the patient is kept unaware. Even where full disclosure is emphasized, telling the truth may be compromised by uncertainties about the course of disease. It is not always easy or possible to discern when a disease has gone beyond reasonable hope of recovery.

The issues of truth-telling and choice are highlighted in a special way in the case of terminally ill children, as we see in "Care of the Dying Child: The Demands of Ethics," by William Bartholome. Most people, including professional caregivers, find it difficult to accept that children die. When a child is terminally ill, then, the emotional weight of coping is especially burdensome. Further, special care is needed to tailor the information disclosed to the child's cognitive level and model of the world. Although it might seem kinder to hide the harsh truth from a child who is terminally ill, this strategy is rarely successful. Seriously ill children tend to be good observers who figure out rather quickly why the adults around them appear concerned and saddened. If the truth cannot reasonably be withheld from children, then, as Bartholome points out, respecting the ill child involves more than simply being truthful.

During the course of life-threatening illness, children often must undergo treatments that can bring pain. What kind of role should a child have in determining what happens to him or her? Should the power to make decisions about medical care be shared with the child-patient? What if the child dissents from the treatment plan that his or her parents advocate? How can such differences be resolved fairly and in the child's best interest? Questions like these make us confront difficult ethical issues. When the limits of medical care are reached, with no further hope of recovery expected, decisions about whether to withhold or withdraw life-sustaining treatments often take center stage. The advances in medicine during this century have not only made it possible for physicians to offer cures where once they could offer only comfort, they have also made it possible to control the timing of death. The names of Karen Ann Quinlan and Nancy Beth Cruzan have come to symbolize the ethical dilemmas that arise from medicine's ability to sustain biological functioning in cases of irreversible coma or persistent vegetative states. But life-sustaining treatment is not always life enhancing.

What constitutes "dignity" in dying? Richard Sandor, in "On Death and Coding," argues that the problem with modern medicine lies not in its awesome power to sustain life, but in the indiscriminate use of that power. All too often, attention is focused on sophisticated machines that monitor heartbeat, respiration, and blood chemistry rather than on the person who is the patient. Yet no matter how sophisticated the technological aids, the object of medical care must always remain the person who is ill. When this fact is seen clearly, death becomes not a biological problem to be overcome but a reality to be accepted. Beyond the science that seeks certainty in the practice of medicine is the art that accepts the mystery of unanswered questions.

Decisions about what constitutes appropriate care at the end of life are made in a social context that includes family members as well as the patient and the medical and nursing team. In "The Story of Mr. and Mrs. Doe," Margot White and John Fletcher describe how an individual's beliefs and values shape what transpires in the clinical setting. Patient autonomy and voluntary choice are complicated by the personalities and communication styles of those participating in treatment decisions. Should a model of autonomy and consent be imposed on patients whose preferred way of encountering the world is otherwise? Consider whether Mrs. Doe was justified in her attempt to protect her husband from the recommendations of the medical staff. Consider also whether your answer might be different if Mr. and Mrs. Doe were members of another culture, one that valued personal autonomy and being fully informed less than it did respecting privacy and protecting the patient from disturbing news.

As we saw in the preceding section of this book, most of us live in a pluralistic cultural environment where one-size-fits-all solutions are less than satisfactory. When standard procedures and practices become rigid, they limit individuals' freedom to confront difficult choices in personally meaningful ways. When these choices relate to profound matters involving life and death, those limits can be acutely frustrating.

This is obvious in the energetic public debates about abortion and euthanasia. The ethical dilemmas arising out of the human encounter with dying and death evoke powerful emotions. Whereas most people do not feel a pressing need to dictate their neighbors' choices of music, food, or cars, decisions that involve life or death—because they are viewed as affecting the whole community—are a different story. And unlike choices that allow us to celebrate our differences, decisions about life and death can cause deep division when they do not match an individual's sense of right and wrong.

Some people argue that the dying person's ability to maintain control over the manner and timing of his or her death is paramount to dying with dignity. Advocates of a right to die typically believe that a person diagnosed with a terminal illness should be able to end his or her life when he or she determines that it is not worth living. Opponents of a right to die, on the other hand, include disparate groups: those who believe that dignity in dying comes through enduring even extraordinary suffering, as well as those who contend that suffering at the end of life can be eliminated or at least made tolerable by the sophisticated use of pain medication and other comfort measures. Each of these views is held by thoughtful and compassionate individuals who seek to define what it means to die with dignity.

Laying aside for the moment the question whether or not one would choose such an action for oneself, if it is permissible to hasten one's own death, is it appropriate for physicians to assist a patient's dying, either directly or indirectly? Charles Dougherty takes up this question in "The Common Good, Terminal Illness, and Euthanasia." When confronted by patients with intractable pain due to terminal illness, physicians and other caregivers find themselves on the horns of a dilemma: How to carry out both the basic commitment to save life and the moral imperative to prevent suffering. It is not always possible to give both goals equal weight; how, then, can choices be made without sacrificing either side of the moral equation? If we view death only as medical failure or moral evil, we neglect the possibility of creating the necessary conditions for a "good" death.

In medical terms, a "good" death involves recognizing the limits of medical intervention and making the comforts of palliative care available to minimize pain. Although some people view suffering as having redemptive value that confers some benefit on the sufferer either in this life or the next, pain reduction is generally viewed as a present benefit not to be lightly dismissed. The goal of reducing pain becomes less universally agreed upon, however, when it includes the possibility, or probability, of ending a person's life. In light of the points mentioned by Dougherty, consider whether you think physician-assisted death is ever morally appropriate and if so under what circumstances. Should there be legal guidelines to regulate the practice of physician-assisted death?

Turning our attention to violent death and suicide, we encounter phenomena that can be viewed as social problems but that also affect us subtly or directly as individuals. Discussion of violence and self-

destructive behavior often focuses on the individual and the effect of a person's death on his or her family and friends. In his discussion of "Horrendous Death," Daniel Leviton broadens this focus to encompass death-related behaviors—war, terrorism, and genocide—that affect large numbers of people. Notice how the categories or types of horrendous death mentioned by Leviton both differ from one another and share certain qualities in common. What role does denial of death play in determining the efforts we make toward preventing horrendous deaths? Can confronting the reality of such deaths stimulate action toward alleviating the suffering they cause?

Expanding on Leviton's discussion of horrendous deaths, the next three articles deal with specific examples of violent death. James Garbarino addresses the impact of war and community violence on children in his essay, "Challenges We Face in Understanding Children and War." A child's own experience of living in a combat zone is conveyed in the excerpt from Zlata's Diary: A Child's Life in Sarajevo by Zlata Filipović. Ice T sheds light on the community violence that occurs in "The Killing Fields" of South Central Los Angeles.

After reading these three selections, take a few moments to recall each of Garbarino's eight challenges to our moral, intellectual, and political resources. The first challenge, for example, points up the difficulty of being able to both feel and think about war. Is it possible to be objectively analytical about war and also emotionally open to the horror and pain that results from it? As you reflect on each of these challenges, consider whether your understanding of violent death has been changed in any way by your studies of death and dying.

Suicide is frequently described as aggression aimed toward oneself. In turning our attention from acts of violence in communities to suicide, Judith Stillion's "Premature Exits: Understanding Suicide" provides a good foundation. She describes a model of suicidal behavior that embraces four risk categories: biological, psychological, cognitive, and environmental. Understanding these risk categories and how they relate to one another is an important step toward reducing the risk of suicide and other self-destructive behaviors.

Notice how some risk factors are influential across the life span while others exert the greatest impact on particular age groups. Similarly, some affect males and females much the same while others exert gender differences. Consider how Stillion's insights can be translated into constructive action for reducing the incidence of self-destructive behaviors.

What specific programs might be implemented within your own community, for example, to increase public awareness about suicide and its prevention?

The effect of social beliefs and perceptions on moderating suicidal behavior is discussed by Kevin Early and Ronald Akers in "'It's a White Thing': An Exploration of Beliefs about Suicide in the African-American Community." Although the suicide rate has been rising among both black and white males over the past three decades, the rate among black males is substantially lower than that among white males. Similarly, the suicide rate among black females is less than half that of white females. Community attitudes toward suicide appear to play a major role in accounting for these differences.

Community attitudes also appear to be a major factor in the incidence of gay and lesbian suicide, although here the attitudes have a negative, rather than positive, effect. In the article "Interpreting the Evidence: Competing Paradigms and the Emergence of Lesbian and Gay Suicide as a 'Social Fact,'" Kathleen Erwin examines how both scientific theories and social attitudes are instrumental in shaping the response to gay and lesbian psychological distress. In reading Erwin's piece, consider the extent to which social forces shape the actions and behaviors of individuals.

In reflecting on social issues related to health care, medical ethics, violence, and suicide, we see how individual behavior shapes the social context, which, in turn, influences personal choices. Social values and practices are in flux, continually adapting to changing circumstances and attitudes. When the stakes involve death, the social fabric can be severely strained as competing ideas about the meaning of life and death vie for acceptance. While it may be true that a little knowledge is a dangerous thing, ignorance is even more perilous. Whether our attention is directed toward broad public policy initiatives or focused more narrowly on our own values and practices, a willingness to confront the reality of death and to recognize its multifaceted impact on our lives is a necessary step toward informed and meaningful choice.

The Health Care System

The Limits of Medical Progress:
A Principle of Symmetry

DANIEL CALLAHAN, PH.D., is co-founder and president of the Hastings Center, a nonprofit organization that conducts educational and research programs on ethical issues in medicine, the life sciences, and the professions. The Center celebrated its twenty-fifth anniversary in 1991. Dr. Callahan says, "Early in my career I decided that I wanted to teach philosophy in a university. However, as time moved on, I felt the field of philosophy was much too detached from the practical problems of the world, and that indeed philosophy should be working more vigorously out in the marketplace, just as Socrates did some twenty-four hundred years ago. About the same time I was thinking about that problem, I became interested in medicine, which seemed to me to provide wonderful issues to deal with in a philosophical way. I began thinking and writing about medicine and its philosophical meaning,

and about the moral problems that advances in biomedicine were generating. This seemed to meet both my personal needs and to open the possibility of making a contribution to a serious field."

Dr. Callahan has served on a number of panels concerned with national policies in the area of scientific and medical ethics, including the Advisory Committee on Scientific Integrity of the U.S. Department of Health and Human Services. In addition to publishing numerous essays and articles, he is the author or editor of more than twenty books focusing on ethical issues, including *Setting Limits: Medical Goals in an Aging Society* (1987) and *The Troubled Dream of Life: Living with Mortality* (1993). The following selection is excerpted from his book *What Kind of Life: The Limits of Medical Progress* (1990).

The principle of symmetry is this: A technology should be judged by its likelihood of enhancing a good balance between the extension and saving of life and the quality of life. Its aim is to promote medical coherence, by which I mean outcomes that foster the rounded well-being of persons, not simply one-dimensional improvements that benefit some aspect of individual well-being at the expense of others. No technology can guarantee a rounded outcome in this sense, but if well developed it can promise a high probability of such a result. That should be the aim in devising it and a standard of judgment in disseminating and financially supporting it.

A healthcare system that develops and institutionalizes a life-saving technology which has the common result of leaving people chronically ill or with a poor quality of life ignores the principle of symmetry. The saving of very low-birthweight babies at the cost of a poor long-term outcome is an example, as is that of using cardiopulmonary resuscitation (CPR) in those cases where the resulting quality of life is likely to be poor. More generally, entitlement programs (such as Medicare) that reward and reimburse well the use of high-technology procedures, but do not well support caring for the lasting damage perhaps done by them or that do not provide long-term care as generously as high-technology care, also by analogy violate the principle of symmetry.

The principle would require the pursuit of research promising an acceptable and balanced *long-term* outcome, not simply an immediate benefit. This would mean giving priority to the development of technologies that promote long-term benefits, that seek a good balance between life extension and quality of life, and that seek also to minimize the impact of illness on those already afflicted. Here are some possible specifications, couched in terms of goals to be pursued:

Pursuing those avenues of medical research that promise a good long-term, overall outcome (at the lowest-general cost, financial and otherwise). Research priorities should be given to those conditions where the state of scientific knowledge and the likelihood of successful clinical application and outcome are the highest over the longest period of time. This principle would imply a bias toward relief of those conditions which are relatively well understood, which predominantly affect children and younger adults, and which promise to enhance the likelihood of avoiding a premature death. Beyond that general priority, the goal should be to pursue research possibilities with the most beneficial long-term results. While this would seem an obvious point, the eager pursuit of such devices as the artificial heart (mainly of value to middle-age males and promising, even if successful, a relatively short enhanced life span of four to five years) indicates that it is in practice far from accepted.

Pursuing those forms of healthcare that strike a good balance between the saving of life and the maintenance of a good quality of life. A powerful proclivity toward acute-care, high-technology medicine has been the mark of the past fifty years or so. This bias has meant the neglect of those conditions that do not shorten life but significantly reduce its quality: arthritis and incontinence among the elderly, as well as poor long-term and home care; inadequate rehabilitation services and financing for the victims of accidents; and genetic anomalies among younger age groups. A primary question always to be asked is: If we are to have available life-saving therapies and technologies, do we also have in place other follow-up therapies and forms of care that help ensure a good long-term quality of life? If the answer to that question is no, then there should be a strong reluctance to disseminate the therapy until such a standard can reasonably be assured. Therapies that promote a good quality of life—hip replacement in the elderly, speech therapy in children—even if they do not extend life, should be given priority in such cases.

Pursuing those forms of healthcare and research that provide the best help for those already born with defects and handicaps; working to reduce the impact of illnesses already incurred. Medicine overreaches itself when it sets as its implicit goal that of curing all diseases and indefinitely forestalling death. Since one consequence, moreover, of an unrestrained effort to hold off death by technological innovation is often that of producing chronic illness and disability in its wake, medical progress of that kind assures the production of still more illness. That cycle can only be broken by developing technology to meet the needs of those who have already survived and whose lives promise long suffering, whether physical or psychological. We should also give priority to those who can be saved by existing technologies over the saving of still more lives by the creation of still more new technologies designed to press beyond present frontiers. We should not, in short, go beyond those frontiers until we know how to improve life for those already existing, but poorly, within the present frontiers. To use a military analogy: If we are going to conduct a war on various diseases, we should not extend our advance beyond our supply lines. That is the classic way of turning victory into defeat.

The Era of the Patient: Using the Experience of Illness in Shaping the Missions of Health Care

STANLEY JOEL REISER

STANLEY JOEL REISER, M.D., M.P.A., PH.D., is the Griff T. Ross Professor of Humanities and Technology in Health Care at the University of Texas Health Science Center in Houston. His interest in the role of the patient in health care developed in connection with his work on the role of technology in shaping medical relationships, the subject of his doctoral dissertation at Harvard. In a number of subsequent works, he has shown that one of technology's main effects is to redirect the attention of physicians from illness as portrayed through the experience of patients to illness as depicted by the data of machines. The ability to portray the composition of body fluids, the molecular makeup of cells, the physiologic motion of organs, and so forth, has drawn physicians away from the life of the patient and absorbed them in studying the life of the body.

Dr. Reiser's interest in the influence of technology reflects a longstanding concern with the development of health care ethics and how people cope with the capabilities of new technologies. In the following article, he describes how the health care ethics and outcomes movements are now directing the attention of the medical world back to the significance of the patient's view of illness. Dr. Reiser hopes that this will result in a better balance between the humanistic and technologic aspects of health care provision in the future.

Dr. Reiser lectures extensively on these issues and is the author and editor of many books, among which are *Ethics in Medicine* (1977), *Medicine and the Reign of Technology* (1978), *The Machine at the Bedside* (1984), and *The Ethical Dimensions of the Biological Sciences* (1993). He is co-editor of *The International Journal of Technology Assessment in Health Care.*

AS WE REACH the last decade of the 20th century, it is possible to recognize the emergence of a medical era that engages the perspectives of patients in the transformation of health care. In many guises and policies, our experiences with illness as patients are becoming keys to changing the health care system. These experiences provide an alternative view of illness from that acquired by health care providers and investigators through their education and work.

This article scrutinizes the events leading to this era; argues that the passive role of patients and consumers in the health care system should be replaced by an active one in which they give health care the benefit of what they have learned about illness; and discusses how the validity of individual experience and reflection on illness has been undermined by the concept of classifying illness into categories called diseases, and by a technological approach to diagnosing and tracking the course of illness. It also examines how these features of modern health care have been challenged by two recent movements, which are connected by their attention to the views of individuals who have encountered illness as patients—the modern medical ethics and outcomes research movements. Finally, it explores new ways a patient- and consumer-based perspective that draws on personal experience with illness can improve health care practice, education, research, and policy, and demonstrates the development of a new stage in health care—the era of the patient.

The Concept of Disease
and the Eclipse of the Patient

The idea of patients as unique beings and thus the significance of their personal experiences with illness were vitally challenged by a concept emerging in the scientific revolution of the 17th century. This concept shifted medical attention from the particular way an individual experienced an illness, to the typical pattern of symptoms displayed by the population it afflicted.

Since the Hippocratic period of the fifth century BC, illness had been depicted as an episode occurring when the relationship among the presumed four basic components of the body called humors was altered. Symptoms were viewed prognostically, indicating whether the illness was getting worse or better. Even though some categories of illness, or diseases, had been described, they were broad and vague. Despite their presence, physicians focused therapeutically on patients as individuals, whose humoral balance they sought to restore, and not on diseases as entities. There was, in effect, one universal illness—humoral disruption—with each person responding uniquely to particular pathology-inducing causes.

This viewpoint about how one got sick was overcome and replaced in the 17th century when the English physician Thomas Sydenham made the discovery and description of diseases the center of medical attention through a precise rendering of their course and development. Sydenham's perspective on illness was a creation of the age of scientific revolution in which he lived. At this time, an intense interest developed in the classification of plants. Scientists devoted great energies to specifying common features of plants, which they used to group them into particular categories. This approach struck Sydenham as applicable to medicine. A brilliant clinician, he searched for and discovered similar patterns of symptoms occurring during the sickness of different patients. Sydenham separated the symptoms of patients into two categories: (1) pathognomonic symptoms—those that were shared among groups of patients and (2) idiosyncratic symptoms—those whose pattern and character were unique to a particular patient.

Sydenham grouped the pathognomonic symptoms into named disease entities, which he believed were as real and tangible as other creations of nature. He wrote: "It is necessary that all diseases be reduced to definite and certain species, and that with the same care which we see exhibited by botanists."[1] In effect, he transformed the individual experiences of illness into the group experience of disease.

This viewpoint initiated in medicine a systematic devaluation of the idiosyncratic features of illness. As the idea of classifying patients into disease categories gradually attracted advocates and became dominant, those symptoms of illness that linked individuals—the pathognomonic signs—became elevated in significance over those symptoms that separated individuals—the idiosyncratic ones. Since Sydenham's time, physicians have sought more to learn how patients are alike than to understand how they are different. This has diminished the value placed by physicians on the unique meanings patients give to their experiences.

The Place of the Patient
in the Technologic Revolution

This way of thinking received a significant boost in the 19th century, when medicine developed new categories of evidence that further reduced the significance of patient-centered views of illness. In this period, physicians continued to rely, as in Sydenham's time, on the patients' experiences of symptoms to define the diseases they had. The building blocks of diseases remained the feelings and sensations perceived by patients and conveyed by them to physicians. But this ownership by patients of the facts that defined disease increasingly appeared to physicians to stand in the way of medicine's scientific advance. The difficulty of confirming the nature and reality of this subjective evidence, the variation in the quality of the evidence caused by the diverse capacities of patients to describe what they felt, and the opportunity for the misrepresentation of this evidence through the flaws of memory or the misleading intentions of the tellers, led physicians to despair about learning what really happened to patients.

Technologies of physical diagnosis such as the stethoscope and ophthalmoscope, introduced in the first half of the 19th century, provided effective remedies for these problems. They permitted physicians to locate and evaluate the sounds and sights of illness themselves. Later in the century, laboratory, graphic, and x-ray diagnosis technologies appeared, which produced numerical and pictorial evidence of illness. These innovations caused physicians to rejoice that a new age was at hand. They finally had acquired the means to gain objective representations of illness that bypassed the interpretative distortions of the patient. They could discern with greater confidence the pathognomonic signs that legitimated the placement of their patients into particular disease categories.[2]

By the yardstick of these new measures, particularly those stated through numbers and pictures, medicine now defined itself as scientific. As the 20th century began, the mark of scientific capability was thought to reside in the capacity of observers to eliminate bias from their judgments. Writing in 1900 in his book *The Grammar of Science,* the mathematician Karl Pearson urged to scientist "above all things to strive at self-elimination in his judgments, to provide an argument which is true for each individual mind as for his own." He declared that evaluating facts, "unbiased by personal feeling is characteristic of what may be termed the scientific frame of mind."[3]

Influenced by this viewpoint, the measurement of patients through scientific tests of their biologic functioning became the mainstay of the 20th-century physician. By the 1940s, Tinsley Harrison, noted diagnostician and editor of an acclaimed textbook of medicine, called attention to "the present-day tendency towards a five-minute history followed by a five-day barrage of special tests in the hope that the diagnostic rabbit may suddenly emerge from the laboratory hat."[4]

This trend toward objectified clinical analysis and the submergence of idiosyncratic responses to illness that thwarted the classification of patients into disease categories removed illness as experienced by the patient from the center of the medical stage. The categories of the physician replaced those of the patient as the focus of analysis. Illness was now disease. The validity of particular symptoms depended on the capacity to state them as quantitative and pictorial indexes. Taken as a whole, developing a portrait of a medical problem was increasingly less the province of the patient, and more the prerogative of the physician. But in the 1950s a movement that focused on the ethics of medicine and the rights of patients challenged this viewpoint.

The Modern Medical Ethics Movement and the Reemergence of the Patient

A tradition of ethical reflection has been a steadfast component of medical study since the development of a corpus of essays on ethics in the Hippocratic literature. Thus, when dilemmas arose in the 1950s and 1960s that required the use of ethical reasoning, physicians initially thought they would find answers from within the existing traditions of medicine. They were mistaken. The novel problems medicine generated in this period made it necessary for physicians to reach out to patients, consumers, courts, legislatures, and social institutions such as religions in an unprecedented way to develop new ethical approaches to medical issues. The sum of these efforts produced the modern medical ethics movement.

Many of these novel problems were created by a group of innovative technologies that rescued patients from life-threatening physiological failures of vital organs. The use of these technologies generated difficult ethical issues, which required patients, families, and communities to be drawn into the ensuing medical discourse. The first of these technologies was the artificial respirator, introduced in the mid 1950s to rescue patients on the brink of death from respiratory collapse. While the technology removed many from that brink, some never got much beyond it and were consigned to lingering—still alive, but no longer aware of surroundings or people and destined never to get better. Trying problems emerged. How to decide whether life supports should be maintained? What ethical standards to apply to this question? And by whom? Family? Physicians? Clergy? Courts? Legislatures? The present or past statements of the patient?[5] In the several decades since the 1950s, these groups have applied their knowledge and values to confront and meliorate this end-of-life quandary. They have clarified pertinent rights and duties and thereby given society an important legacy.

The artificial respirator was soon followed by the artificial kidney, introduced as a clinically effective technology at the Seattle Artificial Kidney Center of the University of Washington in the early 1960s. It also produced ethical dilemmas, but focused more on the problems of allocation. Not enough machines, skilled personnel, or public funds were available in the 1960s to serve the needs of the approximately 75,000 people with chronic renal failure in the United States at risk of dying without this treatment. The Seattle Center, with the public focused on it as the pioneer in the subject, initiated a selection process using panels of community representatives and medical experts to pick recipients of the artificial kidney. The validity of this process and its allocative standards—such as social merit and financial capability—were much debated. This again demonstrated the need for the health care professions and public to work together on the dilemmas raised by technological advances, and the complexity of developing procedures and yardsticks of rationing.[6] This problem was largely resolved in 1972 when federal legislation provided funds for patients needing kidney dialysis and transplantation.

At the time of these events, a civil rights movement was in progress that heightened awareness of rights-sensitive issues throughout society, including medicine. The movement focused society on the hardships of groups deprived of resources and rights necessary to meet medical needs, particularly elderly and indigent persons, and pregnant women. This attention resulted in the passage of the 1965 Medicare and Medicaid Acts, giving the elderly and indigent rights to bundles of medical services, and in 1973 to the *Roe v Wade* Supreme Court decision legalizing the right of women to choose to have an abortion.[7]

This rights-conscious social environment also directed renewed concern toward another vulnerable medical population—the subjects of human studies. Public attention was drawn to this issue by reports in the press of subjects inducted into experiments without being informed of their risks. These revelations were brought together in a 1965 lecture by Henry Beecher, MD, a professor of anesthesiology at Harvard Medical School. Beecher's remarks, later published,[8] along with congressional hearings that revealed human subject problems in the testing of drugs, were important catalysts of a 1966 Surgeon General's ruling. It created institutional review boards at research centers receiving public funds. The institutional review board, which included public representatives, reviewed research protocols to screen out excessive risks to subjects and to assure they contained a clear and complete subject consent document. Institutional review boards thereby have strengthened the role of subjects in the research setting and clarified the responsibilities of investigators.

Among the key changes that emerged from these events of the modern medical ethics movement was a new standing given to the right of individuals to learn about their illness and to help decide on the chosen therapy. Consent and autonomy became highly prized and respected values. Who knew more about the patient than the patient? Who could weigh better the trade-offs of benefits and harms to self in relation to the goals, values, and obligations of life than the subject of an experimental intervention? These insights enhanced the authority of patients and subjects in medical encounters and the authenticity of their views about their illness.

In the last three decades, there have been a number of tangible expressions of this new concern for consulting and listening to individuals when medical decisions are at hand. In the 1960s, as noted, carefully drawn and critically reviewed consent documents for the subjects of scientific investigation emerged. In the 1970s, patient "bills of rights" were issued in hospitals, describing the entitlements to information and actions that a hospitalized patient had.[9] This same decade marked the invention of the living will, a means through which individuals could express their general wishes about medical interventions. This document provided assurance that if an individual were rendered incompetent by illness, the views stated in the living will would be used in deciding medical action.[10] The 1980s witnessed many court cases, a rising feature of the prior decade, which reaffirmed the authority of patients or families acting on their behalf to decide about therapy. These events laid the foundation for patient rights and responsibilities in the United States, a beginning from which they could grow and flourish.

The Outcomes Movement and the Reemergence of the Patient

Increasing the ethical standing of patients to make choices elevated their place in medical discourse and is the hallmark of the modern medical ethics movement. The modern outcomes movement, which developed in the 1980s and made the consequences of a medical intervention to its recipient a major criterion of determining its value, further enhanced the authenticity and authority of the patient's perspective. As a result of the movement, the objective biological standards of evidence, which had formed the foundation of 20th-century medicine, were found to depict the effects of a medical procedure inadequately. Thus, the medical ethics and outcomes movements both drew their strength from the significance they gave to the patient's view of illness and therapy.

Explicit concern with the multiple factors affecting the outcome of therapy initially emerged in the early 20th century through the work of the iconoclastic Boston surgeon E. A. Codman, MD.[11] He asked physicians to keep systematic records that documented the results of their interventions. Clinical actions, other features of a medical facility that could influence patient care such as staff and equipment, and the habits and pursuits of patients themselves all were evaluated in determining the cause of the outcome, or the "end results" as Codman called it. By understanding the factors that produced undesirable end results, Codman acquired a means of preventing future harm. Codman's work failed to attract widespread support from medicine or society: his ideas were too challenging to the established canons of clinical practice. But in the decade of the 1980s, driven by concerns over variations in the way physicians used therapy and the growing costs of health care, a new interest in outcomes measurement appeared that led the patient's view of events to become pivotal. As Kathleen Lohr put it: "The concept of outcome directs attention specially to the patient's well-being; it emphasizes individuals over groups, and the interests of unique patients over those of society."[12] To measure patient views, researchers in this decade produced improved and increased numbers of clinical indices of the health effects of medical interventions. Over 100 instruments to depict the influence of therapies on patient function existed by the end of the decade. They measured characteristics such as physical activities, emotional status, intensity of symptoms, mobility, sleep, social interaction, illness beliefs, and so forth.[13]

A Woods Hole conference of researchers, health care providers, and policy makers convened to review the 1980s experience with outcomes measurement and to chart its future agenda declared: "The role of the patient is increasingly at the center of the outcomes debate."[14] They described a growing effort by hospitals, physicians, and employers to analyze the outcomes of episodes of care. How the patient felt and functioned after therapy and whether the patient could return to work and normal social activities were accepted as the best criteria of whether the treatment succeeded.

Also in the 1980s, health care analyst Paul Ellwood developed an extension of outcomes measurement that he called "outcomes management." He defined it as "a technology of patient experience designed to help patients, payers, and providers make rational medical care–related choices based on better insights into the effect of these choices on the patient's life."[15] Outcomes management pooled evidence from functional measures of patient status and clinical results into a universally accessible, continually updated national database. But its focus and unifying element was tracking and measuring the well-being of patients. In the 1990s, new efforts have emerged to examine the reports of patients about their preferences, values, needs, and experiences, obtained through survey instruments and focus groups. These reports have been used to evaluate the quality and variation of health care interventions and their outcomes, as well as to develop clinical insights into the care of particular patients.[16] Thus, a basic feature of the outcomes movement is the prominence given to the judgment by patients of how a therapy has affected their lives. The movement recognizes that in the final analysis, only the patient can decide if a treatment is successful.[17]

By measuring the success of health care in terms of the experiences and values of patients and consumers, the outcomes movement had been influenced by the ethics movement. Both recognized the subjective views of patients as basic catalysts in changing health care. Now, by building on these events, there are further benefits that the perspectives of consumers and patients can bring to health care practice, education, research, and policy.

Shaping Health Care Practice Through Consumer Consultants

The same rationale that supports the unique subjective views of patients as valid bases of ethical choice and measures of outcome should lead us to consider another innovation in patient care—the consumer consultant.

It is difficult for those who themselves have not endured a particular illness or been part of a family who has faced it to offer advice on what to do. Yet this is what most physicians do for much of their professional lives. They have a great knowledge of illness, but most illness they treat depends on knowledge gained from the outside. Physicians have read about, observed, and cared for patients with specific medical problems. But usually they themselves have not lived through either the illness or the therapy for it. Why should we not ask individuals who have had such experience to be available in an on-call status, to provide advice to patients and physicians having to decide about appropriate care? Why not have consumer consultants?

Such consumer consultants could be trained by hospitals and medical schools to interact with patients and medical staff in making their experience serve the needs of patient care. In many instances, a consumer perspective could be highly significant in helping decide a course of action. What better way for patients to gain insight into how therapy is encountered than from one or more individuals who have already had it? The same applies to decisions families must make for loved ones, such as questions of whether to initiate long-term treatment of a particular chronic illness, undergo a surgical procedure, enter a nursing home, continue intensive care, or donate the organs of a member who has just died. In the last situation, for example, not only can the inner conflict of allowing organ donation be given meaning by persons who went through it, but they can also describe the feelings felt over time that surface only after the decision has been made, feelings that the person making the choice cannot know of.

But the argument can be raised: Might not the special experiences of individual consultants be atypical, or biased? Is it thereby appropriate to introduce their views into a clinical case? The same argument, of course, can apply to physicians and other staff members. They are biased, as we all are, in certain directions. It is such issues that the course of training for individuals to fill the role of consumer consultant must address. For example, consultants should be trained not to approach patients with the objective of persuading them to decide as they did. Rather, the consultants' discussion should be focused on reconstructing the events, issues, and choices they faced in dealing with illness. Further, several consultants with different experiences and perspectives can be available to counsel a given patient. In these discussions, physicians would provide the crucial input of helping patients and families to locate the particular views of consumer consultants in the spectrum of possible interpretations. Similarly, it is essential for medical staff to develop skills to work effectively with the consumer advisers. The experience gained by staff through the medical ethics movement to interact with patients, families, and society over issues of values and rights provides a foundation for this new association of consumers and health care providers.

Occasionally, hospitals or physicians ask patients or the parents of a child who have been through an illness to visit with individuals facing similar choices. Some support groups of former patients also make themselves available for these purposes. But usually requests for these visits are episodic, and the individuals providing advice have not been put through a professionally developed course of education or formally integrated into the clinical routine. In addition, videodisks of patients recapitulating therapeutic decisions are currently being designed to guide the choices of other patients facing similar problems.[18] The videodisks cannot replace the dynamics of human interaction between people sharing ideas, experiences, and feelings. But the two forms of consumer education are complementary. The videodisk is a physician-directed presentation of medical decision making using a structured interview to elicit patient views. The patient-consultant exchange is a nondirected, nonstructured meeting between people that can be wide-ranging in scope and empathic and personal in content.

Influencing Education Through Consumer Instructors

Just as consumers who have sustained illness can be sought to help patients make choices, they can also help teach students about what it's like to be sick and to receive medical care. There is a tradition in medicine of bringing patients with a given illness into the classroom to have their "case" presented. In addition, the patient's history of illness is routinely taken when initiating clinical care, and patients are asked questions about their illness during the course of therapy. But in these settings, they are basically passive participants, responding to queries about what happened to them and how they felt.

Consumer instructors could be trained by medical schools to help students understand illness from the patient's and family's perspective, but with the authority to speak plainly about what they think—a role that is not possible when they are under the authority of physicians and students as cases or patients. It would be meaningful for medical students to listen to patients and consumers as instructors, for this role would invest their views with a special significance. This, in turn, could help students to be more attentive to what patients and their families experience, believe, and need.

Enhancing Research Through Consumer Assessors

It is now common to have consumer representatives on human studies and hospital ethics committees. The principal role that consumers play on such committees is to look past the technically centered perspectives of scientific and clinical experts and bring value-based views to bear on the issues. Even the scientists and clinicians serving on these committees who are not directly involved in the research or clinical issues being considered find it hard to disengage from their learned interests when evaluating problems and defining solutions. As Daniel Yankelovich notes:

> When experts analyze issues, they highlight the technical side. They do so automatically because that is what they are trained to do, paid to do, and can do better than nonexperts. Automatically and unthinkingly, experts play down the value side of issues because from their point of view it muddies the issue and removes it from their fields of competence.[19]

The consumer lacks such technical knowledge or concerns, and thus engages these issues at the level of their ethical and social meanings. The consumer may not be able to assess the implications for science of a hospital protocol or case, but can articulate the meaning of proposed actions for community concerns.

Then, as Yankelovich observes, "once the value questions are settled the issue can be safely returned to experts."[20] This is precisely what happens in human studies and in hospital ethics committees. Once the ethical and social issues are explicated, the protocol or case goes back to the experts for them to engage the complex technical issues in the solution of which they excel.

However, in their committee roles, consumers deal principally with issues after decisions have been made about them by clinicians and investigators. More use should be made of consumers in the research process itself, apart from their role as subjects. To accomplish this, we should devise formal methods to incorporate the insights of consumers and patients into the design of protocols, experiments, questionnaires, and other means of research. The reason for doing this is the same as for placing consumers on committees—to raise the value-based issues so easy for experts to overlook.

We should also consider inserting into research, questions that address treatment as experienced by patients, a perspective on health care that can be called "consumer assessment." A consumer assessment of a clinical technology, for example, would ask questions such as: What sorts of discomfort does the examination cause? What effect does the intervention have on a person's ability to function at the workplace or in the home? How much time does the examination take? Consumer assessment would focus on issues of convenience, pain, anxiety, and influence on work in evaluating medical interventions, areas to which current clinical studies pay insufficient attention.

Changing Health Care Policy Through Competent Consumers

The value-centered orientation of the nonexpert in controversies concerning science and technology provides the main argument for consumer involvement in public discussions of health care policy. The benefit of this perspective has been demonstrated in policy debates concerning cigarette smoking, environmental health hazards, the needs of women in health care, and the use of quality-of-life measures to distribute medical resources. In regard to the last issue, the state of Oregon has used public hearings, opinion polls, and community meetings run by trained volunteers to make public preferences and values a central feature of allocating its limited Medicaid funds among alternative therapies. The focus of the effort is a list of health services, prioritized for funding by outcome yardsticks, such as the quality and length of life, and the cost of different interventions.[21] While there is extensive controversy about the validity of Oregon's allocative formula, its efforts to include consumers in the development of this policy are noteworthy.

More effort is required, however, to directly involve consumers in health care insurance decisions about themselves. There is a widely held view that the complexity of insurance coverage requires experts acting on behalf of consumers to make choices for them about its scope and content. This reasoning is flawed. This is because the range of technical alternatives grows as medical knowledge and technology expand. As a result, experts have increasing difficulty deciding among the interventions that are candidates for benefit packages, which best further the interest of an individual, given the diversity of social, ethical, cultural, and religious values among people. Since consumers understand more than anyone else the meaning of these values to them, insurance choices cannot be left largely to experts. A partnership between the two is needed.

Several means to increase consumer participation in coverage decisions are available, such as separating employer payment from employer management of health insurance funds. Employers, for example, could let employees purchase any plan they wish with their insurance allotment. Having to make choices about

coverage would encourage consumers to learn more about health care costs and alternatives. It would stir the marketplace, as well as physicians, to provide better and more understandable information to assist consumer decision making. Such learning is essential. An uninvolved and thus an unknowledgeable public invites the unwise use of health care resources, a problem that troubles our system. We succeed in other complicated aspects of life to portray the elements of choice in a form the public understands. Why can't we do the same for the coverage decisions of health care?[22]

Implementing Consumer Involvement in Health Care Institutions

Introducing consumers into centers of health education and care will require procedures of integration and tracking. Two steps can be useful. The first is an education and policy committee, which examines the reach and limits of consumer advisers and integrates their efforts with the work of institutional staff. Examples of questions it should consider are: When in the course of an illness or in the design of a research or teaching project should a consumer be called? How to measure and make positive the influence of the consumer advisers on institutional relationships and activities in education, patient care, and research? Will career-related, financial, or other kinds of incentives be needed to implement the work of advisers in hospitals and schools? What steps would enhance the staff's ability to relate to and benefit from the advisers? How should these activities be organized by the institutions and who is to do it? This committee should also create a mission statement for this effort, specifying the goals toward which programs should be directed.

The second step is a periodic review of the activities of consumer advisers, so they may learn from their efforts and create a record for successors. To meet these needs, a monthly case rounds attended by the advisers and professional staff would be useful.[23] It would encompass a case presentation by a consumer adviser of a recent experience, a discussion of issues it raises, and an analysis of decisions taken.

An education and policy committee to orient and write a mission statement for advisers that establishes principles and goals of action for them, and a case rounds to discuss and evaluate what they have done can help assure success of the effort.

Conclusions

The word doctor comes from the Latin verb *docere*—to teach. Developing a capacity to teach consumers to take an active part in practice, education, research, and policy fulfills for medicine a role inherent in its mission, and could greatly increase its knowledge and effectiveness. For much of its history, medicine has viewed the people under its care as passive individuals, as cases, patients, and subjects whom it should help but who themselves have little role in helping medicine. The medical ethics and outcome movements have begun to reverse this view. The additional actions proposed here can make patients and consumers more active voices in health care. By transmitting their experience with illness and critiquing health care practices, consumers bring the perspective of the quintessential medical insiders—themselves—to center stage.

But just as basic, the health care that consumers receive should reflect their individual-ity. This lesson should be given to students in teaching and research settings: that understanding human diversity must be a central goal in acquiring and using medical knowledge. Effort in this area will further the development of a more person-centered and humane health care system. The statesman and author Vaclav Havel recently wrote:

> Things must once more be given a chance to present themselves as they are, to be perceived in their individuality. We must see the pluralism of the world, and not bind it by seeking common denominators or reducing everything to a single common equation. We must try harder to understand than to explain. The way forward is not in the mere construction of universal systemic solutions, to be applied to reality from the outside; it is also in seeking to get to the heart of reality through personal experience.[24]

Havel applied his critique to the politics of the world. But medicine's development has involved similar issues. In constructing diseases we have created population-centered, objective, and statistical interpretations of illness that have devalued the distinctive experience of patients. A patient- and consumer-based perspective on illness makes the individual the focus of attention. As we strive to balance objective and group-based views of sickness with those that portray it through subjective and person-based accounts, the effectiveness and humaneness of health care will proportionately grow.

Hospice: Enhancing the Quality of Life

WILLIAM M. LAMERS JR.

WILLIAM M. LAMERS JR., M.D., is the medical director of Hospice of the Canyon in Calabasas, California. In the late 1960s he wrote a landmark article entitled "Funerals Are Good for People, M.D.s Included," which has since been reprinted widely. During the 1970s, Dr. Lamers was the first physician in the United States to establish a hospice program. This pioneering effort grew out of his own experience in seeking excellent physical and psychological care for three of his contemporaries who had been diagnosed with life-threatening illnesses. Finding none, he established the Hospice of Marin just north of San Francisco.

During the early years of hospice development, Dr. Lamers served as the chairperson of the Standards and Accreditation Committee of the National Hospice Organization. He lectured widely across the United States and in many foreign countries on subjects related to hospice care. His efforts were recognized in 1994 when the National Hospice Organization selected Dr. Lamers to receive its Founders Award. Earlier he was awarded an honorary degree, Doctor of Humane Letters, from the Starr King School of the Ministry. He has received a formal commendation from the California legislature for contributions to community health programs.

Dr. Lamers is a frequent expert witness in cases involving emotional distress related to loss and grief, and he serves on the Bioethics Committee of the Los Angeles County Bar Association. He has written widely on the psychology of loss, hospice care, and hospital bioethics committees.

IN HIS DELIGHTFUL BOOK, *All I Really Need to Know I Learned in Kindergarten,* Robert Fulghum lists some important lessons he learned in kindergarten: "Play fair; don't hit people; when you go out into the world, watch out for traffic, hold hands and stick together."[1]

In kindergarten I learned the phrase, "And they all lived happily ever after." A few months of clinical work in medical school taught me otherwise. Disease and injury take their inevitable toll, often without reason, remission, or fairness. I learned that impaired quality of life can be as destructive as shortened span of life, and can sometimes lead to diminished *quantity* of life. I realized that autonomy diminishes as quality of life is compromised. And I have come to realize that extended life in the face of serious impairment raises difficult ethical issues and provokes questions about the limits of technology.

My earliest recollection of quality of life issues in cancer care dates to my work on a surgery service during medical school in the mid-nineteen fifties. The dermatology clinic of a large hospital referred to us a woman who had a rapidly growing cancer of the face. She was blind, severely crippled with arthritis, and almost totally deaf. The patient lived in continuous darkness and silence in a nursing home. At ninety-nine years of age, she had outlived her family and friends. After examining her, my resident proclaimed, "We're going to cure this woman." She was admitted to our ward and, after preparatory work, brought to the operating room where we removed the cancer and repaired the resulting scar. Following an uneventful recovery she went back to the isolation of her nursing home. At her final check-up in the clinic, my resident was so delighted with the excellent surgical result that he patted her benevolently on the head and loudly proclaimed, "There, there now, mother . . . You can live to be one hundred!" In response she raised a gnarled, arthritic hand and pointed it at us while saying, "And I . . . wish the same on you."

Chronic arthritis, deafness, blindness, and social deprivation (isolation, dependency) seriously compromised the quality of this elderly woman's existence. She did not sense cancer as a further impairment. On the contrary, she saw cancer as a "friend," as a way of obtaining deliverance from an existence that no longer had any meaning. Her religious belief supported hope in an after-life. Cancer, for her, was a natural means of deliverance from this life. She wanted to join her long-deceased husband in the next life. She saw surgery as needless and unwanted. She saw our attempt to rid her of cancer as "meddling," as a way of interfering in her plan to die. She was not depressed, nor was she suicidal. The lesion was not offensive to her or to others. She accepted the reality of her unusually extended existence. Her cancer was not as troublesome to her as it was to her physicians. It is unlikely that her attitude would have changed had we provided her with more information or with counseling.

Her remark, "I wish the same on you," was sage and semi-humorous. She was alerting us to the fact that advanced age is fraught with complications. It was not delivered as a threat. It was free of anger. She was a delightful person who was making a clever response to the prideful remark of her surgeon.

The point is, I don't recall that we even asked whether or not she wanted the surgery. Our benevolent paternalism left little room for her thoughts, wishes and fears. During the nineteen fifties this country enthusiastically declared war on cancer. With new weapons in our medical armamentarium, we wanted nothing to stand in our way. Not even the *quality* of life of some of our patients.

After moving to Marin County in northern California, I came to know a young physician named Chad Calland. Chad had won the coveted gold cane as the outstanding graduate in his medical school class. Early in his practice years, Chad developed chronic membranous nephritis, experienced end-stage renal failure, underwent repeated dialysis and received several renal transplants. During this ordeal, he became a keen observer of the physician-patient relationship, this time from the patient's perspective. In an article published shortly before his death, Chad summarized his experience: "To many patients, the point that is most important is the quality of life. . . . I believe strongly that the patient should have a doctor who is interested in the art of medicine—namely, the *care* of the patient—so that he (the patient) may return to a more 'normal' life, whatever that means to him, not what it means to the doctor."[2]

Out of his ordeal, Chad learned the primacy of the quality of life and determined that its nature is elusive.

Quality of life is a subjective, internal impression; an attitude, a way of conceptualizing reality. We sense what contributes to the quality of our own lives. But we cannot presume to know what constitutes good quality for another person, any more than we can say with certainty, "I know exactly how you feel."

At about the same time that Chad Calland died, one of my fellow psychiatrists, Bob Ott, died of a brain tumor. During our final visit he said, "Bill . . . it's not the length of life that matters, it's the quality."

Early Work in Hospice

In the early 1970s my work with a few dying friends led me to help develop one of the earliest hospice programs in the United States: Hospice of Marin. At the time, I was merely responding to the personal needs of several close friends who had learned they had cancer and were told they were going to die. Each asked me to help. All wanted to be cared for at home . . . against the wishes of their physicians. (At this time—20 years ago—there was *no* care at home for terminal cancer.) Each had recurrent severe pain that was poorly controlled. I spent considerable time with each of them in their homes and witnessed the normal upheavals of grief in one family member after another. Each circumstance made me aware of the importance of attending to detail at the time of crisis. I learned that no single person can be expected to be everything in hospice care. I became intensely aware that excellence of nursing care is central; that psychological crisis successfully resolved can produce dramatic change and growth in a relatively short period of time. I was privileged to work with a dauntless group of health care professionals and laypersons who persevered in developing a home care hospice program.

Later, I worked for several years in hospice development within the framework of a provincial cancer program in Canada. I have also worked and studied in several other countries. It appears to me that the concept we call quality of life knows no national boundaries, no social or ethnic distinctions, no age limits. No matter who or where they are, persons with advanced, incurable illness seek relief, comfort, assurance, and support. They desire the familiar over the new, friend over stranger, calm over turmoil, hope over fear, constancy over change. They want meaning, clarity, and purpose in the midst of confusion and pain. They fear losing their identity, their sense of control, their personal contact.

Norman Cousins alluded to the same concern when he wrote, "Death is not the ultimate tragedy. The ultimate tragedy is depersonalization—dying in an alien and sterile arena, separated from the spiritual nourishment that comes from being able to reach out to a loving hand."[3]

Cancer can be looked at as a paradigm for the human condition. All that live will surely die, including you and me. In this mechanistic, highly technical society, we may try to distance ourselves from the reality of death. When oncologists say, "the patient failed the protocol," they ascribe responsibility for the drugs failure to the patient. Language reflects feeling, in this instance an empathic vacuum, and molds behavior. Charles Aring, my professor

of neurology in Cincinnati, wrote: "A physician unaware of his personal feelings about death and dying by the same token permits them to interfere with his effective treatment of patients. On one hand, indifference has resulted in undertreatment and neglect and, on the other, in overtreatment and an officious striving to keep alive."[4]

Enhanced quality of life for patients requires that physicians not only be technically competent, but that they have an awareness of their own finity that enables them to be involved both objectively and subjectively with patients and families who face incurable illness and death. The physician should strive to see that the patient is more than an impersonal assortment of physical and emotional signs, symptoms, and complaints.

Balfour Mount suggests that the physician's preoccupation with pathophysiology serves as a perceptual blinder that leads to overvaluing technical, scientific, and cognitive factors to the depreciation of affective, psychological, social, and spiritual values. He also says that we tend to overestimate our sensitivity to the needs of others. These problems arise, says Mount, ". . . not through a lack of caring but because we set high occupational goals for ourselves that, for the most part, are irrelevant to the 'personhood' of the patient."[5]

My years as a hospice physician taught me to question some things I had learned in my years of training. I began to question assumptions about the role and training of physicians who care for persons who are dying. I began to research the ethics of health care decisions at the end of life, the cost and availability of excellent palliative care, and the politics of health care planning. I also looked back in time to learn about the origins of current attitudes toward care of persons with incurable illness.

Historical Background

Hospice has a fascinating history, extending back nearly a thousand years to the work of the Knights Hospitaliers of St. John of Jerusalem.[6] Written records tell how the knights hired physicians to diagnose and prescribe for dying persons in an attempt to relieve discomfort. This was at a time when death was seen as a 'door' leading to the next world; dying was simply a necessary part of the journey to eternity.[7]

The hospice concept flowered again in the British Isles a little over a century ago, first in Dublin, later in London. At St. Luke's, "A Home for the Dying Poor" in London, Dr. Barnett used morphine to provide relief from the severe chronic pain present in many of the patients dying of cancer.[8] Dame Cicely Saunders had worked at St. Luke's during her earlier career as a nurse, and it is likely that her emphasis on symptom control dates from this experience. After 20 years of planning, Dame Cicely opened St. Christopher's Hospice in Sydenham, London, in 1967. Hospice concern with the quality of life derives in large part from the St. Christopher's model of excellence in patient care, attention to detail, concern for social, psychological, and spiritual issues, and involvement of the family in decisions and the provision of care.

The hospice concept developed in the United States in the mid-1970s, driven largely by the desire of clinicians to improve the quality of life for patients with incurable illness. These patients were slighted in a health care system that stressed aggressive therapies aimed at cure or rehabilitation, but that seemed to offer disincentives for care aimed at relief of illness. Massive federally funded cancer research programs had begun to provide extended survival to some persons. Yet some who survived did so at the expense of impaired quality of life. Symptoms of protracted pain, nausea, vomiting, skin destruction, weakness, and impaired mobility were compounded by costly hospitalizations. The final common pathway for these patients usually was the nursing home, an option often not met with enthusiasm. For many, hospice home care presented a reasonable and economical alternative.[9]

How People Die

The manner in which people die has also changed. In the pre-antibiotic era, pneumonia was called "the old man's friend." It provided swift and usually not uncomfortable death. In the protocol era of cancer care, there is no such swift and easy deliverance. Deaths have been arbitrarily divided into "hard" and "soft": "soft" deaths (which usually occur outside of health care institutions) include heart attacks, cerebrovascular accidents, and automobile accidents. Hard deaths (like death from cancer and HIV infection) usually involve rigorous treatments, progressive symptoms, physical suffering, and progressive organ and system failure. Psychological stress and social disruption frequently accompany complicated, painful, and expensive, aggressive intervention—and for naught when directed at unattainable cure.

Hospice often offers a balance, a refuge, a place of hope and comfort for those who make the conscious decision to balance quality of existence against the prospect of continued aggressive therapies in the face of diminishing quantity and quality of life, with no hope of cure.

Hospice Imperatives

Fifteen years ago, the number of hospice programs in development in the United States could be counted on one hand. Today there are over 2000 such programs offering palliative care at home or inpatient settings. The continuing growth of hospice suggests that it addresses and meets certain needs in patients, families, and caregivers. I have previously suggested that at least six factors played a role in the rapid acceptance of this hospice concept:

1. *The socio-demographic imperative.* A century ago, death was most common among infants and children. The dying process was brief and usually occurred at home after a short illness, with care provided by friends and family. Today,

most deaths occur in persons over 65 years of age, following a long illness, in some kind of health care institution, with care provided by surrogate care-givers. Our rural heritage with close support systems has given way to urban sprawl, a dispersion of families, and a loss of traditional family and community support systems.

2. *The economic imperative.* The cost of dying has escalated along with advances in science and technology. Health insurance experts have indicated that half the health care expenditures in this country occur during the last year of life. The United States, like other western nations, is experiencing a crisis in funding chronic health care. Hospice offers an economy through use of home care and volunteers without a sacrifice in quality of care or quality of life. Few families can bear the cost of long-term acute hospital care.

We are now in an era of economic limits to health care, limits that raise a number of complex and seemingly insoluble ethical dilemmas. Health care, especially health care for persons of advanced age and those with chronic illness, is rich material for political controversy. We must face the prospect that a combination of laws and economic realities will "pull the economic plug" on whole classes of our society. At the same time we must recognize that economic factors already deprive certain groups in our society of the minimum requisites for illness prevention or health care.

3. *The therapeutic imperative.* Cancer therapies developed since the 1950s offer the promise of extended life and, sometimes, a cure. But therapeutic side effects may add to underlying discomfort and provide a prolonged period of relative disability. For many patients, further therapeutic efforts only aggra-

vate an already impaired quality of existence. Hospice often offers an alternative setting for palliative care when life goes on without reasonable hope of cure or remission. As a physician I can speak to the obvious gains in cancer therapies resulting from protocol-controlled research. At the same time I realize there are limits to what can be gained when treatment offers faint hope at the price of aggravating symptoms.

Informed consent mandates that physicians explain the nature, objectives, and possible complications of procedures to patients in advance of performing the therapy. Informed consent is more than a piece of paper; it should be an on-going process. And for patients with incurable illness, palliative care should always be available and presented as an option. Ruprecht Nitschke learned that children with advanced cancer could make decisions affecting their care. Adults should be afforded the same opportunities.[10]

4. *The thanatologic imperative.* The war on cancer continues. Yet, despite many obvious victories, this year one million new cancer cases will be diagnosed, and half a million persons will die of cancer. We can distance ourselves from death by saying that it is none of our concern, that death happens to old people, to those that do not take care of themselves, to those who pursue dangerous lifestyles. We can dismiss statistics. We can rationalize behavior and deny reality. But when friends or family members or even some of our patients die, we find our usual defenses wanting.

Grief is the sudden and often uncontrollable outpouring of thoughts, feelings, and behavior in response to loss. Grief is resolved through the extended mourning process, often with the assistance of spiritually derived and socially sanctioned bereavement rituals. I have found a statement by Erik Erikson to be very supportive in my work with bereaved persons: "Grief, successfully handled, can serve as the focus for new social and psychological growth."[11] The successful resolution of grief requires what Eric Lindemann called "the great grief work."[12] This includes facing painful realizations and resolutions rather than utilizing avoidance mechanisms like denial, transcendence, and substitution. Some bereaved persons possess the internal and external resources to allow passage through grief with minimal disruption. Others will require lay or even professional assistance.

The impact of death on family members of all ages cannot be dismissed. We are all vulnerable to the loss brought about by death. Those of us who care for persons who are dying must also take responsibility to see that the survivors receive adequate support during bereavement.

Caregivers also grieve the loss of patients to whom they have become attached. Far from being unprofessional in expressing emotion, it is helpful to participate in funerals and other bereavement rituals and to share with one another thoughts and impressions about the person who died.

5. *The analgesic imperative.* A front page story in the *New York Times* last year quoted a survey of recently hospitalized persons in which over 50 percent endorsed the statement, "At some time during this hospitalization I experienced pain that was unendurable."[13]

The major obstacles to pain relief in advanced cancer include inadequate physician education about analgesia, inordinate fear of prescribing narcotics, and lack of clear physician-patient communication about pain.

Extended survival from an illness like cancer carries the potential of severe chronic pain. Methods of dealing with acute pain are generally inappropriate and ineffective when treating chronic pain. Inadequately treated chronic pain tends to increase in severity and gathers to it a host of secondary symptoms, including anxiety, depression, anorexia, insomnia, withdrawal, anger, and thoughts of suicide. Inadequately treated chronic pain erodes the quality of life and, I am quite sure, shortens the quantity of life.

During my training it was generally taught that morphine was not effective as an oral analgesic. Today, the availability of sustained release oral morphine preparations enables us to provide rapid, safe, and continuous relief of chronic pain. Heroin and esoteric narcotic combinations are not necessary. To relieve severe chronic pain requires openness, creativity, clear communication, excellent records, rigorous evaluation, and followup.

We teach our hospice patients to assess the effectiveness of their analgesia by keeping a visual analog scale called the Comfort Control Chart. This chart involves patients in their care, provides a ready means of communicating about symptom management with their physicians and nurses, and provides an excellent graphic record of pain and symptom control.

The multi-modality approach to analgesia includes non-invasive as well as invasive analgesic techniques as indicated. Once continuing analgesia is achieved, many patients can remain pain free on lower doses of narcotics.

There is no longer any excuse for persons with cancer to endure needless pain.

6. *The humanitarian/holistic imperative.* Progress in technology can narrow the physician's focus from the total person to a diseased organ or abnormal

laboratory finding. Patients feel distanced from caregivers by layers of intermediaries. A patient in a cancer center complained to me, "I know who my pharmacist is, but I have no idea who my doctor is." Fragmented and discontinuous care diminishes the quality of life.

Hospice considers the total person in all dimensions: physical, social, psychological, spiritual, and economic.[14] Hospice regards the family as part of the unit of care; they are at once the recipients and the co-providers of care. Abrupt withdrawal of support at the time of death does not coincide with the needs of survivors.

Characteristics of Hospice Care

Hospice care can be described in terms of its priorities. Hospice deals with quality of life by paying constant attention to the changing needs of patients and their families. The following is a list of characteristics that help to describe and define hospice care:

1. *Symptom management takes primacy.* Hospice evaluation and care centers on the needs of the patient and family, beginning with pain and physical symptoms. Successful management of severe chronic pain is the cornerstone of hospice care. Hospice emphasizes relief of pain and physical symptoms through the careful application of recognized therapies by an interdisciplinary team. Hospice assists in the development and maintenance of a supportive human environment for the patient, whether at home or in an inpatient setting. Repeat assessment of symptoms and necessary modification of the plan of care assures emphasis on maintaining quality of life.

2. *Services are readily available.* Hospice recognizes that patient and family needs can change at any time. Home care programs provide 24 hour on-call nursing services. Other members of the hospice team are available as needed. Home care hospice programs have developed contractual arrangements with inpatient units in the event that hospitalization is required.

3. *Care is provided by an interdisciplinary team.* Carefully selected, trained, and supervised hospice volunteers augment the work of health care professionals. The hospice interdisciplinary team is more than a list of names on a sheet of paper; they are an integrated group with clear and open communication working under the direction of the attending physician. They work together throughout the course of care to look for creative ways to meet patient and family needs, to make use of existing community and family resources to ease patient distress.

4. *Patient/family lifestyle is respected.* Saunders has said, "Patients belong to their families, not to us."[15] The patient and family set the tone for care based on open discussion with members of the treatment team. Two patients with the same disease may require quite different management by caregivers. Each person is an individual, and it usually takes time for patients to trust and share their hopes and fears with a member of the hospice team.

5. *Hospice facilitates communication.* Patients deserve clear information in everyday language about their condition and the treatment choices available to them. Communication is the transmission and reception of meaningful messages. Under the stress of serious illness, communication suffers. Hospice strives to improve the level and quality of communication within the patient/family unit as well as among health care providers. At times this borders on an ombudsman role; at other times it involves helping patients recognize their

responsibility in initiating direct communication. Hospice is alert to the tendency of some patients to foster benevolent paternalism in their caregivers.

Ideally, patient decisions affecting care are made on the basis of adequate information and reflection; not out of fear, anger, concern for abandonment or default. Hospice recognizes the need to support patients in their participation in decisions affecting their care. Unrelieved physical and emotional symptoms erode patient autonomy. Hospice strives to relieve symptoms and at the same time to respect patient/family wishes. Hospice encourages the development of reasonable goals for relief of pain and other symptoms.

Twycross suggests that hope is "the possibility greater than zero that an objective can be reached."[16] Reasonable goals enhance the quality of life; unreasonable goals ultimately erode patient/family confidence. Hope can be revised, but trust, once tarnished, is not easily restored. Patients with advanced illness may cling to hope that caregivers deem unreasonable. We sometimes tend to confuse hope with denial, and may feel the urge to force confrontation with a harsh reality that holds no provenance for hope. Hospice is respectful of both hope and reality and recognizes that it is not necessarily pathological to maintain hope even in the face of certain defeat. This attitude stems from hospice's respect for the human spirit and awareness of the importance of intangible, spiritual factors in human existence.

6. *The patient/family is the unit of care.* Hospice strives to preserve the unity of the family as the primary caregivers and support of the patient. The "family" may consist of others than blood relatives: friends, lovers, neighbors. The family is encouraged and taught to assist in providing hands-on care in the home. Conspiracies of silence concerning diagnosis and prognosis are discouraged. Hospice recognizes the need of family caregivers for relief from 24 hour responsibility and offers respite support.

7. *Care in the home is emphasized.* Although some patients may require brief hospitalization during their final weeks or months, most hospice care can be provided in the home. Home care requires excellent symptom management and close attention to detail. It is possible to provide excellent pain management in the home. Care at home mandates family involvement. In the absence of responsible caregivers in the home, it has been found that neighbors, social groups, and hospice volunteers can work with the hospice team to provide excellent palliative care.

8. *Bereavement care is essential.* Impending death provokes a multitude of responses in both the patient and the family. Grief is the normal and spontaneous outpouring of thoughts, feelings, and behavior in response to a loss. Reactions to loss vary greatly depending on a number of circumstances including the ages of the survivors, their participation in providing care, their internal and external support systems, and the character of their prior loss experiences. There is no standard pattern of grieving, no formula that can be universally applied, no standard outcome to be desired. Family history, ethnic background, religion and support systems exert a strong influence on mourning behavior. Children and grandchildren are often overlooked in bereavement support, yet they are quite vulnerable to loss.

Normal grief and bereavement usually do not require professional intervention. Structured social bereavement support programs have proven effective for many survivors. In hospice, bereavement support usually continues through the first year following a death.

Implications for Education

Thirty years ago, medicine was preoccupied with the sanctity of life. Quality of life was a secondary consideration. Life had to be preserved at any cost. Today, in the midst of technologies undreamed of a generation ago, the alternatives are not as clearly defined. Quality of life is of increasing concern. The focus has shifted to an inquiry into the nature of life: What is life? When does it begin? When does it end? Technology is facing a re-examination of the basis of ethical decision making.

Optimal care of seriously ill patients necessarily includes attention to social and psychological concerns. Ten years ago many medical schools taught courses designed to help humanize the dying process. It is disappointing to see that most have abandoned the effort, especially as we face many deaths from HIV infection. Students in medicine and other health care disciplines need formal training that prepares them to address the issue of quality of life in patient care. Hospice has helped to improve the quality of life of many persons with advanced, incurable illness. Our challenge now is to identify the principles that underlie hospice care and see if they can be applied in other areas of health care.

Keeping the Mission

BALFOUR M. MOUNT

BALFOUR M. MOUNT, M.D., is a professor of surgery and director of the Division of Palliative Medicine in the Department of Oncology at McGill University in Montreal. He is the author of over 85 articles and books and producer of a dozen films, videos, and audio tapes focusing on oncology and palliative medicine. He was a visiting professor and attending physician at St. Christopher's Hospice in London, England in 1974. Since 1976, Dr. Mount has chaired the International Congresses on Care of the Terminally Ill held in Montreal. An internationally recognized authority on care of the terminally ill, he has been a lecturer and visiting professor in Great Britain, Norway, Holland, France, Italy, the former Soviet Union, Japan, Australia, and New Zealand.

As the founding director of the pioneering Palliative Care Service at the Royal Victoria Hospital in Montreal, Dr. Mount's work was recognized by the American Journal of Hospice Care in its creation of the Balfour M. Mount Award, which is presented to individuals or programs that demonstrate unique and practical approaches to symptom control for terminally ill patients. His honors include designation as a member of the Order of Canada (1986) and Officier de l'Ordre National du Quebec (1988). He received the Founders Award of the National Hospice Organization in 1990. The following selection is adapted from Dr. Mount's keynote address before the New York Hospice Association in Albany in May 1992.

UNLIKE MANY FIELDS of endeavor where the original concepts have been lost in the sands of time, the foundational thinking that gave rise to the modern hospice movement has been carefully documented and is readily available.

Beginning with "Dying of Cancer" in volume 56(2) of the *St. Thomas's Hospital Gazette* in 1957, Cicely Saunders has produced a remarkable library of lucid writings that provides a detailed analysis of the needs of the dying and their families, and proposes a comprehensive system of care that has become known to the world as "Hospice."

The philosophy underlying hospice was perhaps most succinctly stated in 1948 in the plea of a young dying patient, David Tasma, who told Cicely, "I only want what is in your mind and in your heart." Significantly, this agnostic Polish Jew from the Warsaw Ghetto, who was to become an important catalyst for Cicely's thinking, feelings and subsequent actions, had given voice to the twin pillars of hospice care. The dying need *the friendship of the heart* with its caring, acceptance, vulnerability and reciprocity. They also need *the skills of the mind* embodied in competent medical care. Neither alone is sufficient.[1]

Two seminal papers, "The Need" and "The Scheme" were written by Cicely in June 1959.[2] While later revisions were to extend the net of hospice concern to include teaching, research, and an emphasis on home care, these early documents focused on the need for an inpatient "Home." They provided evidence of the attention to detail, clarity of analysis, and the blending of *a deeply rooted spirituality* and *excellence in medical care* that was to characterize St. Christopher's Hospice.[3]

From the first, Cicely was very aware of both the great potential of hospice and her colleagues' differences in perception. In an address to the British Medical Association at a time when "fighting for life to the very end" was accepted by many as the mandate, Cicely commented, "But to talk of accepting death when its approach has become inevitable is not mere resignation or feeble submission on the part of the patient, nor is it defeatism or neglect on the part of the doctor. Our work then is to alter the character of this inevitable process so that it is not seen as a defeat of living but as a positive achievement in dying; an intensely individual achievement for the patient."[4]

Iron-clad determination, a remarkable memory, an alert mind and a sparkling wit have served Cicely well. Her capacity to listen, *really listen,* to what patients were saying became the womb out of which the insights of hospice were born. In 1963 a patient at St. Joseph's Hospice told Cicely about her pain, "It began in my back, but now it seems as if all of me is wrong. I began to cry for the pills and the injections but I knew that I mustn't. It began to seem as if all the world was against me, nobody seemed to understand. My husband and son were marvelous, but they were having to stay off work and lose their money. It's marvelous to begin to feel safe again." In this sad tale Cicely heard the *whole* patient and the concept of "Total Pain" was born— the *physical pain* invading her whole body; the *emotional pain* of feeling alone; the *social and financial pain* associated with anxiety about her family; the *spiritual pain* already relieved by admission to St. Joseph's.[5]

For Cicely, the absence of further therapy to modify the natural history of the disease and patient or family need define the appropriateness of hospice care, not how many months the patient is expected to live, ability to pay, or the presence of family members who are able to act as caregivers. Cicely would consider the absence of a "primary caregiver" an inconceivable rationale for exclusion from hospice care. Isolation and loneliness in a time of distress, she would argue, make hospice *more,* not less, imperative. For Cicely, hospice care involves meeting people where they are, irrespective of color, creed, sexual orientation, family status or economic resources.

Cicely believes hospice care is physician-intensive. As she likes to say, "It is not a soft option." It stands on a firm foundation of medical competence. And she commented wryly, "I think starting a hospice with volunteers only is very exciting, as long as one or two of the volunteers are doctors."[6]

Reasoned therapy demands careful assessment and accurate diagnosis, which may in turn demand thoughtful investigation. The relevance of investigation is defined by the need for a diagnosis not the cost of the procedure involved.

Cicely sees bereavement support as an essential component of hospice that naturally flows out of the family's place as a central focus of concern. It could never be an optional add-on.

What of hospice management? Cicely's 1990 book, *Hospice and Palliative Care: An Interdisciplinary Approach,* presents a clear picture of hospice management through the operation of an interdisciplinary team; a team that includes the patient as an active member.[7] The goal of management is optimal care. A sense of community is seen as fundamental. In Cicely's words, "It is planned that the staff should form a community, united by a strong sense of vocation with a great diversity of outlook in a spirit of freedom."[8] Cicely shares Bruno Bettelheim's view that, "Community is viable only if it is the outcome of a deep involvement in a purpose which is other than, or above, that of being a community."[9]

What of money? Like management, money, in Cicely's view, is a means to an end, and the end is excellence of care. Both visionary and pragmatist, Cicely bid £27,000 for the property that was to become the site for St. Christopher's, when she had only £500 in the bank.

Her ability to find large sums of money is the envy of professional fund-raisers. When asked her secret she answered, "Never miss an opportunity to tell the tale; never stop saying thank you."[10]

In addition to this simple formula, her biographer Shirley du Boulay, sees four factors as contributors to her enviable track record:

1. Her ability to deliver to potential donors, with clarity, civility and conviction, a message that is both dramatic and filled with hope.
2. Her alliance with patients in fund raising, encouraging them to tell their story.
3. Her personal attitude to money and its purpose. A family friend commented, "She's always been able to collect money because she has such contempt for it." For Cicely, money is never more than a means to excellent inpatient and family care; money is never more than the means to an end.
4. At a deeper level is her faith in a destiny beyond herself that led her to comment, "If we find the pattern we are meant to have, the other things will follow. I really do know that without doubting."[11]

Recently, I was speaking to Cicely on the telephone and she commented that when I called she had been writing a talk she was about to give to the national body of hospice fund-raisers in the United Kingdom. Hoping to collect a fund-raising pearl I asked her what her message to them would be. "Listen to the patient. Listen to the patient. Listen to the patient," was her sage reply.

Hospice Care American Style

Let us turn our attention now to norms of practice here. American hospice has developed along lines that have diverged significantly from the original model. Patient inclusion criteria that include estimated survival, availability of a primary caregiver, and ability to pay have arbitrarily rendered ineligible many who are in great need.

Volunteers have come to define American hospice. Several years after Potter's warning in the *New England Journal of Medicine* that, "A high order of clinical competence is essential if abuse of the hospice is to be avoided,"[12] vol-

untarism had, according to Paradis and Usui, come to define not an *aspect* of American hospice, but the very nature of the thing itself. They state (1987), "The American hospice movement provides an example of organized *voluntary* action focusing on changing aspects of the existing health care system."[13]

Rather than developing as an integrated *part of* the health care system as is the proposed European goal[14] and the goal in Canada, American hospice came to be seen, in Mors' words, as, "an *alternative system* of care."[15]

In preparation for this presentation, a group of New York State hospice directors were asked to comment on "the barriers to keeping a balance of mission and management; to keeping the mission uppermost; to meeting mission objectives."[16] *All* responses started with "inadequate funding." Although some did not get beyond that, six listed other problems. While the small, selected nature of the sample precludes generalization, the problems cited may be familiar and of interest.

As already noted, barriers related to money were most frequently mentioned as the greatest obstacle to keeping the hospice mission. The problem was summed up by one director: "The financial constraints are overwhelming."

Others reflected on the impact of funding constraints: "There is a lack of financial ability to provide some of the high-tech things the patients really need."

One respondent linked financial need to inadequate management: "An important factor in our failure to adequately achieve the hospice mission is our unwillingness to face the necessity of becoming more sophisticated managers and set in motion long range plans to raise sufficient charitable funds. There is a counter trend in some unsuccessful agencies to limit services and complain that reimbursement is not adequate. Successful managers are generally able to share power with a community board that has the talents needed to raise money."

Barriers related to mission were also common, including questions about its definition. As one director commented, "Barriers exist within our own attitudes about what is and is not hospice."

Another director noted, "An original vision which was too narrow artificially restricted patient access, program growth and our ability to change. We need to develop a broader view and more flexibility—about serving children, serving more non-cancer patients, and so forth." Similarly, "The original mission is narrowly and inflexibly defined. I think of this model as 'The Gates of Heaven.' Patients must be just right, families in place, the disease one that the program is comfortable with, etc., etc. Such programs do not grow and over time they find themselves threatened by other providers whom they identify as somehow taking unfair advantage."

The same observer continued, "Another aspect of lack of flexibility is to define any new high-tech treatment 'not hospice' and thus bar its use in all cases, rather than allowing use as appropriate. Part of this is financial, but part is philosophical. Needless to say physicians who insist on this treatment will no longer refer. These decisions are often difficult calls."

The impact of management on mission was also noted. "As the agency grows and founding mothers and fathers are replaced by directors who have been hired from outside of the field, the sense of mission is lost and/or cannot be transmitted to employees."

In some instances specific individuals or attitudes were seen as barriers to meeting the hospice mission. These included the referring physician: "Continuing barriers are set up by some physicians who are not receptive to a holistic approach to end of life issues."

Also seen as barriers were members of the hospice team. As one director commented, "In the beginning my staff was filled with our vision and mission. Now it's 'pay me what I am worth, limit my hours, don't ask me to take on-call. Don't put performance measures on me (that's not hospice), but, treat me like a valued volunteer on the hospice team!' They want the best of both worlds and feel betrayed if they don't get it."

Another director noted the importance of unrealistic goals, "Unrealistic expectations of what we can achieve are a problem. The, 'We're going to fix everything for everybody,' syndrome leads to failure and feelings of inadequacy."

Cultural attitudes were also seen to provide problems: "Cultural barriers to acceptance of good symptom control such as 'The War on Drugs' can be a stumbling block."

Management was directly identified as the problem in a number of observations the hospice directors made. There was repeated criticism of management over-regulation, such as: "Hospice has become very rule-oriented. The rules of the organization are transmitted to new employees rather than the mission." Another commented, "Over-regulation is a major problem. Outside pressures keep us focused on picayune details rather than the bigger picture." In a similar vein a third confessed, "I have to spend my day bean-counting when I should be star-gazing."

Pressures imposed by a system ill-suited to meet the hospice mandate were seen as focusing attention away from the original mission. Such pressures included:

- "The need to maintain a short length of stay which has us using up all our energy chasing emergencies;"
- "Increasing competition (or anticipated competition) for patients;"
- "The necessity of meeting corporate demands by a parent agency that wants to use the same productivity measures used for other departments."

Others were forced to conclude that keeping the hospice mandate as now defined demanded, "more precise prognostication for non-cancer patients," and, "a national data base to better understand parameters of hospice utilization trends."

Finally, one director commented on the problems inherent in team functioning, saying: "Some programs talk 'Team' with implied implications for egalitarian power sharing and decision making, while in reality those with the power hold on to their turf with a ferocious grasp."

It isn't too surprising that we are all having problems in reproducing the example of "balance" so impressively created by Cicely. At the first International Hospice Conference in India, held last November, the final session looked at "Problems in Hospice Care" and compared mission and management difficulties encountered in East and West. Dr. Robert Pye reports that while the differences initially looked vast, "all the problems we encounter, while tinged by a local flavor, are very similar, that is: money/government/bureaucracy/getting mainstream medicine to acknowledge us, etc."[17] Reassuring isn't it?

But is this all we can say? I think not. For there are other messages that are being sent out from every corner of this great land with increasing clarity. Messages about health care delivery that must be acknowledged if this review of mission, money and management isn't to be simply platitudinous.

A New York publishing executive telephoned me regarding some matters of mutual interest. In the course of the conversation she confided, "Our health care system is a nightmare. I could never consider changing my job because of the risk of a lapse in insurance coverage. It has become a factor that rules our lives. Everything you have worked for over a lifetime can be wiped out in a few days if a family member gets sick. When I became pregnant I was afraid to tell anyone until I was sure I was covered. When I did see the obstetrician his secretary informed me the initial consultation fee would be $200 up front, and when I

saw him he said, 'I want to clarify our financial contract before we start. My fee to deliver your baby will be $3500, paid in cash, in advance.' When I told him I had insurance his comment was, 'That's your concern. You apply for it. The fee must be paid in advance.'"

She continued, "A colleague's teenage son has just been found to have a brain tumor. When he had the first seizure his mother was frantic. When the ambulance came, they asked if she was insured before agreeing to take him to the hospital."

Health care as a commodity! Like designer jeans and cosmetics. Money no longer a means to an end, but an end in and of itself.

Nashville legal aid attorney Gordon Bonnyman recounts the experience of a 24-year-old diabetic construction worker named Terry Takewell whose job carried with it no insurance benefits.[18] With his medical record Terry could not buy an individual health insurance policy at any price.

One day after work a neighbor found Terry in poor condition in the trailer where he lived and arranged for him to be taken to the Methodist Hospital in Somerville, Tennessee. The Emergency Room doctor diagnosed acute ketoacidosis and ordered immediate admission. Within the hour, news of the admission had reached the acting hospital administrator. Alarmed at the prospect of the young man adding to the already considerable unpaid hospital bill accrued during previous illness, the hospital official personally went to Terry's hospital room and escorted him out of the hospital, leaving him propped under a tree in the hospital parking lot. When questioned by the indignant neighbor, hospital officials said that the admission had been denied because of the unpaid bills. The neighbor took Terry home to his trailer where he died that night.[19]

What is the relevance of all of this to our assigned topic this morning? One hospital-chain executive observed, when questioned about his denial of treatment to a dying cancer patient, "General Motors isn't expected to give away cars. Grocery stores don't give away food. Why should anyone expect us to give away care to someone who can't pay for it?"[20]

Dear colleagues, that Terry Takewell died is a tragedy beyond measure, but a tragedy of even greater dimensions is found in the myopic comment and closed heart of the hospital executive, and greater still is the tragedy of those of us who have become sufficiently numbed by stories like Takewell's that another one no longer evokes moral outrage.

The recent events in Los Angeles led me to question the validity of a call for moral outrage, and I changed the above text to "moral indignation." But moral outrage is exactly what is called for, both in response to the acquittal of the four police officers who beat Rodney King, and in response to our own inertia when we hear another Terry Takewell story.

The Los Angeles riots were not an indictment of moral outrage. They were an indictment of anarchy and violence—the illegitimate children of moral outrage. What both situations are testimony to, is the need for the true child of moral outrage—justice.

President Bush's criticism of the Canadian health care system on the heels of your kind invitation for me to examine with you the balance between mission, money and health care management, taken together with the facts, begs us not to mince around issues.

Let me be quick to say two things. First, I do not hold up the Canadian health care system as a paragon of perfection. To work in it is to love to hate it. Second, I do not feel comfortable offering these comments, but my minor discomforts can hardly be relevant measured against the scope of the problem and the need to give voice at every opportunity to the ever-increasing torrent of protest from the American middle class. The facts speak for themselves.

Infant mortality rates are considered by the World Health Organization to be one of the most reliable barometers of how well a nation attends to the health needs of its people. The USA ranks 15th among nations according to this criterion. Infant mortality rates among blacks are twice as high as those for whites. An African-American infant is less likely to survive to her first birthday than a child in 28 other countries, including Cuba, Singapore and Bulgaria.[21]

At present, 37 million Americans have no health insurance. That number continues to climb as hyperinflation pushes the cost of insurance above the reach of more and more individuals and employers.[22]

A further group, estimated to be at least as large, is officially classified as "underinsured," that is, their basic health care needs are not covered [23]

"Dumping" is the descriptive term applied when hospitals turn away patients who lack insurance and money. Though it is illegal, a 1987 study published in JAMA [*Journal of the American Medical Association*] estimated that 250,000 emergency patients are dumped each year from American hospitals.[24]

The American Cancer Society reports that cancer survival rates among the uninsured are markedly lower than among those with adequate health coverage.[25]

In addition to the cost in unmet suffering, the current system is associated with worrying dollar costs. For more than two decades health care costs have inflated at twice the rate of personal incomes.[26] Furthermore, projections for the future by two Washington-based advocacy groups, USA Foundation and Citizens Action, predict that health spending per person will more than double the 1980 level by the end of the decade.[27] As a result, more and more of those in the middle class will become uninsured; the number of public hospitals serving the uninsured will continue to drop; and, under pressure of rising costs, states will continue to cut back on their Medicaid programs, as more than 30 are proposing to do this year.[28]

Analysts note that the brunt of this staggering burden is being borne by those in the lower socioeconomic class.[29]

At the same time, commercialized health care as a consumer product generates significant profits for those at the other end of the economic spectrum. In 1990, the mutual funds that outperformed all others were those which invested exclusively in health care stocks.[30] In 1989 the average physician earned approximately $155,800; in 1990 $164,000.[31] Doctor and hospital bills are a leading cause of bankruptcy in the United States.[32]

Is there light at the end of the tunnel? For five reasons I think there is. To begin with, the election of Sen. Harris Wofford in Pennsylvania under the banner of the right to medical care. Second, there is the light being generated by the growing anxiety over access to health care from a middle class already squeezed by recession. Third, health care has become a central issue in the presidential campaign. Fourth, as Watergate demonstrated, your country has a marvelous ability to self-correct that is the envy of the world. When a problem is diagnosed you Americans are pretty good at finding solutions.

Fifth, and in my opinion most significantly, there is light because the American health care system contains an intrinsic catalyst for change and healing—YOU. You entered hospice to promote change; to bring compassion. There can be no more worthy arena for the use of these gifts than the current need for radical health care reform.

But isn't the cost of health care already too high? One might well ask, "If the inflated health care budget is already bankrupting the nation what would happen if we tried to care for the tens of millions of Americans now excluded from the system?" Bonnyman responds, "In fact, America's unique institution of commercialized medicine is far more expensive and less efficient than that of other industrialized nations that provide care to all citizens. Dollars presently wasted on a bloated health care industry are ample, if redirected, to meet the needs of people now being denied care."[33] Once again the facts are thought-provoking.

An estimated 20 percent of US health spending goes into the administration overhead tied to the marketing of thousands of different types of health insurance and their costly associated claims processing bureaucracy.[34]

Hospital costs are inflated by the expenses related to keeping open vacant hospital beds which, in fact, account for more than one third of the national total on any given day.[35]

In spite of the existing national glut of hospital beds, competing hospitals continue to build costly new facilities to "capture better market share."[36]

The padding of insurance claims is generally agreed to be commonplace, significantly adding to health care costs.

What reforms are needed? Effective reform would be characterized by four distinguishing features.[37]

1. *Universality.* Basic health coverage would have to be extended to all citizens with quality of care independent of ability to pay.
2. *Affordability.* Effective cost controls must protect both the individual (against costs related to particular needs such as medications or nursing home care), and the national purse (against spiralling health care inflation).
3. *Accountability.* A reformed health care system should be accountable to the public with built-in incentives that foster primary, preventive and quality care rather than overuse of high-tech invasive medicine. A responsible public with authority for quality control should disarm the potent entrepreneurial legal forces that have been so effective in padding lawyers' incomes and leading

to excessive malpractice insurance costs and settlement awards.

4. *Political feasibility.* Current band-aid reforms recommended by political leaders out of fear that anything more substantial would not be politically feasible must give way to new definitions of what is possible. Reform will become politically viable only when the people find their moral voice and demand change.

There is much to accomplish. Where does one start? The immediate task is to change consciousness, not structures. There are none better equipped to lead in the fight toward consciousness raising than you. For there are none who have experienced more graphically the truth of the observation that the strong need the weak as much as the weak need the strong in the equation of community survival.

A new balance in mission, money and management is needed in your health care system. You're not alone. The secret is, it's needed in ours as well, and in the system in Great Britain, and on, and on.

Many believe that this current "recession" is, in fact, part of a global financial restructuring that has arisen as part of the changing world order. There is an urgent international need for new management answers that will help us ensure economically feasible health care for all as a basic right in each of our countries.

We have a vested interest in your success in this health care revolution. Once again we, your international colleagues, look to you for leadership in problem solving. We wish you good luck and God speed.

Care of the Dying Child: The Demands of Ethics

WILLIAM G. BARTHOLOME

WILLIAM G. BARTHOLOME, M.D., M.T.S., is a professor of pediatrics in the Department of the History and Philosophy of Medicine at Kansas University Medical Center in Kansas City, Kansas. He also chairs the Hospital-Medical Staff Ethics Committee and the Pediatrics Committee at Kansas University Medical Center.

Dr. Bartholome's interest in the care of dying children began during his pediatric residency at the Johns Hopkins Hospital in Baltimore. In 1971 he was involved as a resident in a case that was dramatically reenacted in the film *Who Shall Survive?*, which became one of the first "teaching cases" in the emerging bioethics movement. Since completion of a Joseph P. Kennedy Jr. Fellowship in Medical Ethics at Harvard University Divinity School, Dr. Bartholome has continued his work in pediatric ethics. He served on the Committee on Bioethics of the American Academy of Pediatrics and currently serves as a member of the board of one of the few community-based bioethics centers in the United States, the Midwest Bioethics Center of Kansas City, Missouri.

Dr. Bartholome has lectured at over 300 medical schools, nursing schools, universities, and hospitals in North America and Europe, and he has published widely on topics related to pediatric ethics. The primary commitment that informs his work with dying children is that children who are suffering with chronic, life-threatening, and terminal illnesses have a right to be treated as "developing persons"—persons with a right to know as much as possible about their conditions, a right to participate to the extent of their capacity in health care decision making, and with an emerging capacity to control the course of their health care and their lives. Dr. Bartholome feels strongly that health care professionals, parents, and society at large have profoundly underestimated the knowledge, capacity, and power of children to shape their own lives and destinies—even when they are facing the ultimate challenge, dealing with their own mortality.

WE HAVE COME a long way since the pioneering work of historian Philippe Ariès, anthropologist-philosopher Ernest Becker, and physician Elisabeth Kübler-Ross.[1] Our deeply rooted "denial of death" has been breaking down for over two decades now. We have come to accept our responsibility to care for the dying in a manner that is respectful of their interests, rights, welfare, and dignity. In this country, the dramatic change in our attitudes and practices is most visible in the growth of the hospice movement. Yet almost since the beginning of what some have called the death-and-dying movement in this country, a storm of controversy has surrounded the question of how we are to discharge our responsibilities when the dying person is a child. I would share with you the experiences and thoughts of a father, a pediatrician, a "clinical ethicist." I would also like to begin this essay by acknowledging my enormous debt to the scores of children and parents who allowed me to play the role of a hospice physician to them. By caring enough about me to be my teachers, they provided me the opportunity to discover what it means to care for a dying child.

Provider Problems

Many of the problems involved in responding to the needs of dying children belong to the "big people" involved. Although we have come a long way in accepting the reality of death, most adults in our society still cannot accept the idea of children dying. Old people die. Adults with cancer, heart disease, and strokes die. But it's not natural that children die. It's not the way things are supposed to be. Although we may accept the fact that some infants die and that some children will die sudden, accidental deaths, children should *not* die of diseases. This idea is so unacceptable that many health care professionals in training rule out careers in pediatrics simply because they could not tolerate working with critically ill and dying children.

Parents and providers bring this attitude to their relationships with children, and they see death as the ultimate form of failure. The emotional burden of seeing oneself as having failed to protect an innocent child from this ultimate evil is enormous. Parents and providers expect that they can protect children from such evil or, at least, rescue children who become ill from this fate. When faced with a critically ill child who is not responding to their rescue efforts, they have a powerful need to deny the reality—to see the child as sick but never as terminally ill.

To this day, pediatric health care providers and parents strongly resist using the word *dying*. All too often, the result of this need to deny is that terminally ill children die, but they are rarely seen or treated by their caregivers as dying persons. In order to avoid painful feelings of frustration, impotence, and guilt, providers allow children to die only after they have done everything they could to reverse the course of illnesses. Children continue to die under the full-court press of every intervention known to modern medicine, in desperate attempts to save them. Providers withhold nothing that promises even the most remote hope of benefit. Moreover, most health care providers lack the training and skills needed to provide palliative care to their patients. In fact, few health care professionals receive formal training in the most basic aspects of hospice care.

Finding Terminally Ill Children

As they mount these all-out attempts to rescue critically ill children, providers often overlook a crucial task, namely, identification of terminally ill children who are candidates for hospice care. Whose responsibility is it to "find" terminally ill children? I propose that the burden rests on health care professionals. They are the ones who should determine when a critically ill child has reached the point at which additional attempts to prolong life and prevent death are no longer appropriate. Although the child's parents may recognize this point first, health care professionals are usually in a better position to make the determination.

This task, however, is not just *emotionally* challenging; it is also technically and clinically daunting. There are no widely accepted criteria for health care professionals to use in determining which critically ill patients are actually terminally ill. There are no examinations or blood tests or X rays with which a health care provider can determine that a child is terminally ill. Instead, health care professionals must continually evaluate the condition of the patient and the patient's response to treatment. Although the nature and prognosis of the child's disease may be such that death is a possible or even a probable outcome, the determination of an appropriate point for radically altering the goals of treatment from "curing" to "intensive caring" is both complex and demanding.

For me, the determination rests on four factors in addition to the nature of the child's disease and the prognosis. The first—and least controversial—is the extent to which the treatments are having a measurable effect on the anticipated course of the disease. In terminally ill patients, treatments often are no longer producing any measurable effect. For example, the growth of a child's tumor can no longer be stopped by anticancer drugs. The lungs of a child with cystic fibrosis are just as congested when he is taking antibiotics as when he is not.

The second factor might be called refractoriness, or resistance. Terminally ill patients seem to become progressively refractory to interventions: the dosage or number of drugs needed to achieve a desired effect increases progressively. Providers often have the sense that they are "climbing a mountain of gravel." They are expending a great deal of time, energy, and resources, yet the patient seems only to become more and more dependent on drugs and technology without showing any evidence of improvement.

A third factor might be called the trajectory of the patient. By examining and plotting the child's response to treatment over time, providers can often discern a pattern of the illness and its progressive failure to respond to interventions. The child with leukemia, for example, may have remained in relapse despite the use of three combinations of chemotherapy given over a three-month period. The weakness of the child with muscular dystrophy may have become significantly worse over the course of the past year, during which she was hospitalized five times for treatment of pneumonia compared with twice in the year before.

The final—and most controversial—factor is the providers' own responses to the child and to the feelings they experience in their attempts to treat the child. Nursing staff often become aware of these responses first. For example, they may begin to feel that what they are doing and being asked to do *for* the child is more like something they are doing *to* the child; interventions start to feel more like "torturing" than "treating" the child. Or their willingness to perform painful procedures on their patients hinges on seeing improvement in the child's condition. If providers are willing to undertake this emotionally challenging task of discovering that they have terminally ill patients, they will be able to determine with a reasonable degree of certainty which critically ill patients are candidates for care as dying children.

Problem Identification

Once providers have discovered that they are caring for a terminally ill child, the next major obstacle is sorting out the tangle of "dying problems." First, the encounter with a terminally ill child forces providers to encounter their own death and dying. To state the obvious, the idea of mortality, of one's personal death, is a big problem. Some have argued that it is the ultimate existential problem. Whether they want to see it or not, providers will face their own mortality in the face of the dying child. This is in *no* sense a problem to be solved. The ability to live with one's mortality is a largely impossible goal which must be pursued. To the extent that providers are able to acknowledge that this problem is present in their clinical encounters with dying children, to "own" it as their own problem, they can be more free to get on with the task of responding to the dying child. Second, coming face to face with a dying child triggers in providers—most of whom are also parents—the fear of their own children dying. If they fail to acknowledge and own this problem, they often project it into their encounters with their child patients. The struggle to rescue the ill child becomes the desperate struggle to save their own children from this fate.

The combination of these two problems exacerbates the third problem (described above): the guilt and frustration that providers already feel over letting their child patients die. A fourth problem involves the dying child's parents. Facing the impending loss of a child, parents often turn to health care professionals for help, which places an additional burden on the care provider. Keeping these four problems separate and devising strategies for dealing with them allow both parents and providers to deal with the fifth set of problems: the problems children have with their own dying.

The Reality of the Child

The most daunting problem facing parents and providers who are caring for a terminally ill child is that the person they are caring for lives in a different reality. Today's parents and child health professionals owe an enormous debt to Jean Piaget and a generation of child psychologists who have carried on his work. Thanks to them we now know a good deal about the reality of children and how it differs from adult reality. This understanding forms a bridge between the adult world and the child's world and allows adults to understand children and their problems and needs in facing death.

Take the first word of this seemingly simple sentence: "I will die soon." As adults, we have a fairly well developed sense of self, of what we mean when we use the word *I*. We tend to forget that we only gradually became aware of *self* and distinguished our self from other selves over a long period. As adults, you and I can make sense of the statements "I *have* a body" and "I *am* my body." But the ability to reflect, to think about yourself, or—as my oldest daughter once put it—to "see" a picture of yourself inside your head, is something that rarely develops before the age of six or seven. But even after a child has developed a picture of herself in her head, the child's identity develops only very gradually and is rarely achieved or discovered before late adolescence.

The world of a child is also not neatly divided into animal, vegetable, and mineral. Animate and inanimate are rarely distinguished reliably before age ten. A child's whole world is alive and filled with consciousness. An unfamiliar object like a stethoscope is just as likely to bite as a dog or cat. Needles stick you and hurt you; if you move, they'll hurt you more. Adults also divide the world into fantasy and reality. We know the difference between thoughts and things, dream life and waking life. Not so for kids. The child who dreams of a monster under the bed wants Dad to check under there. If a child wishes Mom were dead—which means nothing more than that she would disappear for a while—and she gets sick, the child feels she probably caused the illness.

What about the second word in our simple statement: "I will die soon"? The concepts of chance and probability can be difficult enough for adults to grasp. But they are virtually absent from the world of a child. The idea of a chance occurrence is foreign to their world. Things don't just happen; everything has an immediate and proximate cause. For example, a sick child feels that somebody or something caused him to get leukemia; somebody must have been angry with him. Furthermore, the intravenous catheter for chemotherapy got infected because he didn't take care of it properly, and now his mother is taking him to the hospital to be admitted for punishment. Worse still, the child believes that it is because he messed up his last catheter that the doctor is ordering (as punishment) an operation to get a new one.

A related problem is the egocentricity of children. When we say that an adult is egocentric, we hope to convey that he or she is inordinately concerned with self. But children have no choice in this matter. They relate everything that happens around them to their own feelings, ideas, and actions. If a child sees his mother crying, he feels he must have done something to upset her. If the doctor who is trying to draw blood is sweating and swearing in frustration at not being able to find a vein, the child patient feels she must be doing something to make her veins hard to find. If the child's parents are crying about the result of his bone marrow test, he must try to cheer them up because he was the one who "failed" this important test. If the doctor and nurse are talking in low voices in the hall outside his room, they must be talking about him.

In addition to this age-related sense of self, children have their own sense of time. What would the word *soon* mean to a dying child? Time for children is not a linear progression of hours, days, months, and years. A child of five or six cannot feel the difference between two weeks and two months. Both are merely a long time. Time is essentially collapsed into the present. If the child is told that her grandmother is coming to visit "soon," she may take that to mean that she should cancel her plan to go to the playroom so she can wait for her grandmother to come. In other words, the idea of having six months to live has no meaning for a child. Not only do young children have trouble with the idea of physical time, but until around age ten, they have no conception of personal time. They have no sense of a lifetime in which to plan and use their time.

Working within this distinctive world, children sort out their experiences in limited categories, using *concretistic* thinking. Having a tumor may mean something like having a big toe or having a baby in your stomach as mothers do or having a new dress. If the nurse says the shot is like a bee sting, the child might expect the nurse to pull a bee out of the drawer and sting him with it. If being dead is like being asleep, the child wants to keep the lights and the TV on in order to stay awake all night.

The Child's Conception of Death

One of the trickiest words for children in the simple sentence "I will die soon" is obviously the word *die*. What in the world might that mean to a child of four or eight or twelve? Would it mean different things to children of different ages or different stages of development? This question has attracted the attention of scores of investigators. As a result, we now know a good deal about how the concept of death develops in children, particularly how this concept evolves in the thinking of healthy children.

In *The Dying Child* by William Easson and in several more recent works that review scores of studies investigators argue that a child's conception of death is linked to stages of cognitive development.[2] For infants and toddlers, who have *sensorimotor intelligence,* death is simply separation. A child of this age would experience separation from a parent through divorce in the same way they would experience the death of the parent. Death means nothing more than "not present to me."

Preschool-aged children use what Piaget called *preoperational thought* and conceive of death as both separation and departure. To be dead is to be "living under unusual circumstances," like in a coffin that is nailed shut and buried in the ground. A child in this age range might well express concerns about lighting arrangements inside the coffin or whether a favorite toy or pet might be allowed to accompany him. Furthermore, to preschool children, death is like sleep, and dead people can feel when individuals visit their graves. Some investigators have argued that children in this age range conceive of death as reversible at least in theory.

Children from the ages of six to ten use *concrete operational thought*. To them, death is real; it can happen to people, and it is irreversible. Some authors argue that children of this age tend to personify death and to think of it in terms of some outside agent.

After this age, and particularly with the development of *formal operational thought* in early adolescence, children conceive of death as involving irreversible decomposition of the body—as the "end of life." In late adolescence, with the development of a sense of self as radically separate and unique, death is also conceived of as the end of personal time, as a cruel personal blow, and as the loss of newly developed intimate relationships.

Although widely accepted, this analysis of the evolution of a child's conception of death has also been challenged on two fronts. One challenge comes from those who feel that the differences between children's conceptions of death and those of adults may have been exaggerated because of misinterpretation of the primary data (structured interviews of children and related instruments) or because of assumptions made about the so-called adult conception of death. One of the more interesting challenges to these stages (called here the standard developmental account) was offered by Gareth Matthews, who points out that "the Standard Developmental Account seems to have as an implication that anyone, adult or child, who believes in the immortality of the soul, let alone the resurrection of the body, is cognitively retarded."[3] Is the belief that personal continuity extends beyond death a child's or an adult's conception? How should one characterize the concept that the dead are living in a special place called heaven? These studies may well have been conducted with the assumption that the most highly evolved conception of death is that it involves physical decompensation and personal annihilation.

The other challenge to this standard developmental account has come from work with populations of sick children. In the past, most studies of child's developing conception of death were conducted in populations of healthy children. But beginning with the ground-breaking work of Myra Bluebond-Langner on children with leukemia,[4] investigators have discovered that the concept of death in many populations of critically ill children does not follow this standard account. Instead, in these populations the conception of death seems related to experience with illness and its treatment rather than to the child's chronological age or stage of cognitive development. These recent challenges should remind health care professionals to use information about the relationship between age and concept of death only as starting points in the dialogue with individual dying children.

Beyond "To Tell or Not to Tell"

Based in part on the differences between the child's world and the adult's world and the early studies of children's conceptions of death, it was common practice during the 1950s and 1960s to shield children—particularly children younger than ten—from the realities of their illnesses. Some providers of care, however, objected to this "conspiracy of silence," asserting that parents would find it very difficult to maintain such an approach, and that children would sense the wall of silence and lose trust in their parents and health care providers. This led to a controversy that lasted almost a decade over whether to tell children the "truth" about their illnesses. Two widely read observational studies conducted in the mid-1960s with populations of children with leukemia challenged this protective approach.[5] It was not until the early 1970s, however, that formal studies of children with life-threatening illness were undertaken.

One of the earliest, undertaken by Eugenia Waechter, involved a population of children between the ages of six and ten with a variety of chronic diseases and a carefully matched control group of children with acute illnesses and children who were normal.[6] The General Anxiety Scale for Children was administered to each child. Each child was also shown a set of pictures and asked to tell a story about the picture. The children's parents were also interviewed. Anxiety scores among children with fatal illnesses were twice as high as scores of other hospitalized children and three times as high as those of healthy children. Children with a poor prognosis related stories that indicated a preoccupation with death in spite of the fact that both parents and providers claimed that no information had been given to the child about the prognosis. And none of these children had directly told parents, providers, or the investigator herself about these feelings. Her study and others that followed confirmed the worst fears of those who had worried about the effects of silence on the child patients. On the other side of the wall of silence, children were struggling to deal with their anxieties, their fears, their preoccupation with mutilation, and above all, their loneliness and sense of isolation.

In the mid-1970s, John Spinetta and Lorrie Maloney published the results of their studies of children with leukemia.[7] Their findings (confirmed by others) led pediatric health care providers and parents beyond the long-standing "to tell or not to tell" debate. Why? These studies documented that in spite of the best efforts to shield young children from the "truth" about their life-threatening illnesses, they managed to discover what was really going on. Even children as young as four years old were able to piece together information from the treatments they were undergoing, from their observations and conversations with other children, from overheard conversations between adults, and from their parents' nonverbal behavior. One of the more disturbing findings was that many school-aged children had actively participated in the conspiracy because they didn't want to burden their distressed parents. Sick children were attempting to parent by protecting their parents.

Truthfulness with Children

Pediatric health care providers and parents have now taken the crucial first step toward truthfulness with child patients. They have accepted the flaws in the conventional approach of shielding or protecting children from the hard truths of their conditions. Children do not need to be shielded or protected from the truth. Furthermore, such efforts actually make things more difficult because they cut children off from the people who can help them understand and deal with what they are experiencing. Nondisclosure, deception, and the all-too-common practice of lying to children have been rejected. Realistically, this now widely accepted standard of openness with children may have resulted as much from the fact that conspiracies are impractical and create difficult

and often noncompliant patients as from any ethical concern with the needs or rights of children to know the truth.

Truthfulness with a child involves a good deal more than the information-dispensing that health care professionals commonly engage in with their adult patients. For one thing, we still have the reality-gulf between the child's world and ours. Young children are likely to encounter significant problems in understanding the information they are provided. Giving them the "facts" or the "truth" about their condition is a dangerous and inadequate method of being truthful.

How, then, are parents and professionals to proceed? The first rule, and the most obvious, is to be aware of self. Communication with a child demands that we as adults become aware of what we are communicating to them before we even start trying! As Fred Rogers ("Mister Rogers") and a host of others have told us, children listen more to what grown-ups do than to what they say. Even small children are astute observers of adult nonverbal communication. Because they have trouble interpreting adult language, they develop the skill of "reading" adult behavior. Not surprisingly, many children are better than adults at reading nonverbal behavior.

Second, we must be sure that we are really ready to be honest with them. Have we sorted through the list of dying problems described above? Are we ready to respond to the problems they have? Children have a built-in skepticism whenever adults approach them. They do not expect honesty. They do not expect adults to take them and their problems seriously.

Third, we must remind ourselves that communication with a child involves a willingness to avoid informing, explaining, and lecturing. Children expect adults to talk "at" them rather than "with" them. In fact, effective communication with them demands that we avoid talking as much as possible. It demands that we listen. It demands that we relinquish control and let them set the agenda for the conversation. Sounds simple. It's not. We are not used to letting children have control of anything, much less a conversation about dying and death.

Fourth, this process demands that we be willing to answer any and all questions the children might have. It means looking for clues to their desire to know and understand more. It means letting them set the pace. Truthfulness with children is a process, not an event. They will come to awareness in their own way and at their own pace. It requires something that few adults have much of—the ability to be patient with them.

And finally, it means seeing our task as *assisting* them in their efforts to come to awareness of their own illness-reality. It is their task. They want to do it, and we must believe that they can do it. Whether we want to or not, we cannot do this for them. John Spinetta and Patricia Deasy-Spinetta have described this process as helping children find ways of "fitting" the awareness of illness, even fatal illness, into their ongoing lives.[8]

When we need to use language in this conversation, it helps to keep in mind the problems children may have with adult language. Obviously, we should avoid references to time as much as possible. We should avoid references to things like chance and probability. We should use simple, concrete language and avoid analogies and similes. Because young children have limited capacity to deal in abstractions, we should avoid references to abstract philosophical, theological, and religious concepts unless we are certain of their "meaning" to the child. My favorite example is that of parents who become upset when conversations about going to heaven and being with Jesus are angrily rejected by children who would just as soon stay home. We also need to be prepared for anxieties, concerns, and fears that may appear irrational or even silly from our adult perspective. We "know," for example, that tumors are not conscious, that they don't decide to grow or to be resistant to chemotherapy. We know, too, that thoughts cannot cause physical changes to take place. We know there are no monsters or bogeymen. But our knowledge of the way the universe is put together is no help to children as they attempt to make sense of their condition.

Beyond Truthfulness: Children as Decision Makers

As demanding and complex as these tasks may sound, they are just the beginning—a giant first step in the process of responding to the dying child. So far, I have described the process of responding to the informational needs of these children, of helping them develop an awareness of the reality of their illness. But respecting them means much more than being truthful. In the course of providing care to these patients, hundreds, if not thousands, of decisions must be made. Most of these decisions will involve interventions into their bodies, interventions intended to influence the course of their diseases, interventions that may profoundly affect their lives. In the context of chronic and potentially terminal illness, these decisions often involve treatments that impose considerable burdens, significant pain and suffering, and disturbing side effects and risks. Moreover, in the context of terminal illness, these decisions often involve withholding or withdrawing treatments, even life-sustaining treatments. What role should the child patient play in making decisions about these interventions?

In the past, parents as guardians made all these decisions in concert with the child's health care providers. This was called *proxy consent*. However, as Langham, Gaylin and Macklin, and others have pointed out, many serious problems are associated with the idea that parents should make these choices.[9] I have argued against the concept of parental consent, particularly against a parent's right to refuse interventions of established benefit to children.[10] One of my major objections to the concept of parental consent in pediatric practice is that it rests on the mistaken idea that children lack the capacity to make decisions about their illnesses and their treatment. On the contrary, children have a right to be treated as developing persons, as persons with a developing capacity for rationality, autonomy, and participation in health care decision making.

The foundation for this right to participate rests on the rapidly expanding literature in developmental psychology on the decisional capacities of children. During the past decade, investigators from a wide variety of disciplines have examined the ability of children to make choices in matters like participating in human-subjects research or receiving chemotherapy for treatment of their cancers, and in a wide variety of other situations.[11] The implications of these findings are profound. First, as philosopher Dan Brock points out, these studies support the presumption of full decisional capacity for children over age fourteen.[12] Second, these studies support the idea that children as young as age seven have developed many of the capacities needed to make good decisions. This is not to say that children in the age range of seven to fourteen should be granted the right of independent consent granted to adolescents and adults. But it is to say that these children are fully capable of participating in the decision-making process.

What should their role be? What should parents and providers do to respect this evolving capacity? The concept that has evolved to describe this new role is called *child assent*. It was first formally incorporated into pediatric practice in federal regulations governing the participation of children in human-subjects research. The National Commission for the Protection of Human Subjects of Biomedical and Behavioral Research recommended that federal regulations require investigators to obtain both the permission of parents to involve their children in research *and* the assent of the child subject.[13] Many child health professionals, and I among them, feel strongly that child assent must become a standard part

of pediatric practice in all decisions involving children from seven to fourteen.

Child Assent

The concept of child assent has four elements. The first (described above in the discussion of truthfulness) consists of assisting the child to develop a developmentally appropriate awareness of the nature of his or her illness. The second involves disclosing to the child the nature of the proposed intervention, whether a diagnostic test or a treatment procedure. Even more important, it involves disclosing to the child what he or she is likely to experience in undergoing the intervention. The third element involves assessing the child's understanding of this information and the factors influencing the child's evaluation. And, finally, assent involves the obligation to solicit the child's expression of willingness to accept the proposed intervention.

An example of this process may be helpful. Mary, an eight-year-old undergoing treatment for leukemia, is coming to the clinic to have an examination, blood test, and a lumbar puncture ("spinal tap"). Her clinic nurse would reinforce the ongoing process of helping Mary to have a developmentally appropriate awareness of the nature of her illness. She might, for example, ask Mary once again to explain to her what was wrong with her or to clarify why Dad had brought her to the clinic that day. She would correct any misinformation, answer any new questions Mary might have, and provide educational materials. Obviously, this essential educational process is one that begins at the time of diagnosis and never ends. Second, both the laboratory technician and the physician would explain to Mary that she needed to have blood drawn and to undergo a spinal tap. They would make sure that Mary understood what she would experience in undergoing these procedures. The lab tech might remind Mary that having a blood test meant having a needle put in your arm for a minute to get some blood out. Third, they would assess the extent of Mary's understanding of the disclosed information and any factors that might be influencing her evaluation. They might, for example, ask Mary to describe what she understood was about to be done and to explain to them why these procedures were being done. And, finally, they would solicit Mary's expression of willingness to have her blood drawn and to undergo a spinal tap. The laboratory technician might ask Mary if she was ready to have her blood test. The physician might inform Mary that he was ready anytime she was ready to go ahead with the spinal tap.

One reason parents and providers resist the concept of child assent is that they fear, and don't know how to respond to, child *dissent*. Although I attempt to be sympathetic to this fear of having to deal with dissenting children, it is important to remember that children are very anxious to please adults and will do almost anything to earn and maintain the love and acceptance of parents and adult providers. I believe that children are extremely reluctant to dissent even when they should! Moreover, children often dissent only temporarily in an effort to gain some control over what is happening to them. Often they are attempting to understand, trying to deal with fear, or expecting something painful. The obligation to solicit assent forces providers and parents to hear and respond to these needs, even if an intervention is temporarily delayed. The obligation to solicit assent also forces providers to acknowledge that manipulation, coercion, and force are to be avoided as much as possible. Even when providers and parents agree that an intervention must be undertaken against the wishes of a child, assent requires that parents and providers explain the need for this procedure, acknowledge that the child is being forced to undergo the intervention against his or her expressed wishes, and apologize for the use of force. Finally, this obligation forces both providers and parents to acknowledge that their interests and needs may be very different from those of the children.

Parents of terminally ill children may be unwilling to let go. They may be willing to try anything to avoid losing their child. In contrast, the child who has been living the illness may be much less willing to make a last desperate attempt. A model of decision making that allows the child patient to participate demands that mechanisms be created and made available to providers, parents, and child patients in such conflict situations. In most hospitals, such mechanisms do exist in case-management conferences, psychological and social service consultation and counseling, and ultimately, review by a hospital-based ethics committee.

The Child as Care Provider

Health care providers and parents, then, must respect the needs of the dying child for information and allow the child an active role in decision making. But the ultimate (and largely unmet) challenge in caring for dying children involves respecting children's developing capacity to care for themselves, to take control of their dying. Hospice workers have discovered that their patients cherish control as the most basic and important ethical value. Dying patients want the care offered and provided by their caregivers, but they want more than anything to be in control of their own dying process. Children use a wide variety of cognitive and behavioral strategies to reduce anxiety, to adapt to the demands of their illnesses and their treatment, and to achieve a sense of mastery and control over what is happening to them. To help them avoid feelings of helplessness and hopelessness, adult providers must find ways to support them in this important task. Allowing children maximum control over what is happening to them dramatically reduces the anxiety and stress of illness-associated pain and treatment procedures. The relief of suffering demands that all care support this sense of control and mastery.

If we wish to allow children to control their dying, we must face the almost universal preference of dying children to die at home. Dying children, just like dying adults, feel that at home they are likely to have more discretion in directing their dying process and in having their desires and needs met. Children also need to be supported in doing the "grief work" of dying. They need to express their own sadness and sorrow at having to leave and to express their anger at having to die. Children also need to participate in planning funeral services and burial arrangements. All these measures help support the coping strategies of dying children and help them to have a sense of living to the end.

The Demands of Respect and Care for the Dying Child

Respect for dying children involves a series of challenges for their parents and health care providers. It means a willingness to acknowledge our limited capacity to rescue them or to protect them from death. It demands that health care providers accept the responsibility for identifying terminally ill children. It means a willingness to respond to their experiences and to the problems they have with their own dying. It means being willing to be truthful and to assist them in developing their own understanding of the reality they face. It demands that we respect their developing capacity for autonomy by allowing them to participate actively in making decisions about appropriate care. And it means supporting them and their coping strategies as they attempt to maintain control over their lives to the end. It means, above all, a willingness and ability to trust that they can manage their own dying, at least as well as "big people."

Medical Ethics and Decision-Making

On Death and Coding

RICHARD S. SANDOR, M.D., is a board-certified psychiatrist in private practice in Santa Monica, California, and an assistant clinical professor at the UCLA School of Medicine. He also serves as the medical director for the Chemical Dependence Center at Saint John's Hospital in Santa Monica and is the president of the California Society of Addiction Medicine.

Other than the usual work of a physician, Dr. Sandor reports that he has had "no special experience with death and dying." Besides "On Death and Coding," he has written two other essays for *Parabola*: "A Physician's Journey" and "The Attending Physician." The following selection was written for the *Parabola* issue on healing. Dr. Sandor describes it as "an attempt to write something that healed, rather than merely writing about healing."

I KNEW A SAGE once. He is, thus far, the wisest man I've known. One night at dinner he asked me, "Do you read much?" "No," I confessed, "I used to, but now I read very little . . . I guess I don't believe I'm going to find what I'm looking for in books anymore." Tongue loosened by the fine Scotch he served, I went on, "Sometimes I'll even find myself having walked into a bookstore, but then almost immediately I begin to doubt that much will come of it, so I walk out without having looked at anything."

"I see," he said. "Debilitating, that, giving up just as you've begun. You see, in truth, you really don't know why you are there. Perhaps there *is* a book you need to find or someone you're supposed to meet. Do you follow me?" And I nodded in agreement without being sure that I really did.

In time, I came to understand that he had diagnosed my condition as an early case of cynicism—the negative side of a new-found professionalism. It seems that in the process of mastering the enormous amount of material required to practice modern medicine, knowledge itself, once a haven from confusion, had become an instrument of bewilderment. I had taken an accidental overdose of information and had lost my appetite for the unknown.

The consequences of this knowledge/malaise became clear to me one day as I was sitting in the hospital cafeteria next to some interns on break from their duties in the Intensive Care Unit. In between bites of macaroni and cheese they were talking about the tough day they were having. The more I tried to ignore their conversation, the more painfully aware of it I became. At the line, "And then this guy coded..." I was involuntarily launched out of my seat and across the room in horror.

I don't imagine there is a television viewer in America who doesn't know what the expression "Code Blue" means. Once upon a time, "Code Blue" was secret hospital language used to page a special team which would try to revive some unfortunate patient whose heart had stopped. Of course, now that everyone knows what it means, the phrase "Code Blue" has lost its power as a euphemism. But in their luncheon lament, those young doctors unwittingly revealed that what once hid the truth from the public, now concealed it from the professionals. Dying, once the central mystery of living, had become for them the trigger for a special job, a "Code Blue." Exactly what happens in the patient's experience at this moment isn't part of the phrase. You might be dying, but to us you are "coding," "have coded," or are "a code."

In all fairness, many grateful people have been revived from the brink of death by the "Code Blue" team—some of them have even been grateful to me. The problem is not that we have such powers but that we use them indiscriminately. Medical practice has become so complex that we've no choice but to reduce much of what we think or do to code, but then somewhere along the way we've forgotten what the code was invented for—why we practice medicine in the first place. One of the

results is that, other than those who work in hospices, fewer and fewer of those who care for the ill know anything about death. We detect subtle disturbances of heart rhythm, manipulate faltering blood pressure to within a few millimeters of mercury, and regulate minute changes in blood chemistry, but what about the person who is dying?

My first encounter with death was different—perhaps just because I hadn't yet developed the professional armor that shields us from unanswered questions. I was taking part in a first-year medical school course called "The Doctor-Patient Relationship." A faction of our faculty, alarmed by the increasing disinterest among students in the *art* of medicine, put together a course in which we interviewed "real live" patients once a week. In the group sessions that followed these interviews, we shared our experiences while the faculty slipped in what they hoped would be antidotes to the deadening trends in medical education.

One Friday night, my assignment took me to the General Surgery floor of Los Angeles County Hospital to talk with an elderly man who'd been struck by a car. He was "under observation" (mine, as it turned out) with a preliminary diagnosis of pelvic fracture. Other, more urgent cases—mostly stab and gunshot wounds—were being whisked to and from the operating theater, hotly attended by the interns and residents. So my patient and I were pretty much left alone.

Mr. Francis wasn't having much pain—certainly not enough to require any "dope," he was quick to assure me. For a man of 64, he was in remarkably good shape. He explained that he owed his good health ("helt," he pronounced it) to the fact that he'd been a boxer in his youth and had maintained the habit of vigorous daily workouts. In addition, he'd eschewed the use of all drugs (prescribed and otherwise), didn't drink or smoke, ate gobs of lecithin studded with vitamin capsules ("You oughta try some, Doc!"), and was careful about the types of ladies with whom he " . . . uh, well, ya know, go wit', Doc—hah!"

My "Doctor-Patient Relationship" interview couldn't have been easier or more pleasant. Mr. Francis regaled me with his stories of a life as foreign to me as the technological wizardry of County Hospital was to him. Several times he began a new tale with the line, "Now, let me tell you something, son. . . ." I was entranced.

Suddenly in the midst of one of these stories, he paused, seemingly confused, and began to pick at the bed sheets—as though he couldn't get them quite right, Then, in a frightened voice, he said, "Hey, it's goin' dark in here—who's messin' wit' da lights?" As he started to try to climb over the bed-rails, I began to panic. What should I do? Stay at the bedside and keep him from falling out, or go for help? In the next moment he fell back into the bed unconscious and I ran to get the interns and residents. When we returned to the bedside, Mr. Francis was pale and still.

The gang of youthful saviors I'd summoned descended upon my friend with an almost voracious violence. And as they stabbed and pounded at Death, I backed away in guilty horror, because it was absolutely clear to me that the battle was already over. After twenty minutes of furious combat, they gave up, and my patient and I were once again alone. Amid the spattered blood, festooned by a tangle of tubes and wires, Mr. Francis looked for all the world like a great whale, harpooned and killed, ready for the flensing. I stood there, weeping in secret and thinking, "Where did he go?" One moment I'd been talking to a man— a lifetime of experience and memory, a way of talking and thinking and feeling, everything it takes to make a man—and then suddenly all that was gone. Where had it gone? I understood that the mangled carcass in the bed was just that, an empty container, but where were the contents?

Quietly, I removed all of the medical paraphernalia, arranged his body in the bed, closed his eyes, and propped his head up with a pillow so his jaw would not hang open. As I pulled a fresh sheet over him, his mouth moved and I jumped back in terror. Had they erred in pronouncing him dead? Quickly, I checked for a pulse, but there was none. Nor was there breath. I ran to tell an intern. With amused condescension he assured me that "reflex" movements like that could continue for as long as thirty minutes after death. So when do we die? I thought. Is awareness wrenched from its vessel in one piece or gradually? Did his consciousness remain in this realm until his body stopped moving? If so, Mr. Francis heard me say good-bye. For one thing was clear: life hadn't stopped, it had just gone somewhere else.

Like Mr. Francis, my father also died at the age of 64, but he never called me "son." I longed for him to. I wanted a wise and patient forester or fisherman for a father, and what I had instead was a brilliant and restless physician/investor who for years could reveal his pride in me only late at night and only to my mother (so she said).

Dad had a sign hung prominently in the living room: "If you're so smart, how come you ain't rich?" And as I look back, I realize I'd applied an alternate version of it to his life: "If you're so smart, how come you ain't happy?" But he was not at all malicious, only flawed, and he did his best. For a long time, I did not know how to love him. The passage of time and my own fatherhood softened the edges of our conflict, and we even learned to enjoy one another while collecting old and rare medical books.

One Saturday he called up wanting me to accompany him to a used book sale in a distant town (he didn't like going to such things alone), and in an uncharacteristic fit of selflessness, I decided not only to go with him, but also to give him my day. No matter what he told me to do, I would obey—a day of whole-hearted service to my father.

Two minutes after we got on the freeway, he started. "Richard, get into the right lane." So I got over, simply, without argument inside or out. Several miles down the road he directed me to get off on what I believed to be the wrong exit, but I didn't argue with him. Twenty minutes later, we were lost. "Do you know how to get to this place?" he said. "Yes, I think so." "Well," (flustered arm waving) "go ahead—get us there." By the time we arrived, he was so shaken by my utter cooperation that he was almost out of instructions. But not quite. "Uh, well, why don't you go around that way, and I'll go this way. See what you find." I replied, "OK, Dad. Whatever you say."

Apparently, in addition to serving my father that day, I was meant to find a book. It turned out to be a first edition of Sir William Osler's *Principles and Practices of Medicine.* My father was ecstatic. Priced at seventy-five cents, we were getting the thing at a hundredth of its value. He was proud of me then, and it made me happy, but I also took my find as a sign from Above that my offering had been accepted. A little over a year later he died of leukemia.

I was with my father frequently towards the end. It was good to be able to care for him at last, but it was hard to watch his world shrinking. At first, he wanted to live to see his youngest child, my sister, graduate from college in June. Then he wanted to make it through the Christmas holidays. Then to Thanksgiving. The last time I was with him, he only wanted to get to the toilet and back under his own power.

There is a death in life the mystics speak of—the death of possessing in favor of being possessed. It's the lesson my wise friend was trying to convey to me at dinner that night. Twice, in attending dying men, what I believed I knew fell away. I saw that two worlds meet at death and that in dying we pass from one we know to another we don't. For Mr. Francis the journey was unexpected and abrupt. For my father it was inevitable and drawn out with pain.

It has been said that all medicines are poisons and that the difference between their power to heal or to destroy lies in dose. But what of the man who gives the medicine? Where is his measure?

The Story of Mr. and Mrs. Doe:
"You Can't Tell My Husband He's Dying; It Will Kill Him"

MARGOT L. WHITE AND JOHN C. FLETCHER

MARGOT L. WHITE, J.D., is a former human rights observer in the Middle East who brought her concerns about treatment of the weak and vulnerable to the arena of medical ethics. Her experiences in the Middle East—where wars, government repression, and poverty engender severe morbidity and high mortality—convinced her that the health of any population is a dynamic indicator of the overall level of human rights enjoyed by that population. Imprisoned for a year as a result of her attempts to organize shipments of medical aid and equipment to the Kurds in northern Iran, she returned to the United States and subsequently attended law school at the University of Virginia (UVa).

While in law school, Ms. White carried out an independent research project at the UVa Health Sciences Center involving an evaluation of participant satisfaction with the process of ethics consultation. "The Story of Mr. and Mrs. Doe" came from this study. Despite the "consultation" format of the ethics service, her research showed that the ethicists were adversarial and confrontational in their approach to conflict resolution. Although the outcome was considered satisfactory from a purely decision making point of view (that is, the decision was usually one that the ethicists and physicians thought best), families and patients expressed considerable unresolved anger and distrust toward the ethicists even while expressing great appreciation to physicians and nurses for the extra time and attention devoted to the patient's situation or the family's dilemma.

After graduating from law school in 1989, Ms. White joined the faculty of the University of Virginia Medical School to teach patient-care law and ethics to medical students, house staff, and faculty. She joined the Ethics Consultation Service and was appointed staff coordinator of the Hospital Ethics Committee, where she developed a style of ethics consultation that relies on mediation and on facilitating communication in a cooperative, non-blaming environment, with an emphasis on listening to people's needs rather

than advocating particular positions or decisions. By far the most common circumstances associated with treatment conflicts are those of terminal illness.

In 1992, Ms. White obtained a grant from the Virginia Foundation for the Humanities and Public Policy to produce a documentary film about the experience of terminal illness as revealed through the stories of patients and families. She is currently on the Board of Directors of Hospice of the Piedmont and maintains a private practice in mediation, including mediation of medical disputes.

Ms. White believes that, although "The Story of Mr. and Mrs. Doe" may have resulted in an ethically "appropriate" decision, the manner in which this conflict was handled was inappropriate. There was a tendency to ridicule Mrs. Doe's avoiding behavior while ignoring her fear and grief about her husband's condition.

JOHN C. FLETCHER, PH.D., is Emily Davie and Joseph S. Kornfeld Professor of Biomedical Ethics at the University of Virginia's School of Medicine in Charlottesville. He is also director of the Center for Biomedical Ethics, founded in 1987. Originally trained as an Episcopal minister, Dr. Fletcher served in parishes in the southern United States from 1957 to 1964. After attending graduate school at the Union Theological School in New York from 1964 to 1966, he conducted research for his dissertation, "A Study of the Ethics of Medical Research," at the Clinical Center of the National Institutes of Health. He then combined a career in theological education with his interests in bioethics until 1977, when he decided to pursue the latter more completely. In 1990, he resigned from the Episcopal ministry for reasons of intellectual honesty, feeling that he could no longer embrace theism or the promises one needs to keep to be an ordained religious leader.

Dr. Fletcher's research interests focus on ethical issues in applied human genetics, fetal and embryo research, new reproductive technologies, cross-cultural issues in medicine, the costs of terminal illness, and clinical ethics. He has published, edited, or co-edited several books and more than 200 articles or chapters on various topics in biomedical ethics. He serves on the editorial boards of three journals in biomedical ethics and two in the areas of human gene therapy and prenatal diagnosis/fetal therapy.

Dr. Fletcher was the first chief of the Bioethics Program of the Clinical Center at the National Institutes of Health (1977–1987). During that time, he was a Founding Fellow of the Hastings Center and a Senior Fellow of the Kennedy Institute of Ethics. He also helped to found the Society for Bioethics Consultation, an organization that assists in studies of the effectiveness of bioethics activities in health care. The following selection is an example of ethics consultation.

THE ETHICS CONSULTATION requested for this patient was the subject of a qualitative research study by the authors to assess the feasibility of evaluating ethics consultations, their impact on patient care, their effect on decision making, and their function in facilitating needed communication. As a result, the thoughts and feelings of each participant in the consultation were available from the research interviews, and the following article is based on those interviews. Mrs. Doe refused us permission to interview her husband after they took him home, and so we do not know how he felt about the ethics consultation at his bedside. All names have been changed, except those of the ethics consultants.

Mr. Doe, a 54-year-old man, was admitted to the university hospital with encephalopathy and suffering from severe and irreversible cirrhosis of the liver. A chronic alcoholic, Mr. Doe had been in declining health since 1980; now his doctors believed he was nearing the end of his life but that he would soon be able to go home. Medicine could do no more for Mr. Doe.

On this day, he lay in his bed, somewhat confused but conscious of his wife as she straightened and folded his bed sheets, tucked and patted his covers, adjusted items on the bedside table, and busied herself with the tasks of caring for and protecting her husband, as she had always done.

Just then, Mrs. Doe noticed young Dr. G at the door, about to enter the room. Mrs. Doe was instantly on guard.

"I've come to talk with your husband," said the young intern.

"What about?" asked Mrs. Doe, blocking the passageway into the room and setting her jaw rigidly.

"We need to talk with your husband about his condition and what he wants." Dr. G suddenly felt anxious about his ability to confront this woman or to pursue the discussion he wanted with "his" patient, despite Mrs. Doe's objections. *Does this woman know that her husband is dying?* he wondered.

"No, I won't let you tell him," said Mrs. Doe, looking defiantly at the young intern. *What could he know about my husband?* she thought. *What do any of these people know about my husband? I won't let them hurt him. These doctors think my husband is going to die, but they mustn't talk like that.*

Dr. G tried again to enter the room, but the stubborn posture of Mrs. Doe was unyielding. He felt perplexed and irritated. He was annoyed at himself for becoming trapped and at Mrs. Doe for denying his role and obstructing his relationship with his patient. Dr. G withdrew into the corridor. *I'll find the resident,* he thought. *She'll know what to do.*

Mrs. Doe watched uneasily as Dr. G disappeared down the hallway. *He's so young,* she thought. *What does he know about anything? They can't just do what they want. He's not theirs, he's mine. I'm the one who takes care of him. I've always protected him. I know what he needs. No one else understands....* And she busied herself with her sleeping husband's bed sheets.

The imposing figure of Dr. Westchester, the attending physician, appeared in the doorway of the visitors' lounge, and Mrs. Doe felt a mixture of awe and apprehension. She tried to listen as Dr. Westchester explained something about ethics, and that we must not feel guilty in the face of difficult decisions, and that these decisions can be made easier by having a meeting, and that there are rules about patients.... Mrs. Doe grew very confused. She didn't want to think about these things. As if through a dense fog, she was aware of people talking around her. She heard them say that her husband's condition was irreversible ... he could die at any moment ... might go into a coma ... need a respirator ... need to decide now.... She didn't want to hear this.

The resident and the intern arranged two meetings over the course of the following week. They needed to make Mrs. Doe recognize not only the physicians' need to talk with her husband about his condition and his wishes regarding terminal care but also her husband's right to be involved in his treatment decisions. She refused to participate. She insisted that any discussion concerning terminal care would significantly harm her husband, that it would "kill him."

Dr. Westchester wondered whether the patient and his wife were uncooperative because the intern and the resident were both young and, in addition, the resident was pregnant. *Perhaps,* Dr. Westchester thought, *these young physicians just can't command the authority that senior clinicians enjoy.*

Meanwhile, Dr. G and Dr. T, the intern and the resident, were increasingly frustrated by Mrs. Doe's obstinacy. They believed that the patient was capable of understanding his situation and participating in the decisions to be made, and they worried that, unless some decisions about the level of treatment were made, Mr. Doe would be readmitted in the near future, in acute crisis and incapable of communicating. Even though Mr. Doe's mental status fluctuated and he was often confused, the resident and the intern believed that he was competent and had lucid periods when they might talk with him about these choices—if only Mrs. Doe would let them.

Dr. T decided to ask for help. She called John Fletcher, PhD, director of the ethics consultation service (ECS), to ask for an ethics consultation. She discussed the problem with the chairman and vice chairman of the department of medicine, both of whom agreed that the patient's right to be consulted about treatment decisions was being overridden by Mrs. Doe. Dr. T was anxious about confronting Mrs. Doe and did not want to alienate her because Mrs. Doe was an integral part of her husband's care. Dr. T wanted help from the ECS in communicating with Mrs. Doe. In particular, she wanted Dr. Fletcher to communicate to Mrs. Doe the importance of her participation in discussions. Dr. T decided to ignore the negative comments she had heard about the "ethics people," who were perceived by some doctors to meddle in decisions that should be made only by physicians. She felt that the staff was facing a genuine dilemma: how to protect this man's right to know his situation and to make his own choices in the face of obstruction from a family member.

Dr. Fletcher suggested a psychiatric consultation to evaluate Mrs. Doe's assertion that knowledge of his terminal illness would kill or seriously harm her husband. Dr. Fletcher's experience suggested that family members who insist on having "everything" done for a dying patient, regardless of the medical benefit and the patient's wishes or best interests, are very often motivated by deeply conflicted emotions toward the patient, which may indicate a need for psychiatric help. Dr. Fletcher's recommendation was sparked by Mrs. Doe's adamant refusal to allow her husband any say in his own treatment.

Dr. G felt that an ethics consultation was not necessary, that he would be able to proceed with his discussion with Mr. Doe. He felt that he had made a serious mistake with the patient's wife but that he should be able to rectify it by himself. All he needed, he felt, was to talk with Mr. Doe alone, and he believed that somehow he would find a way to do this. Dr. G had not been pleased when the resident called an ethics consultation, but now he was curious to see how it would be conducted.

Dr. Bill Broaddus, a neurosurgeon and a member of the ECS, felt that the role of the consultants in this case was to support the medical team's efforts to carry out its duties toward this patient, to persuade Mrs. Doe to participate in the discussion with her husband, and to help the medical team clarify the situation and treatment choices for the patient. He was concerned that if the consultation focused on Mrs. Doe, Mr. Doe's rights would be subordinated to his wife's needs rather than protected from her interference.

Anne Roberts, RN, also a member of the ECS, had for many years cared for alcoholic patients and their families. She was familiar with the dynamics of dependency that are often manifested in such families. Mr. and Mrs. Doe appeared to be locked into a kind of relationship that was not atypical of alcoholic families, and this one had endured for more than 20 years. Mrs. Doe had been making virtually all of her husband's decisions and controlling situations that threatened her relationship to him. Perhaps because of her specialized experience, Ms. Roberts perceived Mrs. Doe's concerns somewhat differently than the other participants in the consultation. She heard Mrs. Doe say not that it would upset her husband to hear that he was dying, but that it would upset *her*. Ms. Roberts felt that the physicians were ignoring the very real fears of Mrs. Doe, who was facing the deterioration of her main purpose in life: caring for her husband and controlling his life. Rather than appreciating that Mrs. Doe was losing the most important relationship of her life, the physicians merely seemed irritated that she was obstructing *their* relationship with her husband.

Dr. Fletcher decided first to meet with the treatment team and to assess the clinical situation, then to meet with Mrs. Doe and to try to persuade her to participate in the discussion with her husband. He assembled the two physicians and the two members of the ECS team in a conference room down the hall from Mr. Doe's room. Dr. Fletcher hoped that the two meetings would result in the implementation of the patient's right to know his prognosis, enabling him to make decisions about what kind of treatment and care he wanted at the end of his life.

Two problems were immediately apparent. As Dr. Fletcher read Mr. Doe's chart, he noted with chagrin that the psychiatric consultant had declared the patient incompetent. This complicated the picture considerably; now the physicians disagreed among themselves about the patient's capacity to make decisions. Apparently, instead of evaluating whether Mr. Doe would be harmed by knowing his terminal diagnosis, the psychiatrist had assumed that the consultation had been requested to evaluate the patient's competence. Perhaps the psychiatric consultation had taken place in one of Mr. Doe's nonlucid periods. At any rate, it did not comport with the observations of his treating physicians.

Dr. G then announced that Mrs. Doe had refused to be present at any meeting with her husband and was still opposed to any discussion at all. Mrs. Doe was in the hallway. Dr. Fletcher left the conference room, telling Dr. T and Dr. G to give him five minutes with Mrs. Doe and then to meet him in the patient's room.

Mrs. Doe fretted and fussed with her bracelets, trying to suppress the dread and anxiety she felt at the sight of so many doctors near her husband's room. She became aware of a tall man with white hair standing next to her.

"Mrs. Doe, I am Dr. Fletcher from the ethics consultation service. We need to talk with your husband, Mrs. Doe," the tall man was saying. "We need your help."

Mrs. Doe began shaking her head. She heard the man talking about "decisions" and telling her that her husband had rights, that he needed to know how sick he was. *No, he doesn't,* she thought. She covered her ears with her hands. *What do these people know about my husband? I don't want to hear this. They can't talk like this. I won't let them. I won't listen.*

To his own surprise, Dr. Fletcher found himself literally shepherding Mrs. Doe back into her husband's room while he verbally appealed to her interest in her husband's comfort. Once in the room, Mrs. Doe seized her purse and retrieved a pill, which she immediately swallowed. She then grabbed some tissues, stuffed them in her ears, and blocked her ears with her hands. Dr. Fletcher lowered her hands and removed the tissues.

Arrayed around Mr. Doe's bedside were Dr. Fletcher, the neurosurgeon and the nurse from the ECS, another nurse, Dr. G, Dr. T, and the reluctant Mrs. Doe. Contrary to the psychiatric consultant's depiction of Mr. Doe, he was partially sitting up, awake, fairly alert, and oriented.

The discussion was a difficult one. There were misgivings at times on the part of virtually all of the participants about the "line" between disclosure of medical recommendations, made repeatedly to ensure comprehension, and subtle coercion of the patient's choice. How "autonomous" can a dying patient be? How "voluntary" is a choice that results from the recommendations of a team of physicians and ethicists? Has the patient's privacy been violated by bringing so many people into his room, which is shared by two other patients? Is the violation justified by the patient's right to full disclosure and respect for his decision-making capacity?

At first, Mr. Doe indicated that he would agree to be "on a machine" if it would help him. The intern explained that it was his decision but that the physicians believed a "do not resuscitate" (DNR) order would be best. "If you think that's best," said Mr. Doe.

"But that's what *they* think," Mrs. Doe said; "they want to know what *you* think." The questions were repeated. Ms. Roberts explained that the patient thought they were asking his permission. Two of the ethics consultants presented Mr. Doe with a hypothetical scenario: if he were brought into the emergency room, would he want to be automatically resuscitated, intubated, put on a machine even though it would not help him? "No," answered Mr. Doe.

"Honey, do you understand they're saying you don't want to be on machines?" asked Mrs. Doe.

"Yes," he replied.

In retrospect, both the intern and the resident in this case acknowledged that they had serious misgivings about the role of the ECS and had been reluctant to call for help. They feared that the ethics team would try to dictate their treatment choices and interfere with medical decisions. Afterward, both expressed gratitude for the support and for the example of effective interaction in a difficult and conflicted family situation. Dr. G said he would be more assertive and confident in addressing a competent patient and that he would invite family members to be present during discussions but would not allow them to veto the patient's decisions or control the patient's access to medical information.

Dr. T said that the ECS consultants had made the physicians more comfortable with full disclosure to Mr. Doe; she said she had learned how to be firm and to insist that patients' rights be respected. It is particularly easy, she felt, to deny incapacitated patients their decision-making rights, even with respect to DNR status. She said she was very surprised at how receptive Mrs. Doe had seemed once the discussion got under way and at how relieved the patient's wife appeared when it was over.

Most self-critical in retrospect was Dr. Fletcher, who commented that his actions toward Mrs. Doe were "the most paternalistic I've ever been." He said that, in a similar situation, he would present a family member with three options: to take part in the discussion with the patient, to substitute another family member in the discussion, or to be absent. He believed that the family member's presence was crucial not only for the sake of the patient but because the family member might have to make future decisions, and such discussions might be one of few opportunities to learn the patient's true wishes about medical treatment. However, Dr. Fletcher would not compel a family member, even a spouse, to be present against his or her wishes.

Mrs. Doe was interviewed by telephone approximately two weeks after she took her husband home. She said she had been against the consultation because she had felt it was "not right" to ask a very sick person to deal with a decision such as DNR status. She insisted that she had not been "bothered" by anything that took place during the bedside discussion, but "to be honest, I was glad when it was over. I was dreading it. Afterwards, I felt much better." Since coming home, she said, neither she nor her husband had referred to the discussion at all. She refused to allow her husband to be interviewed. However, when asked whether she would have wanted such a discussion had she been the patient, she replied: "I guess maybe I would. I have to agree, it *is* the patient's decision. No one else can make it for you."

Mr. Doe suffered a cardiac arrest at his home approximately 10 days after discharge. He was brought to the hospital by rescue squad but died shortly after arrival, with his wife nearby. His previously agreed-upon DNR status was respected.

The Common Good, Terminal Illness, and Euthanasia

CHARLES J. DOUGHERTY

CHARLES J. DOUGHERTY, PH.D., is director of the Center for Health Policy and Ethics at Creighton University. He teaches medical ethics in Creighton's School of Medicine and in its nursing, dentistry, pharmacy, and allied health programs. Dr. Dougherty's interest in the common good has drawn him to ethical issues connected to the health care system and to the debate about health care reform. He has served as an advisor on these issues to Senator Bob Kerrey, the United States Catholic Health Association, the National Health Policy Council, and the Clinton administration's health care transition team.

Dr. Dougherty chairs the Hospital Ethics Committee at St. Joseph Hospital in Omaha. In this capacity, he regularly consults on cases involving the care of terminally ill patients, especially on decisions to withhold or withdraw life-support systems. He is also an advisor to the Ethics and Grievance Committee of the Metro Omaha Medical Society and has been on the board of directors of the Nebraska League for Nursing and the Nebraska AIDS Project. He is currently on the editorial board of *Health Progress* and is a commissioner on the Nebraska Accountability and Disclosure Commission. Dr. Dougherty is a member of the governor of Nebraska's Blue Ribbon Coalition to Study Health Care.

Dr. Dougherty is the author or co-author of numerous articles and five books in the areas of health care and ethics, including *American Health Care: Realities, Rights, and Reforms* (1988) and *Ethics at Work* (1990).

IN ONE SENSE, dying is the most personal and private of all events. Each of us comes to the end of a unique life and dies his or her own death. Along with birth, death sets the natural boundaries of a particular life's trajectory. But unlike birth, the consciousness of death can define a person's plan of life. In existential terms, the consciousness of an inevitable personal death provokes an anxiety that is radically individuating. The fact of my death makes this my life.[1]

Yet no aspect of human experience is wholly personal and private. Like birth, our knowledge of death comes from others. The way we die—when, under what circumstance, and from what cause or reason—is shaped in profound ways by relationships with others and by large social and institutional forces. The symbolic significance attached to death is derived from religious and cultural realities that precede and survive individuals. And it is precisely because death is such an intensely personal and private event, so defining of the individual, that the social arrangements that attend death are so important. What could be more important for society than events that shape individuals?

The character of dying and how the dying are cared for has changed in profound ways in the last several decades.[2] In all of our prior history, death for those who reached adulthood came generally in what is now midlife. It came swiftly, a thief in the night. It came without significant resistance from medicine; little could be done to ward off impending death. Now the situation has changed. Death is generally an event of old age. It typically follows a long pattern of chronic illness and decline. It comes only after exhaustive medical interventions, some of which plainly increase the length and intensity of suffering and all of which increase costs to the health care system.

This change in dying, and especially its impact on the deaths of individuals, has had three effects: to produce a social consensus over the last two generations on a patient's or proxy's right to refuse life-sustaining medical measures, to promote a hospice movement designed to improve the quality of life in dying, and to spur a growing debate over the legalization of doctor-assisted suicide and active euthanasia. What are the social dimensions of these developments, especially the third, since it stands before us as a social choice? Aside from real and projected impacts on individuals, how does our treatment of the terminally ill affect society as a whole? How might changes in social arrangements surrounding dying affect the common good?

These issues are taken up here under three headings. First, some general observations are offered about the notion of the common good. Second, some changes are proposed to better serve the common good in the way dying patients are cared for. Finally, some reasons are developed to show why legalization of doctor-assisted suicide and active euthanasia cannot serve the common good.

The Common Good

Traditionally, the common good has been the key term for articulating and assessing the implications for society as a whole of changes in social practice or public policies.[3] But the notion of the common good is problematic in our society. The idea comes to us from ancient Greco-Roman civilizations and from medieval Europe. Thus, the birth and development of the notion of the common good is derived from civilizations far more homogeneous than contemporary America. The diversity in our society—of races, ethnic groups, religions, languages, culture, and life styles—makes it more difficult for us to understand and assent to the idea that there is some good or goods that are of value to us as members of society irrespective of our many differences.

American politics, especially in the twentieth century, work against generation of a practical consensus on the common good. The checks and balances built into our Constitu-

tion hobble attempts to develop unitary policy visions. Moreover, interest group politics encourage the perception that the public interest is merely the balance struck among competing, highly organized, and well-financed private interests. In other words, Americans tend to think of the common good in descriptive terms instead of normative terms: how the political agenda is set and carried out by the influential few rather than what is best for the nation taken as a whole.[4]

Also, our excessive American individualism has enshrined such a thoroughgoing relativism in our cultural affairs and our intellectual life that we have become deeply skeptical about assertions of ethical goodness or badness that move beyond what any person takes to be good or bad in his or her own experience.[5] Even the most homogeneous societies—say the Athens of Pericles or the Florence of Machiavelli—can have deep disagreements about which choices serve the common good. America is not distinctive in this sense. Our distinctiveness lies in a dogmatic normative relativism pervading our public life: No one has the right to tell anyone else what is good, not only for him or her, but for us. This disposition regards claims about the common good, no matter how modest in substance and style, as arrogant and oppressive.

As a result, surprisingly little has been published on the common good in contemporary scholarly literature.[6] In John Rawls's influential *Theory of Justice,* for example, there are only two brief references to the notion of the *common* good, in spite of considerable attention to theories of the good.[7] Thus, there is no contemporary consensus on the meaning of the notion and little explicit discussion of it.

In spite of these daunting challenges, discussion of the common good is imperative if public policy is to reflect anything more than money, opinion polls, and assertions of individuals' rights. There must be some moment in public life when this question is engaged in its simplest ethical terms: What course of action is best for us? This is especially true when the arena in question—dying and care for the dying—is so important to individuals and therefore to society, the context in which individuals are made. The following brief reflections on the common good are offered in hopes of advancing such a discussion.

The common good is a good for all, not a good for each. The common good is something collective, not simply the sum of what is good for each member of society in a distributive sense. It is a good that pertains to the general social relationships in which individuals seek specific goods. Because the common good is a general good, it may frustrate acquisition of specific goods for individuals.

Traffic lights, for example, plainly serve the common good because they allow for orderly movement through dangerous intersections. They structure social relationships in a way that serves everyone's interests generally. Yet any number of individuals can be frustrated by the order traffic lights impose. It plainly serves the common good to prevent environmental destruction of rivers. The beneficiaries of this application of the common good include generations into the future. But the measures necessary to protect rivers from environmental destruction may thwart goods for others, including the creation of jobs and other economic opportunities. It serves the common good to ban romantic relationships between psychiatrists and their patients because of the emotional vulnerability of psychiatric patients. Yet this ban may frustrate mature and conflict-free romances between some psychiatrists and patients.

In each of these cases an important public good is at stake—safety in transportation, the integrity of our natural environment, protection of the vulnerability of patients—even though other goods legitimately sought by individuals may be frustrated by each of these. Thus, discussion of the common good cannot begin and end with what serves the good of

each and every person in society. Nor can it be left an open question morally whether it is better or not to save lives at intersections, better or not to preserve the environment, better or not to protect the vulnerable from exploitation.

On the other hand, measures that serve the common good must serve the interests of individual persons in general and in the long run. The common good must, as the words themselves suggest, provide a mutual benefit that all can share. So the common good must include goods that serve the interests of individual persons. It cannot be used to violate an individual's basic human rights. This is an especially demanding standard in a society with strong traditions of respect for persons and autonomy. So although the common good is not equivalent to the good of each, no good can be part of the common good if it does not serve the good of most individuals over time.

The tension between serving all but not each and yet respecting individuals can be located more precisely in the social relationships that fulfill or frustrate individual persons. The idea of the common good assumes a social realism: Society is real. It has real effects on the development and particular fates of individual persons. Changes in society can change the development and fates of individuals. These may seem modest and obvious truisms, but they are ignored when exclusive emphasis is placed on individual autonomy. Persons can be considered autonomous ends in themselves from an ethical point of view. From this perspective, they ought to be. But empirically, persons are born into, shaped by, and satisfied or frustrated in networks of concrete means-to-end relationships: people doing things with, for, and to one another. These relationships are themselves configured by social roles and institutional forms. Autonomous agents can be killed at poorly regulated intersections. Individuals who are ends in themselves can be poisoned and denied natural beauty by pollution. Persons with incalculably great individual worth can be psychologically damaged by manipulations in unequal romantic relationships. To know and affirm these truths is to accept the reality of the social context of individual persons.

Two conclusions about the common good can be drawn from these brief observations. First, the common good must be motivated by a dual vision of persons in society. It must assess, on the one hand, what is good for persons considered as individuals. Yet, on the other hand, it must assess what is good for society—including future societies—because social relationships can build or destroy individual persons. Thus, a working definition of the common good might be as follows: The common good is constituted by those general conditions that tend to support the fulfillment of individual persons in real and anticipated societies. The second conclusion follows from the first: Because the common good presumes a social realism and moral concern for relationships and institutional arrangements beyond the individual, claims about the common good will inevitably create tensions in a culture marked by ethical relativism and extreme individualism.

The Common Good and the Terminally Ill

If the common good is composed of the social conditions that tend to fulfill human persons, then any assessment of what measures serve the common good must have two features. It must be contextual, related to the real social conditions of its time and place. But it must also make reference to certain general goods that must be conceived as desiderata of the human condition itself: for example, health, freedom from pain, public order, productive activity, a range of liberty, and support for the pursuit of excellence.

The concerns at stake here are universal: minimizing pain and suffering and increasing the chances of dying in a humane and dignified fashion. But the specific social circumstances of late twentieth century America often frustrate achievement of these goals. Walter Bortz crystallizes the matter: "Dying takes too long and it costs too much."[8] Because it takes too long, excess pain and suffering are created around an already difficult and often tragic set of circumstances. It can take too long because patient wishes to avoid extraordinary or heroic measures are unknown, unsolicited, or disregarded. Providers feel morally (and legally) obliged to do everything to delay death. And dying may take too long in human time when effective pain control measures are withheld and appropriate psychosocial support is unavailable.

Dying costs too much. It is now a significant factor in America's unrestrained health care spending. Up to 28 percent of Medicare spending is devoted to the care of the 6 percent of program enrollees who die each year. Seventy-seven percent of all health care expenses incurred in an individual's lifetime occur in the last 180 days of life.[9] Because so much is spent on the dying, basic health care coverage for the uninsured is made increasingly difficult to obtain, and the package of benefits for those in the Medicaid program more difficult to defend. Moreover, as health care costs escalate, achievement of other social goods in education, transportation, and economic development become jeopardized. These are the opportunity costs of spending nearly a trillion dollars annually on health care in America.

Against this background, the common good can be served by measures that add simplicity and dignity to the process of dying and contain unnecessary spending. The following are some practical measures that might serve to enhance the common good in the care for the terminally ill.

First, the use of home hospice care should be increased dramatically. In spite of significant strides over the last decade, home hospice care still serves too few terminally ill Americans. Many factors account for this. They include a cultural denial of death, poor physician education, medical ideology about fighting death to the last, lack of clear protocols for determining when an illness is terminal, the social logic of referral to specialists in tertiary care centers, and certain federal regulations that make application for Medicare certification unattractive to many hospice organizations. It is also clear that, given the expected dimensions of the need for home hospices in the future, such care will have to rely on wider use of nonprofessional volunteers than ever before. In short, dying should be brought home and put in the hands of family and friends. It should be deinstitutionalized and deprofessionalized.[10]

Second, more aggressive pain management strategies are needed. Dying patients should have access to all drugs, including heroin and marijuana, that show any promise for relieving their pain. Moreover, drugs should be used liberally without fatuous concerns about addiction. Health care providers should be made more aware of the traditional double-effect analysis that permits increasing doses of pain relief even if these measures hasten death, so long as the direct intention is the easing of suffering and not the killing of the patient.

Third, practice protocols and refined use of diagnostic tools such as APACHE scores must be developed in greater detail and used more widely. This will allow for earlier diagnosis of terminal illness and timely referral to hospice care. Following such professional guidelines will help to restrain the use of inappropriate, wasteful, and often unwanted technologies in the care of the dying.

Fourth, the right to refuse extraordinary care must be made universal. The federal government's Patient Self-Determination Act is a good start in promoting the use of advance directives, but it does not go far enough. The next reasonable step is to require by law that all individuals entering hospitals or nursing homes file a living will or name a health care proxy. Society should no longer tolerate individual or family denials that create confusion about what dying patients desire and who is empowered to choose for them when they cannot choose for themselves. Chances are good that more patient control will mean fewer aggressive measures and lower costs. One account suggested that deferring to terminally ill patients' wishes about withholding life-sustaining measures would have saved $55 billion in 1990 alone.[11]

Fifth, policies and practices should be developed to expand the significance of a DNR (do not resuscitate) order beyond its literal translation of withholding frantic attempts to resuscitate a dying patient in crisis. A DNR order should be understood to symbolize acceptance of an inevitable and proximate death. It should trigger withdrawal of all measures not directly related to patient comfort. DNR should mean CMO—comfort measures only—or should be replaced by that new order. Patients with DNR orders should not be kept in ICU beds, where dying is prolonged, expenses multiplied, and loved ones held at arm's length.[12] When DNR orders are written, patients should be sent home for hospice care. If transfer home is not feasible or death is imminent, dying patients should be moved to hospice beds in the hospital, where they can be served by professionals trained in comfort care and where visiting family and friends can have ready and welcoming access.

Sixth, it should be part of the social contract in an advanced society that everyone has access to an appropriate combination of home care, inpatient care, nursing home care, and hospice care, both at home and in nursing homes. Too many of our present long-term care decisions are driven by reimbursement and funding considerations with insufficient attention to the most appropriate locus of care for each patient. Terminally ill patients in nursing homes should not be sent to hospitals in a crisis unless it is to obtain comfort measures.

All nursing homes should have hospice beds and clear protocols, including use of DNH (do not hospitalize) orders, to control pointless hospitalization of dying patients.[13]

Finally, to ensure that these measures benefit everyone, America needs a universal health insurance system that creates enrollment for all Americans in primary, managed care networks. Such networks should have a primary care coordinator whose job it is to see that all enrollees enter the health care system when necessary at the most appropriate site for their care and for the prudent use of health care dollars.[14]

These measures will not ensure that everyone's dying is serene and dignified. But they could significantly improve the current state of affairs and thus serve the common good. They could help create the general social conditions that would support the fulfillment of persons in the dying process. If Americans were assured that every known drug is available to control their pain, that they will be cared for in their homes or in the most appropriate site of care, and that their dying will not be pointlessly extended—if Americans could be assured of this, there would be considerably less energy behind the movement to legalize the direct killing of dying patients.

The Common Good and Killing the Dying

Most of those who oppose legalization of doctor-assisted suicide and active voluntary euthanasia ground their argument explicitly or implicitly in a simple deontic [morally obligatory] foundation: It is wrong to directly intend the death of an innocent human being, including oneself. If it is wrong to kill directly, it is wrong to *assist* in killing directly, even in the voluntary suicide of a terminally ill patient. For most opponents of euthanasia, these claims have a self-evidence difficult to articulate without throwing into question the very

fundamentals of morality. They involve a deep respect for the mystery or sanctity of human life. They entail a commitment to a metaphysical acceptance of fate or of God's will. They express a conviction that it overreaches the human estate to seek to control destiny in such an ultimate fashion.

If these assertions seem too prosaic for such a weighty ethical issue, it is useful to recall the metaethical insight of the intuitionist tradition from Aristotle to the twentieth-century Oxford philosophers.[15] In this view, not everything in ethics can be argued for completely or fully justified on the grounds of reason—there cannot be a reason for every ethical conviction and a reason for that reason and so on, since this would initiate an invidious infinite regress. Instead, there must be some ethical first premises, some moral data, that are simply seen or given in experience. What more obvious candidate for the role of first premise in ethics than a commitment to human life that refuses to accept the directly intended killing of innocent human beings?

But concern for the common good can prescind from this important but difficult element of the debate. A common good perspective must focus on social realities and questions of the public interest. In that light, the following considerations constitute the main elements of the common good argument against legalizing the killing or assisting in the killing of the dying. These are not new arguments, but they are at the heart of the current public policy debate.

First, consider the political and cultural difficulties that stand in the way of achieving the short but ambitious list of changes recommended above to make dying more dignified, humane, and cost-worthy. Now add a new reality: widely available and socially acceptable killing of terminally ill patients. Why bother with raising taxes for ensuring appropriate hospice care for all? Why increase research dollars to develop more effective pain management? Why struggle to improve practice protocols, advance directives, medical orders, and the long-term care system? In short, why take the more difficult road to make dying more humane when there is a social shortcut that terminates dying itself?[16]

This is a serious matter of public policy in the political and economic sense—that is, a matter of sapping the will to invest in the resources necessary to improve the care of dying patients. This surely would happen were assisted suicide and euthanasia to become widely used. Proponents often claim or intimate that recourse to killing would be rare even under the most permissive laws, but there is no good reason to suppose that this would be so. A change in law would change private practice and public expectations. This, in turn, would change our collective moral psychology, making what was previously prohibited more and more socially acceptable, even expected. No doubt it will be part of the future agenda of many of those who favor legalization to remove whatever social stigma may attach to killing the dying so that it is not only permissible but often the right or obligatory thing to do. Our therapy-oriented culture would not want anyone to feel guilty for assisting in or practicing euthanasia. Thus acceptance and recourse to euthanasia would likely grow over time. The first generation after legalization might still feel some powerful moral sentiments against killing in this context; they were raised to think so. This might tend to hold the numbers down at first. But three or four generations later, Americans might come to see this as the way to die. Certainly nothing in the proponents' case for legalization is inconsistent with this future.

Financial pressures may also lead to incentives for active killing by limiting funding for terminal care. Legislators considering the cost of terminal care in the Medicare and Medicaid programs, or private insurers representing premium payers, may well take it as an obligation to encourage a more cost-effective way of dying. Nearly all observers agree that cost pressures will force future adoption of practice protocols based on patient condition, likely outcome, and cost of alternative treatments. If legal and widely acceptable euthanasia is added to this economic pressure, it is hard to imagine a future without practice protocols, a package of basic benefits, reimbursement restrictions, or cost-sharing arrangements that provide de facto incentives for the active killing of terminally ill patients. If this future should come to pass, the freedom to choose that many proponents of legalized euthanasia champion will set the stage for not-so-subtle financial coercions that will determine how many of us die, especially the poor and uninsured or underinsured.

The point that the will to improve dying will be compromised if active killing is legalized is relevant not only to public policy in the broad sense, but also to the social relationships that will be affected by legalized euthanasia. Why should an adult child struggle to support and care for a declining parent when such a facile alternative exists? Why should an aging parent continue to struggle—in fact, how can he or she justify what may come to be seen as the selfishness of continuing to struggle—when others do the "right thing" by their children by having themselves killed? In short, legalization will seriously erode efforts to humanize the dying process and will create its own new coercions. The hard work needed to humanize dying will simply become less and less worth it at the national and familial levels.

It might be said in response that this argument presumes that legalized killing would create new ethical realities but that contemporary medical practice has already sanctioned direct killing in the guise of the removal of ventilators and feeding tubes. There are philosophers aplenty prepared to argue that there is no longer a tenable distinction between allowing someone to die and direct killing.[17] Although there are serious intellectual challenges here and contemporary medical practice has certainly entered a difficult gray zone, the distinction still has merit. The facts of dawn and dusk do not erase the distinction between night and day. There is still at the heart of the matter a profoundly important distinction in moral intention. This distinction is intuitively obvious to many families of dying patients, families prone to say things like: "We don't want to prolong Grandpa's suffering, but we cannot kill him."

Replacement of efforts to make dying more humane with a practice of killing the dying also has a broad cultural significance. It is plainly part of the common good that we should seek moral balance in our public practices, social relationships, and institutions. Virtue or moral excellence lies between excess and deficiency; extremes should be avoided.[18] But there is one extreme in our health care system that has been decried by ethicists and social critics throughout the late twentieth century, namely, fixation on cure to the detriment of care. Euthanasia is the apotheosis of this tendency. Instead of enhancing care for the dying patient, the condition is cured by killing the patient. Legalization will exacerbate this excess and move the health care system further away from balance and moral excellence.

A second common good consideration that counts against legalization of doctor-assisted suicide and euthanasia is the slippery slope concern. There are two moral arguments central to the proponents' case.[19] First is the humanitarian or beneficence-based argument that a doctor-assisted or -caused death will reduce human suffering. There may be cases where the pain experienced in the dying process is simply intractable, though this is a contended claim in the debate.[20] Suffering, of course, is inherently part of the dying process. It can be reduced by care measures typically part of hospice—psychosocial support, maximum family involvement, and spiritual counseling. But suffering in dying can only be eliminated by eliminating death or the dying. It is certainly true that pain and suffering could be lessened in total if the terminally ill died earlier

and more quickly. Killing could be timed to locate the optimal mix of pleasure and pain, happiness and suffering. In theory, legalization could create a world with less pain and suffering than would be the case with continued prohibition of killing.

The second argument is based on autonomy. Competent individuals should have control over their dying as a matter of self-determination. Respect for persons entails the right to be free of paternalistic interference with one's own interpretation and pursuit of the good. In short, whose life is it anyway? Competent adults ought to be free to determine when and how they will die.

Taken together, the beneficence and autonomy arguments ground the claim that terminally ill and competent persons ought to be able to choose doctor-assisted suicide or euthanasia. But note that these two arguments are easily separable. When they are separated, the conceptual slippery slope becomes clear. Development of the pain and suffering argument alone justifies involuntary euthanasia. Why should someone be left in pain and suffering simply because he is not competent to choose death for himself? In fact, isn't it discrimination against persons who are mentally disabled to restrict access to a quick and painless death to persons who are competent?

The slide from voluntary to involuntary euthanasia is not merely a theoretical possibility. At present, Dutch pediatricians are debating proposed guidelines, written by a committee of the Dutch Pediatric Association, that would immunize doctors for performing euthanasia on disabled newborns. "The proposed guidelines recommend that the attending physician decide whether to end the child's life, with approval from the parents and other physicians."[21] The head of the committee estimated that, even without the proposed guidelines, Dutch doctors, who have the most permissive voluntary euthanasia policies in the world, give lethal injections to ten newborns a year.[22] Plainly, legalizing lethal injections for infants would be a step down on the slippery slope from voluntary to involuntary euthanasia. If it is taken, the slide to include other suffering children and incompetent adults would be both small and that much more likely.

On the other hand, the autonomy argument has no inherent link to pain and suffering or even to terminal illness. Suffering or not, terminally ill or not, a person has a right to self-determination. When a competent adult—regardless of somatic health or illness—understands the consequences and freely chooses them, shouldn't he or she have the right to choose death? In other words, is it not insufferably paternalistic to condition the right to choose death on certification of terminal illness, on a requirement of a doctor's consent and cooperation, before an individual can exercise his or her ultimate autonomy? The slope of this argument is a slick, steep grade. At the bottom is an unqualified right to suicide on demand.

Two rejoinders are generally raised against such slippery slope concerns. First, such a moral decline is dismissed as far-fetched. People will not become moral monsters overnight because an ethical prohibition, even a long-standing one, is rejected. But nothing in the slippery slope argument requires that these changes happen quickly, only that they shall happen as a consequence of rejecting the ethical prohibition. Perhaps it will take a generation or two before practice protocols determine when euthanasia is indicated, before third-party payers refuse reimbursement for the care of those who have not been euthanized in the "usual and customary" manner, before the link between suffering and autonomy is uncoupled to legalize both involuntary euthanasia and suicide for the healthy. But when these things happen is not the issue; that they are made likely to happen is the issue.

The second rejoinder brought frequently against the slippery slope is the Dutch example. In Holland, a democratic society has accepted euthanasia without leading to the kind of abuses anticipated in the slippery slope argument. But the Dutch retort is flawed for several reasons. First, as indicated above, Holland may well be moving down the slippery slope by accepting officially the euthanasia of incompetent persons. And there have been other abuses: numbers of acts of involuntary euthanasia and many unreported acts of what may or may not be voluntary euthanasia.[23] Second, there may not have been enough time, enough generations of Dutch citizens and physicians, to reveal the full effects of this policy choice. Physicians and patients have lived with the prohibition against killing, even if imperfectly, for all of the history of Western medicine. It may take longer than a generation before the full effects of losing this moral anchor are evident. Third, Holland has universal health care coverage. This blunts some of the financial incentives that surely would shape euthanasia in America. The gross inequities of our system would pressure America's millions of poor and uninsured toward euthanasia for financial reasons. Finally, Dutch society is significantly more homogeneous than America. Holland is less scarred by extremes of racial and ethnic divisions that would certainly skew patterns of euthanasia in the United States. Can anyone honestly believe that legal euthanasia would not make desired terminal care more difficult to secure for those already underserved in the American system—African Americans, Hispanics, and Native Americans?

The third reason that legalization cannot serve the common good is the negative impact on the doctor-patient relationship when the role of healer becomes conflated with the role of killer. This change would adversely affect the trust the public has in the medical profession. Because of cost pressure and the demand for greater continuity of care, future relations with physicians will probably take place more and more within organized delivery networks not unlike today's HMOs. The structural arrangement responsible for the financial savings of HMOs—prepayment for a covered package of service—is the same arrangement that raises the central moral concern about HMOs, viz., the incentive they have to under-treat. If euthanasia becomes part of the doctor-patient relationship in this context, many patients will ask themselves this question: Is my doctor's advice that there is nothing left for me but euthanasia motivated by my best interest or his, by concern for my suffering or for her delivery network? And, conflicts of interest aside, there will inevitably be this worry: Is my doctor's advice that it is time for euthanasia an expression of concern for me, or of her exasperation with a condition that can't be cured, or of his desire to be done with a case that is no longer medically interesting?

The impact on doctors is worrisome too. Though it may not be so for each doctor, medicine is motivated by a deep compassion for the sick and the dying. Some doctors who advocate legalization are plainly motivated by this compassion. In their practices, they experience the inhumane effects of contemporary dying. Their hope is that some hard cases can be dealt with more humanely by doctor-assisted suicide and active euthanasia. The political agenda of legalization is fostered by the evident professional virtues of these doctors.

But the doctors who advocate legalization today developed their admirable sympathies in a medical world that inherited a clear conviction that killing patients is professionally unethical. When it did occur, it was a private matter in which doctors who believed that killing patients is wrong in general struggled with exceptional cases—and with their own consciences. What of the generations of doctors, most of them quite ordinary men and women, who would be educated after legalization? They would be socialized into a professional ethic that says killing is an acceptable thing, perhaps the right thing, certainly the expected thing. Could they develop the same degree of compassion for suffering and for the dying as doctors of the past? Isn't it more reasonable to suppose that they would increas-

ingly think of suffering as unnecessary, of the natural process of dying as an elective choice, of those who refuse euthanasia as curiosities or fanatics?

There have been multiple critiques of doctors' overly aggressive care for the terminally ill in the last several decades. Will critiques of the future say that doctors behave more appropriately and more compassionately when lethal injections are part of their practice? Or isn't it more reasonable to suppose that critiques of medicine after legalization would center on doctors who inappropriately dispatched their difficult cases, on doctors dulled to the moral drama of killing by its all too quotidian appearance?

One important defense against the undermining of patient trust and the hardening of doctors' attitudes is the personal dimension of the doctor-patient relationship. Patients trust the doctors they know; doctors care about the patients they know. Thus, it can be hoped that the personal core of the therapeutic relationship will safeguard both doctor and patient from the worst consequences of legalization. But how is medical killing most likely to occur? One potential scenario is that most doctors, at least in the first generation of legalized euthanasia, will refuse to accept this new role, will refuse to offer euthanasia as part of their professional care. Because of this and because of the general logic of medical services, the role will then specialize so that some doctors spend a great part or all of their practice as euthanasia experts. These "obitiatrists" may be called in as specialists in hospitals or may operate their own outpatient clinics. This means that euthanasia will occur outside the intimacy and safeguards of a primary care relationship with the same kind of impersonality that is such a widely criticized aspect of our present health care system. The doctor-patient relationship therefore will provide no defense against abuse.

A point often underscored by proponents of legalization in the context of the impact on the doctor-patient relationship is the novelty of contemporary dying. Death can be delayed as never before, resulting in prolongation of pain and suffering. Patients can be locked indefinitely in states of limbo. This is certainly true, and it motivates many of the reforms suggested above. But it is also true that doctors have dealt with dying patients from the beginnings of the profession and have long had at their disposal an array of poisons capable of killing their suffering patients quickly. In other words, while the character of modern dying has surely changed, the general structure of the moral problem of euthanasia is as old as the Hippocratic Oath. Its traditional prohibition has shaped the doctor-patient relationship. Legalization of killing patients would create a profound change in medicine, a change that could bring many other unforeseen and adverse social consequences for the profession and the public it serves.

The common good must be assessed carefully in the debate over legalization of doctor-assisted suicide and euthanasia. This is not just an issue of individual rights or of the difficult deaths of a few. Respect for the common good demands creation and protection of social realities that serve all persons, though they may not serve each. Persons can be best served by adopting measures that make the process of dying more humane and dignified for all of us. In essence, this means adopting a hospice-inspired strategy of accepting death when it is inevitable, providing the best human support to ease suffering, and using every reasonable measure to control pain. But dying is not made more humane and dignified by killing. That "curative" shortcut would undermine efforts to care. Moreover, accepting killing in a few hard cases would set the stage for acceptance of widespread medical killing and would seriously undermine the doctor-patient relationship. In some terribly difficult circumstances, the killing of a dying patient may serve the good of some. But as a public policy, killing cannot serve the common good.

Violence

Horrendous Death:
Improving the Quality of Global Health

DANIEL LEVITON

DANIEL LEVITON, PH.D. is a professor of health education and director of the Adult Health and Development Program (AHDP) at the University of Maryland in College Park. Dr. Leviton developed the AHDP, an intergenerational health promotion and rehabilitation program, and has supervised its spread to seventeen universities in the United States and Israel. This is the only health promotion program with the goal of reducing the probability of "horrendous deaths" by bringing people of diverse backgrounds together to work toward the common purpose of improving health and well-being.

As a doctoral student in the 1960s, Leviton pondered a dissertation topic with his advisor, the late Warren R. Johnson. Observing that Leviton was perhaps every bit as idiosyncratic as himself, Dr. Johnson said, "Make the link between death and health education, as I did with human sexuality." This advice led to a dissertation concerning the perceptual defense of racing car drivers to words related to death and crashes and, in 1968, to the inclusion of topics

related to death and dying in a required health education course. At the conclusion of the course, students rated the topics of death, grief, and suicide second in interest only to human sexuality. A formal course in death education followed, and it continues to attract between 200 and 350 students every semester at the University of Maryland.

Dr. Leviton was a founders and the first president of the Association for Death Education and Counseling. In addition to authoring numerous articles in scholarly journals, he is the editor of *Horrendous Death, Health, and Well-Being* and *Horrendous Death and Health: Toward Action*, both published in 1991. He also serves on the editorial board of *Omega: Journal of Death and Dying*. Much of his spare time is spent coaching his eighteen-year-old son in pursuit of the Holy Grail of baseball pitching—perfect mechanics, and a 90-mph fastball. Both goals are within reach and, hopefully, shall be attained before Dr. Leviton's death. He says, "the spread of the Adult Health and

Development Program throughout the country and overseas is a means of tightening the social fabric and increasing the probability that my kids and yours will live both long and well, enabling all to enjoy the esthetics of a well-pitched baseball on a beautiful, balmy, summer day."

Horrendous-Type Deaths

Thanatology may be viewed at two different levels: the microcosmic and macrocosmic. The field of clinical thanatology (i.e., the study of death) has always been concerned with being helpful to the dying person, the bereaved, and the suicidal. Call this the *microcosmic* level. Emphasis is on the individual and his or her family, caregivers, and so on.

There is another level, the *macrocosmic*, where death affects large populations. This article focuses on two types of macrocosmic death. One genre, called horrendous death, type I (HTD-I) is characterized by being (a) man-made (I use the sexist terminology intentionally); (b) motivated by the desire to kill, maim, injure, torture, or otherwise destroy another; (c) torturous in quality; (d) premature; and (e) deadly to large numbers of people (Table 1).

The second genre is horrendous death, type II (HTD-II) (Table 2). HTD-II differs from HTD-I in that it is caused by people but the deadly motivation to kill another is missing, and the quality of dying may or may not be torturous.

Examples of HTD-I are conventional and nuclear war, homicide, torture, terrorism, genocide, and death as a result of racism. Death by means of vehicular accident; suicide; starvation caused by people; destruction of or poisoning of the environment; and abuse of drugs such as alcohol, tobacco, cocaine, and heroin are examples of HTD-II. An illustration of this is that, say what you might of the tobacco industry, it cannot be accused of wishing to kill any group or individual. In fact, they wish you alive. It is difficult to sell cigarettes to corpses. They are undoubtedly interested in profit. Their motivation differs from that which governs HTD-I.

A third category is labeled Other and includes death as a result of cancer, coronary heart disease, Alzheimer's disease, and other conditions that (a) may or may not be caused by people; (b) cause dying that may or may not be torturous; and (c) affect large numbers of people globally (Table 3). Although important, this category is not discussed in this article.

Table 1

Horrendous Death, Type I

CHARACTERISTICS

1. Man-made
2. Motivation is to kill, maim, injure, or destroy another
3. Style of dying or death is torturous
4. Affects large numbers of people globally

EXAMPLES

1. Nuclear and conventional war
2. Homicide
3. Terrorism
4. Assassination
5. Genocide
6. Man-made hunger and starvation
7. Racism

Table 2

Horrendous Death, Type II

CHARACTERISTICS

1. Man-made
2. Style of dying or death may be torturous
3. Affects large numbers of people globally

EXAMPLES

1. Accidents
2. Suicide
3. Substance abuse
4. Contamination of the physical environment and ecosystem
5. Man-made hunger and starvation where the motivation is not to kill another

Table 3

Other Types of Death

CHARACTERISTICS

1. May or may not be man-made
2. Style of dying or death may or may not be torturous
3. Affects large numbers of people globally

EXAMPLES

1. Disease such as coronary heart disease, cancer, Alzheimer's disease, etc.

All causes of death might be termed *deathogenic.* Thus, HTD-I, HTD-II, and Other causes of death fall under the broader category of deathogenic factors.

Denial of Death

The psychological denial of death is crucial to our concept of eliciting action to reduce the probability of horrendous-type deaths.

As Freud and others have suggested, denial is a universal adaptation to the threat of personal death, that is, annihilation.[1] World War I disillusioned Freud. He was horrified by the eradication of the rules of civilized moral and social conduct, and the brutality with which men could inflict death and suffering upon people whether soldiers or civilians.[2] How could man be so barbaric? Freud's answer was psychological denial of personal death. "Our own death is indeed unimaginable," he wrote. "At bottom no one believes in his own death, or to put the same thing in another way, in the unconscious every one of us is convinced of his own immortality."[3]

Becker agreed when he wrote, "This narcissism is what keeps men marching into point-blank fire in wars; at heart one doesn't feel *he* will die, he only feels sorry for the man next to him."[4]

Yet, Lifton was correct when he observed, "And our resistance to that knowledge, our denial of death, is indeed formidable. . . . But the denial can never be total; we are never fully ignorant of the fact that we die. Rather we go about life with a kind of 'middle knowledge' of death, a partial awareness of it side by side with expressions and actions that belie that awareness."[5]

Governments, like people, tend to deny the fact that horrendous-type death is inimical to health and well-being. *Health, United States, 1986, Prevention Profile,* and other publications of the U.S. Public Health Service and National Center for Health Statistics say little of the health costs of horrendous-type deaths, especially HTD-I. Some mention is made of violent behaviors such as homicide and legal intervention, suicide, accidents, and child and spouse abuse.[6] Whether this is unintentional or intentional is unknown, but the result is the same. Generally, horrendous-type deaths (especially HTD-I) are treated by the governmental health establishment as an aberration, an unmentionable. It is only when one reads such mind-boggling, but objective gems as *The*

State of the World Atlas, and two annual publications, *World Military and Social Expenditures* and *State of the World, 1987* that the enormous economic and health costs of horrendous-type deaths for present and future generations are realized.[7]

Removal of denial of horrendous-type deaths is central to motivating people to act to eliminate those forms of preventable deaths.

Challenges We Face in Understanding Children and War: A Personal Essay

JAMES GARBARINO, PH.D., is president of the Erikson Institute for Advanced Study in Child Development in Chicago. He says, "My interest in children in war zones derives in large measure from coming of age during the Vietnam War. As a college student, I participated in a variety of antiwar activities that brought home to me the barbarous brutality of war and motivated me to seek ways to prevent conflict from becoming violent. I believe my work on children in war zones offers a way to integrate my passion for human rights with my expertise as a child psychologist. My 1991 book, *No Place to Be a Child: Growing Up in a War Zone*, is an important expression of this integration, as is my 1993 book for children, *Let's Talk About Living in a World with Violence*. My visits to war zones around the world—Kuwait, Guatemala, Mozambique, Cambodia—have forced me to confront death as a fact of life for children. My socialization as a person and as a professional impelled me to do something about it."

Dr. Garbarino has served as a consultant to a wide range of organizations, including the National Committee for the Prevention of Child Abuse, the National Institute for Mental Health, the American Medical Association, the National Black Child Development Institute, the National Science Foundation, the National Resource Center for Children in Poverty, and the U.S. Advisory Board on Child Abuse and Neglect. In 1991 he undertook missions for UNICEF to assess the impact of the Gulf War upon children in Kuwait and Iraq, and he has also served as a consultant for programs serving Bosnian and Croatian children.

Dr. Garbarino has been a consultant to television, magazine, and newspaper reports on chil-

dren and families and has served as an expert witness in court cases involving violence and children. In 1981, he received the Silver Award at the International Film and Television Festival of New York for a film he co-authored about adolescent abuse. In 1985, he collaborated with John Merrow to produce "Assault on the Psyche," a videotape program dealing with psychological abuse.

Among the many books authored or edited by Dr. Garbarino are *Troubled Youth, Troubled Families* (1986), *What Children Can Tell Us* (1989), *Children and Families in the Social Environment* (2d ed., 1992), *Towards a Sustainable Society: An Economic, Social, and Environmental Agenda for Our Children's Future* (1992), and *Children in Danger: Coping with the Consequences of Community Violence* (1992).

Dr. Garbarino has received numerous awards and honors for his work. The National Conference on Child Abuse and Neglect honored him in 1985 with its first C. Henry Kempe Award, recognizing his efforts on behalf of abused and neglected children. In 1987 he was elected president of the American Psychological Association's Division on Child, Youth, and Family Services, and in 1989 he received the APA's award for Distinguished Professional Contributions to Public Service. In 1994, the APA's Division on Child, Youth, and Family Services presented him with its Nicholas Hobbs Award.

The following selection is based on a keynote address to the seminar, *The Effects of Armed Conflict and Other Community Violence on Children*, at the Ninth International Congress on Child Abuse and Neglect, Chicago, August 26–28, 1992.

Introduction

Few issues challenge our moral, intellectual, and political resources as does the topic of

children and community violence—war, violent crime on the streets, and other forms of armed conflict. My colleagues and I have invested ourselves in confronting these issues, as we found them in Cambodia, Nicaragua, Mozambique, Israel and Palestine, Kuwait and Iraq, Northern Ireland, and in the Vietnamese detention camps of Hong Kong.[1] As a result, we recognize a series of challenges.

We refer to these issues as "challenges" rather than as "problems" or "risks," because we have come to understand that what matters is how we rise to meet them. If we do rise to them, they can be growth-inducing. If we do not, they can be destructive, debilitating and depressing, of our spirits, of our politics, and ultimately of the quality of life for future generations. There would be no greater abuse and neglect of our children than to fail to meet this challenge.

Challenge #1:
The Challenge of Feeling and Thinking

We can *think* about children and war: the official surveys and estimates that provide objective data on the numbers of children involved in the 30+ wars underway throughout the world and the small scale studies of the impact of armed conflict that demonstrate its effect on nutrition, infant mortality, and the prevalence of Post Traumatic Stress Disorder. We can *feel* about children and war: the often poetic imagery of artists and journalists who convey the suffering of children, the heroism of helpers, the profoundly evil callousness of those who kill, maim, terrorize, and orphan the children. But how do we think *and* feel about the children of war?

Opening ourselves to feeling the pain of children in war tends to shut down our thinking about the "topic," as when we reject any effort to study the differential impact of war experience on different categories of children because we find it abhorrent to "study the obvious," namely that war is bad for children. Vice versa, efforts to take an "objective" and rational perspective often seem callous and surreal, as when we find ourselves thinking about

the number of children who will be injured or killed as "collateral damage" in a bombing raid or the number of maimed children it will take to persuade an enemy to capitulate.

To meet the many other challenges we face in understanding war and children we must face this first challenge. We must force ourselves to both think and feel about the children of war. We must be willing to engage in objective analysis at the same time we open ourselves to the pain and the horror. It is not easy.

Challenge #2:
The Challenge of Replacing Naïve Psychology with an Ecological Perspective on Child Development

Related to the challenge of thinking and feeling is the challenge of naïve psychology. Naïve psychology here refers to a perspective on child development that ignores the importance of the multiple and deep influences on child psychology in favor of a simplistic, narrow view. The challenge is to replace this naïve psychology with an ecological perspective on development, one that recognizes that psychodynamic and behavioral and cognitive and sociobiological influences are at work in mediating the child's response to war and community violence.

Thus, we must do as Anna Freud and her colleagues did in their assessment of World War II on London's children, and see that the basic issues of attachment play themselves out in the new context presented by war, with its increased odds of separation. And we must see that the response of children to war may be represented in the symbolic and indirect ways common to children's expressions of important unconscious elements in "normal times." Likewise, we must recognize and appreciate the power of behavioral processes like modelling (e.g., the parent's coping style) and desensitization (e.g., the child's acclimatization to the day-to-day elements of life under war conditions).

And, we must also see the importance of cognitive and biological development as a basis for the greater vulnerability of younger children (ages 5–10) versus adolescents (11 and older) to Post Traumatic Stress Disorder in response to horrible events.[2] The less developed cognitive frameworks ("schemes" in Piaget's terms) and neurological systems (e.g., brain stem maturation) give the younger child fewer resources with which to manage the philosophical threat and physiological arousal that is trauma.

An ecological perspective insists that when the question is "Does X cause Y?" The answer is, "It depends." The multiple social systems in which biological and psychological processes work themselves out mediate the consequences of those processes.[3] These mediators include the educational system. If it is active and effective in processing the experience of children it can turn the experience of trauma into an opportunity for enhanced human development through a moral and political sensibility made more acute. Nasty and extremist ideologies—be they political or religious—can exacerbate the sense of hurt and injustice experienced by traumatized children and provide a vehicle for converting trauma into rage, violence, and intergenerational patterns of aggression.[4] On the other hand, a philosophy that promotes healing and caring can achieve much that is individually rehabilitative and socially redemptive.[5] What does war mean to children? It depends.

Challenge #3:
The Challenge of Empathy

We who live in safety and security sit across a deep and wide abyss from those who live amidst the terror and insecurity of war and community violence. In her novel *The Gates of Ivory*, Margaret Drabble explores this idea when her characters speak of life in the "Good Times" versus life in the "Bad Times."[6] Cambodia under Pol Pot's regime was the Bad Times. I felt this keenly when I stood amidst the killing fields and touched the tree that was used to murder babies—hundreds and hun-

dreds of them—by smashing their heads against its trunk.

Being trapped in a savagely abusive family is the Bad Times. Living with threat, death, and hopelessness on the streets of a violent community is the Bad Times. Until we make the extreme effort to cross this chasm we cannot be useful to the children of war and community violence. Research on children who have lost a parent reveals this on an individual level.[7] Until adults open themselves fully to the child's pain, they are almost useless to the child as an agent to promote successful mourning and, ultimately, healing. What children can tell us depends, to a large extent, upon what adults are prepared to hear.[8]

Beyond an "attitude" of openness there are important issues of skill and orientation to be confronted in developing an intelligent empathy for the children of war and community violence. We must be effectively attuned to the emotional meaning of their behavior. Studies reveal that only 7 percent of emotional meaning is communicated in the words we speak. More than 50 percent lies in facial expressions, posture, and gestures; nearly 40 percent in tone of voice.[9] At the negative extreme, individuals who are woefully deficient in mastering these modalities may be described as suffering from "dyssemia." Our goal, of course, is to improve our ability to exercise intelligent empathy with children so that each victim may find a therapeutic ally with whom to struggle towards healing.

Challenge #4:
The Challenge of Evil

[When] we look and speak from the perspective of the secular social sciences, we have great difficulty acknowledging and accommodating the reality of evil. Ignorance, yes. Missocialization, yes. Psychopathology, yes. But evil?

And yet our experience of the world of children and war forces us to embrace a concept of evil, of wrongful, horrible badness. What else do we call it when a child is destroyed callously, casually? What term do we use to describe a situation in which deliberate policy or practice seeks to demoralize parents by torturing the child? I can find no other concept that does justice to what I have seen and heard in the war zones of the world.[10]

C. S. Lewis's trilogy on good and evil offers the hypothesis that each culture, along with its particular strengths, contains a susceptibility to a particular form of evil.[11] This new brand of cultural relativism merits serious attention, as does the idea that the United Nations (UN) Convention on the Rights of the Child contains an effort at universalism. The Convention seems to offer a transcultural, international definition of childhood and the meaning of being a child. Certainly the articles that call upon all nations to provide special protection for children caught within the vortex of war do so.

Article 38's provision for special protection for children harkens back to earlier efforts to establish such a notion, an effort to limit the scope of war. Those who violate this protected sphere partake in evil. Recall in Shakespeare's *Henry V* Act IV Scene vii, when the young boys accompanying the English army as "baggage boys" at the Battle of Agincourt have been slain by the French forces in clear contravention to the rules of engagement. As Fluellen says upon discovering the dead boys: "Tis expressly against the law of arms. Tis as arrant a piece of knavery, mark you now, as can be offert, in your conscience, now is it not?" And Gowen responds, "Tis certain there's not a boy left alive, and the cowardly rascals that ran from the battle ha' done this."

The best warriors recognize there must be limits, and that those limits arise most clearly in relation to children. The dramatic acts of sheer evil chronicled by Shakespeare are only part of the story, however. Much more to the point most of the time are the banal evils committed in the context of war. What Hannah Arendt called the "banality of evil" in her analysis of Adolph Eichmann is the more common variety, when ordinary people participate in evil systems or policies because of depersonalization, desensitization, the pressures of peer conformity, and a general lack of moral courage. That is the evil with which most of us must contend—our complicity in evil systems and policies.

Challenge #5:
The Challenge of History

Most of us have internalized a linear and progressive view of history, even if we don't articulate it as such. We think of history as progress. Things get better. Suffering decreases. Evil recedes. Bigotry declines. Intelligence and compassion are ascendant.

I think this is one reason why the civil war in Yugoslavia has been such a disturbing and bitter pill for us to swallow, why we have found it so hard to assimilate into our world view. After the ravages of the two World Wars we believed Europe was all finished with that. Yes, there were NATO troops arranged against Warsaw Pact troops for more than four decades, but the idea of war coming to Europe seemed more and more anachronistic as the years went by. And now this.

While there is a racist and ethnocentric element to this (in the sense that we view Europe as fully civilized while the countries of the Third World are still more or less mired in barbarism), it is more than this. The UN Convention on the Rights of the Child seemed to reflect the idea that progress really was coming to the world—and with European nations in the leading role in bringing it about. And now this. It costs us dearly to accept the idea that history can "backslide." It costs us dearly in our collective self-concept.

Challenge #6:
The Challenge of Identity

Psychological and developmental research focuses more and more on the central importance of identity. A firm and positive sense of who you are is crucial to resilience in the face of stress and trauma. Rejection is a psychological malignancy.[12] What is more, there is a growing recognition that the absence of positive identity—shame—is one of the important well springs of violence.[13]

We face an important challenge in this matter of identity. We face the challenge therapeutically of helping children develop positive personal identity. But the challenge goes beyond that. For the individual to develop positive identity there had best be a social context that nurtures and supports that affirmation. The matter of positive social identity is itself an important concern.

And, rather than being simply the preoccupation of youth (in the sense of an Eriksonian "Identity Crisis") it is the natural issue of a lifetime for the self-aware, for what we must be to understand the paths that can be open to us in wrestling with the children of war, and the war that makes these children. In the preface to his book *Young Men and Fire,* Norman Maclean put it this way: "The problem of self-identity is not just a problem for the young. It is a problem all the time. Perhaps *the* problem. It should haunt old age, and when it no longer does it should tell you that you are dead."[14]

And how do we wrestle with "the problem of self-identity?" We do so by confronting our own culture and society in light of what we see in the culture and society of others. Visiting Brazil more than a decade ago, I was forced to see the problem of children on the streets in a new light, to see the potential for social unravelling that was first being recognized in the United States.[15] Now, more than a decade later, street children in Brazil are being assassinated by death squads and we hear increasing calls for the execution of minors in the United States. Who are we to do this? Where do we look for answers to these questions? One source of answers to the questions of identity lies in the imagery conveyed to us in the mass media—the global mass media—that communicates in counterpoint with traditional culture.

Challenge #7:
The Challenge of Patriarchy

War is a man's game. The impulse to war lies deeply embedded in the masculine psyche— some measure of biological disposition fused with cultural imperative. Survey research in modern societies like the United States reveals that men are overwhelmingly more ready to vote to go to war, with the one exception being the case of efforts to save children from being victimized, where women are actually more likely to vote for war when presented with hypothetical scenarios.

The masculine impulse to welcome aggression is institutionalized in the patriarchal family. Thus, one of the challenges we face in responding to the children of war is to reform the basic relations between men and women, the masculine and the feminine.

UNICEF speaks of "building the smallest democracy at the heart of society." We can echo that message. Just as social justice is the route to genuine political peace, domestic justice and democracy is the path to nonviolence in the family. Peaceful families will help build the social foundation for peaceful societies. And empowering what Carol Gilligan calls "the feminine voice" is an important step down that path that leads to peace for children.[16]

Challenge #8:
The Challenge of War Itself

All the other challenges come down to this: We must look honestly at war. General George Patton is purported to have said words to the effect that "in comparison with war all other forms of human endeavor pale into insignificance." To respond to the challenge of war we must face the truth in Patton's analysis.

Pasternak offers up a character in *Dr. Zhivago* to utter the opinion that "happy men do not volunteer for war."[17] War is exciting and glorious—particularly for the overwhelming majority of participants who do not face combat directly (remember that most soldiers serve in noncombat units such as supply, engineering, administration, etc.). My mother said many times that her years as a teenager in London during World War II were the most exciting time in her life. My father's obvious fondness for his time as a soldier during the same war sent the same message. The reality of that excitement and glory can blind us to the reality of the dark side. So blinded, we are ready to be taken in by those who have something to gain from war, those who will profit from it financially or politically.

There are always those who will tempt us saying that this is really the war to end all wars, that this sacrifice will bring harmony, peace, and justice, that this savagery will save the children. In Dostoevsky's *The Brothers Karamazov,* there is a novel within the novel entitled *The Grand Inquisitor.*[18] As part of presenting it Dostoevsky's protagonist asks, "If you could ensure the future of the world by torturing to death one innocent child, would you agree to make this sacrifice?" We are always being asked to make this sacrifice—usually of someone else's children.

So what is the most appropriate way to look honestly at war? Each of us must have the courage to look at war directly, without the blinders of ideology, and see it for what it is:

killing. As a young man enrolled in an army field training unit, I participated in "night maneuvers" in which my group was to ambush another group of trainees. Before going to take our positions the officers reminded us of the danger involved in shooting our weapons at close range. Even loaded with blanks, as they were, we were told, then shown, that at "point blank" range we could seriously injure someone. We all knew that fact as we set up our positions in the dark forest.

When the attack began "all Hell" literally broke loose. In the midst of it, the exercise became a psychological reality. The young trainee next to me began to scream when his rifle jammed. "They're going to kill us!" he shouted. When my rifle also jammed I joined him in the screaming and the delusion. After working frantically at it, we both were able to clear our weapons. Then, as the "enemy" came over the rise and was in our faces, we both fired "point blank." That's what war really is: kill or be killed. All else submerges in the primal violence of it all.

When asked what the war was like, one young soldier said it simply. "War isn't like anything. It just is." And that's what we must face honestly if we expect to meet the challenge of children and war.

Zlata's Diary: A Child's Life in Sarajevo

ZLATA FILIPOVIĆ

In 1991, just before her eleventh birthday, ZLATA FILIPOVIĆ started a diary that became a´ record of her experiences in Sarajevo during a two-year period marked by war and bloodshed. When she began her diary, Zlata shared the characteristic interests and concerns of young girls everywhere. Six months later, her normal, happy life was shattered by war. Her family's weekend house outside Sarajevo had been destroyed and several of her friends killed while playing in a park. Janine di Giovanni, a journalist who befriended Zlata and her family, recalls Zlata telling her: "I used to dream about the beach, somewhere warm. But when there is shelling, I only think about being safe."

During the summer of 1993, Zlata submitted her diaries to a teacher, who had them published by a small press in Sarajevo. Originally published in Croat with the help of UNICEF, *Zlata's Diary* eventually found its way to a French publisher, who arranged for her family's evacuation to Paris. The French edition became an immediate bestseller, and the diary was translated and published throughout the world, making its author an instant celebrity and an international symbol of the chilling effects of war upon children. Here are eight entries from the American edition of her diary.

Monday, March 30, 1992

Hey, Diary! You know what I think? Since Anne Frank called her diary Kitty, maybe I could give you a name too. What about:

ASFALTINA   PIDŽAMETA
ŠEFIKA   HIKMETA
ŠEVALA   MIMMY

or something else???

I'm thinking, thinking . . .

I've decided! I'm going to call you MIMMY

All right, then, let's start.

Dear Mimmy,

It's almost half-term. We're all studying for our tests. Tomorrow we're supposed to go to a classical music concert at the Skenderija Hall. Our teacher says we shouldn't go because there will be 10,000 people, pardon me, children, there, and somebody might take us as hostages or plant a bomb in the concert hall. Mommy says I shouldn't go. So I won't.

Hey! You know who won the Yugovision Song Contest?! EXTRA NENA!!!???

I'm afraid to say this next thing. Melica says she heard at the hairdresser's that on Saturday, April 4, 1992, there's going to be BOOM—BOOM, BANG—BANG, CRASH Sarajevo. Translation: they're going to bomb Sarajevo.

Love,
Zlata

Monday, April 6, 1992

Dear Mimmy,

Yesterday the people in front of the parliament tried peacefully to cross the Vrbanja bridge. But they were shot at. Who? How? Why? A girl, a medical student from Dubrovnik, was KILLED. Her blood spilled onto the bridge. In her final moments all she said was: "Is this Sarajevo?" HORRIBLE, HORRIBLE HORRIBLE!

NO ONE AND NOTHING HERE IS NORMAL!

The Baščaršija has been destroyed! Those "fine gentlemen" from Pale fired on Baščaršija!

Since yesterday people have been inside the B-H parliament. Some of them are standing outside, in front of it. We've moved my television set into the living room, so I watch Channel I on one TV and "Good Vibrations" on the other. Now they're shooting from the Holiday Inn, killing people in front of the parliament. And Bokica is there with Vanja and Andrej. Oh, God!

Maybe we'll go to the cellar. You, Mimmy, will go with me, of course. I'm desperate. The people in front of the parliament are desperate too. Mimmy, war is here. PEACE, NOW!

They say they're going to attack RTV Sarajevo [radio and TV center]. But they haven't. They've stopped shooting in our neighborhood. KNOCK! KNOCK! (I'm knocking on wood for good luck.)

WHEW! It was tough. Oh, God! They're shooting again!!!

Zlata

Saturday, May 2, 1992

Dear Mimmy,

Today was truly, absolutely the worst day ever in Sarajevo. The shooting started around noon. Mommy and I moved into the hall. Daddy was in his office, under our apartment, at the time. We told him on the intercom to run quickly to the downstairs lobby where we'd meet him. We brought Cicko [Zlata's canary] with us. The gunfire was getting worse, and we couldn't get over the wall to the Bobars', so we ran down to our own cellar.

The cellar is ugly, dark, smelly. Mommy, who's terrified of mice, had two fears to cope with. The three of us were in the same corner as the other day. We listened to the pounding shells, the shooting, the thundering noise overhead. We even heard planes. At one moment I realized that this awful cellar was the only place that could save our lives. Suddenly, it started to look almost warm and nice. It was the only way we could defend ourselves against all this terrible shooting. We heard glass shattering in our street. Horrible. I put my fingers in my ears to block out the terrible sounds. I was worried about Cicko. We had

left him behind in the lobby. Would he catch cold there? Would something hit him? I was terribly hungry and thirsty. We had left our half-cooked lunch in the kitchen.

When the shooting died down a bit, Daddy ran over to our apartment and brought us back some sandwiches. He said he could smell something burning and that the phones weren't working. He brought our TV set down to the cellar. That's when we learned that the main post office (near us) was on fire and that they had kidnapped our President. At around 8:00 we went back up to our apartment. Almost every window in our street was broken. Ours were all right, thank God. I saw the post office in flames. A terrible sight. The firefighters battled with the raging fire. Daddy took a few photos of the post office being devoured by the flames. He said they wouldn't come out because I had been fiddling with something on the camera. I was sorry. The whole apartment smelled of the burning fire. God, and I used to pass by there every day. It had just been done up. It was huge and beautiful, and now it was being swallowed up by the flames. It was disappearing. That's what this neighborhood of mine looks like, my Mimmy. I wonder what it's like in other parts of town? I heard on the radio that it was awful around the Eternal Flame. The place is knee-deep in glass. We're worried about Grandma and Granddad. They live there. Tomorrow, if we can go out, we'll see how they are. A terrible day. This has been the worst, most awful day in my eleven-year-old life. I hope it will be the only one. Mommy and Daddy are very edgy. I have to go to bed.

Ciao!

Zlata

Thursday, May 7, 1992

Dear Mimmy,

I was almost positive the war would stop, but today. . . . Today a shell fell on the park in front of my house, the park where I used to play and sit with my girlfriends. A lot of people were hurt. From what I hear Jaca, Jaca's mother, Selma, Nina, our neighbor Dado and who knows how many other people who happened to be there were wounded. Dado, Jaca and her mother have come home from the hospital, Selma lost a kidney but I don't know how she is, because she's still in the hospital. AND NINA IS DEAD. A piece of shrapnel lodged in her brain and she died. She was such a sweet, nice little girl. We went to kindergarten together, and we used to play together in the park. Is it possible I'll never see Nina again? Nina, an innocent eleven-year-old little girl—the victim of a stupid war. I feel sad. I cry and wonder why? She didn't do anything. A disgusting war has destroyed a young child's life. Nina, I'll always remember you as a wonderful little girl.

Love, Mimmy,
Zlata

Wednesday, May 27, 1992

Dear Mimmy,

SLAUGHTER! MASSACRE! HORROR! CRIME! BLOOD! SCREAMS! TEARS! DESPAIR!

That's what Vaso Miškin Street looks like today. Two shells exploded in the street and one in the market. Mommy was nearby at the time. She ran to Grandma and Granddad's. Daddy and I were beside ourselves because she hadn't come home. I saw some of it on TV but I still can't believe what I actually saw. It's unbelievable. I've got a lump in my throat and a knot in my tummy. HORRIBLE. They're taking the wounded to the hospital. It's a madhouse. We kept going to the window hoping to see Mommy, but she wasn't back. They released a list of the dead and wounded. Daddy and I were tearing our hair out. We didn't know what had happened to her. Was she alive? At 4:00, Daddy decided to go and check the hospital. He got dressed, and I got ready to go to the Bobars', so as not to stay at home alone. I looked out the window one more time and . . . I SAW MOMMY RUNNING ACROSS THE BRIDGE. As she came into the

house she started shaking and crying. Through her tears she told us how she had seen dismembered bodies. All the neighbors came because they had been afraid for her. Thank God, Mommy is with us. Thank God.

A HORRIBLE DAY. UNFORGETTABLE. HORRIBLE! HORRIBLE!

Your Zlata

Monday, June 29, 1992

Dear Mimmy,

BOREDOM!!! SHOOTING!!! SHELLING!!! PEOPLE BEING KILLED!!! DESPAIR!!! HUNGER!!! MISERY!!! FEAR!!!

That's my life! The life of an innocent eleven-year-old schoolgirl!! A schoolgirl without a school, without the fun and excitement of school. A child without games, without friends, without the sun, without birds, without nature, without fruit, without chocolate or sweets, with just a little powdered milk. In short, a child without a childhood. A wartime child. I now realize that I am really living through a war, I am witnessing an ugly, disgusting war. I and thousands of other children in this town that is being destroyed, that is crying, weeping, seeking help, but getting none. God, will this ever stop, will I ever be a schoolgirl again, will I ever enjoy my childhood again? I once heard that childhood is the most wonderful time of your life. And it is. I loved it, and now an ugly war is taking it all away from me. Why? I feel sad. I feel like crying. I am crying.

Your Zlata

Thursday, November 19, 1992

Dear Mimmy,

Nothing new on the political front. They are adopting some resolutions, the "kids" [a popular term for politicians] are negotiating, and we are dying, freezing, starving, crying, parting with our friends, leaving our loved ones. I keep wanting to explain these stupid politics to myself, because it seems to me that politics caused this war, making it our everyday reality.

War has crossed out the day and replaced it with horror, and now horrors are unfolding instead of days. It looks to me as though these politics mean Serbs, Croats and Muslims. But they are all people. They are all the same. They all look like people, there's no difference. They all have arms, legs and heads, they walk and talk, but now there's "something" that wants to make them different.

Among my girlfriends, among our friends, in our family, there are Serbs and Croats and Muslims. It's a mixed group and I never knew who was a Serb, a Croat or a Muslim. Now politics has started meddling around. It has put an "S" on Serbs, an "M" on Muslims and a "C" on Croats, it wants to separate them. And to do so it has chosen the worst, blackest pencil of all—the pencil of war which spells only misery and death.

Why is politics making us unhappy, separating us, when we ourselves know who is good and who isn't? We mix with the good, not with the bad. And among the good there are Serbs and Croats and Muslims, just as there are among the bad. I simply don't understand it. Of course, I'm "young," and politics are conducted by "grown-ups." But I think we "young" would do it better. We certainly wouldn't have chosen war.

The "kids" really are playing, which is why us kids are not playing, we are living in fear, we are suffering, we are not enjoying the sun and flowers, we are not enjoying our childhood. WE ARE CRYING.

A bit of philosophizing on my part, but I was alone and felt I could write this to you, Mimmy. You understand me. Fortunately, I've got you to talk to. And now,

Love,
Zlata

Friday, September 17, 1993

Dear Mimmy,

The "kids" are negotiating something, signing something. Again giving us hope that this madness will end. There's supposed to be a cease-fire tomorrow and on September 21 at Sarajevo airport everybody is supposed to sign FOR PEACE. Will the war stop on the day that marks the change from one season to another???

With all the disappointments I've had with previous truces and signatures, I can't believe it.

I can't believe it because another horrible shell fell today, ending the life of a three-year-old little boy, wounding his sister and mother.

All I know is that the result of their little games is 15,000 dead in Sarajevo, 3,000 of them children, 50,000 permanent invalids, whom I already see in the streets on crutches, in wheelchairs, armless and legless. And I know that there's no room left in the cemeteries and parks to bury the latest victims.

Maybe that's why this madness should stop.
Your Zlata

The Killing Fields

ICE T

ICE T is a musician known worldwide as rap's most articulate spokesman. Credited with inventing LA-style Gangsta Rap, he has sold over 10 million records worldwide and tours extensively in the Americas, Europe, Japan, and Australia. In addition, he has starred in numerous feature films, including *New Jack City*, *Ricochet*, and *Trespass*.

Through music, writing, and public speaking, Ice T calls attention to the troubled state of his hometown, South Central Los Angeles, speaking out on racism, censorship, and other volatile social issues. The following selection is an excerpt from his first book, *The Ice Opinion* (1994), which was published to critical acclaim for its insightful and penetrating analysis of pressing social issues.

I'M NO AUTHORITY on how gang warfare got started, but it's a real war. Lots of people don't see that. They just think it's stupid kids out there shooting at each other. If that's the case, then any war can be regarded as such.

Try to just imagine somebody in your family getting killed by a neighbor, maybe a teenager across the street. The police come to your door, take down the information, and don't do anything about it. Each day after that, you gotta look at these same people. Would you go over there and kill them?

I don't know. Maybe you would, maybe you wouldn't. There's a definite point where a feud begins. Once it starts, it's not easy to stop. You have a little baby my son's age growing up, and he'll put on clothes and somebody will step to him and say, "What is he doing wearing that red shirt?" A Blood—a guy from another gang—may have killed this guy's uncle. So because of this, your kid grows up in the 'hood not wearing a red T-shirt.

I've literally had friends come to my house and question what my baby boy, Ice, was wearing. "Why you putting him in this color? Why he wearing that?" I tell them, "Nigga, Ice ain't tripping with that." And they'll say, "Yeah, yeah. I'm just playing, but why don't you put him in this *blue* shirt?"

The gang scene in Los Angeles is extremely complicated and deep-rooted. The Hispanic gangs have been banging for far more years than any of the black gangs. The black gangs began to form after the Watts riots in '65, after so many brothers were thrown in jail.

I first came in contact with gangs in 1974, when I started going to Crenshaw High School. I saw this one group of guys hanging out together, and I wanted to know what was going on. They were *the* unit. At this point, I unknowingly got connected in with the Crips. When you go to school, and you start hanging out with friends from one neighborhood, this immediately becomes your gang. These guys had come from Horace Mann Junior High School, and they were part of the first generation of black gangs. Across town was a gang called the Brims, which are called the Bloods now. I then started to learn all about the different groups and their idiosyncrasies.

When you live on a certain street, you will always be held accountable for your 'hood if something goes down. In other words, a totally square kid living on 83rd Street knows his street is a Crip street and knows he can't avoid the politics of his 'hood.

The rules of gang warfare are not much different from the U.S. military. If a fight breaks out, and you run, you can get smoked for that.

In the army, you could get sentenced to death. So, the kids who are more blatant with their membership—or in military-speak, gung-ho—gain the rank. In many ways, gangs are playing the same games America plays against other countries. It's a game of superiority being played out on a smaller scale. But it's essentially the same game.

When you see these drive-bys and kids are hitting five or six people on the street, they are retaliating for the murder of one of their boys. I've seen crying men enter cars and when the doors shut, they go out and murder.

If they hit their target when they put in work, most of them will walk. They know that in Los Angeles if you go out and kill another black man, odds are you aren't going to jail. Your case isn't an LAPD priority. It's the old ghetto saying: "A nigger kills a white man. That's murder one. A white man kills a nigger. That's self-defense. A nigger kills a nigger. That's just another dead nigger."

Most of the gang killers are still out there on the street. I meet kids every day who are introduced to me as "the shooter." "This is the shooter. This is our killer." Which means this kid has killed and will kill again. This is not only what he does, it's what he's known for. Sometimes, they won't be much older than fifteen or sixteen years old.

When someone tells me, "This is the shooter," it means he got away with it a few times, and he's not afraid to do it again tomorrow. Getting away with it once is all it takes. In his mind, he's saying, "It's on."

Gangs have been able to get away with so much killing it just continues. The capability for violence in these kids is unimaginable. Last year, five of my buddies died. I don't even go to the funerals anymore. It's just so crazy. There are just so many people dying out there. Sometimes, I sit up with my friends and I think, "There will never be another time on earth where we'll all be together again." A lot of my original crew is dead. You get hard after a

while. You get hard. People on the outside say, "These kids are so stone-faced; they don't show any remorse or any emotion." It's because they are so conditioned. They are conditioned, like soldiers in war, to deal with death. You just don't know what it's like unless you've been around it.

The way to deal with these guys, especially when they're attempting to break out of the gangster mind-set, isn't by threatening them. In Orange County, California, politicians are threatening to crack down hard on gangs. They actually believe if they bully these kids, they will be scared out of gang membership. "Yeah, we'll scare Johnny, and he won't want to be in gangs anymore."

They don't have a clue that by the time a kid joins a gang, he's already lost all fear of what could happen to him. Nothing could be scarier than Johnny's home life and his upbringing. The killing fields have destroyed his spirit and the lives of his friends. If they were smart, they would be exploring the issues that make a kid want to join up in the first place. Why does this kid want to tag on the wall? It's so typical for the government to say, "Let's go after the kid instead of figuring out the reason he's so full of hate. Let's attack Ice T because he wrote 'Cop Killer.' We don't want to explore the reason he might have written it. That's too horrible. That's too complicated."

I never see the elimination of gangs. I would like to see the elimination of gang violence, though. Currently, I'm putting a lot of time and energy into Hands Across Watts, the organization in L.A. trying to see the gang truce through. Many of my friends still live in South Central or Compton, and every other phone call I get is word from the street. I'm what you call a shot caller, so I probably know more about what's going on in the 'hood than the people who live there. I'm paying for funerals and counseling kids to quit killing over colors and streets. I'm their homeboy who made it, and I'm trying to set an example that there are alternatives to violence. I have hope that peace can be instituted.

If you could just get the violence down to a standstill, you'd be left with what the rest of the world calls clubs. In a city this big, you need a group of people around you. When I was in the army, whenever we left the post the sergeants used to tell us to go in a group. "Take a gang," is what they were really saying.

People have got to understand that gang warfare is not something that should be treated like some minor problem. It's gonna take a big truce. It's gonna take negotiations, and it's gonna take money. It will require a lot of effort to get it to end.

Thousands of people have died on each side of this bloody battlefield, and it's not just something that you can snap your fingers and tell people to stop. When you talk to these kids, they are like veterans from war. If you went to Beirut and asked a kid about his life, he wouldn't tell you he's at war. He'd just say, "This is how it is. You know, bombs and shit going off. I grew up with this, so this is how it is."

They are used to death. They are used to despair.

On my song "Colors," I rapped:

My color's death
Though we all want peace
But this war won't end
Till all wars cease.

This gang war is just like any other war. If you think it can be easily stopped, let's go to Northern Ireland and tell them to stop. Let's go to Bosnia and tell them to quit. Don't call it anything less than what it really is. Now, once we accept that, we can begin to deal with it. As long as the media define the fighters as dumb gang members, they are undermining and not really seeing what these kids are going through.

We can say how stupid it is. We can say how ignorant it is, and I'll agree. But understand that you can say that about any war. Regard it as such.

Whenever the U.S. goes to war, there is a reason for it and there is money for it. But in reality, I can see more sense sometimes in this war out here in these streets than in some of the wars people are shipped overseas to from America. They are usually fighting something they don't even understand. They are fighting for a belief system that is American, when these kids are out fighting for somebody who hurt their family. They're on some real shit. Until you've been up and around 250-pound dudes crying while loading guns, you don't know what it's about. You don't know this is real. Why did it happen? I don't know. But the problem, the reality, is somebody's dead, and somebody wants revenge.

But that's just my opinion on the killing fields, who gives a fuck.

Suicide

Premature Exits: Understanding Suicide

JUDITH M. STILLION

JUDITH M. STILLION, PH.D., is a professor of psychology and associate vice chancellor for academic affairs at Western Carolina University, in Cullowhee, North Carolina. Dr. Stillion began her work in death education in 1976, instituting the first course on the psychology of death and dying at her university. Since then she has conducted a series of studies on attitudes toward suicide, work that has received national attention. Dr. Stillion also conducts training of volunteers with Hospice of Jackson County.

Dr. Stillion is a past president of the Association for Death Education and Counseling and continues to serve as that organization's strategic planner. She was named Outstanding Death Educator by ADEC in 1992. She is also a member of the American Association of Suicidology,

the American Psychological Association, and the International Work Group on Death, Dying, and Bereavement.

During the last two decades, Dr. Stillion has authored over fifty articles and chapters dealing with attitudes toward suicide, children and death, the nuclear threat, and gender differences in death and dying. Her first book, *Death and the Sexes: An Examination of Differential Longevity, Attitudes, Behavior, and Coping Skills* (1985), brought together her expertise in the psychology of sex differences and her work in death and dying. *Suicide Across the Life Span: Premature Exits* (1989), co-authored with Eugene McDowell and Jacque May, was the first book to bring a developmental perspective to the study of suicide.

Understanding Suicide: The Western Cultural Context

Suicide is arguably the most complex and the least understood of all human behaviors, although it has been documented through-

out recorded history. The Old Testament describes the suicide of Samson, seemingly a self-inflicted punishment for failing to stand strong in his faith. The New Testament describes the suicide of Judas Iscariot, who killed himself in an attempt to atone for his betrayal of Jesus of Nazareth. Although a few notable suicides, such as those of Socrates (399 B.C.) and Seneca (65 A.D.) resulted from social pressure to make amends for perceived crimes against the state, most willful suicides recorded in early history involve themes of regret and atonement.[1]

Under the influence of the Catholic Church, suicide came to be regarded as sinful. Around 400 A.D., St. Augustine taught that suicide was a sin because it violated the sixth commandment ("Thou shalt not kill") and usurped power over life and death that belonged only to God. Elaborating this view, three Church councils held during the sixth century established specific punishments for suicides. Thus began more than a thousand years of persecution of suicide as a sin, one for which many believed there could be no atonement or forgiveness. Punishment was directed toward both those who committed suicide and their families. The bodies of suicide victims could not be buried in consecrated ground; indeed, it was not unusual for the bodies to be dragged behind carts or buried at crossroads with stakes through their hearts.[2] In some instances, family members of suicides could not inherit estates, and in some sects they could not enter religious orders. By the late 1600s, suicide began to be viewed as a crime against the state. Secular laws were passed describing suicide as a triple crime: murder, high treason, and heresy.[3]

In the mid-eighteenth century, the French physician Merian published the first medical treatise expressing the view that suicide results from emotional illness, thereby ushering in the modern view of suicide from a mental health perspective.[4] By the end of the nineteenth century, this view gained further acceptance through the now-classic work of Emile Durkheim, *Le Suicide,* which postulated the sociological view that suicide occurs as a result of pain individuals experience from not fitting well within their societies.[5]

In the early twentieth century, Sigmund Freud began theorizing about the psychologi-cal roots of human behavior. In *Mourning and Melancholia,* he described suicidal behavior as a result of intrapsychic conflict and suggested that much of the pain experienced by suicidal people results from unresolved struggles among the id, ego, and superego.[6] Later he said that suicidal behavior might also result from anger or aggression turned inward.

While these sociological and psychological approaches represented progress toward understanding suicide, neither was able to capture the complexity of suicidal behavior. Recent work in other areas has helped somewhat. Biological discoveries have added a new dimension to the understanding of suicide,[7] as have studies into the thought patterns[8] and the environmental circumstances of suicidal people.[9] Perhaps equally important, our growing insight about the predictable changes that occur across the lifespan has added to our understanding of suicide.

Despite these developments, suicide remains one of the least understood of all human behaviors. Those considering, attempting, or completing suicide are still viewed negatively by most people. Attitudes toward suicidal people range from pity and compassion to impatience with or contempt for their weakness or mental instability. Current approaches to dealing with suicidal people include ignoring them, treating them as sinners or criminals, counseling them to influence their behavior, treating them with drugs, institutionalizing them against their wills, and helping them to commit suicide.

The Suicide Trajectory: A Model

In order to make sense of this confused situation, researchers and practitioners developed a model that organizes the interactions of the various causal aspects of suicide and sheds light on the act of suicide as carried out by people of different ages while still allowing for the individual differences observed in suicidal behavior. Called the suicide trajectory model (see Figure 1), it asserts that the many causes

Figure 1

The Suicide Trajectory

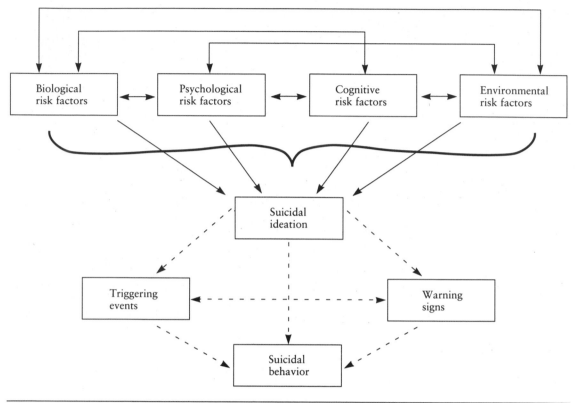

SOURCE: J. M. Stillion, E. E. McDowell, and J. H. May, *Suicide Across the Life Span—Premature Exits* (Washington: Hemisphere, 1989), 240. Copyright © 1989.

of suicide can be sorted into four major categories of risk factors: biological, psychological, cognitive, and environmental.[10]

These risk factors may influence each other, as shown by the interconnecting arrows. As people move through life, they encounter situations and events that add their weight to each risk factor category. When the combined weight of these factors reaches the point where coping skills are threatened with collapse, suicidal ideation—the idea that ending one's life is a solution—is born. Once present, suicidal ideation seems to feed upon itself. It may be exhibited in warning signs; it may also be intensified by triggering events. In the final analysis, however, suicide is attempted because of the contributions of the four risk categories. Understanding any individual suicidal person requires probing into and exposing the experiences that relate to each of these categories. Understanding suicidal risk requires a knowledge of how these risk factors contribute to suicide across the lifespan as well as how predictable life events may increase risk at various stages of the life cycle.

Risk Factors in Suicide

Biological Risk Factors

Evidence of a biological base to suicidal behavior is accumulating from three separate lines of research: research on brain functioning at the cellular level, research into possible genetic bases of suicidal behavior, and research into behaviors associated with being male or female. Much of this research has been carried out with depressed patients who may or may not have reached the point of being suicidal. While nondepressed people may take their lives, most suicidal people report depression as a major symptom. One psychiatrist has estimated that "direct suicide claims the lives of at least 15 percent of depressed patients."[11] Therefore, it is reasonable to review what is known about the biological basis of depression to shed light on suicide.

A growing body of research indicates that neurotransmitters in the brain may play a role in depression and, indirectly, in suicide.[12] The most provocative research for students of suicide has been conducted on serotonin, a substance that is thought to be involved in the regulation of emotion. A deficiency of serotonin has been found in the brains of some people who have committed suicide.[13] In addition, among a group of patients hospitalized for attempted suicide, those who had lower levels of 5-HIAA (a metabolic byproduct of serotonin) were ten times more likely to have died from suicide a year later than were those who had higher levels.[14] This research, although in its early stages, has lent credibility to drug approaches for treating suicidal people.

A second line of research into the biological basis of suicide has tried to tease out possible genetic components by studying identical twins and suicide across generations in the same family. In reviewing this research, Blumenthal and Kupfer cited three intriguing findings.[15] First, data showed that half of a sample of psychiatric inpatients who had a family history of suicide had attempted suicide themselves. A second study reported ten cases of identical twins who both committed suicide but no recorded cases of fraternal twins who both committed suicide. Finally, they cited a study of fifty-seven adoptees who had committed suicide. Among their biological relatives, twelve (4.5 percent) had also committed suicide while none of their adoptive relatives had committed suicide. Among a matched group of fifty-seven adoptees who did not commit suicide, only two (0.7 percent) of their biological relatives (and again none of their adoptive relatives) had committed suicide.

Later work reported by Gold showed a familiar pattern in suicide among the Amish, who have strict religious taboos against suicide.[16] Researchers found a total of twenty-six suicides during the last century in a Pennsylvania Amish group. Of these, 73 percent occurred within four families. The researchers suggested that, since other Amish families experiencing mood disorders did not include suicides, these findings may support a hypothesis for the inheritability of a tendency to suicide. Although this line of research is indirect, it does provide support for a genetic component in suicidal behavior.

The third area of research into biological bases of suicide began with the observation that, in all developed countries that keep suicide statistics, more males complete suicide than do females. Table 1 shows comparative figures for male and female suicide across cultures while Table 2 shows sex differences in suicide across time in the United States. Both tables indicate that death by suicide is three to five times more common among males than females.

Whenever a behavior shows consistent gender differences across cultures and across time, there is reason to suspect that biology may play a role in establishing a threshold or susceptibility for that behavior. A cursory examination of the literature on sex differences

Table 1

Suicide Rates for Selected Countries, by Sex and Age Group

Rate per 100,000 population. Includes deaths resulting indirectly from self-inflicted injuries. Except as noted, deaths classified according to the ninth revision of the *International Classification of Diseases* (I.C.D.).

Sex and Age	United States 1986	Australia 1986	Austria 1987	Canada 1986	Denmark[a] 1986	France 1986	Italy 1985	Japan 1987	Netherlands 1986	Poland 1987	Sweden[a] 1986	United Kingdom[b] 1987	West Germany 1987
MALE													
TOTAL[c]	20.6	19.1	40.1	22.8	35.6	32.9	12.2	25.6	13.9	22.3	27.1	11.6	26.7
15–24 yrs. old	21.7	21.2	29.3	26.9	16.5	16.0	5.2	11.6	8.1	17.8	19.5	9.3	17.6
25–34 yrs. old	25.5	28.3	42.9	32.0	33.2	43.2	9.2	23.7	15.2	30.6	29.4	14.6	24.3
35–44 yrs. old	23.0	23.5	44.8	28.5	50.6	38.1	10.1	29.4	15.3	32.3	33.8	14.6	27.7
45–54 yrs. old	24.4	23.1	54.9	28.1	54.3	46.3	14.8	45.5	19.6	38.5	38.8	15.0	35.2
55–64 yrs. old	26.7	24.6	48.5	27.6	62.2	47.8	22.0	40.5	22.6	35.0	36.1	17.8	37.5
65–74 yrs. old	35.5	27.1	68.1	28.4	52.9	63.5	33.7	42.1	25.5	29.9	39.3	15.8	43.9
75 yrs. old and over	56.0	36.8	125.2	36.3	65.5	121.3	50.0	73.0	42.8	33.2	48.0	20.0	77.2
FEMALE													
TOTAL[c]	5.4	5.6	15.7	6.4	19.9	12.9	4.7	13.8	8.2	4.7	10.1	4.5	11.8
15–24 yrs. old	4.4	5.4	8.1	5.3	5.2	4.6	1.3	6.5	3.6	3.0	7.9	2.1	4.5
25–34 yrs. old	5.9	6.3	10.7	7.5	14.0	10.1	2.7	9.9	9.1	5.7	11.0	3.8	7.8
35–44 yrs. old	7.6	7.5	15.9	8.9	24.6	14.4	4.3	10.9	10.9	6.4	14.6	4.6	10.4
45–54 yrs. old	8.8	10.8	16.8	11.4	36.7	20.2	5.9	16.9	13.6	8.0	15.4	7.6	15.6
55–64 yrs. old	8.4	8.3	22.9	8.9	44.2	21.2	8.8	21.2	13.5	7.7	15.3	7.3	17.4
65–74 yrs. old	7.3	7.6	33.8	9.2	29.3	25.4	11.8	31.1	12.5	7.7	12.7	8.1	23.2
75 yrs. old and over	6.8	6.2	35.4	5.5	26.0	29.5	12.4	53.2	13.0	6.9	8.8	6.9	23.7

NOTE: [a] Based on the eighth revision of the I.C.D. [b] England and Wales only. [c] Includes other age groups not shown separately.

SOURCE: World Health Organization, Geneva, Switzerland, 1988 *World Health Statistics Annual*; U.S. Bureau of the Census (1990). *Statistical Abstract of the United States: 1989*, Washington, DC: U.S. Government Printing Office, p. 838.

Table 2

Suicide Rates, by Sex, Race, and Age Groups: 1970 to 1986

Age	Total[a]			Male						Female					
				White			Black			White			Black		
	1970	1980	1986	1970	1980	1986	1970	1980	1986	1970	1980	1986	1970	1980	1986
All Ages[b]	11.6	11.9	12.8	18.0	19.9	22.3	8.0	10.3	11.1	7.1	5.9	5.9	2.6	2.2	2.3
10–14 years old	.6	.8	1.5	1.1	1.4	2.4	.3	.5	1.5	.3	.3	.7	.4	.1	.4
15–19 years old	5.9	8.5	10.2	9.4	15.0	18.2	4.7	5.6	7.1	2.9	3.3	4.1	2.9	1.6	2.1
20–24 years old	12.2	16.1	15.8	19.3	27.8	28.4	18.7	20.0	16.0	5.7	5.9	5.3	4.9	3.1	2.4
25–34 years old	14.1	16.0	15.7	19.9	25.6	26.4	19.2	21.8	21.3	9.0	7.5	6.2	5.7	4.1	3.8
35–44 years old	16.9	15.4	15.2	23.3	23.5	23.9	12.6	15.6	17.5	13.0	9.1	8.3	3.7	4.6	2.8
45–54 years old	20.0	15.9	16.4	29.5	24.2	26.3	13.8	12.0	12.8	13.5	10.2	9.6	3.7	2.8	3.2
55–64 years old	21.4	15.9	17.0	35.0	25.8	28.7	10.6	11.7	9.9	12.3	9.1	9.0	2.0	2.3	4.2
65 years and over	20.8	17.8	21.5	41.1	37.5	45.6	8.7	11.4	16.2	8.5	6.5	7.5	2.6	1.4	2.4
65–74 years old	20.8	16.9	19.7	38.7	32.5	37.6	8.7	11.1	15.1	9.6	7.0	7.7	2.9	1.7	2.8
75–85 years old	21.2	19.1	25.2	45.5	45.5	58.9	8.9	10.5	16.0	7.2	5.7	8.0	1.7	1.4	2.6
85 years and over	19.0	19.2	20.8	45.8	52.8	66.3	8.7	18.9	17.9	5.8	5.8	5.0	2.8	–[c]	–[c]

[a] Includes other races not shown separately. [b] Includes other age groups not shown separately.
[c] Represents or rounds to zero.
SOURCE: U.S. Bureau of the Census, Statistical Abstract of the United States: 1990 (110th ed.), Washington, 1990.

supports the idea that differences in suicide rates by sex may be related to other sex differences. Human males (as well as the males of other species) display higher levels of aggression at earlier ages than do females.[17] If suicide is viewed as aggression turned inward, it follows that male suicides would outnumber those of females. This line of research gives indirect support for a genetic component in suicidal behavior.

Perhaps the most important biological insight related to suicide can be gleaned from Akiskal and McKinney's work on depressive disorders.[18] These authors maintain that there is always a biological component to true depression. Whether or not the individual inherits a genetic tendency toward depression, when there is sufficient environmental, psychological, or cognitive reasons, the resulting stress is expressed biologically, changing the chemistry of the brain and adding a physical component, which they call the "final, common pathway" to depressive and suicidal behavior. A college student described his dramatic recovery from a serious episode of depression in the following manner: "I knew the minute that the drugs took hold; it was as though someone turned the lights on in a darkened room. My life's situation hadn't changed. I still was hopelessly behind in my courses and my social life was 'caput,' but it didn't seem so grim anymore. I could handle it again. Nothing had changed and yet everything had changed." While not all improvements are as spectacular, the success of drugs in counteracting the biological bases of depression mandates that therapists learn about drugs used to combat depression and work closely with physicians in monitoring the effects of drugs as an adjunct to therapy.

Psychological Risk Factors

Psychological risk factors form the second category that contributes to suicidal behavior. We include within this category such elements as depressed mood (as opposed to clinical depres-

sion, which has already been discussed), feelings of helplessness and hopelessness, poor self-concept and low self-esteem, poorly developed ego defense mechanisms and coping strategies, and existential questions concerning the meaning in life.

Inherent in a diagnosis of depression are the elements of poor self-concept and low self-esteem. Individuals who see themselves positively and value themselves highly are rarely depressed. However, recent research seems to support the idea that hopelessness outweighs depression, poor self-concept, and low self-esteem as the major psychological factor leading to suicide.[19]

Suicidal people have also reached the limit of their coping strategies. The ego defense mechanisms they have learned to use have not been effective, leaving them with overwhelming feelings of hopelessness and helplessness. Those who treat suicidal persons should explore the types of defense mechanisms used in the past and determine why they are no longer effective. New strategies may need to be learned to improve their coping skills.

Finally, depressed and suicidal persons generally struggle at some level with existential issues, questioning the meaning of life. Ronald Maris says, "From the existential perspective under the best conditions life is short, painful, fickle, often lonely, and anxiety generating."[20] For suicidal people, the situation goes beyond that—they often view living as an empty exercise. One suicidal woman expressed it this way: "I don't think I'll ever feel better. But, even if I do, what's the use? It's all illusion anyway. All those people thinking that their little lives mean something. They'll all be dead in 100 years. In 200, nobody will even remember that they lived. What's it all about anyway?" Caregivers must be prepared to face and deal with such nihilism in suicidal people.

Cognitive Risk Factors

Cognitive risk factors are assuming growing importance as we recognize the power our thoughts and words have to maintain or change mental states. This category consists of three major parts.

First is the cognitive level a person has attained. From a Piagetian point of view, we attain understanding of the world gradually, passing through stages that include sensorimotor, preoperational, concrete operational, and formal operation.[21] Understanding a person's position in these stages is important in assessing his or her suicide risk as well as in deciding strategies for treatment.

A second component of cognitive risk factors relates to the messages we tell ourselves about ourselves and how we fit into the world. Meichenbaum identifies these messages as "self-talk" and says that poor adjustment is sustained by negative self-talk while positive self-talk promotes better adjustment.[22]

The third and most important category of cognitive risk factors influencing depression and suicide has been elaborated by Beck and his colleagues as rigidity of thought.[23] Typically, depressed people engage in three types of thinking that may predispose them to suicidal ideation: overgeneralization, selective abstraction, and inexact labeling. Overgeneralization is the tendency to view the world pessimistically, piling negatives upon negatives. Selective abstraction is the tendency to focus on the negative while ignoring or deemphasizing the positive. Inexact labeling occurs when an individual places a negative label upon himself or herself and reacts to the label rather than to the situation at hand. An example of all three types of thinking can be seen in the case of a young male college student who tried to commit suicide by taking an overdose of pills mixed with alcohol. He left a note explaining his reasons for taking his life:

TO WHOM IT MAY CONCERN
Jason Kelvin Joyner
(July 16, 1968–April 30, 1989)
Why?! Because my life has been nothing but misery and sorrow for 20 3/4 years! Going backwards: I thought Susan loved me, but I

suppose not. "I love you Jason" was only a lie. I base my happiness on relationships with girls—when I'm going steady, I'm happy. When a girl dumps me (which is *always* the case), I'm terribly depressed. In fact, over the last 3 years I've been in love at least 4 times seriously, but only to have my heart shattered—like so many icicles falling from a roof. But I've tried to go out with at least 30–40 girls in the last few years—none of them *ever* fell in love with me. My fate was: "to love, but not be loved."

My mother threw me out of the house in March. I guess she must really hate me; she doesn't even write me letters. I think she always hated me.

In high school, and even before that, nobody liked me. They all made fun of me and no girl would ever go to the proms with me.

I haven't anything to live for. Hope? Five years ago I wanted to end my life—I've been hoping for five years. Susan was just the straw that broke the camel's back. I simply cannot take it anymore! I only wanted someone to love; someone who would love me back as much as I loved her.

Yeah, I had pretty good grades, but the way my luck runs, I wouldn't have gotten a job anyway. I got fired over the summer 'cause the boss said, "Jason you don't have any common sense." Gee, that really made my day.

I walk down the streets of Madison and people call out of dorm windows: "Hey, Asshole!" What did I do to them? I don't even know them!

I've been pretty miserable lately (since 1979), so I think I will change the scenery. What's the big deal? I was gonna die in 40 or 50 years anyway. (Maybe sooner: when George decides to push the button in Washington, D.C.!)

Good bye Susan, Sean, Wendy, Joe, Mr. Montgomery, Dr. Johnson, Jack, and everyone else who made my life a little more bearable while it lasted.

—Jason Kelvin Joyner
April 30, 1989

P.S. You might want to print this in the campus newspaper. It would make excellent reading.

There is no doubt that Jason was serious in his suicide attempt. He took over fifty pills of different types, washing them down with bourbon on a Friday night after his roommate had left for the weekend. Only quick action by a resident assistant saved his life. He was taken to a hospital, his stomach was pumped, and he was admitted for psychological examination. On his way from the emergency room to his hospital room, he remarked angrily to a nurse, "Boy, am I a loser! I even mess up when I try to take myself out."

Examining this suicide attempt from a cognitive perspective is instructive. Jason's entire note is a classic example of overgeneralization, as when he writes: "When a girl dumps me (which is *always* the case), I'm terribly depressed." The note goes on to pile negative upon negative by remarking upon his mother's treatment of him, his boss's negative remark prior to firing him, and the fact that even strangers call him names.

Selective abstraction is also seen in the note. In the paragraph about his mother, Jason has chosen to ignore or forget any positive caring that occurred during his childhood and to focus instead on recent events and the lack of letters in reaching the conclusion: "I think she always hated me." A second example can be seen in his deemphasis of the positive factor of good grades, which he links to a negative outcome.

Jason's remark to the nurse is a classic example of inexact labeling. He has forgotten that he has been a good student, that he has coped with life's hardships up to this point in time, and that he has achieved other victories, large or small, over the course of his twenty-two years. All those are gone, replaced with a label evoking utmost disgust and anger: "Loser."[24]

One last point about the cognitive state of many suicidal people is also exemplified in Jason's short note. There are no less than forty-five references to Jason by name or to "me," "my," or "I." The cognitive set of the suicidal individual is characterized by self-absorption, a form of renewed egocentrism so extreme that there is no room for humor or objectivity. Such narrowness of vision is the fertile soil in which suicide ideation flourishes.

Environmental Risk Factors

Environmental factors also influence suicidal behavior. Negative family experiences have been shown to be correlated with suicidal thoughts and behavior.[25] Jason refers to feeling unloved by his mother as an influence on his decision to commit suicide. Among suicidal children, abuse and neglect are common, as is the existence of a turbulent parental relationship. Among suicidal adolescents, parental discord and disorganization are often present in the home. Suicidal adults are much more likely to be living in a discordant home or to be single, divorced, or widowed than to be happily married.[26] Across the lifespan, then, we have evidence that poor home environments are important elements feeding into suicide.

A second environmental factor associated with suicide is the occurrence of negative life events. In Jason's case, being turned down for dates, being fired from his summer job, and being "kicked out" of his home all add to his pessimistic view of the world, his negative self-image, and, ultimately, his suicide attempt.

Loss is a third environmental event affecting the inclination toward suicide. Loss of any kind—whether a relationship, a job, prestige, or a loved one through death—can increase depression. For persons already considering suicide, such losses, especially if they come close together, may be the final blows in destroying the person's weakened or fragmented coping techniques.

A final environmental factor related to suicidal behavior is the easy access to instruments of self-destruction. In Jason's case, he put together a lethal mixture of over-the-counter medications, along with the remnants of several old prescriptions, and washed it down with alcohol. In many suicides, it is the ready availability of firearms that makes a suicide attempt easy and fatal. One authority has gone so far as to point out that the rise in suicide during the last three decades can be accounted for almost entirely by the increase in deaths caused by handguns.[27]

Suicide Ideation

All four of the risk categories discussed above combine to increase an individual's likelihood of attempting suicide. In all but the most impulsive suicides, there is a period of suicidal ideation beforehand. In Jason's case, this period lasted five years, according to his note although he claims to have been feeling miserable for ten years.

Following his attempt, Jason admitted that he had thought through his suicide plans. The day after Susan broke up with him, he went to the drug store and purchased "lots of junk, whatever was the cheapest and had a warning on it that it would make you drowsy or one that warned it shouldn't be taken with alcohol." He had a few painkillers left from an ankle injury a few months before as well as a few sleeping pills prescribed by the college doctor who was treating him for anxiety. He purchased a pint of bourbon, although he usually drank nothing but a beer or two. He even planned the timing of his suicide attempt. He waited until his roommate had left for the weekend and the students in adjoining rooms had gone out for the evening.

Once he had made the plan in his head, it seemed right. He admitted to feeling "such relief that it almost felt like happiness." This feeling of "being right" is typical of suicidal ideation in its advanced stages. While Jason waited for Friday to come, he rehearsed his plan again and again in his mind. When he became upset about something, he had only to think, "Well, by Friday, it will all be over," and he could regain peace of mind. In Jason's case, the semi-euphoric feeling lasted even as he put

on his favorite record, propped himself on the bed, and slowly ingested the lethal mixture of alcohol and pills.

For some, suicidal ideation takes on a compulsive quality. One middle-aged suicidal woman confessed that she "couldn't shake" her suicidal thoughts. They intruded again and again as she went about her everyday tasks, finally taking on the clarity of a vision of a particular place where she could commit suicide by driving over a cliff. The period during which suicidal ideation forms varies from a few minutes to a few years, but it is an intensely important period in the final definition of the suicidal act. The contemplation of the prospective suicide builds upon itself until suicide is seen as "the solution to the problem of life—of having to eat, to breathe, to work, to get up each morning, to shave, to move about, to go to school, to cope with other humans, to experience pain, anxiety, and so on."[28]

Even when suicidal ideation is well advanced, however, some ambivalence generally remains.[29] Although the decision to commit suicide has been made and the details of the suicide plan are complete, the person's ambivalence can be evoked with questions such as What would it take for you to change your mind? What specifics in your life would have to change for you to choose to go on living? Under what circumstances can you see a future for yourself? Such questions may move suicidal persons back from the brink as their essential ambivalence is re-engendered and they are forced to consider possible alternatives for the present and the future.

Triggering Events and Warning Signs

Also shown on the model in Figure 1 are rectangles depicting triggering events and warning signs. These rectangles are connected to the rest of the model by dotted lines because they are not always evident in a suicide attempt. Triggering events can best be understood as "last straw" phenomena. They need not be the worst losses or most dramatic events in a person's life. The crucial element in a triggering event is that it occurs after suicidal ideation has begun. Susan's breaking off with Jason was a triggering event. Jason had broken up with other girls before, but this particular breakup occurred after suicidal ideation was well developed.

Suicidal people may or may not exhibit warning signs. Indeed, Jason's suicide ideation was so complete that he prided himself that no one suspected or could interfere with his plan. However, some warning signs are fairly common among all ages of suicides. These include verbal threats of suicide, self-injurious behaviors, and closure behaviors such as unexpected calls or visits intended as a final goodbye. Warning signs generally become visible following a triggering event or after the decision for death is finalized.

Suicide Across the Lifespan

We have already seen that suicide is not a unitary act. People committing suicide do not all do it for the same reason or in the same way. There are different rates of suicide in different countries as well as between men and women in the same country. At least as important as cultural and sex-related differences are the age differences evident in suicidal behavior. A reexamination of Table 2 attests to the fact that the suicide statistics vary more widely across age groups than across reported time periods. Similarly, Table 1 shows that differences among age groups are at least as great as those among cultures.

As we become more aware of the predictable life stages most people experience, we can examine those stages for developmental events or typical experiences that may increase susceptibility to suicide for people of different ages. Such an examination can help us become aware of questions to ask and areas to probe when dealing with suicidal people of different ages.[30]

Biological Considerations by Age

Childhood suicide is often, though not always, highly impulsive.[31] Children—who have a tendency to act first rather than reflect on the consequences of their action—may try to alleviate their emotional pain by running into traffic or jumping from a high place. Those who work with suicidal children need to be aware that the tendency toward impulsivity may make such children choose highly lethal methods and act out their impulses on the spur of the moment. Therefore, it is important to keep at-risk children in suicide-proof environments.

Puberty brings many hormonal changes. Physically, young adolescents experience a growth spurt and other bodily changes that require them to readjust to their changing body on an almost daily basis. These hormonal changes no doubt spark some of the psychological and cognitive changes that make adolescence such an extremely painful period for many youngsters. Being aware of the many biological changes occurring at this time in life, we should explore and discuss with adolescents issues of sexuality and body image as they contribute to suicidal impulses.

During early adulthood, humans generally experience their peak in biological well-being. Still, for young and middle-aged women, two biological conditions may influence suicidal tendencies. The first, premenstrual syndrome (PMS) has only recently begun to be viewed as a real entity. Rooted in hormonal changes relating to the menstrual cycle, PMS can cause women to feel depressed or anxious, to experience low self-esteem, and even to feel hopeless about their abilities to cope. The second condition, also related to a changing hormonal state, is postpartum depression, or the "baby blues." Postpartum depression can be mild or severe and may last anywhere from a few months to a year after giving birth. Depression, hopelessness, and low self-esteem resulting from PMS or postpartum depression may make women more susceptible to suicide.

During the middle years of life, another biological change, menopause, occurs. Women who have experienced postpartum depression or earlier suicidal urges may once again find themselves confronting a biologically influenced suicidal crisis. Males also face a change of life period called the *climacteric,* marked by decreasing production of the hormone testosterone. While not as apparent or dramatic as female menopause, the climacteric can result in reduced feelings of virility and may lead to depression, especially in males who are experiencing stress in other risk categories. Both sexes begin to notice the biological changes associated with aging: wrinkles, graying of hair, and general decline in physical abilities and youthful attractiveness. These unremitting biological changes may feed into feelings of decreased self-esteem and increased anxiety, resulting in self-concepts that are increasingly negative.

In old age, physical decline can accelerate. Elderly people often develop chronic diseases with accompanying pain and inability to function. Anxiety and depression rooted in these biological changes may become potent factors influencing suicidal behavior. It is important to recognize that the commitment to living may lessen as elderly people develop biological problems. Exploring ways to improve the quality of life may enable elderly people to reject suicide and renew their commitment to life.

Psychological Considerations by Age

Childhood is a time for developing positive feelings of competence. According to Erik Erikson, healthy children build upon positive levels of trust, autonomy, and initiative to develop a strong sense of industry.[32] Children who have been raised in such a way that they develop mistrust, shame, doubt about themselves, and a sense of guilt will have more difficulty developing competence. Such children may develop a basic life stance of inferiority, resulting in poor self-concept and low self-esteem as well as hindering their further psychological growth during adolescence. The sense of inferiority may become so extreme that the child views himself or herself as unworthy or expendable. When this happens, suicidal ideation may be the next step. Children who exhibit feelings of inferiority should be encouraged to attempt activities in which they can succeed and be supported in these attempts. Competence is a powerful antidote to feelings of inferiority.[33]

If we regard adolescence as spanning ages fifteen and twenty-four, we must acknowledge two major psychological conflicts noted by Erikson. First is the question of identity. Young people who have developed a positive sense of industry and solid competence in one or more areas arrive at an adequate answer to the question "Who am I?" more readily than do those who have feelings of inferiority. Much of the angst of adolescence, recognized since G. Stanley Hall's writings in the early part of this century, stems from wrestling with the questions "Who am I?" and "Who do I want to be?"[34] Such questions, coupled with the biological changes discussed earlier, may so overwhelm susceptible adolescents that they feel helpless to answer them and hopeless about their present and future identities and roles in life. They may give up on themselves. Young people should be encouraged to explore their strengths and preferences; supportive listening can nourish their movement toward self-definition.

Beginning in late adolescence and continuing through early adulthood, the main struggle identified by Erikson involves establishing a sense of intimacy with at least one other person. True intimacy results in positive mental health as two people plan and grow together, each invested in the well-being of the other. The opposite of intimacy is isolation. Young adults who fail to develop at least a modicum of intimacy find themselves in a state of psychological isolation that may lead to depression and lowered self-esteem. To counteract this, young adults should be encouraged to probe their sense of intimacy with others. Group therapy and growth groups can be powerful tools to help suicidal young adults explore new ways of being with others and attain the skills necessary to develop intimacy.

In middle adulthood, along with a decline in physical abilities, many people experience a sense of deficiency or inferiority.[35] Taking stock of their progress in life to date, they find that they must give up some of their youthful dreams. Realizing that they will never attain the presidency of the company, have a baby, become a successful rock singer, or reach their secret dream of success, they are susceptible to feelings of stagnation. Erikson theorized that healthy adults in their middle years are generative, contributing to society in meaningful ways. Suicidal adults may no longer have faith in their abilities to make meaningful contributions. They may be bored with their current roles, regretful of roads not taken, and overwhelmed by the feeling that it's too late to begin anew. Psychological stagnation is the mirror image of depression.

Among the elderly, psychological issues include increased feelings of loneliness, passivity, and despair. Erikson pointed out that healthy older people experience a sense of ego integrity, of having lived their lives in a meaningful and positive manner. Unhealthy elderly people, he said, experience despair and disgust, characterized by overwhelming feelings that their lives have been wasted and that nothing has any meaning. Such people risk developing suicidal depression and acting upon it. Reminiscence therapy is a valuable tool for helping suicidal elderly people. In the hands of a skilled practitioner, this approach allows elderly people to reexperience their lives and the decisions they have made, review the conditions under which they made those decisions, and try to find meaningful patterns and values in their experiences.

Cognitive Considerations by Age

Young children have immature conceptions of death; they do not realize that death is final and irreversible.[36] Because of this, there is reason to believe that young children do not fully realize the implications of suicidal behavior. They may expect to wake up and rejoin their families after a brief time.

Another cognitive factor affecting child suicide is the rigidity associated with concrete operational thinking, which characterizes the mental processes of children between six and eleven. Such children view the world in concrete terms: black and white, here and now. They are poor at abstract and hypothetical thinking and are unable to consider multiple outcomes in a problem situation—including the possibility that things might get better. Helping these children means leading them to a deeper understanding of the finality of death as well as finding ways for them to express their pain. Traditional play therapy and art therapy can be effective when combined with the skills of a good listener.

In adolescence, cognitive abilities take a giant leap forward as the young person becomes capable of using formal operational thought. Such thinking permits adolescents to envision different ways of being and to struggle with deep, philosophical questions. However, it may also lead to overly idealistic expectations (for example, of a world where perfect justice prevails) that create disillusionment when they are not met. Perhaps because of their newfound cognitive abilities, adolescents seem prone to renewed egocentrism ("No one has ever felt like I do now; no one understands me"). They tend to see themselves at center stage and may develop extreme self-consciousness, feeling as if they must constantly perform before an imaginary audience.[37] Such a perception may account, at least in part, for the high dependence on peer opinion during adolescence. This is the period in life when suicide by peers or by famous people may lead to copycat or cluster suicides. Many of the intervention approaches in high schools have been initiated because of this phenomenon. Adolescents may also develop an illusion of invulnerability that leads to experimentation with dangerous behaviors such as taking drugs and driving while intoxicated. These behaviors, though not in themselves overtly suicidal, may nevertheless cause death.

During young adulthood, people often experience a cognitive reevaluation of life choices. Described as a "Catch-30" by Sheehy[38] and documented by adult development researchers,[39] this reevaluation seems to be a recognition that one has undeniably entered adulthood and is responsible for the decisions and directions of one's own life. For some, this reevaluation involves setting new goals and directions. For others, it involves ending relationships, leaving secure jobs, or cutting ties with parents or mentors. Such decisions always involve loss and its accompanying emotions of anxiety, depression, and regret. Young adults need to understand that even the most positive decisions for life change carry an emotional cost.

During middle age, a major cognitive change occurs with regard to time. Middle-aged people begin to reckon time not from birth, but as the time left in which to accomplish their goals.[40] Such a shift can lead to a major evaluation of one's experiences directed toward setting one's priorities for the time remaining. It is not unusual to find depressed middle-aged people compulsively reviewing their past decisions, regretting roads not taken, and verbalizing a sense of hopelessness because they feel that it is too late to start making more satisfying choices. Faced with this situation, troubling issues may need to be reframed. For example, a depressed forty-year-old woman who had left nursing school to be married at age twenty told her counselor that she would always regret not becoming a nurse. The counselor, knowing that the woman's children were in college, asked why she did not return to nursing school. The woman replied that the training would take three years and she would be forty-three years old before she got her degree. "Yes," the counselor responded, "but, in three years, you will be forty-three with or without the degree. The choice is yours." People cannot remake or unmake their youthful decisions, but they can move forward, grounded in their life's experience and using current time wisely, to attain the goals they value.

Among the elderly, cognitive shifts include declines in the rate of learning and retrieval from memory of previously learned material although there is disagreement about the rate of such declines and evidence that this decline can be slowed by involvement in life and learning. These declines, coupled with a growing cognitive acceptance of death as a natural and not necessarily negative part of life, may lead elderly people to consider suicide. Indeed, much of the argument about rational suicide comes from and is directed toward the elderly, particularly those who are terminally ill.

Environmental Considerations by Age

For children, the environmental factors with the greatest influence on suicidal inclination are centered in the family. Perhaps the most difficult situation for children, aside from outright abuse and neglect, is to experience confusion over role definitions, a situation that often occurs when there is drinking or drug abuse by parents. Children find themselves coping with adult responsibilities beyond their years; in effect, becoming a parent to their own parents as well as to younger siblings. The strain and anger children experience in this kind of situation, coupled with their helplessness to change the situation, may promote suicidal behavior as an attempt to escape. Outside the home environment, repeated failure in school may also predispose a child to depression by feeding a growing sense of inferiority rather than a healthy concept of industry.

In adolescence, although the quality of family life is important, events and experiences outside the home take on relatively greater importance. Peers become especially important, and loss of peer approval can be devastating to an adolescent's self-concept. Experimentation with alcohol or other drugs, when combined with the dramatic hormonal changes taking place in these years, may exacerbate the turbulence of this period of life. If addiction occurs, the adolescent's emerging identity is further compromised by feelings of being out of control. Also, since many of the drugs taken by adolescents are depressants, they can accentuate suicidal feelings.

In young adulthood, marital problems and occupational problems are often involved in suicidal depression. Women with young children in the home seem at high risk for depression, especially if they have few outside contacts and little support from a husband or boyfriend.[41] Men faced with unemployment or downward occupational mobility experience higher levels of depression than men who are not in those circumstances.[42] A third factor influencing depression in both sexes is increased mobility.[43] Although people of every age may move, young adults move more often than people of other ages. The dislocation and inevitable loss of relationships and sense of place can be powerful negative environmental factors. Finally, a new environmental influence on the suicide rate among young adults is knowing that one has AIDS or testing positive for HIV. Although AIDS affects people of all ages, it is most prevalent among young adults. In one study the suicide rate among people who have tested HIV-positive was 66 times higher than the suicide rate for the general population.[44]

In middle adulthood, many normative losses occur. Most middle-aged adults experi-

ence the deaths of their parents as well as the deaths of friends and other family members. The empty nest or child-free home also becomes a reality, requiring a redefinition of parenting. Middle-aged adults may be less involved in social activities as they no longer participate in child-related obligations such as PTA, school plays and recitals, and the like. A shift toward interiority, coupled with a cognitive change in time perspective, may cause middle-aged adults to be increasingly ego-absorbed. This is also the period when alcoholism begins to exert a drastic influence on suicide rates. The risk of suicide among alcoholics has been estimated to be 58-85 times greater than that for nonalcoholics.[45]

Among the elderly, environmental factors feeding into suicide potential include the loss of a spouse, retirement, moving to a smaller home, the death of a friend, chronic illnesses, and so on. Although these are normative events (that is, they are to be expected given the current state of medicine and cultural attitudes), they are nonetheless powerful experiences that affect the older person's well-being and self-concept. Taken together with other losses, they constitute a pattern of cumulative loss that is inevitable in old age. These losses may occur in such rapid succession that the elderly person cannot work through one before being confronted with the next. It is easy to see why feelings of hopelessness and helplessness result. Loneliness and isolation are also powerful factors relative to elderly suicide,[46] as is lack of financial security. Double suicides, which occur as a result of suicide pacts, are more common among the elderly than in any other age group. It is important to realize that, in old age, there is less warning about suicide, fewer attempts compared to completions, and the highest fatality of all age groups. Simply put, elderly persons do not talk about suicide; they do it. Thus, the challenge in working with this age group involves being alert to indirect signs of impending suicide (such as putting one's affairs in order) and striving to keep the balance of comfort and discomfort on the side of a decision for life.

Summary

Understanding the four categories of risk factors that contribute to suicide (biological, psychological, cognitive, and environmental) can help illuminate suicidal behavior. Knowing something of the developmental stages and normative events that occur at various points across the lifespan provides additional insight toward assessing the potential for suicide.

Models of behavior are, in themselves, neither good or bad, right or wrong. If they provide useful guidance to people who want to understand a given phenomenon, then they are worthwhile. By systematically exploring the four categories of risk factors, paying special attention to how these factors affect people at various ages and developmental stages, the suicide trajectory model can guide us toward a better understanding of suicide and of the suicidal person. Probing suicidal ideation and scanning for warning signs or triggering events typical for people at various ages may enable us to predict more accurately who is at risk for suicide. In these ways, the suicide trajectory model may serve as a finer screen for sifting and examining information from troubled people and may thereby enhance our understanding of those who are considering premature exits from the stage of life.

"It's a White Thing"—An Exploration of Beliefs about Suicide in the African-American Community

KEVIN E. EARLY AND RONALD L. AKERS

KEVIN E. EARLY, PH.D., is an assistant professor of sociology at Oakland University in Rochester, Michigan. He specializes in criminology, corrections, deviance and social control, and substance abuse. With his father in the Air Force, Dr. Early spent his childhood in Japan and Brazil as well as the northeastern United States. He earned a baccalaureate in history and political science from Dillard University in 1982, then obtained a master's degree and certificate in Latin American and Iberian Studies from Vanderbilt University. Dr. Early's next move was to Lisbon, Portugal, where he studied under a research grant from the Portuguese government and earned a diploma from the Faculdade de Letras of the Universidade de Lisboa. Returning to the United States in 1986, he earned a master's and Ph.D. in sociology from the University of Florida. He has more than five years of experience in the areas of mental health and corrections.

His involvement in death and dying came about serendipitously as a graduate student at the University of Florida when he read about a number of suicide cases in the Gainesville area. While the suicides were not in any way unique, he observed that none of the victims was African American. Investigating further, he discovered that an overwhelming majority of the suicide cases in the state were white, with African Americans comprising only a small percentage. Realizing that African Americans did in fact commit suicide, he didn't understand why the rates of suicide were low, particularly when one considers the effects of racism and other socioeconomic factors on the African-American community. One hypothesis that he offered was that churches within the African-American community had a greater influence than did their counterparts among white Americans and thus provided amelioration of social forces that would otherwise lead to suicide. With this in mind, he began his research.

In addition to publications in the area of death and dying, Dr. Early is co-author of

Nameless Persons: Legal Discrimination Against Non-Marital Children in America (with Martha T. Zingo, in press) and other publications focusing on race relations. His book, *Religion and Suicide in the African-American Community* (1992), has been compared to the work of Elliot Liebow in *Talley's Corner*, an award-winning study. This book and the article reprinted here deepen our understanding of the lives of African Americans and are significant contributions to our knowledge about suicide in the African-American community.

RONALD L. AKERS, PH.D., is a professor of sociology and director of the Center for Studies in Criminology and Law at the University of Florida. He is former president of the Southern Sociological Society and of the American Society of Criminology. He is a fellow of the American Society of Criminology, which awarded him its Sutherland Award.

Dr. Akers's research and teaching interests revolve around the sociology of deviant and criminal behavior. He has conducted research and published on a variety of topics including delinquency, adolescent substance use, smoking behavior, elderly alcohol behavior, prison inmate systems, the exclusionary rule in criminal trials, juvenile justice, and, most recently, the impact of Hurricane Andrew on crime and social control in the Miami area. He is best known as the author of the social learning theory of criminal and deviant behavior, which he and a colleague first formulated in the 1960s. This innovative theory is expounded in his book *Deviant Behavior: A Social Learning Approach,* first published in 1973 and now in its third edition. In addition to that book and numerous journal articles, he is author of *Law and Control in Society* (1975), *Drugs, Alcohol, and Society* (1992), and *Criminological Theories* (1994).

Dr. Akers's interest in understanding suicide grew out of his theoretical, research, and teaching involvement in the sociology of deviant behavior. A unit on the sociology of suicide has long been included in his courses on deviance, and three chapters of *Deviant Behavior* are devoted to the topic, including a social learning explanation of suicidal behavior. The intriguing question of why black rates of suicide are so much lower than white rates and the sociocultural context for this difference is part of the longstanding sociological interest in understanding religious, class, gender, racial, ethnic, and other differences in suicide rates.

THE LOW BLACK suicide rate is well documented. There has been an increase in black male suicides in the past two decades, but until the mid-1980s that was matched by an increase in suicides among white males. The differences in suicide between younger black and white males has never been large and may be getting smaller. Nevertheless, overall the white suicide rate is nearly double the black suicide rate. The ratio of white male to black male suicide rates is 1.75:1, and the suicide rate among white women is more than double the rate for black women.[1] It is this persistent difference in rates of suicide across racial groups that has been the focus of sociological interest in suicide in the black community. The question raised by this difference is, Why is there relatively little black suicide?

Factors in Black Suicide

The question is raised because there seem to be reasons to expect higher levels of suicides among blacks. Durkheim's brief reference to suicide and slavery would suggest that "fatalistic" suicide should be high in the black community.[2] According to anomie theory, relative deprivation and blocked opportunity (conditions found in the lower-class and black community) produce strain, stress, and alienation leading to all forms of deviance.[3] All of the usual indices of anomie or social disorganization (e.g., dysfunctional families, powerlessness, high illegitimacy rate, alienation, unemployment, blocked opportunity) are found disproportionately among the black community. Feelings of powerlessness and oppression have long been offered as reasons why blacks commit suicide.[4] To the extent that perceptions of powerlessness permeate the black community, the suicide rate should be higher than it is.

"Family deficit" theory also suggests that black suicide rates should be high. The frequent absence of a male role model in the black family is seen as one such deficit. The role of black females as head of households is hypothesized to maximize the propensity toward suicide.[5] For black youths the absence or loss of a "sensitive, strong, loving masculine father figure causes psychological damage and leads to suicide."[6] Davis proposes that suicide among African Americans is likely to occur with the weakening of the relational, communal, and family system and that "the likelihood of suicide is increased without important support systems."[7]

Suicide Buffers
in the African-American Community

What sustains a relatively low black suicide rate in the face of these conditions that would predict higher rates? One answer is that those in lower status in society (blacks) tend to direct aggression outward, while higher status persons (whites) direct aggression inward.[8] The answer most frequently given in the literature, however, is a general "buffering hypothesis." This hypothesizes that black suicide is lower, in part, because of the role played by religion and the family in the African-American community in ameliorating or buffering social forces that might otherwise promote suicide. Billingsley, Stack, Allen, Martin, and McAdoo all look at the family, church, and social support systems they believe help insulate African Americans from suicide.[9] This perspective is also adopted by Rutter, who used the term protective factors.[10] Woodford proposed that experiences with urbanization, segregation, and racism have helped to buffer African Americans from suicide by producing adaptability.[11] Davis hypothesized that:

> For blacks, the stresses and anxieties that might lead to suicide have often been offset by strong family and communal ties. Effectively denied all other mechanisms to compensate for rejection and abuse, blacks have in the past used their families, communities, and institutions (i.e., churches, social clubs, fraternal organizations, etc.) to develop positive and functional forms of response to recurrent stressful social situations. The black community, in effect, has functioned as a protective society, providing participation and purpose, a sense of belonging, and the possibility of cooperative and self-help approaches to problems.[12]

As stated in the literature the hypothesis remains nonspecific as to just what it is about the church, family, or other institutions in the African-American community that has provided or could provide suicide buffering. We propose that there are both social and cultural dimensions to any suicide buffering effect that may be found. The social dimension relates to the extent to which social relationships and responsiveness to one another provide social support countering suicide situations and motivations. The cultural dimension refers to the normative climate, the values and norms shared by the church, family, and other institutions in the African-American community. Research has not yet identified the empirical content of either of these dimensions.

The purpose of this paper is to report an exploratory, qualitative investigation of the content of the cultural/normative dimension. The study was designed to find what, if any, religious beliefs there are in the African-American community that might serve a sui-

cide-buffering function.[13] Specifically, we report a study of normative views of suicide, contrasted with views of other deviant acts such as drug abuse and crime, reported by religious leaders in one community. The study did not have comparative data from the white community and therefore was not an effort to directly test the buffering hypothesis or to explain differences in white and black suicidal behavior. Rather, the study attempted to identify the content of religiously based antisuicide beliefs to gain a greater understanding of black cultural perceptions of suicide.

The Centrality of the Church in the African-American Community

Our emphasis here on the religiously based meanings of suicide is taken from the literature portraying the central role the church plays in the black community. Gibbs, for instance, maintains that the church has "traditionally been the central axis around which the rest of the community revolved."[14] For African Americans, the church "has served as a refuge for blacks from racial discrimination and social oppression,"[15] as well as the conferrer of status, center of organization, and center of protest.[16] C. Eric Lincoln vividly described the unique place of the church in the black community:

> The Church is the spiritual face of the Black community, and whether one is a "church member" or not is beside the point in any assessment of the importance and meaning of the Black Church. Because of the peculiar nature of the Black experience and the centrality of institutionalized religion in the development of that experience, the time was when the personal dignity of the Black individual was communicated almost entirely through his church affiliation. The Black Church, then, is in some sense a "universal church," claiming and representing all Blacks out of a long tradition that looks back to the time when there was only the Black Church to bear witness to "who" or "what" a man

was as he stood at the bar of his community. The Church still accepts a broad-gauge responsibility for the Black community inside and outside its formal communion. "The Church" is still in an important sense "the people," and the Church leaders are still the people's representatives.[17]

Feagin offered a similar description of the importance of the black church.[18] Staples and Wilmore argued that religious participation is a major way that morals, ethics, self-definition, and cultural traditions of blacks are expressed.[19] If these perspectives on the black church are correct, the moral and social views promulgated by the church leaders should influence the values in the larger black community. Is the social meaning of suicide reflected in religious views such that, if the church does have the significance attributed to it, would be expected to work against black suicide? If the normative buffering is specific to suicide, how and why does it differ from the view of other forms of deviance and life-threatening behavior such as violence, other dangerous crimes, and drug abuse?

Methodology

The study was conducted in 1991 in a southeastern standard metropolitan statistical area (SMSA) of about 84,000 with 21% African Americans. The data were collected by the first author in face-to-face interviews with black pastors. There are a total of 37 black churches located in the area, and 30 pastors agreed to take part in the study. The pastors were interviewed as informants, as persons strategically located in the community to provide information, insight, and contacts within that community. Therefore, they were asked their own opinions and were asked to comment on beliefs about suicide in the general community.

The interviews were loosely structured and undisguised, lasting about 1-1/2 hours each. The interviews were divided into two main sections. The first section covered: (a) The pastor's views as leader of the church and the stated position of his or her church on suicide; (b) The pastor's assessment of the role of the church and religion in the African-American family and community; (c) The extent to which the pastor teaches and preaches on suicide-relevant topics; and (d) The definition and meaning of suicide and its causes and assessment of why there are few suicide deaths in the African-American community. The second part of the interview asked the pastors to respond to two vignettes depicting cases of suicide and attempted suicide and two vignettes depicting cases of crime and substance abuse (see Appendix A). Each vignette was succeeded by four to seven follow-up questions that were designed to elicit pastors' judgments and attitudes about several issues related to the nature of suicide and life-threatening behavior depicted in the vignettes and the role that the black church could play or had played in dealing with these social issues.

None of the pastors reported direct experience with cases of suicide, and therefore assessment of actual cases could not be used. The vignettes allowed us to explore what the stated reactions and assessments would have been if the pastors had encountered such cases. They also served to compare views on suicide with those on other deviant behavior such as violence and drug abuse.

The Church's Role in the Black Community

Not surprisingly, the pastors offer strong support for the contention in the literature iterated above that the church serves unifying and leadership functions in the black community. They point to the black church as an institution that has provided social and cultural integration for black Americans and has interacted with the black family to provide resiliency under stressful conditions.

[Interview 08269010] The church has played a major role because it has been the Bible of the black community from slavery time to now. The thing that has held us together has been the church and prayer. The church has been the social hall. It's been the place of contact. It's been the place to where the meeting of the minds take place. I see the suicide rate very low in our community compared to others because of the role that the church has played. It has helped blacks understand. It has built self-esteem. It has helped educate them as to what would happen and the result of suicide. The belief of heaven and hell really existed. The facts of eternity. The facts of lost people and saved people. I think that the part that the church has played in training, developing and creating the minds of our young people has been a vital part of really holding the community together.

(Interview 08269010] The church is the black person's life. That's where most of everything is taken care of anyway. Our politics is taken care of at church. That's when we decide who to vote for. In education, the pastor tells you to get back in school. In economics, bills are even discussed with the pastor. Religion is the fiber of our community. . . . It is what's holding us together.

[Interview 07149001] Well, first of all, the black church is our only communication. The black people have nothing else. They don't have any women's clubs. They don't have any decent recreational facilities. Ah . . . they don't have any Jaycees or business clubs. Whereas, the white community has all kinds of outlets where they can express themselves and let off their steam. The black people only have the church.

Beliefs About Suicide, Drug Abuse, and Crime

The pastors' perceived significance of the church in the community does not guarantee

that its stand on suicide is widely shared in the black culture, and our research did not include a community survey. However, as we have seen, the literature strongly supports this perception, and it seems reasonable to assume that the norms and attitudes expressed by the pastors are reflected to some extent in the larger community. Those norms, as articulated by the pastors in this study, condemn suicide on religious grounds and define it as so alien to the black experience, religious and secular, that willingness to commit suicide runs directly counter to all that is implicit in what it means to be African American. They articulate differentiations between suicide and other deviant acts such as drug abuse.

The pastors defined suicide as "willful, premeditated, and not in accord with a sound judgment" and a "nonproductive act whereby a person takes his or her own life." However, some also referred to self-injurious behavior such as drug use as forms of suicide.

[Interview 08119007] Substance abuse is a form of suicide. It might be a slower form of suicide, but it's suicide. Once you start doing it, it's suicide. The finality of suicide is physical death, but suicide begins when you start doing substances, crack, cocaine, you know, marijuana. Those are smaller symptoms of suicide that lead up to the finality.

[Interview 08099006] Suicide includes drugs because when you look at our circumstances that we are faced with in our society, so many of our young people are really committing suicide through drugs.

However, this fusing together of suicide and other self-injurious acts seems primarily to have been an effort on the part of the pastors to show that one can be self-destructive without really intending to be. Once having said this, they quickly moved to distinctions between this "slow suicide" and "actual" or "real" suicide that they maintained throughout the interviews. They did see a difference between intended suicide as the deliberate and immediate taking of one's own life and other actions such as drug use. The pastors obviously did not consider them to be the same thing because they reported no knowledge of suicides or suicide attempts in their congregations; yet they said they knew directly of cases of drug and alcohol abuse. Moreover, the pastors' responses to the vignettes clearly distinguished between suicide as deliberately ending one's life and engaging in alcohol/drug abuse. The latter is viewed as very wrong but an understandable response to the socioeconomic and political condition of blacks in American society; suicide, however, is still defined as unthinkable.

In the view of the pastors, the black church unequivocally condemns suicide as unforgivable sin. "Man is not the giver of life. Hence, man has not the authority to take life." "The Lord giveth and only the Lord taketh away."

[Interview 08269010] We don't condone suicide. We condemn it to the maximum. We believe that most people that commit suicide never [get the chance before dying] to ask for forgiveness.

[Interview 07289001] God did not put us here to determine our own conclusion of life and taking it upon ourselves to make quick exits. That, Biblically, is not an approved act of God. It's unpardonable sin. One who commits suicide goes to hell and is unpardoned for their sin.

[Interview 09089015] If you take your own life, why, it's a lost cause not only in this life but in the life to come. I feel like blacks really consider this even more so that they have a soul that they must give an account for.

[Interview 09119017] Black people believe in a heaven and hell. We've been taught, as black people, that if you kill yourself you automatically go to hell.

This definition of suicide as a sin that is unpardonable is combined with the view that suicide runs counter to black "soul." The soul represents the gift of life. The soul is tied to the black experience not only spiritually, but has worldly, cultural, and traditional dimensions. If one is to insure one's soul a proper place in heaven after death, it is important to live life as productively as possible despite life's many obstacles. Obstacles should not be a deterrent to life, but an encouragement to struggle. To struggle with the help of God is believed to enhance the quality of life and to make the individual resilient to pressures that would otherwise cause suicide. The soul belongs to God and is entrusted to the individual who is ultimately held accountable. To the extent that this norm of accountability for one's own life and soul is transmitted in both sacred and secular versions throughout the community, it could act as one of the normative suicide buffers.

The pastors were not asked direct general questions about their views on and explanations of other forms of deviance in the black community as they were about suicide, but those views were clearly stated in response to the third and fourth vignettes about alcohol/drug abuse and murder, respectively (see Appendix A).

[08099006, VS3.1.] Now this young man is . . . without employment and he have taken a habit of drinking, using various drugs, and his family members are members of the same church. . . . I have been faced with situations basically of that same nature. . . . Because as we know, that is what is causing so many of our black young men to be destroyed today.

[07149002, VS3.2.] Son, let me tell you. This behavior is bad business. It's typical of what is happening to our black men. I preach against this all the time. With the black family losing some of its power 'cause of all these material things. . . . Ernest's behavior is not right, but it's what's happening out there in the world.

[061299001, VS3.1.] Of course alcohol and drug abuse is a major problem. . . . Probably the influence of his friends—they have more influence on him than probably his family has over him. . . . Well, doing what he is doing is wrong . . . but that's a good one because I am dealing with that particular issue right now in the community where we are. Unless we change the environment, change the demand for what he is doing he knows is wrong then we are not going to help the person.

As reported by these pastors, there is no doubt that the black church condemns the use of alcohol and drugs, but note there is a subtle shift from the way in which suicide is condemned. This shift does not seem to be in the degree to which suicide and drug abuse are condemned. Rather, it appears to be the extent to which there are references to conditions or uncontrollable factors that may move one to crime and drugs. The behavior is unacceptable, but understandable because of the system and social conditions, unemployment, lack of education, influence of friends, and so on. "Messin' with drugs is bad business and is a kind of suicide, but times being the way they are—no jobs and all—are killin' our young black men." "There is no excuse for this here young man hanging out there doin' drugs, but what can someone who don't have an education and a job do?" "It's a sin, but who is going to work for minimum wage when they can make 100 times that much standin' on a corner lookin' out for the man?" This same perceptual shading is evident in the assessment given of the vignette depicting a homicide by a youngster with a history of crime (see Appendix A). The pastors were unanimous in condemning the behavior and viewing it as extremely serious, but as with the case of drug abuse, they tended to offer plausible explanations of it.

[07149002, VS4.1.] This behavior is unacceptable, son. It seems to be what we are seeing more and more of in our community. . . . Our situation as a race has created this kind of thing . . . our people don't have the kind of money white folks have. . . . We don't have the clubs and parks for our kids. . . . That's why it is so important for the church to assist these mothers and fathers with their families.

[09039011, VS4.1.] As always, people's responses or reactions have some basis in the deficiency or lack of something that people want. . . . By no means is it justifiable. I am trying to say that perhaps the root of his behavior is a combination of a lot of things. A lot of ramifications if you will. I am trying to show how some things can lead up to, way back there, not having had any parental guidance say from a father.

The pastors' basic views of crime, murder, and drug abuse are similar to their basic view of suicide; they are all sin. However, they tend to assess violence and substance abuse as stemming from environmental factors, societal conditions, economic deprivation, and failure to provide black families with the services and benefits that are afforded to white families. The pastors neither excuse nor justify violent behavior against others or the self-destructive behavior of alcohol and drug abuse. But they see them as explicable in the face of deprivation, while suicide is inexplicable in the face of the same deprivation.

Suicide Is a "White Thing"

This is not to say that the informants had no conception of the social causes of suicide, because when asked specifically to elaborate on this point, their replies were very sociological. All of the pastors pointed out that suicide is a very infrequent pulpit topic and most did not ever preach on it. They saw this lack of direct pastoral attention to the issue as a natural outcome of the low level of suicide in the black community. There are many pressing spiritual and social problems that need frequent addressing from the pulpit, but suicide is not one of them.

The pastors were asked directly why they believed that suicide is less of a problem for the African-American community and why suicide occurs infrequently. Their explanations for black suicide are consistent with the deprivation and deficit theories noted above, namely that the person committing suicide has experienced a breakdown in religious and family ties and stress associated with the assimilative effects of racial integration that is seen as undermining the internal integration of the black community. As we have seen, the specifically religious norms on the unexcusable and inexplicable nature of suicide may be one element buffering against these suicide-inducing pressures.

But the pastors' responses reflect a fusion of these religious norms with secular norms. The message in their assessments is that suicide, in addition to being unholy and sinful, is almost a complete denial of black identity and culture. It is assumed that suicide is outside the black experience. It is simply not done. In the revealing words of the first pastor interviewed, which inspired the title of this paper, "suicide is a white thing."

Suicide is viewed as a white thing not simply because of its recognized greater statistical frequency among whites. Rather, the phrase captures the idea that suicide is antithetical to black culture. This was communicated to the interviewer and first author, who is black, not only by the first pastor but by several others in subsequent interviews. They insisted that he should not even have to ask questions related to blacks and suicide because suicide is a white thing, not a black thing. "As a rule blacks don't kill themselves . . . you should know this already." "Well, being black you should know that black people want to live." "You should know that suicide is somethin' that occurs over there, on the other side of the tracks." "We

want to live, son . . . we want to get there . . . you should know this."

The belief against suicide is so much an assumed part of being black that the pastors were, therefore, a bit surprised to have the question asked, especially by another black person. It is not just an assumed part of being a black religious person. It is assumed to be an inherent part of being black, period. The pastors knew that the interviewer is a religiously committed, active participant in his own church and that the topic at hand was religious beliefs on suicide. Nevertheless, they did not express surprise at the question coming from a religious person; they expressed surprise at the question coming from a black person. They did *not* say, "You should know that, you're a Christian." Rather they said, "You should know that, you're black." The truth is that the interviewer himself took it so much for granted, and was so focused on the content of the religious norms themselves, that no explicit questions about this cultural assumption of "it's a white thing" were in the interview schedule. To maintain commonality across the interviews, no explicit questions on the issue were added, even after it became transparent in the first interview. Yet, the same reactions of surprise at a black person asking the question of why the suicide rate is low in the black community, as well as the occurrence of unsolicited expressions of the basic incompatibility of suicide with the black experience and culture as contrasted with white culture, were common in the interviews.

All of the pastors presented the view that there are unique features of black culture that render some of the same difficulties and problems that might lead to suicide by whites less of a suicide threat for African Americans. The belief is that having to deal historically and currently with economic, political, and social deprivation has made black Americans more resilient against these problems. Indeed, one of their worries was that racial integration, in spite of all its other benefits, may break down some of that resiliency because it may foster blacks taking on white culture and attitudes about suicide.

[Interview 07179003] The suicide rate being so low among blacks goes back to the strength that we have as a culture. It goes back to the value systems that we were taught and even having been taught those value systems. We never get away from them. We have always been aware of what our roles were. We have always been aware of what our strengths were. Our strengths have overpowered our weaknesses. That has made us bold up, brace our shoulders back, and stand firm. In a sense, allow the bullets to bounce off. The bullets hurt, but we've been taught to stand strong.

[Interview 09049013] I think in this case it goes back to our culture. We have been taught down through the years that we as a people don't do these kinds of things . . . committing suicide. As a boy growing up I never knew anything about blacks committing suicide until integration came about and I believe black America then began to take on the traits, if you will, of white America.

[Interview 09229020] We as a race have always been used to hardships. We are more used to hardships than whites. Suicide was always more prevalent among whites than it was blacks. I personally believe that if black folks are killin' theyself it's because of the integration. We've gotten where we're communicating closer with whites every day.

Of course, suicide is condemned by whites as well, and the specifically religious beliefs of white Christians regarding suicide probably do not differ much from the religious beliefs of black Christians expressed by the pastors in this study.[20] However, the concept that whites are fundamentally different in terms of their response to stress is clearly articulated by the pastors in this study. Through the "struggle" black Americans have developed a culture of

resilience to behavior that would otherwise be self-destructive.

[Interview 07149002] It is a low down shame for people to take their lives. That is something I could never quite understand. . . . That's just something our people don't do. I am from the South. Been here all my life. We grew up on the land with values. Nobody took from their neighbor and nobody took themselves out. . . . My mama and dad struggled all their life and their people before them struggled. None of them ever thought about killin' themselves. I have struggled ah . . . you know son . . . we been strugglin' all of our lives. The greater the sufferin' ah . . . you know . . . ah . . . what we going to get will be better in heaven. That's what the ole time preachers said. That's what my people always said . . . ah . . . and so we always coped with whatever the deal was.

[Interview 08099006] Well, on suicide, as I look at it, in the white race, seem'ly they— their views on life is different from the black American, and seem'ly if they are not able to carry out their objectives in life, to me, they gets in a more pressure stage, and they're certain to commit suicide more fastly, to my belief.

The pastors portrayed blacks as being a more religious people than their white counterparts. Additionally, blacks were described as being able to endure more hardships and not succumb to the despair and despondency that leads to suicide. The black experience in America is one of struggle. Survival represents hope and the promise of a better life after death. The church unifies black Americans around a common tradition shaped out of suffering. The church is a source of strength, identity, coping skills, and a reason for living. Thus, the pastors identified secular as well as religious norms forming a cultural buffer against suicide in the black community to keep suicide from having become a black thing. Suicide is excluded as contradictory to what it means to be black. Whites may do it, but blacks do not.

Summary and Conclusions

The most common explanation for the relatively little black suicide proposed by scholars is that the black church and family ameliorate social forces that might otherwise lead to suicide. We have referred to this as the buffering hypothesis and noted that it leaves unspecified what it is that does the buffering. The principal goal of this study was to investigate what some of these buffers might be.

Thirty pastors in one community in a southeastern state were interviewed to elicit their observations and views on suicide in the black community as compared to other forms of deviance such as crime and drug abuse. According to the pastors, the church is a refuge, problem-solver, and moral voice of the black community. They describe the church as central to the black experience, which is consistent with what sociologists of race and ethnicity have been saying for a long time. Assuming the importance of the black church in the larger community as asserted by these pastors and as stated in the literature, we have tentatively identified religiously based beliefs with the potential for countering suicide.

The pastors condemned suicide as an unpardonable sin. Theologically, they defined it as an unpardonable sin "against God's perfect will." Suicide does nothing for the "soul" except place it in peril of eternal damnation. The church recognizes no justification for suicide. Crime and drug abuse were also strongly condemned as immoral, but the pastors seemed to offer explanations of them that differ somewhat from the unequivocal condemnation of suicide. They tended to place some blame on the "system" and hence deflected some of the responsibility away from the individuals. They would not condone or overtly excuse criminal and drug behavior, but given

the circumstances that many blacks faced (e.g., economic, political and social deprivation) they could "understand" how a black person could succumb to these behaviors. Those same circumstances, while recognized as sometimes being factors connected to the act of suicide, were never referred to as making suicide understandable or lessening the individual's responsibility. While our research has uncovered these differences in pastoral perceptions of suicide and other deviance, we have not determined the extent to which these beliefs are shared by the black community at large or differ enough from white perceptions that they account for the lower black suicide rate. That determination awaits further research.

Our research has uncovered another dimension of the pastors' beliefs about suicide to which future research should pay particular attention, namely the perception of suicide as inherently contradictory to the black experience and a complete denial of black identity and culture. The pastors reasoned, "Why talk about suicide? [Not concentrating on suicide in sermons] is not an oversight, it just is not a problem." Problems that might lead to suicide by whites do not pose a threat to black Americans. Blacks have developed an apparent resilience to direct self-destructive behavior. To struggle and endure hardships toughens one to withstand sorrows and religious faith offers hope and the promise of a better life. Suicide is seen as peculiar to white America "across the tracks." Black Americans may get involved in crime and drug abuse, but "to our credit at least we don't kill ourselves. That's a white thing."

We know that crime is disproportionately intraracial. Indeed, 92% of violent crime completed against black victims is committed by black offenders.[21] How do we make sense of this in light of the low rates of black suicide? Why are black citizens so violent toward one another, while so hesitant to commit suicide? Adequate answers to these and similar questions would take us well beyond the scope and data in this paper. At this point any explanation is speculative, but the issue needs at least to be recognized and addressed.

We have suggested here that part of the difference may lie in the religiously based perception (at least partially affecting perceptions in the whole community) that suicide is never justified and never forgivable, while other forms of deviant adaptations are viewed as understandable in light of the injustices and oppression of blacks in American society. Suicide is the ultimate, unforgivable, and unredeemable offense. Abuse of alcohol and drugs, participation in the drug trade, and even violence, although strongly condemned, are not viewed as inexplicable, unforgivable, or unredeemable.

Other possibilities are suggested by the frustration-aggression hypothesis that those in higher status will direct aggression inward while lower-status groups such as African Americans direct the aggression outward.[22] This does not explain why the aggression is directed disproportionately toward others in the same low status. It may be that while the frustration has its roots in the racism of the larger system, the aggression is directed at intraracial targets closer at hand. Similarly, the anomie/strain hypothesis that less access to legitimate opportunity motivates some blacks to turn to innovative and retreatist adaptations in crime and drugs may apply.[23] This and other sources of strain may lead to angry aggression, again with those closer at hand becoming victims.[24]

We recognize, of course, that this discussion of religious perceptions of suicide, other forms of deviant behavior, and other possible explanations of the suicide/crime conundrum really raises more questions than it answers. None of these possibilities, for instance, answers the following questions: Why are both suicide and violence toward other blacks higher for males than females? Are both viewed as more unforgivable for women than men? Why are both suicide and crime higher for black youth? Do differences in normative prohibitions against suicide and crime apply differently by age?

Why do status position and frustration leading to suicide or to violence vary by age and sex? Why are status frustration and strain so disproportionately directed toward other blacks? Is it simply a matter of proximity?

Raising questions, of course, is in the nature of exploratory research. We regard all of what we report here as tentative, the results of searching for the religious and secular meanings attached to suicide in the black community. Further research with systematic samples and inclusion of other types of data collection is needed to show to what extent the exploratory findings and alternative explanations given here can be substantiated.

The limitations of the study are obvious. It is a small-scale, qualitative investigation in one southern community. It provides no direct comparison with white informants and does not include a sample of the general black population.

Other factors in black suicide beyond buffering of moral norms and values are not examined in this study. Therefore, there is no claim to have provided a test of the buffering hypothesis. However, the study has provided evidence of a religiously influenced social meaning of suicide as unacceptable, perhaps even unthinkable, for the vast majority of black Americans. This permits us to go beyond the general hypothesis of the suicide-buffering function of the religious institution in the black community found in the literature to propose the following specific hypothesis: The condemnation of suicide as wrong and as an unthinkable contradiction of black culture is sufficiently pervasive in the black community that it helps to keep the rate of suicide low.

Appendix A

Vignette 1

A church mother you have known for years has changed since her husband of 40 years committed suicide after learning he had prostate cancer. She stays relatively to herself, has dropped out of church activities, has lost weight, and appears unkempt. At first you thought her behavior was typical of mourning, but it has now been well over a year since her husband's demise and she appears to be getting worse instead of better.

1. What would you say about her husband's suicide?
2. How do you define this person's suicide?
3. How should the church respond to the widow?
4. Where would you start in handling the situation?
5. As a clergyman, in what context would you talk to this person?
6. What step or action would you likely take to help get this woman redirected or reintegrated into the church family?
7. Suppose you could have encountered her husband before his suicide. What would you have said and done?

Vignette 2

A 15-year-old has reacted badly to his parents' divorce some months ago. Always extroverted, the child is now quiet and withdrawn. In school the child isolates himself from his peers and has dropped off the basketball team. His friends avoid him and his grades have dropped. His father was always active in his life, and you suspect he feels abandoned by him. His mother, with whom he lives, tends to let him alone to do whatever he wants. The boy has told a school counselor that he is tired of living and that he would like to go to a problem-free place far away where he can find ultimate peace. The child insists he is the reason that his parents aren't living together. He believes the divorce would not have occurred if his parents really loved him. Frustrated, the boy has come to you to tell you of his attempts to find a way to "escape from it all." Crying and rolling up his sleeves slowly, he reveals scars where he has slashed his wrist several times.

1. What is your analysis of the problem?
2. Talk to me about suicide as you would talk to this boy.
3. How would you as a pastor approach this boy's mentioning of suicide?
4. How would you evaluate the seriousness of the situation?

Vignette 3

Ernest is a 28-year-old, single, unemployed man who has a problem with alcohol and multiple drug abuse (marijuana, quaaludes, and crack). Ernest grew up in the church. He was baptized, sang in the youth choir, and always attended Sunday school and church services with his family. His family is still an active part of your congregation. Ernest, on the other hand, spends most of his time drinking very heavily with only several short periods of being sober. Ernest is still living at home with his parents. According to his mother, he comes and goes as he pleases. Ernest has been arrested several times by the local police and his driver's license was suspended more than a year ago for driving while intoxicated. When Ernest is sober he makes an occasional appearance in church. However, when he is "high" he gets together with his old friends who, like him, misuse alcohol and drugs. Ernest needs help and his parents have asked you to intervene.

1. How would you evaluate the seriousness of the situation and what would you do about it?
2. How would you evaluate Ernest's behavior?
3. What steps or action would you take as pastor to redirect or reintegrate Ernest into the church family?
4. Talk to me as you would talk to Ernest.

Vignette 4

Charles is an 18-year-old young man who has just been arrested and charged with the murder of another young man. Charles grew up in the black community in a southeastern city where he lived with his mother, a member of your church, and five siblings. Charles never knew his father as his father abandoned his mother when he was an infant. As the oldest of six children, Charles spent most of his time caring for his younger brothers and sisters while his mother worked as a janitor in a downtown bank. Charles was an average student in high school until he dropped out in his junior year. He claims that he dropped out of school for good reasons. Frustrated, Charles began acting out at home and stealing from his mother's purse. Finally, Charles' mother told him to either get a job or go back to school where he could get his diploma. Unable to get a job, Charles got involved in law violations.

1. How would you evaluate Charles' behavior?
2. How would you evaluate the seriousness of Charles' situation?
3. In your role as a clergyperson, how would you approach this situation?
4. What steps would you take or action would you likely take to redirect the youth into the church family?

Interpreting the Evidence:
Competing Paradigms and the Emergence
of Lesbian and Gay Suicide as a "Social Fact"

KATHLEEN ERWIN

KATHLEEN ERWIN, M.P.H., is a doctoral candidate in the Medical Anthropology Program, Department of Anthropology, at the University of California, Berkeley. Prior to pursuing graduate studies, she worked in the areas of women's health and international health and development. She has been involved in health projects in the United States, China, and Brazil.

Her interest in gay and lesbian suicide began during her master's studies in community health education at the University of California. At the time, Ms. Erwin was conducting research into the social factors affecting alcohol use and mental health among Native Americans as part of her work at a Native American health agency in northern California. She was also involved in research on gay and lesbian mental health. It quickly became apparent that the issue of suicide figured prominently in both topics, and the following essay stemmed from this confluence. It is part of a larger research project exploring the relationships among identity, sexuality, and mental health among gay, lesbian, and "third gender" Native Americans.

While conducting her research, Ms. Erwin was particularly moved by the personal accounts of Native American lesbians and gay men, who experience intense personal trauma due to societal prejudices. Reviewing the literature, what struck her was that many brief references alluded to the frequency and severity of gay and lesbian suicide, yet very few explored the issue as a product of cultural and historical, rather than solely individual, circumstances. Ms. Erwin wrote "Interpreting the Evidence" to examine the production of scientific knowledge within a specific historical and social context. Her hope is that this essay will elaborate new questions and directions for further research and action, thereby contributing to the social acceptance and psychological well being not only of gays and lesbians, but of all people who are stigmatized because of their supposed differences.

Ms. Erwin's current doctoral research, funded by a fellowship from the National Science Foundation, addresses the historical and cultural production of concepts of gender and sexuality among women in an entirely different cultural and historical context: urban China in the late twentieth century.

THE REMOVAL OF homosexuality from the Diagnostic and Statistical Manual in 1973 signaled that the American Psychiatric Association no longer considered homosexuality a psychopathology. Despite this change in definition, however, studies continue to show significantly higher rates of depression, substance abuse, and attempted suicide among lesbians and gay men than among heterosexuals in the United States. This apparent contradiction has been explained in terms of "the myth and fact of gay suicide."[1] The "myth" refers to the discredited but still popular belief that the inherent psychopathology of gay people makes them suicidal; the "fact," to the more contemporary belief that self-destructive behavior among many gays and lesbians in the United States is due to social isolation and the internalization of negative stereotypes.

What are the origins of the myth of gay pathology in U.S. and Western European societies, and how did it come to be widely accepted as an explanation for gay and lesbian psychological distress? What were the forces that revealed this explanation as mythical, and how have new explanations, which view the causal agent as external to the individual, come to be formulated in Western societies? This article attempts to address these questions in order to illuminate how historical and political forces have shaped our contemporary social and medical understanding of, and response to, gay and lesbian psychological distress, and how emerging explanations offer new hope for prevention of mental "dis-ease" among gays and lesbians.

Indicators of Psychological Distress Among Gays and Lesbians

Rates of attempted suicide and suicide mortality among gays and lesbians in the United States are extremely difficult to ascertain, due to incomplete and inaccurate reporting. Many gays and lesbians are not "out" as gay and, even among those who are, their deaths may not be reported as suicide due to the stigma attached to both homosexuality and suicide.[2] Because of this invisibility and underreporting, studies of suicide and attempted suicide among gays and lesbians make no claims to be representative of the gay population nationwide, in terms of gender, age, ethnicity, or distribution. Nevertheless, the accumulated evidence, summarized below, indicates that self-destructive behavior is disturbingly—and disproportionately—high among American gays and lesbians.

In 1977, Jay and Young conducted a study of over 5,000 lesbians and gay men in the United States and Canada, ranging in age from 14 to 82. They reported that 40 percent of gay men and 39 percent of lesbians had attempted or seriously considered suicide; of those who attempted suicide, 53 percent of the men and 33 percent of the women said their homosexuality was a factor.[3] Another study, published in 1978 by Bell and Weinberg, surveyed 575 white gay men, 111 black gay men, 229 white

lesbians, and 64 black lesbians. Bell and Weinberg found that significantly higher percentages of gays than heterosexuals had attempted or seriously considered suicide. The figures were consistent across race and gender: 37 percent of white gay men compared to 13 percent of white heterosexual men; 24 percent of black gay men compared to 2 percent of black heterosexual men; 41 percent of white lesbians compared to 26 percent of white heterosexual women; and 25 percent of black lesbians compared to 19 percent of black heterosexual women.[4]

The proportion of suicides and attempted suicides among gay youth is especially startling. In the Bell and Weinberg study, over half of the lesbians and gay men who had attempted suicide had done so at age 20 years or younger, 36 percent of the black lesbians' and 32 percent of the black gay men's attempts occurred before age 17, while 21 percent of the white lesbians' and 27 percent of the white gay men's occurred by that age.[5] More recently, in 1989, Gibson found suicide to be the main cause of death among gay and lesbian youth, accounting for at least 30 percent of all adolescent suicides (while gays are generally estimated to represent only 10 percent of the population).[6] Gibson and others have calculated the risk of suicide among gay and lesbian youth to be three to six times that of heterosexual adolescents.[7]

High rates of alcoholism and other drug abuse are also reported among gays and lesbians, and have been associated with many of the suicide attempts. Studies indicate that approximately 30 percent of gay men and lesbians could be considered "alcoholic," "heavy" or "excessive" drinkers, or "alcohol dependent."[8] In a 1973 study of 230 white middle-class people, including 89 gay men, 57 lesbians, 40 heterosexual men, and 44 heterosexual women, Saghir and Robins found that 35 percent of lesbians and 30 percent of gay men were alcohol dependent at some point in their lives, compared with 5 percent of heterosexual women and 20 percent of heterosexual men.[9] Gays and lesbians also frequently report feelings of self-hatred, isolation, depression, and low self-esteem.[10]

These data point to high levels of emotional distress among gays and lesbians, but they do not explain the origin of the distress. Up to the contemporary period, such findings were seen as evidence that homosexuality was immoral and inherently pathological; feelings of self-hatred and self-destructiveness result from recognition of one's own immorality or pathology. Charges of immorality were drawn from early Judeo-Christian writings, which were interpreted as condemning same-sex relations. Theories of homosexual pathology became dominant in the nineteenth and early twentieth centuries as part of a larger shift from religious to "scientific" explanations of human behavior. In the last quarter century, researchers and gay and lesbian activists have challenged the religious and medical explanations, proposing instead that oppressive social conditions are the root cause of gay and lesbian suicide and psychological distress. Critically examining these competing paradigms demonstrates how historical, social, and political forces have been instrumental in shaping the scientific and medical response to gay and lesbian psychological distress to the present day.

Homosexuality and Suicide as Sin

In the Judeo-Christian tradition, homosexuality has long been seen as sinful and immoral, but not for the reasons often invoked today. The Jewish proscription on homosexuality in ancient times was directed specifically at males, who faced the death penalty for homosexual acts, while female homosexuality seemed unproblematic. This distinction arose because the proscription was not aimed at eliminating homosexuality, per se, but rather at discouraging Jews from attending Canaanite temples where the holy men engaged in sexual acts with other men who came to worship.

Because the Canaanite holy women engaged in heterosexual acts, lesbianism was not similarly problematized in early Judaism.[11] By 1270 A.D., however, these religious proscriptions had become naturalized, and French legal codes included laws prohibiting both male and female homosexual acts, upon penalty of death.[12]

Religious and secular laws against homosexual acts, which are still widely enforced today throughout many parts of the world, imply that sinful or weak people *choose* to engage in homosexual acts due to lasciviousness and immorality. Suicide within this framework, then, results when the person—faced with burning at the stake, public humiliation, or personal shame—chooses instead a second immoral act, that of taking his or her own life.[13] While the religious model does not medicalize or pathologize homosexuality, Judeo-Christian tenets have nevertheless strongly influenced the response by the modern medical, psychiatric, and public health professions to both homosexuality and the psychological distress with which it is associated.

Homosexual Suicide and Scientific Inquiry in the Nineteenth Century

The religious interpretation of homosexuality and homosexual suicide first began to be challenged in the nineteenth century. Fueling the challenges were rapid social and economic changes, including a shift to industry as the primary mode of production. The consequent influx of single men and women into urban areas led to greater exploration of alternative lifestyles, growth of female and male prostitution, and the establishment of specific geographically defined homosexual neighborhoods. The increasing visibility of homosexual behavior led to a new intellectual dialogue regarding the causes of male homosexuality in particular. These inquiries shifted the focus from viewing homosexuality as a religious concern to viewing it as a medical and biological one, and led to the emergence of the "homosexual" as a social category and topic of scientific discourse. This shift can be seen as part of a larger social trend of secular institutions using "reason" to actively challenge the dominance of the Christian church in a variety of areas newly investigated by "science."[14]

Competing for supremacy in late nineteenth century European thought were two main theories of homosexuality. One posited that homosexuality was a nonpathological, "natural," and harmless variation, and the other labeled it a mental disorder, or "sickness," in which suicidal tendencies were not uncommon. Both of these perspectives challenged the idea that homosexual acts were "chosen sin" or criminal, and thus contested the dominance of the Christian church over sexual matters.[15] Moreover, both drew upon prevailing notions of biological determinism. Thus, even though the "homosexuality as harmless" proponents intended to diminish the stigmatization of homosexuals, they subscribed to the biological premise that also lay at the heart of the sickness hypothesis.

Beginning in the 1860s, the theory of homosexuality as an innate, nonpathological variation was promoted by social reformers such as Karl Ulrichs, Havelock Ellis, Edward Carpenter, Edward Stevenson, and Magnus Hirschfeld.[16] Karl Ulrichs, himself a homosexual and an attorney, did not see homosexuality itself as a cause of psychological distress or suicide.[17] Indeed, he saw homosexuals (whom he termed "Urnings") as mentally healthy, and believed they not only were harmless, but perhaps even particularly valuable for their combined male and female qualities.[18] Later, Ellis, Hirschfeld, Carpenter, and Stevenson embraced these views and joined Ulrichs in advocating the repeal of laws prohibiting homosexual acts.

The competing formulation, viewing mental distress and suicidality as manifestations of homosexual pathology, found one of its strongest advocates in the well-respected Austrian psychiatrist Richard von Krafft-Ebing. A leading proponent of the medical model, Krafft-Ebing believed a heritable defect resulting in an abnormal nervous system could be traced in sexually "pathological" individuals. This pathology resulted in higher rates of mental abnormalities, suicide, and violence among sexual "perverts" than among other men.[19] Thus, Krafft-Ebing argued, for their own protection and that of society, perverts should be institutionalized in asylums.

As a psychiatrist who studied homosexuality among the mentally ill, rather than in the general population, it is not surprising that Krafft-Ebing came to these conclusions—nor was it surprising to his contemporary adversaries. Ulrichs, critiquing the medical-pathological theories advocated by such heterosexual doctors, complained in 1879: "My scientific opponents are mostly doctors of the insane . . . for example, Westphal, v. Krafft-Ebing, Stark. They have observed Urnings in lunatic asylums. They have apparently never seen mentally healthy Urnings. The published views of the doctors for the insane are accepted by others."[20]

Despite Ulrichs' protestations, the medical-pathological interpretation had become dominant by the early twentieth century. It dovetailed with the then-popular Darwinian view of sexual intercourse as evolving purely for the purposes of reproduction.[21] Moreover, it did not pose a direct threat to religious proscriptions against homosexual acts. Supported by medical doctors and scientists, Krafft-Ebing's theories held sway over the "unscientific" theories advocated by homosexuals and other "social reformers."

Although these two competing formulations, both presupposing the fundamentally individual nature of homosexuality, took center stage in the scientific and social debates of the late nineteenth century, the seeds of an alternative formulation were also being sown. Emile Durkheim's landmark sociology treatise,

Suicide, published in 1897, posited that suicide was not an individual phenomenon, but a "social fact" that could be explicated through sociological methods.[22] Despite its importance to the development of sociology, Durkheim's thesis was not extended to the question of homosexual suicide, which came to be viewed as a medical and psychological "fact" rather than a social one. It took nearly three-quarters of a century before the social facts underlying homosexual suicide received serious scientific attention.

Psychoanalytic Theory and Homosexual Suicide

It was in this highly charged context of competing theories and contested disciplinary boundaries that Sigmund Freud, in the early twentieth century, proposed his still controversial psychoanalytic theories of homosexuality and psychopathology. Challenging the biological basis of mental conditions, Freud proposed that sexuality, and in turn homosexuality, was primarily the product of early psychological development and familial relations, rather than neurological defects. While he conceded that in some cases homosexuality could be inborn, he contended that when psychoanalytic facts were considered, "the supposition that nature in a freakish mood created a 'third sex' falls to the ground."[23]

Freud believed that certain neuroses were associated with homosexuality, and could be traced to abnormal psychological development and the reversal of the Oedipal complex for both men and women.[24] With regard to homosexual suicide specifically, in "The Psychogenesis of a Case of Homosexuality in a Woman," published in 1920, Freud noted that an attempted suicide was the precipitating event leading to the woman's therapy. While the woman attributed her suicide attempt to rejection by another woman, Freud interpreted it as "wish-fulfillment" and "self-punishment." That is, he saw the suicide attempt as moti-

vated by the frustrated wish of the girl to have a child by her father, and a death wish for one or both of her parents that had been turned upon herself.[25] Thus, the suicide attempt was neither a manifestation of an innate neurological defect (as Krafft-Ebing might have supposed), nor an expression of the woman's deep grief; rather, it demonstrated the continuing enactment of the Oedipal drama gone awry in a female homosexual.

Initially, Freud's theories on human sexuality were sharply criticized as unscientific. However, over time, psychoanalytic theory became widely accepted, and by the 1930s in the United States, it had become the foundation for seeing homosexuality as psychopathological.[26] This interpretation derived from the strong Christian tradition in the United States, as well as the American emphasis on individualism, that is, the belief that individuals' conditions are largely determined by their individual characteristics. Moreover, medicalization, rather than criminalization, was considered a much more humane and liberal treatment of social deviants, as it still is in many quarters today. It was in response to many of Freud's basic tenets that more recent alternative theories to the concept of homosexuality as sickness have been developed.

Challenging the Pathological Models of Gay Suicide

The political upheavals of the 1960s and 1970s created a new social and intellectual climate for challenging the pathological basis of "deviance" and psychological distress among many oppressed groups. With respect to homosexual suicide specifically, these challenges led to a shift from emphasis on pathology to a focus on the social conditions that produce psychological distress among homosexuals.

The gay liberation movement that developed in the United States in the 1970s was largely responsible for the development of the concept of a "gay identity," based on the status of being a sexual minority.[27] Activists strove to challenge the widely accepted psychoanalytic notion that homosexuality was a sickness resulting from childhood trauma. Instead, echoing Ulrichs' and Ellis's nineteenth century theories, many claimed that homosexuality was a healthy, natural outcome on the spectrum of sexual possibilities. Thus, homosexuality itself —whether innate or fixed early in a child's development—is neither a sin nor a sickness, and cannot be forcibly changed or cured. These claims were supported by the findings of Kinsey and other sex researchers in the 1950s and 1960s, who found a wide range of diversity in sexual behavior, and found bisexual and homosexual behavior to be much more common than previously believed.[28]

Gay activists and medical professionals recognized that gays and lesbians suffer from high rates of suicide and attempted suicide, substance abuse, and other self-destructive behavior. Given these same facts, what is striking is that they reframed the issue of psychological distress and self-destructiveness as one in which the proximate cause was feelings of isolation and self-hatred, and the ultimate cause lay in society's intolerance. The feelings of self-hatred come from both internalized and external homophobia, that is, negative attitudes toward homosexuality and gay people.[29] Thus, echoing Durkheim's thesis of the previous century, homosexual suicide was reframed as a "social fact," rather than an individual psychological one.[30]

The Social Facts:
Psychological Effects of Heterosexism

According to this construction, gays and lesbians grow up in a homophobic society in which they learn that homosexuality is immoral and sick, concepts drawn from the religious and early medical-psychological theories. At some point in their lives, varying from person to person, they come to realize they are different from most other people based on their erotic and emotional attractions to people of the same biological sex. By this time, however, they have already internalized society's homophobia. As role models, most gays and lesbians have only the media's negative stereotypes of sick, sinful, "effeminate" men or "masculine" women. When they try to tell their families, they are often rejected and/or sent to psychotherapy to be "cured." Moreover, they must continue to "come out" throughout their lives, if they want themselves and their significant relationships recognized. They may face discrimination in the workplace, in housing, and in other social and economic arenas. Faced with lack of role models, fear of public disclosure, negative self-image, familial rejection and, most recently, fear and deep grief in the face of the AIDS epidemic, many become self-destructive.[31]

Although the term "homophobia" is still commonly used to refer to isolated or individual-level demonstrations of negativism toward gays and lesbians, more recently, the term "heterosexism" has begun to replace "homophobia" in describing the myriad ways in which society discriminates against sexual minorities. Heterosexism incorporates both the idea of dislike of homosexuality and gay people, and the societal and institutional-level discrimination against gays and lesbians. It shifts the focus from blaming prejudiced individuals for their "homophobia" to placing the onus on larger social institutions and values. In addition, this term draws a parallel with other forms of discrimination, like racism and sexism.[32]

Viewing heterosexism as the primary underlying cause of mental distress among gays and lesbians holds two implications for "treatment." The first is that the ultimate cause of the disease, heterosexism, must be actively addressed through efforts to change the laws, institutions, and attitudes that oppress homosexuals. The second is that the proximate causes of mental distress—that is, feelings of isolation, shame, negative parental response, and other manifestations of stigmatization—must be addressed through responsive forms of individual, group, and family counseling, which recognize not only the environmental causes of the distress but also that all aspects of psychological distress may *not* necessarily be related to one's experience as gay.[33]

Despite the removal of homosexuality from the Diagnostic and Statistical Manual III, many medical professionals continue to have heterosexist attitudes that impede their ability to recognize and correctly diagnose psychological problems among gay and lesbian clients.[34] Others continue to seek evidence of neurological abnormalities to explain the "cause" of homosexuality.[35] As a result of these attitudes and ingrained biomedical beliefs, the psychological problems of many gay and lesbian clients continue to go untreated or mistreated. In a study of psychiatrists, Kourany found that "the magnitude of [psychiatrists'] lack of exposure to [homosexual youth] suggested that they either did not recognize or did not want to treat these patients."[36] Moreover, lesbians and gay men continue to cite fear of heterosexist response as a primary reason for not getting adequate health care.[37]

Ongoing Challenges to Explicating Gay and Lesbian Suicide

Even among those who accept the premise that psychological distress among gays and lesbians results from societal heterosexism, many find this formulation a necessary, but insufficient, explanation for gay and lesbian suicide. This critique is based on the recognition of the immense social, economic, and cultural diversity among lesbians, gays, and others who engage in same-sex sexual activity in the United States. Thus, the formulation of heterosexism as the sole root of psychological distress is too narrow, and ignores other kinds of oppression experienced by many sexual minorities. Moreover, continuing research in the field of sexuality shows that not even all

lesbians and gay men agree on what it means to themselves to be "homosexual" or "gay"—despite restrictive legal definitions focused specifically on particular behaviors. These critiques form the basis for continuing exploration of the social determinants of gay and lesbian suicide.

Lesbians and the Women's Movement

Throughout the modern period, theories of causation regarding female homosexuality, also used to explain psychological distress among lesbians, have for the most part been patterned after the theories developed by men to explain male homosexuality and psychological distress. Thus, both Ulrichs and Krafft-Ebing believed that female homosexuals were the mirror images of the male homosexuals upon whom they based their theories. Along similar lines, Freud's theory of human sexuality, both heterosexual and homosexual, relies on the male-centered notion of "penis envy," which differentially affected men and women. This conflation has served not only to obscure the existence of lesbians in history, but more importantly, for the purposes of understanding lesbian suicidality, it has also obscured the social conditions that contribute to psychological distress among lesbians.

Recognizing this oversight, lesbians, particularly white lesbian feminists, have challenged both the long-standing conflation of lesbianism with male homosexuality, as well as the notion that heterosexism alone accounts for the oppression and psychological distress they may experience in this society. They argue that their identity as women is as central to their life experience as their identity as lesbians. Some have sought more fluid definitions of their sexuality, such as "woman-identified women" and "political lesbians."[38] Rich argues that lesbians see their oppression as linked to men's control over women's sexuality and reproduction.[39]

In the realm of lesbian mental health, these arguments suggest that the economic and social oppression lesbians experience as women is as critical to their feelings of self-worth as is their experience as lesbians. This point is graphically illustrated in the alarming statistics on suicide attempts among women (as compared with men) cited earlier in this article. It implies that prevention of psychological distress among lesbians must come through addressing sexist attitudes and structures, as well as heterosexist ones.

Gay and Lesbian People of Color

For people of color in the United States, membership in particular ethnic minority groups may be central to their identity, and they often feel marginalized by racism in both the gay movement and the larger society. They may come from families and communities where the norms and expectations of men and women are different from those in the dominant culture. These cultural norms have also shaped their experiences with heterosexism and psychological distress.

When youth of color experience racism in the larger society, they often turn to their families and communities for support and role models.[40] However, gay and lesbian youth of color are frequently rejected by their families when they "come out." Moreover, some youth come from cultures that have even stricter sex role expectations than does the dominant culture. In order to "come out," these youth must leave their families and reject their cultures to fit into the predominantly white gay culture of urban America. The psychological stress of familial rejection and cultural alienation in an already hostile social environment often leads to increased levels of psychological distress.[41]

Alternative Constructions of Sexuality

Cultural differences can also provide an avenue for exploring dominant constructions of sexuality, and for creating, or recreating, alternative understandings of sexual diversity that challenge heterosexism. For example, recent scholarship by anthropologists and

Native Americans, especially gay and lesbian American Indians, has rekindled interest in the traditional "berdache" and "amazon" roles found in many Native American tribes.[42] The berdache was a biological male who expressed "feminine" attributes that were understood to be endowed by the Creator in a dream or vision. Girls might also express the "masculine" attributes of amazons. A child found to have these special attributes was given special social roles and responsibilities throughout life, including, in many cases, that of the marital or sexual partner of others of the same biological sex (who were not berdache or amazon). Recent research has indicated that these beliefs have not died out among Native Americans and, in fact, in some cases are reemerging along with the resurgence of Indian identity and pride.[43] Many other cultural groups maintain traditional attitudes and values regarding identity and sexuality that differ greatly from the Western European religious, medical, and psychological views dominant in the United States.[44] These varying cultural constructions of same-sex relationships both provide alternative possibilities for understanding same-sex relations and highlight the significant role of social attitudes in shaping identity, self-esteem, and mental health.

The very definitions of lesbian and gay "identity" in contemporary Euro-American culture have also been challenged by the now burgeoning research on sexuality in many disciplines and by the self-proclaimed sex radicals of the 1990s; these alternative constructions likewise have implications for mental health.[45] For instance, although the terms "gay" and "lesbian" generally refer to people whose primary emotional and erotic attachments are to people of the same biological sex, often a disjuncture exists between people's behavior and their identity. The distinction between behavior and identity raises important questions with respect to the impact of heterosexism on mental health. For instance, does a married man who occasionally engages in homosexual sex, but considers himself straight, face the same kind of oppression as a self-identified gay man? Does a woman who is celibate and "passes as straight," but considers herself a lesbian, face the same kind of oppression as a lesbian who is engaged in an openly gay relationship? Do gays and lesbians whose behavior challenges dominant gender roles experience more psychological distress and opposition than those who conform to dominant gender roles? How these identities, as well as behaviors, differently impact the mental health of different individuals is still very poorly understood.[46]

Most recently, the term "queer," utilized to ridicule homosexuals in the past, has been reclaimed by many radicals. Popularized by the radical gay organization, Queer Nation, "queer" has become a challenge to restrictive categories such as "lesbian," "gay," or "bisexual," which are seen as separating and marginalizing people rather than highlighting their shared oppression. Instead, queer includes all people who have been marginalized by society, and who refuse to assimilate to mainstream norms, again introducing the concept of "choice" into the notion of sexual orientation.[47]

As for its implications for mental health, the 1990s radicals' view of oppression as inclusive of all marginalized groups, rather than fragmented among different groups, is useful, since it draws attention to the need for broad social change to address feelings of low self-worth, isolation, and suicide affecting many marginalized groups in the United States. At the same time, it is necessary to acknowledge that different forms of oppression do affect groups and individuals differently, as evidenced by the racism, sexism, and heterosexism experienced by lesbians of color, for instance.

New Directions for Public Health and Social Science Research

Research in sexuality and sexual identity, and their implications for mental heath, is still rela-

tively new, especially research that takes into account social intolerance as the ultimate causal agent in psychological distress. The continuing challenges to this formulation highlight the historical, social, and cultural specificity, as well as fluidity, of current conceptions of homosexual suicide.

One problematic arena concerns the kind of published research that informs theory and practice. Although homosexuality is increasingly becoming a topic of academic research and debate, there is a noticeable paucity of reference to gay suicide in the public health and mental health literature.[48] Despite the occasional token article found in many journals, the vast majority of articles examining the relationship between sexual identity, mental health, and suicide appear in such journals as *The Journal of Homosexuality*. Research on suicide among gay people of color and lesbians is especially scant, as most articles on homosexual suicide focus primarily on the experiences of white gay men.[49] Given the high rates of gay and lesbian suicide, the neglect of gay and lesbian suicide in academic journals points to a high degree of heterosexism.[50]

A second topic for critical reflection by social scientists, practitioners, and researchers involves the definitions, assumptions, and methodologies that form the foundations of scientific inquiry, and shape our understanding of human behavior. In the area of gay and lesbian suicide, this means continually questioning underlying assumptions about the relationships between mental health and sexual identity, and exploring new methods of understanding the complexity of human behavior and its changing cultural meanings. Such exploration raises new challenges and questions for researchers, including: How does one measure the impact of heterosexism on a person's mental health, and how does one measure the cumulative effects of multiple oppressions? Can the effect of one oppression ever be separated from another oppression among people who are multiply oppressed? How do cultural ideas about gender and gender roles differently affect the mental health of those who challenge those roles and of those who do not—even if both are "gay," or if *neither* identifies as gay? Moreover, how can we better understand the cultural and social institutions or individual qualities and actions that mitigate the effects of oppression? Research in the fields of sociology, anthropology, social epidemiology, and social psychology has begun to tackle these questions through predominantly qualitative methods and approaches that more actively involve community members in research design and implementation.[51] Efforts in this direction must be developed and expanded in order to broaden the base of knowledge that informs social, scientific, and public health theories.

Conclusion

The phenomenon of disturbingly high rates of homosexual suicide and psychological distress has long been recognized, although only in recent decades has it come to be studied as such. In order to better understand the social and medical response to this public health issue, this article has examined contending theories of gay and lesbian suicide, from biblical times to the present, that have dominated European, and later North American, thought. The religious, medical, and psychological theories share a common emphasis on problematizing *individual* psychology or physiology as the root cause of homosexual suicide. In contrast, more contemporary social theories that

emerged in the 1970s have located the cause of gay and lesbian suicide and psychological distress in the oppressive forces of an unjust and intolerant society.

These strikingly divergent approaches to explaining high rates of lesbian and gay psychological distress highlight the extent to which scientific research and theories are shaped by historical, political, social, and cultural processes. Placing the religious and medical theories in their historical context and critically examining their underlying assumptions illuminates the origins of the myth of homosexual suicide and the reasons for its persistence in some quarters today. Similarly, the historical and political forces of the last two decades have led to the emergence of new theories that challenge the myth of gay and lesbian suicide, and begin to incorporate issues of gender, cultural, and class diversity into our understanding of gay and lesbian mental health. Adopting this latter framework calls for a radical restructuring of the fields of psychology and public health, away from the blame-the-victim approach that sees psychological problems as rooted in the individual, rather than in society. Moreover, critical reflection on these contemporary views points toward provocative new directions for social science and public health research.

Acknowledgments—Special thanks to Nancy Krieger and Karen Franklin for their inspiration, assistance, and thoughtful editing, and to Vern Bullough and an anonymous reviewer for their helpful comments in revising this article.

The Health Care System

Jeanne Quint Benoliel. "Health Care Providers and Dying Patients: Critical Issues in Terminal Care," *Omega: Journal of Death and Dying* 18, no. 4 (1988): 341–63. A pioneer in the care of terminally ill patients, Benoliel looks at three main areas of concern: the education of those who provide terminal care, the stresses associated with such care, and the organizational structures and institutional values that influence how care is provided. Benoliel notes that the profit motive, which emphasizes efficiency and a patient-as-product orientation, creates a climate that does not favor innovative changes.

John O. Caldwell, I. O. Orubuloye, and Pat Caldwell. "Underreaction to AIDS in Sub-Saharan Africa," *Social Science and Medicine* 34, no. 11 (1992): 1169–82. This account offers an instructive look at how communities shape initiatives and priorities in public health programs. Beliefs about the causes of death and social attitudes about sharing private information are important influences on how people respond to health crises. Beliefs about the role of fate or destiny and life after death, may play an even more critical role. This applies to our own responses to death and dying, not only in the obvious case of AIDS, but with respect to such issues as infant mortality, which occurs at a higher rate in the United States than in most other industrialized countries. What causes people in our nation to underreact to some public health issues?

Melvin Konner. *Medicine at the Crossroads: The Crisis in Health Care.* New York: Pantheon, 1993. Going beyond the headlines telling us health care in the United States needs repair, Konner points out that the problems are not altogether new nor can they be solved solely by governmental action or decisions made by physicians and other caregivers. Current dilemmas are addressed in an engaging style, laced with illuminating stories, providing excellent coverage of the doctor-patient relationship, the allocation of health care resources, the search for "magic bullet" cures, genetic engineering and reproductive technologies, AIDS, medical quality assurance and outcomes assessment, life-span extension and care of the aged, and the right to die.

Balfour Mount. "Whole Person Care: Beyond Psychosocial and Physical Needs," *American Journal of Hospice and Palliative Care* 10, no. 1 (1993): 28–37. Although the concept of caring for the whole person has long had advocates, medical care tends to be focused almost exclusively on the body. In correcting this imbalance, suffering needs to be viewed within a framework that takes account of the whole person. This piece is an inspiration and a challenge toward acknowledging the interrelationships among body, mind, and spirit.

Sherwin B. Nuland. *How We Die: Reflections on Life's Final Chapter.* New York: Alfred A. Knopf, 1994. Tales of individuals' deaths are used to explain how and why people die. These stories and explanations not only further our understanding of the distinctive features of various causes of death—heart disease, cancer, AIDS, accident, murder, and suicide—they increase our appreciation for life and living.

Carol Pogash. *As Real as It Gets: The Life of a Hospital at the Center of the AIDS Epidemic.* New York: Birch Lane Press, 1992. Focusing on the unfolding daily dramas at San Francisco General Hospital, journalist Carol Pogash describes the impact of AIDS on patients and their caregivers. As we read the individual human stories of fear and compassion, we begin to grasp the tragic reality that lies behind the medical, social, ethical, and political issues of AIDS.

Avery D. Weisman. "Appropriate Death and the Hospice Program," *The Hospice Journal* 4, no. 1 (1988): 65–77. The conditions that nurture the likelihood of achieving an "appropriate death" are discussed here by the man who pioneered the use of the term. "An appropriate death," says Weisman, "has been defined as a death one might choose, had one a choice." The success of the hospice concept is due in significant measure to the perception that it provides an environment that helps people die appropriate deaths.

Medical Ethics and Decision Making

George J. Annas. "The Health Care Proxy and the Living Will," *New England Journal of Medicine* 324 (25 April 1991): 1210–13. This essay examines the historical context of the living will and its limitations, as well as recent moves toward laws implementing health care proxies, which allow competent persons to designate someone to make treatment decisions if the signer becomes unable to make them.

Lisa Belkin. *First, Do No Harm.* New York: Simon and Schuster, 1993. Belkin, a medical reporter for the *New York Times,* takes the reader through one summer at a Houston hospital, telling the stories of doctors, patients, families, and hospital staff members as they confront high-tech medicine and its extraordinary capacity to sustain life. The work of hospital ethics committees is highlighted as the challenges of medical ethics are described in vivid, human terms.

Howard Brody. "Assisted Death: A Compassionate Response to Medical Failure," *New England Journal of Medicine* 327 (5 November 1992): 1384–88. Is it ever morally appropriate for physicians to assist a patient's dying? What should be the stance of the law toward physician-assisted death? Increasingly, these questions are the subject of public debate, both by private citizens and in legislative chambers. Brody suggests that resolving the dilemma might involve neither outright prohibition of assisted death nor its establishment as standard policy.

Courtney S. Campbell. "Body, Self, and the Property Paradigm," *Hastings Center Report* 22, no. 5 (September–October 1992): 34–42. Do I *own* my body? May I allow for its commercial exploitation in the marketplace? Is it ethically permissible to exchange a kidney or an eye for monetary reward? Given the scarcity of organs and lengthy waiting lists for transplantation, is it a reasonable option for society to make organ donation a commercial venture to increase the incentive for such donations? In a straightforward fashion, Campbell explores the concept of the body as property and discusses how our understanding of this concept affects efforts to supply organs to those who need them.

Arthur L. Caplan. *If I Were a Rich Man, Could I Buy a Pancreas? and Other Essays on the Ethics of Health Care.* Bloomington: Indiana University Press, 1992. In addition to the title essay, which provides a lucid examination of problems in the current system of allocating organs for transplantation, Caplan tackles some of the most pressing issues in medical ethics, including animal and human experimentation, advances in reproduction and genetics, chronic illness and aging, and trade-offs between technology and cost-containment. Of special interest are his opening essays on the nature of applied ethics in health care and his answer to the question, "Moral experts and moral expertise: Does either exist?"

Renee C. Fox and Judith P. Swazey. *Spare Parts: Organ Replacement in American Society.* New York: Oxford University Press, 1992. Known for their studies of medical experimentation and organ transplantation, Fox and Swazey trace the rapid expansion of such procedures during the 1980s. The questions that transplantation raises in the "medical commons" are highlighted in an account of the Jarvik-7 artificial heart. For admirers of their work, the last chapter is especially poignant. In it, Fox and Swazey give their reasons for leaving a field of study in which they have been active for many years as medical anthropologists. The account of their "final journey" deserves careful consideration by citizens and policymakers alike, as they raise issues about the limits of technology and the distribution of medical resources.

Harold L. Klawans. *Life, Death, and In Between: Tales of Clinical Neurology.* New York: Paragon House, 1992. This personal account of a physician's experiences illuminates the process of arriving at a diagnosis and making decisions about medical care in life-or-death situations. In the context of these stories, Klawans poses questions that are not easily answered: When is a hopelessly ill and comatose patient considered dead? Should doctors fight to extend a life that cannot be saved? When is prolonging life just prolonging the final agony? Emphasizing the patient's role in making such decisions, Klawans helps us explore the edges of life and death.

Violence

James Garbarino, Nancy Dubrow, Kathleen Kostelny, and Carole Pardo. *Children in Danger: Coping with the Consequences of Community Violence.* San Francisco: Jossey-Bass, 1992. The meaning of danger in their lives is explored through accounts of children living in war zones from Mozambique to Cambodia to Israel and Palestine as well as in the inner city of Chicago. How does living in chronic danger affect children's experiences of exploration, growth, and development? The answer: "It threatens the very core of what they need to make a go of their lives." This is an important look at the effects of violence in children's lives, as is the earlier work by Garbarino, Kostelny, and Dubrow, *No Place to Be a Child: Growing Up in a War Zone* (Lexington, Mass.: Lexington Books, 1991).

Susan Goodwillie, ed. *Voices from the Future: Our Children Tell Us About Violence in America.* New York: Crown, 1993. Produced through interviews by members of Children's Express, this is the story of violence in the lives of children and adolescents as told in their own words. We hear stories of violence at home and in the streets, at school and in jail; violence that results from disputes over turf, racism, and homophobia. Accounts of how children cope with violence are found alongside expressions of hope that things can change for the better.

Christie W. Kiefer. "Militarism and World Health," *Social Science and Medicine* 34, no. 7 (1992): 719–24. War does not come cheaply. Preparing for conflict causes the diversion of resources, suppression of dissent, environmental damage, and, often, crime and terrorism. These effects are pronounced in less developed nations, where the impact on poor people is manifested in ill health and increased mortality. Kiefer defines the various meanings of the word *militarism* and shows how its consequences for health are both serious and pervasive. Is the trade-off between military and health expenditures worth the sacrifice?

Kody Scott. *Monster: The Autobiography of an L. A. Gang Member.* New York: Atlantic Monthly Press, 1993. The violence and mayhem of everyday life in South Central Los Angeles is depicted in this chronicle of a world where there is risk even in crossing the street and where any slight, real or imagined, may be met with retribution in a constant war for turf and respect. Earning the nickname "Monster" for acts of violence that repulsed even fellow gang members, Scott runs the gauntlet of juvenile hall, probationary camp, Youth Authority, and various jails and prisons, including Soledad and San Quentin. He wrote this account from his cell in solitary confinement at Pelican Bay, a maximum-security state prison in California.

Debra Umberson and Kristin Henderson. "The Social Construction of Death in the Gulf War." *Omega: Journal of Death and Dying* 25, no. 1 (1992): 1–15. The Gulf War was notable for the absence of death in military and media reports. When death was mentioned, euphemisms ("collateral damage") were used to create a sense of distance and encourage denial. How do you construct a social reality whereby the deaths that occur in the context of war become acceptable? Umberson and Henderson examine the psychological and social mechanisms that facilitate acceptance of combat and of the deaths, on both sides, that inevitably occur.

Suicide

Silvia Sara Canetto. "She Died for Love and He for Glory: Gender Myths of Suicidal Behavior," *Omega: Journal of Death and Dying* 26, no. 1 (1992–1993): 1–17. Studies show that women attempt suicide more often than men while men complete suicide more often than women. Further, women are said to engage in suicidal behavior for love, men for pride and performance. Canetto looks at whether these perceived differences have any basis in reality. Might our shared assumptions influence the suicidal choices made by women and men?

Fred Cutter. *Art and the Wish to Die.* Chicago: Nelson-Hall, 1983. Making use of extensive illustrations, Cutter combines art history with suicidology in this presentation dealing with themes of self-injury in art. From the earliest surviving work of self-injury in the visual arts (a

portrayal of the death of Ajax in 540 B.C.E..),
Cutter has identified over a thousand examples
of this artistic theme in Western, Eastern, and
indigenous cultures. Historical and cross-cultural attitudes toward suicide and its prevention
become evident as one notes the changing depiction of self-injury through the ages and across
cultures.

Glen Evans and Norman L. Farberow. *The Encyclopedia of Suicide.* New York: Facts on File,
1988. A reference book that's also interesting to
read, this volume includes an extensive section
on the history of suicide by Farberow and thorough coverage in encyclopedic form of the important topics related to suicide and self-injury.
Sources of information about suicide and its prevention are listed in an appendix.

Herbert Hendin. "Psychodynamics of Suicide with
Particular Reference to the Young," *American
Journal of Psychiatry* 148, no. 9 (September
1991): 1150–58. To understand suicide risk and
behavior, we must become familiar with the psychodynamics of suicide. This is particularly
important when interacting with young people
who threaten suicide or engage in suicidal behavior. This article, written for clinical professionals,
offers an overview of the main points about the
mental and emotional components of suicide.

Edwin S. Shneidman. "Some Controversies in
Suicidology: Toward a Mentalistic Discipline,"
Suicide and Life-Threatening Behavior 23, no. 4
(1993): 292–98. Widely acknowledge as the
"father of suicidology," Shneidman argues in this
paper that mental pain (which he terms *psychache*) has a life of its own and deserves to be
recognized as separate from the organic
processes of the brain, "the organ that cradles
the processes of the mind." Without discounting
the value of knowledge about the sociocultural
or biological factors that influence suicide,
Shneidman maintains that the human impulse
toward self-destruction is a decision of mind to
stop the psychache, and suicidologists must not
lose sight of this fact. Shneidman brings his considerable wit and intelligence to bear on the
"philosophic war" between dealing with the
mental pain that leads to suicide and merely
masking its symptoms with drugs.

part three

Personal Dimensions of Loss

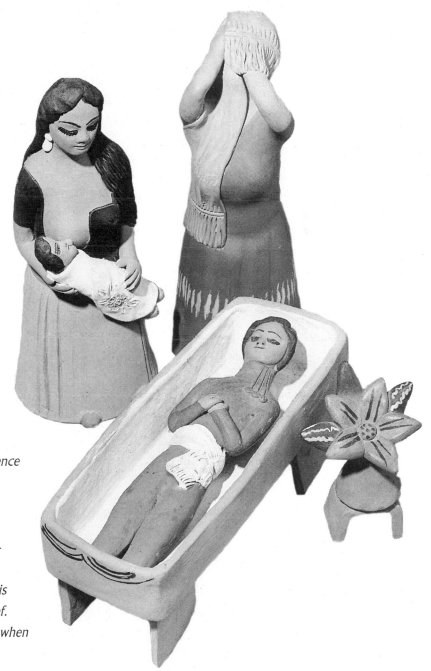

*H*aving examined dying and death in the contexts of culture as well as social institutions and values, we now take a closer look at the impact of death on individuals and families. Everyone has experienced some kind of loss. Relatively few people, however, pay attention to the nature of grief by consciously investigating its dynamics and processes. Yet doing so can help people deal with the losses that inevitably accompany human life.

Unfortunately, when attention is given to grieving, it is often confined to interpreting the experience in terms of a stage-based model of grief that is prone to being misunderstood. Having heard about various stages of grief—denial, bargaining, and acceptance, for example —people sometimes assume that this model constitutes the whole of grief. They become surprised or worried when their own experience does not match the theory. In fact, there is no single right way to grieve. The response to loss varies widely among individuals and across cultures.

Our world view is important in conditioning our understanding of grief. In recent times, the predominant Euro-American view has been that successful grieving means breaking emotional ties between the bereaved and the deceased, which frees the bereaved person's emotional or psychic energy to be reinvested in new relationships and activities. This view of grief is quite different from the romanticist understanding that prevailed in the last century, as Margaret Stroebe and her colleagues point out in "Broken Hearts or Broken Bonds: Love and Death in Historical Perspective." In this earlier world view, the death of a beloved person was a defining event in the life of the survivor, signaling the beginning of what was often a lifelong memorialization of the deceased. Intimate relationships were not easily broken.

This fidelity to memories of the deceased is found not only in nineteenth-century expressions of grief, but in a great many cultures, both past and present. Indeed, despite theories of grief that may suggest otherwise, there is growing recognition that maintaining emotional bonds with a deceased loved one is common among bereaved persons in modern societies as well.

In "Grief: Re-forming Life's Story," John Kelly explains how the death of a loved one requires survivors to reconstruct their life stories. Central to our life stories are images of ourselves and our relationships. Rather than severing our ties to the deceased, adapting to loss means incorporating it into our ongoing life story. Examples of this process are described by Dennis Klass in "Solace and Immortality: Bereaved Parents' Continuing Bond with Their Children," as well as in the article by Phyllis Silverman, Steven Nickman, and William Worden, "Detachment Revisited: The Child's Reconstruction of a Dead Parent."

The death of a child is usually experienced by parents as an irreparable loss. One does not "get over" such a loss; one finds ways to live with it. Klass notes that the continuing interaction with an inner representation of the dead child is, for many parents, a source of comfort and solace. This seems true not only for parents whose child has died, but also for survivors of other types of bereavement.

As Silverman and her colleagues found in their study of children whose parents had died, developing an inner construction of the deceased may in fact contribute to healthy coping. Bereaved individuals frequently are counseled to disengage or separate from the deceased; "holding on" or perpetuating his or her memory is often viewed as thwarting good adjustment. That view is now being replaced by an understanding that the goal of grief work may be rather to accommodate *the loss.*

Think of the losses in your life; did the messages communicated by family and friends echo the conventional wisdom of getting over the loss and going on with your life? Or did these messages reflect the value of retaining memories of the person who died and his or her significance to you? Mementos and keepsakes that link our memories with the deceased can be touchstones for expressing grief and for recalling to mind affection for a dear friend or family member. Accommodating loss, making room for it, acknowledges the importance of a cherished relationship.

Unhealthy grief is more likely to occur when survivors are inhibited in expressing their grief. In the article "Disenfranchised Grief," Kenneth Doka explains how a person may experience a loss but not have a socially recognized right, role, or capacity to grieve. This disenfranchisement of the survivor's right to grieve is frequently evident in circumstances involving homosexual couples and extramarital relationships, as well as bereavements related to prenatal death (such as abortion and miscarriage), the deaths of friends or business associates, and the deaths of beloved pets. A friend's death, for instance, can be a significant loss, yet social institutions and businesses rarely provide avenues for survivors to grieve over such deaths. While someone whose close relative dies may get time off from work and temporary respite from other routine duties of daily life, someone whose friend or coworker dies is unlikely to receive such support. In these situations, without opportunities to openly express grief or otherwise publicly acknowledge the reality of the loss, the bereaved person suffers.

Similarly, even though people experience strong bonds with their pets, the death of a pet is rarely viewed as a significant loss. In "Bereavement and Companion Animals," Avery Weisman points up an irony: the virtues of pet ownership are praised while grief over a pet's death is trivialized. The notion that such losses are not truly significant is heard in the phrase "You can get another one." (A similar message is communicated when bereaved parents who have experienced miscarriage or stillbirth are told, "You can have another child.") However well-intentioned, such advice fails to acknowledge the significance of this relationship, this *loss.*

When social support is absent or minimized, the normal processes of mourning may be complicated. Healthy adaptation to loss becomes more difficult. In considering Doka's and Weisman's discussions of disenfranchised grief, notice the variables that influence the degree of social support available to survivors. You may recall situations you have lived through or observed in which the emotional response to loss was minimized or discounted because it didn't fit someone's idea of appropriate behavior or because the loss wasn't seen as a socially sanctioned occasion for grief.

Social support is important whenever significant relationship bonds are altered by death. Stephen Fleming and Leslie Balmer describe how individuals who experience similar losses benefit from coming together to assist one another through grief. In their account of "Bereaved Families of Ontario: A Mutual-Help Model for Families Experiencing Death," Fleming and Balmer describe an excellent example of the social support networks available to help individuals deal with bereavement. In the Ontario program, activities are tailored to help bereaved parents as well as children and young adults who have suffered the death of a sibling or parent. As with most such groups, mutual sharing and support form the centerpiece of the organization's activities. Support groups with similar aims can be found in many communities; referrals to these organizations can be obtained from health care agencies and other social service providers.

We sometimes fail to appreciate how humor alleviates emotional pain and provides a breathing space in the midst of suffering. In "Humor and Critical Incident Stress," Mary Hall and Paula Rappe relate how humor is an important means of coping for emergency personnel, who act as first responders to various catastrophic events. When we understand the part that humor plays in the range of coping mechanisms people use to confront experiences of loss, even so-called gallows humor takes on a certain respectability. Jokes that might be characterized as "sick" can be useful to individuals coping with the aftermath of disasters, helping them keep a positive attitude despite demoralizing and traumatic circumstances. Humor also provides relief from the intense grief experienced in the context of more personal loss. The suffering caused by the death of a family member, for example, is lightened as survivors recall comic traits or funny incidents associated with the deceased, thereby giving momentary relief to an experience that seems unbearable.

In exploring personal reactions to loss, we have so far dealt mostly with experiences related to bereavement. We must also address the multiple losses experienced by the person facing his or her own death due to terminal illness. The dynamics of grief, its variety of expression, and the range of mechanisms for coping with loss are poignantly realized when we consider the impact of a diagnosis that implies one has only a short while to live. Despite knowing that our lifespan is limited, we rarely contemplate our own mortality in terms of months or years. Yet that is precisely the situation facing the person who has been told his or her illness is life-threatening.

We err when we treat a person as a dying *person and neglect the fact that he or she is also a* living *person. As we learn in "To My Readers," Harold Brodkey's account of his own life-threatening illness, there can be a number of ups and downs, of advances and setbacks, as the nature of an illness changes over time. Despite the death sentence of a fatal prognosis, knowing that one has only a short time to live can stimulate thinking about the meaning of one's life and lead to creative activity in the time left. Personal accounts of living with life-threatening illness often mention that facing the prospect of death can lead to a renewed appreciation of intimate relationships and a willingness to make the most of the moment.*

In more melodramatic interpretations, this ability to draw positive lessons from the worst circumstances may become a caricature — dying as beautiful. Although there can be experiences of beauty and grace in dying, these shining moments do not comprise the whole story. Physical debility, discomfort, pain, frustration, anger, questioning, regret, and loss are also part of the composition. Some of these themes run through Brodkey's description of his life with AIDS.

Despite the multiple losses that typically accompany terminal illness, the trajectory of disease prior to death can be a period of intimacy and promise, as we see in Janmarie Silvera's "Crossing the Border." The desolation of the setting is echoed in the bony frailty of a woman near death. Yet the atmosphere inside the tiny room exudes warmth as mother and daughter share an easy familiarity. Without denying the reality of suffering or loss, Silvera shows us that it is possible to find pleasure in simply sharing the moment. This story also points up how the familiar roles of parent and child may be reversed when debilitating illness makes the child the caregiver.

Just as stage-based theories for coping with bereavement are being replaced by models that provide a more accurate representation of how people actually grieve, new models of how people cope with dying are emerging. The notion of a progression through stages is being replaced by a focus on the tasks confronting the dying person. Charles Corr's description of "A Task-Based Approach to Coping with Dying" introduces recent theoretical developments. Highlighted in this model are four primary dimensions of coping with dying: physical, psychological, social, and spiritual. Within each of these dimensions, there is a corresponding set of tasks that an individual may or may not choose to pursue at any given time. The use of a comprehensive framework like this encourages us to relate to dying persons holistically and helps us embrace all the dimensions of human life. Without such understanding, it is altogether too easy to engage in generalization or selective focusing, either of which can result in failure to see the individual before us as a unique, whole person.

As you read and reflect on the selections in this part of the book, take time to think about the losses you have experienced in your life. Notice the similarities and differences in your experiences compared to those described here. What kind of social support was available to you? Did friends and members of your family view some losses as more significant than others? Did these perceptions match your own experience? In our relationships with bereaved persons, we must recognize that one person's notion of what constitutes a significant loss may not apply to someone else. In taking care not to impose our own model of appropriate grieving on others, we should remember that we are endowed with two ears and one mouth. A willing listener can be a welcome source of comfort to grieving and dying persons. Even when we have learned a great deal about loss and grief, keep in mind that no one has all the answers.

The Experience of Grief

Broken Hearts or Broken Bonds:
Love and Death in Historical Perspective

MARGARET STROEBE, MARY M. GERGEN, KENNETH J. GERGEN,
AND WOLFGANG STROEBE

MARGARET STROEBE, PH.D., has a research appointment in the Department of Clinical and Health Psychology, University of Utrecht, The Netherlands. MARY M. GERGEN, PH.D., is an associate professor at Penn State University's Delaware County Campus in Media, Pennsylvania. KENNETH J. GERGEN, PH.D., is Mustin Professor in the Department of Psychology, Swarthmore College, Swarthmore, Pennsylvania. WOLFGANG STROEBE, PH.D., is a professor in the Department of Psychology at the University of Utrecht.

As two married couples who are close friends, the Stroebes and Gergens embarked on research into bereavement together more than fifteen years ago. Their partnership began with a serendipitous walk in a cemetery in the heart of the Black Forest, when seeing the death dates on the tombstones of married couples prompted a question: Was one's life threatened by the loss of a mate? The outcome of that discussion, based on data gathered from the tombstones in the driving rain, was their first joint publication. Thereafter, meetings in Paris, Swarthmore, Tubingen, Brighton, Cancun, Wengen, and Utrecht, among other sites, refined and extended their ideas.

MARGARET STROEBE is the only purist of the group; she has confined her academic interest to the area of bereavement. She is co-author, with husband Wolfgang, of *Bereavement and Health: The Psychological and Physical Consequences of Partner Loss* (1987) and editor of *Handbook of Bereavement: Theory, Research, and Intervention* (with Wolfgang and Robert O. Hansson, 1993).

The other three authors have diverse interests and perspectives within psychology. WOLFGANG STROEBE is a social psychologist with interests in organizational and health psychology. He is editor of the *European Review of Social Psychology* (with Miles Hewstone) and of the *European Textbook of Social Psychology* (1988, with Hewstone, Geoffrey Stephenson, and Jean Paul

Codol), and author, with Margaret Stroebe, of *Social Psychology and Health* (in press).

KENNETH GERGEN is often regarded as an iconoclast. His publications include *Toward Transformation in Social Knowledge* (1982), *The Saturated Self: Dilemmas of Identity in Contemporary Life* (1991), and *Realities and Relationship* (1994). His major theoretical work is within the social constructionist domain, which emphasizes the idea that society is actively and creatively produced by human beings rather than merely given or taken for granted.

MARY GERGEN, an iconoclastic sympathizer, is involved in feminist/postmodern interests within psychology and is currently writing a book on this theme. She is editor of *Feminist Thought and the Structure of Knowledge* (1988) and is co-editing (with Sara Davis) a book of readings on feminist psychology.

Have I forgot, my Only Love, to love thee,
Severed at last by Time's all-wearing wave?
—Emily Brontë

ONE OF THE chief characteristics of psychological inquiry in the present century has been the search for robust laws of human nature. In their attempts to emulate natural scientists' claims to broad covering laws, psychological researchers have aimed at formulating general principles of human functioning. This universalizing tendency is strongly evident in all domains of psychology, including the mental health professions. Both researchers and practitioners have used their observations to support claims of the broadest scope, hoping to generate insight into the "basic" processes of depression, drug dependency, stress disorders, and the like, and to establish optimal treatment programs for various forms of dysfunction.

Although such a universalizing approach is highly optimistic in its promise of incremental knowledge and reliable programs of counseling or treatment, there has been recurrent doubt about its basic assumptions.[1] Specialists in community mental health, family therapy, and social work, in particular, have drawn increasing attention to the ways in which various problems, including the very definition of the problematic, are generated in particular social milieus or conditions.[2] These conclusions strongly suggest that patterns of action, including their meanings and significance, are, at least in part, socially constituted, and thus subject to historical and cultural change. Similar conclusions have been reached in many investigations across the social sciences.[3] For example, on the basis of her review of the cross-cultural literature on depression, Lutz proposed that the disorder is not universally recognized and in some cultures does not appear to exist.[4]

Although sensitivity to culturally constructed components of dysfunctional behavior and ameliorative action is increasing, the relevance to specific mental health practices is far less apparent. What implications does viewing dysfunctional behavior as culturally and historically contingent have for matters of daily practice and policy development within the mental health professions? Are caregiving strategies and therapeutic practices subject to historical and cultural limitations? Does each new generation require new forms of support and treatment? If people of one subculture or generation consider a given form of action appropriate and acceptable, are those who fail to share their views justified in viewing such action as a problem in need of attention? All such questions gain focal significance in this context.

These issues are complex and multifaceted. In the present article we explore the dimensions of one particular area of central concern to many health care researchers and therapists—reactions to the loss of a loved one, and the associated processes of grieving. In so doing we both demonstrate the concrete significance of a cultural constructionist view and suggest a possible alternative to currently prevailing practices.

We first consider the predominant Western view of grief and grief intervention strategies that are embedded in what we view as *modernist* practices. This view is contrasted with evidence from other cultures and then with the *romantic* conception of grief, which was most popular in the previous century but is still a mainstay of cultural life. As we argue, the romantic view is threatened by modernist practices. At the same time, theory and results from recent research and analysis challenge the modernist orientation, and are used to demonstrate ways in which the romantic view can be sustained. Finally, we consider this conflict in a postmodern context.

Breaking Bonds in the Twentieth Century

Scholars frequently have used the term *modernist* to characterize the cultural zeitgeist of contemporary Western society, in contrast with that of the preceding century, which has often been described as *romanticist*. Among the chief attributes of cultural modernism are an emphasis on reason and observation and a faith in continuous progress.[5] The modernist approach to life is one that emphasizes goal directedness, efficiency, and rationality. In psychology, modernism has given rise to the machine metaphor of human functionality. When applied to grief, this view suggests that people need to recover from their state of intense emotionality and return to normal functioning and effectiveness as quickly and efficiently as possible. Modernist theories of grief and related therapeutic interventions encourage people who have experienced loss to respond in just this way. Grieving, a debilitating emotional response, is seen as a trouble-

some interference with daily routines, and should be "worked through." Such *grief work* typically consists of a number of tasks that have to be confronted and systematically attended to before normality is reinstated.[6] Reducing attention to the loss is critical, and good adjustment is often viewed as a breaking of ties between the bereaved and the dead.

The belief in the importance of severing ties from a deceased loved one found early and important expression in Freud's work.[7] Freud conceptualized love as the attachment (cathexis) of libidinal energy to the mental representation of the loved person (the object). When the loved person dies, the libidinal energy remains attached to thoughts and memories of the deceased. Because the pool of energy is limited, the cathexis to the lost object has to be withdrawn in order for the person to regain these energy resources. The ties to the loved object are severed by a process of energy detachment that Freud termed *hypercathexis*. Freud saw the psychological function of grief as freeing the individual of his or her ties to the deceased, achieving gradual detachment by means of reviewing the past and dwelling on memories of the deceased. This process is complete when most of the energy is withdrawn from the lost object and transferred to a new one. Those who fail to hypercathect remain emotionally stunted.

A more fully developed modernist view was offered by John Bowlby. Consider his reaction to C. S. Lewis's classic case study, *A Grief Observed*.[8] Lewis described his overwhelming feelings of grief and frustration as he attempted to make sense of the death of his wife. Just two years after the book's publication, Lewis also died. By contemporary standards of mental health, Lewis's reactions seem excessive; his preoccupation with the loss of his wife may have even hastened his own demise. As Bowlby wrote, Lewis's account

> suggests a man whose feeling life had
> become . . . inhibited and suppressed during

childhood and who had grown up, as a result, to be intensely introspective. . . . His frustration [was] . . . due to the systems mediating his attachment behavior having become deactivated after his mother died when he was nine.[9]

In Bowlby's view, grief is conceptualized as a form of separation anxiety, the motivation for which is to restore proximity to the lost object. In the case of death, a permanent separation, the attempt to restore proximity is inappropriate or nonfunctional. The dysfunctionality does not prevent the attempts from occurring, and only gradually do they become extinguished. This takes place through a sequence of phases, sometimes alternating from protest and anger through to despair when hope that the lost person will return is gradually abandoned.[10]

Like psychoanalytic theory, which focuses on the importance of relinquishing ties, Bowlby's work suggests that bonds with the deceased need to be broken for the bereaved to adjust and recover. Relevant counseling or therapy programs are designed to help achieve this process of withdrawal. Those who retain ties are considered maladjusted. This general assumption that ties with the deceased need to be severed is referred to in this article as the *breaking bonds* hypothesis.

Other modernists have written of the need for a grieving person to gain a new identity; again, the theme is one of achieving independence from the deceased. The title of an article by Golan, "Wife to Widow to Woman," expressed this succinctly.[11] More elaborate is the title of Judith Viorst's volume, *Necessary Losses: The Loves, Illusions, Dependencies and Impossible Expectations That All of Us Have to Give Up in Order to Grow.*[12] Parkes has written at length on processes of identification in bereaved people, particularly widows, pointing out how the old identity that relies heavily on the deceased person gradually dissolves and is replaced by a new and different one.[13] Sanders described the task of "letting go" the tie to the loved one as a necessity for the resolution of grief work, and for the "rebuilding of a life with new rewards and reinforcements."[14] Sociologist Helena Lopata has written extensively on the need for widows to develop new identities.[15]

The breaking bonds hypothesis receives further support from the literature on counseling and therapy for the bereaved.[16] Principles of grief counseling and therapy follow the view that, in the course of time, bereaved persons need to break their ties with the deceased, give up their attachments, form a new identity of which the departed person has no part, and reinvest in other relationships. People who persist in retaining a bond with their deceased loved one are in need of counseling or therapy. Worden, a leading authority on grief intervention, maintained that the bereaved may need counseling or therapy to achieve emotional withdrawal from the deceased and reinvest in other relationships.[17] In his view, one of the major hindrances to the completion of grief is holding on to the past attachment rather than letting go and forming new ones. Even more extreme are two syndromes described by Gorer—*mummification* and *despair*—wherein grief remains intense and sometimes permanent.[18] Cases of mummification are characterized by an incessant dwelling on the deceased and retention of the life routine as it was before that person's death. Despairing grief is said to be accompanied by "flat" emotion and social isolation; the tie to the deceased may be clung to in the absence of alternative social relationships.

In line with both theoretical formulations and counseling practices, researchers consistently identify "relationship to the spouse" as one of the major risk factors for poor bereavement outcomes. Parkes and Weiss described two major causes of pathological grief, which stem from problematic marital bonds.[19] One of these, following Freud, is called the *ambivalent grief syndrome*. This refers to a relationship in which elements of love and hate coexisted, conflicts were frequent, and divorce or separation may have been contemplated. After loss the bereaved may still be attached to the deceased, by insecurely so. Another syndrome, called the *chronic grief syndrome,* follows the termination of a relationship characterized as highly dependent or clinging.

It is noteworthy that aspects of a closely bonded marital relationship have been identified not only as a cause of pathology, but as a major contributor to poor adjustment among the bereaved in general. Lopata found disorganization in widowhood to be related to previous marital roles.[20] Those widows who had been intensely involved in their husband's lives and who were psychologically as well as socially dependent on them had greater problems in adjustment than those who were more autonomous.

As we see, the prevailing view of grief within the professions emphasizes the importance of breaking bonds and the problematic implications of deeply dependent relationships.[21] Proper bereavement requires that ties with the deceased be relinquished, and counseling and therapy programs are designed to further this breaking of ties. From this it follows that those persons who are independent and autonomous in marriage will encounter less difficulty in breaking their bonds and thus will have a less problematic experience of grief.

Grief in Other Cultures

Although the breaking bonds orientation appears from a modernist perspective to have implications of universal scope, its spatiotemporal limitations become apparent when it is viewed in cultural contrast. A brief survey of non-Western cultures reveals that beliefs about the value of continuing bonds with the deceased vary widely. In sharp contrast with

Western conventions, the maintenance of ties with the deceased is accepted and sustained by the religious rituals of Japan. Yamamoto, Okonoji, Iwasaki, and Yoshimura compared the courses of grief among a small sample of Japanese widows with those of British counterparts.[22] Adjustment among the Japanese widows was comparatively better. The authors attributed this to the belief in both the Shinto and Buddhist religions (to which most of the Japanese widows belonged) that contact should be maintained with the deceased. In both religions the deceased join the ranks of one's ancestors. As Yamamoto explained, "The ancestor remains accessible, the mourner can talk to the ancestor, he can offer goodies such as food or even cigars. Altogether the ancestor . . . remains with the bereaved."[23] This cultivation of continued contact with the deceased is facilitated by the presence in nearly all homes of an altar dedicated to the family ancestors. Offering food at the altar of a loved one would be classified as pathological by most Westerners, who would fear that the bereaved was fixated in the grief process and had failed to relinquish the tie to the deceased. However, in the Japanese case, such practices are fully normal.

In sharp contrast with both the Japanese and the Western patterns of grief are those of certain Native American tribes. Among the Hopi of Arizona, for example, the deceased are forgotten as quickly as possible, and life is carried on much as usual. As Mandelbaum explained, the bereaved may well feel the pain of loss, but "they give themselves over to no overt transport of grief."[24] This habit is congenial with their beliefs about the afterworld: The Hopi believe that contact with death brings pollution, and they are afraid of death and of the dead person, whose spirit becomes a depersonalized entity. Supernatural spirits are not Hopi and do not have the characteristics of deceased relatives or friends. They are greatly to be feared. As Mandelbaum described, "The

Hopi go to great lengths to make sure that the dichotomy of quick and dead is sharp and clear. Many rites having to do with spirits conclude with a ritual device which breaks off contact between mortals and spirits."[25] Mandelbaum gave a vivid illustration of Hopi attitudes toward the deceased. He had taken a photo of a young girl, whom he later learned had died. On a subsequent visit to the village he presented her mother with an enlarged copy, and was surprised to have his gift returned. As he later learned, the reason for the return was that the photo reminded the woman too much of her daughter. As Mandelbaum described it, "The sovereign desire is to dismiss the body and the event."[26]

Detailed descriptions of differing cultural prescriptions and their effects on grief are found in the recent work of the Norwegian anthropologist Unni Wikan.[27] In an insightful analysis, Wikan has explored the experiences and expressions of grief in two Muslim societies, in Bali and in Egypt. That grief is debilitating is clearly accepted in both societies, but Wikan described entirely different ways by which the two come to terms with loss. In Egypt, the bereaved are encouraged to dwell profusely on their grief, surrounded by others who relate similarly tragic accounts and express their own sorrow. They show their compassion and love for the bereaved by ceaseless mournful tirades and emotional outpourings. Wikan pointed to the "cathartic significance" of such recurrent tales. One can conclude that, among Egyptian Muslims, little attempt is made to block memories or to break ties with the deceased. In Bali, the pattern of grieving is entirely different. The bereaved are enjoined to contain their sorrow, even to laugh and be joyful. They may be made to feel that they are doing others an injustice if they do not do so. Generally speaking, no overt signs of retained bonds with the deceased are evidenced, but should they be, they are harshly judged. One Balinese man who expressed his grief in an "excessive" manner was stigmatized as mad (*gila*) and was ridiculed each time the incident was discussed.

The picture that emerges from these cultural descriptions is far different from prevailing twentieth-century Western culture. In none of the cases described above (and there are many more) do we find evidence of Western forms of "proper grieving." In some cultures people hold tight to those who are dead; in others they try quickly to relinquish all ties. In all cases the result, in general, is normal adjustment within the culture.

Grief in the Romantic Age

Given broad cultural differences in patterns of grieving and adjustment, further questioning of our own patterns is appropriate. Is it possible that the breaking bonds orientation, naturalized and universalized by Western practices of research and therapy, is largely a product of contemporary times? And if the prevailing view is the product of the modern age, what is being overshadowed? If alternative views of death and mourning have previously proved rich resources in the culture, does not the hegemony of the present view threaten their existence? To the extent that the professional view of proper mourning becomes accepted as normal, then previous orientations become irrelevant—if not deviant.

This possibility gains significant credibility when one begins to survey cultural reactions to death even a century ago. In bold contrast with the modernist modes, the romantic view of life held sway. Whereas modernists hold scientific rationality as the critical ingredient of successful human functioning, romanticists believed in the centrality of "the deep interior"—mysterious forces or processes, beyond consciousness, somewhere toward the center of one's being and one's life.[28] Many felt that the deep interior was occupied by the human spirit or soul, the source of love, creative inspiration, and the powers of genius. Romanticists placed love at the forefront of human endeavors, and praised those who would abandon the "useful" and the "functional" for the sake of a loved one. Romanticists saw marriage as a communion of souls, a family as bonded in eternal love, and friendship as a lifetime commitment.

Within the romanticist context the concept of grief was far different from the modern one. Because close relationships were matters of bonding in depth, the death of an intimate other constituted a critical point of life definition. To grieve was to signal the significance of the relationship, and the depth of one's own spirit. Dissolving bonds with the deceased would not only define the relationship as superficial, but would deny as well one's own sense of profundity and self-worth. It would make a sham of a spiritual commitment and undermine one's sense of living a meaningful life. In contrast with the breaking bonds orientation of modernism, in romanticism valor was found in sustaining these bonds, despite a "broken heart."

Some of the most expressive indicators of the broken heart mentality are found in nineteenth-century poetry. For William Barnes, the memory of his deceased wife was constantly present:

In every moaning wind I hear thee say
sweet words of consolation . . .
I live, I talk with thee wheree'er I stray.[29]

And echoing a common theme in romanticist writings, he concluded,

Few be my days of loneliness and pain
Until I meet in love with thee again.[30]

For Emily Dickinson, these impassioned memories were borne out in actions. As she wrote,

The grave my little cottage is,
where "Keeping house" for thee

I make my parlour orderly
And lay the marble tea.[31]

The, echoing again the belief in a spiritual reuniting, we find,

For two divided, briefly,
A cycle, it may be,
Till everlasting life unite
In strong society.[32]

Poetic writings of the time provide some of the most dramatic expressions of the broken heart mentality; another glimpse of its manifestations in daily life is given in Paul Rosenblatt's volume, *Bitter, Bitter Tears: Nineteenth Century Diarists and Twentieth Century Grief Theories*.[33] Rosenblatt examined accounts of grief as revealed in 56 diaries from the nineteenth century. As these diaries indicated, not only was there little evidence of breaking bonds, but the prevailing attempt was to hold fast to the departed loved one. This holding fast was accomplished in numerous ways. There are many instances in the diaries of striving to sense the presence of the deceased; some dreamed of the lost person, whereas others had compelling impressions of the deceased actually being present, as of old, in habitual settings. As Rosenblatt noted, the "sense of presence, like sorrow and other aspects of grief, can return repeatedly."[34] Praying for someone dead maintained the same caring relationship that was present before the loss. Similarly, prevalent references to a reunion in heaven reflected a continuing aspiration to resume, rather than break, contact with the deceased. Some families used child naming as a way of bringing back the presence of the deceased. Rosenblatt also found evidence of a phenomenon that we report on later in the context of twentieth-century bonds with the deceased, namely, using the wishes of the lost one as a guide to action. Finally, a common recourse for the grieving was to try to retain ties through spiritualism. The belief that one could communicate with the spirits of the dead through seances and spirit mediums became popular in the mid-nineteenth century, and many diarists recorded taking part in these rituals.

It should also be noted that these attempts to maintain the relationship with the deceased were not merely the expressions of an appropriately delimited period of mourning. Rather, they continued for long durations. As Rosenblatt concluded from this study of diaries, grief was felt "quite possibly as long as one lives."[35]

Unrelinquished Relationships in Contemporary Society

Do inhabitants of twentieth-century Western culture, although dominated by modernist views, continue a romance with romanticism? Surely there is much in popular culture—in film, television, music, and the like—to suggest that this is so. And do those who retain ties to romanticism confront more severe problems of adjusting to grief, as might be suggested by the breaking bonds orientation? The Tubingen Longitudinal Study of Bereavement has provided evidence relevant to these questions.[36] Among this sample of young widows and widowers, it was evident that many demonstrated romanticist tendencies to maintain their ties, despite the modernist emphasis on breaking bonds. Even after two years, more than two thirds of the sample planned to continue in their previous (prebereavement) life-styles as much as possible, and only a handful of respondents reported looking ahead to changes in their lives. Likewise, only a small minority (17 percent) said they were seeking a new partner. These results indicate that many of the widowed persons were not planning a major break with their pasts, rather that they were integrating the loss experience into their life-styles and trying to carry on much as before.

More specific information about the persistence of ties with the deceased was also available. When asked about the perceived presence of the deceased, nearly one third of the sample agreed that they still sensed their spouses' presence, and searched for them even after two years. The extent to which the deceased partner was used as a model for decision making and other behaviors was assessed. These results indicated that the deceased continued to have strong psychological influences over the way the widowed organized and planned their lives. For example, well over half "consulted" the deceased when having to make a decision. One widow said, "I gain great comfort knowing that this is exactly what Paul would have wanted me to do."

Very similar results have recently been reported by Shuchter and Zisook for an American sample. These authors detailed a number of ways in which the relationship to a deceased spouse is cherished and even nurtured. Just as was found in the Tubingen Longitudinal Study, these authors concluded that ties are not broken, but strongly held.

> The empirical reality is that people do not relinquish their ties to the deceased, withdraw their cathexis, or "let them go." What occurs for survivors is a transformation from what had been a relationship operating on several levels of actual, symbolic, internalized and imagined relatedness to one in which the actual ("living and breathing") relationship has been lost, but the other forms remain or may even develop in more elaborate forms.[37]

Silverman and Worden noted similar attempts by children who have lost a parent to maintain a sense of the deceased in their current life, and to connect with the parent by talking to him or her, keeping mementos, visiting the grave, and thinking about the parent.[38]

These observations suggest that romanticist styles of attachment remain robust in significant sectors of the adult population and that the broken heart orientation to loss seems no more or less conducive to poor adjustment than are dispositions more congenial to breaking bonds. One may argue, of course, that these results are specific to a population in a specific culture—that is, that they are both historically and culturally limited. But to argue this is simply to underscore our central thesis: The grieving process is indeed imbedded within cultural traditions, and to approach the therapeutic or counseling setting with a universalist (and more specifically a modernist) preference for breaking bonds is not only to undermine existing patterns of culture, but to throw into question the normalcy or emotional adequacy of an otherwise unproblematic segment of the population.

Additional support for the pervasiveness of the romantic or broken heart reaction of maintaining ties, and its relationship to adjustment to loss, comes from a different culture. Consider recent findings from a study by Rubin of parents of sons who died during two Israeli wars, 4 or 13 years previously.[39] Although adverse effects characterized the bereaved for many years following loss, difficulties associated with functioning and overt areas of behavior subsided over time; the bereaved parents went about their daily activities much as usual, somatic complaints were no longer excessive, and their psychological adjustment seemed normal. However, on a deeper level, the parents remained very involved with their sons. The picture Rubin painted is one of intense involvement and strong valuation of the bereaved parents with this private relationship, often to the detriment of relationships they had with living children, relatives and friends. For example, the parents idealized the lost son in ways that were not apparent among a control group of parents whose sons were still alive but had recently left home. Thus, despite apparent adjustment, the effect of loss on the inner lives of the parents did not subside. Rather, there was a persisting preoccupation and retention of very close ties even when there was a reduction in the more overt signs of grieving and problems of functioning. As Rubin concluded, bereaved parents of adult

sons show virtually no change in their preoccupation with the deceased over the years.

By current standards, these parents failed to break their bonds properly, and the result appears to be a life preoccupied with the dead, at the expense of the living. From the modernist perspective, the tragedy of death is compounded: Not only are the sons lost to them, but in significant ways, their families are as well. However, for those who retain a romanticist worldview, the breaking of bonds would approximate sacrilege. It would be to degrade the significance of their son, the cause for which he had died (their cause as well), and the significance of their relationship with him. To be sure, it is a suffering, but it is a suffering that validates the very significance of their lives. Is this pathology or purpose? It depends on the sociocultural setting.

Bereavement in Postmodern Perspective

To return to the more general issue, inquiry into grieving suggests that diverse groups of people engage in different patterns of action and share different meaning systems within which their actions are understood. Thus, actions deemed aberrant, maladjusted, or pathological in one cultural milieu may be fully acceptable in another. We have seen how the repetitious reciting of mournful stories, weeping, and wailing are normal reactions in one culture, whereas smiling and making jokes in the face of a loss are acceptable reactions in another. Treatment designed in one culture to "correct" or "repair" the actions of the other would at best appear to be insensitive, and at worst a form of cultural (or historical) imperialism. What are the implications of this line of reasoning for research and therapy concerned with grief? Are there forms of therapy that are more sensitive to cultural and social variations? Are there means by which attention can be focused on the better strategies for helping someone in distress?

The present account grows out of a newly developing consciousness, which may be termed *postmodern*. That is, when the relativity of the modernist perspective is recognized (here against the backdrop of romanticism), modernism loses its power of persuasion. In effect, we thus move beyond the modernist commitment and recognize the possibility of multiplicity in perspective. This shift toward multiplicity of voice is hardly unique to the present analysis, and by most standards would be considered a constituent feature of postmodern consciousness more generally.[40]

However, recognition of the possibility of variations in perspectives does not itself lead to unequivocal conclusions concerning the future of grief research and therapy. At the outset we find that any evaluation of research and therapeutic outcomes can only be made from within some cultural framework. Thus, the negative functions of holding on to a relationship with the dead are fully compelling as long as one remains in the modernist perspective. Within this tradition, retaining ties may be symptomatic of emotional problems and mental illness, and may even lead to premature death: Building a life around a broken heart is contraindicated. Yet, from within the romanticist framework, there is much to be said on behalf of retaining ties. Parents of the Israeli war dead reveal the ennobling aspects of keeping strong ties to the dead, even if difficulties are incurred in their relations with the living. Each perspective yields its own outcomes, and suffers its own limitations. Therapeutic outcomes would be similarly affected.

If definitive resolution is beyond our grasp, what alternatives then lie before us? Let us consider three possibilities. First, attention may be given to means of *conceptual integration*. That is, rather than sustaining the disparate conceptions of grief—along with their accompanying theories and practices—we might seek means of integrating or combining them in some fashion. There are good prece-

dents for such synthesis. Psychoanalytic theory borrowed heavily from romanticism in its conception of unconscious forces, and combined it with a theory of ego functioning, a mainstay of subsequent modernism. The result was a more enriched and compelling theoretical edifice. It is not our attempt, in the present context, to offer an integrative theory of bereavement. However, for purposes of illustration, consider the implications of Mary Gergen's conceptual analysis of "social ghosts."[41] Social ghosts are defined as real or fictitious persons with whom individuals conduct imaginal interactions over time; they are the cast of characters with whom we engage in imaginal dialogues. Gergen detailed a variety of positive functions that these relationships play in people's lives. For example, social ghosts provide models for action, offer attitudinal perspectives, and lend esteem and emotional support to those who engage with them.

Romanticists may favor the concept of social ghosts, which suggest that it is both normal and emotionally sustaining to retain and nurture images of the deceased. Similarly, in their concern with social efficacy, modernists may also find the view sustaining. In this case the concept of social ghosts expands the range of significant others with whom relations should be effective, adding an internal dimension of the social world. In addition, the existence of social ghosts may have useful outcomes for ongoing interaction. Also supportive of this conclusion is Rosenblatt and Meyer's discussion of internal dialogues with a deceased person.[42] As they argued, such dialogue serves the positive function of helping the bereaved clarify thoughts, deal with unfinished and emergent relationships, and prepare for the future.

A second outcome of postmodern consciousness for theory and therapy is an invitation toward *culturally embedded practices*. That is, rather than attempting conceptual integration, one may approach the culture with an appreciation for its rich texture of possibilities. Thus, researchers would not attempt to generate conclusions of universal proportion; even the attempt to characterize a culture as a whole may be considered too generalized. Rather, researchers might profitably be concerned with the enormous variations in forms of bereavements. Rather than attempting to generalize, they would search for an appreciative understanding of grief in all its varieties. On the therapeutic level, this would mean curtailing the search for ideal therapeutic procedures and focusing instead on tailor-made treatments. This would require a highly sensitive receptivity—an open listening to the client voice, for the reality and values of its sustaining subculture. At the same time, this option would invite educating for alternatives. It might prove desirable to teach clients that there are many goals that can be set, many ways to feel, and no set series of stages that they must pass through—that many forms of expression and behavioral patterns are acceptable reactions to loss. The stoic widower may need to learn to cry out over his loss at times, and the weeping widow to put her husband's wishes aside as she becomes the financial manager of her estate. The key concepts are growth, flexibility, and appropriateness within

a cultural context. Awareness of a need for such multiplicity is just beginning to penetrate the field of bereavement research.[43] We support this endeavor.

Finally, a postmodern orientation toward grief theory and therapy invites an *expansion of responsibility*. A psychologist committed to either the romantic or the modernist view has a sense of moral or social responsibility that is constrained by a particular set of practices. The sense of choice is muted. A therapist committed to a Rogerian interpretation need not worry about the morality of not choosing to practice as a Freudian or behaviorist. In this sense, as the psychologist develops a postmodern consciousness, the range of viable perspectives is vastly increased.[44] One becomes aware that assumptions of health and adjustment are by-products of cultural and historical processes. Similarly, one realizes that theories of personal deficit harbor implicit systems of value, favoring certain ideals over others. More generally, theories and therapeutic practices favor certain forms of cultural patterns over others. For good or ill, they move the society toward or away from certain ends. Effectively, this is to urge a substantial broadening of self-reflective dialogue within the field.

Grief: Re-forming Life's Story

JOHN D. KELLY

JOHN D. KELLY is the coordinator of pastoral care and bereavement in the Palliative Care Service at Providence Hospital in Washington, D.C. A retired civil servant, he is active in community and church affairs and is an ordained deacon in the Archdiocese of Washington. In 1979, the Rev. Mr. Kelly responded to a call from a neighbor to see her terminally ill husband, though he did not know what to do or say. Through his contact with this man, he discovered the world of the terminally ill and those who work within it. As a member of the Citizens' Advisory Board of Providence Hospital, he soon began advocating for establishment of a hospice. He worked with the Hospital's Center for Life department to develop a hospice-style volunteer program within the acute-care environment, and subsequently served as coordinator of the volunteer program for seven years, prior to the establishment of the Palliative Care Service in 1987.

IF WE CONSIDER the reality of our lives as stories, then both the griever and the caregiver will have more positive goals in working through the grief process.

> Tell me a story. A story of where we are and how we got here and the characters and roles we play. Tell me a story, a story that will be my story as well as the story of everyone and everything about me, a story that brings us together in a . . . community.[1]
> —Berry, 1990 (1)

In a recent show on the TV series *Matlock*, Julie, the prosecuting attorney and "significant other" to Ben Matlock, is pursued via binoculars and phone calls by a person who is terrifying her. She is so disturbed by his tactics and persistence that at one point she cries out, "All I want is to get my life back." Eventually, of course, the case is resolved and Julie, in great relief, says to Ben, "Let's go home."

We could read that as: "Give me back the story of my life as it was before all this."

The notion of life as story has existed for as long as people have been able to communicate. The hieroglyphics of ancient Egypt depicted stories of human relations and events of those times. For the Judeo-Christian culture the story of creation in Genesis is the beginning of the story of "the action of God in the course of human events"[2] carried out through all of the Old Testament: the story of Adam and Eve; of Job (often used as an example in grieving interactions)[3]; of Jonah; and of Lot and his wife. In other cultures there are other stories of the first people on earth.[4] Through myth and story we have traced our cultural history, e.g. the *Iliad* and the *Odyssey*, the knights of the middle ages; our national history, e.g. Paul Bunyan, John Henry, cowboys, and gold miners; and our family history, e.g. our forefathers' travels to the New World, the trials and victories of our immigrant parents and grandparents, and the stories of our families as slaves and as freed men and women.

The story of our own lives is in a sense our image of ourselves and our relationships. Based on the facts of births, meetings, associations, schools, graduations, loves, marriages, relocations, jobs—any number of facts—it is how we form these facts and how we view our relationships that enable us to form our story. But, as Ervin Polster points out, the story is much more than the narrowness of the facts involved.[5] I am one of a family of five children, raised by loving parents, struggling through a depression, off to a war, college, marriage, family, death, remarriage. My story of each of these events is not the story of my siblings, nor are theirs mine. Yet for all of us many of the facts are the same. The same holds true for my children and their respective stories; the same, for everyone.

For each of us, keeping our lives and our relationships intact, as we know them, is very important. So important that any change, unless approved or controlled by us, comes as an impact which requires our adjustment, a changing in the way we view our lives and the relationships which make our lives what they are. A change in the "story" of our lives is necessary.

The trauma of a loss, particularly the loss of a loved one, takes its toll in a variety of forms.[6] We lose our appetite, our ability to concentrate, our interest in people or things. We go sleepless. We're angry, we cry, we withdraw. We grasp at what appear to be comforting straws in the wind only to find that they quickly bend and break.

Then, in the normal process, we begin to affirm the loss, accepting its reality. We begin to take the grief into ourselves. It becomes a part of us, altering our lives. Rather than manifesting this through a withdrawal from the deceased emotionally, psychologically, or spiritually, the deceased remains much a part of our lives, but in a different way.[7] He or she takes another form in our life's story.

Pictures are always important to story, and a picture of our relationships can be compared to the basic structure of any unit, the atom with its nucleus and rings. In this case these would represent the different levels of relationship to people, work, hobbies, etc. So we can use our capacity to "picture" this unit as the comparison is described.

As the nucleus, the griever is surrounded by relationships. They vary in the degree to which they inform and affect the life of the griever. Ring one would be the close familial type; ring two other friends, caring and cared for enough to influence and support (to receive from and give on a mutually willing basis); ring three—present but less connected; ring four; and so on.

While this structure points to relationships on the social level, we must be aware that most relationships function on several levels, i.e. social, psychological, and spiritual. These levels commingle in such a way that each shares with and informs the others. It is this commingling which gives each person a wholeness, a unity, and which gives each relationship that particular level of identity with another.

For the purpose here we can assume the death of a significant person is in ring one. What happens? The grief process begins and the "tasks of mourning" are started.[8] The first two tasks take place much as Dr. Worden describes them. We begin to accept the reality of the loss and experience the pain of grief. But it seems to me that Task III, "to adjust to an environment in which the deceased is missing," and Task IV, "withdrawal and reinvestment" need some modification.[9] The environment is not one in which the deceased is "missing." It is important to recognize that the relationship, while final in the form the griever knew it, takes on a new reality within the griever's life story. The deceased is gone in body, but is not gone from the mind or the life of the griever and probably never will be. The work of mourning is to adjust to the awareness and acceptance of this new role that the departed person takes in the grieving relationship. Mourning then becomes more than "the adaptation to loss."[10] The process must involve the incorporation of the loss of this person in the form he or she was known, into life's story in a new form.

So too for Task IV. There is not so much an emotional withdrawal from the deceased as there is the acceptance of the deceased in the re-formed story. Arriving at this stage enables the griever to invest his or her time, energy, and effort in all of the other relationships which exist or may come into being, but again in a new way. It is the work of grieving which, with the support of others, identifies the new substance of these relationships.

Not only does the relationship between the deceased and the griever change, but all other relationships in the griever's structure also change. A spouse discovers relational changes with the children, with the siblings of the departed person, with those with whom they shared a relationship. Many people other than the spouse may find that each of their relationships within this structure is changing. For the moment, then, we must consider that each life story must be re-formed.

While we must assist the griever in recognition of the reality of the loss and its effects on the griever, we must remember that within the structure of the griever's story the departed person takes on a new meaning, a new essence. The relationship takes a new form, *but it is still there.*

Engel states that, "For the mourner . . . the main work of grief goes on intrapsychically."[11] Included in this working process we must consider the psychic elements of wonder, and awe, and the sense of the spiritual and the numinous.[12] The former two are usually connected to the developmental stage of children and are never lost to us. Unrecognized, perhaps, or at least subdued in most of us—due to what I would call cultural denial—these elements are nonetheless present and assist greatly in the building and re-forming of our stories. Polster gives a chapter over to "Fascination."[13] While he is discussing this as a quality in the caregiver, I would call this "wonder" in the griever. The phrases he attributes to his patients I suggest were spoken from the sense of awe and wonder.[14]

The sense of the spiritual and the "capacity for the numinous" are usually associated only with a specific belief or religion.[15] I believe, however, that they are basic human qualities upon which faith and religious beliefs are built and which inform our personalities.[16]

As heir to and participant within the Judeo-Christian tradition, these capacities should make me aware, through Jesus Christ, of the presence of the God of the Israelites in all creation and, especially, in all people and in the eternalness of life. For some other cultures these capacities lead people to establish their identities with great things in nature,[17] several gods,[18] or different singular god-man relationships.[19] But the capacities are there in all peoples.

Engel points out further that it has been the poets alone who "have come close to grasping the essential psychological verities" of the loss due to the death experience.[20] Perhaps this is because that capacity for wonder and awe and the sense of the spiritual and the numinous are best expressed in poetic or romantic language—the language which is the best for telling stories.

Awareness of the involvement of these elements in the grief process enables the caregiver to encourage the griever to talk, to tell the story of the relationship as it has been. The caregiver can expect to hear that "I will never see Grandma again." "He is gone, my life is over." "If only I could speak to her once more." It is important that while these expressions of feeling not be denied *per se,* the notion of what I will call "continuity of presence" should be kept alive for the griever. The bereaved should be given permission to feel the presence of the deceased in their lives.[21] "No, you won't see Grandma as you knew her, but she will still be present to you." "Your life is not really over, and though he is gone as he was he will be with you always." "Feel free to speak to her once more, and feel that she will know you are doing so." These are appropriate and reassuring responses.

Helpful, also, is the drawing out from the griever of anecdotes and vignettes of the relationships. Some will be bitter, some will be sweet, but all can help in returning to the griever the sense of control over the story and over his or her life.

This element of control is most important—I should say critical—to the grief process. Control by the griever is critical to recovery. Through the re-forming process the sense of unity and wholeness comes to the griever's new life story. The healing of the griever's damaged image of his or her life and self is completed. Healthy relationships with the deceased are established. [22] Only by recovering the sense of unity and wholeness to life's story can the healing of the damaged image of ourselves and our lives be completed. Only then can we again feel in control.

The pitfalls to the grief recovery process are no less present when the objectives are viewed from the perspective of re-forming life's story. The difficulties inherent in experiencing the "normal" grief process are there, but there also are the dangers of complications, of delayed or unresolved grief.[23] Intense identification with the deceased, to the point of not allowing for new relationships or a "new story" to form, denial of the grieving process, "throwing oneself" into living—these are but some of the dangers. The caregiver in these situations should be alert to the symptoms of these conditions and be able to distinguish uncomplicated from complicated grieving and make appropriate suggestions and referrals for more intensive therapy.[24]

In helping the griever to re-form life's story to involve the new integrations of the deceased and the adjustment of all relationships, the caregiver aids in restoring unity and wholeness to an acceptable degree. The work of investing in other relationships can then go on.[25] If the griever is not able to do this, then the story will be re-formed *for* him or her and he or she will not have control. It is our work, then, to help the bereaved "open the covers of [their] lives," confront their situations "painful or pleasurable," and thus help in re-forming the story.[26]

So Julie can't really "get her life back" as it once was, and our stories—our lives—never will be the same. But with support through the grief process, those whom we lose can be taken into our lives in a new form, and our grief, sufficiently processed, can help us to become new whole persons. Librarian Linda Neal Boyce is quoted as saying that stories "tell us where we've been and where we're going. They tell us who we are."[27]

Solace and Immortality:
Bereaved Parents' Continuing Bond with Their Children

DENNIS KLASS

DENNIS KLASS, PH.D., is a professor in the Department of Religion at Webster University in St. Louis, Missouri. His involvement in death and dying came about unwittingly when, as a graduate student in the psychology of religion at the University of Chicago in the fall of 1968, he answered an advertisement for a research fellow to assist in the chaplain's office at the University Hospital. After getting the position, he learned that it involved working with a psychiatrist whose seminar was sponsored by the chaplaincy. The psychiatrist turned out to be Elisabeth Kübler-Ross, and her book *On Death and Dying* was published soon after Klass began working with her. As a graduate student, Klass realized that qualitative data about how people relate to questions of meaning in their lives is relatively easy to obtain and that, with respect to death and dying, every question is ultimately religious.

After taking a teaching position at Webster, Dr. Klass began offering courses in death and dying. In 1979, he and Audrey Gordon pub-lished *They Need to Know: How to Teach Children About Death*. Having written a book with *children* and *death* in the title, he was asked to assist with a series of monthly meetings of parents whose children had died. Dr. Klass says: "It became clear to me that nobody knew much about parents whose kids died. I think it's a very lucky researcher who finds a group where the basic questions have not been asked, where you can make a contribution, and where you really like the people you are studying." When a couple from this group decided to form a chapter of The Compassionate Friends in St. Louis in 1979, Dr. Klass was asked to be the professional advisor; he has been with the group ever since.

In 1992, the National Board of The Compassionate Friends honored Dr. Klass with its Appreciation Award, which is given to an individual who is not a bereaved parent. Dr. Klass's findings concerning parental bereavement have been published in numerous articles and in his book *Parental Grief: Solace and Resolution* (1988).

IN THE SORROW of grief humans need to be consoled. The defining characteristic of solace is the sense of soothing. To console means to alleviate sorrow or distress. Solace is that which brings pleasure, enjoyment, or delight in the face of hopelessness, despair, sadness, and devastation.

This essay looks at consolation within the resolution of the grief of parents whose children have died. It grows out of a long-term ethnographic study of a local chapter of The Compassionate Friends, a self-help group of bereaved parents.[1] The ten-year study has resulted in a large body of materials that can be used to understand parental grief and the interactions within The Compassionate Friends chapter. Materials include: interviews with bereaved parents, writings by members in chapter newsletters, and notes from meetings.

When a child dies, the parent experiences an irreparable loss, for the child is an extension of the parent's self.[2] While one of the psychological tasks of parenting in modernity is to separate the child from the self so the child can be experienced as a separate being,[3] such separation is seldom complete. When a child dies, a part of the self is cut off. Many parents find the metaphor of amputation useful. In a meeting a father said, "It is like I lost my right arm, but I'm learning to live as a one-armed man." A parent who seems to have had experience with amputees wrote in a newsletter article:

For the amputee, the raw bleeding stump heals and the physical pain does go away. But he lives with the pain in his heart knowing his limb will not grow back. He has to learn to live without it. He rebuilds his life around his loss. We bereaved parents must do the same.

Like amputation, parental bereavement is a permanent condition. The hopes, dreams, and expectations incarnate in the child are now gone.

Bereaved parents do find some resolution to their grief, in the sense that they learn to live in their new world. They "re-solve" how to be themselves in a family and community in a way that makes life meaningful. They learn to grow in those parts of themselves that did not die with the child. They learn to invest themselves in other tasks and other relationships. But somewhere inside themselves, they report, there is a sense of loss that cannot be healed. A bereaved father wrote in a newsletter:

If grief is resolved, why do we still feel a sense of loss on anniversaries and holidays and even when we least expect it? Why do we feel a lump in the throat even six years after the loss? It is because healing does not mean forgetting and because moving on with life does not mean that we don't take a part of our lost love with us.

A part of them is missing and their world is forever diminished. It is that part of the self which seeks consolation. How do parents find consolation for their irreparable loss?

The Nature of Solace

Horton finds that the majority of people have a history of solace that they nurture.[4] Most adults can easily identify a solace-filled object to which they repair when they need soothing: a memory of a special place or person, a piece of music or art, an imagined more perfect world, a sense of divine presence. Horton finds that solace is necessary for the individual who can live in a society. Psychopathic criminals, he says, have no solace in their lives. Horton finds that the earliest solace is the transitional object[5] such as a child's security blanket, which helps the child explore new situations and adjust to unfamiliar environments.[6] Horton says that in adults these objects are no longer transitional, for they are important in the adult's ongoing life. Solace is experienced as blended inner and outer reality. There is a noetic quality in this reality that is self-validating. While the content of solace may have rational characteristics, the truth and comfort of solace are neither provable nor challengeable.

A recurring pattern in The Compassionate Friends is that parents find long-term solace in continuing interactions with an inner representation of their dead child. Inner representation can be defined following Fairbairn as: (a) those aspects of the self that are actualized in interaction with the deceased person, (b) characterizations or thematic memories of the deceased, and (c) emotional states connected with those parts of the self and with those characterizations and memories.[7] Phenomena that indicate interaction with the inner representation of a deceased person are a sense of presence, hallucinations in any of the senses, belief in the person's continuing active influence on thoughts or events, or a conscious incorporation of the characteristics or virtues of the dead person into the self.

These phenomena may be experienced in altered states of consciousness. Parents often use phrases like: "It was in a dream, but it was different than other dreams." The phenomena may also be experienced in ordinary states of consciousness and accepted as part of the everyday world. Interaction may be consciously sought or it may seem to come unbidden. Interaction with the inner representation of the dead may be continuous with the self as the characteristics or virtues of the dead are incorporated into the self-representation. Or the interaction may seem apart from the self-representation as the parent says that having such thoughts and feelings is "just not like me."

The inner representation of the dead child has the character of both outer and inner reality. It is not simply an objective presence, for the meaning of the experience is strongly personal. Neither can it be said to be simply subjective. Many parents in the study argue strongly against reducing the experience to a psychic reality, or as one person said, "Don't tell me that this is just in my head." Yet at the same time they are usually able to grant that the meaning of the child's presence is very personal and not generalizable to other people's lives.

The message and meaning of the interaction with the inner representations of dead children are self-evident to the bereaved parent. It does not matter to the parents in the study whether, with the help of the spirits of the dead, parapsychologists can bend spoons. Their children appear, act, speak, and influence. The intense meanings they feel within the bond with their child are quite apart from rational proof or disproof.

Inner representation of the dead are not simply individual phenomena, but they are maintained and reinforced within families and other social systems. The dead child is often a part of the bond within the continuing family and is an integral element of the bond between members of The Compassionate Friends. Parents consciously work to maintain the inner representation of the child. Several families do this by including the picture of the dead child on family portraits made after the child's death. Others do it by consciously evoking the memory of the child in significant situations. In The Compassionate Friends, the sense of oneness with other bereaved parents and within the bonds to the dead child can be seen in the "TCF Credo," which has been adopted by the National Board of TCF and which is recited on special occasions such as holiday memorial services, national, and regional meetings.

> We reach out to each other with love, with understanding and with hope. Our children have died at all ages and from many different causes, but our love for our children unites us. . . . Whatever pain we bring to this gathering of The Compassionate Friends, it is pain we will share just as we share with each other our love for our children.[8]

Literature on Inner Representations of the Dead

Extent of the Phenomena

There is ample evidence from research on Western cultures that the inner representation of the deceased continues as an active part of the life of the survivor, even though it has little sanction within the dominant scientific world view. At present, the inner representation of Elvis Presley plays an active part in many people's lives and within some social systems.[9] Lehman, Wortman, and Williams found that four to seven years after an accidental death 90 percent of widows and widowers and 96 percent of bereaved parents said that during the past month memories, thoughts, or mental pictures of the deceased had come to their mind.[10] Kalish and Reynolds found that 44 percent of a random sample said they had experienced or felt the presence of someone who had died.[11] The dead appeared and spoke in 73.6 percent of the experiences, the dead were psychologically felt in 20.3 percent, and there was a sense of touch in 6 percent. Rees found that 46.7 percent of the Welsh widows he interviewed had occasional hallucinations for several years.[12] Most common was the sense of the presence (39.2 percent), followed by visual (14 percent), auditory (13.3 percent), and tactile senses (2.7 percent). Glick, Weiss, and Parkes found among widows a persistent continuing relationship with the inner representation of the dead husband.[13] They report:

> In contrast to most other aspects of the reaction to bereavement, the sense of the persisting presence of the husband did not diminish with time. It seemed to take a few weeks to become established, but thereafter seemed as likely to be reported late in the bereavement as early.

Cross Cultural Differences and Continuities

There are wide cultural variations in what is considered to be the appropriate place of the inner representation of the dead in the family and other social systems. Yamamoto and his colleagues claim that because Japanese religion (both Shinto and Buddhist) involves ancestor worship, which encourages the mourner to maintain contact to the deceased, mourning is different in Japan than in the West.[14]

There are also some obvious continuities across cultures in the phenomena by which inner representation of the dead are manifest. Matchett reports three instances of Hopi women having visions of recently deceased people.[15] The mental state he describes is not different from that in bereaved parents:

> The experience to be described is neither truly seance nor truly dream, but appears to represent a mental state with some similarities to both. The apparition is real enough to the beholder to be conversed with, to be described in great visual detail, and even at times to be struggled with physically. However, it is clear to the beholder, even during the experience, that this presence with which he argues and struggles as if it were "real" occurs somewhere outside the usual definition of reality.

Functions of the Inner Representation of the Dead

There have been some studies of how inner representations function in the lives of sur-

vivors, though often this aspect is not central to the investigation, or the sample has been very small. Among widows, Silverman argues that maintaining a changed relationship with the inner representations of deceased spouses allows the widows to find stability in time.[16] Lopata finds what she calls "husband sanctification," which allows the widow to "continue her obligation to the husband to remember him, yet break her ties and re-create herself into a person without a partner."[17] Moss and Moss claim that the sanctified inner representation of the dead spouse is a factor in the relationship between elderly widows and widowers when they remarry.[18] Goin, Burgoyne, and Goin find widows, even after remarriage, renew the bond with their dead husband as they decide to have a face-lift operation.[19] Among children whose parent has died, Tessman finds that children "preserve the relationship psychically and continue to make use of whatever mixture of affection and guidance emanated from the parent."[20] Bushbaum finds that the inner representation of the dead parent is essential to the child's development.[21] College women, Silverman finds, reintegrate the dead parent into each new developmental stage.[22]

Inner Representations of the Dead in Contemporary Grief Theory

These experiences of bereaved parents run contrary to most contemporary understandings of the healthy resolution of grief, which hold that the inner representation plays no or only a slight role in the survivor's life after the resolution of grief. The two classic models of grief come from Bowlby and his followers and from the psychoanalytic group. The Bowlby model expects that after a period of emotionally searching for the deceased, survivors should let go of the inner representation, and resume normal functioning, albeit in changed social roles.[23] The psychoanalytic model expects that mourning should detach the ego from the affective bond with the deceased and that the inner representation is transformed into an identification that enriches the ego or self-representation.[24]

Models of grief that try to go beyond the Bowlby and psychodynamic models do not find a positive place for the inner representation in the resolution of grief either. Brice in his paradoxical model of parental grief finds that his subjects

> painfully came to see that, while they retained a psychical representation of their child, they had irretrievably lost their child's external presence—something of which their mental images were, alas, a poor copy.[25]

Brice says one of the difficulties that parents have with the experience of presence is that they fear insanity. Although Brice mentions his contact with The Compassionate Friends, he does not seem to have seen that with social validation of the sense of presence bereaved parents no longer accept the label of insanity. Sanders notes that sensing the presence or actually seeing the dead person "brought a sense of comfort," but she understands the experiences to be the "cognitive counterpart of yearning."[26] Thus she is saying that interaction with the inner representation of the dead child is wish fulfillment rather than a positive element in resolution.

The contemporary theoretical difficulties are seen in Rando's attempt to synthesize the literature of clinicians. She says:

> The single most crucial task in grief is "untying the ties that bind" the griever to the deceased individual. This does not mean that the deceased is forgotten or not loved; rather, it means that the emotional energy that the mourner had invested in the deceased is modified to allow the mourner to turn it towards others for emotional satisfaction.[27]

"Emotional energy" is a problematic concept at best, so the idea of "modified" energy explains very little. Rando gives no way the dead can remain loved and remembered, yet have the emotional energy modified except as "rituals, anniversary celebrations, prayers, commemorations, memorializations, and healthy identification."[28] She does not show the mechanisms by which energy modification takes place. Further, she does not say how rituals and these other factors function in the resolution of grief, nor does she give any definition or examples of "healthy identification."

There is a minority voice in the literature that is more congruent with this study. Rubin finds that breaking bonds with the dead is not the function or measure of successful grief:

> It is in the nature of the relationship of the bereaved to the deceased that is the best determination of whether the mourning has been resolved. . . . The greater the comfort and fluidity with which one can relate to the representations (memories, fantasies, feelings) of the deceased—the more one can refer to "resolution" of the loss.[29]

The Question of Pathology

In many contemporary theories of grief, the widespread continued interaction with the inner representations of dead children seem to be pathological, for beginning with Freud, theorists have understood the purpose of grief as relinquishing the lost object so that new attachments in the present can be formed. Failure to sever the bond has been defined as pathological grief. This is not the venue for a full discussion of the unexamined assumptions and lack of data upon which this definition of pathology is based. The author has discussed the issue previously, especially with regard to Bowlby and his followers,[30] but a few comments can indicate the problems with this view of pathology. The most powerful clinical argument for this definition of pathological grief is the link some researchers have established between depression and the unresolved grief of children for deceased parents. Tennant, however, in a detailed review of this body of research concludes:

> Parental loss has all too readily been accepted as a significant risk factor in adult psychopathology. However a reasonable scrutiny of the empirical findings reveals their fragility. . . . there is no evidence that parental death is a significant risk factor for depression.[31]

The definition of the healthy resolution of grief as severing bonds with the dead does not stand the test of cross-cultural nor of comparative historical analysis. Stroebe, Gergen, Gergen, and Stroebe in a historical study show that the definition is an artifact of modernism that values goal directedness, efficiency, and rationality:

> In psychology, modernism has given rise to the machine metaphor of human functionality. When applied to grief, this view suggests that people need to recover from their state of intense emotionality and return to normal functioning and effectiveness as quickly and efficiently as possible.[32]

Modernism, they note, is a reaction against romanticism in which continuing bonds to the dead were valued and nurtured.

That is not to say that inner representations of dead children, like any significant attachment, do not on occasion become twisted in psychopathology. To understand the etiology of pathology in grief, it is useful to look again at the classic work of Lindemann and Cobb.[33] They do not find causal factors in the processes the bereaved undertake to resolve grief. Rather, Lindemann and Cobb find that persons with a prior history of psychopathology or with a social support system loaded with guilt and conflict are likely to exhibit pathology in their grief. Thus pathology in grief is a function of other pathology.

There have been studies of the destructive possibilities of socially maintained inner representations, though less study of the construc-

tive possibilities. Maintaining the inner representation in the form of "replacement children" can be a heavy burden on the child who is expected to live someone else's life.[34] Family systems therapists have focused on the ways in which families can get "stuck" by not publicly mourning losses so the family can reorganize without a "ghost" in the family.[35] On a more positive note, though on a smaller scale, Rynearson shows how making the inner representation a party to the social system of psychotherapist and client helps the survivor resolve grief in a healthy way.[36] Going somewhat further, Mogenson suggests:

> While more investigation should be undertaken, it may be that maintaining the bond with the dead prevents pathology. When relationships to the dead are maintained it makes it less likely that their images will be reincarnated in the form of projections which distort our relationships to other people. . . . A heart that grieves, a heart that communes with the dead in reverie, is immune to falling in love on the rebound. By welcoming the ghosts the bereaved may find themselves to be no longer haunted by them.[37]

Inner Representation as Solace

What forms of relationship to a dead child do parents maintain as solace in their lives? Three common ways among members of The Compassionate Friends are linking objects, religious ideas and devotion, and memory. In the descriptions of these three types of relationships that follow, we consider both the solace that individuals find and how shared solace-bearing inner representations are a part of the bonds within families and communities.

Linking Objects

Linking objects are objects connected with the child's life that link the bereaved to the dead; in so doing, they evoke the presence of the dead.[38] Six years after his child's death, a father wrote a birthday letter to him:

> I haven't been able to part with the bicycle cart that I bought for you and your sister a few weeks before you died. It's never used anymore but I keep it in my study at home. . . . I still see your smile as you sat there holding our puppy. . . . Your little wind-up toy, the one of Donald Duck sitting in a shoe, sits on top of the file cabinet in my study. I feel close to you when I'm close to your favorite things.

The sense of smell is particularly intimate. Parents often report that they hold their children's clothes which still have the scent of the child. One mother who miscarried wrote that it is not the usual newborn scent that links her to her child.

> So the flowers I place upon his grave
> Are the only scent I know.
> So when I smell a flower
> My son always comes to mind.

The linking object need not be small toys or fast-fading flowers. A father whose daughter had died five years earlier said:

> It's that old pick-up truck. She used to ride around in it with me. She would lean against me on the seat. It has almost 200,000 miles on it, but I am not going to sell it. By now I probably couldn't get anything for it anyway. I told the boys they could work on it and use it if they got it going. But I'll never sell the truck because I can sit in there and feel my daughter. It's great.

The linking object is a self-validating truth to the parent that, though the child is dead, yet the child lives. One parent had many memories of being at the beach with her child. They would look for sand dollars, which the boy saved. Her memory of those times also include natural mystical experiences[39] in which her bond with nature and with the child are inter-

twined. In a newsletter article she wrote that the child "was especially awed by the setting sun and as we walked the beaches, always he would stop and watch the sun go down—I did too! I was so happy with him."

> In February I went to Padre Island and one lonely evening I walked the beach alone —just the sand, the sea, a beautiful setting sun, the screeching gulls, God and me. It was there I begged Him to show me a sign that E. lives—to "please send me a sand dollar." I knew that it was not the season for sand dollars. Even the local people had told me that they had not seen sand dollars since last summer. But I only wanted just one sand dollar— just one! Watching the fading sunset and listening to the roar of the waves, darkness began to fall, so I turned to go back when there by my feet, the waves pushed up one lone sand dollar—a small but perfect sand dollar!
>
> That is exactly the way it happened and I cannot begin to tell you the feelings I had. My prayer had been answered.

The answer to her prayer for a sign that the child still lives is the linking object of the sand dollar. Now that she has had the intense experience of finding the sand dollar, the memory of this experience can be evoked and the memory itself can serve as a linking object.

If the linking object is rich enough, it can serve as an enduring, communally shared symbol. For this to happen, the object must have a cultural meaning by which the parent can connect personal solace to that provided within the social reality. One family in the study found the child's presence at a place in a national park the child had spontaneously called "just like heaven." One couple share a linking object that has an often unrecognized cultural symbolism. Asked, "Do you ever sense that C. is still around?" the mother answered:

> Every time I see a mourning dove.
> Mourning doves are magnificent. The day

after C. died, Cliff and I were sitting in the den looking out the window and there was a mourning dove on the porch. I didn't know what it was at the time, so I got out my bird book and looked it up. It is m-o-u-r-n-i-n-g dove, not m-o-r-n-i-n-g. It was so ironic because here I'd just lost a daughter and I'm getting out my bird book to look for mourning doves. It was phenomenal that we would see a mourning dove when we were mourning. It's got to mean something, right? So the two of us took this as, "This is C. C. is with the dove." Then, a few days later, there were two doves there. Cliff decided that it was C. telling him that she had a friend with her. It's really fascinating because I'll find myself thinking about her and I'll look around and see the mourning dove. That has become a symbol of C. It was on the year anniversary when we were going to the cemetery and Cliff said, "I wish I could see a mourning dove." So I said, "Come over here, there is usually a mourning dove over here." And I'll be damned if there wasn't a mourning dove on the wire. He said, "That's a sign. Now I can go to the cemetery."

Religious Devotion

Linking objects can have a numinous sense[40] about them, for they function like relics of the saints in which "any personal possession or part of a person's body . . . can carry the power or saintliness of the person with whom they were once associated and make him or her 'present' once again."[41] The numinous feeling is clearer in the many people who sense the presence of the child in their religious experience of prayer, ritual, and religious ideation. Religion as used here is the individual's sense of connectedness to that which transcends death.[42] The inner representation of the child is merged with something bigger, but something of which, in the deeper reaches of the psyche, the parent feels a part. Religion can be provided within an institutionalized frame-work. One mother wrote a letter to her dead daughters describing the sense of presence at Catholic Mass.

> Every time I attend the sacrifice of the Mass, at the part where our Blessed Lord comes into our hearts, I feel so close to your angelic presence. What a devine experience! The only problem is that it doesn't last long enough. If only the others could share these feelings.

Religion can also be outside churches or theology. Parents feel the presence of the child within their bonds with the whole world. On her child's birthday, one mother wrote a letter as if from the child.

> I would have been twenty today, bound by earthly constraints. Do not cry, Mom. I am forever, I am eternal, I am ageless. I am in the blowing wind, the first blades of grass in the spring, the haunting cry of the owl, the shriek of the hawk, the silent soaring of the turkey vulture. I am in the tears of those in mourning, the laughter of little children, the pain of the dying, the hopelessness of the homeless. I am the weightless, floating feeling when you close your eyes at night; I am the heaviness of a broken heart. . . . Like an invisible cocoon I surround you. I am in the moonlight, the sunbeams, the dew at dawn. . . . Do not cry. Remember me with love and laughter and yes, with pain. For I was, I am, and I will always be. Once T., now nameless and free.

The child's presence comes within a sense of the uncanny, a feeling often associated with religious belief and practice.[43] In one newsletter account, the uncanny appears twice, first as a dream that seems a premonition, and second as an unaccounted-for physical event. A few months before she was murdered, the daughter told her mother of a dream in which she was looking in the window at the family gathered for Christmas.

On Christmas morning, while we were opening the gifts (which the daughter had made) my husband told me to look out the window. There are two rocking chairs on the porch and one was rocking back and forth. My husband reached over and held my hand, and it was at that moment I remembered what M. had told us about her dream, and I realized then that her dream had become a reality. M. was still with all of us and was indeed content at watching the family she loved so much sharing the joy of Christmas together.

Almost all the parents in the study feel that the child is in heaven. The inner representation of the child as in heaven is held tightly by some parents in the initial shock and disbelief of grief, even before they can develop a sense that they have an active interaction with the child. The separation from the child seems too much to bear for many parents, so even as they feel that their child is nowhere to be found in this world, they retain hope that they will join their child after death. A mother wrote a newsletter early in her grief, before she had put together an integrated inner representation of the child:

There's a hole in me. You see, a part of me is missing. I keep looking for my son, and all I find are bits and pieces of him—something he wrote, a picture he took, a book he read, a tape he made, something he drew— but there is an emptiness in me that these bits and pieces cannot fill, that nothing will ever fill. . . . My son is gone and he is not coming back. I will have to go to him and someday I will.

Such a feeling early in the grief often gives way to a more immediate interaction with the inner representation in a way that, while the hope of reunion after the parent's death is retained, there is a sense of a bond with the child in heaven, which is consoling. This is true even with those for whom heaven is not part of their theology. Knapp found that bereaved par-

ents could not sustain a belief that there is no afterlife for their child.[44] Several people in the study felt the child to be with another significant person who had died. One woman whose father had died four years before her child reported:

It was hard after my father died because I always had this sense that I didn't know where he was. But I was busy with L. because she was so sick all the time. After L. died I was really bothered that I didn't know where she was and that somehow that meant that I didn't know she was safe. That lasted two years. One day I started crying and I realized I wasn't just crying for L. I was missing my father. And suddenly I just thought, "Daddy is taking care of L. She is OK because she is with him and that's where he is. It is like they are together." That sounds so simple-minded. I don't believe in heaven or afterlife. I think we just live on in memory. But it just feels like I don't have that worry about either of them any more. I know they are together.

Within a social system, sharing a religious sense in the bond with the inner representation of a dead child has a quite common form. Ethnic, racial, or political membership is often infused with religious feelings. Indeed, for many people, God and country feel as one. All peoples encourage a strong bond with the dead hero or martyr. Among the symbols that bind a nation together are the internalized representations of its young who died that the nation could have its land, its freedom, its king, its religion, its form of government, or its economic power. Lincoln's address at Gettysburg offers solace to the parents of those buried there, and at the same time it bonds the citizens to the war dead and to the abstract ideals on which the nation was founded. Such solace can, or course, be used destructively. In some pathological cultural systems or in historical situations in which there has been a regression to what Wilber calls mythic membership, blood must be answered by blood.[45] In the name of those fallen for the cause, other people's children may be killed with impunity.[46] It is difficult to stop a cycle of violence when each side merges the solace of the inner representations of dead children with a religious feeling of peoplehood and with a drive for revenge that feels as if it has divine sanction.

Memories

Bereaved parents can find solace in memory. Unconflicted and peaceful memory is often at the end of a difficult process of separating self-representation from the inner representation of the child. Memories are at first very painful, for they are reminders of the loss. One mother reflected on the discovery that letting go of the pain did not also mean letting go of the child.

> You know, I remember being afraid that someday I would wake up and my feeling of being bonded to K. wouldn't be there. I thought that when the pain left, she would be gone too. But now I find that I hope the memories will come. The times in the hospital are not what I remember. I remember the good times, when she was well. Sometimes I just look at her pictures and remember when we took them. I never know when I will look at the pictures, but I feel better afterwards.

This use of memory as solace seems similar to what Tahka calls "remembrance formations." He says once the remembrance formation

> has been established, its later calling back to mind, reminiscing about it and dismissing it again from the mind, are invariably experienced as activities of the self taking place exclusively on the subject's own conditions. Although it is experienced as a fully differentiated object representation, no illusions of its separate and autonomous existence are involved. In contrast to fantasy objects pos-

sessing various wish-fulfilling functions, it includes the awareness that nothing more can be expected from it and therefore, in its fully established forms, it has chances for becoming the most realistic of all existing object representations.[47]

A poem in a newsletter makes the point more gracefully.

> Memories are the
> perennials that
> bloom again
> after the hard winter grief
> begins to
> yield to hope.

Memory can be a part of everyday life. The quiet times remembering the dead child have about them a somewhat forbidden quality, but the memory time becomes a personal ritual around which to build a day.

> Sometimes I pretend, when no one's around,
>   that you are still home,
>   creating you own special sound—
>   the car, the stereo, singing in the shower.

Such thematic memories—that is memories that catch the essence of the individual child—take the parent out of the present and to a time when the world was better.

> I can still envision the surprised, happy look on his face that Christmas when he opened a gift and found a silver vest and pants to wear when he played his bass guitar with his beloved band. . . . I remember when he took me out to eat one Mother's Day, just he and I. . . . how handsome he was in his tux and top hat and how he introduced his date for the prom . . . how proud we all were at his graduation when he gave the welcome address. . . . Wonderful memories are something that no one can take away. Some memories just won't die.

Often it is the emotional states attached to the thematic memories that carry the quality of solace. Writing nearly twenty years after the death of her daughter, a mother reflected on her memory of a beginners' ballet recital.

> I can't remember the details of that afternoon. . . . But I remember the feeling, somewhere between laughter and tears. I remember loving that small, beautiful person, my child. I remember my sense of admiration for her, and a fittingly stifled flood of pride. . . . I have forgotten so many things, but I remember the feeling. Always the feeling.

Memory binds family and communities together. In The Compassionate Friends, the members do not remember each other's children as living, for it was the death of the children which brought members to the group. But the solace of memory is important in the group's bond. The group has developed rituals that express the bond with the child as part of the bonds within the community. Such rituals give permission to each parent to hold the inner representation without conflict. A significant portion of national and regional meetings are devoted to ritual activity, such as boards with pictures of the dead children. The holiday candlelight memorial service is the largest gathering of the local chapter. Many of the members, including "alumnae" who no longer attend meetings, bring the child's siblings, grandparents, uncles, aunts, or family friends. The memory of the child is thus included in the holiday and in the family circle. As the children's names are read the parents and those who have come with them rise and light a candle. A liturgy adopted from *Gates of Prayer*, a Jewish prayer book, is a central part of the memorial service.

> *In the rising of the sun and in its going down,*
>   *We remember them;*
> *In the blowing of the wind and in the chill of winter,*
>   *We remember them;*

> *In the opening of buds and in the warmth of summer,*
>   *We remember them;*
> *In the rustling of leaves and the beauty of autumn,*
>   *We remember them;*
> *In the beginning of the year and when it ends,*
>   *We remember them;*
> *When we are weary and in need of strength,*
>   *We remember them;*
> *When we are lost and sick at heart,*
>   *We remember them;*
> *When we have joys we yearn to share,*
>   *We remember them,*
> *So long as we live, they too shall live, for they are now*
>   *a part of us as*
> *We remember them.*[48]

Solace and Immortality

This essay has looked at three ways in which the inner representation of the child is a solace-giving, ongoing part of the parent's inner world and social world: linking objects, religious devotion, and memories. In each of those ways, the child remains immortal, in the sense that the inner representation of the child remains a real, living presence in the parent's inner and social world.

Most psychosocial thinking about immortality is from the self's point of view. Individuals fear annihilation of the self and compensate, as one psychoanalytic scholar finds, by a "regression to the union of the archaic idealized omnipotent figure in the death-transformation passage to the 'new existence' . . . based on symbiosis with the undifferentiated god."[49] The death of a child brings a most difficult grief in this culture because the sense of selfhood involved in parenting is a central part of the being. The bond reaches back to the parent's own infancy and the bond with the parent's own parents and it reaches forward to the hopes for the completion of the self that children represent. The death of the child is the death of a part of the self. But the child is also not the self. The parents must still live in a poorer world. The child's immortality need not be so regressive.

The continuing interaction with the inner representation of the dead child in bereaved parents seems to support Lifton's idea that the sense of immortality is not compensation or denial and therefore not pathological. Lifton finds that the sense of immortality is "man's symbolization of his ties with both his biological fellows and his history, past and future."[50] The parents' bond with the child already symbolizes the parents' ties to their biological, personal, and cultural history. Bereaved parents often remind each other, "When your parent dies, you lose your past. When your child dies, you lose your future." Solace is required for living in that poorer world. The immortal inner representation of the child maintains the bonds to history and future, to biology and culture symbolized by the living child.

Winnicott notes that art and religion seem to grow out of the blended inner and outer reality first seen in the child's transitional object.[51] The language of one mother writing in the newsletter shows that she already knew the part of herself where she now feels connected to her child.

> I cannot open my eyes to see his smile. I close my eyes and listen to my heart, for it is there that he lives. I must dig deeper inside myself to a place that I ever knew existed to feel the joy this child brought.

In many of his sonnets Shakespeare asks how a dead friend or lover can live on. He seems finally to settle upon the immortality of his own art, for if he can join the reality of the deceased to the "eternal lines" of the poem, the dead person is made immortal.[52] Thus Shakespeare locates the immortality of the dead in his art much the way bereaved parents locate their dead children in their experience of solace.

> And every fair from fair sometime declines,
> By chance or nature's changing course untrimm'd;

> But thy eternal summer shall not fade
> Nor lose possession of that fair thou owest;
> Nor shall Death brag thou wander'st in his shade,
> When in eternal lines to time thou growest:
> So long as men can breath or eyes can see,
> So long lives this and this gives life to thee. (Sonnet 18)

For their parents, dead children do not lose possession of that fairness they embodied, nor do they wander only in Death's shade. They have lived just the summer, but their summer does not fade; it remains eternal in a part of the parent's psyche and in the social system where the parent feels most at home. The parents find solace in linking objects that evoke the presence of the dead, in religious ideas and devotion which merge the child with other death-transcending connections of the parent's life, and in memories by which time can drop away and the parent can return to the world when it was a better place. So long lives this in the inner and social world of bereaved parents, this gives life to their children who have died.

Such immortality is not the only immortality available after a child dies. For example, passing of genetic material is a universal form of immortality. Shakespeare recognizes:

> But were some child of yours alive at time,
> You should live twice; in it and in my rhyme.
> (Sonnet 17)

Human efforts to create external symbols of immortality feel less sure, and in the end less meaningful, than the immortality bereaved parents find in the solace-filled bond with their child.

> Not marble, nor the gilded monuments
> Of princes, shall outlive this powerful rhyme;
> But you shall shine more bright in these contents

Than unswept stone, besmeared with
sluttish time. . . .
So, til the judgement that yourself arise,
You live in this, and dwell in lover's eyes.
(Sonnet 60)

The immortal children are present in the
same world in which the parent lives, not in
another world. Harper says:

There are persons whom we cannot think
of except as being alive. They seem to resist
destruction, even when dead. . . . Around
them, even remembering them, whether away
for a while or permanently, we feel the whole
world a more vibrant as well as more interesting place.[53]

In a new life that sometimes feels neither sure
nor safe, the immortal child provides a solace-
filled reality that feels both inside and outside
the self, that does not change, and the truth of
which cannot be challenged.

Clinical Implications

The resolution of a parent's grief is adaptation,
growth, and change, not recovery of the way
he or she was before the death. Parents now
live in a different world with a self that has
been changed. The change in the world is that
a child, their child, has died. Among the
changes in the self is the transformed inner
representation of the now-dead child. What,
then, is the role of the clinician in grief support
groups or counseling? Clinical issues may be
(a) stress in everyday life after the death of the
child, (b) difficulties in transforming the inner
representation of the child, or (c) ensuring that
the inner representation of the child is held in
as healthy a way as possible.

With parents whom The Compassionate
Friends describe as "well along in their grief,"
the nature and mode of the inner representation can be determined with questions like:
"Who is C. to you right now?" "How are you
still in touch with C.?" "Where is C. for you
now?" "What role does C. still play in your

life?" Most parents whose grief is well toward
resolution can give a rather full answer to
these questions and often can discuss problems
they are having in managing the relationship
with the inner representation of the child. This
information enables the clinician to share the
client's world in order to deal with whatever
issues are at hand. Because some phenomena
in the interaction with dead children fall outside socially accepted reality, parents may
monitor their answer in terms of the perceived
attitude of the questioner.

Bereaved parents who are, as The Compassionate Friends describe it, "new in their grief"
or "early in their grief," will usually not be
able to answer the questions to their own satisfaction; and indeed, many answer the question
in terms of absence or of the lack of connection. In this case, the clinician makes the inner
representation part of the bond with the client.
The clinician gets to know the child through
photographs, art work, or stories of the child.
It is not unusual for parents to bring linking
objects into the consulting room. After the
child is established as a social reality and the
early issues of grief are navigated, parents
begin to discuss the problems of living, the
meanings of life, and the meaning of the death
partly in terms of the meaning of the child
now. Often at this time, the clinician will hear
reports of visitations or interchanges with the
child, and will begin to hear reports of the
solace those interactions bring.

There are two especially difficult clinical situations involving the inner representation of
the child. The first is when the inner representation is not shared in the client's natural support networks. There are a variety of reasons
the inner representation may not be shared.
After miscarriage often family and friends do
not regard the fetus as a child, while the parent
has already bonded with a whole set of hopes
and expectations. When a married couple is a
birth-parent and a stepparent, conflict may
ensue if the stepparent has not deeply bonded
to the child and, thus, does not share the birth-

parent's inner representation of the dead child. There are also parents who are unusually isolated from social networks, and parents whose child died in such a socially unacceptable way that the parent is cut off from social support. When the inner representation is not a social reality, it is difficult to use it for solace. In these cases, referral to The Compassionate Friends or other grief support groups is often effective. When referral does not work, the therapist and the client can form the community in which the inner representation can become real.

The second difficult situation is when the inner representation becomes intertwined in individual or family pathology. In these cases, clinicians can work with the individual and family using the same theories and techniques they would use if the bond were with the living child. When the child is maintained as a frozen entity in the family system, the issue is flexibility. As the family can be helped to be more flexible, the inner representation will take a healthier place in the new dynamics. If a parent has so identified with the child that the whole selfhood was dependent on the child, the thera-

peutic issue is differentiation. When differentiation is achieved, the inner representation will provide solace rather than being a reminder of the parent's unfulfilled narcissistic bond.

In the easiest clinical situation, the clinician is called upon to validate the parents' experiences of interaction with the inner representation of their dead child. The clinician's authority can be used to normalize the experience. Learning that such experiences are normal and common often relieves a great deal of stress and thereby allows the parent to accept the solace being offered by the inner representation of the child.

Bereaved parents in The Compassionate Friends remain in active interaction with the inner representations of their dead children. As clinicians learn to understand how these immortal children take their place in the parents' lives, and how the inner representations give solace in the face of irreparable loss, the clinician can more effectively help parents deal with the stresses in their lives and untangle whatever pathologies present themselves.

Detachment Revisited:
The Child's Reconstruction of a Dead Parent

PHYLLIS R. SILVERMAN, STEVEN NICKMAN, AND J. WILLIAM WORDEN

PHYLLIS R. SILVERMAN, PH.D., is a professor at the Institute of Health Professions and an associate in social welfare in the Department of Psychiatry at Massachusetts General Hospital and Harvard Medical School. Her work with the widowed began in 1965 when Gerald Caplan asked her to develop a preventive intervention program that would decrease the risk of a widowed person developing emotional problems. She accepted the assignment with great reluctance since she generally closed her eyes when she went by cemeteries and was not good at coping with issues of bereavement. She allowed herself to be recruited because she could satisfy her interest in developing relevant preventive interventions for populations at risk.

In the following three years, she met her future husband, acquired an instant family of three children, had two children, completed her doctorate, and wrote her first paper, in which she proposed the concept of widow-to-widow social support as the most appropriate intervention for the newly widowed. When she came up for air, the program was launched. It has become a model for mutual help programs and support groups in the United States and abroad. Dr. Silverman has worked in the areas of bereavement and mutual help ever since. She has also learned to accept the reality of death and to keep her eyes open.

As she ran her widow-to-widow demonstration project, Dr. Silverman wondered if the children of widows were not having a more difficult time than they. She became co-principal investigator and project director of Mass General's now-completed Child Bereavement Study, a longitudinal study of the impact of the death of a parent on school-age children.

Dr. Silverman has served as consultant to several task forces on bereavement and primary prevention convened by the National Institute of Mental Health, and she has consulted with hospices, hospitals, and social agencies in the United States and abroad on bereavement, mutual help,

and prevention. She is the recipient of the 1991 Presidential medal from Brooklyn College, City University of New York, for her outstanding contributions to the fields of bereavement and social welfare. She spent the 1993–1994 academic year at the School of Social Work at Haifa University in Israel as a Senior Research Fulbright Fellow. In Israel, she is directing a study of children's reactions to the death of a parent similar to the one she completed in the United States and is comparing the reactions of children in the two countries.

Dr. Silverman has published extensively in professional journals and her books include *Helping Each Other in Widowhood* (1975), *Mutual Help Groups: A Guide for Mental Health Professionals* (1978), *Mutual Help Groups: Organization and Development* (1980), *Helping Women Cope with Grief* (1981), *Widow-to-Widow* (1986), and *Widower: When Men Are Left Alone* (1987).

STEVEN NICKMAN, M.D., is director of the Adoption and Custody Unit in the Department of Child Psychiatry at Massachusetts General Hospital and a clinical assistant professor at Harvard Medical School. He describes himself as a "child psychiatrist in general practice—a lot of therapy, some medications, some family counseling, and evaluations for courts." He first became interested in loss through a personal experience which led him and his wife to adopt. When his son began to express sadness and confusion about adoption, Dr. Nickman read everything he could find about the losses adoptees experience which resulted in his book *The Adoption Experience,* a resource for junior high and high-school age adoptees. Meanwhile, he had also been doing divorce custody evaluations for courts, and this led to the writing of a second book for school-age children, *When Mom and Dad Divorce.*

When Dr. Silverman initiated her research on childhood bereavement, she invited Dr. Nickman to be a consultant. They had collaborated earlier on an adoption research proposal and on the surrogacy case of "Baby M." Drs. Nickman and Silverman believe that there are similarities in adoption, divorce, and bereavement; in all these situations, children need the help of an adult to form an internal picture of the person who is absent or less available than before.

J. WILLIAM WORDEN, PH.D., is a clinical psychologist specializing in the area of life-threatening illness. During the 1960s, while providing mental health services to the fine arts community— primarily actors and musicians—Dr. Worden attended a social gathering at which the chief of psychiatry at Boston University suggested that he might enjoy meeting Dr. Avery Weisman, who was then beginning studies of the psychosocial aspects of terminal illness. Having read Herman Feifel's landmark book, *The Meaning of Death,* and with an academic background in existential philosophy, education, and theology as well as psychology, Dr. Worden found Dr. Weisman's work intriguing and engaging. In 1968 he joined Dr. Weisman at Harvard in establishing the Omega Project, a series of NIH-funded studies on the psychosocial aspects of terminal illness, cancer, suicide, and bereavement. Their pioneer-

ing work in this area included receiving the first research grant funded by the National Cancer Institute to study the psychosocial aspects of cancer.

Dr. Worden has been actively involved in hospice care, having served on the initial board of advisors for the Connecticut Hospice, and he is currently a consultant to the Hospice of Pasadena, California. He was a founding member of the International Work Group on Death, Dying, and Bereavement (IWG) and of the Association for Death Education and Counseling (ADEC). He was awarded the Clinical Practice Award by ADEC in 1993.

Dr. Worden is co-director of the Child Bereavement Study at Massachusetts General Hospital, where he was recently honored for twenty-five years of service, and he holds academic appointments at Harvard Medical School and the Rosemead Graduate School of Psychology in California. He is well-known for his book *Grief Counseling and Grief Therapy*, a widely used text that has been translated into several foreign languages, and is the author of *Personal Death Awareness* and co-author of *Helping Cancer Patients Cope*. His research has been published in medical and psychiatric journals.

THE OBSERVATION THAT children maintain a connection to deceased parents is not new.[1] However, there are different interpretations of this observation and different theories about the nature of the connection. In their studies of parents whose children had died, Klass and Rubin concluded that remaining connected to the deceased seems to be a necessary part of the bereavement process— that it is adaptive and facilitates an accommodation to the death.[2] Lifton described strategies that mourners used to provide the deceased with "symbolic immortality."[3] Others have reported that for successful mourning to take place, the mourner must disengage from the deceased, that is, let go of the past.[4] This experience of the deceased is often thought of as symptomatic of psychological

problems.[5] In her study of bereaved preschool children attending a therapeutic nursery school, Furman noted that it is important for children to loosen their ties to their deceased parents and suggested that therapists should encourage detachment behavior.[6] This formulation has its roots in Freud's observations that patients best resolved their grief when they gradually withdrew the mental energy they had extended toward the lost love object and reinvested this energy in new relationships.[7]

The conceptualizations that prescribe detachment were drawn primarily from clinical interactions with troubled people. Thus, they may be based on a sample that is overly representative of individuals who had recourse to relatively primitive defense mechanisms, such as denial. These people, who may have experienced greater than normal difficulty in accepting the reality of the death, were more likely to exhibit an inappropriate investment in the past.[8] The present paper, based on interviews with children who had lost a parent, is an attempt to broaden our understanding of the bereavement process and the ways in which the deceased is experienced by a nonclinical population.

In the psychoanalytic literature on children, efforts to maintain a connection to the deceased parent are seen as internal representations of the dead parent.[9] Identification and internalization are considered processes that the bereaved use to keep an aspect of the deceased with them forever.[10] These inner representations are described as unchanging. Dietrich and Shabad emphasized the paradoxical character of the inner representation of the deceased: one that is both frozen in time and timeless—immortalized and lost simultaneously.[11] Schafer regarded a bereaved child's inner representations of the lost parent as persisting unmodified and inaccessible to secondary-process thinking.[12]

The concept of internalization, however, does not fully describe the process that bereaved children undergo. What the authors observed was more colorful, dynamic, and interactive than the term *internalization* suggests. In fact, this inner representation was not buried in the unconscious or stable over time. The child was aware of the inner representation, and the representation seemed to change with time as the child developed. Playwright Robert Anderson used the word *relationship* to describe his experience of the deceased, as did such researchers as Klass and Rubin.[13]

Rizzuto observed that the process of constructing inner representations involves the whole individual and that these representations are not static, but grow and change with the individual's development and maturation.[14] She also noted the importance of the role of others in the construction of inner representations of significant people in her subjects' lives. Construction, she suggested, is partly a social activity. This observation is supported by the findings of Rosenblatt and Elde, who studied bereaved families and found that grief work included maintaining connections with memories of the deceased.[15] Mourners kept these memories "alive" by remembering, both in solitude and in the company of others, while integrating their memories into the present and into relationships with others.

A helpful family environment has positive facilitating effects. While individual family members have their "internalization," or inner representation of the deceased, the family as a whole may also have communal or shared representations, which may be experienced by individual members as existing or proceeding from outside the self; these can be altered as people and relationships change. Klass made a similar observation about the importance of others in helping bereaved parents maintain an active "relationship" with their dead children.[16]

An analogous situation may occur with the disclosure of the fact of adoption to a child who was placed in infancy.[17] How well the adoptive parents are able to remain in touch with the child's developing internal representation of the birthparents can affect the child's self-esteem, personality development, and overall level of functioning. How well the adoptive parents help their child build a realistic representation of the birthparents that is compatible with the child's changing ability to understand is also a factor. With a child who is adopted later, the experience is similar to that of the bereaved child because the child is old enough to remember his or her birthparents.

The authors propose that it may be normative for mourners to maintain a presence and connection with the deceased and that this presence is not static. Just as the adopted child faces the question, "How could they give me up?" and deals with the birthparents' motivation over a period of years, so the bereaved child must deal with how and why the parent died and what the parent's presence may have been like had it continued over time. One cannot deal with a loss without recognizing *what* is lost.

The construction of the lost parent is an ongoing cognitive process. The nature of the construction of the deceased is connected to the child's developmental level, with particular reference to children's changing ability to know themselves and to know others.[18] For example, a critical developmental shift takes place when a child moves from seeing others in terms of how these others can meet his or her needs to seeing others as people with needs of their own and with whom some reciprocity is required for a relationship to be sustained. Although the deceased does not change, the child's ability to understand a given set of information about this person will change as the child matures.

The word *construction* derives from the Latin *struere,* to make something out of component parts; to construe is to analyze or set out logically the figurative aspects of a thing. In the psychological literature, constructivism refers to a theoretical position that regards persons or systems as constituting or constructing their own reality.[19] The authors see the child's attempt to maintain a connection to a dead parent as an active effort to make sense of the experience of loss and to make it part of the child's reality.

Data to be reported in this paper, drawn from a longitudinal study of the impact of a parent's death on school-age children, suggest a process of adaptation and change in the post-death relationship and the construction and reconstruction of new connections. On the basis of these observations, the authors posit that learning to remember and finding a way to maintain a connection to the deceased that is consistent with the child's cognitive development and family dynamics are aspects of an accommodation process that allows the child to go on living in the face of the loss. The pres-

ent paper investigates the elements from which this connection is made and describes what the connection looks like phenomenologically.

Child Bereavement Study

The Child Bereavement Study is a prospective study of children aged 6–17, one of whose parents has died. Families representing a range of socioeconomic and ethnic backgrounds were recruited from communities in the greater Boston area; 70 percent of the families were Catholic, reflecting the large concentration of Roman Catholics in this region. Interviews were conducted in the family home with each child and with the surviving parent at four months, one year, and then two years after the death.[20]

Seventy families with 125 children were interviewed. There were an almost equal number of boys and girls in the sample, with an average age of 11.6 years. Seventy-two percent of the children had lost a father and 28 percent a mother. The average age of the surviving parent was 41 years, with a range of 30 to 57 years for the surviving mothers and 33 to 50 years for the surviving fathers. In the case of 58 percent of the children (34 boys and 38 girls), the parent had died after a long illness.

For most couples (91 percent), this was their only marriage, and the mean length of their marriage had been 17 years. The modal number of children was two. In nine of the families, the child who participated in the study was an only child.

Family incomes after the death ranged from less that $10,000 a year to more than $50,000, with a median income range of $20,000–$29,000. Before the death, men were the primary breadwinners in the families. Many women worked part time outside the home, providing the family with a second income.

Data presented in this paper were taken primarily from the first two semistructured research interviews with these bereaved children and their surviving parents at four months and then at one year after the death. Where appropriate, data from the third interview were used. All the interviews were taped; if a tape was not transcribed, the authors listened to it. These interviews included questions regarding the parent's death, the child's mourning behavior, and the child's thoughts about the deceased, in part informed by one of the author's prior research on bereaved children.[21]

Additional qualitative data were drawn from the children's responses to the Child's Understanding of Death questionnaire.[22] The analysis of date followed that recommended by Strauss,[23] leading to the development of a theory of the bereavement process that is grounded in the data.[24] The authors studied a sample of these interviews to identify themes and then read additional records to determine whether the same themes were present.[25] The remainder of this paper describes the elements from which a connection to the deceased is constructed.

Awareness of Death

The children's responses were initially examined to see if their efforts to connect with the deceased were the consequences of a faulty understanding of the concept of death. Findings from research on nonbereaved children raise questions about the age at which a child understands the irreversibility and finality of death.[26] These bereaved children, regardless of their age, seemed aware of the meaning of death. One seven-year-old girl had no doubt about the finality of her father's death: "Sometimes I want to talk to him, but I go to sleep fast so I won't think about his being gone." A ten-year-old said: "He's not with me, and it hurts."

It was with great difficulty that these children accustomed themselves to the fact that their parents were dead. The contrast between presence and absence often seemed too diffi-

cult for them to contemplate, and their discomfort was apparent. In response to the standardized question, "What does it mean when someone dies?" a ten-year-old boy said, "I can't think about that." It seemed impossible to think that his father was gone. Some children, especially those whose parents died suddenly, talked about the shock they felt when they heard the news.

Their new reality required an understanding of death that is not typical of nonbereaved children of the same ages. A 12-year-old girl whose mother died after a long illness said that she could not talk about her mother because it "simply hurts too much." She added: "However, I don't want her to come back and be in such pain." When asked how he felt after his father's death, one 13-year-old boy said plaintively: "I don't know. . . . I just know he's not here anymore." The connection to the deceased cannot be dismissed as merely a way of denying the finality of the loss. The special tension in these children was clear. Although they were aware that their parents were dead, they experienced their parents as still existing in themselves and in their world. This duality caused cognitive dissonance for some and may have accounted for some of the inarticulateness seen shortly after the loss.

Strategies of Connection

Five categories were identified that reflect the child's efforts to maintain a connection to the deceased parent during this period: (1) making an effort to locate the deceased, (2) actually experiencing the deceased in some way, (3) reaching out to initiate a connection, (4) remembering, and (5) keeping something that belonged to the deceased. The majority of the children reported some activity in each area. There seemed to be no significant relationship between the type of death or the gender or age of the child and any of these responses. These aspects are discussed next, along with anecdotal data from interviews with the children.

Locating the Deceased

When asked where they thought the dead parent was presently, most of the children were able to locate the deceased. Of the 125 children, 92 (74 percent) believed in a place called "heaven" and that once dead, this was where their parents were; the other 33 (26 percent) were uncertain what they believed. There was no relationship between a child's age and his or her belief about an afterlife, nor was there any relationship between a child's belief system and how frequently the child dreamed or thought about the dead parent.

Although 70 percent of the sample were Roman Catholic and Catholic theology encourages children to believe in the existence of heaven and in a life after death, there was no statistical relationship between the children's expressed beliefs and their religious background. Many non-Catholic children shared a similar belief system in which their parents had some form of existence in a place called "heaven." Even children in their early teens, who were otherwise developmentally and cognitively sophisticated, did not always distinguish between the state of being of the spirit and the body. Many continued to endow the deceased, now residing in heaven, with concrete attributes of a living person, e.g., that dead people see, hear, feel, and move. Others acknowledged a difference between the body that was buried and the soul that was in heaven, but they still endowed the soul with living qualities of vision, hearing, and mobility.

By contrast, matched nonbereaved control children were less likely to endow a deceased person with living attributes. Locating the deceased in a distant place (heaven) seemed to help the bereaved children make sense of their experience: although the deceased cannot see, feel and move *here*, they may be able to do so in the place to which they have gone (a place that cannot be seen from here).

The words of a 14-year-old Catholic boy whose father died reflected this belief:

> I want my father to see me perform. If I said a dead person can't see, then I would not be able to have my wish that he see what I am doing. I believe that the dead see, hear, move. Don't ask me how, I just believe it. Heaven is a mysterious place. My father is with all the other relatives that died.

Belief in heaven allowed this boy to maintain a sense that his father was still in his life. A 17-year-old Jewish girl, two years after her father died, was clear about the permanency and finality of death, as would be expected, given her age. In her religious education the concept of heaven or an afterlife was not mentioned. However, in her response to a question about whether the dead can see or hear, she said:

> Yes, the dead can see and hear. It's what I would *like* to think, so he could hear comforting words and . . . that maybe he can see significant events in my life.

A similar cognitive construction was made by a 15-year-old girl who both saw her father in heaven and recognized that some of what she was experiencing was of her own making:

> I think heaven is not a definite place. . . . I know I'm not imagining him . . . it's not as if I actually see him standing there, but I feel him and, like, in my mind I hear his voice.

Experiencing the Deceased

Believing that their dead parents were watching them was an extension of this construction of the parents being in heaven and provided these children with yet another way of connecting with their dead parents. Of the 125 children, 101 (81 percent) felt that their deceased parents were watching them, and of those who felt watched, 71 (57 percent) were "scared" by this feeling. These children's uneasiness was related to their fear that their dead parent might not approve of what they were doing. As an 11-year-old boy said:

> I sometimes think he is watching me. It scares me because sometimes he might see me do something he wouldn't like. Like, it's weird . . . it's not scary . . . like if you're doing something, like if someone's watching you, you don't do it, if it's bad. You don't do it if someone's watching.

This boy saw his father in the role of disciplinarian, and his feelings about his father included experiencing him as a helpful external control to supplement his incompletely formed superego. A teenage girl talked about how important good grades were for her mother. She said almost playfully that she could imagine her mother "yelling in heaven if I didn't do well in school."

In contrast, a child who did not have a good relationship with her father pictured him in a dream with a mean facial expression, but she could not make out his attitude toward her with any certainty. The dream frightened her and seemed to reflect an aspect of their relationship before his death that was not affirming of the child. It is apparent that, whether the parent was a disciplinarian, a nurturer, or one whose response might be unpredictable, the child experienced the parent in a way that reflected aspects of their relationship before the death.

Some children experienced their parents as communicating with them in a benevolent way that reflected the parents' status as spirits. One nine-year-old boy saw flashing colored dots in his bedroom at night and said he liked to think that it was his mother trying to be in touch with him. When he asked his father if it was possible, his father allowed the possibility and did not try to rationalize the experience away. An adolescent girl noticed a puff of wind blowing open the door of a restaurant where both she and her mother had worked and

thought of it as her mother's presence coming to visit. This perception became a standing, good-natured joke between her and the others working in the restaurant.

Another way of experiencing the deceased was through dreams. Many children (56 percent, $N = 69$) dreamed about their parents and, for almost all of them ($N = 63$), the parents were alive in the dreams. As one child put it:

> I dreamed he met me on the way home from school and that he hugged me. When I woke up, I felt so sad that I won't have that anymore.

Even though the children felt sad when faced with the fact that their parents' presence was only a dream, some children found these dreams comforting:

> When I wake up from these dreams, I know she's gone, but when I dream, it feels like she is there and it's reality.
>
> I'm not sure but I hear his voice at night. It's probably in my dreams. He tells me he likes what I did, that I did real good.

Experiencing the deceased in this way tempered the pain and provided an occasion for the child to get parental approval: "It feels good to remember, to feel that he is still part of the family."

Children who found their deceased parents available to them in this way attributed some initiative to the parents and saw themselves as recipients. At some level, they knew that this construction was probably coming from something within themselves. This understanding may be similar to what Weisman called "middle knowledge": a partial awareness of the reality of death that forms the best compromise between an unpleasant truth and a wished-for state of events.[27]

Reaching Out to the Deceased

Children also took some initiative to keep a connection. Visiting the cemetery was one way of actively seeking a place where they could "find" the deceased. For many, the cemetery was the place where they had the last contact with their parents. A 12-year-old girl whose mother had died said: "I go to the cemetery when I feel sad and I need someone to talk with." "Going to the cemetery makes me feel close." A 15-year-old boy, who passed the cemetery on his way home from school, stated:

> I don't talk about it much, but I stop by
> to visit about once a week. I tell him about
> my day and things I've done.

Speaking to the deceased was another way of bringing the parent into the child's life. Seventy-one children (57 percent) spoke to their deceased parents. The initiative to choose the place was clearly with the child. A teenage girl said: "I say 'Hi, how are you?' when I go by her picture in the house." A 10-year-old boy reported: "In my mind, I talk to him; I tell him what I did today, about the fish I caught and that I did real good." Although 43 percent ($N = 29$) of these children, mostly younger, felt they received an answer, they were not usually able to tell us what their parents said. A 15-year-old girl remarked: "It's not that I heard him, but in my head I felt he said, 'You'll be OK. Carry on.'" A 16-year-old described her experience one year after her mother died:

> My mother was my friend. I could talk
> to her about anything. I talk to her, but she
> can't respond. She doesn't tell me what to do,
> but like she helps me—I can't explain it.

The ability to take an active role in relation to the death of their parents was reflected in the children's answers to the question, "What advice would you give another child who had lost a parent?" Some children could not answer this question and responded, "I don't know" or "I can't think of anything." These were the same children who did not dream about or talk to their deceased parents. They did not seem to have a place, as yet, for the deceased in their lives. The majority of chil-

dren, however, did have suggestions, and most counseled fortitude. They said they would advise another child "not to let it get you down all the time" and that "it's possible to carry on." They also said, "It's best to think about the person who died and to remember the good times that you had." "Just think of them as often as you can." "It helps to go to the cemetery a lot to let them know." These responses reflected the ability of some children to organize their experience and to reflect on what would be helpful to others in the same plight.

Waking Memories

The dead parents were present in the children's waking thoughts as well. These waking thoughts involved both reflection and memory. At the four-month interview, 90 percent of those responding were still thinking about their deceased parents at least several times a week. When asked what they thought about, most children remembered in fairly literal and concrete terms what they did with their parents. A 15-year-old girl whose mother had died said: "I think about the stupid little things we did together." A seven-year-old said, in remembering her father: "I think about all the things that he used to bring me and how he used to flip me over."

A few children reported that they still could not believe the death was real and sometimes forgot their parents had died. Others, reflecting on their new reality, thought about how hard it was to get along without their parents and wished for them to come back. Such reflections were painful and contrasted to the comforting memories that some children counseled a hypothetical bereaved child to call upon.

Linking Objects

Having an object belonging to the deceased was an important means of maintaining a link to him or her. *Linking objects,* a term used by

Volkan, refers to an aspect of the relationship or an object from that relationship that keeps the mourner living in the past.[28] A more positive link or connection can be found in the concept of *transitional objects*—those that connect one realm of experience with another.[29] These transitional objects provide comfort while one is engaged in the initial mourning process. Of the 125 children, 95 (77 percent) had something personal that belonged to their dead parents. They acquired these objects in different ways. Often it was something the deceased had given them or something belonging to the deceased that the child had taken after the death. Sometimes their surviving parents had given the objects to them or told them they could take what they wanted from the deceased parents' possessions. For the most part, the children kept these items either on their person or in their rooms. One teenage girl said: "It makes me feel good to wear his shirt to school." Another girl said: "I carry his key chain; it makes me feel good . . . the way some people use crystals or whatever."

As the first year of mourning progressed, some of these transitional objects became less powerful for the children and took on more of the characteristics of "keepsakes."[30] A 13-year-old boy took his father's baseball hat and his cologne right after he learned that the father was dead. He did not understand why he did so, but he just reached out and took what was there and put it in his room. A year later both objects were still in his room. The hat now hung in a remote corner, rather than on the bedpost. Two years after the death, the boy was not sure what had happened to the hat. However, he said that he was reassured by his feeling that his father was always with him, making sure that "I am safe and stuff."

Role of the Surviving Parent

As was noted earlier, the authors see the process of constructing a connection to the deceased as part of an ongoing family dialogue. Not every parent was prepared to talk about the deceased, however. One father, who was primarily concerned with keeping his family going, remarked that his children had forgotten how often they were angry with their mother for being so involved outside the home. He acknowledged that he would listen to the children, but had little patience for their reminiscences. These children finally discovered that they could talk with each other about their mother and thus felt less frustrated with their father's silence.

On the other hand, some parents were eager to talk, but were met with resistance from the children. As one boy said, "I know my father would listen, but I don't want to talk." One year later, the boy remarked: "Talking makes me sad, but it is better than thinking about it alone. My father listens, and it really helps."

A 10-year-old boy whose sadness was clear and who could not talk about his father told the interviewer that his mother helped him to develop a positive memory of his father:

> She says we'll pray every night for Daddy and that he'll be able to see me. She says we have to remember Daddy outside in the sunshine laughing, not like he looked when he died. I asked if Daddy can help me now, if he'll always be with me. Mom said yes.

The children seemed to be comforted by being reminded of their dead parents, even when such reminders did not come from direct conversations with their surviving parents. Although he did not share his reaction with his mother, one 14-year-old commented: "It makes me feel good when I hear my mother talking to someone about how nice my father was."

Changes Over Time

By the second interview, some children who initially had reported no relevant dreams and who seemed to have little or no connection with the deceased found it easier to remember. An 11-year-old girl reported during the first interview that she did not dream about her mother, and she could not describe her to the interviewer. She was unable to concentrate at school because of her thoughts about her mother's absence. She did not possess anything that had belonged to her mother. Her sadness was palpable. She could not talk about her feelings, and she did not feel close to anyone in the family with whom she could talk about her mother.

By the end of the first year, this girl began to dream. She wanted to keep the dreams private, but said they went back to before her mother died. She visited the cemetery, where she talked to her mother; in her head, she could hear her mother's voice, giving her good advice. She took some of her mother's jewelry and kept it in her room. Her schoolwork improved, and her sadness seemed less pervasive. She talked to her friends and her father about her mother and what her mother was like:

> This Christmas was hard, but I got through it because I got used to it. Just looking at her picture is hard because I miss her. I think about whether or not she can see me and she can hear me. Is she happy? I hear her voice in my head telling me it's OK. I talk to my friends I can trust and to my dad because he loved her, too, and understands what I am going through.

It is not clear if this girl was better able to confront the loss and tolerate sad feelings because she found a way of connecting with her deceased mother or if being able to tolerate her feelings enabled her to connect with her mother.

Discussion

This paper has described an aspect of the bereavement process in children: the establishment of a set of memories, feelings, and actions that the authors have called "constructing" the deceased. This inner representa-

tion or construction leads the child to remain in a relationship with the deceased, and this relationship changes as the child matures and as the intensity of the grief lessens. The concept of identification is insufficient to describe what was observed. A child may construct a sense of the deceased and develop an inner representation of that person that does not involve (at either a conscious or an unconscious level) becoming like that person. Memorializing, remembering, and knowing who died are active processes that may continue throughout the child's entire life. Rubin noted that there seems to be a relationship between the comfort and fluidity with which the bereaved can relate to the representations of the deceased and their ability to cope effectively with the loss.[31] Although the intensity of the relationship with the deceased must diminish with time, it does not disappear. This is not a matter of living in the past, but rather recognizing how the past informs the present.

These findings suggest a shift in our understanding of the bereavement process. Bereavement should not be viewed as a psychological state that ends or from which one recovers. The intensity of feelings may lessen and the child may become oriented more to the future that to the past, but a concept of closure that requires a determination of when the bereavement process ends does not seem compatible with the view suggested by these findings. The emphasis should be on negotiating and renegotiating the meaning of the loss over time, rather than on letting go. While the loss is permanent and unchanging, the process is not. Thus bereavement should be understood as a cognitive, as well as an emotional, process that takes place in a social context of which the deceased is a part.

Children's cognitive processes include their ability to experience complex feeling states, as well as their inborn qualities and their intellectual and social development. Piaget observed that development involves a push toward greater mastery of one's situation.[32] In Kegan's view, mastery emerges as children construct and reconstruct their world to find greater coherence and new meanings that can unify memories and feelings into a temporary coherent whole that prevails until the child moves to the next stage of development.[33] The ability to call up memories of specific events; abstractions concerning the nature of past interactions; and, on the highest level, descriptions of the deceased's personality, likes, and dislikes depends on the child's level of development.

Accommodation may be a more suitable term than *recovery* or *closure* for what takes place as a result of a death in the family. However, in this context, accommodation should not be viewed as a static phenomenon. Rather, it is a continuing set of activities—related both to others and to shifting self-perceptions as the child's mind and body change—that affect the way the child constructs meaning. In this process, the child seeks to gain not only an understanding of the meaning of death, but a sense of the meaning of this now-dead parent in his or her life. To do so requires the development of a common language for talking about the death and the person who died.

When an experience is re-created in language, it may lose in immediacy, but it is more likely to be kept in memory. Critical to representation in language is the family's use of ritual that could legitimate the construction of an inner representation of the deceased. Most non-Western cultures have rituals that help their members acknowledge and cope with loss and with the sense of the deceased.[34] The need for such rituals is acknowledged less in contemporary Western thinking and worldviews. We may need to look anew at rituals that facilitate dialogue and other kinds of relationships to the past.

The interview data reported in this paper have identified ways in which the child maintains a connection to the deceased parent. These data challenge the traditional clinical practice of encouraging the bereaved to disengage from the deceased. In facilitating mourning, those who work with children may need to focus on how to transform connections and place the relationship in a new perspective, rather than on how to separate from the deceased.

Recognizing Hidden Sorrow

Disenfranchised Grief

KENNETH J. DOKA

KEN DOKA, PH.D., is a professor of gerontology at the College of New Rochelle in New York. He became interested in the study of death and dying quite inadvertently. Scheduled to do a practicum in a facility that housed juvenile delinquents, he discovered that his supervisor had changed the assignment. Instead, Doka found himself counseling dying children and their families at Sloan-Kettering, a major cancer hospital in New York. This experience became the basis of two graduate theses, one in sociology entitled "The Social Organization of Terminal Care in Two Pediatric Hospitals," and the other in religious studies entitled "Pastoral Counseling to Dying Children and Their Families." (Both were later published.) His doctoral program pursued another longstanding interest: the sociology of aging. In 1983, Dr. Doka accepted his present position at the College of New Rochelle where he specializes in thanatology and gerontology.

Active in the Association for Death Education and Counseling since its beginnings, Dr. Doka was elected its president in 1993. In addition to articles in scholarly journals, he is the author of *Death and Spirituality* (with John Morgan, 1993), *Living with Life-Threatening Illness* (1993), and *Disenfranchised Grief: Recognizing Hidden Sorrow* (1989), from which the following selection is excerpted. His work on disenfranchised grief began in the classroom when a graduate student commented, "If you think widows have it rough, you ought to see what happens when your ex-spouse dies."

Introduction

Ever since the publication of Lindemann's classic article, "Symptomatology and Management of Acute Grief," the literature on the nature of grief and bereavement has been growing.[1] In the few decades following this seminal study, there have been comprehensive studies of grief reactions,[2] detailed descriptions of atypical manifestations of grief,[3] theoretical and clinical treatments of grief reactions,[4] and considerable research considering the myriad variables that affect grief.[5] But most of this literature has concentrated on grief reactions in socially recognized and sanctioned roles: those of the parent, spouse, or child.

There are circumstances, however, in which a person experiences a sense of loss but does not have a socially recognized right, role, or capacity to grieve. In these cases, the grief is disenfranchised.[6] The person suffers a loss but has little or no opportunity to mourn publicly.

Up until now, there has been little research touching directly on the phenomenon of disenfranchised grief. In her comprehensive review of grief reactions, Raphael notes the phenomenon:

> There may be other dyadic partnership relationships in adult life that show patterns similar to the conjugal ones, among them, the young couple intensely, even secretly, in love; the defacto relationships; the extramarital relationship; and the homosexual couple. . . . Less intimate partnerships of close friends, working mates, and business associates, may have similar patterns of grief and mourning.[7]

Focusing on the issues, reactions, and problems in particular populations, a number of studies have noted special difficulties that these populations have in grieving. For example, Kelly and Kimmel, in studies of aging homosexuals, have discussed the unique problems of grief in such relationships.[8] Similarly, studies of the reactions of significant others of AIDS victims have considered bereavement.[9] Other studies have considered the special problems of unacknowledged grief in prenatal death,[10] [the death of] ex-spouses,[11] therapists' reactions to a client's suicide, and pet loss.[12] Finally, studies of families of Alzheimer's victims and mentally retarded adults[13] also have noted distinct difficulties of these populations in encountering varied losses which are often unrecognized by others.

Others have tried to draw parallels between related unacknowledged losses. For example,

in a personal account, Horn compared her loss of a heterosexual lover with a friend's loss of a homosexual partner.[14] Doka discussed the particular problems of loss in nontraditional relationships, such as extramarital affairs, homosexual relationships, and cohabiting couples.[15]

This article attempts to integrate the literature on such losses in order to explore the phenomenon of disenfranchised grief. It will consider both the nature of disenfranchised grief and its central paradoxical problem: the very nature of this type of grief exacerbates the problems of grief, but the usual sources of support may not be available or helpful.

The Nature of Disenfranchised Grief

Disenfranchised grief can be defined as the grief that persons experience when they incur a loss that is not or cannot be openly acknowledged, publicly mourned, or socially supported. The concept of disenfranchised grief recognizes that societies have sets of norms— in effect, "grieving rules"—that attempt to specify who, when, where, how, how long, and for whom people should grieve. These grieving rules may be codified in personnel policies. For example, a worker may be allowed a week off for the death of a spouse or child, three days for the loss of a parent or sibling. Such policies reflect the fact that each society defines who has a legitimate right to grieve, and these definitions of right correspond to relationships, primarily familial, that are socially recognized and sanctioned. In any given society these grieving rules may not correspond to the nature of attachments, the sense of loss, or the feelings of survivors. Hence the grief of these survivors is disenfranchised. In our society, this may occur for three reasons.

1. The Relationship Is Not Recognized

In our society, most attention is placed on kin-based relationships and roles. Grief may be disenfranchised in those situations in which the relationship between the bereaved and deceased is not based on recognizable kin ties. Here the closeness of other non-kin relationships may simply not be understood or appreciated. For example, Folta and Deck noted, "While all of these studies tell us that grief is a normal phenomenon, the intensity of which corresponds to the closeness of the relationship, they fail to take this (i.e., friendship) into account. The underlying assumption is that closeness of relationship exists only among spouses and/or immediate kin."[16] The roles of lovers, friends, neighbors, foster parents, colleagues, in-laws, stepparents and stepchildren, caregivers, counselors, co-workers, and roommates (for example, in nursing homes) may be long-lasting and intensely interactive, but even though these relationships are recognized, mourners may not have full opportunity to publicly grieve a loss. At most, they might be expected to support and assist family members.

Then there are relationships that may not be publicly recognized or socially sanctioned. For example, nontraditional relationships, such as extramarital affairs, cohabitation, and homosexual relationships have tenuous public acceptance and limited legal standing, and they face negative sanctions within the larger community. Those involved in such relationships are touched by grief when the relationship is terminated by the death of the partner, but others in their world, such as children, may also experience grief that cannot be acknowledged or socially supported.

Even those whose relationships existed primarily in the past may experience grief. Ex-spouses, past lovers, or former friends may have limited contact, or they may not even engage in interaction in the present. Yet the death of that significant other can still cause a grief reaction because it brings finality to that earlier loss, ending any remaining contact or fantasy of reconciliation or reinvolvement. And again these grief feelings may be shared by others in their world such as parents and children. They too may mourn the loss of "what once was" and "what might have been." For example, in one case a twelve-year-old child of an unwed mother, never even acknowledged or seen by the father, still mourned the death of his father since it ended any possibility of a future liaison. But though loss is experienced, society as a whole may not perceive that the loss of a past relationship could or should cause any reaction.

2. The Loss Is Not Recognized

In other cases, the loss itself is not socially defined as significant. Perinatal deaths lead to strong grief reactions, yet research indicates that many significant others still perceive the loss to be relatively minor.[17] Abortions too can constitute a serious loss,[18] but the abortion can take place without the knowledge or sanctions of others, or even the recognition that a loss has occurred. It may very well be that the very ideologies of the abortion controversy can put the bereaved in a difficult position. Many who affirm a loss may not sanction the act of abortion, while some who sanction the act may minimize any sense of loss. Similarly, we are just becoming aware of the sense of loss that people experience in giving children up for adoption or foster care,[19] and we have yet to be aware of the grief-related implications of surrogate motherhood.

Another loss that may not be perceived as significant is the loss of a pet. Nevertheless, the research shows strong ties between pets and humans, and profound reactions to loss.[20]

Then there are cases in which the reality of the loss itself is not socially validated. Thanatologists have long recognized that significant losses can occur even when the object of the loss remains physically alive. Sudnow for example, discusses "social death," in which the person is alive but is treated as if dead.[21] Examples may include those who are institutionalized or comatose. Similarly, "psychological death" has been defined as conditions in which the person lacks a consciousness of existence, such as someone who is "brain dead."[22]

One can also speak of "psychosocial death" in which the persona of someone has changed so significantly, through mental illness, organic brain syndromes, or even significant personal transformation (such as through addiction, conversion, and so forth), that significant others perceive the person as he or she previously existed as dead.[23] In all of these cases, spouses and others may experience a profound sense of loss, but that loss cannot be publicly acknowledged for the person is still biologically alive.

3. The Griever Is Not Recognized

Finally, there are situations in which the characteristics of the bereaved in effect disenfranchise their grief. Here the person is not socially defined as capable of grief; therefore, there is little or no social recognition of his or her sense of loss or need to mourn. Despite evidence to the contrary, both the very old and the very young are typically perceived by others as having little comprehension of or reaction to the death of a significant other. Often, then, both young children and aged adults are excluded from both discussions and rituals.[24]

Similarly, mentally disabled persons may also be disenfranchised in grief. Although studies affirm that the mentally retarded are able to understand the concept of death[25] and, in fact, experience grief,[26] these reactions may not be perceived by others. Because the person is retarded or otherwise mentally disabled, others in the family may ignore his or her need to grieve. Here a teacher of the mentally disabled describes two illustrative incidences:

> In the first situation, Susie was 17 years old and away at summer camp when her father died. The family felt she wouldn't understand and that it would be better for her not to come home for the funeral. In the other situation, Francine was with her mother when she got sick. The mother was taken away by ambulance. Nobody answered her questions or told her what happened. "After all," they responded, "she's retarded."[27]

The Special Problems of Disenfranchised Grief

Though each of the types of grief mentioned earlier may create particular difficulties and different reactions, one can legitimately speak of the special problem shared in disenfranchised grief.

The problem of disenfranchised grief can be expressed in a paradox. The very nature of disenfranchised grief creates additional problems for grief, while removing or minimizing sources of support.

Disenfranchising grief may exacerbate the problem of bereavement in a number of ways. First, the situations mentioned tend to intensify emotional reactions. Many emotions are associated with normal grief. Bereaved persons frequently experience feelings of anger, guilt, sadness and depression, loneliness, hopelessness, and numbness.[28] These emotional reactions can be complicated when grief is disenfranchised. Although each of the situations described is in its own way unique, the literature uniformly reports how each of these disenfranchising circumstances can intensify feelings of anger, guilt, or powerlessness.[29]

Second, both ambivalent relationships and concurrent crises have been identified in the literature as conditions that complicate grief.[30] These conditions can often exist in many types of disenfranchised grief. For example, studies have indicated the ambivalence that can exist in cases of abortion,[31] among ex-spouses,[32] significant others in nontraditional roles,[33] and among families of Alzheimer's disease victims.[34] Similarly, the literature documents the many kinds of concurrent crises that can trouble the disenfranchised griever. For example, in cases of cohabiting couples, either heterosexual or homosexual, studies have often found that survivors experience legal and financial problems regarding inheritance, ownership, credit, or leases.[35] Likewise, the death of a parent may leave a mentally disabled person not only bereaved but also bereft of a viable support system.[36]

Although grief is complicated, many of the factors that facilitate mourning are not present. The bereaved may be excluded from an active role in caring for the dying. Funeral rituals, normally helpful in resolving grief, may not help here. In some cases the bereaved may be excluded from attendance. In other cases they may have no role in planning those rituals or in deciding whether even to have them. Or in cases of divorce, separation, or psychosocial death, rituals may be lacking altogether.

In addition, the very nature of the disenfranchised grief precludes social support. Often there is no recognized role in which mourners can assert the right to mourn and thus receive such support. Grief may have to remain private. Though they may have experienced an intense loss, they may not be given time off from work, have the opportunity to verbalize the loss, or receive the expressions of sympathy and support characteristic in a death. Even traditional sources of solace, such as religion, are unavailable to those whose relationships (for example, extramarital, cohabiting, homosexual, divorced) or acts (such as abortion) are condemned within that tradition.

Naturally, there are many variables that will affect both the intensity of the reaction and the availability of support. All the variables—interpersonal, psychological, social, physiological—that normally influence grief will have an impact here as well. And while there are problems common to cases of disenfranchised grief, each relationship has to be individually considered in light of the unique combinations of factors that may facilitate or impair grief resolution.

Implications

Despite the shortage of research on and attention given to the issue of disenfranchised grief, it remains a significant issue. Millions of Americans are involved in losses in which grief is effectively disenfranchised. For example, there are more than 1 million couples presently cohabiting.[37] There are estimates that 3 percent of males and 2–3 percent of females are exclusively homosexual, with similar percentages having mixed homosexual and heterosexual encounters.[38] There are about a million abortions a year; even though many of the women involved may not experience grief reactions, some are clearly "at risk."

Disenfranchised grief is also a growing issue. There are higher percentages of divorced people in the cohorts now aging. The AIDS crisis means that more homosexuals will experience losses in significant relationships. Even as the disease spreads within the population of intravenous drug users, it is likely to create a new class of both potential victims and disenfranchised grievers among the victims' informal liaisons and nontraditional relationships.[39] And as Americans continue to live longer, more will suffer from severe forms of chronic brain dysfunctions.[40] As the developmentally disabled live longer, they too will experience the grief of parental and sibling loss. In short, the proportion of disenfranchised grievers in the general population will rise rapidly in the future.

It is likely that bereavement counselors will have increased exposure to cases of disenfranchised grief. In fact, the very nature of disenfranchised grief and the unavailability of informal support make it likely that those who experience such losses will seek formal supports. Thus there is a pressing need for research that will describe the particular and unique reactions of each of the different types of losses; compare reactions and problems associated with these losses; describe the important variables affecting disenfranchised grief reactions;[41] assess possible interventions; and discover the atypical grief reactions, such as masked or delayed grief, that might be manifested in such cases. Also needed is education sensitizing students to the many kinds of relationships and subsequent losses that people can experience and affirming that where there is loss there is grief.

Bereavement and Companion Animals

AVERY D. WEISMAN

AVERY D. WEISMAN, M.D., is a professor of psychiatry emeritus at Harvard Medical School; a senior psychiatrist at Massachusetts General Hospital; and a training-supervising analyst at the Boston Psychoanalytic Society and Institute.

Long recognized as a pioneer in the psychosocial study of cancer, thanatology, and consultation-liaison psychiatry, Dr. Weisman is certified in psychiatry, neurology, and psychoanalysis. For most of his career, he has been associated with the Massachusetts General Hospital, where for many years he was principal investigator of Project Omega, a multidisciplinary study of coping and vulnerability among cancer patients. With Dr. Thomas Hackett, he established a psychiatric consultation service at Mass General, one of the first of its kind.

During the 1960s, Dr. Weisman was associated with the origins of what eventually became *Omega: Journal of Death and Dying,* having written an article entitled "Birth of the Death People" for the inaugural issue of its mimeographed predecessor. He is credited with introducing the concept of "middle knowledge" as applied to persons with terminal illness and their intimates. This concept denotes a state of knowledge characterized by both *knowing* and *not knowing* as the possibility of death is confronted. Another of Dr. Weisman's concepts—

one that has been adopted widely, especially in the hospice movement—is summed up in the felicitous phrase "appropriate death." In an interview published in *Omega* in 1993, Dr. Weisman reiterated his understanding of the "good" or "appropriate" death as one embracing the qualities of awareness, acceptance, timeliness, and propitiousness. This latter quality, says Dr. Weisman, "means to die a death one can live with in terms of the values one has supported and in terms of the groups whose respect and regard matter most."

Dr. Weisman has received numerous honors and awards from various societies, organizations, and hospitals. In recent years, the Foundation of Life-Threatening Behavior and Loss established a lectureship in his name. In 1992, the consultation-liaison service at Massachusetts General Hospital became the Avery D. Weisman, M.D., Psychiatry-Consultation Service.

Dr. Weisman is the author of over 100 professional publications, including *The Existential Core of Psychoanalysis: Reality Sense and Responsibility* (1956), *On Dying and Denying* (1972), and *The Coping Capacity: On the Nature of Being Mortal* (1984). His latest book, *The Vulnerable Self: Confronting Ultimate Questions*, was published by Insight/Plenum in 1993.

CONSIDERING THE ENORMOUS length of time that humanity has been linked to animals, for working, guarding, hunting, or companionship, it is strange that studies of bereavement have rarely emphasized the death of a significant animal as a precipitant of mourning or deep bereavement. Occasionally, popular periodicals do refer to pet loss, and there are a few professional books designed for the general public which describe the potential problems following pet death. While the subject has not been ignored by specialists in veterinary medicine and animal behavior, research reports

are scarce and tend towards the anecdotal.[1] Psychotherapists do not seem to take pet loss seriously, judging by sparse articles, and in professional discussions, the topic of companion animal grief is often greeted with a smile, as if there is a tacit consensus that bereavement following animal death is only a displacement from a serious prior loss to a more trivial and transient current episode. Besides these psychological surmises, however, the public at large has little idea of how disruptive the death of a companion animal may be. Consequently, those suffering such a loss are understandably hesitant to admit the depth of their grief even to mental health professionals.

Background

Almost two years ago, facing a certain amount of free time as a result of being retired from the practice of psychoanalysis and clinical thanatology, I volunteered to work at the Animal Rescue League of Boston. My qualifications did not include any direct experience with veterinary medicine or animal behavior, but I did have an interest and some experience in dealing with bereavement and terminal illness.

The Animal Rescue League of Boston is a highly respected and venerable institution dedicated to the humane care of animals for over ninety years. Facilities include a shelter for unwanted animals, an adoption section enabling people to acquire pets at a reasonable cost, a veterinary clinic, and a law enforcement branch that investigates cases of cruelty and mistreatment. Throughout the organization the staff is experienced and devoted to animal welfare. My services, though vague, were welcomed and I was given permission to look around and see where I might best fit in.

One of my early observations was that euthanasia, the humane practice of putting animals to sleep, is a universally distressing problem that even the most experienced staff members hardly ever become accustomed to. Although nationwide thousands of unwanted or incapacitated cats and dogs are destroyed in this way each year, the emotional consequence of performing many such euthanasias is a strong source of burnout, along with other symptoms, emotional and physical.

The shelter section annually accepts hundreds of animals, some of which are strays and others, family pets. Although many of the latter are turned over to an uncertain fate with great reluctance by owners, others are given up in an off-hand if not callous manner. Since pets may be abandoned in this way even after years of living in a household, I thought about the wide range of emotional responses to parting.

There were a few people who wept openly, and some kissed their pet goodbye before releasing them to certain euthanasia. I wondered what decides how distressed or depressed pet owners will become. How does animal loss bereavement compare with mourning for a person who dies? To what extent does the death of a companion animal disrupt everyday life and its remaining relationships?

I set up a bereavement counseling program for owners mourning the death of a companion animal. Referrals came from a newspaper advertisement in the Pets section. It said, in part, "If you have lost a pet or are anticipating the loss of a pet, you don't have to go through it alone." The ad offered professional counseling and gave a phone number.

Parenthetically, the term "pet" is frowned on, as if it is "too petty" and condescending to fit a companion animal. But the designation "companion animal" favored by professionals, seems too awkward for general use. "Domestic animal" is inaccurate because it might refer to cows and chickens, and "household animal" is hardly any better. Bereaved owners are not helpful in this respect because they usually refer to the dead animal by given name or some other affectionate sobriquet. Because I cannot resolve the name problem, I will merely use familiar terms for convenience, without any preference.

Assessment and Management

Practically all the referrals came from the newspaper or through occasional telephone inquiries, none from the shelter. Perhaps troubled owners delegated someone else to bring in their pet or postponed euthanasia for a long time until the pet died at home.

The individual assessment was rather informal but conducted with manifest compassion for the importance of the death, just as I might with any other mourner. I got information about this pet, previous pets, names, breed, ownership, terminal illness or accident, euthanasia, if any, disposition of the body, time since death, and so on, and encouraged as full a description as possible. The session went into other deaths, family history, marriage, work, and any information that was relevant to the primary problem—the recent death of a companion animal. The method might conveniently be called "existential" in that I focussed on the here-and-now, without attempting any psychodynamic clarification of latent conflict.

Clients spoke freely and with relief; the discovery of acceptance and respect for their bereavement was in itself appreciated. There was a general reluctance to tell others about their bereavement, because they feared criticism, condescension, or curt suggestions such as "Get another cat," "After all, it's only a dog." Their resentment could be compared with mourners who are told, "Never mind, you'll get married again," or "You're better off without that bother." Clients felt that their grief was both exceptionally strong and abnormally tenacious, and they wept accordingly, as if confessing something unmentionable. Most people apologized for crying.

The first session often turned out to be enough, although I saw some for a second time. I invited several to join a support group. These groups have met about every three weeks, and attendance is optional. Some clients drop out after a month or so, having adopted another pet, while others no longer feel it necessary. A loyal core continues, however. There was an occasional client in whom the pet loss is only a most recent loss, and who showed signs of more serious personality problems. For these clients, I suggested regular counseling and referred them elsewhere.

Common Themes

Loss of a companion animal after many years of mutual devotion is an unqualified occasion for bereavement. While I have little information about owners who voluntarily give up or abandon pets after an equal amount of time and show negligible remorse or sadness, I propose only that human relationships that end in death also vary in depth and duration of grief. Were there not established rituals, ceremonials, and cultural expectations about so-called normal grief in human death, I would not be surprised to find a vast range of bereavement responses there too, from indifference to rejoicing, including conventional sadness and sense of loss.

The person-animal bond, or better, the person-pet bond, is in my opinion as authentic as any other relationship characterized by mutuality and love. The unique characteristics of the companion animal and its owner have been described often. While the animal is usually considered to be most dependent, the dependence may often go in the opposite direction as well. Other people could leave, one woman said, but she had implicitly assumed that her dead dog would never leave, like a devoted child who does not grow up and never leaves home.

There was empathy for the suffering of the companion animal and additional personal suffering from deciding whether to opt for death through euthanasia or for a few more days of sickness. The distinctly unambivalent relationship with the pet, plus an abundant perception of love and unqualified acceptance, rendered the rest of life after the loss pretty bleak until, in some cases, another animal could be introduced.

I have emphasized how much owners personalized their pets, attributing a level of understanding, empathy, and mutuality almost never found in human relationships except under idealized circumstances. In a person, such qualities would be superhuman. Personalization extended to disposition of the remains. As a rule, ashes were kept, or the pet was buried in an animal cemetery, sometimes with prayers, religious medals, and ceremony. Some owners speculated about the after-life of their companion animal and wondered whether the animal might return in another form.

Almost without exception, owners at first regretted giving consent for euthanasia, despite illness, invalidism, or senescence. This was not an indictment of euthanasia, however, but an expression of how guilty owners felt about invoking their power of life and death, as if it had been a betrayal not a gift or release from suffering.

Flashbacks were common, usually focussing on the penultimate moments prior to death. These were sights of suffering and sounds of anguish. Dreams occurred but, strangely, were about other animals, not the lost pet. What remained after the animal's death along with grief was a sense of barrenness, since many owners valued their pet more than friends or relatives. There was little left to substitute, even for people with children or spouses at home.

The Animal-Human Bond

There have been learned essays on the animal-human bond, but the mere number of cat and dog owners should confirm that the relationship is not only variegated and diffuse but deep and primitive. Legal evolution has gone from regarding animals as mere property and not capable of experiencing pain to more modern viewpoints that appreciate the gift of life and oppose even reasonable animal experimentation.

Worth reviewing, however, are the various unique contributions that companion animals, apart from hunting and guarding, contribute to humanity. It takes no great insight to see that pets provide structure, organization, steadiness, and a sense of purpose for many people, particularly those living alone who do not have a regular schedule or source of other relationships.

But the relationship offered by companion animals is not confined to the lonely and purposeless. Traditionally, pets are part of the family group. Pet ownership is very welcome, of course, to those without work or purpose, but it is no panacea for loneliness, isolation,

and alienation. Moreover, companion animals are notoriously indifferent to status, wealth, looks, or any other value that the rest of society uses to judge its members. There have been several reports of the use of pets to facilitate psychotherapy or to reach otherwise inaccessible patients. But this is another matter, not directly related to bereavement.

One of the reputed advantages of pet ownership, often cited by animal literature and devotees, is that cats and dogs give much more in return than what they require. A place to sleep, food, exercise, and a little attention are often enough, although, regrettably, many pet owners fail to provide even these. A companion animal is said to be constant and devoted, loyal and unambivalent. If true—and I am sure there are exceptions—the gains of ownership exceed the deficits and detractions.

Many owners were reluctant to hand their pets over to euthanasia, regardless of indications. This did not mean that they continued to feel misguided or regretful. They were deeply aware of their animal's trust and dependence and seemed to know that the animal wanted to live. The power of life over death, and the choice of death, particularly killing something you love, caused much consternation that sometimes continued, as if they had actually executed their companion, not bestowed a gift that released them from suffering.

Another question raised by this study is what makes the human-animal bond so difficult to acknowledge when death occurs. Here and there, of course, there are exceptions: condolence cards, cemeteries, even large bequests for animal care. For the most part, however, custom does not approve of mourning for a lost pet. Along with other examples of illicit love and forbidden mourning, Doka has called this *disenfranchised grief.*[2]

In our culture, the only permissible bereavement, established by custom, ceremony, and ritual, results from the death of a family member. We have no established way of mourning for a good friend, and certainly none for an unacceptable relationship, such as that between homosexuals, adulterous love affairs, and so on. But, like these, a pet-person bond deserves open acknowledgment and respect. I surmise that one reason for not doing so is that bereavement of this kind might imply that the animal has human characteristics and attributes, such as feelings, wishes and fears, pain and pleasure, or even a soul. Negative attitudes towards pet bereavement are acknowledged at the same time as people praise the value of animal ownership, calling it "Pure friendship," "Absence of ambivalence," and "Total acceptance." The animal bond seems to be necessary for the human, although city living makes it very difficult. If we could put cultural prejudice aside for a moment, the genuine bereavement that follows death for some owners suggests that it might be the "animal model" for studies of human bereavement.

Conclusions

Information gathered from a pet loss counseling program has demonstrated that the depth of a human-animal bond often exceeds that between a person and close kith and kin. Because the relationship is authentic, normal, often deep and enduring, bereavement following death of a companion animal may be very distressing and persistent.

Clients coming to the counseling program tended to have their pets for long periods, averaging fifteen years. They described a unique bond of companionship and communication not experienced with other people, family, or friends. Nevertheless, brief counseling, individually or in a support group, proved to be helpful, as marked by reduction in mourning symptoms or by adoption of another animal.

Contemporary customs do not approve of mourning a pet; at best, it is indulged. In fact, mourning is sanctioned mainly for family members, regardless of the relationship with friends. Future studies of bereavement might investigate questions about pet/animal bereavement and its implications for human-human bonding. This could conceivably broaden the limits we now impose and permit mourning more appropriate to the grief we feel.

Social Support for Survivors

Bereaved Families of Ontario:
A Mutual-Help Model for Families Experiencing Death

STEPHEN J. FLEMING AND LESLIE BALMER

In addition to his private practice, STEPHEN FLEMING, PH.D., is a professor and chair of the Department of Psychology at Atkinson College of York University in Toronto. Dr. Fleming's interest in issues related to trauma and grief arose out of his psychological practice as he witnessed the anguish and the courage of those living with loss.

In 1978, he was approached by the Bereaved Families of Ontario (BFO)—a fledgling mutual-help organization for families who have experienced the death of a child—to assist in developing their various programs. Thus began a rich and rewarding relationship that continues to this day.

Dr. Fleming has lectured widely in Canada, the United States, and Europe. He is an expert witness in litigation involving trauma, consults with numerous hospices and palliative care programs, and teaches graduate and undergraduate courses on the psychology of death at York University.

In addition to sitting on the editorial boards of the *Journal of Palliative Care* and *Death Studies,* Dr. Fleming's current research interests include exploring the distinctive features of grief and clinical depression, distinguishing anticipatory and conventional grief, developing a grief process model of child sexual abuse survival, and identifying mediating factors in adolescent adjustment to sibling loss.

LESLIE BALMER, PH.D., maintains a private practice in psychology and consults to numerous organizations, including Bereaved Families of Ontario; Discoveries Child and Family Centre, a therapeutic center for preschool-aged children at risk for developmental delay; and T.L.C. Foster Homes, which provides long-term care to latency-aged boys (ages six to twelve) in a family milieu.

Dr. Balmer's clinical and research interest in the area of bereavement began in 1987 when she volunteered as a facilitator of children's groups at Bereaved Families of Ontario. While working with her cofacilitators, most of whom were adolescents who had a sibling who had died, she became aware that the case-presentations she read in the literature didn't have much positive to say about outcomes. This literature did not match her own experience with these young people, whom she saw as wise beyond their years. Thus she became interested in this topic, which led to her doctoral dissertation and a paper cowritten with Dr. Fleming.

Dr. Balmer has lectured in Canada, the United States, and Europe on bereavement issues and special populations such as preschoolers, school-aged children, adolescents, and developmentally delayed adults.

The following selection is based on a presentation by Drs. Fleming and Balmer in 1992 at an international conference on children and death held in Edinburgh.

THE BEREAVED FAMILIES of Ontario, Metropolitan Toronto chapter (BFO),[1] is a mutual-help organization originally established in 1978 to assist families when a child dies. Within a few years, however, BFO expanded its mandate to include children, adolescents, and young adults who had suffered the death of a parent or sibling. The aims of this organization are: (a) to offer a support program for parents at the death of a child and for children, adolescents, and young adults who have suffered the loss of a sibling or parent; (b) to provide appropriate referrals when indicated; and (c) to educate the public and professionals alike on the nature and dynamics of grief and how death affects families.

Organizational Structure

Figure 1 depicts the various offices, positions, and committees of BFO. The Board of Direc-

Figure 1

Bereaved Families of Ontario Organization Chart

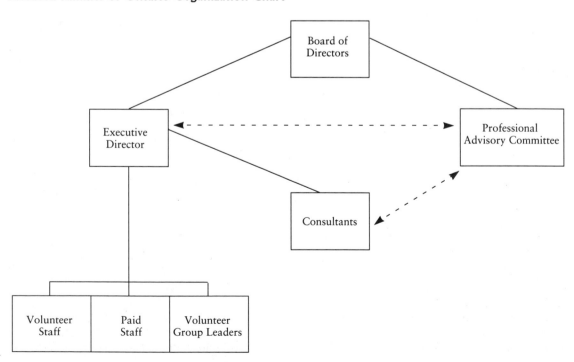

tors is composed of approximately fifteen members, 50 percent of whom are bereaved parents. This body is responsible for all aspects of BFO's functioning including fundraising, budgeting, program development, staffing, and administration.

The executive director is a bereaved parent. This person is very much the administrative heart of the organization. More specifically, in conjunction with the board, the Professional Advisory Committee, and the professional consultants, the executive director has numerous responsibilities including office staffing, organization of all mutual-help groups, the daily financial operation of BFO, coordinating family nights, and the selection and training of group leaders.

The Professional Advisory Committee (PAC) is composed of individuals with expertise in the area of bereavement. These volunteers represent such professions as psychology, psychiatry, nursing, medicine, social work, sociology, and the clergy. In effect, members of the PAC are the chairpersons of the various subcommittees that oversee the functioning of BFO (the committees responsible for program delivery, community outreach, research and program development, and other activities). The executive director and the consultants are ex-officio members of the PAC.

Responsibilities of the PAC include:

♦ Ongoing supervision of group leaders
♦ Preparation, implementation, and evaluation of the training program for prospective group leaders
♦ Evaluating proposals from parties interested in doing research within the organization
♦ Participating in and contributing to public awareness and education on behalf of BFO
♦ Ongoing evaluation and development of programs

The BFO employs two consultants. One is a mental health professional—currently the position is filled by a pastoral counselor—responsible for the day-to-day issues of a clinical or program nature. This consultant is available for ongoing consultation with the executive director and group leaders, organizes and implements the training program and the continuing education workshops for group leaders, supervises those leaders who are facilitating groups, secures ongoing group supervision, attends family nights, and functions in a public relations capacity for BFO. The second consultant is responsible for the multicultural outreach program of BFO, as there are chapters in the Chinese and Portuguese communities and communication with the First Nation, East Indian, and Hispanic communities.

Staff perform three principal functions: operating the BFO offices, handling public relations and education duties, and facilitating the various bereavement groups. For the most part, staff are bereaved parents who volunteer their time at BFO; there are, however, a bookkeeper, an administrative assistant, and a secretary who are paid. There are approximately ninety bereaved-parent or young adult group leaders and thirty professionals who provide supervision on a voluntary basis for the bereaved parent groups.

Activities and Programs

The most succinct manner of describing the various BFO programs is to illustrate what might happen when a bereaved parent contacts the office whether as a result of media exposure, word of mouth, professional referral, or our outreach program (speaking engagements, workshops, and so on). Figure 2 illustrates this process.

Frequently, at the death of a child, it is all too easy for the survivor to withdraw and become reclusive. We encourage the caller to make his or her way to our office; BFO volunteers do not make home visits.

Bereaved persons who choose not to be formally involved in the BFO group program are asked if their names might be added to our

Figure 2

BFO Participation Process

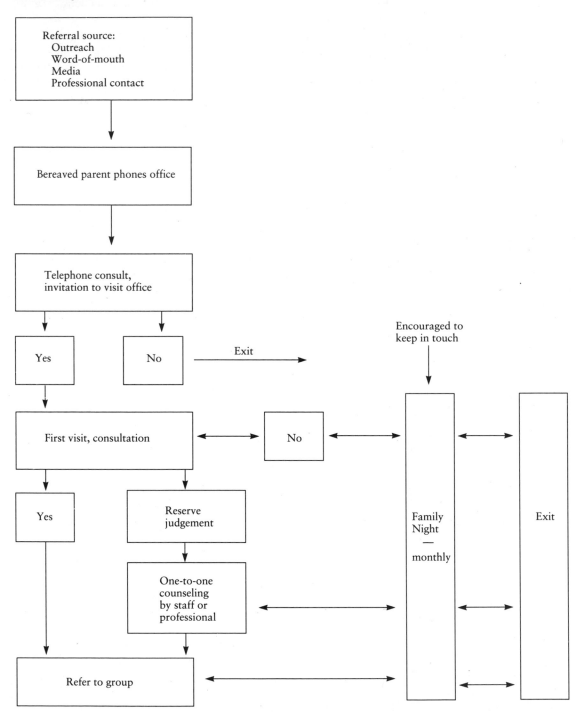

mailing list, enabling them to receive the monthly calendar of events, the semiannual newsletter, and material on upcoming special events. In addition, they are encouraged to attend any of the monthly family support nights in which three or four group leaders address selected topics (such as men's grief, the grief of siblings, or coping with the holidays).

For those wishing to enter a formal group, an initial interview is scheduled with a bereaved parent experienced in conducting these screening assessments. There are three possible outcomes of this initial interview: (a) the parent enters one of the groups, (b) he or she elects not to proceed into a group, or (c) the interviewer reserves judgment as to the parent's suitability for a group and suggests referral either to the BFO consultant or to an outside agency or counselor. The principal criteria for exclusion from a group include clinical depression, suicidal intent, and substance abuse. Of course, these individuals are encouraged to participate in all other programs and activities of the BFO. Such individuals may contact BFO at a later date and enter a group at that time (after consultation with their therapist or counselor). In practice, the number of interviewees not admitted to a group is very small; a considerably larger number decides that the group format is not for them.

When a bereaved child or adolescent is being considered for a group, the interview is not conducted with him or her but rather with the parent. A bereaved young adult desiring to join a group is interviewed individually by a trained person of similar age.

Bereaved parents may select from a number of groups:

- Bereaved mothers
- Bereaved fathers
- Bereaved couples
- Mixed (bereaved mothers or fathers attending individually, that is, without their spouses or partners)
- Bereaved parents of infants (mothers, mothers and fathers, and couples groups)

In addition, BFO offers groups for bereaved children, adolescents, and young adults who have suffered the death of a parent or sibling. All parental groups offered by BFO are supervised by mental health professionals with expertise in group processes and adjustment to loss. Since professionals are involved as cofacilitators in the children's, adolescents, and young adults groups, there is no professional supervision.

Bereaved Parents Groups

Each twelve-week bereaved parents group has approximately six to eight participants. Each meeting is co-led by trained, bereaved parents and lasts approximately two hours. Although there are suggested topics for each weekly meeting, the cofacilitators are encouraged to be flexible and spontaneous in the consideration of such issues as:

- The dying and death of the child
- The funeral
- Guilt and anger
- Spirituality
- Relationship with one's spouse
- Surviving siblings
- The extended family
- Ongoing parenting
- Work
- Packing clothes; memories
- Saying "goodbye" (group termination)

At the conclusion of each group, there is an exit interview with each participant in which they are requested to evaluate the leaders, the most important and least important topics, and the impact of the group on them personally. In addition, participants—who have been observed over the duration of the group experience—may be approached at this time to consider leadership training or volunteering in some other capacity.

Infant Loss Program

The Infant Loss Program began in September 1985 after numerous requests from bereaved mothers desiring to share the experience of a miscarriage, a stillbirth, a newborn death, or a sudden infant death. All bereaved mothers and fathers wishing to participate in this ten-week experience undergo an initial screening interview prior to admission to a mothers group, a mixed group, or a couples group.

Many of the weekly themes in the infant loss groups are similar to those of other groups; however, they also tend to reflect the unique experiences of this group of participants. Variations include:

- Circumstances of the death and whether the parent had the opportunity to see or hold the child
- Whether there are pictures of the child
- Whether the cause of death is known
- The reaction of family and friends
- Whether the child was named
- Replacement needs (future pregnancy)

At the conclusion of the group, each participant receives an exit interview that evaluates the group, as is done for the bereaved parents' groups.

Bereaved Children's Program

Children's groups were established in 1985 to provide a safe environment in which children who had suffered the death of a sibling or parent could freely express their thoughts, feelings, and experiences related to their loss. All groups are cofacilitated by a professional therapist who has training and experience working with children and by a bereaved adolescent or young adult who has completed the leaders' training program. The groups currently run for approximately eight weeks, with each session lasting about ninety minutes.

Prior to the group's first session, the coleaders meet with all the parents as a group to discuss the children's reactions to the loss, explain the group process, discuss what to expect in terms of one's responses as they progress through the group, and provide resource material on children's grief.

Making extensive use of nonverbal modes of expression (visual art, plasticine or clay modeling, music, and movement), the group explores the following themes:

- *Getting acquainted.* Outline of the rules and format of the group and introduction of the death of a family member as a common theme.
- *Commemoration.* Each child brings pictures or memorabilia associated with the deceased.
- *The funeral.* What happened and how did you feel?
- *Family.* Changes in the family since the death (or at the time of and following the death).
- *Other people.* What has it been like with friends and at school?
- *Open topic.*
- Unfinished business and goodbyes.

Upon completion of the final session, the therapist and coleader meet individually with the child and his or her parent or parents. At this time, the child has the opportunity to express, verbally or with the assistance of their artwork, the impact of the group experience. The child then leaves the room and the therapist concludes the interview with the parent or parents by discussing his or her assessment of the child's grief response, sensitive areas of concern, and suggestions for followup intervention if appropriate.

Bereaved Adolescents and Young Adults Groups

Adolescents and young adults who have experienced the death of a parent or sibling are eligible to participate in a mutual-help group. All potential young-adult group members are interviewed by a person of similar age who has participated in such a group and completed the

BFO leaders' training program. This interview elicits information regarding the family; circumstances of the death; changes in mood, weight, and appearance; motivation; reactions of and toward friends; and suicide ideation and suicide attempts. With bereaved adolescents, a group interview is also held with their parents prior to their commencing the group experience.

Adolescence is an era of the self, as the young person looks at others from his or her own perspective. It is, therefore, essential that there be a mental health professional as one of the group's leaders to point out the legitimacy of other perspectives. This professional coaxes empathy and respect for differences while the bereaved adolescent coleader offers credibility with accounts of his or her own pain and the struggle to overcome it.

Although adolescents and young adults meet separately, their groups function in much the same manner. Currently, there are eight sessions (once per week) of approximately two hours each. The last session is a dinner at a local restaurant chosen by the group. The first five meetings are theme oriented; the last two are open to issues arising from the previous sessions.

Typically, the format is:

1. *Introduction to the group.* Each participant recounts the circumstances of his or her loved one's death.
2. *The funeral.* Before proceeding with this topic, participants show pictures of their deceased family members, then thoroughly discuss the funeral and its impact.
3. *Friends and workmates.* Participants are often angry at the perceived abandonment by their friends and colleagues.
4. *School, work, future.*
5. *The family.* Participants discuss changing roles of parents and children. The issues of guilt and anger toward parents

along with one's impotence to assuage the pain of grief are discussed.
6. *Open topics.*
7. *Open topics (continued) and beginning of termination.* In addition to open discussion of topics chosen by the participants, sessions 6 and 7 include discussion of the impact of participating in the group. These two sessions are also devoted to a written evaluation of the group experience. This is an individual response to a series of questions probing the functioning of the group and cognitive, affective, and behavioral changes that have occurred.
8. *Farewell dinner.*

Leaders' Training Program

A unique, innovative feature of the BFO is the use of selected and trained bereaved adolescents, young adults, and parents as group facilitators. To be a full-fledged group leader is a lengthy, time-consuming process. All potential candidates begin as members of a group, at the conclusion of which they are interviewed by the consultant, and, if selected, they are invited to participate in leadership training.

Training programs for potential group leaders are conducted semiannually. Coordinated by the professional consultant and using the skills of the PAC members, participants attend four one-day training sessions. There is both theoretical and experiential exposure to such topics as:

- The dynamics of grief (both complicated and uncomplicated varieties)
- Infant loss
- Spirituality and grief
- The family system, grief, and intimacy
- Sibling grief
- Self-help group processes
- The bereaved parent as group leader

At the conclusion of the training program, two evaluations are undertaken. In the first, the executive director reassesses the suitability of the participant for further work as a trainee. This interview focuses on the person's communication skills and sensitivity to individual and group dynamics. In the second instance, the participants evaluate the training program itself.

If the person continues to be willing and the assessment is favorable, he or she then moves to the next phase of training, namely, working as a coleader in conjunction with an experienced group leader or a professional (for example, in an adolescent or children's group). At the conclusion of this phase, there is yet another assessment; only at this time is the individual considered as a full-fledged group leader. We recognize that using bereaved parents as group leaders presents risks; however, there are also definite and powerful benefits. To minimize the risks, the training program is an arduous one.

In addition to facilitating the groups themselves, group leaders are also asked to (a) consult weekly with their supervisor, (b) keep accurate, updated records of all group meetings (and telephone contact with members of their group), (c) mail notes on the death anniversary dates of their group members (while the group is in session), (d) attend family night meetings, (f) conduct exit interviews for their group, and (g) participate in education programs offered periodically by BFO.

Conclusion

This paper has provided an overview of the nature and function of the BFO, a mutual-support organization developed to assist families experiencing death. In addition to considering the goals and objectives of BFO and its organizational structure, the various program offerings were discussed. These groups are designed to facilitate the grieving process, emancipate the bereaved person from crippling attachments to the deceased, assuage fears that one is "going crazy," educate the survivors about the nature and dynamics of grief to normalize their experience, and promote the usual curative qualities found in groups (the installation of hope, altruism, group cohesiveness, catharsis, and insight).

There are two unique features of BFO worthy of mention. First, BFO's group programs are facilitated by selected and trained bereaved parents and young adults. Second, this model involves the use of mental health professionals in a variety of capacities, including supervision, public awareness, and group facilitation. Nevertheless, BFO remains a mutual-help organization uncontaminated by an association with any institution or professional group. It is important that this nonaligned position be maintained and that grief be perceived as a normal, natural response to the loss of a loved one and not a pathological phenomenon demanding professional intervention.

Humor and Critical Incident Stress

MARY N. HALL AND PAULA T. RAPPE

MARY N. HALL, a Licensed Clinical Social Worker, is an associate professor emerita at the University of West Florida in Pensacola. She is a certified death educator and grief counselor with an active practice in loss and grief counseling. Her interest in learning and teaching about death, dying, and grief was sparked in 1970 when she saw Elisabeth Kübler-Ross interview a dying woman with a child of the same age as her own daughter. She subsequently designed and taught a highly successful course on death and dying at the university, and she has provided instruction to law enforcement recruits, nurses, hospital staff, hospice volunteers, and a host of other groups, including widowed persons and emergency services personnel.

Mrs. Hall has been a frequent presenter at national professional meetings, where her topics have included death notification, imagery and grief, and organ transplantation, among others. As an outcome of her research into hope and the trajectory of dying in the late 1970s, she became impressed with the importance of humor as an adjunct to hope. In addition to speaking on this topic at meetings of the Association for Death Education and Counseling and the American Association for Therapeutic Humor, Mrs. Hall finds that humor serves to keep a balance in her personal and professional life. As "Absorbine Junior," she is an active member of a clown ministry.

Mrs. Hall is a graduate of advanced training in critical incident stress debriefing and a member of both the Association for Death Education and Counseling and the International Critical Incident Stress Foundation. Her work has been published in professional journals for death studies, law enforcement, and social work education.

PAULA T. RAPPE, also a Licensed Clinical Social Worker, is an assistant professor of social work at the University of West Florida. Married to a veteran of the Vietnam War, she and her husband became involved in the uses of critical incident stress debriefing as a preventive to posttraumatic stress disorder among emergency services workers. She has been a member of the Pensacola Critical Incident Stress Debriefing Team since 1988 and for the past two years has been state clinical coordinator for critical incident stress debriefers in Florida.

Mrs. Rappe has seen firsthand how humor can be a constructive means for coping with chaos and disaster. Herself a survivor of the ravages of Hurricane Camille in Biloxi, Mississippi, in 1969, she was a first-responder following Hurricane Andrew in Homestead, Florida, in 1992.

Mrs. Rappe has spoken at national and international forums and is a member of the International Critical Incident Stress Foundation. She and Mrs. Hall are currently engaged in ongoing research into the functions of humor in critical incidents, a study that has become international in scope.

The wisest men that e'er you ken
have never dreamed it treason
To rest a bit and jest a bit
And balance up their reason
To laugh a bit and chaff a bit
And joke a bit in season.
　　　　　　　　　—Anonymous

THIS PAPER ADDRESSES dual functions served by humor and laughter in the management of stress among emergency service personnel. First response to catastrophic and disastrous events in our communities is given by an assortment of paramedics, EMTs, firefighters, law enforcement officers, ambulance drivers, emergency room staffs, dispatchers, and others. Raphael, Taylor and Frazer, Titchener, Mitchell, and others have observed that certain events prove especially traumatic for first responders.[1] These issues, producing extraordinary emotional response in emergency personnel, have led to the development of crisis support systems in many areas to assist these first responders and prevent more severe traumatic stress problems.

Since Biblical times, it has been believed that a "merry heart doeth good like a medicine."[2] Scholars of humor from Freud's day forward contend that humor has a very significant part to play in our human dealings with stressful events. In a 1928 paper, Freud wrote that "humor is a sort of defense mechanism that allows people to face a difficult situation without becoming overwhelmed with unpleasant emotions."[3] Certainly, Norman Cousins, both in his *Anatomy of an Illness* and his later writings, developed further the notion that positive emotions, light laughter, and good humor help promote wellness even in the face of extremely serious problems.[4] This is certainly not an American phenomenon alone. An anthropologist, fictionalizing an actual field investigation, described a village reunion in Africa after a terrible disease ravaged the population. A young child named "Accident" limped about miming the handicaps and symptoms which heralded the approach of the deaths of the victims. The villagers at the gathering responded by convulsing with uproarious laughter. The anthropologist asked if the villagers must not at such a time either laugh or go mad.[5]

Jim Boren, who ran for president on the "humor ticket" in 1992, agrees with the anthropologist. He reports, after a humor tour with representatives of Eastern European nations, that similar laughter-evoking commentaries in times of great disaster characterize those populations as well. He brings three examples from Chernobyl. One is a cartoon of Don Quixote tilting at a nuclear reactor with his faithful squire garbed in a gas mask. A second is a quote under a cartoon which reads, "Well, if you want fried chicken, just hold it out the window a minute." A third explains the reasons that dried and withered apples

from Chernobyl are selling better than round and rosy ones from Moscow. The caption says, "We are buying them for our bosses."[6]

All of us know of the somewhat drastic and "black" kind of humor that gives rise to comments like "John-John's fourth birthday present, Jack-in-a-box" or "Christa McAuliffe did not shower before she got on the shuttle to the moon because she knew she would wash up on shore." These gross sounding stories apparently serve a purpose in helping us deal with terrible and terrifying events.

In 1985, John Abraham presented a paper at the ADEC Conference listing twelve functions of humor in death-related situations. Among them were the functions of "raising us for a moment above the awfuls," enabling us to talk about what otherwise could not be mentioned, and being the "great leveler," keeping us humbly laughing about *ourselves* in a time of catastrophe.[7]

Serious Life Event Minimizer

Lefcourt and Martin utilized six different instruments to study humor and its relationship to stressful circumstances. Their focus was upon humor as a potential moderator or minimizer of serious or adverse life events. Two findings from their studies were that: (a) humor helps us keep a positive perspective—we don't win every round, but it's still all right; and (b) we can protect ourselves with humor even from the threat of insanity at such a time.[8]

In the last two decades, we have become much more familiar, especially through television, with the kinds of catastrophes—both manmade and natural—that can take their toll on an individual's adjustments. Examples of this kind of event include the supper club fires, tornadoes, the Hyatt Skywalk collapse, plane crashes, hurricanes, Hiroshima, combat in Vietnam, the Holocaust, volcanic eruptions, and the toxic exposure of people at Love Canal.

What makes an event a catastrophe? According to Charles Figley, editor of *Trauma and Its Wake,* three things must characterize an event to make it catastrophic and severely traumatic. The first is that it happens suddenly and without warning; second, there is a perceived sense of great danger to ourselves or to someone we care deeply about; and finally, the event is emotionally overwhelming—there is so much sensory overload and overstimulation that ordinary defenses cannot handle it.[9]

The generally accepted explanation for traumatic neurosis rests on notions of the overloading of the mental systems and functioning, on how the individual perceives the experience, and on the ineffectiveness of support after the fact. Overloading means that massive stimuli or excitations from the external events break through the stimulus barrier, flooding and disorganizing the ego's functions. The process of reorganization and restoration of ego function can occur normally. It is something like the awakening from a nightmare, only taking a much longer period of time. There are varying degrees of success in restoration and occasionally the trauma produces drastic changes in the individual.

The authors concur that humor, laughter and joking serve very important functions in terms of the capacity of the confronted human being to deal with the disaster at the time it is occurring. We also are convinced that humor and laughter can help the individual who has *had* affective disruption and is suffering from post-traumatic decline (as described by Tichener) to recover from system overload, to mobilize coping forces, and to heal at last from the shock.[10]

Social support networks have an important effect on the psychosocial recovery from disaster. Without them the victim is increasingly vulnerable to a variety of physical and mental health problems. As Susan Solomon notes in "Mobilizing Social Support Networks," among the individuals most in need of this support are disaster relief workers.[11]

When rescue and response personnel are called to the scene of a disaster or major catastrophic emergency, they walk into an environment that is filled with pandemonium, confusion, pain, fear, shock, and noise. The intensity of what they must cope with depends upon the severity of the disaster. They must immediately set to work rescuing people in danger, treating the injured, and providing comfort and support to the bereaved. They must carry out these tasks amid horrifying sights and sounds; they must act quickly in the face of pain, fear, and in some cases, hostility from those they are trying to help.

Shared Personality Traits

Emergency service personnel are high achieving individuals who do not like to fail, and sometimes describe themselves as "adrenaline junkies."[12] Whenever the alarm goes off, there is the possibility of high tension and danger, and also the potential for optimum performance under the most extreme kinds of stress. At such times, a combination of significant stressors can lead to serious physical illness or emotional problems in these response personnel. These stressors include being exposed to distressing and unexpected sights, sounds, smells, and feelings; difficult working conditions (for example, lights in your face and not on the patient); many types of personnel occupying the same space; reporters or photographers hanging over your shoulder; and more.

Helping personnel are particularly vulnerable if they have had loss of a personal friend or injury to themselves or people they love, particularly traumatic stimuli, or failure of the mission that can possibly be blamed on human error. The death of a coworker can be considered one of the most catastrophic things that can happen in its ability to create depth and duration of strong emotion. Out of 255 firefighters involved in one fire which resulted in the loss of three firemen, twenty-five required professional counseling for a period of up to two years. The emergency response team can often become more of a family than one's own family after teams work together over time. As one EMT says, "The comradeship of EMS, law enforcement, and fire folks surpasses a family bond."

In communities that are essentially rural, critical incidents—especially those involving more than one casualty—are particularly high stressors due to the likelihood of emergency responders knowing both the victims and the survivors.

Most response personnel who deal with "guts and gore" on a daily basis are likely to have developed some protective strategies, but even the most experienced will find some events difficult to deal with. Following a San Diego air crash in 1978 in which 145 people lost their lives, 250 body bags had to be used to recover between 10,000 and 15,000 body parts. Nine years later, thirty-six persons who were in the recovery operations were still having problems dealing with what they had to take care of at the crash site.[13] One of the aftereffects of seeing such carnage is what Lifton has called the "death imprint," which causes severe feelings of anxiety, vulnerability, being out of control, and being overwhelmed.[14] There is medical evidence that blood values change in individuals who have listened over a period of time to persons crying out in pain.

In 1980, Dunning and Silva began suggesting that rescue organizations should implement stress debriefing programs for the prevention of stress symptoms among disaster relief workers.[15] It began to be more evident that emergency workers could be trained to offer emotional support to one another, discourage unrealistic self-expectations, offer acceptance and understanding of the on-scene or delayed stress responses, and demonstrate appreciation for the efforts of their fellow workers. It was believed that if this was done within forty-eight hours following a disaster it

would be extremely helpful in preventing more serious post-traumatic difficulties down the road.

The Pensacola CISD Program

The authors have been involved with the development and continuance of a critical incident stress debriefing (CISD) team in Pensacola, Florida. Begun in our area by three paramedics, despite resistance by others who felt that expressing feelings was a weakness, the Pensacola group followed the Jeffrey Mitchell model, and has now been debriefing emergency crews since 1987.[16] The urgency to move ahead with the project came to a climax when a member of the EMT "family," a Vietnam veteran, took his own life. There are thirty-one trained volunteers now on call to handle debriefings. The team works on a rotational basis, and volunteers are screened before being recruited. The victims of the traumatic experience, the emergency responders, are given an immediate opportunity to talk about the event in specific and thorough detail, including all of the responses felt—humorous and otherwise. A structured format is used, offering a sense of security so that the emergency responders can revisit the event. Debriefings consist only of those people who were on the scene, not management—unless they were actually present. There is no critique involved and procedures are not evaluated. Participation is voluntary. Handouts are given; they discuss normal reactions, the usual duration of the stress response, and techniques of resting and seeking respite that may help to lessen the intensity of the response. Mental health clinicians support these debriefings, which are preventative in nature. Facilitating a debriefing with mentally healthy people after a traumatic event is significantly easier than dealing with post-traumatic symptoms after the EMS worker begins to suffer them.

What part does humor play? In the course of debriefings, and afterwards, team members observe that humor about the terrifying event is one of the most common ways of dealing with a tragedy. Only two examples are offered here, but they are typical of interchanges shared at debriefings.

A young highway patrolman joined with others in hot pursuit of a speeding motorcycle rider. The speed and danger of the chase had so overpowered a brand new patrol driver that he pulled to one side and allowed this patrolman to follow the speeding cyclist. Hot pursuit is in itself a frightening experience. Even more startling was the visualization of the motorcyclist missing a turn, striking a concrete highway divider, his body splitting into two parts, and his lower body including all intestines splattering against a lamppost. When a reporter rushed up on the scene, the highway patrolman quotes himself as saying, "At least I know one thing for sure, he'll never have the guts to run from me again."

Another macabre bit of humor had to do with the excessive avoirdupois of a woman in full cardiac arrest for whom the side of a building had to be knocked out so that she could be lowered ten stories on the platform of a hook-and-ladder truck. As she swayed on the platform, the paramedic, who himself is not a small person, laughed with his partner about the "difficult extrication" as they swayed ten stories above the sidewalk, still doing compressions to keep the obese individual alive. He quotes himself as having said to the family, "extrication is a little difficult this time." To which the family said, "But she's not having trouble with her teeth!"

Humor Acts as Filter

These are examples of responses honestly given at a time of great trauma. It helps those who are frightened and feeling overpowered to maintain their composure sufficiently to proceed with the task at hand. If you have ever sat with a veteran of combat and heard the "war stories" told many months or even years after the event, you are aware that humor is a very large part of the filter through which these events are observed. Waving the detached arm of a dead victim at a particularly bothersome newspaper reporter can be important in helping the first responder to feel in control of the situation, even though it seems gross or insensitive to the average bystander. The rescue workers at the mass suicide of more than 900 men, women, and children in Jonestown saw humor as a valuable support during the stress. "To tell the truth, the only way me and my friends found to keep one sane was to joke around so much and to keep laughing, even if it meant making fun of the bodies. . . . During the Jonestown detail, the grosser the joke, the better."[17]

Another function of humor, laughter, and play for the emergency service responder comes later in the scenario. Susan Solomon promotes the significance of social support as a treatment for recovery from disaster and a promotion of lessening vulnerability to physical and mental health problems resulting from repeated exposure to disaster.[18] In 1990, the Pensacola CISD team began hosting an annual February conference for all area emergency service personnel called "Hearts and Sirens." A significant feature of this meeting is the strong encouragement to laugh and play and to recover the childlike joy that each individual can experience in a socially supportive group. Emergency response is a serious business in many ways, but there is definitely a need for the reuniting of the emergency service "family" as well as the members' own families, by structured encouragement to play together. Utilizing the techniques of Matt Weinstein and the Play Fair group,[19] a mental health practitioner/humorist interacts with the group and shares with the members techniques of playing in nonthreatening and supportive ways. The tension relieving and socially supportive games that we have used include much touching, hugging, and childlike role modeling. For example, "Pretend you are a litter of puppies or kittens playing on the grass in the sunshine." Sensory experiences of softness are offered (stuffed animals to be held and stroked), as are "clean jokes" and noncompetitive team games.

Humor Distances Horror and Rebonds "Family"

The results have clearly been some rebonding, some healing of lingering pain and grief in the first response family exposed to multiple trauma. It is our conviction that these two functions of humor—the distancing from horrors and the later rebonding of the "family"—can be powerful instruments in caregiving for emergency service personnel.

The first responders are a special breed of people, carrying out special tasks in a complicated society. We need to take good care of those who are taking such good care of us and on whom we depend in catastrophic and cataclysmic circumstances. Offering the realization that one is loved, supported, cared for, and respected—as well as offering one's jokes—can be an important feature of this social support. Future research should certainly include exploration of ways in which we can carry out this support even more effectively.

Coping with Life-Threatening Illness

To My Readers

HAROLD BRODKEY

HAROLD BRODKEY is the author of the novel *The Runaway Soul* (1991) and several collections of shorter fiction, including *First Love and Other Sorrows* (1958; 2d ed., 1986), which won one of the literary world's most coveted prizes, the Prix de Rome; *Women and Angels* (1985); and *Stories in an Almost Classical Mode* (1988). Much of his latest book, *Profane Friendship*, was written in Venice during 1992 at the invitation of the Consorzio Venezia Nuova, a group charged with saving the city's heritage. Mr. Brodkey is also a frequent contributor of poetry, essays, and fiction to the *New Yorker*, *Esquire*, *Vanity Fair*, *Partisan Review*, and *Paris Review*, among other periodicals, and his work has been anthologized in numerous books. Mr. Brodkey's writing has been characterized as "unparalleled in American prose fiction since the death of William Faulkner."

When Brodkey was seventeen months old, his mother became ill. She died six months later from an infection possibly caused by an illegal abortion. Writing in *New York* magazine (1988), Dinitia Smith says that the death of his mother "remains the determining trauma of Brodkey's life. It preoccupies him still, and much of his work is an effort to remember her." At the age of two, Brodkey was adopted by his father's second cousin and her husband. Then, when he was nine, his adoptive father suffered either a heart attack or a stroke and remained an invalid until his death, which occurred when Brodkey was fourteen. The previous year his adoptive mother had become ill with cancer. Brodkey has said about this period in his life, "In one year, I had two parents who were dying," and Smith comments that "to this day, their names seem to have an almost talismanic significance for him."

In addition to the Prix de Rome, Mr. Brodkey's work has won the National Magazine award for fiction (1974), the Pushcart Prize (1975), and the O'Henry prize for best American short story (1978). He lives in New York with his wife, Ellen Schwamm. Since 1987, he has been a staff writer for the *New Yorker*, where the following selection was originally published.

I HAVE AIDS. I am surprised that I do. I have not been exposed since the nineteen-seventies, which is to say that my experiences, my adventures in homosexuality, took place largely in the nineteen-sixties, and back then I relied on time and abstinence to indicate my degree of freedom from infection and to protect others and myself.

At first, shadows and doubts of various kinds disturbed my sleep, but later I felt more certainty of safety. Before AIDS was identified, I thought five years without noticeable infection would indicate one was without disease. When AIDS was first identified, five years was held to indicate safety. That changed. Twenty years now is considered a distance in time that might indicate safety, but a slight number of AIDS cases are anomalous; that is, the delay in illness is not explicable within the assumed rules, even under the most careful, cynical investigation. It doesn't matter much. I have AIDS. I have had *Pneumocystis carinii* pneumonia, which almost killed me. Unlikely or not, blood test, T-cell count, the fact that it was *Pneumocystis* means I have AIDS and must die.

There it is. At the time I was told, I was so ill, so racked with fever and having such difficulty breathing, that I hardly cared. I was embarrassed and shamed that the people who cared for me in the hospital had to take special precautions to protect themselves. Then as the fever went down I suppose my pride and sense of competition took over. When someone from social services showed up to offer counsel, I found that bothersome, although the counsellor was a very fine person, warm and intelligent. I suppose I was competitive with or antagonistic toward the assumption that now my death would be harder than other deaths, harder to bear, and that the sentence to such death and suffering was unbearable.

I didn't find it so. I didn't want to find it so. Granted, I am perverse. But my head felt the doom was bearable. My body hurt. I haven't felt even halfway human for eight or nine weeks now, until the last two or three days. It was as if I had walked through a door into the most unstable physical state of wretched and greatly undesirable discomfort possible.

But, of course, blindness and dementia are worse states. And my parents suffered excruciatingly with heart trouble and cancer. Also, I was not, am not, young. I am not being cut down before I have had a chance to live. Most important, I was not and am not alone. On the second day, when the truth was known, my wife, Ellen Schwamm, moved into the hospital with me. When we began to tell the family, no one rejected me. No one. I am embarrassed to be ill and to be ill in this way, but no one yet has shown disgust or revulsion. I expect it. But in the hospital AIDS is a boring thing for interns, it is so common. And outside it arouses, at least in New York, sympathy and curiosity. I do get the feeling I am a bit on show, or rather my death is and my moods are. But so what?

So far the worst moments, in terms of grief, came about when I was visited by my grandson, aged four, a wide-faced blond, a second child, bright, and rather expert at emotional warfare. I hadn't seen him in four months, and he looked at me snottily and said, "I don't remember *you*." I said, "I used to be a pink-and-black horse." He looked at me, thought or reacted, then grinned and said, "I remember you now," and came over and took my hand and generally didn't leave my side. But the horror was I had no strength to respond or pretend after only a short while, less than an hour. I am not able to be present for him and never will be anymore. That led to a bad twenty-four hours. But that can hardly be uncommon, and I had already felt a version of it toward Ellen, although less intense, because I am able to be there in some ways still, and can find some sort of robot strength in myself still if I have to.

My doctor, who is very able and very experienced, is surprised that I am not more depressed. He says cheerfully that I am much more upset than I realize. He credits some of the medicines with shielding me, my mood, and warns me that severe unhappiness is coming, but so far it hasn't come. I have resisted it, I suppose. And my wife is with me every moment. I feel cut off from old age, it's true, but that's not like someone young feeling cut off from most of his or her possible life.

In my adult life and in my childhood, I was rarely, almost never ill, but when I was, it was always serious, and nearly fatal. I have been given up by my doctors three times in my life and for a few minutes a fourth time. This time is more convincing but otherwise it is not an unfamiliar or unexplained territory.

I was a hypochondriac, but for a good reason—I could take no medicine, none at all, without extreme, perverse, or allergic reactions. Essentially I never got sick. I was gym-going, hike-taking, cautious, oversensitive to the quality of the air, to heat and cold, noise and odors, someone who felt tireder more quickly than most people because of all these knife-edge reactions, someone who was careful not to get sick, because my allergic reactions to medicines made almost any illness a drastic experience.

I had an extremely stable baseline of mood and of mind, of mental *landscape*. Well, that's gone; it's entirely gone. From the moment my oxygen intake fell to about fifty per cent and the ambulance drivers arrived in our apartment with a gurney and with oxygen for me to breathe, from that moment and then in the hospital until now, I have not had even one moment of physical stability. I am filled off-and-on with surf noises as if I were a seashell, my blood seems to fizz and tingle. I have low and high fevers. For a day I had a kind of fever with chills and sweats but with body temperature *below* normal, at 96 degrees. I have choked and had trouble breathing. I have had pleuritis, or pleurisy, in my right lung, an inflammation of the thoracic cavity which feels like a burning stiffness of the muscles and which hurt like hell if I coughed, moved suddenly, or reached to pick something up.

And, of course, one can die at any moment or discover symptoms of some entirely new disease. My life has changed into this death, irreversibly.

But I don't *think* the death sentence bothers me. I don't see why it should more than before. I have had little trouble living with the death-warrant aspect of life until now. I never denied, never hysterically defined the reality of death, the presence and idea of it, the inevitability of it. I always knew *I* would die. I never felt invulnerable or immortal. I felt the presence and menace of death in bright sunlight and in the woods and in moments of danger in cars and planes. I felt it in others' lives. Fear and rage toward death for me is focussed on resisting death's soft jaws at key moments, fighting back the interruption, the separation. In physical moments when I was younger, I had great surges of wild strength when in danger, mountain climbing, for instance, or threatened in a fight or by muggers in the city. In the old days I would put my childish or young strength at the service of people who were ill. I would lend them my will power, too. Death scared me some, maybe even terrified me in a way, but at the same time I had no great fear of death. Why should it be different now? Ought I to crack up because a bluff has been called?

As with other children, when I was very young, death was interesting—dead insects, dead birds, dead people. In a middle-class, upper-middle-class milieu, everything connected to real death was odd, I mean in relation to pretensions and statements, projects and language and pride. It seemed softly adamant, an undoing, a rearrangement, a softly meddlesome and irresistible silence. It was something some boys I knew and I thought we ought to familiarize ourselves with. Early on, and also in adolescence, we had a particular, conscious will not to be controlled by fear of death—there were things we would die rather than do. To some extent this rebelliousness was also controlled; to some extent we could choose our dangers, but not always. All this may be common among the young during a war; I grew up during the Second World War. And a lot was dependent on locality, and social class, the defense of the sexual self or the private self against one's father or in school.

Having accepted death long ago in order to be physically and morally free—to some extent—I am not crushed by this final sentence of death, at least not yet, and I don't think it is denial. I think my disbelief weeks ago gave way to the *maybe so* of the onset of belief. I am sick and exhausted, numbed and darkened, by my approximate dying a few weeks ago from *Pneumocystis,* and consider death a silence, a silence and a privacy and an untouchability, as no more reactions and opinions, as a relief, a privilege, a lucky and graceful and symmetrical silence to be grateful for. The actual words I used inwardly read ambiguously when written out—*it's about time* for silence.

I'm sixty-two, and it's ecological sense to die while you're still productive, die and clear a space for others, old and young. I didn't always appreciate what I had at the time, but I am aware now that accusations against me of being lucky in love were pretty much true and of being lucky sexually, also true. And lucky intellectually and, occasionally, lucky in the people I worked with. I have no sad stories about love or sex.

And I think my work will live. And I am tired of defending it, tired of giving my life to it. But I have liked my life. I like my life at present, being ill. I like the people I deal with. I don't feel I am being whisked off the stage or murdered and stuffed in a laundry hamper while my life is incomplete. It's my turn to die—I can see that that is interesting to some people but not that it is tragic. Yes, I was left out of some things and was cheated over a lifetime in a bad way but who isn't and so what? I had a lot of privileges as well. Sometimes I'm sad about its being over but I'm that way about books and sunsets and conversations.

The medicines I take don't grant my moods much independence, so I suspect these reactions, but I think they are my own. I have been a fool all my life, giving away large chunks of time and wasting years on nothing much, and maybe I'm being a fool now.

And I have died before, come close enough to dying that doctors and nurses on those occasions said those were death experiences, the approach to death, a little of death felt from the inside. And I have nursed dying people and been at deathbeds. I nearly died when my first mother did; I was two years old. As an adult, at one point, I forced myself to remember what I could of the child's feelings. The feelings I have now are far milder. My work, my notions and theories and doctrines, my pride have conspired to make me feel as I do now that I am ill.

I have always remembered nearly dying when I was seven and had an allergic, hypothermic reaction coming out of anesthesia. When I was thirty, a hepatitis thing was misdiagnosed as cancer of the liver, and I was told I had six weeks to live. The sensations at those various times were not much alike, but the feeling of extreme sickness, of being racked, was and is the same as is the sense of the real death.

I have wondered at times if maybe my resistance to the fear-of-death wasn't laziness and low mental alertness, a cowardly inability to admit that horror was horror, that dying was unbearable. It feels, though, like a life-giving rebelliousness, a kind of blossoming. Not a love of death but maybe a love of God. I wouldn't want to be hanged and it would kill my soul to be a hangman but I always hoped that if I were hanged I would be amused and superior, and capable of having a good time somehow as I died—this may be a sense of human style in an orphan, greatly damaged and deadened, a mere sense of style overriding a more normal terror and sense of an injustice of destiny. Certainly, it is a *dangerous* trait. I am not sensible. . . . At all times I am more afraid of anesthesia and surgery than I am of death. I have had moments of terror, of abject fear. I was rather glad to have those moments. But the strain was tremendous. My feelings of terror have had a scattered quality mostly, and I tended to despise them as petty. I have more fear of cowardice and of being broken by torture than I do of death. I am aware of my vulnerability, of how close I come to being shattered. But next to that is a considerable amount of nerve—my blood parents and real grandparents were said to have been insanely brave, to have had an arrogant sang-froid about their courage and what it allowed them to do. They had, each of them, a strong tropism toward the epic. My mother, before I was born, travelled alone from near Leningrad to Illinois in the nineteen-twenties, a journey that, at her social level, took nearly two months; the year before, her older brother had disappeared, perhaps murdered. My father once boxed a dozen men in a row one evening on a bet and supposedly laid all the women under thirty who lined up afterward. Another time, better attested, with two other men, he took on a squad of marching local Nazis in St. Louis, twenty-five or thirty men, and won.

I myself am a coward, oversensitive, lazy, reclusive, but the mind and spirit have their requirement of independence; and death can't help but seem more bearable than a stupid life of guilt, say.

Is death other than silence and nothingness? In my experiences of it, it is that disk of acceptance and of unthreading and disappearance at the bottom of the chute of revenant memories, ghosts and the living, the gantlet of important recollections through which one is forced in order to approach the end of one's consciousness. Death itself is soft, softly lit, vastly dark. The self becomes taut with metamorphosis and seems to give off some light and to have a not-quite-great-enough fearlessness toward that immensity of the end of individuality, toward one's absorption into the dance of particles and inaudibility. Living, one undergoes one metamorphosis after another—often, they are cockroach states inset with moments of passivity, with the sense of real death—but they are continuous and linked. This one is a stillness and represents a sifting out of identity and its stories, a breaking off or removal of the self, and a devolution into mere effect and memory, outspread and not tightly bound but scattered among micromotions and as if more wind-blown than in life.

People speak of wanting to live to see their grandchildren marry, but what is it they will see? A sentimental ceremony or a real occasion involving real lives? Life is a kind of horror. It is O.K., but it is wearing. Enemies and thieves don't lay off as you weaken. The wicked flourish by being ruthless even then. If you are ill, you have to have a good lawyer. Depending on your circumstances, in some cases you have to back off and lie low. You're weak. Death is preferable to daily retreat.

Certainly people on the street who smile gently at me as I walk slowly or X-ray attendants calling me *darling* or *lovey* are aware of this last thing. A woman I know who died a few years back spoke of this in relation to herself. She hated it. I don't want to talk about my dying to everyone, or over and over. Is my attitude only vanity—and more vanity—in the end? In a sense, I steal each day, but I steal it by making no effort. It is just there, sunlight or rain, nightfall or morning. I am still living at least a kind of life, and I don't want to be reduced to an image now, or, in my own mind, feel I am spending all my time on my dying instead of on living, to some satisfying extent, the time I have left.

Not constantly but not inconstantly either, underneath the sentimentality and obstinacy of my attitudes, are, as you might expect, a quite severe rage and a vast, a truly extensive terror, anchored in contempt for you and for life and for everything. But let's keep that beast in its gulf of darkness. Let's be polite and proper and devoted to life now as we were earlier in our life on this planet.

One of the things that struck me when I was first told that I had AIDS was that I was cut off from my family inheritance of fatal diseases—the strokes and high blood pressure and cancers and tumors of my ancestors. My medical fate is quite different; I felt a bit orphaned yet again, and idiosyncratic, but strangely also as if I had been invited, almost abducted, to a party, a sombre feast but not entirely grim, a feast of the seriously afflicted who yet were at war with social indifference and prejudice and hatred. It seemed to me that I was surrounded by braveries without number, that I had been inducted into a phalanx of the wildly-alive-even-if-dying, and I felt honored that I would, so to speak, die in the company of such people.

Really, I can say nothing further at this point. Pray for me.

Crossing the Border

JANMARIE SILVERA is a learning-disabled re-entry student in nursing at a community college in California. She was thirty-two years old when her mother died, the same age her mother had been when Ms. Silvera was born.

Ms. Silvera says, "A lot of life changes have developed for me out of my mother's illness and death. One of these is my desire to work in health care. As a caretaker for my mother, especially at the clinic in Mexico where a lot of the 'nursing' duties are turned over to family members, I became aware of my talent and affinity for being present with those, not just my mother, who were in the midst of life-threatening illness. Although I am not sure what field of care I will wind up in, I know that I am on the right path."

Ms. Silvera lives in a rural area where she raises Dalmatians, grows roses, and enjoys seeing the stars at night.

HER SOFT, GREY-BLUE eyes stare endlessly into space, as the color of the room dims with nightfall. I'm too tired to get off my bed and turn on the light, so we lay in silence, watching each other fade. Our tiny beds are separated by two night tables and an overstuffed chair, which I sometimes drag across the room so she can look out the picture window. The picture window is the one thing that keeps us sane. It's our only escape from this room. I spend every other week here, twenty-four hours a day. My mother has spent months here.

The window covers the entire east wall. It overlooks a large patch of hard dirt, covered with low shrubs which were probably once green, but now in the Mexican heat have been dried to a brittle golden brown. We never see any people navigating across this stretch, but the remnants of bottles, paper, and trash mark our view with great regularity, leading us to believe that perhaps this is part of their trek made at night to cross the Mexican border into California.

Off to the right squats a Catholic school. Its yard faces us and offers afternoons of lively schoolgirls practicing their native folk dances. We watch them twirling their bright skirts, weaving lines of laughing colors across our otherwise muted landscape. The tinny sound of a mariachi band floats from the P.A. system and mingles with the clapping of their young hands, reminding us that life is still fresh and holds promise for those outside the cancer clinic. We secretly covet that promise, as if it were our own.

To the left runs a battered road which disappears between two high cliffs. Somewhere in the gap between them, Mexico becomes California.

Her bony hands, that only months ago were full and strong, play back and forth across her smooth, hairless head. I know she's worried by the way she chews her lower lip, as her brow furrows and knits.

"What are you thinking?" I ask. The sound of my voice snaps her back to the room.

"Oh, nahsing reely," she says in her heavy Danish accent. "What time is my radiation tomorrow?"

"Seven A.M.," I answer casually. I don't mention that her radiation has always been at seven A.M., six days a week for the last five weeks. Radiation to the brain kills more than just cancer cells.

"Have I eaten today?"

"You ate a few bites. I'll get us some dinner soon."

"Do I have to take some pills?" Her questions and confusion make her seem both very old and very young at the same time.

I can't see her well because of the darkness. I hear her labored breath. I close my eyes and listen to her silent fear.

"Oh, my God," she whispers.

"What is it?" I try to sound calm, but I'm afraid some new agony has found her.

She points to the window. A huge, luminous full moon is starting to blossom between the cliffs.

"Help me sit up." She reaches her spindly arms toward me, like a child who wants to be held.

I slowly, gently raise her skeleton of a body and adjust her array of pillows, some to cushion her, some to prevent her from tipping over. Her bed seems to be getting bigger, but then I realize it's because she's diminishing.

The room begins to shimmer as the moon creeps softly higher. I see my mom's eyes, which dominate her emaciated skull, light up for the first time in months.

"I'm not afraid to die," she assures me. "I'm just afraid of going on like this."

I sit on the bed and hold her hand as the light fills the room.

"I'll miss you so much if you die," I say to her.

"I know." She squeezes my hand. "But I'll visit you in your dreams."

The moon is a full and perfect circle, perched above the cliffs. It's so close I can see its spongy texture. I can imagine how tender and warm it would be to touch.

My mother sighs, not the sad sigh I've heard so much recently, but a sigh full of life. I see the awe illuminated on her face.

"Zis is za most beautiful moon I've ever seen," she says, filled with pure joy.

I watch the moon, but I also watch my mom, a tiny, bald woman. Her ears seem too large, hanging there on either side of her head. A smile of wonderment dances across her face. Her brow is smooth and calm. She seems to be breathing in the glow of the moon. She is absolutely beautiful.

"It's taking such a long time," she murmurs with enchantment. "Have you ever seen such a slow moon?"

A Task-Based Approach to Coping with Dying

CHARLES A. CORR

CHARLES A. CORR, PH.D., is a professor in the School of Humanities, Southern Illinois University at Edwardsville, and a volunteer with Hospice of Madison County, Illinois. Dr. Corr began teaching about death and dying in the fall of 1975. Since then, he has taught courses on children and death; hospices; death education; and loss, grief, and bereavement. He came to this work as a result of an opportunity to help establish an interdisciplinary course in death studies.

Dr. Corr volunteered at the first hospice program in the St. Louis area during the winter of 1978 and at St. Luke's Nursing Home (now St. Luke's Hospice) in Sheffield, England, during that summer. He later led two-week work-study trips to St. Luke's each summer from 1979 to 1987. Dr. Corr has been associated with the Madison County chapter of The Compassionate Friends, the Dougy Center, and the National Donor Family Council of the National Kidney Foundation. He has been a member of the boards of directors of the Association for Death Education and Counseling (1980–1983), the Illinois State Hospice Organization (1981–1984), and the International Work Group on Death, Dying, and Bereavement (1987–1993), serving as chairperson of that organization from 1989 to 1993.

In addition to writing more than fifty articles and chapters, Dr. Corr's publications include *Death Education: An Annotated Resource Guide* (Vol. I, 1980; Vol. II, 1985); *Hospice Care: Principles and Practices* (1983); *Helping Children Cope with Death: Guidelines and Resources* (2d ed., 1984); *Childhood and Death* (1984); *Hospice Approaches to Pediatric Care* (1985); *Adolescence and Death* (1986); *Sudden Infant Death Syndrome: Who Can Help and How* (1991); and *Death and Dying, Life and Living* (1994). Dr. Corr's professional work has been recognized by awards from the Association for Death Education and Counseling (1988) and Children's Hospice International (1989); five Book-of-the-Year Awards from the *American Journal of Nursing;* and Research Scholar (1990), Outstanding Scholar (1991), and Kimmel Community Service (1994) awards from his university.

THERE IS A pressing need to develop new and better theoretical models for explicating coping with dying. In recent years large strides have been made in learning about coping with bereavement.[1] During this period new theoretical models in the field of bereavement have helped to improve analyses of grief and mourning, have proved useful for those coping with loss, and have guided enlightened efforts to help bereaved persons. One noticeable feature of many of these models is their emphasis on phases or processes in mourning, rather than stages. Two of the most interesting and promising of the new models have employed task-based approaches,[2] and Attig has argued for the importance of viewing grieving as an active process.[3]

In the area of coping with dying, the principal paradigm is more than twenty years old.[4] The model is constructed around a stage-based approach to understanding coping with dying. Inadequacies in this model have been identified in the literature and by some of the most knowledgeable and sophisticated clinicians in the field.[5]

Many have been sensitive to the criticisms of the Kübler-Ross model. They recognize that a stage-based approach, especially when used in ways not in accord with its author's intentions, can erect obstacles to individualization, risking stereotyping vulnerable individuals who are coping with dying. Accordingly, in their teaching and clinical practice many have moved away from this model. The model lingers on, however, in popular folk wisdom and in literature that touches on the field from another subject area.[6]

It is not sufficient to criticize flawed theoretical models or even to set them aside. Constructive alternatives to inadequate theoretical models need to be developed. A perfect model is beyond reach, and there are no absolute guarantees against misuse of any theoretical model. Nevertheless, we must strive to create better models and to describe them in ways that minimize the likelihood of misunderstanding.

Constructive work is begun by looking, not only to the bereavement literature, but also to what has been learned in recent years about dying and coping. For example, the modern hospice movement has given rise to improved care for dying persons and their family members in many parts of the world.[7] In addition, a number of insightful scholars have contributed in important ways to our understanding of the experience of dying.[8] Active discussions about coping in recent years have focused on good and bad coping.[9] However, except for two helpful little books,[10] not much attention has been directed to basic processes in coping with dying. There remains a compelling need to reexamine central theoretical models for coping with dying.

It is time to begin thinking about new models, new ways of organizing thinking about coping with dying, and to make proposals as to the shape such models might take. In particular, any model in this area—new or old—should do four things: (a) provide a basis for *understanding* all of the dimensions and all of the individuals involved in coping with dying; (b) foster *empowerment* for those who are coping with dying by emphasizing the options available to them as they live out what is often a difficult time in life; (c) emphasize *participation* or the *shared* aspects of coping with dying—those aspects whereby people draw together in small communities and assist each other in interpersonal networks; and (d) provide *guidance for care providers and helpers,*

whether they are professionals, volunteers, or family members. These are the tests of a good model for coping with dying, and they are the tests my own proposal must meet: understanding, empowerment, participation, and guidance for helpers.[11]

The remainder of this article is divided into three principal parts:

1. Some brief comments about the nature of a task-based approach.
2. An outline of four primary dimensions of coping with dying, which define four primary areas of task work.
3. An argument as to why this new perspective should be adopted—which depends upon some thoughts about the nature of coping and an analysis of four advantages that apply to a task-based approach.

What Is a Task-Based Approach?

Tasks represent work that may be undertaken by those who are coping. Like household chores, tasks may or may not be addressed (in various ways and degrees) as individuals find them appropriate: One day the individual decides to cut the lawn; another day to put it off; and a third day, to cut only the front lawn. Similarly, in coping with dying: One day the individual wants to be surrounded by loved ones; another day, to be left alone; and a third day, to be in the company of one special person.

Many task-based accounts insist upon the urgency of their proposed tasks. These accounts appeal to developmental or situational frameworks to describe tasks as essential to satisfactory progress in resolving the challenges of life. In coping with dying, however, all must live out their own lives. "Killing me softly with his song" is to be regretted in all aspects of life; it is a special tragedy in coping with dying.[12] There is no single right way to cope with dying, although there may be better, worse, and even unacceptable modes from the standpoint of each of those involved. A task-based model approaches people from their perspectives and their coping tasks.

For this reason, I prefer to describe tasks in coping with dying as mainly discretionary, although I realize that some may be more or less necessary and others may recommend themselves more insistently. It has been said that no one is dying twenty-four hours a day. If so, then at one time a specific task may be important; at another time, it may be set aside or given less priority in the complex business of coping.

As long as one is alive, it is always possible to return from time to time to tasks of this sort. However, the overall work any individual takes up in coping with dying is never fully completed as long as the individual lives. Progress may be made in one's work with certain tasks; perhaps sometimes one can even be so fortunate as to complete specific pieces of business. The task work in coping with dying described here is part of the ongoing business of living. It is never completed; it merely ends with the individual's death.

Situational tasks, such as those involved in coping with dying, are undertaken within the larger context of lifespan developmental tasks; coping with dying occurs within the warp and woof of an individual's entire life. In one sense, developmental tasks are fundamental markers in human living; in another sense, they are simply a part of the overall context within which one's coping with dying must take place.

What Is Task Work in Coping with Dying?

Four Primary Dimensions in Coping with Dying

A task-based approach centers on the tasks confronting individuals coping with dying. There are four primary areas in which such tasks present themselves. These are: (1) the physical; (2) the psychological; (3) the social;

and (4) the spiritual. Consider for a moment how recognition and attention came to these four dimensions.

The hospice and death awareness movements arose from the realization that *dying patients are living human beings;* terminally-ill patients are not merely extreme examples of malfunctioning lungs or of defective kidneys—they are living persons.[13] This is a point that is so simple and basic it may appear to be obvious, but it is not obvious in the practice of many aspects of health care around the world, even today.[14]

If dying patients are living human beings, then the focus must be on the person, not merely the disease. In the first place, it is important, but not sufficient, to consider the *physical* dimensions of death-related experiences. So people began to speak also of *psychological* and *social* dimensions in living and dying. Taken together, these are *psychosocial* aspects of living and dying.

Recognition of psychosocial dimensions in living and in dying was an important step forward. Those who like to invent new terms combined physical and psychosocial dimensions in speaking of the *biopsycho-social*—a clumsy term with a commendable motive. But this, too, is not enough. In addition to physical and psychosocial dimensions of care, the hospice movement has also advocated respect for the spiritual dimensions of human life. Indeed, one could argue that the modern hospice movement is rooted in a broadly spiritual foundation.[15]

Spiritual dimensions of hospice care have not always been defined with precision. Hospice care recognizes that each person coping with dying is a unique and valuable being. It also strives to achieve a sense of wholeness, integration, or integrity in living and dying. This includes, but is not necessarily the same as, *religious* dimensions of life in which the term is employed to indicate denominational or sectarian organizations and practices. For example, the hospice movement has sought to respect all religious orientations, including agnosticism or atheism. Hospice care does not impose any particular religious or spiritual values; it fosters continued opportunities to actualize spiritual values by individuals who are coping with dying and bereavement.

Any account of living human beings, and particularly one that has to do with human beings who are coping with dying, must respect all four of these fundamental dimensions.[16] These four dimensions include everything and omit nothing. Anything less is insufficient.

Four Primary Areas of Task Work

Each of these four dimensions can be understood as the foundation for a primary area of task work in coping with dying. These *four primary areas of task work* can be described as follows:

1. To satisfy *bodily needs* and *minimize physical distress* in ways that are consistent with other values.
2. To maximize *psychological* security, autonomy, and richness in living.
3. To sustain and enhance those *interpersonal attachments* significant to the person concerned and to address the *social implications* of dying.
4. To identify, develop, or reaffirm sources of *spiritual* energy and in so doing foster *hope*.

Physical Dimensions—Physical aspects of coping with dying primarily concern *meeting bodily needs* and the *minimization of physical distress*. Fundamental bodily needs involve nutrition, hydration, and elimination, as well as obtaining shelter from the elements. Minimization of physical distress undoubtedly relates to management of pain, but also to nausea, vomiting, constipation, and other corporeal sources of distress.

One might think that an emphasis on pain relief and the control of distressing physical symptoms would be a concern of all medical and health care systems. In a sense, this is true, but it was precisely the lack of adequate relief of distressing symptoms among patients with terminal illness that stimulated the development of early hospice programs.[17] This deficiency may have evolved for many reasons: a tendency to withdraw from dying persons because of a sense of frustration or inadequacy, a fear of failure, or concerns about one's own mortality; inadequate understanding of pain and other symptoms; misplaced fears of addiction; or an overemphasis on cure-oriented interventions associated with distressing side effects. Whatever the reasons, reforms in palliative care—the management of distressing symptoms—were clearly needed. The modern hospice movement deserves credit for contributing to improvements in these aspects throughout our health care system.

There is a *prima facie* need to insist on focusing on the physical aspects of coping with dying; Maslow described some needs as being more fundamental than others.[18] This is why Lack wrote: "We hear far too much about counseling for the dying patient and not enough about giving the physical care."[19] This is not an attack on counseling; it is a plea for attention to the fundamental physical needs of those who are dying.

At the same time, one must take into account *other values* that may take precedence over physical dimensions for an individual who is coping with dying. Anyone who addresses physical dimensions in care of the dying quickly realizes how these people are affected by anxiety, their need for a sense of security, and their need for relations with others. These are psychological (or psychosocial) concerns. Their importance is evidenced in a study conducted by Parkes that contrasted management of distressing physical symptoms at home and in hospital. Parkes noted that "people dying at home were much more likely to remain mobile and in clear consciousness than patients dying in hospital, but they were also likely to suffer more pain."[20] Thus, "home can be the best place or the worst place to die."[21] Whether or not one chooses home care depends upon what options are available but also upon what one regards as most important in coping with dying. Some dying persons experience more pain at home than they might experience in a hospital but nevertheless choose to remain at home. This represents a choice in which relative primacy is not given to physical aspects of coping. The point is not to advocate this particular ranking of priorities, but only to note that physical aspects of coping with dying may not always have absolute primacy over other dimensions.

Psychological Dimensions—Psychological aspects of coping with dying center on maximizing three features of life: security, autonomy, and richness. To be *secure* is to be as free as one can be from anxiety, fear, or apprehension. Ordinarily, humans feel secure because they appreciate that they are in a safe situation, or because they believe that they are able to manage the situation at hand. In fact, while security and safety are usually related roughly as subjective and objective aspects of one's position, they are not necessarily correlated. The baby that cries at night may be insecure, even though it is actually quite safe. Parents who pledge that "everything is OK" may provide their child with a sense of security, even though they make an assertion that may not be accurate in a dangerous universe. The hospice pledge not to abandon dying persons and their families frequently contributes to a sense of security, although it does not minimize the dangers encountered in confronting the experience of dying and the reality of death.

Autonomy is the feature of life encompassing the human's ability to be self (*auto*) governing (*nomous*). To be in control of one's own life, to the degree this is possible, is a high priority for many human beings, even if they occasionally transfer responsibility for decision making to others. Autonomy sometimes requires individuals to strive continuously to contend with challenges in living and to assert their own dominion over events that impinge on their lives. Autonomy is supported to the degree that others value the uniqueness of the individual in question.

Richness in living describes the texture of a human life. It designates that which makes life satisfactory or bountiful. What richness will mean for individuals must be left to their determination. One person might prize serenity and the absence of threat; another might choose activity, creativity, and a degree of risk or danger.

Social Dimensions—Social aspects of coping with dying have two central features: relations with other people as individuals and as members of groups or with society as a whole. For the first of these, the cardinal area of task work in coping with dying is to sustain and enhance *interpersonal attachments significant to the person in question*. Interpersonal attachments are honored because humans are social creatures. In the midst of the challenges of coping with dying, it is critical, however, that they be the interpersonal attachments valued by the person in question, not those whom others think that person should value. The network of interpersonal attachments significant to a dying person may shrink or change in nature as death draws close.

The group or *corporate aspect* of social dimensions of coping with dying is an inescapable feature of life. Americans profess to prize independence, but in fact all are interdependent. Individuals are always implicated in both personal and communal networks. In coping with dying, as in all other aspects of human life, one is never fully disconnected or uninvolved in relationships with social groups surrounding one's life. There are many of these collective systems; they include families, tribes, cultures, guilds, congregations, and governmental entities. Even in dying, one is obliged to address the demands of these enveloping social organizations, just as in coping with dying one may wish to call upon the resources such social entities make available. Often, economic concerns are an important feature of these social dimensions of coping with dying.

Spiritual Dimensions—Spiritual aspects of coping with dying essentially involve those sources from which one draws spiritual vigor and vitality. These sources depend upon the individual's fundamental values and moral commitments. Spirituality encompasses acceptance, reconciliation, self-worth, meaning, and purpose in living. Thus, spirituality concerns achieving what Erikson called "integrity" or a sense of wholeness.[22]

For many, this is connected with some formal or informal religious focus in life, but this is not true for everyone, and it is not the whole story for anyone. Spirituality includes not just those persons, places, objects, or events designated as holy or sacred but anything having to do with the life of the human spirit. In dying, meaning in one's life may be sought through a process similar to what Butler called "life review" in elderly adults.[23]

The spiritual dimension in living also concerns *hope,* a key element in coping. Dying persons and others who are coping with dying need not be without hope. They can, in fact, be hopeful—full of hope—in ways that are often a source of awe to those around them. At bottom, hope involves faith and trust (again, not just in a formally religious sense). In contrast to wishing, hope is grounded in reality.

As the process of coping with dying is worked through and lived out, the object or focus of one's hope may alter. For example, hope may be directed toward cure or salvation, but it may also focus on relief from one's own distress, the welfare of others, living until some significant date or event (for example, a holiday or the birth of a grandchild), an opportunity to achieve reconciliation with an estranged relative, or influencing what will happen after death (for example, planning the funeral, making financial provisions for the family, donating creative achievements to charity). In order to determine how hope is or might be embodied in individuals, we must listen to people carefully and identify with them their definition of meaningfulness in living.

Each of these four dimensions defines an *area* of task work, not a list of individual tasks. These four areas arise from understanding what it is to be a living human and what is involved in a comprehensive program of care. They mark out universal areas of possible task work in coping with dying, not merely generalizations. In order to be applied to the particular circumstances of a concrete individual, these four task areas become the main headings for a list of specific tasks that could be undertaken by the person in question.

Why Adopt a Task-Based Approach to Coping with Dying?

The foregoing is the new theoretical model proposed for describing coping with dying. The following is a description of the advantages of adopting such a model, an argument on behalf of this new conceptual framework.

Coping with Dying

Dying and coping with dying are, or often can be, human experiences. Some dying trajectories are so swift and unexpected they provide little opportunity for anything distinctively human in the experience. But often dying is not like this. Dying that arises from degenerative diseases typical of mortality in our society usually takes time (often weeks, months, or even years) and frequently can be anticipated or predicted in some degree. If this were not true, Kübler-Ross could not have spoken of death as "the final stage of growth."[24]

Dying can often be incorporated into a distinctly human portion of the journey through life. The process of seizing control of events is called *coping,* a popular term in contemporary society. It is fashionable to talk about good or bad coping, about coping that is helpful or hurtful, productive or counterproductive, satisfactory or unsatisfactory. There are various forms of coping, and they can have various outcomes—especially from different points of view.

But thinking about coping needs to be deeper and more fundamental. The issue does not merely concern methods, tactics, or outcomes of coping. What, in fact, is coping? When is someone coping? What is involved in coping with dying?

Coping encompasses more than just reacting to or defending against the events and challenges of life. Coping involves an awareness of events and challenges, plus efforts to contend with them. According to Lazarus and Folkman, coping can be defined as "constantly changing cognitive and behavioral efforts to manage specific external and/or internal demands that are appraised as taxing or exceeding the resources of the persons.[25] Further, Weisman suggested coping "is positive in approach; defending is negative."[26] Defensive reactions are, at best, just one portion of the full spectrum of coping processes. Essentially, coping involves efforts to manage what occurs in one's life, to achieve a livable balance insofar as it is possible. Coping may be provoked by fear, anxiety, or threat but also by much more pleasant, if unusual, opportunities and challenges. In Selye's language, stress can lead to creativity, just as it can lead to burnout.[27] There is stress in living and in dying; the issue is how to deal with that stress, how to cope.

Coping with dying is not merely a role in living; it encompasses the whole of an individual's life, and it is not confined merely to the dying person. It applies to all individuals who are drawn into the experience of dying: the dying person, family, and friends (taking "family" here to mean those significant others who are united to the person by blood, marriage, or other forms of more or less deliberate decision); and those involved in providing care to the dying person.

How do we identify all of the ways in which each of these individuals is coping with dying? There is no shortcut; we must be present to each of these individuals in ways that are characterized by active listening, careful observation, sensitive assessment, and ongoing reassessment. No one can hope to know *a priori* how any individual is coping without actually making the effort to find out the concrete circumstances. We must listen actively to each individual coping with dying.

Advantages of a Task-Based Approach

A task-based approach contributes to improved understanding, empowerment, participation, and guidance for helpers in coping with dying.

Improved Understanding—First, a task-based approach takes into account not only feelings or psychosocial responses but all the dimensions of human life. It provides a holistic perspective, in contrast to one that merely attends to selected segments or aspects of the person's life.

Second, a task-based approach is firmly grounded in two important features:

1. That which applies universally to all human beings (four primary areas of task work: physical, psychological, social, and spiritual).
2. That which applies uniquely to each individual (the specific, concrete tasks facing only that person and that the person chooses to undertake or set aside).

In this way, a task-based approach rejects broad generalizations that have an initial and superficial attractiveness. The problem with generalizations is that they obscure the distinctive qualities of the individual and do not achieve universal validity.

Third, a task-based approach explicitly recognizes coping undertaken by all of the individuals—the dying person, family members or friends, and care providers—involved in a particular experience of dying. In each of these ways, a task-based approach provides an improved foundation for understanding coping with dying.

Empowerment—In contrast to stages or phases, tasks are meant to empower individuals coping with dying. Individuals can decide which tasks are important to them, how and when, if at all, they will be addressed, and so on. There is much that seems to be and truly is out of control in dying, but if the individual can make choices about which tasks will be undertaken, then he or she has not lost all influence over this important process. In a voice that speaks from the abyss of the Nazi death camps, Viktor Frankl wrote: "everything can be taken from a man but one thing: the last of the human freedoms—to choose . . . one's own way."[28] Anything that contributes to empowerment of vulnerable people is particularly important.

Theoretical models that emphasize or suggest passivity in coping with dying are undesirable. If one only reacts to what is happening or passes mysteriously from one stage to another, then one is truly a "patient," someone beset and dominated by the events of life, someone acted upon by forces outside one's own authority. As a passive spectator, one has not yet begun to exercise control, take charge, or actively influence the course of one's life. In this way, autonomy gives way to anonymity, the personal yields to the impersonal, and humans are dehumanized. In the words of Ted Rosenthal, "being invisible I invite only generalizations."[29]

As noted earlier, a task-based approach does not concentrate upon that which is oblig-

atory ("must") or normative/prescriptive ("should" or "ought"). Instead, it emphasizes choices among possible tasks. In this way, it avoids the twin pitfalls of linearity and directedness that are prominent risks in any stage-based approach. The language of stages should never be used unless one means to identify intervals or periods in a linear process. Stages are like marks on a gauge that record a rise and fall in temperature or in the depth of a river. They allow for movement forward and backward, but they do not constitute a model sufficiently flexible to account for the dynamic features of coping with dying.

Further, stage-based models often take on a sense of directedness or obligation in the hands of those who use them. A student once asked if there were stages that individuals had to go through when they were coping with dying. Are we in danger of not dying in the "right" way? Can one really "fail" dying? Insistence that one ought to cope with dying in a particular way risks disempowering the very people who most need empowerment.

Participation—Tasks enhance participation or sharing in the life that remains to be lived. A task-based approach is not confined solely to dying persons. It describes tasks to be undertaken by three broad groups of people: individuals who are dying or who have a life-threatening illness; their family members and friends; and their caregivers, whether professional or lay.

This offers two advantages. First, it extends the understanding of the scope of coping with dying to include all of the people who are involved in this coping. Second, it recognizes the many layers of complexity in coping.

The second point draws attention to the fact that each individual has at least two sets of tasks in coping with dying. The first set of tasks concerns the individual's own needs; the second set concerns relationships with others who are bound to the individual in an interrelated network. Some tasks are undertaken (or set aside) for oneself; others are undertaken (or set aside) on behalf of others. A task-based approach explicitly recognizes the willingness or unwillingness of each coping individual to take part in a caring community. All of these people are, or can be, individuals who are coping with dying. This sharing in the lives and tasks of others is an unavoidable feature of coping with dying.

Guidance for Helpers—A task-based approach gives direction to all of those who are involved in helping an individual who is coping with dying. This occurs because the tasks the individual is addressing can also be seen as guidelines for helping. When one has chosen certain tasks in coping with dying, it becomes the responsibility of helpers to consider whether or how they can best assist in the fulfillment of those tasks. For example, a dying person may want to remain at home or to visit that home one last time. Helpers who are able to contribute to making that possible honor the person and the person's associated tasks.

Of course, it may not always be possible to actualize a particular task. Sometimes a perceived task may, in fact, be counterproductive for the individual in question or hurtful to others. Helpers who decline to assist with a particular task (for example, the determination to end one's own life) or who encourage an individual to reconsider the choices among tasks retain their own autonomy as decision makers. The point is this: in all of these examples, the helper's autonomy is informed and focused by the structure of a task-based approach.

A model that is content to identify reactions to the threat of dying confines itself mainly to recognition and understanding. Once the reaction has been identified, the model has nothing further to say. Once someone is told that the individual is in the stage of "bargaining," a stage based model provides no guidance as to how one should deal with it. In this framework, it seems to be enough merely to give a name to the reaction. Beyond that, helpers are left in an essentially passive state; they acknowledge or accept the reaction but are not guided as to how they should or might work with it.

Active participation by willing helpers within the coping process deserves more encouragement and guidance. Potential caregivers must be shown not only how to understand the ways in which an individual is coping, but also how they might assist with the constructive aspects of that coping. A task-based approach provides guidance needed by helpers. Here again, a task-based approach fosters awareness of the individual and sensitivity to the interactive processes involved in coping with dying; a task-based approach emphasizes the dynamic tension between individual and community characteristic of human existence. At the same time, it cautions helpers not to overwhelm vulnerable persons by confusing their tasks with those of the helpers.

Conclusion

Any model of coping with dying must provide a descriptive, theoretical framework for understanding, empowering, sharing with, and helping individuals who are coping with dying. All models set out to simplify in order to clarify. In so doing, they must be careful not to falsify or distort the experiences they represent. When it comes to coping with dying, models must leave individuals free to live out their own experiences during the living/dying interval—as, of course, they always are, whatever is said about them in grand theories.

The Experience of Grief

John DeFrain. "Learning About Grief from Normal Families: SIDS, Stillbirth, and Miscarriage," *Journal of Marital and Family Therapy* 17, no. 3 (July 1991): 215–32. Why did this happen? How long will the pain last? Am I losing my mind? Where can I find help? These are among the questions that family members commonly pose when an infant dies. Individuals who have experienced such losses can teach us a great deal about grief and how to survive the tragedies that occur in our own lives.

Julie Fritsch, with Sherokee Ilse. *The Anguish of Loss.* Long Lake, Minn.: Wintergreen Press, 1988. Through a series of sculptures that evolved out of the need to express her pain following the death of her son just before his birth, Fritsch presents a visual expression of grief and sorrow. Photographs of the sculptures are juxtaposed with Fritsch's writings. Working through the loss by sculpting became a way to release her feelings; these pieces, in turn, have become a vehicle for helping others.

Bob Krizek. "Goodbye Old Friend: A Son's Farewell to Comiskey Park," *Omega: Journal of Death and Dying* 25, no. 2 (1992): 87-93. When the home of the White Sox closed, Krizek attended the last game played at the old baseball stadium both as a social scientist recording the thoughts and feelings of others and as a son reconnecting with memories of and feelings for his father. Although the upper-deck seats where he and his father had shared many games were not very good by the usual standards, to Krizek they were "sacred." In that park, in those seats, the memories and feelings endured. What happens to our associations and emotional investments when physical connections with our past are destroyed?

Marian Osterweis, Fredric Solomon, and Morris Green, eds. *Bereavement: Reactions, Consequences, and Care.* Washington: National Academy Press, 1984. In this study commissioned by the National Institute of Medicine, grief is examined from psychosocial and biological perspectives, with the aim of determining the health consequences of bereavement and assessing various interventions designed to ease both the acute pain and the longer-term effects of grief. Of special interest are sections on bereavement reactions throughout the lifespan and on the biology of grieving.

Therese A. Rando. "The Increasing Prevalence of Complicated Mourning: The Onslaught Is Just Beginning," *Omega: Journal of Death and Dying* 26, no. 1 (1992–1993): 43–59. Using the term *complicated mourning* in preference to other designations (such as pathological, neurotic, maladaptive, unresolved, abnormal, dysfunctional, or deviant mourning), Rando examines situations in which grief as a series of processes has somehow become "complicated." She suggests that complicated mourning is increasing due to the types of death now occurring, the characteristics of the relationships severed by these deaths, and the personality and resources of contemporary mourners.

Kathleen M. Wright, Robert J. Ursano, Paul T. Bartone, and Larry H. Ingraham. "The Shared Experience of Catastrophe: An Expanded Classification of the Disaster Community," *American Journal of Orthopsychiatry* 60, no. 1 (1990): 35–42. When an airliner crashed on takeoff from Gander, Newfoundland, killing 248 members of the 101st Airborne Division, who were the bereaved? Most immediately, of course, they were the parents, spouses, and children of those killed. Friends, more distant kin, and others in the military and civilian communities were also deeply affected. Less readily identified, perhaps, were numerous service and support personnel who served as escorts and honor guards for the bodies of the deceased, chaplains, morgue workers, transport crews, grave registration personnel, and volunteers in the recovery operation. Applying a model of "circles of involvement," the authors invite us to expand our definition of the community that feels the impact of death or disaster.

Recognizing Hidden Sorrow

Norbert Elias. *The Loneliness of the Dying*. New York: Basil Blackwell, 1985. In contrast to the past, most people now die in hospitals and other medical institutions, often alone and lonely. As lifespan has increased, death is further postponed. For a variety of social and personal reasons, death is often pushed behind the scenes. This can be a bitter experience for the dying, who nevertheless feel they must hide their sorrow. In an essay that ranges through history as well as the social sciences and embraces his own encounter with dying, Elias offers an intimate examination of dying and death in modern societies.

Nathan R. Kollar, "Rituals and the Disenfranchised Griever," in *Disenfranchised Grief: Recognizing Hidden Sorrow*, edited by Kenneth J. Doka (Lexington, Mass.: Lexington Books, 1989), 271–85. What happens to us when normal expectations for funerals and other mourning rituals are not met? Our grief is disenfranchised, and we lose a valuable opportunity for moving through a pattern of activity that can lessen the pain of grief. Beginning with an excellent presentation on the nature of postdeath ritual and its goals, Kollar focuses on social barriers that tend to keep disenfranchised grievers from acknowledging their grief through ritual—and he discusses ways of overcoming these barriers. Kollar's analysis of the purpose of funerals and other death rites and his creative suggestions for alternatives to the standard forms are not only for those whose grief is disenfranchised, but for everyone who wishes to have the benefits of postdeath ritual.

Patricia R. Krysinski. "Coping with Suicide: Beyond the Five-Day Bereavement Leave Policy," *Death Studies* 17 (1993): 173–77. As a former public school principal and administrator, Krysinski helped employees deal with the deaths of students and loved ones. She had read the literature on grief and felt competent to provide care and support to others. When her husband committed suicide, however, she realized that her prior understanding of grief was only part of the story. The death of a loved one is incapacitating, and recovery takes longer than the time permitted for bereavement leave.

J. William Worden. "Grieving a Loss from AIDS," *Hospice Journal* 7 (1991): 143–50. Among the determinants that influence the intensity and course of grief is the type of death. Worden examines several features of an AIDS death that bear on survivors' reactions. These include the stigma associated with the disease, a lack of social support for persons in nontraditional relationships, fear of contagion or guilt about transmitting the virus to one's partner, the untimeliness of death at a young age, the progressive physical and mental deterioration that often precedes the death, and the frequent presence of neurological complications such as dementia that may cause survivors to feel that they lost the person they once loved long before death actually occurs. Worden discusses these factors in detail, with case examples, and suggests strategies for intervention.

Social Support for Survivors

Dana Cable, Laurel Cucchi, Faye Lopez, and Terry Martin. "Camp Jamie," *American Journal of Hospice and Palliative Care* 9, no. 5 (1992): 18–21. What happens when twenty-six bereaved children are paired with caring adults, many recovering from losses themselves, in an idyllic mountain setting? Just such an experiment was tried by Hospice of Frederick County, Maryland, and the event led to a few surprises and many magical moments for participants.

Karen M. Freehill. "Critical Incident Stress Debriefing in Health Care," *Critical Care Clinics* 8, no. 3 (1992): 491–500. When we think about social support for grieving, often neglected are medical staff and other health personnel who are affected by patient death and other traumatic experiences in the course of their professional duties. The term "critical incident stress" has been coined to describe the effect of patient death, contact with severely injured children, multiple casualties from disasters, death or serious injury of a coworker in the line of duty, and other such occurrences. Debriefing, taking time for those affected to talk about the event, can reduce distress. Freehill, herself a former emergency services worker, provides guidelines for making the most of debriefing sessions following traumatic events.

Kathleen R. Gilbert and Laura S. Smart. *Coping with Infant or Fetal Loss: The Couple's Healing Process*. New York: Bruner-Mazel, 1992. Examining the healing process of twenty-seven couples who experienced miscarriage, stillbirth, or the death of their infant, this book tells the stories of how these parents dealt with their loss and with each other. How can parents who are grieving individually reach out to each other and provide solace? In a world disrupted by tragedy, how do couples engage one another in a dance of grief that allows them to take turns comforting and being comforted? For grieving couples, social support begins at home. Gilbert and Smart explore the dynamics of the healing process for couples and suggest outside sources that can lend strength to the couple's own efforts at mutual support. The interested reader may also wish to consult Laura Smart's "The Marital Helping Relationship Following Pregnancy Loss and Infant Death," *Journal of Family Issues,* 13, no. 1 (1992): 81–98.

Irving G. Leon. "Perinatal Loss: Choreographing Grief on the Obstetric Unit," *American Journal of Orthopsychiatry* 62, no. 1 (1992): 7–8. In many hospitals a phenomenal change has occurred in the recent past concerning how they handle the death of a newborn on the ward. Instead of whisking the baby away from the stunned parents and telling them to forget the loss and try to have another baby as soon as possible, hospital personnel are more likely to encourage expression of parental grief. Parents are given opportunities to name, embrace, and make photographs of the deceased baby. Leon suggests that a closer look is needed at the script caregivers may be following in these situations. Improvisation (genuine communication) may be lost when well-meaning "grief counselors" have set ideas about what bereaved persons should be doing and feeling.

Paul C. Rosenblatt. "Grief: The Social Context of Private Feelings," *Journal of Social Issues,* 44, no. 3 (1988): 67–78. Although the psychology of grief focuses on individuals, Rosenblatt reminds us that grief occurs in the context of social relationships and culture. For the grieving person, interactions with others can be painful as well as comforting. Of particular interest is Rosenblatt's discussion of the value of social support in the context of brief interactions, thereby bridging the apparent emotional gap between the grieving person and others.

Hans Sande. "Palestinian Martyr Widowhood: Emotional Needs in Conflict with Role Expectations," *Social Science and Medicine* 34, no. 6 (1992): 709–17. Social support for the bereaved is usually viewed as a kind of benevolent, even altruistic, action taken to lessen the grieving person's pain and confusion following a death. This look at the role expectations placed on martyr widows—women whose husbands died while fighting in military operations or from torture while imprisoned—brings a fresh perspective to the definition of social support in bereavement. Is community involvement in shaping the grief experience necessarily helpful to the bereaved themselves?

Phyllis R. Silverman and J. William Worden. "Children's Understanding of Funeral Ritual," *Omega: Journal of Death and Dying* 25, no. 4 (1992): 319–31. Should children be allowed (or encouraged) to attend funerals of loved ones? In this study, 120 children who experienced the death of their parents, most of whom also attended the funeral, were asked about their view of funeral ritual. Their answers shed light on the issue of whether funerals provide social support and comfort for children as well as adults.

Coping with Life-threatening Illness

Judith Ahronheim and Doron Weber. *Final Passages: Positive Choices for the Dying and Their Loved Ones*. New York: Simon and Schuster, 1992. Patients and their families will benefit from this guidebook through the thicket of issues arising from dealing with terminal illness. Ahronheim and Weber present current information about managing pain and other symptoms, hospice care, eliciting information from physicians and other health care personnel, safeguarding legal rights through the use of living wills and powers of attorney, financial planning, understanding and treating depression, weighing suicide and euthanasia, and expressing feelings about death.

Sandra L. Bertman. *Facing Death: Images, Insights, and Interventions*. New York: Hemisphere, 1991. Using material from the visual arts; excerpts from poetry, fiction, and drama; and examples from popular culture, this presentation gently brings us to appreciate the issues that confront the dying and those who care for them.

Anatole Broyard. *Intoxicated by My Illness*. New York: Clarkson Potter, 1992. The author of this affecting work died in 1990 of prostate cancer, which had been diagnosed fourteen months earlier. During his illness, Broyard wrote the essays and journal entries that are printed, along with several earlier pieces, in this slim volume. His observations about coping with illness and about current American attitudes toward death and dying are informed by his belief in the importance of dying with style. In coming to terms with his fate, Broyard writes: "I understood that life itself had a deadline—like the book I had been working on." He argues for making "a game, a career, even an art form" of opposing the limitations imposed by illness.

Kenneth J. Doka. *Living with Life-Threatening Illness: A Guide for Patients, Their Families, and Caregivers*. New York: Lexington Books, 1993. Emphasizing the experience of *living* with illness, Doka provides a comprehensive view of life-threatening illness from the crisis of diagnosis through various treatment possibilities to recovery or the prospect of impending death. Ways of coping with and managing the challenges of serious illness are clearly explained, and practical suggestions are given for improving the lives of patients, family members, and caregivers.

David B. Morris. *The Culture of Pain*. Berkeley: University of California Press, 1991. Is pain simply a medical problem? Is its relief only a matter of finding the right combination of drugs, ointments, or surgery? For those who know firsthand the discomfort and pain of life-threatening illness, these are not idle questions. The question of how best to manage pain becomes uppermost when efforts to cure are dispensed with in favor of palliative or comfort care. "This is a book," says the author, "about the meanings we make out of pain." It goes beyond conventional boundaries to explore the full scope of pain as shaped by both mind and culture.

Albert Lee Strickland and Lynne Ann DeSpelder, "Communicating About Death and Dying," in *A Challenge for Living: Dying, Death, and Bereavement*, edited by Inge B. Corless, Barbara B. Germino, and Mary Pittman (Boston: Jones and Bartlett, 1994). Encounters with dying and death present special challenges to us as communicators. Sensitive and caring communication is an essential component of physical care. Learning to recognize the range and styles of nonverbal and verbal communication is important in helping patients and families cope with terminal illness and loss.

part four

Death in Life

*T*he impact of death on human behavior is far-reaching, affecting the shape and tenor of our lives in a variety of contexts: cultural, social, and personal. Efforts to deny the reality of death must inevitably be unsuccessful. Death is part of life.

As befits an age of scientific investigation, innumerable studies and clinical reports have added to our storehouse of information about how people grieve and how people confront and cope with the prospect of dying. The net of understanding is being cast ever wider, and we are beginning to appreciate both the diversity and the universality of human responses to death and dying. To the extent that the door has been opened and death allowed at least part way out of the closet, we have learned that our lives are enhanced, not diminished, when we face the facts of death. Knowledge increases our ability to cope with dying, grief, and loss.

The benefit of this openness about death and dying is evident in the movement to establish programs of hospice and palliative care and in innovative approaches to home care that make it possible for terminally ill patients to enjoy the companionship of family and friends rather than spending their last days in an impersonal institutional environment. Educational programs within schools and in other settings have furthered public understanding of the dynamics of grief and its expression.

This greater openness about dying and death has not met with unanimous approval, however. Are issues involving death and dying private matters that have no place in public discourse? Voices have been raised against the "evils" of death education. Of particular concern to many critics of death education is the fear that it undermines family values and diminishes respect for life. According to this view, public discussions about the ethical issues involved in withdrawing or withholding life-sustaining treatment may make such actions more acceptable. Similarly, there is concern that talking about suicide may cause some individuals, especially young people, to kill themselves. Is such criticism valid?

In the article, "Is Death Education a 'Nasty Little Secret'? A Call to Break the Alleged Silence," Patrick Dean examines some of the major criticisms lodged against death education and concludes that, given the reality of our lives in the twentieth century, the question is not whether death education should be taught, but how. Death education takes place in a variety of settings, sometimes in rather haphazard fashion. For instance, it may consist of a spontaneous and unplanned discussion in response to the unexpected death of a classmate. In such situations, teachers do their best to muddle through in ways that answer students' questions without creating additional anxiety. At other times, death education may be tacked on to a curriculum unit in health science or other subject without first ascertaining whether the teacher has adequate and appropriate preparation to deal with the issues that arise. In yet other circumstances, a well-meaning teacher who has recently "discovered" death education may want to bring it into the classroom, not realizing the range of academic and human relations skills needed to successfully carry out such an aim. In examining the diverse settings in which death education takes place, we need to consider how to improve its quality. Dean makes some specific suggestions in this regard that deserve careful thought.

Hannelore Wass takes up this theme in "Visions in Death Education," adapted from a keynote address presented to the Association for Death Education and Counseling. In tracking the evolution of death education from the pioneering efforts made by a few scholars and clinicians, Wass notes that the field's rapid growth has not been accompanied by a clear

sense of continuity or common tradition, qualities that are crucial for
the stability of a new scholarly discipline. Further, few mechanisms are
in place for ensuring that minimal standards in the training of death
educators are met. Consequently, the quality of instruction varies,
sometimes falling far short of what was envisioned by the field's
founders. This is a matter of real concern to many leading practitioners.

Death education has a broad appeal. There are courses at all educational levels as well as programs for health professionals and for the
general public. Clearly, the level of discussion about dying and death has
reached peaks unanticipated just a short time ago. But it is difficult to
assess or evaluate the impact of all this talk and instruction. There is as
yet no clear consensus about the goals of death education or of the so-
called death-awareness movement. Few would argue against increased
awareness of techniques for managing pain or other aspects of terminal
care when that awareness leads to improved care and comfort for dying
patients. Nor is there much argument about the benefit of community
programs promoting suicide prevention. In both of these areas, the
practical application of efforts related to death education and awareness
is obvious.

But should the goal of death education be to reduce anxiety about
death, to make death a more comfortable experience for people? Here
the situation becomes murky and ill-defined. While there are undoubtedly many instances in which it is beneficial to reduce the level of such
anxiety, particularly when it is debilitating or causes dysfunction,
a healthy fear or respect for death is not to be discarded lightly.
Devaluation of death can lead to devaluation of life. We become too
comfortable about death when we accept uncritically the "horrendous
deaths" due to violence, war, and environmental disaster that are all too
characteristic of our time. Envisioning the future of death education,
Wass notes that death education is about "fears and terrors and retaining one's sanity in a world of war, terrorism, and the threat of total
destruction," as well as about "life, its quality, meaning, preciousness,
and beauty."

Education about dying and death can prepare us for the inevitable
experiences of loss in our lives. It can make us better aware of our
choices with respect to such matters as terminal care, funeral rites,
styles of grieving, and social support. It can encourage us to stop automatically turning away from the subject of death and instead to consider its meaning in our lives. As we contemplate the meaning of death

and recognize that loss is profoundly woven into the fabric of human existence, we acknowledge not only the painful loss of those who are dear to us but also our own mortality. As illustrated in "The Mortal King," a Chinese folk tale retold by Allan Chinen, this acknowledgment can be interpreted in life-enhancing ways.

When we reflect deeply on the impermanence of our existence and the inevitability of our own death, we naturally experience grief. Such mourning is associated with the "grief for oneself" experienced by individuals who are terminally ill and near death, but it occurs in other contexts as well. Thomas Attig calls our attention to this fact in "Coping with Mortality: An Essay on Self-Mourning." Bereavement, for example, can give rise to an intensely personal search for meaning with respect to the central questions of life and death. As in the ancient epic story of Gilgamesh, the death of a loved one causes us to recognize our own mortality. Various milestones of life, such as approaching middle age or retirement, are frequently accompanied by a pressing need to confront issues involving mortality.

The struggle to come to terms with impermanence and limitation may occur at various times and in varying intensities throughout a person's life. Perhaps you have been provoked to reflect on such matters as a result of taking a course on death and dying or reading this book: How do these issues apply to me? In thinking about your experiences, consider whether your encounter with death and dying has caused you to reconsider issues of life and living as well. Confronting our mortality sometimes leads us to evaluate and even reorient ourselves in relation to our aims and purposes in life.

Facing death clearsightedly deepens appreciation for life. It also fosters increased empathy and compassion for others. We exist not only as individuals, but also as members of communities. In "The Limits of Self-Interest," Alfred Killilea discusses how the wider community of which we are part can benefit from ending the denial of death and instead affirming a place for it in our lives. How might your own insights about dying and death be extended from personal application to touch upon the shared life of the community? Making room for death in our lives helps us recognize that materialistic ambition and affluence alone do not create a society that is truly wealthy. The prevailing ideology of acquisition and winning, Killilea says, "seems piteously irrelevant to the real life events that try people's hearts and souls."

When we read or hear accounts of persons who have faced life-threatening illness, we often find some common themes: The encounter with death can bring renewed zest for living; and it often results in valuing relationships more and things less. These themes are evident in the life stories recalled by Sandra Bertman in "Bearing the Unbearable: From Loss, the Gain." Through the biographies of individuals like Reverend Bryant and Ted Rosenthal, we learn that people can maintain their characteristic humanity, integrity, and connectedness even in the midst of hopelessly incurable disease and its attendant suffering.

No one is immune to the ravages of disease and death. As persons who experience grief when loved ones die and who are ourselves mortal, this statement cannot be seriously contested. But it is not the final word about the human condition. Despite unbearable loss, there can be renewal of love and community. This lesson from our study of death and dying is worth recalling as we go about our lives.

Death Education for Living

Is Death Education a "Nasty Little Secret"?
A Call to Break the Alleged Silence

PATRICK VERNON DEAN

PATRICK VERNON DEAN, M.ED., is director and founder of the Milwaukee Bereavement Center, where he works with clients on issues related to loss, healing, and personal growth. He also serves as a critical incident stress debriefer for police, fire, and emergency medical personnel and as a specialist with the district attorney's Crisis Response Unit in Milwaukee, providing on-scene crisis intervention to survivors and families following violent crime. Asked how he became involved in working with issues of loss and grief, Mr. Dean says, "I feel that my interest in death and dying, life and living, began the day I was born and I expect it to last until the day I die . . . and perhaps beyond."

In the early 1980s, Mr. Dean was an innovative public-school teacher who became involved in the study of death and dying through the experiences of his students in the classroom. During one school term, his students learned about childhood cancer by raising funds for a peer with cancer, sending her to Disneyland through the auspices of the Make-a-Wish Foundation. He holds certification from the National Center for Death Education and is a member of the International Association of Trauma Counselors. Mr. Dean is currently pursuing his doctorate in child and adolescent studies with an emphasis on the developmental perspectives of grief throughout the lifespan.

IN THE VERNACULAR of the 1990s, death education has been "outed." At least that's what its critics claim. They say death education has been done surreptitiously, hidden from the eyes of parents. Now these guardians of our public institutions have shed light on this "nasty little secret."[1] The most visible attack on death education originated in the late 1980s and was carried out by Phyllis Schlafly and the Eagle Forum, which produced a videotape intended to expose its "evils."[2] According to Schlafly, death education not only undermines parents' relations with their children, it also contributes to depression and even suicide among young people. In an article published in the *Brooklyn Spectator,* Schlafly characterized death education as "one of the nasty little secrets of public school education."[3]

Whereas Schlafly apparently sees the relationship between parents and educators as adversarial, my experience during a decade of public school teaching was quite opposite. With very few exceptions, I found that parents and teachers share the goal of acting in children's best interests. The parent-teacher relationship reflects more a meeting of the minds than the battleground envisioned by Schlafly.

The claim that classroom discussions of death have led to suicide by students is simply spurious. Following the illogic of such reasoning, we would have to believe that discussions of drunk driving lead to increased drinking. In fact, students who participate in courses about death and dying are likely to be more alert to the danger signs of suicide and to make the comment, as did a Long Island student, that she "no longer would ignore a friend who expressed thoughts of suicide but would talk to him seriously about his feelings."[4] Those involved in death education hold to the view that problems are not made worse by talking about them; rather, problems occur when people feel they cannot talk about a troubling issue. In dealing with issues that may provoke anxiety, the psychological maxim holds true: If it's mentionable, it's manageable.

Even a cursory analysis reveals that much of the criticism of death education is ill-founded and biased. Nevertheless, such criticisms do call attention to legitimate concerns about how death education is taught and the qualifications of those who teach it. Death education is not to be undertaken as a haphazard enterprise, engaged in at the whim of someone with an interest in death. Responsible education dictates that formal curriculum guidelines be established and that teachers meet certain qualifications, including specific preparation in the subject matter. In this respect, death education should meet standards similar to those applied to other subjects in the curriculum.

If death education has been the bastard child of the curriculum hidden in the closet, as some of its critics suggest, we may owe a debt of gratitude to those critics for giving us an opportunity to highlight the importance of death education as preparation for living. Rather than allowing the critics to characterize the study of death as morbid, death educators should take the lead, proclaiming that education about death and dying is in fact education about life and living. In this sense, death education should be termed "life and loss education." Anyone working in the field of death education, counseling, and care is acutely aware of the truth in the adage: "The unexamined life is not worth living." Only through awareness of our lifelong losses and appreciation of our mortality are we free to be in the present, to live fully. When you encounter the label "death education," think of it as "life/loss education." I have found that the people involved in "life/loss education" are not morbid and ghoulish folks, but rather intensely life-affirming.

Grappling with questions of life, loss, and death has occupied human consciousness since the dawn of time. People have relied on culture and religion to help provide answers, and they have relied on family and friends to provide comfort when their lives are visited by death. While interest in death is not new, the present shape of this interest does exhibit some innovative features.

The Origins of Death Education

Although the origins of the current death awareness movement can be variously noted, it is generally agreed that the pioneering efforts began in the 1940s and 1950s. These efforts resulted in important achievements that broadened our knowledge of dying and death, laying the foundation for the multistoried, many-roomed edifice that we see today. It was not until the 1960s and 1970s, however, that discussion of grief and loss moved beyond academic and professional circles. Herman Feifel's *The Meaning of Death,* published in 1959, brought together authorities from various disciplines and represented a multitude of viewpoints related to dying, death, and bereavement. It showed that death was a topic for public as well as scholarly consideration. Ten years later, Elisabeth Kübler-Ross's *On Death and Dying* ignited the spark of widespread public discussion of death. It became a springboard for seminars, workshops, and college courses.

During the 1970s, a variety of groups were organized with the express purpose of providing social support to dying and grieving persons. (Here one thinks of such groups as The Compassionate Friends, various widow-to-widow groups, Make Today Count, and the Shanti Project of San Francisco.) The hospice movement, an import from England growing out of the pioneering work of Cicely Saunders, was transplanted onto American soil to stimulate new ideas and techniques in care of the dying. Professional organizations such as the Forum for Death Education and Counseling (formed in 1976 and renamed the Association for Death Education and Counseling ten years later) provided an arena for sharing information and techniques across a whole range of issues concerned with death education, counseling, and care.

During the late 1960s and throughout the 1970s, there was a veritable explosion in the number of courses on death and dying offered at the college level, most of them full-semester courses. Scholarly journals devoted to the subject—notably *Omega* and *Death Studies* (formerly *Death Education*)—became commonplace in college and university libraries, as did periodicals like *Thanatos* and *Bereavement.* While courses in death and dying are found in various academic disciplines (with the

majority within departments of health and psychology), death education generally embraces a multidisciplinary approach that includes insights from both the social sciences and the humanities. Although this approach provides inherent richness and intellectual stimulation, it tends to make death education "an academic orphan."[5] Courses may be either jealously claimed in turf battles over enrollment or summarily dropped when the budgetary axe falls during times of fiscal constraint. Still, formal death education is more firmly established at the college and university level than it is in elementary and secondary schools.

In elementary schools, death education usually takes place as postvention in the context of "teachable moments," as, for example, when the class hamster dies or when students are exposed to more widely recognized tragedies like the explosion of the space shuttle *Challenger.* In middle and high schools, death education may be integrated into traditional curricula (literature, for example) or, again, be handled as postvention following the death of a classmate.

A recent nationwide survey sponsored by the Association for Death Education and Counseling found that only about 11 percent of schools from pre-kindergarten through twelfth grade offered formal courses in death education, with 17 percent offering education about grief or grief-support programs and 25 percent having suicide prevention programs.[6] Of the few programs offered, most are part of health education and last two weeks or less. These sporadic, isolated efforts are inadequate to meet the need for death education.

The Growing Need for Death Education

With frightening increases in student-against-student violence, skyrocketing suicide rates among the young, and the damaging effects of AIDS, schools are necessarily on the front lines with respect to the serious social problems that confront us all, children as well as adults. Schools can also be our best defense in combating such social ills. The death of a person from suicide or from AIDS often has a ripple effect in communities, spilling over into its classrooms. Judy Stillion, a past president of the Association for Death Education and Counseling (ADEC), has pointed out that "the increase in youth suicides is heightening awareness of the need for education in death and dying, while the rise of AIDS is telling teachers that death may strike the classroom at any time."[7]

Fifty percent of our students will endure parental divorce. Violence and drug use are epidemic in many schools. It is a sad reality of the 1990s that many elementary children find drug syringes and bullet casings on the playground along with their swings and sandboxes. These myriad losses must be addressed if a child is to effectively concentrate on the academic tasks at hand. Our future rests squarely on the educational gestalt of our children.

More teacher training is required to meet our children's needs. The ADEC study cited above found that opportunities for teacher inservice education regarding dying and death are sorely lacking. It is obvious, and a critical point in any discussion of death education, that one cannot adequately teach what one hasn't learned oneself. ADEC now offers a systematic program of certification courses for teachers and other professionals, yet only a comparative handful of professionals have availed themselves of this useful preparation. Rather than abandoning death education as the critics urge, however, it would be better to mandate requirements and qualifications for teachers that would safeguard the beneficial results of death education.

While educators universally lament yet another area of responsibility being foisted on them when classroom time is already at a premium, the harsh reality is that the issues dealt with in death education (that is, life education) are having an impact on the nation's class-

rooms as never before in our history. Ignoring this reality is not the answer. Schools spend tens of millions of dollars on programs for at-risk youth. A grieving child or adolescent, as any classroom teacher can attest, is definitely at-risk in terms of academic and social performance. How best, then, to teach the crucial knowledge that can help children and adolescents cope with experiences of loss? We must teach the teachers.

Teaching the Teachers

This moves the debate from *whether* we should teach death and loss to *how* best to teach it. Clearly, everyone concerned—students, parents, and teachers—will benefit from refining the present catch-as-catch-can system. The problem has less to do with determining appropriate course content than with addressing its distribution and application. Stillion has listed three necessary qualifications for teachers involved in death education:

1. They must have training in handling their own feelings about death, dying, and loss, and they must comprehend the meaning that these experiences bring to life.
2. They must be familiar with the professional literature in death studies.
3. They must be able to sensitively integrate knowledge about loss with a student's developmental level.[8]

To serve the varying needs of the diverse population represented by K–12 students, teachers must understand and be able to apply developmentally appropriate instruction.

To accomplish these goals, three things must be done. First, we must standardize the K–12 curriculum for death education and professionalize its delivery to students. The expertise for accomplishing this already exists. A national task force on death education under the auspices of the Association for Death Education and Counseling recently completed a three-year study of present policies and practices across the country.[9] In 1992, the International Work Group on Death, Dying, and Bereavement published a comprehensive, fourteen-point statement of assumptions and principles concerning death and loss education.[10] This statement, reflecting leading-edge thinking from the finest practitioners of the art around the world, should form the cornerstone of any plan for death education in our nation's schools. In concert with a cadre of ADEC-certified consultants, work could begin at the state level to institute this curriculum. Approval from state Parent-Teacher Associations (PTAs) could be sought, and plans could incorporate an opt out clause (as with current sex education policy) that allows parents who object to the curriculum to pull their children from the course.

Second, death education should be required in programs of teacher training. In this way, all new teachers nationwide would be prepared to meet the challenge of teaching loss issues that are sure to be encountered in the twenty-first century.

Finally, for teachers who are now licensed, existing requirements for continuing education should be enhanced to provide an opportunity for them to attain skills in this area. This training is especially germane in an era of single-parent and blended families and alternative life styles. We ask and expect teachers to wear many hats for the many roles kids expect them to play—teacher, counselor, friend, confidant. Teachers must be prepared to play these roles effectively.

The difficult experience of outing is often seen in retrospect as the storm before the calm—no more nasty little secrets. Someday soon, when the program outlined here is implemented and death education is viewed, rightly, as life and loss education, we may find ourselves thanking our detractors for calling attention to present deficiencies and saying, "Thanks, Ms. Schlafly, you've done us all a favor."

Visions in Death Education

HANNELORE WASS

HANNELORE WASS, PH.D., is a professor emerita of educational psychology at the University of Florida in Gainesville, where in the early 1970s she developed and then taught two graduate courses on death: "Psychosocial and Educational Aspects of Death" and "Issues in Childhood and Death." Currently she is planning to offer a graduate course on death and loss from a gender perspective. Dr. Wass came to the study of death and dying in the late 1960s when she noticed her own anxieties and lack of skills in counseling students who came to her with personal problems involving death, from Vietnam-related deaths to the loss of a pet. She gained information through extensive reading and study and by interacting with people involved in death-related work.

In 1976 she conducted the first national conference on death and dying to be held in the South; it was attended by over 500 persons. At that time, Dr. Wass also began to pursue research on attitudes toward death in older adults and on children's and adolescents' thoughts and understandings of death and their perceptions of violent death in the media.

Her primary concern through the years has been to help people of all ages cope with death effectively. She views education as a primary vehicle to make this possible. As founding editor of the journal *Death Studies*, she has had a key role in shaping the field of thanatology. Her published work in the area of death includes more than one hundred papers and ten books, including *Childhood and Death* (1984); *Helping Children Cope with Death: Guidelines and Resources* (2d ed., 1984); *Death Education: An Annotated Resource Guide* (Vol. I, 1980; Vol. II, 1985); and, most recently, *Dying: Facing the Facts* (3d ed., 1995).

Dr. Wass is a charter member of the Association for Death Education and Counseling. In 1987, she received the Association's Contributions to the Field Award, and her efforts were again recognized by ADEC in 1991 by means of a Special Contributions Award marking her retirement as editor of *Death Studies*. The following selection is adapted from a keynote address presented by Dr. Wass to ADEC's 1985 annual meeting.

WE IN DEATH EDUCATION need to take a close look at what we are and are not doing, where we are going, if anywhere, and where we might or should be going and why.

I will start with a quotation: "Death education in the United States can now be considered as fully developed with instructional programs firmly in place at all educational levels." Where could this statement have come from? Well, it's not a declaration by a deluded death educator. It's from a book published last fall in Germany titled *Die Begleitung Sterbender—Theorie und Praxis der Thanatotherapie*,[1] or, translated somewhat freely, *Walking with the Dying—Theory and Practice of Thanatotherapy*. My first reaction when reading this statement was shock. "It can't be. The authors are fools." But I know better. I know them by correspondence. The authors and editors are not naive about us. The book is co-edited by two widely recognized psychotherapists; one has professional positions in five countries and commutes among France, the Netherlands, Switzerland, Austria, and West Germany. Still, I am puzzled about this statement. Is our literature so romantic? It is a splendid reputation. I wish it were deserved.

Now that we've had an outside view, let's do an internal audit. In 1977, Van Pine chronicled the history of the death education movement in an article published in the inaugural issue of *Death Education.*[2] His update covering the years 1976 to 1985 subsequently appeared in *Death Studies.*[3] Pine identified three distinct phases in the development of death education, with three distinct groups of death educators in each phase.

The first group were the pioneers. They produced the initial knowledge, charted the territory, plowed the field, sowed the seeds. They included such people as Robert Fulton, Herman Feifel, Richard Kalish, Robert Kastenbaum, Daniel Leviton, and Jeanne Quint-Benoliel.

The second group shaped the field further. They spread the word, taught more courses, organized conferences, started the Association for Death Education and Counseling (ADEC), and also added to the knowledge base. In this group Pine lists Elisabeth Kübler-Ross, Melvin Krant, Sandra Bertman, Earl Grollman, Colin Murray Parkes, and Gene Knott, among others.

Pine called the third group of death educators *nouveau arrivée.* Unfortunately, and this is my own observation, there is no direct lineage from the first group to the third. The first group, the intellectual grandparents of the movement, was small in size. They talked a lot to each other (maybe to themselves, too), and they were mentors. They produced many of those in the second group. Although some of those in the second group joined ADEC or helped nurture its beginnings, many others worked alone. And they didn't seem to do much mentoring. Thus, no clear sense of continuity or of a common tradition emerged. The third group, the newcomers, were mostly women who brought comparatively little knowledge, but big hearts. (There were also men with heart.)

Some say these new people jumped on the bandwagon, but that strikes me as the wrong metaphor. If there was a bandwagon, I don't think it was going very fast, so there was no need to jump. You just climbed on. Nor do I believe there was any band. There was no great fanfare. It wasn't a joyride either. Death educators were considered even weirder and more morbid in those days than they are today. I think people have been climbing on and off that so-called wagon over the past few years, so there is not even a stable third group. This lack of stability and continuity is of course not helpful when you are trying to establish a field.

Let us now examine what we have accomplished. First, a word about evaluation. It is very difficult to assess the overall progress of death education in this country. Any evaluation is open to criticism. This is because we have to rely on judgment, and that depends largely on the sorts of phenomena we admit as evidence. Ours is a large society and the field is not only multifaceted but is itself a complex matrix of interrelated fields, some central, some peripheral, but all contributing to the configuration. We have no established system of recordkeeping; there are no reliable means or measures; there is little accountability and virtually no quality control. We are likely to see things through rose-tinted glasses. It is natural to do this, but I will try to step back a bit and view the record more objectively. I will consider what we have done by way of death education for five groups: the general public, elementary-school children, high-school students, college students, and health professionals.

Death Education in Public Settings

I don't think there have been any major changes in outlook and attitude toward death on the part of the general public. With all our talking and writing we may have merely achieved what Bob Kastenbaum terms "a more sophisticated level of denial." In fact, there are still too many occasions that show death denial today to be the same old death denial it was two decades ago. We still have an absolute taboo on the word *death* in our nursing homes and in many of our hospitals. Not long ago I visited a friend in a hospital in Tampa. While near the nursing station I overheard a supervisor saying to a young man (apparently a new intern): "Death and dying are dirty words in our facility. I won't have you use them while you are with us. Our patients expire. Is that clear?" My first reaction to such statements is shock. I think of Geoffrey Gorer, who wrote: "Death is viewed as pornographic." But that was twenty years ago! We like to think that those types of death deniers are extinct, but unfortunately they are very much still with us.

Consider Bob Fulton's findings of diminished mourning by adult children. Consider also his findings of a decrease in ceremonial grief expression by society at large. Thus, diminished mourning may well be the dominant pattern. Are these not symptoms of death denial? What attitudes about the value of a person's life do we transmit to our young? What kinds of models of love, care, and dignity do we present to them? Is this not a hidden curriculum of unintentional but nonetheless powerful death education? Fulton and others note that children are often still kept from attending funerals, so they may not even learn the *forms* of our rituals.

Even vicarious experiences may not be available. We recently did a study of over 1500 commercial television drama programs occupying 1400 hours of prime time and weekday afternoons. There were about 300 incidents of one or more deaths, four-fifths of them caused by violence. Yet, intense grief reactions were portrayed in less than 10 percent of these instances. Only nine funerals were shown. Isn't it offensive to see death stripped of its awesome essence? Isn't that also death denial? Death is natural, but it's not trivial. Television gives a distorted picture of death in most of its programming. At the same time, television brings news of horrendous deaths into the living room. Children spend more time in front of the television set than they do in school. And, based on a study I'm doing with Judy Stillion, it seems that after age ten children increasingly watch the news and other informational programs.

There are other signs of death denial. As a society we deny the reality of the nuclear threat. We have stockpiled enough nuclear warheads to destroy all life on this earth several times over. Too terrible to ponder? That's denial too. We have a nickname for nuclear warheads. We call them *nukes*. It sounds almost friendly. New euphemisms have been created for us. What's more comforting than the thought that, in place of earth-based warfare, we'll have "Star Wars"? It's a magic phrase. We picture ourselves sitting in a movie house or at home watching extraterrestrial homing vehicles, rocket pods, smart rockets, and other weapons yet to be invented do their devastating work out in space. Our good earth is wonderfully protected, and we are merely spectators.

Worse than minimizing death is an attitude of apathy toward it. People sometimes take the position that the world will end by nuclear war and that it could happen anytime. When the students at Brown University exhibited their awareness of the nuclear threat by requesting that the administration stockpile cyanide pills for use if a nuclear war occurred, Robert Coles, the Harvard psychiatrist, reported the reaction of a blue-collar worker: "These spoiled rich kids. Everyone else is going to suffer a slow death and they want a quick way out."

A student who is doing a doctoral dissertation on European and American children's images of war and peace wants to have sixth graders take pictures reminding them of peace and of war, and then have them comment on their photos. She went to a number of school officials and all of them turned down her proposal. One official said, "War and peace are controversial issues; we don't want to put these burdens on our students." Another said, "Our curriculum is already crowded; we haven't got the time to play around with cameras"!

We know our young are concerned about war, murder, and nuclear destruction. Since 1975, the Institute of Social Research at the University of Michigan has done annual surveys of the attitudes of high-school students toward nuclear war. Consistently, about 30 percent of these students report that they are "worried" or "very worried" about a nuclear war. With whom can they discuss these fears? It's usually not their parents, nor their teachers. Their peers are often equally worried.

Since the death penalty was reinstated, one third of all executions in the United States were carried out in Florida—twelve men. The first execution, in 1979, galvanized the media. Yet, not one of the forty high-school teachers I interviewed on the subject discussed the death penalty in their civics or social studies classes. It's a "controversial" subject. What do our young people think about it? Why are we afraid to discuss it and to let youngsters take a position? We are, after all, a democratic society, aren't we? Death education for the public is death education for parents, educators, other helping professionals, and children. We have not done at all well at this level.

Death Education in Elementary Schools

Despite dedicated efforts by many individuals, as well as a sizable literature to guide and prod, death education has never really been accepted at the elementary-school level. The available survey data suggest that between 1 percent and 5 percent of elementary teachers deal with the subject in any planned way. Further, the manner in which death-related crises are handled in the schools is related more to a teacher's personality, level of comfort with the topic, style of teaching, skill in interpersonal communication, empathy, and the like than to

any special preparation. I know of no college of education that requires a course on death in its curriculum for prospective teachers.

Most elementary-school teachers, parents, and school officials do not see any merit in death education of whatever sort for children. Many of them still cling to the myth that this subject will do psychological harm to children, or they believe that children are not interested in death and know nothing about it. Yet the scholarly literature on the subject is clear. By age seven, most children recognize that death is an irreversible event.

Ideally, death education should be unobtrusively integrated into the elementary-school curriculum where it fits naturally. At the very least we should teach teachers what to do when death-related incidents occur. Death denial is so massive that, in many crisis situations in the classroom, persons from outside the school—nurses, counselors, school psychologists, or professors from the college campus, if there is one nearby—are called in. Death is definitely extracurricular.

Many stories could be told illustrating this fact. Let me share my most recent story. Susie is in first grade. One morning about a month ago she stood before her classmates during "show and tell." She had nothing to show but something very important to tell. She said, "My brother Jamie died." The teacher was completely unprepared, and her response was silence. She pretended that she hadn't heard and motioned to another child. But Susie was determined. She repeated, this time more loudly, "My brother Jamie died." Now all the children heard, and they looked expectantly to the teacher, then to Susie, then back to the teacher. But the teacher appeared petrified. By now Susie demanded that the teacher pay attention to what she had to say. She screamed the statement at her teacher who promptly came to life, for now she was on familiar ground. She took Susie by the hand and said, "We do not shout in the classroom," and she walked her out of the room.

What lessons do we teach our children when adults are so traumatized and ineffectual when death invades the classroom?

Death Education in High Schools

We have done better at the high-school level than in the elementary school, but much remains to be done. Health educators have been most successful in bringing death education into the high schools. One survey indicates that, in New York state, 14 percent of health educators in the high schools teach a unit on death, and another 64 percent incorporate the subject into related subject areas. But, in fairness to those who teach other high-school disciplines, we should remember that health is a national preoccupation, and teaching students about death can provide a powerful stimulus for their learning to keep themselves alive through healthful living. It is easier to carry out death education with such motivation. Similar stimuli appear to be absent in other parts of the high-school curriculum. Very little death education takes place in the biological and social sciences or the humanities or in such practical courses as home economics and family development.

Those of us who believe that death education for our children and adolescents is important are distressed with this apparent apathy on the part of teachers and parents. There are 90,000 public and private elementary and high schools in our country and over 46.5 million students enrolled in them. What missed opportunities for essential learning!

The current trend in our schools is "Back to Basics," and those are not the basics of life and death. Schools have always been vulnerable to public pressure. Right now computer literacy is "in." Perhaps the trend will change. John Naisbitt in his book *Megatrends* suggests that every high-technology trend is accompanied or followed by an opposing one: Tech touch/People touch.[4] He uses the development of lifesaving medical technologies and the concurrent development of hospices as illustration. I don't see that happening in our schools. I don't think we can sit and wait. Too many of our adolescents are concerned about questions of life and death. Many are worried about nuclear destruction, mass starvation, homicide, and death in other forms. We must give our youngsters opportunities to talk, to share their fears, anxieties, and frustrations. We must give them opportunities to share ideas about possible solutions, to debate alternatives. We must also give them opportunities to do concrete things: write letters to their congressional representatives or to their local newspapers.

Death Education at the College Level

What about the death and dying course at the college level? A national survey taken in the mid-1970s showed that 1,000 undergraduate courses were being offered in four-year degree-granting colleges and universities. Since that time, this figure has probably more than doubled. Courses have also been developed in community colleges. Altogether we have about 3,200 colleges and community colleges with an enrollment of about 15 million students. Courses in death and dying are popular. If they are a fad, they have not been a passing fad. Judging from the vigorous competition in the textbook market, it seems clear that courses at the college level have become generally accepted. What is less certain is the quality of instruction, which is at best uneven, a matter about which I'll say more momentarily.

Death Education in the Health Professions

Several national surveys of medical and nursing schools done in the 1970s indicate that some sort of death education was part of the curricula in most of them, usually in the form of a few lectures or discussions. Only about 5 percent required a course on death. I don't know how much progress has been made since then. My guess is that it has been very modest. Yet, if the published literature is any indication, death education for health professionals has been growing steadily.

Of course, our shining success has been the hospice movement. Here a small group of pioneers has taught caregivers about the needs of terminally ill persons and their families so well and with so much compassion that they have galvanized their students into action. Against all odds, without the help of the mainstream health care system, they have proved that it's possible to set up alternative structures and practices for terminal care. Two thousand hospices in the United States testify to this success. I have not yet seen any studies that systematically evaluate the quality of that care, but I know that people in the hospices are among the most dedicated and compassionate I have ever known.

The hospice movement is one aspect of what appears to be a widespread trend toward moving much health care back into the home. Hospitals will become intensive care facilities, and those who are acutely ill will be treated in outpatient clinics. The family or surrogate family will be expected to provide most of the primary care. More people will die at home. That has implications with respect to death education for both health professionals and the public.

One other trend I see emerging is toward focusing death education of health professionals on specific and more directly job-related aspects, such as psychosocial dynamics and care of the terminally ill and their families, medical ethics, patients' rights, and bereavement and grief. It is interesting to note in this context that hospice people call their efforts "hospice training," not "death education." This more narrow conceptualization of death education is characteristic also of continental

Europe and Scandinavia as the field is evolving in these countries.

There are, of course, benefits from specialization. For one, it is easier for students to become familiar with an existing body of knowledge when an area of study is narrowly defined. In addition, specialization promotes the development of theory and research that can be applied by practitioners. As it happens, the psychosocial dynamics of terminal illness and bereavement are currently two of the most active research areas in thanatology (the other, of course, is and has been suicide). The trend toward specialization also has drawbacks, however. It almost certainly means that the larger sociocultural and global contexts are neglected. That is regrettable.

Teacher Preparation

I've said that we have failed miserably in death education at the elementary-school level. There is another outstanding failure to which I must point. We have failed to establish any means or mechanisms for systematic training and screening of death educators at any level. There are some exceptions. One is the program at the master's level at Brooklyn College in New York developed by David Meagher. There are also educational situations whereby leaders in the field work with individual students to plan and carry out a systematic program of study. Still other aspiring death educators follow a comprehensive program of self-training or independent study. We wouldn't have a field of death education if we did not have many dedicated, informed, and effective teachers. But there are individuals who enter the field with none of these characteristics, and there is at present no mechanism in place to stop them.

This phenomenon is perhaps most pronounced at the continuing education level. Any adult anywhere in the country can teach a seminar, a workshop, or a course to a group of unsuspecting adults as long as the participants don't ask for educational credits or want proof of the instructor's credentials. All you have to do is print up a brochure and call yourself a thanatologist. Just recently I met a woman who introduced herself to me as a "Certified Nurse-Educator-Thanatologist." I don't know how she finds the time. I asked where she received her certificate, and she told me it was at a two-day intensive workshop conducted by Dr. WHO?, a "Certified Psychologist-Diplomate in Clinical Thanatology."

I know we cannot control outright fraud, and I know diplomas and doctorates and other titles can be bought. But even among some of our colleagues, there are those who seem to think that two workshops are sufficient preparation for being a death educator. Even a full-semester course does not a death educator make! If we argue otherwise, we do not appreciate the complex and sensitive nature of the subject, and we belittle our field.

Beginnings and Successes

There is no doubt that death education has evolved into a professional field. It may be amorphous, and we may have death educators who *are* because they say so. Actually some like to call themselves "thanatologists." That term has a better ring to it. Doesn't it imply a higher status? But, in any event, death education is a recognized field of study and practice. We have scholarly journals, a national organization with local and regional chapters. We hold annual conferences and sponsor workshops. We publish our conference proceedings as well as newsletters. Recently, the Association for Death Education and Counseling set in motion a certification procedure for death educators and counselors. So, yes, we have a field of death education. We just need to tell the world that it exists and why it's needed.

We have a *vision* of a broad program of death education, a program of *death education for all.* Three general goals apply across all educational levels, and they have been articu-

lated by many of the pioneers and leaders in the field. They are: (1) to receive information, (2) to develop and improve coping capacities and skills, and (3) to clarify and cultivate one's values.

I think that these goals apply at four levels: the individual, the family or close community of which one is a member, the society, and the world. For instance, whether I obtain information about the dynamics of grief, learn to cope constructively with fear, or understand that nutritious food is important to my health, I first use this learning on behalf of myself and my intimate group, then for colleagues and neighbors, and finally for the people of my country and all people of the world. The critical component is that I transcend self-interest and become concerned for others. Such altruism includes the leap from a parochial to a global view. This is the kind of death education that is relevant. It concerns us and our world today.

Several of the newer or revised textbooks include sections that deal with global threats and megadeath. Robert Fulton led the way in his book *Death and Dying: Challenge and Change.* Other writers followed suit, including Edwin Shneidman, Richard Kalish, and Lynne DeSpelder and Albert Strickland.

Thus, we have a *new vision* of death education. It has dawned on us that death education is an appropriate domain for dealing with the inhumanities of our time, the "horrendous deaths" related to holocaust, chemical and other warfare, homicide, starvation, poisoning of the air, and nuclear threat. To me, this dawning vision is the single most hopeful sign, a new focus on the future: *trying to ensure that there will be one.*

Toward Fulfilling Our Vision

So what is my vision for the future? It's that we will have high-quality death education, in the broadest sense, in this country such that the quotation with which I began this piece will be an accurate description.

To conclude, I would like to offer some thoughts concerning a description of effective death education and its requisites:

- Death education requires teachers who are authentic, self-confident, sensitive, responsive, optimistic—think of all good attributes.
- Death education requires teachers who confront their own mortality.
- Death education involves the affective as well as the cognitive domain. The art is to strike a proper balance between the two.
- Death education is practical. When done rightly, it results in behaviors that help, whether the helping is directed towards oneself or others.
- Death education requires motivation. Personal experience is an important datum, but it is only *one*. Personal experiences are helpful, but they do not transform us into death educators.
- Death education requires thorough knowledge of the literature and the ability to differentiate between fact and myth. Lack of knowledge compromises the quality of death education.
- Death education requires basic knowledge about scientific study to the extent that the educator becomes an informed consumer of research, sees its usefulness (when there is any), and can translate it into educational action.
- Death education requires responsibility and intellectual honesty. It takes courage to admit when there are no clear answers or when one is ignorant.
- Death education requires constant

study. The field of thanatology is complex and multidisciplinary, and its research literature is voluminous and growing, and there are still great gaps in our knowledge.
- Death education requires basic communication skills.
- Death education requires at least some minimum of skill in helping individuals with death-related problems and, as appropriate, guiding them to professional helpers.

If you think I am trying to discourage anyone from becoming a death educator, let me assure you that I'm not. It's just that we need good people in the field. I have tried for the past fourteen years to become a good death educator. I am still trying.

I want to invite and encourage people to become death educators, aware of the enormous challenge that's involved. But if Maslow, Combs, Rogers, and all the other third-force psychologists are correct, and I think they are, then human beings have a basic need to become adequate, to realize their full potential, and to reach beyond their own narrow spheres. Death education deserves persons with such motivations.

Finally, as you all know, death education is about life—its quality, meaning, preciousness, and beauty. Death education is about fears and terrors and retaining one's sanity in a world of war, terrorism, and the threat of total destruction. Death education is about loss, hurt, and suffering. Death education is about love, care, and compassion. It is about helping and healing.

Acknowledging Our Mortality

The Mortal King

ALLAN B. CHINEN

ALLAN B. CHINEN, M.D., was born in Honolulu and earned degrees in biology, philosophy, and medicine from Stanford University. He is a psychiatrist in private practice and an associate clinical professor of psychiatry at the University of California in San Francisco. Dr. Chinen first became interested in death and dying issues during college when exploring existentialist philosophers. He says, "During medical school, I began working with fairy tales after a series of vivid visions came to me while meditating or jogging. These images were the endings to fairy tales with older men and women as protagonists." After writing down the stories, he figured that people must have created similar stories over the years and started looking for traditional folk tales about midlife and aging. He found a treasure trove of long-forgotten stories dealing with death, dying, and spiritual development in maturity.

Dr. Chinen is a diplomate from the American Board of Neurology and Psychiatry and a member of the board of directors of the Association for Transpersonal Psychology. He has presented lectures, workshops, and seminars nationally. In addition to numerous articles and chapters in scholarly works, his writings include *In the Ever After: Fairy Tales and Psychological Development in the Second Half of Life* (1989), *Beyond the Hero: Classic Stories of Men in Search of Soul* (1993), and *Once Upon a Midlife: Classic Stories and Mythic Tales to Illuminate the Middle Years*, published by Jeremy P. Tarcher in 1992, from which the following selection is excerpted.

ONCE UPON A TIME, a king went riding with his friends. They stopped atop a mountain to rest. The King surveyed the countryside and then smiled with pleasure. His land was rich, his people prospered, and he felt justifiably proud of his realm. Then a terrible thought struck him. "I will die one day, and lose all this!" the monarch declared.

His companions paused and then echoed the King's lament. "Aye, dying is cruel," they murmured, thinking of what they would lose—families, wealth, and honor. Only one lord among them said nothing.

"I wish we could live forever!" the King exclaimed. "That would be wonderful!"

His nobles nodded in agreement, but the silent lord laughed softly. The other nobles glanced curiously at their companion.

The King went on. "Think of all the hunting and feasts we could enjoy! We would never have to worry about growing old." The nobles sighed, picturing the delights of immortality. The bold lord laughed again.

His companions turned to him. "What is amusing about death? Do you spurn the wish for immortality?" they demanded, but the laughing lord said nothing.

The King ignored the interruption. "To live forever as we are now, in the prime of life— what greater boon could a man enjoy? An eternity of happiness!" he exclaimed.

The lords nodded again, and murmured approval, but the other noble chuckled once more. This time the King turned to the laughing lord. "What is the reason for your humor?" the King demanded. "I see nothing comical about death or immortality!"

The noble bowed to his monarch and said, "I do not mean to offend you, Sire. But I thought of what life would be like if we all lived forever as you suggested." The lord paused. "Why, then, all the heroes of history would still live among us—the king who first unified the land, the law-giver who brought peace, the great sages with all their wisdom, and the holy prophets of our people." Again, he paused. "Compared to them, we would be peasants, fit only to plough the fields! And you, my lord," he turned to the King, "would no doubt be a clerk in the provinces!"

The King stared at the impertinent lord, and all the other peers held their breaths. Then the King laughed long and hard. "You are wise and brave, my friend," the King said. "But you speak the truth."

The King turned to the other nobles and said, "For encouraging me in my vanity, I penalize you two draughts of wine each!"

The King embraced the laughing lord. "As for you, my friend," the monarch decreed, "whenever I lament the thought of my own death, you must cry out, 'A clerk! A clerk!'"

Coping with Mortality: An Essay on Self-Mourning

THOMAS ATTIG

THOMAS ATTIG, PH.D., is professor and chair of the Department of Philosophy at Bowling Green State University in Ohio. His interest in death and dying evolved out of his academic studies in existential philosophy as well as his own experience with death in his large extended family. In 1974, he developed and taught his first course in death and dying as applied philosophy in the College of Health and Human Services to educate students in the helping professions. Among his many published articles are "Relearning the World: Toward a Phenomenology of Grieving," "On the Importance of Conceiving of Grieving as an *Active* Process," and "Grief and Personal Integrity"; his forthcoming book *Grieving: Relearning the World* conveys many of his insights about the nature of grief.

Additionally, Dr. Attig has published and lectured on death education, death themes in popular music, and suicide intervention. He also serves in Ohio courts as an expert witness in wrongful death cases. He received the Association for Death Education and Counseling's Service Award in 1987 and assumed the presidency of that organization in 1995.

The dark background which death supplies brings out the tender colors of life in all their purity.
—George Santayana

IN HIS MOVING BOOK *Voices of Death,* Edwin Shneidman defines *self-mourning* as "mourning for oneself as one is dying."[1] He refers to the terminally ill bewailing their pending nonexistence, bemoaning the partial losses experienced in present illness and decline that render them less than they used to be, grieving over the pending loss to the world of memories and wisdom accumulated during lifetimes now about to end, and mourning for what might have been had there been more time. He urges that this self-mourning is (a) an important aspect of the "death work" of the last days of dying, (b) a healthy sign of proper self-respect, and (c) especially poignant since the dying know their talents and (sometimes secret) aspirations best of all.

In this paper I explore extending the idea of self-mourning to all humans (not simply those who are terminally ill) who reflect on their personal mortality and struggle to cope with their own finiteness. These reflections and struggles have features and significance that are strikingly parallel to the experiences of the terminally ill to which Shneidman calls attention. How, then, can the idea of self-mourning shed light on the existential challenge of coping with life in the shadow of death?

In what follows I explore analogies that suggest that coming to terms with our own finiteness is a grieving process, first, considering the impact of confrontation with mortality (another person's or one's own), and, second, considering four major tasks faced by both grieving persons and lifelong self-mourners while underscoring the centrality of concerns with finiteness, impermanence, uncertainty, and vulnerability in both experiences.

The Impact of Confrontations with Mortality

Those who suffer losses are affected in all dimensions of their lives. Grief is at once physical, emotional-psychological, intellectual-spiritual, and social. This pervasive impact can shake the foundations of self-understanding and orientation in the world and pose significant challenges to personal integrity and to the perceived meaningfulness of continued living.

There are striking similarities between this impact in grief and bereavement and in facing squarely the prospect of one's own death.

Consider first the emotional impact. Feelings of sadness, loneliness, isolation, alienation, longing, fear, anxiety, anguish, dread, frustration, anger, helplessness, hopelessness, inconsolability, guilt, and depression are common to many experiences of both types. So, too, are the perceptions of threat and vulnerability, of being out of control, and of powerlessness and insignificance. The ebb and flow of emotions, variations in intensity, unusual juxtapositions of contrary feelings, confusion, overlapping, persistence, and unbidden character of the onslaught of emotion are comparable. In the personal mortality case, it may be harder for those affected to recognize the connection between these emotions and their first recognition of their own mortality. While it may be less common for one first confronting his or her personal mortality to experience emotion with the white-heat intensity of fresh grief over the death of another, this is not an unimaginable possibility. If there is a consistent discrepancy of this type, it may derive from built-in, protective, psychological, repressive responses to perceived threats to one's own very existence. The prospect of our own mortality is not easily taken in.

Consider now the physical concomitants of grieving and confronting one's own mortality. Crying, tightness in the throat, agitation, disruption of sleep patterns, nightmares, restlessness, enervation and loss of motivation for daily routine tasks, stomach upset, loss of appetite, and changes in eating pattern are recognizable possible components of both experiences. Again, the connections may be less conscious in the case of recognizing mortality. The shock and numbness often experienced at the onset of bereavement may at first blush seem unmatched in the typical encounters with personal mortality. Most comparable may be those encounters with mortality that are forced and where avoidance of reality is more difficult

(for example, experiences where life is immediately threatened, where one has a close call with death). Shock and numbness are common components of such experiences. Recent speculative literature, at least partially confirmed, has endeavored to connect more serious and long-range physical changes to unresolved grief, including increased instances of gastrointestinal illnesses, heart attacks, strokes, and even cancers. I would confidently speculate that comparable connections can be found linking such serious physical consequences to unresolved self-mourning.

Both grieving and self-mourning include great struggle with central questions about life, death, and the meanings of each. Why do persons die? Why must this particular person die? Why must I die? Why must some die before fulfilling the promise of their lives? How is meaningful living compatible with this death? How are meaningful life and suffering compatible? How am I to sustain a sense of meaning and purpose in life? Is there life after death? If there is, or if there isn't, what are the implications for the meaning of the life I know? The struggle for reorientation following the death of another is very much a struggle to find satisfactory and sustaining answers to these and similar questions or to find the means to living without answers in uncertainty. Similarly, for self-mourners, these questions become something more than simple intellectual curiosities as individuals experience the subjective significance of what is at stake in the quest for answers. Interestingly, thanatologists acknowledge the convergence of these two spiritual crises in recognizing that one of the most distressing features of bereavement can be the reminder of personal mortality that grieving frequently entails.

Bereavement often has profound social consequences as new tensions are introduced into personal relations, especially within the family. The problems are rooted in, among other things, differences in (a) coping styles and patterns; (b) need for diverse personal interactions; (c) communication patterns; (d) emotional experiences and patterns of emotional expression; and (e) intellectual and spiritual accommodation to loss. Similarly, self-mourners undergo significant transformations in their orientation to the world in general and, more particularly, in their relationships with others. Their coping with finiteness is in many ways a function of the quality of interaction with others as they choose either to broach the subject or to hold their silence. In response, on the one hand, others may be supportive in the struggle because they are not distracted by their own grief, but on the other hand they may have difficulties in being supportive, given the widespread cultural patterns of denial and avoidance of death and the tendencies of reminders of personal mortality to arouse anxiety and discomfort. Rethinking the meaning of life often entails significant shifts in patterns of interaction with others. Consider but one example: the typical midlife crisis which involves a near full-faced acknowledgement of the prospects of personal mortality, often entailing upheaval in personal relationships.

Grieving poses a challenge to personal integrity as the bereaved are affected in virtually all dimensions of their lives. Thus, the impact of bereavement profoundly affects the whole person. As they grieve, persons let go of what is no longer viable in their lives, learn again to trust what is still viable, and strike out in new directions. This grieving process transforms them as they become persons with new daily life patterns and altered and redirected life histories. Similarly, persons are affected in virtually all dimensions of their lives by serious and sustained self-mourning. Lifetime reflective dialogue with death entails shifts in values, hopes, expectations, desires, motivations, and attendant life patterns comparable to the shifts entailed by the deepest grief. Such lifelong struggle toward accommodation to personal finiteness and fragility can be profoundly self-transforming. Indeed, those who are more self-

consciously aware as they grieve or self-mourn report parallel and often pervasive changes in their patterns of caring and involvement in the world as they experience their surroundings, their fellows, and themselves anew in the penetrating light of their encounters with death.

The Tasks Entailed by Coming to Terms with Death

Consider now the analogies between the major tasks of grieving and self-mourning. William Worden has usefully and persuasively outlined four major tasks of grieving: (a) acknowledging the reality of loss, (b) finding the means to effectively express emotion, (c) saying appropriate goodbyes to and loosening attachments to those who have died, and (d) relearning life in a world where the dead are absent.[2] Comparable tasks confront those who would sustain rather than ignore the struggle to come to terms with their own inevitable death.

Acknowledging the reality of personal finiteness is a daunting task. The typical patterns of fight or flight and their many variations are found here, as in the case of grieving. In both cases, persons struggle with the reality of human existence as small and insignificant, constantly buffeted by change and impermanence, vulnerable to suffering and shrouded in uncertainty. Acknowledging these features of their lives and affirming the potential meaningfulness of this fragile existence do not come easily, and the temptations to avoid the subject and to live as if one could live forever are great. Ernest Becker has written of the profound implications of the pervasive patterns of "the denial of death" in shaping individual and cultural life.[3] The alternatives to a gentle but firm affirmation of this human condition include fantasy, self-deception, or self-denial, which can only entail loss of self-esteem and depreciation of just how precious, however fragile, life can be. Those who refuse to accept their own finiteness court frustration, resentment, and bitterness at every turn. Just as the bereaved must acknowledge the reality of the death of the other in order to begin to reorient themselves to the world as it is (that is, profoundly changed), so self-mourners must acknowledge the reality of their own inevitable death to begin to reorient themselves to personal existence as it is (that is, profoundly different for its being pervasively finite and limited).

Just as the bereaved must fight through the emotional pain of grieving, so the self-mourner must fight through the emotional distress of coming to terms with the prospect of having to die one day. Finding the opportunity and means to effectively express emotions is difficult in large measure due to the pervasive cultural taboos surrounding the expression of negative emotions in general and of emotional distress concerning death in particular. The difficulties may be compounded further by cultural suppression of concern about one's self as opposed to concern for another. Moreover, patterns of psychological repression often make it difficult for individuals to recognize that their distress, while apparently aroused by other matters (for example, in ordinary bereavement), is symbolically connected to distress over personal mortality.

Saying goodbyes and loosening attachments to the deceased are analogous to the letting go of or modifying those values, hopes, expectations, and aspirations that are untempered by acknowledgment of personal mortality. Personal integrity, if it is to be attained at all, must be achieved in finite time. Choices must be made about which cares and involvements are the most important, and they must be interwoven into distinctive life patterns. Self-mourning requires acknowledging the challenge to personal integrity that these existential choices represent. Loosening attachments entailed by some choices in order to realize the values entailed by others is a constant and often painful concomitant of life in the shadow of death. Just as the bereaved are forever different for having cared for the deceased and struggle to continue to love the deceased in their absence, self-mourners are forever different for having seriously entertained options now forsaken and struggle to continue to appreciate values now only marginally realized in lives decisively different for the choices made. Meaning in life is hard won to the extent that it is within persons' control at all, and it is possible to die having failed to find it or even having failed to recognize the urgency of seeking it. Robert Lifton has written of the profound implications of struggles to achieve a sense of "connection," with transcendence as a vital component of these struggles for personal integrity and meaning of life.[4] His writings are filled with insights into the difficulties and implications of letting go of the aspiration to live forever. Just as the bereaved can come to a fuller appreciation of the value of relationships with others, however fleeting, so self-mourners can come to fuller appreciation of the value of their precious capacities to flourish, however temporarily.

Many authors, including Worden and Parkes and Weiss have urged that grieving is very much a process of "relearning the world."[5] I have written elsewhere of this process as entailing reorientation to physical surroundings, personal relationships, and one's own self.[6] The power of this way of thinking about grieving should not be underestimated. Relearning, as with all learning, is an active process that requires both time and effort. Just as no one can learn for another, so no one can grieve for another. If it is indeed a world that is to be relearned, it is easy to see how complex and difficult grieving is. Finally, grieving is largely a process of finding appropriate meanings. Consider the similarities in coping with personal mortality. Self-mourners reevaluate the opportunities, challenges, and obstacles to life projects that various features of the physical world represent and acknowledge their own limitations in confronting them. In their social environment, self-mourners acknowledge that all beginnings have endings, all personal attachments bring eventual separations, and all commitments come only with attendant risks. Self-mourners acknowledge that there is only a finite and indefinite amount of time available within which to achieve personal integrity and to find meaning in life as they experience the existential urgency attendant to major life choices. This self-mourning is an active process that requires both time and effort. Indeed, it is a lifelong struggle. It is an individuating affair, as self-mourners realize that death must be faced alone. Thinking of self-mourning as a "relearning of the world" strikingly captures the complexity and difficulty of the many processes involved. Finally, self-mourning is centrally a process of finding meaning for one's own finite and fragile existence.

The bereaved complete the tasks of grieving neither all at once nor once and for all. Because it is an entire experiential world within which the bereaved must be reoriented, they do not encounter that world all at once. Rather, the bereaved commonly experience fresh episodes of grief when they find them-

selves in new circumstances in which they are once again reminded that the world is different for the person's having died. They also commonly experience fresh episodes of grief when they find themselves at later stages in life where the death now comes to have new and different meanings for them. In like manner, the self-mourner's task of grieving over his or her own eventual death is accomplished neither all at once nor once and for all. Encounters with finiteness and limitation, change and impermanence, uncertainty and vulnerability take place at quite diverse locations, within widely varied personal interactions, in disparate moments of self-awareness and reflection, and across all stages of lifespan development. Just as grieving varies in intensity over the coarse of a single bereavement and from bereavement to bereavement, so self-mourning varies in intensity throughout one's life history, as self-mourners bring ever-developing or changing selves to ever-new encounters with the prospects of dying one day.[7]

The Politics of Being Mortal

ALFRED G. KILLILEA

ALFRED G. KILLILEA, PH.D., is professor of political science at the University of Rhode Island.
He began studying, writing, and teaching about death and dying after attending a campus lecture by Elisabeth Kübler-Ross in 1974. He says, "I was struck by how powerfully the denial of death in American culture described in that lecture impacts on political ideas and practices. Kübler-Ross's directness and pluck provoked me to explore how the avoidance of limits in modern capitalist culture seems to mandate an avoidance of the subject of death."

Dr. Killilea's book *The Politics of Being Mortal* (1988) is one of very few studies of the potential *political* repercussions of a wider acceptance of mortality in American society. The book argues that a greater awareness of our mortality would provide a much-needed catalyst for change in our politics away from narcissism and nationalism. It traces how, from John Locke to the present, a politics and economics based on growth for the sake of growth have required silence about human vulnerability. Our confrontation with death, Killilea maintains, goads us to question our roles as mere acquirers and to take more seriously the need for greater equality and community in our society.

In charting how we can come to terms with death and how profoundly our attitudes toward death affect our attitudes toward politics, Dr. Killilea concludes that the most valuable spur to the examined life extolled by Socrates is the knowledge that we will die. He says, "The only revision of this thesis since publication of the book stems from the hard-won realization that accepting one's own death is relatively easy compared to accepting the loss of someone very close. Both efforts to cope with death confirm that life always involves struggle and that the personal relationships that make any life worthwhile are diminished by a politics of self-interest and the attempt to deny death."

The Limits of Self-Interest

While I thought I was learning how to live, I was learning how to die.
—Leonardo da Vinci

RATHER THAN THREATENING to deprive life of all meaning, death deepens an appreciation of life and the capacity of every person to give life to others. This is no mere cerebral thesis. It is an idea whose implications are as broad as they are urgent and have a force that is emotional as well as logical. Some insightful points that Glenn Tinder makes about evaluating ideas in his book *Political Thinking* have great relevance:

> An idea is living and important only so far as it brings us into relationship with ourselves and with reality, so far as it pulls things together. . . . Feeling necessarily plays a great part in searching for the truth. Much that must be pulled together does not have the definite and conscious form of a fact or an idea. A great idea is one that symbolizes and unifies not only facts and beliefs that are clearly present to consciousness but also intuitions and impulses that have not been focused on and given form. The idea that does this is exciting.[1]

If our intellects have been uneasy with the gaps and avoidances in our traditional treatment of death, our *feelings* have begun to convulse in response to the unsoundness and irrelevance of ideas about life and about death that do not bring the one into relationship with the other. In appreciating the power and excitement in an idea that brings death into phase with attitudes about life, we should look again at how our society both discourages and lays the seedbed for the germination of such ideas.

What has prepared the ground in the feelings and emotions in Western society for new ideas about death and human vulnerability is the emotional toll exacted by the old images we have accepted of both death and life. The old image of death has been horrifying and menacing. The gaunt visage glimpsed has been that of a Grim Reaper whose indifferent scythe is no respecter of seasons and capriciously cuts down new life as well as old. This view of death as the canceler and spoiler of life has forced us to try to hide from and deny death by absorbing ourselves in a peculiar image of life. We have seemed convinced that we could avoid the nightmare by never sleeping, so our image of life could not be a placid one of measured effort and rest but one of a restless contest or quest that demanded all of our energies and commitments to constant activity and growth. Without ever really considering what the point of it all was, we became absorbed in a contest to expand ourselves and those attached to us. In the effort to conquer nature and to surpass in wealth and power as many other people as we could, we felt a respite from the nightmare and a fragile sense of power.

But if our image of death has been a nightmare for us, our image of life that excludes death and achieves power and freedom has become an illusion. With a focus on expanding power and self-interest, modern Western culture since Adam Smith has achieved dazzling economic and technological results. In our increasing enthusiasm for competition for status and celebration of self-interest as the genie that has made possible all of our inventions and conveniences, we have slid into a number of critical oversights. For one, we ignore the unevenness of our splendid inventions and the fact that self-interest can divert our ingenuity into finding new fragrances for the perfume industry or lightweight throw-away cigarette lighters rather than wrestling with a 50 percent drop-out rate in urban schools. In our giddiness about the power of self-interest, we have ignored the point in John Stuart Mill's caution that "one person with a belief is a social power equal to ninety-nine who have only interests."

A classic example of our extravagant expectations of the compensations of self-interest can be seen in a *New York Times* column in which William Safire recites an "Ode to Greed." Always brash and provocative, Safire becomes fervent in this attempt to demonstrate that it is only by exhorting the wealthy to greed that the needy will be effectively helped:

> Greed is finally being recognized as a virtue. Dressed in euphemism—"the profit motive" or "growth incentives" or "the entrepreneurial spirit"—our not so deadly sin turns out to be the best engine of betterment known to man.
>
> The world has learned that to concentrate on divvying-up diminishes us all, while scrambling to help ourselves helps others; without Greed, there is no wherewithal for Generosity.
>
> By hustling to improve our station, by indulging the desire for necessities that becomes a lust for luxuries, by competing to make our pile bigger, we engage in the great invisible handshake that enlarges pies, lifts all boats and enriches us without impoverishing our neighbor.[2]

It is revealing that Safire rests his case on citing examples of the inefficiencies in state control rather than examples of how the achievements of greed trickle down "[to lift] all boats." The fact is, as in our discussion of John Locke, there is a built-in brake on how much the greed for more in one class can alleviate the needs of another class; for having more, once one gets past necessities and security for the future, is not interesting unless others have less. This is what Edmund Burke meant when he said "the characteristic essence of property... is to be *unequal*"[3] and what Ernest Becker was pointing to when he claimed that the allure of gold is that it separates us from other people.

But besides being ineffective as a feeder of the needy, society's unleashing of a "lust for luxuries," which seems so natural and innocuous to Safire and many others, is increasingly disturbing the good-life dreams of those who heed this siren call. Individuals and societies alike, whose singular ambitions are material growth and affluence, are becoming more aware every day of how vulnerable they are to the disillusioned and disaffected people and nations who do not compete successfully. Terrorism is proving a vicious, destructive, and, alas, effective threat for spoilers who are resentful at what they perceive as the avarice and arrogance of these eager accumulators. We are all increasingly hostages to desperate people and their states of mind. Any social theory that today focuses our attention on the interests of those with "the entrepreneurial spirit" and ignores the interests, attitudes—and fury —of everyone else is not only blindly elitist but unrealistic and dangerous.

Quite apart from the state of mind of those who can't compete in the pursuit of "more," however, the celebration of self-interest does perhaps its greatest damage to the states of mind of the very people who buy into this ambition for competition. Adam Smith and William Safire may be right in arguing that competition for a bigger pile increases, however indifferently, the gross national product, but they seem never to consider what it does to the competitors themselves. They celebrate a tragic, Faustian swap of productivity for purpose, of quantity for quality, and, in Mill's terms, of interest for belief. The biggest toll in the invitation to getting and spending is that it forbids us to glance at that limited side of our nature manifested by death, the side that would question the significance of a bigger pile. Unconfronted and unexamined, death is forced to remain as a nightmare that intrudes upon us indirectly but pervasively in feelings of insecurity. This insecurity infects even our most precious relationships. We push our children from the cradle to achieve and excel because we are so unsure of what the future holds for either them or ourselves. Because we are presented with a portrait of human behavior that emphasizes how everyone is trying to get ahead of everyone else, we can rely on no one else for comfort and support.

It is interesting that the one time in life when we come closest to recognizing this insecurity and to questioning our priorities and absorptions is called a mid-life *crisis*. It's called a crisis because we seem to lose our grip and stray from normalcy by abruptly noticing that our individual life is at least half gone and by coming close to admitting the nightmare into our consciousness. In our society enough of us get through this crisis to maintain productivity and Little League championships, but in the process we glimpse what a price individuals pay to maintain "growth incentives" and how our dream of life is not securely insulated from our nightmare of death. As Christopher Lasch makes clear, much of the drive in the culture of narcissism is fueled by a determined avoidance of the subject of aging and death.

Fortunately for us, however, death will not be denied. It continues to assert itself and continues our opportunity to catch sight of how insignificant is the issue of how big our pile is. Of course giving death its due is not the only way of coming to realize the emptiness of a culture built upon greed. One dramatic example of the chaos and weakness of a society where self-interest rules can be seen in the "Crisis Relocation Instructions," published by the Federal Emergency Management Agency. These instructions, meant to be distributed to citizens when our country is on the brink of nuclear war, have provoked much derision for their bizarre tone of normalcy as they advise evacuees to remember to take with them to shelters their insurance policies, wills, credit cards, and post office change-of-address cards. But amid the macabre humor of these instructions are some vital lessons on what any society needs to survive.

One paragraph of the instructions that has been largely ignored by commentators is titled "Postattack Situation." Here citizens receive the following dispassionate reminder: "A major problem in the postattack situation would be the control of exposure to fallout radiation. Yet, to do essential work after a massive nuclear attack, many survivors must be willing to receive much larger radiation doses than are normally permissible. Otherwise work that would be vital to national recovery could not be done."[4]

What is stunning about this statement is that it comes from unsentimental realists who do not shrink from preparing for nuclear war, presumably because nations and people in the "real world" are too self-interested to avert provocation and catastrophe. Yet these realists, who would think it utopian for people to yoke their egos and self-interest to avoid nuclear war, are nevertheless forced to expect people *after* such a war to sacrifice all concern for individual survival on behalf of society's survival. Given the minuscule chances for *any* survivors of "a massive nuclear attack," one can only lament that these realists do not challenge people's egos and short-range interests on behalf of society *before* a nuclear war, the only time they can realistically promote survival.

This example seems to underline both our unexamined acceptance of the rule of self-interest and the realization, by even those most reluctant to acknowledge it, that in crises societies cannot survive if people are not accustomed to transcend their self-interests. There are a variety of circumstances like this in which we can perceive rationally the limits and contradictions in a society's promoting greed and self-interest among its citizens, but at no time are these contradictions more evident, both rationally and emotionally, than when we truly acknowledge our mortality. Face to face

with the reality of death, we see and feel the absurdity of finding self-esteem or consolation or refuge in how large our pile of possessions is. In the light, rather than the proverbial shadow, of death, we see the true terms of the bargain offered by an economy driven by greed: the growth and productivity of the system at the expense of the individual's finding meaning in life and acceptance of death. We can hardly wonder why societies that accept the spur of greed should promote the denial and avoidance of death.

Yet the denial of death that has been prevalent for almost a century in our society is already beginning to soften. A burgeoning literature on death and dying, death education classes, the hospice movement, and a greater honesty by physicians with patients are just some of the developments that are pushing our society away from the denial of death. These developments did not have a spontaneous generation but are reminders that, in spite of the imperatives of their economic system, Americans have never bent entirely to the incentives of self-interest. Right alongside the hustling Horatio Algers, promotion-hungry narcissists, and Madison Avenue's push to frantic consumption (perhaps best captured in the ever-youthful beer ad: "Who says you can't have it all?") has been the steadfast resolve of generations of people from all economic strata not to be bought away from some activity that was vital to them. Whoever does something for its intrinsic value as opposed to what or where it can get him or her, whoever delights in anything from Bach to frisbee simply for the enjoyment of the activity puts a crimp in the incentive of greed and is, in some degree, receptive to regarding life in qualitative, rather than quantitative and materialistic, terms. The millions of people who play in community orchestras, who volunteer their time in hospitals, who play recreational sports and can be contented losers, who backpack into nature to find a richness that could never be purchased—these people are evidence that the incentive of greed does not simply own the soul of America. Many of these same people do find a real tension between the unacquisitive side of their lives and their roles in the marketplace as producers and consumers. I do not suggest that people should be angelically devoid of all self-interest, but only that the persistent appeal to greed as the dominant human motivation beckons people to a lonely and artificial obsession. It is not a purpose to live or die for.

Given the mixture of motives in most people's lives, to hope for a greater acceptance of mortality is not to advocate revolution. Rather, it is to build on needs and desires already in people, and to insist that the promotion of unlimited acquisition cannot be allowed to preempt the need everyone has to come to terms with death. The long-range economic fallout of such a priority would hardly be disastrous. The market system would continue to operate, but without the artificial demand for the extraneous and the extravagant, whose only utility is the appearance of superiority they bestow on competitive accumulators. Instead of feeding the illusion that the advantaged people in our society are self-made and have no responsibilities to a larger community, an economy with new qualitative priorities would produce to fulfill human needs across the population rather than concentrating on the privileged elite. It is one of the great self-righteous and blinding myths of that elite that people will work hard and economies will be productive only when there are material, individual rewards for effort and work. Since a

crucial part of our liberation from the numbing fear of death is the realization that death does not exterminate us if we give life to others, there are inducements for us to labor more tirelessly and to produce more valuable goods than the incentives of individual economic gain could ever achieve.

A liberation from the fear of death can also point us toward a greater democracy and toward an iron will to put an end to nuclear weapons. With these developments we would not be on our way to a new Jerusalem but would become a society freed from dire threats to its survival in the desperation it has tolerated in the lives of its "losers" and in the hollow prizes it has accorded its alleged "winners." Such a society would not be a utopia, for we would still have to face disasters and disappointments, pathos and tragedy. We would also have to contend with age-old individual inclinations to avarice, pride, and greed. But the big difference is that society would not be cheering on the temptation to egoism; instead it would be concretely reassuring people that such defensiveness is no more necessary than spending our lives hiding from death.

In short, people would be able to relax a bit and feel a calm empowerment in diverting their energies to meet real needs. They would know that death testifies to life's fragility and pain but that it finally does not mock life. They would know that death prods us to value life and our precious power to share life with others.

Afterword

ON OCTOBER 26, 1987, seven weeks after I completed the revised manuscript for this book, our sixteen-year-old daughter, Mari, was in an accident on her way to school and was killed. Since so many of the ideas in this book were inspired by the pleasure and joy

I took in Mari's life and that of her brother Joe, I am moved to share two insights forced on me by the experience of losing Mari.

I argue in the book that although death causes enormous grief and pain it does not extinguish the meaning and significance of any person's life. The existence of every one of us affects others' lives, and this spiritual effect ripples through time to all future generations, despite the fact that we die and our bodies return to nature. I have not changed anything in the book in the two months since my daughter's death, and I would certainly not change this central argument. I have a deepened awareness of how cold and cruel fate can be and of how excruciatingly lonely and joyless the world can appear, a condition gentled at times by generous, comforting friends. I nevertheless know viscerally that my daughter remains a part of me and that her life will always affect my priorities and commitments. I do not shrink from the pain that I now know bereaved parents never lose, because the pain is a confirmation of my closeness with my daughter and the continuing evidence of her wonderful spirit. And I know that she will continue in the lives of many friends and family members. Her classmates in a crowded architectural drawing class insist on keeping her stool and drawing table unoccupied. In the future, long after they have perhaps stopped thinking of the shy, perceptive young woman they lost in their senior year, they may make choices that arise from a deeper respect for beauty and humane values because Mari touched their lives at a formative time.

The second insight I have to share is also a point that is treated theoretically in the book but has been seared into my emotions in the aftermath of my daughter's death. I find it incredible that so many people in our society seek fulfillment and meaning in their lives by competing for a larger pile of possessions. The only thing that has allowed my wife and me to bear so far the loss of our child is the conviction that she knew that we loved her and that we know that she loved us. The ideology of quantity, of increase, of winning that one hears so much trumpeted in America today seems piteously irrelevant to the real life events that try people's hearts and souls. I can only conclude that this ideology has no place for people who lose loved ones—that is for the "losers"—and it has no place for death. The significance of the struggle between those who would deny death and those who would affirm love—and the risk, indeed certainty, of suffering and grief that comes with love—has never seemed more momentous to me than in the last two months. The struggle seems to be about sanity itself. To acquire more and to love less is no protection from death. With a pained vision of a mountain of my own smashed precautions, I know that death will have its way whatever we do. But in spite of the agony and bitter tears it exposes us to, all of my recent education discovers that there is one power that can stand up to death, and that is love.

Bearing the Unbearable: From Loss, the Gain

SANDRA L. BERTMAN

SANDRA L. BERTMAN, PH.D., is a professor of humanities in medicine and founding director of the Program in Medical Humanities at the University of Massachusetts Medical Center, where she teaches in both the medical school and the graduate school of nursing. Her extensive experience ranges from training therapists in grief counseling to preparing physicians, nurses, and other frontline staff working with chronic and life-threatening illness.

Dr. Bertman is internationally known for her lectures and interactive workshop presentations, and her unique integration of the visual and expressive arts. Her media credits include the documentary films *Dying*, which aired on public broadcasting stations in 1976 and brought the voices of persons living with life-threatening illness to the attention of a wide public, and *Harbor of Hope* (1993). She has also written numerous articles and the book *Facing Death: Images, Insights, and Interventions* (1991).

In 1988, Dr. Bertman received the University of Massachusetts Award for Distinguished Professional Public Service for her work in the psychology of death and dying, with particular mention of her integration of the humanities and medicine. The awards committee observed that Dr. Bertman made the "unmentionables and unmeasurables" an important part of medical education. In 1989 she received the American Journal of Hospice Care Award for extending her classroom and counseling techniques to patients, families, and staff in hospice, hospital, nursing homes, and other therapeutic settings. She was named Outstanding Death Educator by the Association for Death Education and Counseling in 1991.

Of her current work, Dr. Bertman says that perhaps most exciting is her involvement in "care for the caregiver" workshops, ongoing support for nurses on the wards, and retreats designed to provide renewal and support for nurses. She is also developing programs on the language of grief and the art of consolation, the changing images of AIDS, and the cross-cultural experience of aging, illness, and death.

At the Threshold of Death

Even though the doctor has told me that I didn't have long to live, I'm living some of the greatest moments in life. If I should use a name—I don't think that Rockefeller could be as happy a man as I am.

Diagnosis: cancer, Reverend Bryant[1]

And when they told me I might have a remission my hopes went crashing to the ground.

Diagnosis: leukemia, Ted Rosenthal[2]

How can two men living with the dread disease, cancer, make such statements? What are they telling us? Either they're naive, stupid, denying or lying. Only fools, madmen or saints face death so brazenly. How could anyone who has been told there is no further treatment to arrest or remove one's malignancy mouth such nonsense?

In fact, neither man initially or consistently displayed such mien. When the Reverend first heard of cancer metastases to his liver, his agitated demeanor underscored his concern. He asked about all the medical treatments he could think of—surgery, chemotherapy, radiation—to be reassured that the physician had exhausted every possible option. Ted Rosenthal, after being told he had five months left to live, felt the same as being told he would die that very afternoon, which would be preferable, he tells us, because at least he'd be spared the emotional and physical agonies that accompany the trauma of a cancer sentence.

The Reverend adjusted quickly to his fate, refocusing his energies and concerns. He tells us God gives us cancer so we'll take stock of life, pause, and appreciate what we have. In the documentary film, *Dying,* Reverend Bryant does just that. We witness his "life review," his memories and reveries. We revisit the south of his childhood, where he had his first barbeque, and we walk with him through the cemetery where his parents are buried. We relive some special moments of courtship and intimacy with his cherished wife. And with him, we live a lifetime in a moment as he teaches a grandson the prayer of grace.

In the documentary film *How Could I Not Be Among You,* Ted Rosenthal's thinking becomes so reconsidered he does not fear living under the Damoclean sword for six months, but rather a remission. If he were given a reprieve from cancer, which the remission would be, he'd lose a precious, new-found sensitivity and ability to live in the present moment. He talks of being able to experience his environment so differently:

I could see the birds for the first time in my life. Instead of just looking at the birds and just saying, "Ah yes, birds," I could see them, without calling them birds; without seeing them as being something. I could see the sky. I could see the clouds. . . . It was just an open, full, rich feeling.

Both men are testament to the fact that terminal illness may provide momentary paralysis and subsequent heightened awareness that removes the tarnish from the routines of daily living while providing a sense of timelessness and peace—a kind of eternity in the now. Perhaps there is an irony that in seeing things, suddenly, as if for the last time, one not only savors them as the Reverend does, but, as in the case

of Rosenthal, sees them, as if for the first.[3] The poet Emily Dickinson puts it this way:

By a departing light
We see acuter, quite,
Than by a wick that stays.
There's something in the flight
That clarifies the sight
And decks the rays.[4]

Neither man turned his face to the wall and gave up the ghost without a struggle. Nor did either man view death as welcome relief from pain and suffering. Both underwent harrowing effects of palliative treatments and struggled with physical deterioration to hang on to every additional moment of life. Weak with paralysis and a stroke's aftermath, the Reverend smiles feebly at his wife, telling her, "You got to keep fighting." And after bouts of chemotherapy and nausea, "to the extent they can prolong your life," says the poet, Rosenthal, "dying's beautiful."

Sometimes the "departing light" is balked at by family members and friends. In the poem "Virginia,"[5] by Karen Swenson, anger at a friend's fate of cancer is spewed out at surgeons who, desperately trying to save her life, are viewed almost as butchers, relentlessly dismembering or hacking away at the victim's womanhood: one breast amputation follows the other, then the removal of the ovaries and pituitary gland ("the module/whose function they weren't sure of./It is a matter of taking out the fuse/so the lights won't go on.") The bitter tones of the poem are balanced by those of wonder and admiration for Virginia's stance in light of all these procedures. This woman gets on with life. Hiding her wounds behind a prosthesis, she sounds very much like the Reverend and poet when she speaks of what it means to be living with death:

It gives life salt, not depending
on any other time to make up your tense,

and days become what they always
should have
been pungent with the present.

The speaker comes to understand why Virginia keeps returning for biopsies and invasive operations. Virginia is cut back to the bone, but the ironic paradox is she is not at all diminished: "the more they minus/the more multiples there are."

Sometimes the "departing light" highlights unrecognized conflicts and allows for their peaceful resolution. Such is the case for the protagonist of Tolstoy's classic novella, *The Death of Ivan Ilych*.[6] When the man of the title is able to let go of the pretensions of his life and face the reality of terminal cancer, his "life review" painfully exposes the sham of his days. Ilych is confronted with what he was not, that is, a caring, concerned, empathic father and husband. On his deathbed, for the first time in his life, Ilych understands his son's tears and feels pity for his family's plight. For Ilych, this new-found empathy is what ultimately relieves his physical and mental agonies, silences his screaming, and is, for him, healing. We are told in place of death there is light. His former fear of death is replaced by a fulfilling sense of well-being. Acting so as not to hurt his family, he releases them and frees himself (and the reader) from these sufferings:

"What joy! . . . Death is finished," he said to himself "It is no more." He drew in a breath, stopped in the midst of a sigh, stretched out, and died.

In "Last Words of My English Grandmother"[7] we have quite a different scenario. The poet and physician, William Carlos Williams, comes to see his grandmother's gesture of "turning one's head to the wall" and ending the fight for life as a defiant and unmistakable act of assertion. Worn out by sickness and age, a person may experience the length of days more as a punishment than a privilege.

Despite her protests, Williams's grandmother is forced into an ambulance and rushed to the hospital. Focusing for the last time on a vista of trees outside the ambulance window, this nearly blind old woman states aloud, "I'm tired of them" and "rolled her head away."

Another instance of willful death is presented in the photo-journal *Gramp*,[8] a family's three-year documentation, in picture and diary notation, of Gramp's deterioration and death at home. For this gentle old man, rolling his face to the wall is his refusal to eat or drink. Gramp makes this position clear when he removes his dentures, handing them to a grandson with the explanation that he won't need them anymore. He spits back his spoon feedings, (im)patiently waiting for death. As the grandsons write in the introduction, during that time they learned a lot about Gramp and one another, but even more about themselves. When the ordeal of caring for a senile, incontinent grandfather was finally over, they were surprised not to feel the expected sense of relief. Instead, one grandson describes a tinge of emptiness:

a feeling that we would miss the craziness
he brought into our lives—but, most of all,
I felt an enormous amount of respect for
this tough old coal miner. "You pulled it off,
Gramp," I thought. "You really pulled it
off."

The Amputation Becomes an Acquisition

Death is not the only threat to the fortress of one's body or one's sense of well-being. The specter of loss of a body part or body function can elicit overwhelming anxieties. What does it mean to be crippled, to lose a colon and void feces and urine through a new hole some place on your abdomen, or to undergo amputation of a breast that is a badge of femininity, maternity and womanness in most societies?

In "Cancer's a Funny Thing," a physician with rectal carcinoma composes a "public poem," as he calls it, deliberately to induce cancer patients to be operated on early and be cheerful about it.[9] He uses light rhyme to gloss over the traumatic body alteration ("So now I am like two faced Janus/The only god who sees his anus") and the embarrassments caused by leakage and odor of the colostomy ("And hope, as soon as I am able,/To make it keep a fixed time-table.") Never veering from this verse pattern, he minimizes or diffuses the fact that cancer is painful and, perhaps, even fatal:

I know that cancer often kills,
But so do cars and sleeping pills;
And it can hurt one till one sweats,
So can bad teeth and unpaid debts.

Confronting the malignancy with humor is a mature and, indeed, literal defense in James Dickey's serious poem, "The Cancer Match."[10] Told medicine has no hope to offer, the protagonist of this work stages his own war with the thing growing within by pitting it against his positive attitudes—his inner resources:

. . . Swarm over him, my joy, my laughter,
my Basic Life
Force! Let your bright sword-arm stream
Into that turgid hulk, the worst
Of me, growing:
Get 'im, O Self

He cuts the cancer down to size with one-upsmanship and surprises, by matching it with whiskey in the boxing ring of his body and by throwing it off step ("They are fighting,/Or are they dancing?") We all know who will be the ultimate victor ("I don't have all the time/In the World, but I have all night"); but for the speaker, and for us, the victory of just this one bout is exhilarating.

Humor is more than "defense" or momentary shift of perspective for Norman Cousins.

In his autobiographical book, *The Anatomy of an Illness As Perceived by the Patient*,[11] "laugh therapy," as he calls it, was instrumental in the cure of his crippling and irreversible disease. Like Dickey, Cousins musters his affirmative emotions to war against his body chemistries. Where Dickey called on drink as ally in this venture, Cousins summoned funny movies such as Marx Brothers and "Candid Camera" spoofs:

It worked. I made the joyous discovery that ten minutes of genuine belly laughter had an anesthetic effect and would give me at least two hours of pain-free sleep.

Cousins's view of heavy mirth, literal body shaking laughter, as "a good way to jog internally without having to go outdoors" though charming, has been the butt of medical controversy.[12] We shall not debate the physiological or biomedical benefits of laughter here. What all three of these works do demonstrate, nonetheless, is an ability to confront the anxieties associated with loss and death by creating moods in which other positive emotions can be released to restore, regenerate, and even enhance one's physical and mental health.

In Karl Shapiro's poem, "The Leg,"[13] tears of grief rather than paroxysms of laughter are the mechanisms used to confront loss. Waking from anesthesia, the protagonist comes to the realization that his leg has been amputated. He grieves for his leg "as a child cries whose puppy is mangled under a screaming wheel." Moving from the depths of despair to consideration of life without his limb, he explores the rehabilitation possibilities of limping, prosthesis and wheelchairs. Using a bit of "laugh therapy," and, like Dickey whose cancer is a boy with boxing gloves and Cousins whose innards jog, he personifies his leg, equipping it with playful obstinance and sense of humor. But the trauma of the separation is not to be minimized. He continued to identify with his missing leg. Preoccupied with ways of keeping it alive, he assesses the question of adjustment from its point of view: "he is its injury, the leg is his orphan." He must "cultivate the mind of the leg" in order to help it [him?] let go. Finally, after being able to pray for its peace, he is able to face the idea of his leg's death not with the tearful anguish of a child whose puppy was dreadfully mangled or with preoccupying fantasies of the lost leg's whereabouts and loneliness, but "quietly."

By the final stanza, the loss is transcended. No mention is made of the leg. Ebullient in tone, the amputee has a new sense of himself as well as a sense of creative relatedness to God and the Cosmos:

> The body, what is it, Father, but a sign
> To love the force that grows us . . .
>
> That if Thou take me angrily in hand
> And hurl me to the shark, I shall not die!

Shapiro never accuses the leg of suddenly or in some unexpected way betraying him. He feels fright and tenderness; he trembles and cries. But even when the prosthesis is unable to be fitted, the protagonist speaks of his stump as friend, intelligent, with a sense of humor and a mind of its own.

In Audre Lorde's *The Cancer Journals*, waiting for the results of the biopsy, the author grows angry at the breast in question, blaming it for her plight.[14] She attributes malicious motives to it and is uncomfortable with this heretofore cherished part of herself:

> as if it had become already separate from me
> and had turned against me by creating this
> tumor which might be malignant. My breast
> had suddenly departed from the rules we had
> agreed upon to function by all these years.

The support and assurances of friends and family do not assuage the psychic pain or feelings of being untouchable and unlovable as she investigates how she and others in her world can live with a new, foreign physical self. Feeling so alone and vulnerable she even considers refusing the surgery. After the mastectomy, Lorde recalls her own experience of making love to her one-breasted lesbian lover, remembering the hesitation and tenderness she herself felt as she touched the deeply scarred hollow of another where a breast used to be.

Unlike Virginia, Lorde cannot carry on bravely as if she were not now different by hiding her scars behind soft foam or silicone. Coerced by hospital personnel into wearing a prosthesis, Lorde considers the justifications for false breasts which, she argues, are not even as functional as dentures that help one chew or artificial limbs that allow one to manipulate or walk. She sees the mask of prosthesis as a cosmetic sham and trivializing for the single-breasted woman. Her arguments suggest this emphasis on physical pretense and facade of normalcy and cheerfulness actually retards the adaptive process by forcing one to mourn the loss of her breast in secret "as if it were some crime of which she were guilty." She writes in her journal that she cannot wear the prosthesis because it feels like a lie more than merely a costume and that facing the truth of the loss and its ramifications is prerequisite.

Like Rosenthal and Shapiro, the idea of having cancer or losing a part of one's self seems much more traumatic before the operation and amputation. Facing the magnitude of the loss she equates the pain with being "at least as sharp as the pain of separating from [her] mother. . . . But I made it once before, so I know I can make it again." She makes it by weeping, raging, despairing, testing lovers, internalizing and, finally, seeing the experience as enhancing. In tones almost as eulogistic as Shapiro's she concludes:

> At times I miss my right breast, the actual-
> ity of it, its presence, with a great and poig-
> nant sense of loss. But in the same way, and
> just as infrequently, as I sometimes miss
> being 32, at the same time knowing that I

have gained from the very loss I mourn. . . . I would never have chosen this path, but I am very glad to be who I am, here.

After Death

The story *Gifts* by Deena Linett is a conversation between a brother and sister the night following their mother's death.[15] Or rather it is a monologue of the sister; a reliving of the details of the deathwatch and its aftermath, from the mother's vomiting blood and paroxysm of dying, to her father's shocking invitation to personally prepare the body for burial. Her father tells of the orthodox Jewish tradition of washing their own dead: "It's a last act of loving kindness. I plan to do this for your mother. Would you like to help me?"

The remainder of the story is her recollections of the ritual experience: her terror upon seeing her dead mother in the funeral home, her fears she'll scream or faint and be a disappointment to her father.

As Linett becomes absorbed in the procedure of washing and dressing the body, the distasteful chore becomes an honorable act. Her revulsion to the literal physicality of death vanishes; "How could I be afraid of her body that gave me life? . . . She looked beautiful." The daughter who couldn't bear to enter the bedroom at the moment of death ("I knew I ought to go in, but I couldn't"), who prayed her doctor-brother would arrive earlier to give the injections and handle the washing of the corpse (". . . you've handled dead people before. Why couldn't we wait for you?") has changed. The young woman comes to feel a strength in herself that she never thought she had "just because I helped him prepare her that way." She concludes her tale to her brother with gratitude and praise for her mother: "She gave me everything. . . . Even in death she gave me these gifts."

The valley of the shadow of death is not walked through alone. Spencer, in *Faerie Queen,* corroborates the therapeutic value of company: "He oft finds med'cine who his griefe imparts."[16] Sorrow unshared, as suggested by Shakespeare on more than one occasion, can even produce bodily harm. In *Titus Andronicus,* "like an oven stopp'd," sadness concealed, "doth burn the heart to cinders where it is."[17] And in *Macbeth:* "Give sorrow tongue/The grief that does not speak/Whispers the o'erfraught heart/and bid it break."[18]

Epilogue: A Sense of Identity

A common thread in many of the scenarios described herein is connectedness, affinity with all mankind; past, present, alive, dead. To repeat the oft-quoted words of the poet and priest, John Donne, "No man is an island."[19] The Reverend Bryant, a religious man, touches base with his dead ancestors and sings joyfully of his connection with Christ ("Jesus died for me!"). Ted Rosenthal comes to feel an expansiveness in his self-definition. Who he heretofore was ("himself or an extension of what's in his hip pocket"), now embodies "the infinite potential of the whole race. Man; first man; last man; all man." He describes his sense of connectedness as a drug high, "a good trip."

Going one step further than Ivan Ilych, Rosenthal experiences a new-found empathy with the pain of unrelated others. He urges us, in his poetry, to love our mothers, lovers, neighbors, even strangers. He seems to imply we are all kindred spirits in that all persons shall be touched by illness, sorrow and death. . . .

A thirteenth-century Christian philosopher has said the shell must be cracked apart if what is in it is to come out. The only way to know the kernel is to break the shell.[20] In coming to terms with the realities of the trauma of loss and death, none of the persons or characters cited above were themselves destroyed. Quite the contrary: after experiencing the full gamut of the grief process, denial, anger, sadness, fear, despair, something quite new was created from their sorrow.

Growth is not as automatic or vegetative as the growth of mighty oaks from tiny acorns. A cracked shell may result in a withered kernel. Exposure to death and grief is not enough. Dying and grieving must be actively engaged in, not passively endured. The seed of grief must be planted in fertile soil, watered, nurtured and tended to.

In choosing how to confront their respective fates, these persons chose their very characters. Reverend Bryant, Lorde, and the protagonist of "The Leg" did not win in the sense of reversing the inevitable, but they asserted their humanity and integrity in the face of the overwhelming onslaughts presented by the specter of loss. They have borne the unbearable. Self-pity does not end up as self-disparagement for Ilych or for the English grandmother. Both Rosenthal and Ilych develop a new sense of love and communion with all who have suffered. The survivors, Gramp's family and Linett, discover new self-knowledge and with it, dividends of self-pride. And we, the readers and viewers of their worlds, exposed to their fresh new perceptions, are enriched. Through them, we strengthen our own connections with the human family. Vicariously, we revise our concepts and reform our own beings, emerging, as they have, from the situation of loss, with gain.

Death Education for Living

Thomas Attig. "Person-Centered Death Education," *Death Studies* 16, no. 4 (1992): 357–70. Attig describes a humanities-based approach to death education that emphasizes storytelling as well as reflection on what it means to be a person and to respect persons, thereby preparing students for the real-life circumstances in which they find themselves. The acquisition of information about death and dying, though important, is outweighed by helping students reflect upon the *meaning* of the information. More than simply learning facts, death education is about exploring subjective truths; that is, truths that make a difference in shaping lives, informing interactions with others, and grounding a sense of meaning and purpose in living.

Inge B. Corless, Barbara B. Germino, and Mary Pittman, eds. *Dying, Death, and Bereavement: Theoretical Perspectives and Other Ways of Knowing.* Boston: Jones and Bartlett, 1994. This collection of essays focuses on such topics as home and hospice care, theories of grief and complications in mourning traumatic death, psychosocial variables in the experience of dying, suicide, and other social and cultural aspects of experiencing death.

International Work Group on Death, Dying, and Bereavement. "Education about Death, Dying, and Bereavement," in *Statements about Death, Dying, and Bereavement by the International Work Group on Death, Dying, and Bereavement* (London, Ont.: IWG, 1994). An international organization composed of clinicians, researchers, and educators, the IWG is a catalyst for formulating policies and principles in the field of death and dying. Its statements address three aspects of death education: in society at large, for professionals in health care and human services, and for volunteers and nonprofessionals. In each instance, the aim is to establish guidelines and provide a framework for carrying out responsible education about life-threatening illness, dying, death, and bereavement.

Robert Kastenbaum and Beatrice Kastenbaum, eds. *The Encyclopedia of Death.* Phoenix: Oryx Press, 1989; New York: Avon Books, 1993. A useful starting point in any research project as well as a concise one-volume work addressing many of the central topics in the study of death and dying, this reference work offers a broad range of information without claiming to be all-inclusive. The interested reader will find coverage of such topics as the biomedical aspects of death, hospice care and trajectories of dying, deathbed scenes, anticipatory grief, cryonic suspension, and much more. The very fact that an encyclopedia of death is in print says much about the changing nature of attitudes toward death within the past few decades.

Robert G. Stevenson, ed. *What Will We Do? Preparing the School Community to Cope with Crises.* Amityville, N.Y.: Baywood, 1994. This collection examines the scope and effects, including both the potential benefits and possible risks, of programs designed to help students cope with crises such as death from accident, illness, suicide, homicide, violence, and war. Included are specific steps that can be taken to prepare communities to cope with future crises and to assist young people and others when crisis occurs. Also see, by Stevenson and others, the anthology *Curing Death Ignorance: Teaching Children about Death in the Schools* (Philadelphia: Charles Press, 1994), which examines the ongoing debate about the capability of schools to teach about death and the wisdom of developing such instruction.

Acknowledging Our Mortality

Daniel Callahan. *The Troubled Dream of Life: Living with Mortality.* New York: Simon and Schuster, 1993. By candidly exploring his own life and the lives and deaths of loved ones, Callahan provides a framework for understanding mortality in the context of personal and social issues. Despite the public debate about dying with dignity, we have been reluctant to think about death itself, thereby distancing ourselves from the more basic question, What should be the meaning of death in our lives? Death is not simply an avoidable accident. In shifting the way we think about death in our own lives, we need to recognize the importance of self-understanding as well as the place of death in nature. Only then can we find fresh and insightful ways of living with mortality.

James P. Carse. *Death and Existence: A Conceptual History of Human Mortality*. New York: John Wiley and Sons, 1980. Guided by the thesis that death does not rob life of its meaning but rather makes life's meaning possible, Carse looks at what ten major conceptual traditions tell us about death, grief, and freedom. While each tradition has its unique approach to understanding the meaning of death, virtually all agree that denying our mortality locks us into an airless spiritual trap. In denying death we will have denied life. See also, by Carse, *Finite and Infinite Games: A Vision of Life as Play and Possibility* (New York: Ballantine, 1986).

Ernest J. Gaines. *A Lesson Before Dying: A Novel*. New York: Knopf, 1993. Set in a small Cajun Louisiana community in the 1940s, this story of death and identity reveals the strength of the human spirit and the human capacity for heroic response in the most extreme circumstances. A man who doesn't want to be involved reluctantly comes to the aid of another man who is condemned to die. Despite their differences and their settled belief that they are both pawns in a hopeless situation, they find resources within themselves for continuing the struggle against futility even to the point of death.

Donald Hall. *Life Work*. Boston: Beacon Press, 1993. When Hall, a prize-winning poet and author of several dozen books, began this account of his work as a writer, he meant it to be a testimony to the pleasures of craft. Halfway through the writing, he was diagnosed with cancer. Although his work had always been done "in defiance of death," now the more immediate prospect of dying becomes a powerful stimulus simply to "get done what you can." This is an intimate account of the life-changing result of one man's encounter with mortality.

Bernice L. Neugarten and Dail A. Neugarten. "Policy Issues in an Aging Society," in *Adult Years: Continuity and Change*, edited by Martha Storandt and Gary R. VandenBos (Washington: American Psychological Association, 1989), 143–67. No matter what your age, it is a fact of biological life that you are aging. The United States is itself an aging society in which the proportion of old to young is increasing rapidly. Does the specter of an aging society portend disaster? How will the economy support large numbers of retirees? If you find such questions troubling, you are not alone. This article provides a good starting point for understanding what these changes will mean over the near future and into the twenty-first century.

Adrian Tomer. "Death Anxiety in Adult Life: Theoretical Perspectives," *Death Studies* 16, no. 6 (1992): 475–506. Fear of death, death concern, and nonspecific distress about death are often subsumed under the generic term *death anxiety*. Death is viewed as a threat to the realization of the basic goals one hopes to accomplish in life. In this study, Tomer looks at a number of philosophical and psychological approaches, seeking to provide a perspective on the causes of death anxiety and its meaning in human life.

notes and references

Part I: Cultural Contexts

Confronting Death

ROBERT KASTENBAUM, "Reconstructing Death in Postmodern Society," *Omega: Journal of Death and Dying* 27, no. 1 (1993): 75–89. Reprinted, in slightly revised form, by permission of the author and Baywood Publishing Co. Copyright © 1993.

Notes

1. R. Kastenbaum, *Death, Society, and Human Experience,* 4th ed. (New York: Macmillan/Merrill, 1991).
2. M. Foucault, *The Archeology of Knowledge* (New York: Pantheon, 1972).
3. H. Lawson and L. Appignanesi, eds., *Dismantling Truth: Reality in the Postmodern World* (London: Weidenfeld and Nicholson, 1989).
4. T. W. Adorno, "Theses on the Sociology of Art," *Working Papers in Cultural Studies* 2 (1972): 121–28.
5. M. Horkheimer, "The End of Reason," in *The Essential Frankfurt School Reader,* ed. A. Arato and F. Gebhart (1941; reprint, New York: Continuum, 1990).
6. J. Derrida, *On Grammatology* (Baltimore: Johns Hopkins University Press, 1976).
7. M. Ryan, *Marxism and Deconstruction* (Baltimore: Johns Hopkins University Press, 1982).
8. M. E. Metchnikoff, *The Nature of Man* (New York: G. P. Putnam and Sons, 1903).
9. R. Park, "Thanatology: A Questionnaire and a Plea for a Neglected Study," *Journal of the American Medical Association* 58 (1912): 1243–46.
10. R. S. Woodworth and H. Schlosberg, *Experimental Psychology,* rev. ed. (New York: Henry Holt, 1954).
11. J. Piaget, *The Construction of Reality in the Child* (New York: Basic Books, 1954).
12. V. R. Pine, "The Age of Maturity for Death Education: A Socio-Historical Portrait of the Era 1976–1985," *Death Studies* 10 (1986): 209–32.
13. G. W. Davidson and L. W. Zimmerman, eds., "Human Remains: Contemporary Issues," *Death Studies* 14 (1990): whole issue.
14. L. Tolstoy, *The Death of Ivan Ilych* (1886; reprint, New York: New American Library, 1960)
15. E. Kübler-Ross, *On Death and Dying* (New York: Macmillan, 1969)
16. R. Kastenbaum and C. Normand, "Deathbed Scenes as Expected by the Young and Experienced by the Old," *Death Studies* 14, no. 3 (1990): 201–17.
17. R. A. Moody, *Life After Life* (Atlanta: Mockingbird Books, 1975); and K. Ring, "Near-Death Experience," in *Encyclopedia of Death,* ed. R. Kastenbaum and B. K. Kastenbaum (Phoenix: Oryx Press, 1989), 193–96.
18. R. Kastenbaum, "'Safe Death' in the Postmodern World," in *A Safer Death,* ed. A. Gilmore and S. Gilmore (Plenum: New York, 1988), 3–14.
19. D. Umberson and K. Henderson, "The Social Construction of Death in the Gulf War," *Omega: Journal of Death and Dying* 25, no. 1 (1992): 1–15.
20. D. L. Kozak, "Dying Badly: Violent Death and Religious Change among the Tohono O'odham," *Omega: Journal of Death and Dying* 23, no. 3 (1991): 207–16.
21. Ibid.

HERMAN FEIFEL, "Psychology and Death: Meaningful Rediscovery," *American Psychologist* 45 (April 1990): 537–43. Reprinted courtesy of the author.

Notes

1. See, for example, G. T. Fechner, *The Little Book of Life After Death* (1836; reprint, Boston: Little, Brown, 1904); G. S. Hall, "Thanatophobia and Immortality," *American Journal of Psychology* 26 (1915): 550–613; and W. James, *The Varieties of Religious Experience* (Boston: Longmans, Green, 1910).
2. A. Toynbee, A. K. Mant, N. Smart, J. Hinton, S. Yudkin, E. Rhode, R. Heywood, and H. H. Price,

Man's Concern with Death (New York: McGraw-Hill, 1968).

3. H. Feifel, ed., *New Meanings of Death* (New York: McGraw-Hill, 1977).

4. H. Feifel, "Philosophy Reconsidered," *Psychological Reports* 15 (1964): 415–20.

5. Ibid.

6. H. Feifel, "Attitudes Toward Death: A Psychological Perspective," *Journal of Consulting and Clinical Psychology* 33 (1969): 292–95.

7. Ibid.

8. See, for example, I. E. Alexander, R. S. Colley, and A. M. Adlerstein, "Is Death a Matter of Indifference?," *Journal of Psychology* 43 (1957): 277–83; H. Feifel, "Attitudes of Mentally Ill Patients Toward Death," *Journal of Nervous and Mental Disease* 122 (1955): 375–80; and H. Feifel, "Older Persons Look at Death," *Geriatrics* 11 (1956): 127–30.

9. H. Feifel, "Death," in *Taboo Topics,* ed. N. L. Farberow (New York: Atherton Press, 1963), 12.

10. S. Potter, *The Theory and Practice of Gamesmanship* (New York: Holt, Rinehart, and Winston, 1970).

11. Feifel, "Death," 11–13.

12. See R. Kastenbaum and R. Aisenberg, *The Psychology of Death* (New York: Springer, 1972); K. R. Eissler, *The Psychiatrist and the Dying Patient* (New York: International Universities Press, 1955); J. Hinton, *Dying* (Baltimore: Penguin Books, 1967); E. Kübler-Ross, *On Death and Dying* (New York: Macmillan, 1969); C. M. Parkes, *Bereavement: Studies of Grief in Adult Life* (New York: International Universities Press, 1972); A. D. Weisman, *On Dying and Denying: A Psychiatric Study of Terminality* (New York: McGraw-Hill, 1972); R. Fulton, ed., *Death and Identity* (New York: John Wiley and Sons, 1965); B. G. Glaser and A. L. Straus, *Awareness of Dying* (Chicago: Aldine, 1965); J. Quint-Benoliel, *The Nurse and the Dying Patient* (New York: Macmillan, 1967); J. Choron, *Death and Western Thought* (New York: Collier, 1963); and G. Gorer, *Death, Grief, and Mourning* (New York: Doubleday, 1965).

13. C. W. Wahl, "The Fear of Death," in *The Meaning of Death,* ed. H. Feifel (New York: McGraw-Hill, 1959), 16–29.

14. W. H. Gillespie, "Some Regressive Phenomena in Old Age," *British Journal of Medical Psychology* 36 (1963): 203–9; and H. Searles, "Schizophrenia and the Inevitability of Death," *Psychiatric Quarterly* 35 (1961): 634–65.

15. Feifel, *New Meanings of Death*; and H. Feifel and V. T. Nagy, "Another Look at Fear of Death," *Journal of Consulting and Clinical Psychology* 49 (1981): 278–86.

16. H. Feifel and A. B. Branscomb, "Who's Afraid of Death?," *Journal of Abnormal Psychology* 81 (1973): 82–88.

17. H. Feifel and V. T. Nagy, *Coping with Life-Threat and General Life Conflict: Two Diverse Beasts* (Ann Arbor: University of Michigan, 1986; ERIC Document Reproduction Service No. ED 266 362); H. Feifel and S. Strack, "Coping with Conflict Situations: Middle-Aged and Elderly Men," *Psychology and Aging* 4 (1989): 26–33; H. Feifel, S. Strack, and V. T. Nagy, "Degree of Life-Threat and Differential Use of Coping Modes," *Journal of Psychomatic Research* 31 (1987): 91–99; H. Feifel, S. Strack, and V. T. Nagy, "Coping Strategies and Associated Features of Medically Ill Patients," *Psychosomatic Medicine* 49 (1987): 616–25; and R. L. Silver and C. B. Wortman, "Coping with Undesirable Life Events," in *Human Helplessness: Theory and Applications,* ed. J. Garber and M. E. P. Seligman (New York: Academic Press, 1980), 279–375.

18. Feifel, *New Meanings of Death.*

19. C. Saunders, "Dying They Live: St. Christopher's Hospice," in Feifel, ed., *New Meanings of Death,* 153–79.

20. Feifel, *New Meanings of Death*; and R. Fulton and D. J. Gottesman, "Anticipatory Grief: A Psychosocial Concept Reconsidered," *British Journal of Psychiatry* 137 (1980): 45–51.

21. Feifel, *New Meanings of Death.*

22. Weisman, *On Dying and Denying.*

23. Parkes, *Bereavement.*

24. Kübler-Ross, *On Death and Dying*; and J. Bowlby, *Loss: Sadness and Depression* (New York: Basic Books, 1980).

25. Weisman, *On Dying and Denying.*

26. Feifel, *New Meanings of Death.*

27. Ibid.

28. Feifel, "Death."

29. Feifel, "Attitudes Toward Death."

30. Ibid., 294.

31. Feifel, *New Meanings of Death,* 354.

32. Ibid.

33. Feifel and Nagy, "Another Look at Fear of Death"; R. Kastenbaum and P. T. Costa, "Psychological Perspectives on Death," *Annual Review of Psychology* 28 (1977): 225–49; and R. Schulz, *The Psychology of Death, Dying, and Bereavement* (Reading, Mass.: Addison-Wesley, 1978).

34. Feifel, "Attitudes Toward Death."

35. Feifel, "Philosophy Reconsidered."

36. Feifel, *New Meanings of Death,* 11.

37. Ibid.

CHARLES E. ROSENBERG, "What Is an Epidemic? AIDS in Historical Perspective," *Daedalus: Journal of the American Academy of Arts and Sciences* 118, no. 2 (Spring 1989): 1–17. Excerpt, pages 9–14, reprinted by permission of the American Academy of Arts and Sciences. Copyright © 1989.

Notes

1. One might also note the desire to specify implausibly explicit beginnings—and clothe them with moral meaning. Compare the expository and narrative function of Camus's rat [in the novel *The Plague,* which Rosenberg discussed in the portion of the article before this extract] with the role played by Gaetan Dugas, the antisocial and hypersexual airline steward of Randy Shilts's recent best-seller *And the Band Played On: Politics, People, and the AIDS Epidemic* (New York: St. Martin's Press, 1987). A rodent vector obviously provides the occasion for a rather differently nuanced moral agenda. One can hardly blame a rat.

2. Even scientists can, and doubtless do, understand seemingly objective statements at several levels simultaneously. "When certain immunologists suggest that predisposition to AIDS may grow out of successive onslaughts on the immune system—it may or may not prove to be an accurate description of the natural world. But to many ordinary Americans (and perhaps a good many medical scientists as well) the meaning lies in another frame of reference. . . . The emphasis on repeated infections explains how an individual had predisposed him or herself. The meaning lies in behavior uncontrolled." And suitably punished. See Charles E. Rosenberg, "Disease and Social Order in America: Perceptions and Expectations," *Milbank Quarterly* 64 (supp. 1) (1986): 52.

3. The spread of AIDS through the blood-banking and processing system represents an instance of this category of intervention—one in which the transmission of a disease can be limited or halted without inducing behavioral change in prospective victims.

4. The layman's persistent belief in contagion through casual contact despite the reassuring words of medical authority reenacts another traditional element in the history of epidemic disease.

5. Compare Allan M. Brandt, *No Magic Bullet, A Social History of Venereal Disease in the United States Since 1880, with a New Chapter on AIDS* (New York: Oxford University Press, 1987). On "syphilis of the innocent," see L. Duncan Bulkley, *Syphilis in the Innocent . . . Clinically and Historically Considered, with a Plan for the Legal Control of the Disease* (New York: Bailey and Fairchild, 1894). There are a good many other parallels between AIDS and syphilis, such as the proposed criminalization of the knowing transmission of the disease. Changed attitudes toward female sexuality have, however, altered presumptions of female "innocence" and responsibility.

6. The contrast with the very gradual elucidation of such protean clinical entities as syphilis, tuberculosis, and rheumatic fever is instructive. Although AIDS may seem to have appeared suddenly in the public consciousness, as a biological phenomenon it has been extremely slow in developing, certainly in comparison with other virus diseases such as measles and influenza.

7. *New York Times,* 23 August 1988, A14.

8. And, needless to say, it underlines as well the often less than adequate preparation of medical personnel for dealing with fatal illness. That AIDS is infectious as well as almost invariably fatal provides an exacerbating element that differentiates it from the great majority of chronic life-threatening ills.

9. The epidemic has illustrated the geographical integration of society as well; AIDS has made clear North America's relationship with other countries and continents. Our traditional habit of largely ignoring African health conditions may be a luxury we can no longer afford.

10. Rosenberg, "Disease and Social Order," 35–36, 53.

11. Albert Camus, *The Plague,* trans. Stuart Gilbert (New York: Alfred A. Knopf, 1952), 35, 278.

JACK LULE, "News Strategies and the Death of Huey Newton," *Journalism Quarterly* 70, no. 2 (Summer 1993): 287–99. Reprinted by permission of the author. Copyright © 1993 by Jack Lule.

Notes

1. See for example, Report of The National Advisory Commission on Civil Disorders, Otto Kerner, director (Washington, D.C.: U.S. Government Printing Office, March 1968); George P. Hunt, "The Racial Crisis and the News Media: An Overview," in *Race and the News Media,* eds. Paul Fisher and Ralph Lowenstein (New York: Frederick Praeger, 1967), 11–20; William L. Rivers and Wilbur Schramm, "The Negro and the News: A Case Study," *Responsibility in*

Mass Communication, rev. ed. (New York: Harper & Row, 1969), 175–89; Jack Lyle, ed., *The Black American and the Press* (Los Angeles: Ward Ritchie Press, 1968).

Also see, Vernon A. Stone, "Trends in the Status of Minorities and Women in Broadcast News," *Journalism Quarterly* 65 (Summer 1988): 288–93; Judee Burgoon, Michael Burgoon, David Buller, Ray Coker, and Deborah Coker, "Minorities and Journalism: Career Orientations Among High School Students," *Journalism Quarterly* 64 (Summer–Autumn 1987): 434–43; Ellis Cose, "The Quiet Crisis: Minority Journalists and Newsroom Opportunity: A Report from the Institute for Journalism Education," *APME Minorities Research Committee* (San Francisco: Associated Press Managing Editors Association, 1985).

2. Peter Braham, "How the Media Report Race," in *Culture, Society and the Media,* eds. Michael Gurevitch, Tony Bennett, James Curran and Janet Woollacott (New York: Methuen, 1982), 268–86; Jannette L. Dates and William Barlow, eds., *Split Image: African Americans in the Mass Media* (Washington, D.C.: Howard University Press, 1990); Paula Johnson, David Sears, and John McConahay, "Black Invisibility, the Press and the LA Riot," *American Journal of Sociology* 76 (January 1971): 713–17; Richard Lentz, *Symbols, the News Magazines, and Martin Luther King* (Baton Rouge: Louisiana State University Press, 1990); David Paletz and Robert Dunn, "Press Coverage of Civil Disorders: A Case Study of Winston-Salem, 1967," *Public Opinion Quarterly* 33 (1969–70): 340–45; also see, Todd Gitlin, *The Whole World Is Watching* (Berkeley: University of California Press, 1980), 290–91; David L. Paletz and Robert M. Entman, *Media, Power, Politics* (New York: Free Press, 1981); Pamela J. Shoemaker, "Media Treatment of Deviant Political Groups," *Journalism Quarterly* 61 (Spring 1984): 66–75, 82.

3. Herbert J. Gans, *Deciding What's News* (New York: Pantheon Books, 1979), 295; and Carolyn Martindale, "Selected Newspaper Coverage of Causes of Black Protest," *Journalism Quarterly* 66 (Winter 1989): 964.

Also see Carolyn Martindale, *The White Press and Black America* (Westport, Conn.: Greenwood Press, 1986); Stuart Hall, "Deviance, Politics, and the Media," in *Deviance and Social Control,* eds. P. Rock and M. McIntosh (London: Tavistock, 1974); J. Halloran, P. Elliott, and G. Murdock, *Demonstrations and Communication: A Case Study* (Hammondsworth, England: Penguin, 1970); Gitlin, *Whole World Is Watching;* Paletz and Entman, *Media, Power, Politics;* and Shoemaker, "Deviant Political Groups."

4. Previous discussions that touch on media coverage of Newton and the Panthers can be found in Earl Anthony, *Picking Up the Gun: A Report on the Black Panthers* (New York: Dial, 1970); Michael Arlen, *An American Verdict* (Garden City, N.Y.: Doubleday, 1973); Black Panther Party, *All Power to the People: The Story of the Black Panther Party* (Oakland, Calif.: People's Press, 1970); Edward Epstein, "The Panthers and the Press," in *Between Fact and Fiction: The Problem of Journalism* (New York: Vintage, 1975), 33–77; G. Louis Heath, *Off the Pigs! The History and Literature of the Black Panther Party* (Metuchen, N.J.: Scarecrow Press, 1976); Gene Marine, *The Black Panthers* (New York: Signet Books, 1969), 67–76; Gilbert Stuart Moore, *A Special Rage: A Black Reporter's Encounter with Huey P. Newton's Murder Trial, the Black Panthers and His Own Destiny* (New York: Harper & Row, 1971); Bobby Seale, *Seize the Time: The Story of the Black Panther Party and Huey P. Newton* (New York: Random House, 1970); and Gail Sheehy, *Panthermania: The Clash of Black Against Black in One American City* (New York: Harper & Row, 1971).

5. Much of the following biographical information is taken from Moore, *A Special Rage;* Seale, *Seize the Time;* and Huey P. Newton, *Revolutionary Suicide* (New York: Harcourt, Brace, Jovanovich, 1973).

6. He embraced the doctrine of black self defense preached by Malcolm X: "It doesn't mean that I advocate violence, but at the same time I am not against using violence in self defense. I don't even call it violence when it's self defense; I call it intelligence." Malcolm X, *Malcolm X Speaks: Selected Speeches and Statements* (New York: Merit, 1965), 8. The line continues to inspire debate, crowing the finale of Spike Lee's film of racial politics, *Do the Right Thing.*

7. They flipped a coin; Seale won the right to be president and Newton became minister of defense.

8. The relationship between the Panthers and New York social circles was satirized in Tom Wolfe, *Radical Chic and Mau-Mauing the Flak Catchers* (New York: Farrar, Straus, 1970).

9. He was convicted of a lesser charge, voluntary manslaughter. This conviction was overturned on appeal and after two mistrials, charges were dropped. Excellent accounts of Newton's trial are given in Moore, *A Special Rage;* Arlen, *An American Verdict;* also see Murray Kempton, *The Briar Patch: The People of the State of New York v. Lumumba Shakur et al.* (New York: E. P. Dutton, 1973).

10. See Paul Chevigny, *Cops and Rebels: A Study of Provocation* (New York: Pantheon, 1972). Epstein, "The Panthers and the Press," discusses press coverage of confrontations between police and the Panthers and the evidence of a conspiracy between the FBI and state police against the Panthers. COINTELPRO, the FBI plan to disrupt the Panthers and other U.S. opposi-

tional groups, is discussed in William Keller, *The Liberals and J. Edgar Hoover* (Princeton: Princeton University Press, 1989); Athan Theoharis, *The Boss: J. Edgar Hoover and the Great American Inquisition* (Philadelphia: Temple University Press, 1988); Richard Gid Powers, *Secrecy and Power: The Life of J. Edgar Hoover* (New York: Free Press, 1987); also see David Garrow, *The FBI and Martin Luther King, Jr.: From "Solo" to Memphis* (New York: W. W. Norton, 1981).

11. His dissertation was entitled, "War Against the Panthers: A Study of Repression in America."

12. The next day, Tyrone Robinson, 25, was arrested and charged with murder. An Associated Press wire report said the killing was an attempt by Robinson "to make a name for himself in the Black Guerilla Family, a drug-running prison gang." See "Suspect in Newton Shooting Held," Associated Press, 27 August 1989.

13. The newspapers analyzed were *Atlanta Constitution, Houston Post, Kansas City Times, New York Times, Los Angeles Times, San Francisco Chronicle, St. Louis Post-Dispatch, The Tribune* of Oakland, *Tulsa World, USA Today, Wall Street Journal,* and *Washington Post.* The dates examined were 22 and 23 August 1989.

Ten papers carried the story on the front-page, a testimony to Newton's enduring status; the two other papers, the *Washington Post* and *USA Today,* noted the death on the front page but placed the story inside.

Seven of the newspapers relied upon some combination of Associated Press and other wire service reports for their lead accounts; most of these papers supplemented the lead report with staff sidebars. Five of the papers, the *San Francisco Chronicle, The Tribune, Los Angeles Times, Washington Post,* and *USA Today,* used accounts attributed solely to their own staffs.

14. The following discussion is drawn from Burke's work in *Language as Symbolic Action* (Berkeley: University of California Press, 1966); *A Grammar of Motives* (Berkeley: University of California Press, 1969); *Dramatism and Development* (Barre, Mass.: Clark University Press, 1972); *The Philosophy of Literary Form* (Berkeley: University of California Press, 1973); "Dramatism," in James Combs and Michael Mansfield, eds. *Drama in Life* (New York: Hastings House, 1976), 7–17; *Permanence and Change,* 3d ed. (Berkeley: University of California Press, 1984).

15. Burke, *Philosophy of Literary Form,* 1.

16. Ibid., 89.

17. Ibid., 302. The strategies of texts, Burke notes, do not necessarily correspond to strategies of authors. Texts are products of cultural conventions, editorial restrictions, and other forces that may be partially unconscious and not fully understood by writers or their editors. For Burke, the question is not what does the author mean to say but: What does the text mean?

18. Carey relies on Burke's work in much of "The Communications Revolution and the Professional Communicator," *The Sociological Review Monograph* 13 (January 1969): 23–38; "Journalism and Criticism: The Case of an Undeveloped Profession," *The Review of Politics* 36 (April 1974): 227–49; "A Cultural Approach to Communication," *Communication* 2 (1975): 1–22; "The Press and the Public Discourse," *The Center Magazine* 20 (March–April 1987): 4–32; *Communication as Culture: Essays on Media and Society* (Boston: Unwin Hyman, 1989).

19. Carey, "Journalism and Criticism," 245.

20. Carey calls the reporter a *broker in symbols;* see "The Communications Revolution," 27.

21. Again, the notion of strategy does not ask what did the reporter mean to do but instead: How does the report accomplish its message? How does the report put forth its meaning?

22. Irony as "strategy" does not necessarily mean irony was used consciously by reporters or editors. Intent is not at issue; the possible meanings of news language is at issue.

23. "Black Panthers Leader Dies on Turf Where Work Began," *Kansas City Times,* 23 August 1989, A1.

24. "Huey Newton Found Shot to Death in Part of City Where He Began," *New York Times,* 23 August 1989, A15.

25. "Huey Newton, Head of Black Panthers, Found Shot to Death," *New York Times,* 23 August 1989, A1.

26. Paul Clancy, "Ex-'Panther' Slain," *USA Today,* 23 August 1989, A2.

27. "Huey Newton Slain; He was '60s Apostle of Black Militancy," *Atlanta Constitution,* 23 August 1989, A1.

28. Harry Harris, "The Final Chapter: Police Suspect Drugs Involved," *The Tribune,* 23 August 1989, A1.

29. Lori Olszewski and Rick DelVecchio, "Huey Newton Shot to Death in West Oakland," *San Francisco Chronicle,* 23 August 1989, A1.

30. Olszewski and DelVecchio, "Newton Shot to Death," *San Francisco Chronicle,* p. A1.

31. Ibid.; "Huey Newton Slain; Led Black Panthers," *St. Louis Post-Dispatch,* 23 August 1989, 1.

32. Cynthia Gorney, "Huey Newton, Cofounder of Black Panthers, Slain in Oakland," *Washington Post,* 23 August 1989, A6.

33. Ibid.

34. "Black Panthers Co-Founder Newton Dies in Shooting," *Houston Post,* 23 August 1989, A1.

35. "Huey P. Newton," *Wall Street Journal,* 23 August 1989, A1.

36. Mark A. Stein and Valarie Basheda, "Black Panther Founder Huey Newton Is Killed," *Los Angeles Times,* 23 August 1989, A1.

37. "Huey Newton," *New York Times,* A1.

38. Stein and Basheda, "Huey Newton Is Killed," *Los Angeles Times,* A1.

39. Harris, "Final Chapter," *The Tribune,* A1.

40. "Huey Newton Slain," *St. Louis Post-Dispatch,* 1.

41. Gorney, "Huey Newton," *Washington Post,* A6.

42. Harris, "Final Chapter," *The Tribune,* A1.

43. Olszewski and DelVecchio, "Newton Shot to Death," *San Francsico Chronicle,* A1.

44. Gorney, "Huey Newton," *Washington Post,* A6; William Brand and Larry Spears, "Friends and Foes Remember Newton: 'Visionary,' 'Thug,'" *The Tribune,* 23 August 1989, A2; "Huey Newton Slain," *St. Louis Post-Dispatch,* A18.

45. Olszewski and DelVecchio, "Newton Shot to Death," *San Francisco Chronicle,* A1.

46. Brand and Spears, "Friends and Foes," *The Tribune,* A2.

47. Clancy, "Ex-'Panther' Slain," *USA Today,* A2. The report was making a caustic allusion to the Panthers' support from liberal groups in the 1970s and Tom Wolfe's satirizing of that support in *Radical Chic and Mau-Mauing the Flak Catchers.* The disenchanted member of the "radical chic" is identified in the report as David Horowitz, former editor of *Ramparts* and author of *Destructive Generation: Second Thoughts about the '60s* (New York: Collier, 1989).

48. Gorney, "Huey Newton," *Washington Post,* A6.

49. "Black Panthers Co-Founder," *Houston Post,* A1.

50. "Huey Newton Slain," *Atlanta Constitution,* A1.

51. Dennis Hevesi, "Huey Newton Symbolized the Rising Black Anger of a Generation," *New York Times,* 23 August 1989, A15.

52. "Troubled Life of Huey Newton," *San Francisco Chronicle,* 23 August 1989, A12.

53. The site description is taken from the *Los Angeles Times.* As discussed below, the *Times* was the only newspaper to report the memorial scene. Stein and Basheda, "Huey Newton Is Killed," *Los Angeles Times,* A1, A3.

54. "A passerby pauses by some flowers that had been left at the spot where Huey Newton was slain in Oakland," *San Francisco Chronicle,* 23 August 1989, A1; *The Tribune* ran a small, one-column, uncaptioned photograph of a similar scene, 23 August 1989, A3.

55. Jacqueline Cutler, "People Remember Leadership and His Past," *The Tribune,* 23 August 1989, A2.

56. Stein and Basheda, "Huey Newton Is Killed," *Los Angeles Times,* A1, A3.

57. "Unidentified man lays flowers at spot where Huey Newton was slain," *Los Angeles Times,* 23 August 1989, A3.

58. Stein and Basheda, "Huey Newton Is Killed," *Los Angeles Times,* A3.

59. Burke, *Philosophy of Literary Form,* 1; and Carey, "Journalism and Criticism," 245.

60. Gitlin, *Whole World Is Watching,* 2; see also Stokely Carmichael and Charles Hamilton, *Black Power: The Politics of Liberation in America* (New York: Random House, 1967), 2–32; Robert F. Williams, "Every Freedom Movement Is Labeled 'Communist,'" in *Black Power: The Radical Response to White America,* ed. Thomas Wagstaff (Beverly Hills: Glencoe Press, 1969), 105–11.

61. Gitlin, *Whole World Is Watching.*

62. Marine, *The Black Panthers,* 69.

63. Moore, *Special Rage,* 258.

64. Burke, *Philosophy of Literary Form,* 89–90, 301–4.

65. Heath, *Off The Pigs!,* ix. A chapter in Martin Lee and Norman Solomon's *Unreliable Sources: A Guide to Detecting Bias in News Media* (New York: Carol Publishing, 1990) contains a brief paragraph that supports this study; these authors, too, charge the news media with bias in reporting Newton's death. The full notation on page 56 reads:

> When former Black Panther Party leader Huey Newton was gunned down in Oakland, stories and obituaries about Newton omitted important facts about his political history.
>
> According to the *Miami Herald,* "The Panthers eventually died out because of infighting, arrests, deaths, imprisonments and differing philosophies" among leaders of the group. The article made no reference to the FBI's COINTELPRO program which secretly targeted the Black Panther Party for destruction. Nor did the *Herald* mention the assassination of key party leaders, including Fred Hampton, who was murdered in bed by Chicago police.

Multicultural Perspectives on Death and Dying

NANCY SCHEPER-HUGHES, *Death Without Weeping: The Violence of Everyday Life in Brazil* (Berkeley: University of California Press, 1992). Excerpts from pages 268–69, 286–91, 400, 403–6, and 416–33 reprinted by permission of the author and the Regents of the University of California. Copyright © 1992.

Notes

1. Carolina Maria De Jesus, *Child of the Dark* (trans. of *Quarto de Despejo,* 1960; New York: Dutton, 1962), 108.

2. Elie Wiesel, *From the Kingdom of Memory: Reminiscences* (New York: Summit Books, 1990), 174.

3. *United Nations Convention on the Rights of the Child,* 1989.

4. Denise Levertov, "What Were They Like?" in *Poems, 1968–1972* (New York: New Directions, 1987), 123.

5. Lawrence Kohlberg, *The Philosophy of Moral Development: Moral Stages and the Idea of Justice* (San Francisco: Harper & Row, 1981).

6. Carol Gilligan, *In a Different Voice: Psychological Theory and Women's Development* (Cambridge, Mass.: Harvard University Press, 1982).

7. Garrett Hardin, "Living on a Lifeboat," *BioScience* 24, no. 10 (1974): 561–68.

8. Gilberto Freyre, *The Mansions and the Shanties: The Making of Modern Brazil* (trans. of *Casa-Grande e Senzala,* 1933; Berkeley and Los Angeles: University of California Press, 1986), 58.

9. Gilberto Freyre, *The Masters and the Slaves: A Study in the Development of Brazilian Civilization* (trans. of *Sobrados e Macombos,* 1936; Berkeley and Los Angeles: University of California Press, 1986), 144.

10. Ibid., 388.

11. Euclides Da Cunha, *Rebellion in the Backlands* (trans. of *Os Sertões,* 1904; Chicago: University of Chicago Press, 1944), 113.

12. See George M. Foster, "The Ritual Death in Spanish America," in *Culture and Conquest: America's Spanish Heritage* (New York: Viking Fund, 1960), 143–66; John Schechter, "Corona y Baile: Music in the Child's Wake of Ecuador and Hispanic America, Past and Present," *Revista de Música Latino Americano* 4, no. 1 (1983): 1–80; John Schechter, *Velorio de Angelito/Baquiné/Wawa Velorio: The Emblematic Nature of the Transcultural, Yet Local, Latin American Child's Wake,* Latin American Studies Working Papers, no. 3 (Santa Cruz: University of California, 1988); James Belote and Linda Belote, "Suffer the Little Children: Death, Autonomy, and Responsibility in a Changing Low Technology Environment," *Science, Technology, and Human Values* 9, no. 4 (1984): 35–48; Luis Arturo Dominguez, *Velorio de Angelito,* 2d ed. (Caracas: Ediciones del Ejecutivo del Estado Trujillo, Imprenta Oficial Estado Trujillo, 1960); Rodolfo Lenz, "Velorio de Angelito," in *Antologiá Ibérica Americana del Folklore,* ed. Félix Coluccio (Buenos Aires: Guillermo Kraft, 1953), 115–18.

13. Roger Bastide, *The African Religions in Brazil* (Baltimore: Johns Hopkins University Press, 1978).

14. Freyre, *Masters and Slaves,* 388.

15. Schecter, "Corona y Baile."

16. Marilyn Nations and Linda-Anne Rebhun, "Angels with Wet Wings Can't Fly: Maternal Sentiment in Brazil and the Image of Neglect," *Culture, Medicine, and Psychiatry* 12 (1988): 141–200.

17. Freyre, *Masters and Slaves,* 388.

18. Dominguez, *Velorio de Angelito,* 31.

19. See Alfredo Ebelot, *La Pampa: Costumbres Argentinas* (Buenos Aires: Alfer and Vays, 1943); and Baldomero Lillo, "El Angelito," in *Relatos Populares* (Santiago de Chile: Nascimento, 1942), 219–34.

20. See Donald Woods Winnicott, *The Child, the Family, and the Outside World* (London: Penguin, 1964), 167–72.

21. John Bowlby, "Childhood Mourning and Its Implications for Psychiatry," *Journal of American Psychiatry* 118 (1961): 481–98; John Bowlby, "Processes of Mourning," *International Journal of Psychoanalysis* 42 (1961): 317–40; John Bowlby, *Loss: Sadness and Depression* (New York: Basic Books, 1980); Elisabeth Kübler-Ross, *On Death and Dying* (New York: Macmillan, 1969); Robert Jay Lifton, *Death in Life* (New York: Touchstone, 1967); Robert Jay Lifton, "Preface," in Alexander Mitscherlich and Margaret Mitscherlich, *The Inability to Mourn* (New York: Grove, 1975), vii–xv; and Robert Jay Lifton, *The Broken Connection: On Death and the Continuity of Life* (New York: Simon and Schuster, 1979).

22. See Sigmund Freud, "Mourning and Melancholia," in *The Standard Edition of the Complete Psychological Works of Sigmund Freud,* vol. 14, ed. and trans., J. Strachey (London: Hogarth, 1957), 244–45; Bowlby, *Loss: Sadness and Depression;* and Lifton, *Death in Life.*

23. Marshall Klaus, personal communication.

24. Bowlby, *Loss,* 113–24.

25. J. Johnson, M. J. Cunningham, S. Ewing, D. Hatcher, and C. Dannen, *Newborn Death* (Omaha, Neb.: Centering Group, 1982).

26. Ibid., 1.

27. Ibid., 4.

28. Ibid., 8.

29. Bowlby, *Loss,* 139.

30. Helene Deutsch, "Absence of Grief," *Psychoanalytic Quarterly* 6 (1937): 12–22.

31. Bowlby, *Loss,* 139.

32. Lifton, "Preface," vii.

33. Renato Rosaldo, *Ilongot Headhunting, 1883–1974: A Study in Society and History* (Palo Alto, Calif.: Stanford University Press, 1980).

34. Catherine Lutz, *Unnatural Emotions* (Chicago: University of Chicago Press, 1988).

35. Repression refers to the pushing away from consciousness the unpleasant awareness of one's own (morally disallowed) aggressive or sexual impulses.

Denial is a defense mechanism that concerns disturbing perceptions of the real world, of external reality. If allowed to permeate the consciousness, such perceptions cause unbearable anxiety or profound displeasure. Instead, the individual may reframe the experience as minor and inconsequential through a turning away from, or a denial of, the reality itself. It is a way of protecting the self. I am not denying the existence of individual defense mechanisms or neuroses. But I am uncomfortable when psychodynamic concepts are applied to normative, cultural institutions and to collective ways of thinking and feeling. I am as reluctant to label all the women of the Alto do Cruzeiro who "fail" to grieve the death of their infants as manifesting a psychological condition of "denial" or "shellshock" or "posttraumatic stress" as of labeling all those adults who easily enter into "dissociative" religious possession and trance (whether devotees of Xango or evangelical Protestantism) as "hysterics." Reliance on such psychological terminology diminishes the human condition. Moreover, it serves as a shortcut (or short-circuit) analysis that allows one to think that the task of understanding is completed when it has only just begun.

36. See, for example, Ira Glick, Robert Weiss, and Colin Murray Parkes, *The First Year of Bereavement* (New York: John Wiley and Sons, 1974), 263–65; and Thomas Scheff, *Catharsis in Healing, Ritual and Drama* (Berkeley and Los Angeles: University of California Press, 1979).

37. See Gail Kligman, *The Wedding of the Dead* (Berkeley and Los Angeles: University of California Press, 1988); and Paul Rosenblatt, Patricia Walsh, and Douglas Jackson, *Grief and Mourning in Cross-Cultural Perspective* (New Haven, Conn.: HRAF Press, 1976), 26–27.

38. See Susan Sontag, *Illness as Metaphor* (New York: Farrar, Straus, and Giroux, 1979).

39. Nations and Rebhun, "Angels with Wet Wings," 158.

40. Ibid., 160.

41. Ibid., 158.

42. Ibid., 141.

43. I am not so radical as to suggest that there are no constituted human drives for sex, attachment, and so on; rather, I mean to say that as compared with other species, human instinctual rituals are remarkably insecure and transient. Humans are not social automatons; it is our freedom from specific behavior patterns—our biological as well as our cultural "openness"—that represents our evolutionary heritage. While we have instinctual needs, the "objects" of our drives and the timing of our desires are shaped by experience and culture.

44. Lutz, *Unnatural Emotions*; Lila Abu-Lughod, *Veiled Sentiments: Honor and Poetry in a Bedouin Society* (Berkeley and Los Angeles: University of California Press, 1986).

45. Rosaldo, *Ilongot Headhunting*.

46. Renato Rosaldo, "Grief and a Headhunter's Rage: On the Cultural Force of Emotion," in *Text, Play, and Story*, ed. Steven Plathner and Edward Bruner (Washington: American Ethnological Society, 1983), 180.

47. Ibid., 179.

48. Thomas Gregor, "Infants Are Not Precious to Us: The Psychological Impact of Infanticide Among the Mehinaku Indians," Stirling Prize paper, annual meeting of the American Anthropological Association, Phoenix, November 1988, 6.

49. Ibid., 3.

50. Ibid., 6.

51. Ibid.

52. Ibid., 19.

53. Rosaldo, "Grief and a Headhunter's Rage."

JOSEPH M. KAUFERT AND JOHN D. O'NEIL, "Cultural Mediation of Dying and Grieving Among Native Canadian Patients in Urban Hospitals," in *Coping with the Final Tragedy: Cultural Variation in Dying and Grieving,* ed. David R. Counts and Dorothy A. Counts (Amityville, N.Y.: Baywood, 1991), 231–51. Adapted by permission of the authors and Baywood Publishing Co. Copyright © 1991.

Notes

1. P. Palgi and H. Abramovitch, "Death: A Cross-Cultural Perspective," in *Annual Review of Anthropology* no. 13, ed. B. Siegel (Palo Alto, Calif.: Annual Reviews, 1984), 385–417.

2. B. G. Glaser and A. Strauss, *Awareness of Dying* (Chicago: Aldine, 1965).

3. B. G. Glaser and A. Strauss, *Time for Dying* (Chicago: Aldine, 1968).

4. J. Kaufert and W. Koolage, "Role Conflict Among Culture Brokers: The Experience of Native Canadian Medical Interpreters," *Social Science and Medicine* 18 (1984): 283–86.

5. Ibid.

6. J. Kaufert, J. O'Neil, and W. Koolage, "Cultural Brokerage and Advocacy in Urban Hospitals: The Impact of Native Language Interpreters," *Sante, Culture, Health* 3, no. 2 (1985): 2–9.

7. E. Kübler-Ross, *On Death and Dying* (New York: Macmillan, 1969).

8. Kaufert and Koolage, "Role Conflict Among Culture Brokers."

9. E. Goffman, *Asylums: Essays on the Social Situation of Mental Patients and Other Inmates* (Garden City, N.Y.: Anchor, 1961).

10. I. K. Zola, "Medicine as an Institution of Social Control: The Medicalizing of Society," *Sociological Review* 29, no. 4 (1973): 487–504.

11. A. Strauss, S. Fagerhaugh, B. Suczek, and C. Wiener, *The Social Organization of Medical Work* (Chicago: University of Chicago Press, 1986).

12. Kübler-Ross, *On Death and Dying.*

13. J. D. O'Neil, "Referrals to Traditional Healers: The Role of Medical Interpreters," in *Health Care Issues in Northern Canada,* ed. D. Young (Edmonton: Boreal Institute Press, 1988), 29–38.

14. A. I. Hollowell, *Culture and Experience* (Philadelphia: University of Pennsylvania Press, 1955).

15. A. I. Hollowell, "The Passing of the Midewiwin in the Lake Winnepeg Region," *American Anthropologist* 38 (1936): 32–51.

CHRISTOPHER L. HAYES AND RICHARD A. KALISH, "Death-Related Experiences and Funerary Practices of the Hmong Refugee in the United States," *Omega: Journal of Death and Dying* 18, no. 1 (1987–1988): 63–70. Reprinted by permission of the authors and Baywood Publishing Co. Copyright © 1987.

Notes

1. V. L. Bengston et al., "Statum Contrasts and Similarities in Attitudes Toward Death," *Journal of Gerontology* 32 (1977): 76–88; R. A. Kalish and D. K. Reynolds, *Death and Ethnicity: A Psychocultural Study* (Los Angeles: University of Southern California Press, 1976; reprint, Farmingdale, N.Y.: Baywood Publishing, 1981); K. B. Bryer, "The Amish Way of Death," *American Psychologist* 34 (1979): 255–61; J. Moore, "The Death Culture of Mexico and Mexican Americans," *Omega: Journal of Death and Dying* 1 (1970): 271–91; P. Osuna and D. K. Reynolds, "A Funeral in Mexico: Description and Analysis," *Omega: Journal of Death and Dying* 1 (1970): 249–69; A. C. Hill, "The Impact of Urbanism on Death and Dying Among Black People in a Rural Community in Tennessee," *Omega: Journal of Death and Dying* 14 (1983–1984): 171–86; and T. F. Garrity and J. Wyss, "Death, Funeral, and Bereavement Practices in Appalachian and Non-Appalachian Kentucky," *Omega: Journal of Death and Dying* 7 (1976): 209–28.

2. C. Baldwin, *Capturing the Change* (Santa Ana, Calif.: Immigrant and Refugee Planning Center, 1982).

3. W. E. Garrett, "No Place to Run: The Hmong of Laos," *National Geographic,* January 1974, 78–111; T. Vang, *The Hmong of Laos* (Hawthorne, Calif.: Cultural Friendship Center, 1981).

4. Y. Dao, "Why Did the Hmong Leave Laos?" in *The Hmong in the West,* ed. D. Olney (Center for Southeastern Asian Refugee Studies Project, University of Minnesota, 1982), 3–18; and *Newsweek,* 1 December 1977.

5. Dao, "Why Did the Hmong Leave Laos?"

6. R. J. Lifton, *Death in Life: Survivors of Hiroshima* (New York: Random House, 1967).

7. T. Des Pres, *The Survivor* (New York: Oxford University Press, 1976); and H. Epstein, *Children of the Holocaust* (New York: G. P. Putnam's Sons, 1979).

8. C. L. Hayes, "A Study of the Older Hmong Refugees in the United States" (Ph.D. diss., University Microfilms, 1984); and R. J. Kastenbaum, "Death and Bereavement in Later Life," in *Death and Bereavement,* ed. A. H. Kutscher (Springfield, Ill.: C. C. Thomas, 1969).

9. *Science,* 29 May 1981.

10. A. D. Weisman and T. P. Hackett, "Predilection to Death," *Psychomatic Medicine* 23 (1961): 232–56; and R. A. Kalish, "Non-medical Interventions in Life and Death," *Social Science and Medicine* 4 (1970): 655–65.

11. Vang, *The Hmong of Laos;* Hayes, "Study of Older Hmong Refugees"; G. Betts, "Social Life of the Miao Tsi," *Shanghai Journal* 2 (1899); L. Barney, "The Hmong of Northern Laos," *Indochinese Refugee Education Guides* (Washington: Center for Applied Linguistics, 1967); and W. Geddes, *Migrants of the Mountains* (Oxford: Clarendon Press, 1976).

12. Barney, "The Hmong of Northern Laos."

13. H. Chindarsi, *The Religion of the Hmong Njua* (Bangkok: Dompong Press, 1976).

14. Barney, "The Hmong of Northern Laos."

RONALD K. BARRETT, "Contemporary African-American Funeral Rites and Traditions," from *Death, Grief, and Funeral Ritual in the African-American Experience* by Ronald K. Barrett. Forthcoming. Published by permission of the author. Copyright © 1994 by Ronald Keith Barrett.

Notes

1. Ronald K. Barrett, "Psychocultural Influences on African American Attitudes Towards Death, Dying, and Funeral Rites," in *Personal Care in an Impersonal World,* ed. John Morgan (Amityville, N.Y.: Baywood Press, 1993), 378–413.

2. Jonathan Olumide Lucas, *Religions in West Africa and Ancient Egypt* (Lagos: Nigerian National Press, 1970), 263–76; Elaine Nichols, ed. *The Last Miles of the Way: African-American Homegoing Traditions, 1890–Present* (Columbia: South Carolina State Museum, 1989).

3. Hylan Lewis, "Blackways of Kent: Religion and Salvation in *The Black Church in America,* ed. Hart M. Nelson, Raytha L. Yokley, and Anne K. Nelson (New York: Basic Books, 1971), 100–18; Frank S. Mead and Samuel S. Hill, *Handbook of Denominations in the United States,* 8th ed. (Nashville: Abington, 1985); Julia C. Furtam, ed., *Black Americans Information Directory,* 1992–93 (Detroit: Gale Research, 1992), 131–56.

4. Jerome Taylor, "Proposal for a Taxonomy of Racism," *Bulletin of the Menninger Clinic* 35 (1971): 421–28; Jerome Taylor, "One Hundred and Forty-four Conceptual Varieties of Racialism: Research Strategies and Practical Implications" (unpublished paper, 1971); Ronald K. Barrett, "A Study of Attributed Responsibility as a Function of Internal-External Locus of Control and Interracial Person" (master's thesis, University of Pittsburgh, 1974); and Francis Terrell, "The Development of an Inventory to Measure Aspects of Black Nationalism Ideology" (Ph.D. dissertation, University of Pittsburgh, 1972).

5. Nichols, *Last Miles of the Way.*

6. Ibid.

7. Hans Abrahamsson, *The Origin of Death: Studies in African Mythology* (Uppsala, Sweden: Almgvist, 1951); Lucas, *Religions in West Africa;* Vincent Mulago, "Vital Participation: The Cohesive Principle of the Bantu Community," in *Biblical Revelation and African Beliefs,* ed. Kwesi Dickson and Paul Ellingsworth (London: Butterworth Press, 1979), 137–58; and Kofi Asare Opoku, "African Perspectives on Death and Dying," in *Perspectives on Death and Dying: Cross-Cultural and Multi-disciplinary Views,* ed. Arthur Berger et al. (Philadelphia: Charles Press, 1989), 14–23.

8. John S. Mbiti, *African Religions and Philosophy* (London: Heinemann, 1969); Lucas, *Religions in West Africa;* Georges Balandier and Jacques Maquet, eds., *Dictionary of Black African Civilization* (New York: Leon Amiel, 1974); Ronald K. Barrett, "Psychocultural Influences on African American Attitudes."

9. Lucas, *Religions in West Africa;* Ikenga Emefie Metuh, *God and Man in African Religion: A Case Study of the Igbo of Nigeria* (London: G. Chapman, 1982).

10. Nichols, *Last Miles of the Way;* Dominique Zahan, *The Religion, Spirituality, and Thought of Traditional Africa,* trans. Kate E. Martin and Lawrence M. Martin (Chicago: University of Chicago Press, 1979).

11. Lucas, *Religions in West Africa.*

12. Ibid.; Mulago, "Vital Participation."

13. Alan Lomax, "The Homogeneity of African and Afro-American Musical Style," in *Afro-American Anthropology: Contemporary Perspectives,* ed. Norman E. Whitten and John F. Szwed (New York: Free Press, 1970), 181–202.

14. Lucas, *Religions in West Africa.*

15. Edward G. Parrinder, *African Mythology* (London: Paul Hamlyn, 1967); Lucas, *Religions in West Africa;* Nichols, *Last Miles of the Way;* Barrett, "Psychocultural Influences on African American Attitudes."

16. Lucas, *Religions in West Africa;* Mulago, "Vital Participation," Opoku, "African Perspectives on Death and Dying."

17. Barrett, "Psychocultural Influences on African American Attitudes."

18. Lucas, *Religions in West Africa;* Nichols, *Last Miles of the Way;* Barrett, "Psychocultural Influences on African American Attitudes."

19. Richard R. Kalish and David K. Reynolds, *Death and Ethnicity: A Psychocultural Study* (Farmingdale, N.Y.: Baywood Press, 1981).

20. Howard C. Raether, "The Place of the Funeral: The Role of the Funeral Director in Contemporary America," *Omega: Journal of Death and Dying,* 2 (1971): 151–53.

21. Ibid.; Cynthia Connor, "Archaeological Analysis of African-American Mortuary Behavior," in Nichols, ed., *Last Miles of the Way,* 51–55.

22. Barrett, "Psychocultural Influences on African American Attitudes."

23. Ronald K. Barrett, "Urban Adolescent Homicidal Violence: An Emerging Public Health Concern," *The Urban League Review* 16, no. 2 (1993): 67–75.

24. Ronald K. Barrett, "African-American Homicide and Suicide: A Closer Look at Who Is at Risk," *The American Black Male* (Part I) 3, no. 2 (April–May 1991): 4–8; and (Part II) 3, no. 3 (June–July 1991): 4–6.

25. David G. Mandelbaum, "Social Uses of Funeral Rites," in *The Meaning of Death,* ed. Herman Feifel (New York: McGraw-Hill, 1959), 189–217.

26. Lucas, *Religions in West Africa;* Elizabeth A. Fenn, "Honoring the Ancestors: Kongo-American Graves in the American South," in Nichols, ed., *Last Miles of the Way,* 44–50; Herbert U. Fielding, "Mourning and Burying the Dead: Experiences of a Lawcountry Funeral Director," in Nichols, ed., *Last Miles of the Way,* 56–58.

27. Nichols, *Last Miles of the Way;* Barrett, "Psychocultural Influences on African American Attitudes."

28. Lotta R. Thomas, "Litany of Home-Going/Going Forth: The African Concept of Time, Eternity and Social Ontology," in Nichols, ed., *Last Miles of the Way,* 65.

29. Jack Goody, *Death, Property, and the Ancestors: A Study of the Mortuary Customs of the LoDagaa of West Africa* (London: Stock, 1962); Lucas, *Religions in West Africa;* Igor Kopytoff, "Ancestors as Elders in Africa," *Africa,* 41 (1971): 129–42; Zahan, *Religion, Spirituality, and Thought of Traditional Africa;* Opoku, "Death and Immortality in the African Religious Heritage," in *Death and Immortality in the Religions of the World,* ed. Paul Badham and Linda Badham (New York: Paragon House, 1987), 9–23.

30. Kalish and Reynolds, *Death and Ethnicity,* 94–119.

31. Nichols, *Last Miles of the Way.*

References

DeSpelder, Lynne Ann, and Albert Lee Strickland. *The Last Dance: Encountering Death and Dying,* 3d ed. Mountain View, Calif.: Mayfield, 1992.

Fulton, Robert. "The Sacred and the Secular: Attitudes of the American Public Toward Death, Funerals, and Funeral Directors." In *Death and Identity,* edited by Robert Fulton, 89–105. New York: John Wiley and Sons, 1965.

Green, Jennifer, and Michael Green. *Dealing with Death: Practices and Procedures.* New York: Chapman and Hall, 1992.

Idowu, E. Bolaji. *African Traditional Religion: A Definition.* London: SCM Press, 1973.

Jackson, Maurice. "The Black Experience with Death: A Brief Analysis Through Black Writing." *Omega: Journal of Death and Dying* 3, no. 3 (1972): 203–9.

Mbiti, John S. *Introduction to African Religion.* London: Heinemann, 1975.

Nangoli, Musamaali. *No More Lies About Africa: Here Is the Truth from an African.* East Orange, N.J.: African Heritage, 1988.

Parrinder, Edward G. *African Traditional Religion.* London: SPCK, 1962.

Pinkney, Alphonso. *Black Americans.* Englewood Cliffs, N.J.: Prentice-Hall, 1969.

Rosenblatt, Paul C. "Grief in Cross-Cultural and Historical Perspective." In *Death and Dying: A Quality of Life,* edited by Patricia F. Pegg and Erno Metza, 11–18. London: Pitman Press, 1981.

Part II: Social Issues

The Health Care System

DANIEL CALLAHAN, "The Limits of Medical Progress: A Principle of Symmetry," from *What Kind of Life: The Limits of Medical Progress* (New York: Simon and Schuster, 1990). Excerpt, pages 164–67, reprinted by permission of the author and Simon and Schuster. Copyright © 1990.

STANLEY JOEL REISER, "The Era of the Patient: Using the Experience of Illness in Shaping the Missions of Health Care," *Journal of the American Medical Association* 269, no. 8 (February 24, 1993): 1012–17. Reprinted by permission of the American Medical Association. Copyright © 1993.

Notes

1. T. Sydenham, "Medical Observations Concerning the History and Cure of Acute Diseases," in *The Works of Thomas Sydenham, M.D.,* vol. 1, trans. R. G. Latham (London: Sydenham Society, 1848–1850), 15.

2. S. J. Reiser, *Medicine and the Reign of Technology* (New York: Cambridge University Press, 1978).

3. K. Pearson, *The Grammar of Science,* 2d ed. (London: Adam and Charles Black, 1900).

4. T. R. Harrison, "The Value and Limitation of Laboratory Tests in Clinical Medicine," *Journal of the Medical Association of Alabama* 13 (1944): 381–84.

5. Pope Pius XII, "The Prolongation of Life," *The Pope Speaks* 4 (1958): 393–98.

6. D. Sanders and J. Dukeminier, "Medical Advance and Legal Lag: Hemodialysis and Kidney Transplantation," *UCLA Law Review* 15 (1968): 366–80.

7. *Roe v. Wade,* 410 U.S. 116 (1973).

8. H. K. Beecher, "Ethics and Clinical Research," *New England Journal of Medicine* 274 (1966): 1354–60.

9. American Hospital Association, "Statement on a Patient's Bill of Rights," *Hospitals* 47 (1973): 41.

10. S. Bok, "Directions for Care at the End of Life," *New England Journal of Medicine* 295 (1976): 367–69.

11. D. Neuhauser, "Ernest Amory Codman, M.D., and End Results of Medical Care," *International Journal of Technology Assessment in Health Care* 6 (1990): 307–25.

12. K. M. Lohr, "Outcome Measurement: Concepts and Questions," *Inquiry* 25 (1988): 37–50.

13. Canadian Medical Association, *Quality of Care: Issues and Challenges in the U.S.: A Literature Review* (Ottawa: Canadian Medical Association, 1992).

14. R. Geigle and S. B. Jones, "Outcomes Measurement: A Report from the Front," *Inquiry* 27 (1990): 7–13.

15. P. M. Ellwood, "Outcomes Management: A Technology of Patient Experience," *New England Journal of Medicine* 318 (1988): 1549–56.

16. T. L. Delbanco, "Enriching the Doctor-Patient Relationship by Inviting the Patient's Perspective," *Annals of Internal Medicine* 116 (1992): 414–17; and P. D. Cleary, S. Edgman-Levitan, M. Roberts, et al., "Patients Evaluate Their Hospital Care: A National Survey," *Health Affairs* 10 (Winter 1991): 254–66.

17. Beecher, "Ethics and Clinical Research"; and Bok, "Directions for Care."

18. S. Dentzer, "Doctor Wennberg's Uncertainty Principle," *Dartmouth Alumni Magazine,* May 1991, 16–26.

19. D. Yankelovich, *Coming to Public Judgment: Making Democracy Work in a Complex World* (Syracuse: Syracuse University Press, 1991).

20. Ibid.

21. *Evaluation of the Oregon Medicaid Proposal* (Washington: Office of Technology Assessment, 1992).

22. S. J. Reiser, "Consumer Competence and the Reform of American Health Care," *Journal of the American Medical Association* 267 (1992): 1511–15.

23. S. J. Reiser, "Administrative Case Rounds: Institutional Policies and Leaders Cast in a Different Light," *Journal of the American Medical Association* 266 (1991): 2127–28.

24. V. Havel, "The End of the Modern Era," *New York Times,* 1 March 1992, 15.

WILLIAM M. LAMERS, Jr., "Hospice: Enhancing the Quality of Life," *Oncology* 4, no. 5 (May 1990): 121–26. Reprinted by permission of *Oncology.* Copyright © 1990.

Notes

1. R. Fulghum, *All I Really Need to Know I Learned in Kindergarten* (New York: Villard Books, 1988).

2. C. Calland, "Iatrogenic Problems in End-Stage Renal Failure," *New England Journal of Medicine* 287, no. 7 (1972): 334–36.

3. N. Cousins, *A Celebration of Life* (New York: Harper and Row, 1974).

4. C. Aring, *The Understanding Physician* (Detroit: Wayne State University Press, 1971).

5. B. M. Mount, "Caring in Today's Health Care System," *Canadian Medical Association Journal* 119 (1978): 303–4.

6. S. Stoddard, *The Hospice Movement: A Better Way of Caring for the Dying* (New York: Stein and Day, 1977).

7. E. Hume, *Medical Work of the Knights Hospitalers of St. John of Jerusalem* (Baltimore: Johns Hopkins University Press, 1940).

8. G. Goldin, "A Protohospice at the Turn of the Century," *Journal of the History of Medicine and Allied Sciences* 36, no. 4 (1981): 383–415.

9. W. M. Lamers, "Hospice Care in North America," in *Cancer, Stress and Death,* ed. S. B. Day (New York: Plenum Publishing, 1986).

10. R. Nitschke, G. Humphrey, G. Bennett, et al., "Therapeutic Choices Made by Patients with End-Stage Cancer," *Journal of Pediatrics* 101, no. 3 (1982): 471–76.

11. E. Erikson, *Childhood and Society* (New York: Norton, 1950).

12. E. Lindemann, "The Symptomatology and Management of Acute Grief," *American Journal of Psychiatry* 101 (1944): 141–48.

13. D. Goleman, "Physicians Said to Persist in Undertreating Pain and Ignoring the Evidence," *New York Times,* 31 December 1987, B5.

14. Stoddard, *Hospice Movement,* Appendix C.

15. C. Saunders, personal communication, 1978.

16. R. Twycross, "How Whole Is Our Care?" remarks made at Seventh International Congress on Care of the Terminally Ill, Montreal, October 18, 1988.

BALFOUR M. MOUNT, "Keeping the Mission," *American Journal of Hospice and Palliative Care* 9, no. 5 (September–October 1992): 32–37. Reprinted, in slightly revised form, by permission of the author and the *American Journal of Hospice and Palliative Care.* Copyright © 1992.

Notes

1. S. du Boulay, *Cicely Saunders: The Founder of the Modern Hospice Movement* (London: Hodder and Stoughton, 1984), 172.

2. Ibid., 86.

3. Ibid., 90–91.

4. Ibid., 174.

5. Ibid.

6. C. Saunders, personal communication, 1978.

7. C. Saunders, *Hospice and Palliative Care: An Interdisciplinary Approach* (London: Edward Arnold, 1990).

8. du Boulay, *Cicely Saunders,* 100.

9. B. Bettelheim, *Home for the Heart* (London: Thames and Hudson, 1974); cited in du Boulay, *Cicely Saunders,* 135.

10. du Boulay, *Cicely Saunders,* 126.

11. Ibid., 126–27.

12. J. F. Potter, "A Challenge for the Hospice Movement," *New England Journal of Medicine* 302 (1980): 53–55.

13. L. F. Paradis and W. M. Usui, "Hospice Volunteers: The Impact of Personality Characteristics on Retention and Job Performance," *The Hospice Journal* 3, no. 1 (1987): 3–30.

14. S. Ahmedzai, review of V. Mor and S. Masterson-Allen, "A Comparison of Hospice vs. Conventional Care of the Terminally Ill Cancer Patient," *Oncology,* July 1990, 94–96.

15. V. Mor and S. Masterson-Allen, "A Comparison of Hospice vs. Conventional Care of the Terminally Ill Cancer Patient," *Oncology,* July 1990, 85–91.

16. C. Selinske, personal communication: results of informal survey of New York State hospice directors, March 1992.

17. R. Pye, "The First International Hospice Conference in India," *West Australia Palliative Care Newsletter* 38 (1991): 6.

18. G. Bonnyman, "Moral Malpractice," *Sojourners* 21, no. 3 (1992): 12–17.

19. "Equal Access to Health Care: Patient Dumping," a hearing before a subcommittee of the Committee on Government Operations, House of Representatives, 100th Cong., 22 July 1987, 14–16; Z. M. Hill, testimony before the Human Resources and Intergovernmental Relations Subcommittee of the House Committee on Government Operations, 100th Cong., 22 July 1987, 17; and *Wall Street Journal,* 29 November 1988, 1.

20. Bonnyman, "Moral Malpractice."

21. *The Health of America's Children: Maternal and Child Health Data Book* (Washington: Children's Defense Fund, 1989), 18.

22. Congress Research Service, Library of Congress, *Health Insurance and the Uninsured: Background Data and Analysis,* Energy and Commerce Committee print no. 100–X, 1988; U.S. Bipartisan Commission on Comprehensive Health Care, *Final Report: A Call to Action* (Washington: U.S. Government Printing Office, 1990), 21–23; and Office of Management and Budget, "Introductory Statement: The Problem of Rising Health Care Costs," presented before the Senate Finance Committee, 16 April 1992, 6–8.

23. P. Farley, *National Health Care Expenditures Study: Who Are the Underinsured?* (Washington: National Center for Health Services Research, 1984), 20.

24. D. Ansell and R. Schiff, "Patient Dumping: Status, Implications, and Policy Recommendations," *Journal of the American Medical Association* 257, no. 11 (1987): 1500–1502.

25. *Cancer and the Poor: A Report to the Nation* (Atlanta: American Cancer Society, 1990), 7.

26. E. Peden and M. Lee, "Output and Inflation Components of Medical Care and Other Spending Changes," *Health Care Financing Review* 14, no. 2 (1991): 75–81; and Bipartisan Commission, *Final Report,* 38.

27. *The Growing Threat to the Family Budget* (Washington: Families U.S.A. Foundation, 1991).

28. G. Bonnyman, results of July 1992 survey of the states, personal communication with D. Super, attorney, National Health Law Program, Washington; and *The States and the Poor: How Budget Decisions in 1991 Affect Low Income People* (Washington: Center

on Budget and Policy Priorities and Center for the Study of the States, 1991), 31–44.

29. Bipartisan Commission, *Final Report,* 42, 43.

30. "How Stock Funds Performed Last Year," *USA Today,* 7 January 1991, B3.

31. G. Pope and J. Schneider, "Trends in Physician Income," *Health Affairs* 11, no. 1 (1992): 181–94; and S. Rich, *Washington Post,* 21 May 1992.

32. Bonnyman, "Moral Malpractice."

33. Ibid.

34. S. Woolhandler and D. Himmelstein, "The Deteriorating Administrative Efficiency of the U.S. Health Care System," *New England Journal of Medicine* 324 (1991): 1253–58; and U.S. General Accounting Office, *Canadian Health Insurance: Lessons for the U.S.,* GAO/HRD 91–90 (Washington: U.S. Government Printing Office, June 1990).

35. *Hospital Statistics, 1985 Edition* (Chicago: American Hospital Association, 1985).

36. P. Ginsburg and D. Koretz, "Bed Availability and Hospital Utilization: Estimates of the 'Roemer Effect,'" *Health Care Financing Review* 5, no. 1 (1983): 87–92.

37. Bonnyman, "Moral Malpractice."

WILLIAM G. BARTHOLOME, "Care of the Dying Child: The Demands of Ethics," *Second Opinion* 18, no. 4 (April 1993): 25–39. Reprinted by permission of the Park Ridge Center for the Study of Health, Faith, and Ethics; Chicago. Copyright © 1993.

Notes

1. Philippe Ariès, *Western Attitudes Toward Death: From the Middle Ages to the Present* (Baltimore: Johns Hopkins University Press, 1974); Ernest Becker, *The Denial of Death* (New York: Free Press, 1973); Elisabeth Kübler-Ross, *On Death and Dying* (New York: Macmillan, 1969); and Elisabeth Kübler-Ross, *On Children and Death* (New York: Macmillan, 1983).

2. William Easson, *The Dying Child* (Springfield, Ill.: Charles C. Thomas, 1970); see also Susan Carey, *Conceptual Change in Childhood* (Cambridge, Mass.: M.I.T. Press, 1985); and Mark W. Speece and Sandor B. Brent, "Children's Understanding of Death: A Review of Three Components of a Death Concept," *Child Development* 55 (1984): 1671–86.

3. Gareth B. Matthews, "Children's Conceptions of Illness and Death," in *Children and Health Care: Moral and Social Issues,* ed. Loretta M. Kopelman and John C. Moskop (Boston: Kluwer Academic Publishers, 1989), 133–46.

4. Myra Bluebond-Langner, *The Private Worlds of Dying Children* (Princeton: Princeton University Press, 1978).

5. Albert J. Solnit and Morris P. Green, "The Pediatric Management of the Dying Child, Part II: The Child's Reaction to the Fear of Dying," in *Modern Perspectives in Child Development,* ed. Albert Solnit (New York: International Universities Press, 1963), 145–56; and Joel Vernick and Myron Karon, "Who's Afraid of Death on a Leukemia Ward?" *American Journal of Diseases of Children* 109 (1965): 393–97.

6. Eugenia H. Waechter, "Children's Awareness of Fatal Illness," *American Journal of Nursing* 71 (1971): 1168–72.

7. John J. Spinetta and Lorrie J. Maloney, "Death Anxiety in the Out-Patient Leukemic Child," *Pediatrics* 56 (1975): 1034–37.

8. John J. Spinetta and Patricia Deasy-Spinetta, eds., *Living with Childhood Cancer* (St. Louis: C. V. Mosby, 1981).

9. Paul Langham, "Parental Consent: Its Justification and Limitations," *Clinical Research* 27 (1979): 349–58; and Willard Gaylin and Ruth Macklin, *Who Speaks for the Child? The Problems of Proxy Consent* (New York: Plenum Press, 1982); see also Norman Fost, "Parents as Decision Makers for Children," *Primary Care* 13 (1986): 285–93.

10. William G. Bartholome, "A New Understanding of Consent in Pediatric Practice," *Pediatric Annals* 18 (1989), 262–65.

11. Gary B. Melton, G. P. Koocher, and M. J. Saks, eds., *Children's Competence to Consent* (New York: Plenum Press, 1983).

12. Dan W. Brock, "Children's Competence for Health Care Decisionmaking," in *Children and Health Care: Moral and Social Issues,* ed. Loretta M. Kopelman and John C. Moskop (Boston: Kluwer Academic Publishers, 1988), 181–212.

13. National Commission for the Protection of Human Subjects of Biomedical and Behavioral Research, *Report and Recommendations: Research Involving Children* (Washington: U.S. Government Printing Office, 1977).

Medical Ethics and Decision Making

Notes

1. Martin Heidegger, "Being and Time," in *Existentialism,* ed. Robert C. Solomon (New York: Modern Library, 1974), 116.

2. See generally L. Tad Cowley et al., "Care of the Dying: An Ethical and Historical Perspective," *Critical Care Medicine* 20 (1990): 1473.

3. See, for example, John A. Oesterle, *Ethics: The Introduction to Moral Science* (Englewood Cliffs, N.J.: Prentice-Hall, 1957), 198; and Michael Novak, *Free Persons and the Common Good* (Lanham, Md.: Madison Books, 1989).

4. Compared, for example, to France, where *l'etat* is thought to embody the common good and interest groups are viewed as self-serving. See David Wilsford, *Doctors and the State: The Politics of Health Care in France and the United States* (Durham, N.C.: Duke University Press, 1991), 56.

5. Charles J. Dougherty, "The Excesses of Individualism," *Health Progress* (January-February 1992): 22.

6. Recent books include Gary J. Dorrien, *Reconstructing the Common Good: Theology and the Social Order* (Maryknoll, N.Y.: Orbis Books, 1990); Novak, *Free Persons and the Common Good;* and Marcus G. Raskin, *The Common Good: Its Politics, Policies, and Philosophy* (New York: Routledge and Kegan Paul, 1986).

7. John Rawls, *A Theory of Justice* (Cambridge, Mass.: Harvard University Press, 1971), 233, 246.

8. Walter M. Bortz II, "The Trajectory of Dying: Functional Status in the Last Year of Life," *Journal of the American Geriatric Society* 38 (1990): 146.

9. James R. Webster and Celia Berdes, "Ethics and Economic Realities: Goals and Strategies for Care Towards the End of Life," *Archives of Internal Medicine* 150 (1990): 1795.

10. On hospice care see C. Brooks, "A Comparative Analysis of Medicare Home Care Cost Savings for the Terminally Ill," *Home Health Care Services Quarterly* 10 (1989): 79; Cathy C. Cutchins, "Making Room for Hospice," *Geriatric Nursing* (May–June 1991): 144; Olga Lechky, "In a Greying Canada, Hospice Care Is the Wave of the Future," *Canadian Medical Association Journal* 145 (1991): 1152; Jill Rhymes, "Hospice Care in America," *Journal of the American Medical Association* 264 (1990): 369; Robert J. Miller, "Hospice Care as an Alternative to Euthanasia," *Law, Medicine, and Health Care* (Spring-Summer 1992): 127; and Robert J. Miller, "Ethics and the Hospice Physician," *American Journal of Hospice and Palliative Care* (January-February 1991): 17.

11. Peter A. Singer and Fredrick H. Lowy, "Rationing, Patient Preferences, and the Cost of Care at the End of Life," *Archives of Internal Medicine* 152 (1992): 478, 479.

12. M. Campbell and B. Field, "Management of the Patient with Do Not Resuscitate Status: Compassion and Cost Containment," *Heart and Lung* 20 (1991): 345–48.

13. For an example of a nursing home-based hospice, see Cutchins, "Making Room for Hospice." See also Kathleen Nolan, "Do-Not-Hospitalize Orders: Whose Goals? What Purpose?" *Journal of Family Practice* 30 (1990): 31.

14. See generally Charles J. Dougherty, "Ethical Values at Stake in Health Care Reform," *Journal of the American Medical Association* 268 (1992): 2409.

15. See H. Pritchard, "Does Moral Philosophy Rest on a Mistake?" in *Readings in Ethical Theory,* 2d ed., ed. Wilfred Sellars and John Hospers (New York: Appleton-Century-Crofts, 1970), 86, describing the main insight of intuitionism.

16. American Geriatric Society Public Policy Committee, "Voluntary Active Euthanasia," *Journal of the American Geriatric Society* 39 (1991): 826; and Miller, "Hospice Care as an Alternative," 131.

17. See, for example, James Rachels, "Active and Passive Euthanasia," *New England Journal of Medicine* 292 (1975): 78, and the rejoinder in Thomas L. Beauchamp and James F. Childress, *Principles of Biomedical Ethics,* 3d ed. (New York: Oxford University Press, 1989), 136–50.

18. This is Aristotle's "Golden Mean." See Aristotle, *Nichomachean Ethics,* trans. Terence Irwin (Indianapolis: Hackett, 1985), 41–52.

19. See Daniel J. Callahan, "Aid-in-Dying: The Social Dimensions," *Commonweal,* supp. (September 1992): 12.

20. Miller, "Hospice Care as an Alternative," 128.

21. "Dutch Pediatricians Move to Address Infant Euthanasia," *American Medical News,* 14 September 1992, 6.

22. Ibid.

23. Carlos F. Gomez, "Euthanasia: Consider the Dutch," *Commonweal,* supp. (September 1992): 5.

Violence

DANIEL LEVITON, "Horrendous Death: Improving the Quality of Global Health," in *Horrendous Death, Health, and Well-Being,* ed. Daniel Leviton (New York: Hemisphere, 1991). Excerpt, pages 17–19, reprinted by permission of the author and Hemisphere Publishing Co. Copyright © 1991.

Notes

1. R. Lifton, *The Broken Connection* (New York: Simon and Schuster, 1979); W. Meissner, "Impending Nuclear Disaster: Psychoanalytic Perspectives," in *Psychoanalysis and the Nuclear Threat,* ed. H. Levine, D. Jacobs, and L. Rubin (Hillsdale, N.J.: Analytic Press, 1988), 89–110; and H. Segal, "Silence Is the Real Crime," in Levine, Jacobs, and Rubin, eds., *Psychoanalysis and the Nuclear Threat,* 35–58.

2. S. Freud, "Thoughts for the Times on War and Death," in *Civilisation, War, and Death: Sigmund Freud,* ed. J. Rickman (London: Hogarth Press, 1968), 1–25.

3. Ibid., 15.

4. E. Becker, *The Denial of Death* (New York: Free Press, 1973), 2.

5. Lifton, *Broken Connection,* 17.

6. National Center for Health Statistics, *Health, United States, 1986* (Washington: U.S. Government Printing Office, 1986).

7. M. Kidron and R. Segal, *The State of the World Atlas* (New York: Simon and Schuster, 1981); R. Sivard, *World Military and Social Expenditures, 1985* (Washington: World Priorities, 1985); and L. Brown, W. Chandler, C. Flavin, J. Jacobson, C. Pollock, S. Postel, L. Starke, and E. Wolf, *State of the World, 1987* (New York: W. W. Norton, 1987).

JAMES GARBARINO, "Challenges We Face in Understanding Children and War: A Personal Essay," *Child Abuse and Neglect* 17, no. 6 (1993): 787–93. Reprinted by permission of Elsevier Science, Ltd., Pergamon Imprint, Oxford, England. Copyright © 1993.

Notes

1. See J. Garbarino, "The Experience of Children in Kuwait: Occupation, War, and Liberation," *Child, Youth, and Family Services Quarterly* 14, no. 2 (1991): 2–3; J. Garbarino, *Toward a Sustainable Society: An Economic, Social and Environmental Agenda for Our Children's Future* (Chicago: Noble Press, 1992); J. Garbarino, N. Dubrow, K. Kostelny, and C. Pardo, *Children in Danger: Coping with the Consequences of Community Violence* (San Francisco: Jossey-Bass, 1992); J. Garbarino, K. Kostelny, and N. Dubrow, *No Place to Be a Child: Growing Up in a War Zone* (New York: Lexington/Macmillan, 1991); and J. Garbarino and E. Menvielle, *Interviews with Vietnamese Minors in Detention Camps in Hong Kong* (Chicago: Erikson Institute, 1992).

2. J. Davidson and R. Smith, "Traumatic Experiences of Psychiatric Outpatients," *Journal of Traumatic Stress Studies* 3, no. 3 (1990): 459–75.

3. Garbarino and Associates, *Children and Families in the Social Environment,* 2d ed. (Hawthorne, N.Y.: Aldine, 1992).

4. P. Greven, *Spare the Child: The Religious Roots of Punishment and the Psychological Impact of Physical Abuse* (New York: Alfred A. Knopf, 1991).

5. Garbarino, Kostelny, and Dubrow, *No Place to Be a Child.*

6. M. Drabble, *The Gates of Ivory* (New York: Viking, 1991).

7. E. Furman, *A Child's Parent Dies* (New Haven, Conn.: Yale University Press, 1974); and M. Wolfenstein, *Loss, Rage, and Repetition: Psychoanalytic Study of the Child* (New York: International Universities Press, 1969).

8. J. Garbarino, F. Stott, and the Faculty of the Erikson Institute, *What Children Can Tell Us: Eliciting, Interpreting, and Evaluating Information from Children* (San Francisco: Jossey-Bass, 1989).

9. S. Nowicki and M. Duke, *Helping the Child Who Doesn't Fit In: Deciphering the Hidden Dimensions of Social Rejection* (Atlanta: Peachtree Publications, 1992).

10. See Garbarino, *Toward a Sustainable Society;* and Garbarino, Kostelny, and Dubrow, *No Place to Be a Child.*

11. C. S. Lewis, *Out of the Silent Planet* (New York: Macmillan, 1944); *Perelandra* (New York: Macmillan, 1944); and *That Hideous Strength* (New York: Macmillan, 1946).

12. J. Garbarino, E. Guttman, and J. Seeley, *The Psychologically Battered Child: Strategies for Identification, Assessment, and Intervention* (San Francisco: Jossey-Bass, 1986).

13. J. Gilligan, "Shame and Humiliation: The Emotions of Individual and Collective Violence," paper presented at the Erikson Lectures, Harvard University, Cambridge, Mass., 23 May 1991.

14. N. Maclean, *Young Men and Fire* (Chicago: University of Chicago Press, 1992).

15. Garbarino, *Toward a Sustainable Society.*

16. C. Gilligan, *In a Different Voice: Psychological Theory and Women's Development* (Cambridge, Mass.: Harvard University Press, 1982).

17. B. Pasternak, *Doctor Zhivago* (New York: Alfred A. Knopf, 1991).

18. F. Dostoevsky, *The Brothers Karamazov* (New York: Modern Library, 1929).

Suicide

Notes

1. J. M. Stillion, E. E. McDowell, and M. J. May, *Suicide Across the Life Span: Premature Exits* (New York: Hemisphere, 1989).

2. N. Farberow, ed., *Suicide in Different Cultures* (Baltimore: University Park Press, 1975).

3. Even as recently as 1860, we find an account of a man who was resuscitated after having cut his throat in a suicide attempt only to be hanged for attempting suicide; see A. Alvarez, *The Savage God: A Study of Suicide* (New York: Random House, 1970).

4. J. Merian, "*Sur la crainte de la mort, sur le mepris de la mort, sur le suicide, memoire*" ("About the Fear of Death, About Contempt for Death, About Suicide, Recollection"), in *Histoire de l'Academie Royale des Sciences et Belles-Lettres de Berlin,* vol. 19 (1763); see E. Esquirol, *Mental Maladies: A Treatise on Insanity* (1838; reprint, New York: Hafner, 1965).

5. E. Durkheim, *Suicide,* trans. J. A. Spaulding and G. Simpson (1897; reprint, Glencoe, Ill.: Free Press, 1951).

6. S. Freud, "Mourning and Melancholia," in *The Standard Edition of the Complete Psychological Works of Sigmund Freud,* vol. 14, ed. and trans., J. Strachey (London: Hogarth, 1961), 243–58.

7. See, for example, M. Asberg, L. Traskman, and P. Thoren, "5–HIAA in the Cerebrospinal Fluid: A Biochemical Suicide Predictor," *Archives of General Psychiatry* 33 (1976): 1193–97; and M. Asberg and L. Traskman, "Studies of CSF 5–HIAA in Depression and Suicidal Behavior," *Experiments in Medical Biology* 133 (1981): 739–52.

8. See, for example, A. T. Beck, A. Rush, B. Shaw, and G. Emery, *Cognitive Therapy of Depression* (New York: Guilford Press, 1979).

9. See, for example, R. W. Maris, *Pathways to Suicide: A Survey of Self-Destructive Behaviors* (Baltimore: Johns Hopkins University Press, 1981).

10. Stillion, McDowell, and May, *Suicide Across the Life Span.*

11. M. S. Gold, *Good News About Depression* (New York: Bantam Books, 1986).

12. Asberg and Traskman, "Studies of CSF 5–HIAA"; C. M. Banki and M. Arato, "Amine Metabolites, Neuroendocrine Findings, and Personality Dimension as Correlates of Suicidal Behavior," *Psychiatry Research* 10 (1983): 253–61; and J. J. Schildkraut, "The Catecholamine Hypothesis of Affective Disorders: A Review of Supporting Evidence," *American Journal of Psychiatry* 122 (1965): 509–22.

13. Asberg, Traskman, and Thoren, "5–HIAA in Cerebrospinal Fluid."

14. Ibid.

15. S. J. Blumenthal and D. J. Kupfer, "Generalizable Treatment Strategies for Suicidal Behavior," in *Psychobiology of Suicidal Behavior,* ed. J. J. Mann and M. Stanley (New York: New York Academy of Sciences, 1986), 327–40.

16. Gold, *Good News About Depression.*

17. R. Unger, *Female and Male Psychological Perspectives* (New York: Harper and Row, 1979); E. E. Maccoby and C. M. Jacklin, *The Psychology of Sex Differences* (Palo Alto, Calif.: Stanford University Press, 1974); K. B. Hoyenga and K. T. Hoyenga, *The Question of Sex Differences* (Boston: Little, Brown, 1979); J. Money and A. Ehrhardt, *Man and Woman, Boy and Girl* (Baltimore: Johns Hopkins University Press, 1972); R. W. Goy and J. A. Resko, "Gonadal Hormones and Behavior of Normal and Pseudohermaphrodetic Non-human Female Primates," in *Recent Progress in Hormone Research,* ed. E. Astwood (New York: Academic Press, 1972); B. Svare and R. Gandelman, "Aggressive Behavior of Juvenile Mice: Influence of Androgen and Olfactory Stimuli," *Developmental Psychobiology* 8 (1975): 405–15; and G. Mitchell, *Sex Differences in Non-human Primates* (New York: Van Nostrand Reinhold, 1979).

18. H. S. Akiskal and W. T. McKinney, "Depressive Disorders: Toward a Unified Hypothesis," *Science* 218 (1973): 20–29.

19. R. D. Wetzel, "Hopelessness, Depression, and Suicide Intent," *Archives of General Psychiatry* 33 (1976): 1069–73; R. D. Goldney, "Attempted Suicide in Young Women: Correlate of Lethality," *British Journal of Psychiatry* 139 (1981): 382–90; and A. E. Kazdin, N. H. French, A. S. Unis, K. Esveldt-Dawson, and R. B. Sherick, "Helplessness, Depression, and Suicidal Intent Among Psychiatrically Disturbed Inpatient Children," *Journal of Consulting and Clinical Psychology* 51 (1983): 504–10.

20. Maris, *Pathways to Suicide,* xviii-xix.

21. J. Piaget and B. Inhelder, *The Psychology of the Child* (New York: Basic Books, 1969).

22. D. Meichenbaum, *Stress Innoculation Training* (Elmsford, N.Y.: Pergamon Press, 1985).

23. Beck, Rush, Shaw, and Emery, *Cognitive Therapy of Depression.*

24. As an aside, males seem to view suicide attempts more negatively than do females; see J. White and J. M. Stillion, "Sex Differences in Attitudes Toward Suicide: Do Males Stigmatize Males?," *Psychology of Women Quarterly* 12 (1988): 357–66.

25. E. W. Bock and I. L. Webber, "Social Status and Relational Systems of Elderly Suicides: A Reexamination of the Henry-Short Thesis," *Suicide and Life-Threatening Behavior* 2 (1972): 145–59; B. D. Garfinkel, A. Froese, and J. Hood, "Suicide Attempts in Children and Adolescents," *American Journal of Psychiatry* 139 (1982): 1257–61; and C. R. Pfeffer, *The Suicidal Child* (New York: Guilford Press, 1986).

26. J. B. Stephens, "Suicidal Women and Their Relationships with Husbands, Boyfriends, and Lovers," *Suicide and Life-Threatening Behavior* 15 (1985): 77–89.

27. R. W. Hudgens, "Preventing Suicide," *New England Journal of Medicine* 308 (1983): 897–98.

28. R. W. Maris, "Suicide Intervention: The Existential and Biomedical Perspectives," in *Suicide: Understanding and Responding,* ed. D. Jacobs and H. N. Brown (Madison, Conn.: International Universities Press, 1989), 450.

29. E. S. Shneidman, *Definition of Suicide* (New York: John Wiley and Sons, 1985).

30. For a more complete discussion, refer to Stillion, McDowell, and May, *Suicide Across the Life Span.*

31. Pfeffer, *Suicidal Child.*

32. E. H. Erikson, *Identity and the Life Cycle* (New York: International Universities Press, 1959).

33. R. White, "Motivation Reconsidered: The Concept of Competence," *Psychological Review* 66 (1959): 297–333.

34. G. S. Hall, *Adolescence* (New York: Appleton, 1904).

35. D. J. Levinson, D. Darrow, E. Klein, M. Levinson, and B. McKee, *The Seasons of a Man's Life* (New York: Alfred A. Knopf, 1978).

36. M. Nagy, "The Child's Theories Concerning Death," *Journal of Genetic Psychology* 73 (1948): 3–27; H. L. Swain, "Childhood Views of Death," *Death Education* 2 (1979): 341–58; H. Wass and C. Corr, *Childhood and Death* (Washington: Hemisphere, 1984); and H. Wass and J. M. Stillion, "Death in the Lives of Children and Adolescents," in *Dying: Facing the Facts,* ed. H. Wass, F. M. Berardo, and R. A. Neimeyer (Washington: Hemisphere, 1988), 201–8.

37. D. Elkind and R. Bowen, "Imaginary Audience Behavior in Children and Adolescents," *Developmental Psychology* 15 (1979): 38–44.

38. G. Sheehy, *Passages: Predictable Crises of Adult Life* (New York: Dutton, 1976).

39. See, for example, R. L. Gould, *Transformations: Growth and Change in Adult Life* (New York: Simon and Schuster, 1978).

40. See, for example, J. W. Santrock, *Adult Development and Aging* (Dubuque, Iowa: William C. Brown, 1985).

41. G. W. Brown and T. Harris, *Social Origins of Depression* (London: Tavistock, 1978).

42. W. Breed, "Occupational Mobility and Suicide Among White Males," *American Sociological Review* 28 (1963): 179–88; Maris, *Pathways to Suicide;* and E. H. Powell, "Occupation, Status, and Suicide: Toward a Redefinition of Anomie," *American Sociological Review* 23 (1958): 131–39.

43. D. Hull, "Migration, Adaptation, and Illness: A Review," *Social Science and Medicine* 13 (1979): 25–36.

44. P. M. Marzuk, H. Tierney, K. Tardiff, E. M. Gross, E. B. Morgan, M. Hsu, and J. J. Mann, "Increased Risk of Suicide in Persons with AIDS," *Journal of the American Medical Association* 259 (1988): 1333–37.

45. A. Roy and M. Linnoila, "Alcoholism and Suicide," in *Biology of Suicide,* ed. R. Maris (New York: Guilford Press, 1986), 162–91. The rate of suicide for alcoholics has been estimated to be around 170 per 100,000 population; see C. Miles, "Conditions Predisposing to Suicide: A Review," *Journal of Nervous and Mental Disease* 164 (1977): 231–46. The typical alcoholic suicide can be described as a middle-aged male between forty-five and fifty-five years old who is currently drinking and who has been abusing alcohol for two or more decades; see B. Barraclough, *Suicide: Clinical and Epidemiological Studies* (London: Croom Helm, 1987).

46. A. R. Darbonne, "Suicide and Age: A Suicide Note Analysis," *Journal of Consulting and Clinical Psychology* 33 (1969): 46–50; and M. Miller, *Suicide After Sixty: The Final Alternative* (New York: Springer, 1979).

KEVIN E. EARLY AND RONALD L. AKERS, "'It's a White Thing'—An Exploration of Beliefs About Suicide in the African-American Community," *Deviant Behavior* 14, no. 4 (1993): 277–96. Reprinted by permission of the authors and Taylor and Francis, Inc. Copyright © 1993.

Notes

1. See Department of Health and Human Services, *Statistical Series, Annual Data, 1990: Series E-21: Vital Statistics of the United States,* vol. 2: *Mortality* (Washington: Public Health Service, National Center for Health Statistics, 1992), part A.

2. Emile Durkheim, *Suicide: A Sociological and Statistical Study,* trans. John A. Spaulding and George Simpson (1897; reprint, Glencoe, Ill.: Free Press, 1951).

3. Robert K. Merton, *Science, Technology, and Society in Seventeenth-Century England* (Bruges, Belg.: Saint Catherine Press, 1938).

4. Charles Prudhomme, "The Problem of Suicide in the American Negro," *Psychoanalytic Review* 25 (1938): 187–204, 372–91; Robert Davis, "Suicide Among Young Blacks: Trends and Perspective," *Phylon* 41 (1980): 223–29; Craig B. Little, *Understanding Deviance and Control* (Itasca: F. E. Peacock, 1983); Jewelle T. Gibbs, *Young, Black, and Male in America* (Dover: Auburn House Publishing, 1988); and James Moss, "Hurling Oppression: Overcoming Anomie and Self-Hatred," in *Black Male Adolescents: Parenting and Education in Community Context,* ed. Benjamin P. Bowser (New York: University Press of America, 1991), 282–97.

376
Notes and References

5. Robert Davis, "Black Suicide in the Seventies: Current Trends," *Suicide and Life-Threatening Behavior* 9 (1979): 131–40; Robert Davis, "Black Suicide and the Relational System: Theoretical and Empirical Implications of Communal and Family Ties," *Research in Race and Ethnic Relations* 2 (1980): 43–71; Robert Davis, "Black Suicide and Social Support Systems: An Overview and Some Implications for Mental Health Practitioners," *Phylon* 43, no. 4 (1982): 307–14; and Davis, "Suicide Among Young Blacks."

6. Herbert Hendin, "Black Suicide," *Archives of General Psychiatry* 21 (1969): 407–22.

7. Davis, "Suicide Among Young Blacks," 228.

8. Andrew F. Henry and James F. Short, *Suicide and Homicide* (New York: Free Press, 1954).

9. Andrew Billingsley, *Black Families in White America* (Englewood Cliffs, N.J.: Prentice-Hall, 1968); Carol Stack, *All Our Kin* (New York: Harper and Row, 1974); Walter Allen, "Black Family Research in the United States: A Review, Assessment and Extension," *Journal of Comparative Family Studies* 9 (1978): 168–89; Elmer P. Martin, *The Black Extended Family* (Chicago: University of Chicago Press, 1978); and Harriette McAdoo, *Black Families* (Beverly Hills: Sage Publications, 1981).

10. Michael Rutter, "Resilience in the Face of Adversity," *British Journal of Psychiatry* 147 (1985): 598–611.

11. J. Woodford, "Why Negro Suicides Are Increasing," *Ebony* 20 (1965): 89–100.

12. Davis, "Suicide Among Young Blacks," 228.

13. The terms black, black American, and African American will be used interchangeably.

14. Gibbs, *Young, Black, and Male,* 352.

15. Ibid.

16. Robert Staples, *Introduction to Black Sociology* (New York: McGraw-Hill, 1976); Gibbs, *Young, Black, and Male;* C. Eric Lincoln and Lawrence H. Mamiya, *The Black Church in the African-American Experience* (Durham, N.C.: Duke University Press, 1990); and Hans A. Baer and Merrill M. Singer, *African-American Religion in the Twentieth Century* (Knoxville: University of Tennessee Press, 1992).

17. C. Eric Lincoln, *The Black Church Since Frazier* (New York: Schocken Books, 1974), 116.

18. Joe Feagin, *Race and Ethnic Relations,* 3d ed. (Englewood Cliffs, N.J.: Prentice-Hall, 1989).

19. Staples, *Introduction to Black Sociology;* and Gayraud S. Wilmore, *Black Religion and Black Radicalism,* 2d ed. (Maryknoll: Orbis Books, 1983).

20. The reference to Christian beliefs here should not be taken to mean that other faiths adhered to by blacks such as Islamic or Jewish faiths would take a different stance on suicide. In this community the only black churches are Christian.

21. Bureau of Justice Statistics, *Criminal Victimization in the United States, 1991* (Washington: U.S. Department of Justice, 1992).

22. Henry and Short, *Suicide and Homicide.*

23. Merton, *Science, Technology, and Society.*

24. Robert Agnew, "Foundation for a General Strain Theory of Crime and Delinquency," *Criminology* 30 (1992): 47–88.

KATHLEEN ERWIN, "Interpreting the Evidence: Competing Paradigms and the Emergence of Lesbian and Gay Suicide as a 'Social Fact,'" *The International Journal of Health Services* 23, no. 3 (1993): 437–53. Reprinted by permission of the author and Baywood Publishing Co. Copyright © 1993.

Notes

1. E. Rofes, *"I Thought People Like That Killed Themselves": Lesbians, Gay Men and Suicide* (San Francisco: Grey Fox Press, 1983); and S. G. Schneider, N. L. Farberow, and G. Kruks, "Suicidal Behavior in Adolescent and Young Adult Gay Men," *Suicide and Life-Threatening Behavior* 19, no. 4 (1989): 381–94.

2. The terms "lesbian" and "gay" are culturally and historically specific terms that should not be applied uniformly to all people who engage in same-sex sexual relations. In Europe and North America, from the 19th century to the present, the term "homosexual" came to refer to people engaging primarily in same-sex sexual relations. In this article, I use the terms "gay" and "lesbian" to refer to male and female "homosexuals" in contemporary American society.

3. K. Jay and A. Young, *The Gay Report: Lesbians and Gay Men Speak Out About Sexual Experiences and Lifestyles* (New York: Summit Books, 1979), 729.

4. A. P. Bell and M. S. Weinberg, *Homosexualities* (New York: Simon and Schuster, 1987), 451.

5. Ibid.

6. P. Gibson, "Gay Male and Lesbian Youth Suicide," in *Report of the Secretary's Task Force on Youth Suicide,* vol. 3: *Prevention and Interventions in Youth Suicide,* DHHS Publication no. 89–1623 (Washington: U.S. Government Printing Office, 1989).

7. Ibid.; Schneider, Farberow, and Kruks, "Suicidal Behavior"; and G. Remafedi, J. A. Farrow, and R. W. Deisher, "Risk Factors for Attempted Suicide in Gay and Bisexual Youth," *Pediatrics* 87, no. 6 (1991): 869–75.

8. R. J. Kus, "Alcoholism and Non-acceptance of Gay Self: The Critical Link," *Journal of Homosexuality* 15, no. 1–2 (1988): 25–41; and M. T. Saghir and E. Robins, *Male and Female Homosexuality: A Comprehensive Investigation* (Baltimore: Williams and Wilkins, 1973), 118–19, 276–77.

9. Saghir and Robins, *Male and Female Homosexuality.*

10. Rofes, *"People Like That"*; Schneider, Farberow, and Kruks, "Suicidal Behavior"; Jay and Young, *The Gay Report;* Bell and Weinberg, *Homosexualities;* Gibson, "Gay Male and Lesbian Youth Suicide"; Remafedi, Farrow, and Deisher, "Risk Factors"; Kus, "Alcoholism and Non-acceptance of Gay Self"; Saghir and Robins, *Male and Female Homosexuality;* R. F. C. Kourany, "Suicide Among Homosexual Adolescents," *Journal of Homosexuality* 13, no. 4 (1987): 111–17; and A. D. Martin, "Learning to Hide: The Socialization of the Gay Adolescent," *Adolescent Psychiatry* 10 (1982): 52–65.

11. L. Crompton, "The Myth of Lesbian Impunity: Capital Laws from 1270 to 1791," *Journal of Homosexuality* 6, 1–2 (1980–1981): 11–22.

12. Ibid.; and V. L. Bullough and M. Bullough, *Sin, Sickness and Sanity* (New York: Garland, 1977).

13. Rofes, *"People Like That,"* 3.

14. V. L. Bullough, *Homosexuality: A History* (New York: Garland, 1979); H. C. Kennedy, "The 'Third Sex' Theory of Karl Heinrich Ulrichs," *Journal of Homosexuality* 6, no. 1–2 (1980–1981): 103–11; J. Weeks, *Sex, Politics and Society: The Regulation of Sexuality Since 1800* (New York: Longman, 1981); J. Weeks, *Sexuality and Its Discontents* (London: Routledge and Kegan Paul, 1985), 61–95; and R. C. Lewontin, S. Rose, and L. J. Kamin, *Not in Our Genes: Biology, Ideology and Human Nature* (New York: Pantheon Books, 1984), 37–51.

15. Bullough, *Homosexuality;* and Kennedy, "'Third Sex' Theory of Ulrichs."

16. K. H. Ulrichs, *Inclusa: Anthropological Studies in the Sexual Love Between Men,* trans. M. Lombardi (Los Angeles: Urania Manuscripts, 1979); H. Ellis, *Sexual Inversion* (Philadelphia: F. A. Davis, 1901); E. Carpenter, *Homogenic Love and Its Place in Free Society* (London: Redundancy Press, 1980); E. Carpenter, *The Intermediate Sex: A Study of Some Transitional Types of Men and Women* (New York: Mitchell Kennedy Press, 1912); E. Stevenson, *The Intersexes: A History of Similisexualism as a Problem in Social Life* (New York: Arno Press, 1975); M. Hirschfeld, *Sexual Anomalies and Perversions, Physical and Psychological Development and Treatment: A Summary of the Works of Professor Dr. Magnus Hirschfeld, Compiled as a Humble Memorial by His Pupils* (London: Torch, 1948).

17. Kennedy, "'Third Sex' Theory of Ulrichs."

18. Bullough, *Homosexuality;* and Kennedy, "'Third Sex' Theory of Ulrichs."

19. Rofes, *"People Like That,"* 6.

20. Kennedy, "'Third Sex' Theory of Ulrichs," 108.

21. Weeks, *Sexuality and Its Discontents.*

22. Emile Durkheim, *Suicide* (1897; reprint, New York: Free Press, 1951); and J. Selkin, "The Legacy of Emile Durkheim," *Suicide and Life-Threatening Behavior* 13, no. 1 (1983): 3–14.

23. S. Freud, "The Psychogenesis of a Case of Female Homosexuality," in *Sexuality and the Psychology of Love,* ed. P. Rieff (1920; reprint, New York: Macmillan, 1963), 158.

24. Ibid.; Bullough, *Homosexuality;* S. Freud, "Certain Neurotic Mechanisms in Jealousy, Paranoia and Homosexuality," in Rieff, ed., *Sexuality and Psychology of Love,* 160–70; D. Altman, *The Homosexualization of America* (Boston: Beacon Press, 1982); C. S. Hall and G. Lindzey, *Theories of Personality* (New York: John Wiley and Sons, 1978), 31–73; and N. Chodorow, *The Reproduction of Mothering, Psychoanalysis and the Sociology of Gender* (Berkeley: University of California Press, 1978).

25. Freud, "Case of Female Homosexuality," 149.

26. D. Klaitch, *Woman to Woman* (New York: Simon and Schuster, 1978). There is some controversy over whether or not Freud saw homosexuality as inherently pathological, and indeed Freud's writings are somewhat contradictory on this point (see Freud, "Case of Female Homosexuality" and "Certain Neurotic Mechanisms"; Altman, *Homosexualization of America;* and K. Lewes, *The Psychoanalytic Theory of Male Homosexuality* [New York: Simon and Schuster, 1988]). Freud argued that everyone was innately bisexual and had at least some latent homosexual desires, and that homosexual acts should be decriminalized. However, his belief that homosexuality resulted from childhood trauma, and should be cured through psychoanalysis, has been pointed to as evidence that Freud did see homosexuality as pathological.

27. Weeks, *Sex, Politics and Society;* L. Faderman, *Odd Girls and Twilight Lovers: A History of Lesbian Life in Twentieth Century America* (New York: Columbia University Press, 1991); and J. D'Emilio, *Sexual Politics, Sexual Communities: The Making of a Homosexual Minority in the United States, 1940–1970* (Chicago: University of Chicago Press, 1983).

28. Altman, *Homosexualization of America;* and Klaitch, *Woman to Woman.*

29. Rofes, *"People Like That"*; Gibson, "Gay Male and Lesbian Youth Suicide"; Remafedi, Farrow, and Deisher, "Risk Factors"; Martin, "Learning to Hide"; G. Herek, "Beyond 'Homophobia': A Social Psychological Perspective on Attitudes Toward Lesbians and Gay Men," *Journal of Homosexuality* 10, no. 1–2

(1984): 1–21; and G. Herek, "The Context of Anti-Gay Violence: Notes on Cultural and Psychological Heterosexism," *Journal of Interpersonal Violence* 5, no. 3 (1990): 316–34.

30. J. Saunders and S. M. Valente, "Suicide Risk Among Gay Men and Lesbians: A Review," *Death Studies* 11 (1987): 1–23.

31. Rofes, *"People Like That"*; Gibson, "Gay Male and Lesbian Youth Suicide"; Herek, "Beyond 'Homophobia'"; Herek, "Context of Anti-Gay Violence"; A. D. Martin and E. S. Hetrick, "The Stigmatization of the Gay and Lesbian Adolescent," *Journal of Homosexuality* 15, no. 1–2 (1988): 163–83; R. C. Savin-Williams, "Coming Out to Parents and Self-Esteem Among Gay and Lesbian Youth," *Journal of Homosexuality* 18, no. 1–2 (1989): 1–35; and S. G. Schneider, et al., "AIDS-related Factors Predictive of Suicidal Ideation of Low and High Intent Among Gay and Bisexual Men," *Suicide and Life-Threatening Behavior* 21, no. 4 (1991): 313–28.

32. Herek, "Beyond 'Homophobia'"; and Herek, "Context of Anti-Gay Violence."

33. Gibson, "Gay Male and Lesbian Youth Suicide"; R. D. Fowler, ed., "Section on Psychology in the Public Forum," *American Psychologist* 46, no. 9 (1991): 947–74; and R. Simon, ed., "Special Feature on Gays and Lesbians in Therapy," *Family Therapy Networker* 15, no. 1 (1991): 26–60.

34. Ibid. (both); Kus, "Alcoholism and Non-acceptance of Gay Self"; and Kourany, "Suicide Among Homosexual Adolescents."

35. See, for example, the recent controversial research of S. LeVay ("A Difference in Hypothalamic Structure Between Heterosexual and Homosexual Men," *Science* 253 [1991]: 1034–37) and L. S. Allen and R. A. Gorski ("Sexual Orientation and the Size of the Anterior Commissure in the Human Brain," *Proceedings of the National Academy of Science* 89 [1992]: 7199–202). Both studies hypothesize causal links between homosexuality and structures in the brains of gay men who died of AIDS. Although some medical researchers argue that proof of a biological basis for homosexuality would reduce prejudice against lesbians and gays (see D. Perlman, "Brain Cell Study Finds Link to Homosexuality, Tissue Differs Between Gay and Straight Men," *San Francisco Chronicle*, 30 August 1991, A1; and C. Petit, "Evidence of Difference in Brains of Gay Men, Study Bolsters Biological Basis of Sex Roles," *San Francisco Chronicle*, 1 August 1992, p. A1), critics counter that "scientific" evidence of biological difference would lead only to renewed efforts to "cure" the "deformed" brains of gays (and lesbians?).

36. Kourany, "Suicide Among Homosexual Adolescents," 114.

37. P. E. Stevens and J. M. Hall, "A Critical Historical Analysis of the Medical Construction of Lesbianism," *International Journal of Health Services* 21, no. 2 (1991): 291–307.

38. T. Marotta, *The Politics of Homosexuality* (Boston: Houghton Mifflin, 1987); A. Rich, "Compulsory Heterosexuality and the Lesbian Existence," in *The Signs Reader: Women, Gender and Scholarship,* ed. E. Abel and E. Abel (Chicago: University of Chicago, 1983), 139–68; and C. Golden, "Diversity and Variability in Women's Sexual Identity," in *Lesbian Psychologies: Explorations and Challenges,* ed. Boston Lesbian Psychologies Collective (Urbana: University of Illinois Press, 1987), 19–34.

39. Rich, "Compulsory Homosexuality."

40. B. Tremble, M. Schneider, and C. Appathurai, "Growing Up Gay or Lesbian in a Multicultural Context," *Journal of Homosexuality* 17, no. 3–4 (1989): 253–67.

41. Ibid.; Gibson, "Gay Male and Lesbian Youth Suicide"; Saunders and Valente, "Suicide Risk"; M. Riggs, "Tongues Untied" (video recording) (San Francisco: Frameline, 1989); and W. L. Williams, *The Spirit and the Flesh: Sexual Diversity in American Indian Culture* (Boston: Beacon Press, 1986).

42. Williams, *Spirit and Flesh;* W. Roscoe, ed., *Living the Spirit: A Gay American Indian Anthology* (New York: St. Martin's Press, 1988); E. Blackwood, "Sexuality and Gender in Certain Native American Tribes: The Case of Cross-Gender Females," *Signs: Journal of Women in Culture and Society* 10, no. 1 (1984): 27–42; and W. Roscoe, "Bibliography of Berdache and Alternative Gender Roles Among North American Indians," *Journal of Homosexuality* 14, no. 3–4 (1987): 81–171. The anthropological term "berdache" was introduced by early French observers, who borrowed it from the Persian word for passive homosexual. Williams and others have used the term "amazon" to describe the female berdache (see Williams, *Spirit and Flesh* and Roscoe, "Bibliography of Berdache"). These Euro-American terms are used here for the sake of convenience. Roscoe ("Bibliography of Berdache") has complied a comprehensive list of indigenous terms.

43. Williams, *Spirit and Flesh;* Roscoe, *Living the Spirit;* and K. Erwin, "Mental Health Issues in the Context of Culture, Race and Sexuality: A Preliminary Study of Gay and Lesbian Native Americans," unpublished paper, University of California, Berkeley, May 1991.

44. S. Nanda, *Neither Man Nor Woman: The Hijras of India* (Belmont, Calif.: Wadsworth, 1990); J. Robertson, "Gender-bending in Paradise: Doing 'Female' and 'Male' in Japan, *Genders* 5 (1989): 50–69; P. Caplan, ed., *The Cultural Construction of*

Sexuality (London: Tavistock, 1987); E. Blackwood, ed., *Anthropology and Homosexual Behavior* (New York: Haworth Press, 1986 [reprint of special issue of *Journal of Homosexuality* 11, no. 3–4, 1986]); M. W. Ross, J. A. Paulsen, and O. W. Stalstrom, "Homosexuality and Mental Health: A Cross-Cultural Review," *Journal of Homosexuality* 15, no. 1–2 (1988): 131–52.

45. Herek, "Beyond 'Homophobia'"; and Herek, "Context of Anti-Gay Violence."

46. Gibson, "Gay Male and Lesbian Youth Suicide"; Remafedi, Farrow, and Deisher, "Risk Factors"; Herek, "Beyond 'Homophobia'"; Herek, "Context of Anti-Gay Violence"; Saunders and Valente, "Suicide Risk"; and Ross, Paulsen, and Stalstrom, "Homosexuality and Mental Health."

47. A. Berube and J. Escoffier, "Queer Nation," *Out/Look: National Gay and Lesbian Quarterly* (Winter 1991): 12.

48. Fowler, "Section on Psychology"; and J. M. McGinnis, "Suicide in America—Moving Up the Public Health Agenda," *Suicide and Life-threatening Behavior* 17, no. 1 (1987): 18–30.

49. Schneider, Farberow, and Kruks, "Suicidal Behavior"; Remafedi, Farrow, and Deisher, "Risk Factors"; and Saunders and Valente, "Suicide Risk."

50. Saunders and Valente, "Suicide Risk"; C. R. Fikar and M. Koslap-Petraco, "Pediatric Forum: What About Gay Teenagers?," *American Journal of Diseases of Children* 145 (1991): 252; and G. Herek et al., "Avoiding Heterosexist Bias in Psychological Research," *American Psychologist* 46, no. 9 (1991): 957–63.

51. Gibson, "Gay Male and Lesbian Youth Suicide"; Herek, "Context of Anti-Gay Violence"; Golden, "Diversity and Variability"; Tremble, Schneider, and Appathurai, "Growing Up Gay or Lesbian"; Williams, *Spirit and Flesh*; G. Herdt, "Representations of Homosexuality: An Essay on Cultural Ontology and Historical Comparisons, Parts 1 and 11," *Journal of the History of Sexuality* 1, no. 3 (1991): 481–504, and 1, no. 4 (1991): 603–32; N. Krieger, "Racial and Gender Discrimination: Risk Factors for High Blood Pressure?" *Social Science and Medicine* 30, no. 12 (1990): 1273–81; and W. Roscoe, "Making History: The Challenge of Gay and Lesbian Studies," *Journal of Homosexuality* 15, no. 3–4 (1988); 1–40.

Part III: Personal Dimensions of Loss

The Experience of Grief

MARGARET STROEBE, MARY M. GERGEN, KENNETH J. GERGEN, AND WOLFGANG STROEBE, "Broken Hearts or Broken Bonds: Love and Death in Historical Perspective," *American Psychologist* 47, no. 10 (October 1992): 1205–12. Reprinted by permission of the authors and the American Psychological Association. Copyright © 1992.

Notes

1. M. Foucault, *Madness and Civilization,* trans. R. Howard (New York: Vintage Books, 1965); and N. Rose, *The Psychological Complex: Politics and Society in England 1869–1939* (London: Routledge and Kegan Paul, 1985).

2. See S. McNamee and K. J. Gergen, *Social Construction and the Therapeutic Process* (London: Sage, 1992).

3. E. Badinter, *Motherlove, Myth and Reality* (New York: Macmillan, 1980); M. Carrithers, S. Collins, and S. Lukes, eds., *The Category of the Person* (Cambridge, Eng.: Cambridge University Press, 1985); A. Corbin, *The Foul and the Fragrant* (Cambridge, Mass.: Harvard University Press, 1986); and R. A. Shweder and J. G. Miller, "The Social Construction of the Person: How Is It Possible?" in *The Social Construction of the Person,* ed. K. J. Gergen and K. E. Davis (New York: Springer-Verlag, 1985), 42–72.

4. C. A. Lutz, *Unnatural Emotions* (Chicago: University of Chicago Press, 1988).

5. K. J. Gergen, *The Saturated Self: Dilemmas of Identity in Contemporary Life* (New York: Basic Books, 1991).

6. For more detailed discussions of the grief work hypothesis, see M. Stroebe and W. Stroebe, "Does 'Grief Work' Work?" *Journal of Consulting and Clinical Psychology* 59 (1991): 57–65; and M. Stroebe, "Coping with Bereavement: A Review of the Grief Work Hypothesis," *Omega: Journal of Death and Dying* 26, no. 1 (1992–1993), 19–42.

7. S. Freud, "Trauer und Melancholy" ["Grief and Melancholy"], *Internationale Zeritschrift für Artzliche Psychoanalyse* 4 (1917): 288–301.

8. C. S. Lewis, *A Grief Observed* (London: Faber, 1961).

9. J. Bowlby, *Attachment and Loss,* vol. 3: *Loss: Sadness, and Depression* (London: Hogarth Press, 1980), 241–42.

10. J. Bowlby, *Attachment and Loss,* 3 vols. (Harmondsworth, Eng.: Pelican Books, 1971, 1975; London: Hogarth Press, 1980).

11. N. Golan, "From Wife to Widow to Woman," *Social Work* 20 (1975): 369–74.

12. J. Viorst, *Necessary Losses: The Loves, Illusions, Dependencies and Impossible Expectations That All of Us Have to Give Up in Order to Grow* (London: Simon and Schuster, 1986).

13. C. M. Parkes, *Bereavement: Studies of Grief in Adult Life* (1972; reprint, London: Penguin, 1986).

14. C. Sanders, *Grief: The Mourning After* (New York: John Wiley and Sons, 1989), 94.

15. H. Lopata, "On Widowhood: Grief Work and Identity Reconstruction," *Journal of Geriatric Psychiatry* 8 (1975): 41–55; H. Lopata, *Women as Widows: Support Systems* (New York: Elsevier, 1979); and H. Lopata, "Support Systems of American Urban Widowhood," *Journal of Social Issues* 44 (1988): 113–28.

16. For a recent review, see B. Raphael and K. Nunn, "Counseling the Bereaved," *Journal of Social Issues* 44 (1988): 191–206.

17. W. Worden, *Grief Counseling and Grief Therapy: A Handbook for the Mental Health Practitioner* (New York: Springer, 1982).

18. G. D. Gorer, *Death, Grief and Mourning in Contemporary Britain* (New York: Doubleday, 1965).

19. C. M. Parkes and R. Weiss, *Recovery from Bereavement* (New York: Basic Books, 1983).

20. H. Lopata, *Widowhood in an American City* (Morristown, N.J.: General Learning Press, 1973); and Lopata, *Women as Widows.*

21. It should be noted that seldom do the writings of a single author remain consistently tied to a period of paradigm. Thus, within the works of Parkes, Gorer, Worden, and Raphael, for example, romanticist concepts and options are sometimes voiced as well.

22. J. Yamamoto, K. Okonoji, T. Iwasaki, and S. Yoshimura, "Mourning in Japan," *American Journal of Psychiatry* 126 (1969): 74–182.

23. J. Yamamoto, "Cultural Factors in Loneliness, Death, and Separation," *Medical Times* 98 (1970): 181.

24. D. G. Mandelbaum, "Social Uses of Funeral Rites," in *The Meaning of Death,* ed. H. Feifel (New York: McGraw-Hill, 1959), 201.

25. Ibid., 202.

26. Ibid., 203.

27. U. Wikan, "Bereavement and Loss in Two Muslim Communities: Egypt and Bali Compared," *Social Science and Medicine* 27 (1988): 451–60; and U. Wikan, *Managing Turbulent Hearts* (Chicago: University of Chicago Press, 1991).

28. Gergen, *Saturated Self.*

29. J. Stallworthy, ed., *Penguin Book of Love Poetry* (New York: Penguin Books, 1973), 361–62.

30. Ibid.

31. T. J. Johnson, ed., *Emily Dickinson: The Complete Poems* (London: Faber and Faber, 1970), 706–7.

32. Ibid.

33. P. Rosenblatt, *Bitter, Bitter Tears: Nineteenth Century Diarists and Twentieth Century Grief Theories* (Minneapolis: University of Minnesota Press, 1983).

34. Ibid., 126.

35. Ibid., 59.

36. See M. Stroebe and W. Stroebe, "Who Participates in Bereavement Research? A Review and Empirical Study," *Omega: Journal of Death and Dying* 20 (1989): 1–29; Stroebe and Stroebe, "Does 'Grief Work' Work?"; W. Stroebe and M. Stroebe, "Determinants of Adjustment to Bereavement in Young Widows and Widowers," in *Handbook of Bereavement: Theory, Research, and Intervention,* ed. M. Stroebe, W. Stroebe, and R. O. Hansson (New York: Cambridge University Press, 1993), 208–26; W. Stroebe, M. Stroebe, and G. Domittner, "Individual and Situational Differences in Recovery from Bereavement: A Risk-Group Identified," *Journal of Social Issues* 44 (1988), 143–58.

37. S. Shuchter and S. Zisook, "The Course of Normal Grief," in Stroebe, Stroebe, and Hansson, eds., *Handbook of Bereavement,* 23–43.

38. P. Silverman and W. Worden, "Children's Reactions to the Death of a Parent," in Stroebe, Stroebe, and Hansson, *Handbook of Bereavement,* 300–316.

39. S. Rubin, "The Death of a Child Is Forever: The Life Course Impact of Child Loss," in Stroebe, Stroebe, and Hansson, *Handbook of Bereavement,* 285–99.

40. See analyses by S. Connor, *Postmodernist Culture: An Introduction to Theories of the Contemporary* (New York: Basil Blackwell, 1989); and Gergen, *Saturated Self.*

41. M. M. Gergen, "Social Ghosts: Opening Inquiry on Imaginal Relationships," paper presented at the Ninety-fifth Annual Convention of the American Psychological Association, New York, August 1987.

42. P. Rosenblatt and M. Meyer, "Imagined Interactions and the Family," *Family Relations* 35 (1986): 319–24.

43. See, for example, Stroebe, Stroebe, and Hansson, *Handbook of Bereavement.*

44. H. Anderson and H. Goolishian, "The Client Is the Expert: A Not Knowing Approach to Therapy," in *Social Construction and the Therapeutic Process,* ed. S. McNamee and K. J. Gergen (London: Sage, 1992), 117–36.

JOHN D. KELLY, "Grief: Re-forming Life's Story," *Journal of Palliative Care* 8, no. 2 (Summer 1992): 33–35. Reprinted by permission of the *Journal of Palliative Care.* Copyright © 1992.

Notes

1. T. Berry, *The Dream of the Earth* (San Francisco: Sierra Club Books, 1988).
2. J. L. McKenzie, *The Two-Edged Sword* (Garden City, N.Y.: Image Books, 1966).
3. H. S. Kushner, *When Bad Things Happen to Good People* (New York: Dell, 1983).
4. S. Feldman, ed., *African Myths and Tales* (New York: Dell, 1963).
5. E. Polster, *Every Person's Life Is Worth a Novel* (New York: W. W. Norton, 1990).
6. J. W. Worden, *Grief Counseling and Grief Therapy* (New York: Springer, 1982).
7. Ibid.
8. Ibid.
9. Ibid.
10. Ibid.
11. G. L. Engel, "Grief and Grieving," *American Journal of Nursing* 9 (1964): 93–98.
12. Spiritual: "the immaterial or sensual part of a person . . . providing one's personality with its inward structure, dynamic drive and creative response to the demands it encounters in the process of becoming" (*Webster's Dictionary,* 1966); Numinous: [a sense of] a dynamic or creative force; a sense of the presence of the divinity (*Webster's Dictionary,* 1966).
13. Polster, *Every Person's Life.*
14. Ibid.
15. Berry, *Dream of the Earth.*
16. M. Amenta, "Nurses as Primary Spiritual Care Workers," *The Hospice Journal* 4, no. 3 (1988): 47–55.
17. V. Deloria, Jr., *God Is Red* (New York: Dell, 1963).
18. Berry, *Dream of the Earth.*
19. Feldman, *African Myths and Tales.*
20. Engel, "Grief and Grieving."
21. With apologies to Dr. Phyllis Silverman, who used a similar expression in her presentation to the Conference on Bereaved Children and Their Families, Washington, D.C., 6 October 1990. While her remarks were in the context of the bereaved child, they seem to be applicable to all grievers.
22. T. A. Rando, *Grieving: How to Go on Living When Someone You Love Dies* (New York: Free Press, 1988).
23. Ibid.
24. Worden, *Grief Counseling and Grief Therapy;* and T. A. Rando, Workshop: Therapeutic Interventions, Grief and Mourning, Baltimore, 1991.
25. Worden, *Grief Counseling and Grief Therapy.*
26. Polster, *Every Person's Life.*
27. Ibid.

DENNIS KLASS, "Solace and Immortality: Bereaved Parents' Continuing Bond with Their Children," *Death Studies* 17, no. 4 (1993): 343–68. Reprinted, in slightly revised form, by permission of the author and Taylor and Francis, Inc. Copyright © 1993.

Notes

1. D. Klass, *Parental Grief: Resolution and Solace* (New York: Springer, 1988).
2. T. Benedek, "Parenthood as a Developmental Phase," *American Psychoanalytic Association Journal* 7 (1959): 389–417; and T. Benedek, "Discussion of Parenthood as a Developmental Phase," *Journal of the American Psychoanalytic Association* 23 (1975): 154–65.
3. M. Elson, "Parenthood and the Transformations of Narcissism," in *Parenthood: A Psychodynamic Perspective,* ed. R. S. Cohen, B. J. Cohler, and S. H. Weissman (New York: Guilford Press, 1984), 297–314.
4. P. C. Horton, *Solace, the Missing Dimension in Psychiatry* (Chicago: University of Chicago Press, 1981).

5. D. W. Winnicott, "Transitional Objects and Transitional Phenomena," *International Journal of Psychoanalysis* 34 (1953): 89–97; and D. W. Winnicott, *Playing and Reality* (New York: Basic Books, 1971).

6. R. H. Passman, "Arousal Reducing Properties of Attachment Objects: Testing the Functional Limits of the Security Blanket Relative to the Mother," *Developmental Psychology* 12 (1976): 468–69; and R. H. Passman and P. Weisberg, "Mothers and Blankets as Agents for Promoting Play and Exploration by Young Children in a Novel Environment: The Effects of Social and Nonsocial Attachment Objects," *Developmental Psychology* 11 (1975): 170–77.

7. W. D. Fairbairn, *An Object-Relations Theory of the Personality* (New York: Basic Books, 1952).

8. *TCF Credo*, Oakbrook, Ill.: The Compassionate Friends, 1983.

9. R. A. Moody, *Elvis After Life: Unusual Psychic Experiences Surrounding the Death of a Superstar* (Atlanta: Peachtree Publishers, 1987).

10. D. R. Lehman, C. B. Wortman, and A. F. Williams, "Long-term Effects of Losing a Spouse or Child in a Motor Vehicle Crash," *Journal of Personality and Social Psychology* 52 (1987): 218–31.

11. R. A. Kalish and D. K. Reynolds, *Death and Ethnicity: A Psychocultural Study* (Farmingdale, N.Y.: Baywood Publishing, 1981).

12. W. D. Rees, "The Bereaved and Their Hallucinations," in *Bereavement: Its Psychosocial Aspects*, ed. Bernard Schoenberg et al. (New York: Columbia University Press, 1975), 66–71.

13. I. O. Glick, R. S. Weiss, and C. M. Parkes, *The First Year of Bereavement* (New York: John Wiley and Sons, 1974), 147.

14. J. Yamamoto, K. Okonoji, T. Iwasaki, and S. Yoshimura, "Mourning in Japan," *American Journal of Psychiatry* 125 (1969): 1661–65.

15. W. F. Matchett, "Repeated Hallucinatory Experiences as a Part of the Mourning Process Among Hopi Indian Women," *Psychiatry* 35 (1972): 185–94.

16. P. R. Silverman, *Widow-to-Widow* (New York: Springer, 1986), 185.

17. H. Z. Lopata, *Women as Widows, Support Systems* (New York: Elsevier, 1979), 126; see also H. Z. Lopata, *Widowhood in an American City* (Cambridge, Mass.: Schenkman, 1973).

18. M. S. Moss and S. Z. Moss, "The Image of the Deceased Spouse in Remarriage of Elderly Widow(er)s," *Journal of Gerontological Social Work* 3, no. 2 (1980): 59–70.

19. M. K. Goin, R. W. Burgoyne, and J. M. Goin, "Timeless Attachment to a Dead Relative," *American Journal of Psychiatry* 136, no. 7 (1979): 988–89.

20. L. H. Tessman, *Children of Parting Parents* (New York: Jason Aronson, 1978), 42.

21. B. C. Bushbaum, "Remembering a Parent Who Has Died: A Developmental Perspective," *The Annual of Psychoanalysis*, vol. 15 (Madison, Conn.: International Universities Press, 1987), 99–112.

22. P. R. Silverman, "The Impact of Parental Death on College-Age Women," *Psychiatric Clinics of North America* 10, no. 3 (1987): 387–404.

23. J. Bowlby, *Attachment and Loss*, vols. 1–3 (New York: Basic Books, 1969, 1973, 1980); C. M. Parkes, *Bereavement: Studies in Grief in Adult Life* (New York: International Universities Press, 1972); C. M. Parkes and R. S. Weiss, *Recovery from Bereavement* (New York: Basic Books, 1983); B. Raphael, *The Anatomy of Bereavement* (New York: Basic Books, 1983); and J. W. Worden, *Grief Counseling and Grief Therapy: A Handbook for the Mental Health Practitioner* (New York: Springer, 1982).

24. V. D. Volkan, *Linking Objects and Linking Phenomena* (New York: International Universities Press, 1981); V. D. Volkan, "The Scope of Depressive States," in *Depressive States and Their Treatment*, ed. V. D. Volkan (Northvale, N.J.: Jason Aronson, 1985), 1–17; V. D. Volkan, "Psychotherapy of Complicated Mourning," in Volkan, ed., *Depressive States and Their Treatment*, 271–95; V. Tahka, "Dealing with Object Loss," *Scandinavian Psychoanalytic Review* 7 (1984): 13–33; D. R. Dietrich and P. C. Shabad, eds., *The Problem of Loss and Mourning: Psychoanalytic Perspectives* (Madison, Conn.: International Universities Press, 1989); E. Furman, *A Child's Parent Dies: Studies in Childhood Bereavement* (New Haven, Conn.: Yale University Press, 1974); and E. N. Jackson, *Understanding Grief: Its Roots, Dynamics, and Treatment* (New York: Abingdon Press, 1957).

25. C. W. Brice, "Paradoxes of Maternal Mourning," *Psychiatry* 54 (1991): 1–12.

26. C. M. Sanders, *Grief: The Mourning After* (New York: John Wiley and Sons, 1989), 70.

27. T. A. Rando, *Grief, Dying, and Death: Clinical Interventions for Caregivers* (Champaign, Ill.: Research Press Company, 1984), 19.

28. Ibid., 78.

29. S. S. Rubin, "The Resolution of Bereavement: A Clinical Focus on the Relationship to the Deceased," *Psychotherapy* 22, no. 2 (1985), 231–32.

30. D. Klass, "John Bowlby's Model of Grief and the Problem of Identification," *Omega: Journal of Death and Dying* 18 (1987), 13–32.

31. C. Tennant, "Parental Loss in Childhood: Its Effect in Adult Life," *Archives of General Psychiatry* 45 (1988): 1049.

32. M. Stroebe, M. M. Gergen, K. J. Gergen, and W. Stroebe, "Broken Hearts or Broken Bonds: Love and Death in Historical Perspective," *American Psychologist* 47, no. 10 (1992): 1206.

33. E. Lindemann and S. Cobb, "Neuropsychiatric Observations After the Coconut Grove Fire," in *Beyond Grief: Studies in Crisis Intervention,* ed. E. Lindemann and E. Lindemann (New York: Aronson, 1979).

34. A. C. Cain and B. S. Cain, "On Replacing a Child," *Journal of the American Academy of Child Psychiatry* 3 (1964): 443–56; S. Johnson, "Sexual Intimacy and Replacement Children After the Death of a Child," *Omega: Journal of Death and Dying* 15 (1984): 109–18; C. Legg and I. Sherick, "The Replacement Child—A Developmental Tragedy: Some Preliminary Comments," *Child Psychiatry and Human Development* 70 (1976): 113–26; and E. O. Poznanski, "The 'Replacement Child': A Saga of Unresolved Parental Grief," *Journal of Pediatrics* 81, no. 6 (1972): 1190–93.

35. F. Walsh and M. McGoldrick, eds., *Living Beyond Loss: Death in the Family* (New York: W. W. Norton, 1991).

36. E. K. Rynearson, "Psychotherapy of Pathologic Grief: Revisions and Limitations," *Psychiatric Clinics of North America* 10, no. 3 (1987): 487–99.

37. G. Mogenson, *Greeting the Angels: An Imaginal View of the Mourning Process* (Amityville, N.Y.: Baywood Publishing, 1992), 20.

38. Volkan, *Linking Objects and Linking Phenomena.*

39. See R. Hood, "Eliciting Mystical States of Consciousness in Semistructured Nature Experiences," *Journal for the Scientific Study of Religion* 16, no. 2 (1977): 155–63.

40. R. Otto, *The Idea of the Holy,* trans. John W. Harvey (New York: Oxford University Press, 1923).

41. L. E. Sullivan, "Death, Afterlife, and the Soul," in *Selections from the Encyclopedia of Religion,* ed. Mircea Eliade (New York: Macmillan, 1987), 51

42. D. Chidester, *Patterns of Transcendence: Religion, Death, and Dying* (Belmont, Calif.: Wadsworth, 1990).

43. See L. Dawson, "Otto and Freud on the Uncanny and Beyond," *Journal of the American Academy of Religion* 58, no. 2 (1989): 283–311.

44. R. Knapp, *Beyond Endurance: When a Child Dies* (New York: Schocken, 1986).

45. K. Wilber, *Up from Eden* (Boulder: Shambhala, 1981).

46. S. Jacoby, *Wild Justice, the Evolution of Revenge* (New York: Harper and Row, 1983).

47. Tahka, "Dealing with Object Loss," 18.

48. *Gates of Prayer: The New Union Prayer Book* (New York: Central Conference of American Rabbis; London: Union of Liberal and Progressive Synagogues, 1975).

49. G. H. Pollock, "On Mourning, Immortality, and Utopia," *Journal of the American Psychoanalytic Association* 23, no. 2 (1975): 341.

50. R. J. Lifton, "On Death and the Continuity of Life: A 'New' Paradigm," *History of Childhood Quarterly* 1, no. 4 (1974): 685.

51. Winnicott, "Transitional Objects and Transitional Phenomena"; and Winnicott, *Playing and Reality.*

52. E. Hubler, *The Sense of Shakespeare's Sonnets* (Princeton, N.J.: Princeton University Press, 1952).

53. R. Harper, *On Presence: Variations and Reflections* (Philadelphia: Trinity Press International, 1991), 89.

PHYLLIS R. SILVERMAN, STEVEN NICKMAN, AND J. WILLIAM WORDEN, "Detachment Revisited: The Child's Reconstruction of a Dead Parent," *American Journal of Orthopsychiatry* 62, no. 4 (October 1992): 494–503. Reprinted by permission of the authors and the American Orthopsychiatric Association, Inc. Copyright © 1992.

Notes

1. J. Bowlby, *Attachment and Loss,* vol. 3: *Loss: Sadness, and Depression* (New York: Basic Books, 1980); D. R. Dietrich and P. C. Shabad, *The Problem of Loss and Mourning* (Madison, Conn.: International Universities Press, 1989); S. C. Jacobs, T. R. Koston, S. Dasl, and A. M. Ostfeld, "Attachment Theory and Multiple Dimensions of Grief," *Omega: Journal of Death and Dying* 18 (1987): 41–52; D. Klass, *Parental Grief: Solace and Resolution* (New York: Springer, 1988); J. B. M. Miller, "Children's Reactions to the Death of a Parent: A Review of the Psychoanalytic Literature," *Journal of the American Psychoana-lytic Association* 19 (1971): 697–719; M. S. Moss and S. Z. Moss, "The Image of the Deceased Spouse in Remarriage of Elderly Widowers," *Journal of Gerontological Social Work* 3, no. 2 (1981): 59–70; M. Osterweis, F. Solomon, and M. Greene, eds., *Bereavement: Reactions, Consequences, and Care* (Washington: National Academy Press, 1984); S. S. Rubin, "The Resolution of Bereavement: A Clinical Focus on the Relationship to the Deceased," *Psychotherapy: Theory, Research, Training and Practice* 22 (1985): 231–35; P. R. Silverman, *Widow to Widow* (New York: Springer, 1986); S. M. Silverman and P. R. Silverman, "Parent-Child Communication in Wid-

owed Families," *American Journal of Psychotherapy* 33 (1979): 428–41; and J. W. Worden, *Grief Counseling and Grief Therapy: A Handbook for the Mental Health Practitioner,* 2d ed. (New York: Springer, 1991).

2. Klass, *Parental Grief;* and Rubin, "Resolution of Bereavement."

3. R. J. Lifton, *The Broken Connection: On Death and the Continuity of Life* (New York: Simon and Schuster, 1979).

4. E. Furman, "Children's Patterns in Mourning the Death of a Loved One," in *Childhood and Death,* ed. H. Wass and C. Corr (Washington: Hemisphere Publishing, 1984), 185–203; and V. D. Volkan, *Linking Objects and Linking Phenomena* (New York: International Universities Press, 1981).

5. Dietrich and Shabad, *Problem of Loss and Mourning;* and Miller, "Children's Reactions."

6. E. Furman, *A Child's Parent Dies: Studies in Childhood Bereavement* (New Haven, Conn.: Yale University Press, 1974).

7. S. Freud, "Mourning and Melancholia," in *The Standard Edition of the Complete Psychological Works of Sigmund Freud,* vol. 14, ed. and trans. J. Strachey (1917; reprint, London: Hogarth Press, 1957), 237–58.

8. Furman, *Child's Parent Dies;* and Volkan, *Linking Objects.*

9. Dietrich and Shabad, *Problem of Loss and Mourning;* E. Jacobson, "The Return of the Lost Parent," in *Drives, Affects, and Behaviors,* vol. 2, ed. M. Schur (New York: International Universities Press, 1965), 193–211; G. Rochlin, "Loss and Restitution," *Psychoanalytic Study of the Child* 8 (1959): 288–309; G. Rochlin, *Griefs and Discontents: The Forces of Change* (Boston: Little, Brown, 1965); R. Schafer, *Aspects of Internalization* (New York: International Universities Press, 1968); and M. Wolfenstein, "The Image of the Lost Parent," *Psychoanalytic Study of the Child* 28 (1973): 433–56.

10. Furman, "Children's Patterns in Mourning"; and Volkan, *Linking Objects.*

11. Dietrich and Shabad, *Problem of Loss and Mourning.*

12. Schafer, *Aspects of Internalization.*

13. R. Anderson, "Notes of a Survivor," in *The Patient, Death and the Family,* ed. S. B. Troop and W. A. Green (New York: Charles Scribner's Sons, 1974), 73–82; Klass, *Parental Grief;* and Rubin, "Resolution of Bereavement."

14. A. M. Rizzuto, *The Birth of the Living God: A Psychoanalytic Study* (Chicago: University of Chicago Press, 1979).

15. P. Rosenblatt and C. Elde, "Shared Reminiscence About a Deceased Parent: Implications for Grief Education and Grief Counseling," *Family Relations* 39 (1990): 206–10.

16. Klass, *Parental Grief.*

17. S. L. Nickman, "Loss in Adoption: The Importance of Dialogue," *Psychoanalytic Study of the Child* 40 (1985): 365–98.

18. R. Kegan, *The Evolving Self: Problem and Process in Human Development* (Cambridge, Mass.: Harvard University Press, 1982); and J. Piaget, *The Construction of Reality in the Child,* trans. M. Cook (New York: Basic Books, 1954).

19. K. J. Gergen, "The Social Constructionist Movement in Modern Psychology," *American Psychologist* 40 (1985): 266–73.

20. P. R. Silverman and J. W. Worden, "Children's Reactions to the Death of a Parent in the Early Months After the Death," *American Journal of Orthopsychiatry* 62 (1992): 93–104.

21. P. R. Silverman, "The Impact of the Death of a Parent on College Age Women," *Psychiatric Clinics of North America* 10 (1989): 387–404; and Silverman and Silverman, "Parent-Child Communication."

22. S. Smilansky, *On Death: Helping Children Understand and Cope* (New York: Peter Lang, 1987).

23. A. L. Strauss, *Qualitative Analysis for Social Scientists* (Cambridge, Eng.: Cambridge University Press, 1987).

24. B. Glaser and A. Strauss, *The Discovery of Grounded Theory* (Chicago: Aldine Publishing, 1967.

25. Strauss, *Qualitative Analysis.*

26. R. Lonetto, *Children's Conceptions of Death,* vol. 3 (New York: Springer, 1980).

27. A. Weisman, *On Dying and Denying: A Psychiatric Study of Terminality* (New York: Behavioral Publications, 1972).

28. Volkan, *Linking Objects.*

29. D. W. Winnicott, "Transitional Objects and Transitional Phenomena," *International Journal of Psycho-Analysis* 34 (1953): 89–97; and Worden, *Grief Counseling and Grief Therapy.*

30. Worden, *Grief Counseling and Grief Therapy.*

31. Rubin, "Resolution of Bereavement."

32. Piaget, *Construction of Reality.*

33. Kegan, *Evolving Self.*

34. P. C. Rosenblatt, R. P. Walsh, and D. A. Jackson, *Grief and Mourning in Cross-Cultural Perspective* [machine-readable data file]. Human Relations Area Files, 1976; and Silverman and Silverman, "Parent-Child Communication."

Recognizing Hidden Sorrow

KENNETH J. DOKA, "Disenfranchised Grief," in *Disenfranchised Grief—Recognizing Hidden Sorrow,* ed. Kenneth J. Doka (Lexington, Mass.: Lexington Books, 1989). Excerpt, pages 3–11, reprinted by permission of Lexington Books, imprint of Macmillan, Inc. Copyright © 1989.

Notes

1. E. Lindemann, "Symptomatology and Management of Acute Grief," *American Journal of Psychiatry* 101 (1944): 141–49.

2. See, for example, I. Glick, R. Weiss, and C. M. Parkes, *The First Year of Bereavement* (New York: John Wiley and Sons, 1974); A. Bowling and A. Cartwright, *Life After a Death: A Study of the Elderly Widowed* (New York: Tavistock, 1982); and C. M. Parkes and R. Weiss, *Recovery from Bereavement* (New York: Basic Books, 1983).

3. See, for example, V. Volkan, "Typical Findings in Pathological Grief," *Psychiatric Quarterly* 44 (1970): 231–50.

4. See, for instance, J. Bowlby, *Attachment and Loss,* vol. 3: *Loss: Sadness and Depression* (New York: Basic Books, 1980); and W. Worden, *Grief Counseling and Grief Therapy* (New York: Springer, 1982).

5. See, for example, B. Raphael, *The Anatomy of Bereavement* (New York: Basic Books, 1983); and T. Rando, *Grief, Dying and Death: Clinical Interventions for Caregivers* (Champaign, Ill.: Research Press, 1984).

6. A term suggested by Austin Kutscher (private communication).

7. Raphael, *Anatomy of Bereavement,* 227.

8. J. Kelly, "The Aging Male Homosexual: Myth and Reality," *The Gerontologist* 17 (1977): 328–32; D. Kimmel, "Adult Development and Aging: A Gay Perspective," *Journal of Social Issues* 34 (1978): 113–31; and D. Kimmel, "Life History Interview of Aging Gay Men," *International Journal of Aging and Human Development* 10 (1979): 237–48.

9. A. Heinemann et al., "A Social Service Program for AIDS Clients," paper presented to the Sixth Annual Meeting of the Forum for Death Education, Chicago, October 1983; and S. Geis, R. Fuller, and J. Rush, "Lovers of AIDS Victims: Psychosocial Stresses and Counseling Needs," *Death Studies* 10 (1986): 43–54.

10. R. J. Corney and F. T. Horton, "Pathological Grief Following Spontaneous Abortion," *American Journal of Psychiatry* 131 (1974): 825–27; J. Wolff, P. Neilson, and P. Schiller, "The Emotional Reaction to a Stillbirth," *American Journal of Obstetrics and Gynecology* 101 (1970): 73–76; L. Peppers and R. Knapp, *Motherhood and Mourning* (New York: Praeger, 1980); J. Kennell, M. Slyter, and M. Klaus, "The Mourning Response of Parents to the Death of a Newborn Infant," *New England Journal of Medicine* 283 (1970): 344–49; and T. A. Helmrath and G. M. Steinitz, "Parental Grieving and the Failure of Social Support," *Journal of Family Practice* 6 (1978): 785–90.

11. K. Doka, "Loss upon Loss: Death After Divorce," *Death Studies,* 10 (1986): 441–49; and S. Scott, "Grief Reactions to the Death of a Divorced Spouse," paper presented to the Seventh Annual Meeting of the Forum for Death Education and Counseling, Philadelphia, April 1985.

12. W. J. Kay et al., eds., *Pet Loss and Human Bereavement* (New York: Arno Press, 1984).

13. P. S. Lipe-Goodson and B. I. Goebel, "Perception of Age and Death in Mentally Retarded Adults," *Mental Retardation* 21 (1983): 68–75; R. Clyman, C. Green, J. Rowe, C. Mikkelson, and L. Ataide, "Issues Concerning Parents After the Death of Their Newborn," *Critical Care Medicine* 8 (1980): 215–18; and R. B. Edgerton, M. Bollinger, and B. Herr, "The Cloak of Competence: After Two Decades," *American Journal of Mental Deficiency* 88 (1984): 345–51.

14. R. Horn, "Life Can Be a Soap Opera," in *Perspectives on Bereavement,* ed. I. Gerber, A. Weiner, A. Kutscher, D. Battin, A. Arkin, and I. Goldberg (New York: Arno Press, 1979).

15. K. Doka, "Silent Sorrow: Grief and the Loss of Significant Others," *Death Studies* 11 (1987): 455–69.

16. J. Folta and G. Deck, "Grief, the Funeral and the Friend," in *Acute Grief and the Funeral,* ed. V. Pine, A. H. Kutscher, D. Perctz, R. C. Slater, R. DeBellis, A. I. Volk, and D. J. Cherico (Springfield, Ill.: Charles C. Thomas, 1976), 239.

17. Raphael, *Anatomy of Bereavement.*

18. B. Raphael, "Psychosocial Aspects of Induced Abortion," *Medical Journal of Australia* 2 (1972): 35–40A.

19. Raphael, *Anatomy of Bereavement.*

20. Kay et al., *Pet Loss and Human Bereavement.*

21. D. Sudnow, *Passing On: The Social Organization of Dying* (Englewood Cliffs, N.J.: Prentice-Hall, 1967).

22. R. Kalish, "A Continuum of Subjectively Perceived Death," *The Gerontologist* 6 (1966): 73–76.

23. K. Doka, "Crypto Death and Real Grief," paper presented to a symposium of the Foundation of Thanatology, New York, March 1985.

24. Raphael, *Anatomy of Bereavement*.

25. Lipe-Goodson and Goebel, "Perception of Age and Death."

26. Edgerton, Bollinger, and Herr, "Cloak of Competence."

27. H. Goldstein, private communication.

28. Lindemann, "Symptomatology and Management of Acute Grief"; and Worden, *Grief Counseling and Grief Therapy*.

29. See, for example, Kelly, "Aging Male Homosexual"; Geis, Fuller, and Rush, "Lovers of AIDS Victims"; Peppers and Knapp, *Motherhood and Mourning*; Doka, "Crypto Death and Real Grief"; Doka, "Loss upon Loss"; and L. Miller and S. Roll, "A Case Study in Failure: On Doing Everything Right in Suicide Prevention," *Death Studies* 9 (1985): 483–92.

30. Worden, *Grief Counseling and Grief Therapy*; Raphael, *Anatomy of Bereavement*; and Rando, *Grief, Dying and Death*.

31. Raphael, "Psychosocial Aspects of Induced Abortion."

32. Doka, "Loss upon Loss"; and Scott, "Grief Reactions to the Death of a Divorced Spouse."

33. Doka, "Silent Sorrow"; and Horn, "Life Can Be a Soap Opera."

34. Doka, "Crypto Death and Real Grief."

35. See, for example, Kimmel, "Adult Development and Aging"; Kimmel, "Life History Interview of Aging Gay Men"; Doka, "Silent Sorrow"; and Horn, "Life Can Be a Soap Opera."

36. Edgerton, Bollinger, and Herr, "Cloak of Competence."

37. I. Reiss, *Family Systems in America* (New York: Holt, Rinehart and Winston, 1980).

38. J. Gagnon, *Human Sexualities* (Glenview, Ill.: Scott, Foresman, 1977).

39. One can also speak of "disenfranchising deaths." In some cases the cause of death creates such shame and embarrassment that even those in recognized survivor roles (such as spouse, child, or parent) may be reluctant to avail themselves of social support or may feel a sense of social reproach over the circumstances of death. Death from a dreaded disease like AIDS and certain situations surrounding suicide and homicide are illustrations of disenfranchising death. Each carries a stigma that may inhibit even survivors in recognizably legitimate roles from seeking and receiving social support.

40. R. Atchley, *Social Forces and Aging,* 4th ed. (Belmont, Calif.: Wadsworth, 1985).

41. As has been stated, some of these variables will be common to all losses. Others, such as the degree to which a loss is socially recognized, publicly sanctioned, openly acknowledged, or replaceable, may be unique to certain types of disenfranchised grief.

AVERY D. WEISMAN, "Bereavement and Companion Animals," *Omega: Journal of Death and Dying* 22, no. 4 (1990–1991): 241–48. Adapted by permission of the author and Baywood Publishing Co. Copyright © 1991.

Notes

1. B. Fogle and D. Abrahamson, "Pet Loss: Survey of Practicing Veterinarians," *Anthrozoos* 13, no. 3 (Winter 1990): 143–50; W. Kay et al., eds., *Pet Loss and Human Bereavement* (Ames: Iowa State University Press, 1984); W. Kay et al., eds., *Euthanasia of the Companion Animal* (Philadelphia: Charles Press, 1988); and H. Nieburg and A. Fischer, *Pet Loss: A Thoughtful Guide for Adults and Children* (New York: Harper and Row, 1982).

2. K. Doka, ed., *Disenfranchised Grief* (Lexington, Mass.: Lexington Books, 1989).

Social Support for Survivors

STEPHEN J. FLEMING AND LESLIE BALMER, "Bereaved Families of Ontario: A Mutual-Help Model for Families Experiencing Death." Based on a paper presented at the Second International Conference on Children and Death, Edinburgh, September 1992. Published by permission of the authors. Copyright © 1994 by Stephen J. Fleming and Leslie Balmer.

Notes

1. The Metropolitan Toronto chapter is but one of many groups comprising the Bereaved Families of Ontario, a provincial governing body. However, for ease of discussion, the abbreviation BFO will refer to the Toronto chapter and not the provincial organization.

MARY N. HALL AND PAULA T. RAPPE, "Humor and Critical Incident Stress," *The Forum: Newsletter of the Association for Death Education and Counseling* 17, no. 5 (September-October 1992): 11–14. Adapted by permission of the authors and the Association for Death Education and Counseling. Copyright © 1992.

Notes

1. Beverly Raphael, *When Disaster Strikes* (New York: Basic Books, 1986); A. J. W. Taylor and A. G. Frazer, "The Stress of Post-Disaster Body Handling and Victim Identification Work," *Journal of Human Stress* 8 (December 1982): 4–12; James L. Tichener, "Post-Traumatic Decline: A Consequence of Unresolved Destructive Drives," in *Trauma and Its Wake,* vol. II, ed. Charles Figley (New York: Brunner-Mazel, 1986), 5–6; and Jeffrey T. Mitchell, "Recovery from Rescue," *Response Magazine* (Fall 1982), 7–10.

2. Proverbs, 15:13.

3. S. Freud, "Humor," *International Journal of Psychoanalysis* 9 (1928): 1–6.

4. Norman Cousins, *Anatomy of an Illness* (New York: W. W. Norton, 1979.

5. Herbert M. Lefcourt and Rod A. Martin, *Humor and Life Stress* (New York: Springer-Verlag, 1986), 125–26.

6. Jim Boren, "American/Russian Humor," unpublished work (1991).

7. John Abraham, "Jest Death," *The Forum: Newsletter of the Association for Death Education and Counselling* (July 1985), 11.

8. Lefcourt and Martin, *Humor and Life Stress,* 123–24.

9. Charles R. Figley, "Traumatic Stress: The Role of the Family and Social Support System," *Trauma and Its Wake,* vol. II, ed. Charles Figley (New York: Brunner-Mazel, 1986), 41–42.

10. Tichener, "Post-Traumatic Decline," 5–6.

11. Susan D. Solomon, "Mobilizing Social Support Networks in Times of Disaster," in Figley, ed., *Trauma and Its Wake,* vol. II, 251.

12. Larry Rappe, "Rescue Personnel in Disasters," unpublished paper (1990), 1.

13. Taylor and Frazer, "Stress of Post-Disaster Body Handling," 4–12.

14. Robert J. Lifton, *Death in Life: Survivors of Hiroshima* (New York: Random House, 1967), 481.

15. C. Dunning and M. Silva, "Disaster-Induced Trauma in Rescue Workers," *Victimology: An International Journal* 5, nos. 2–4 (1980): 287–97.

16. Mitchell, "Recovery from Rescue," 7–10.

17. David R. Jones, "Secondary Disaster Victims," *American Journal of Psychiatry* 142, no. 3 (1985): 306.

18. Solomon, "Mobilizing Social Support Networks," 234.

19. M. Weinstein and J. Goodman, *Play Fair* (San Luis Obispo, Calif.: Impact Publishers, 1980).

Coping with Life-Threatening Illness

HAROLD BRODKEY, "To My Readers," *The New Yorker,* 21 June 1993, 80–82. Reprinted by permission of the author. Copyright © 1993 by Harold Brodkey.

JANMARIE SILVERA, "Crossing the Border." Published by permission of the author. Copyright © 1994 by Janmarie Silvera.

CHARLES A. CORR, "A Task-Based Approach to Coping with Dying," *Omega: Journal of Death and Dying* 24, no. 2 (1991–1992): 81–94. Reprinted, in slightly revised form, by permission of the author and Baywood Publishing Co. Copyright © 1992.

Notes

1. M. Osterweis, F. Solomon, and M. Green, eds., *Bereavement: Reactions, Consequences, and Care* (Washington: National Academy Press, 1984); C. M. Parkes, *Bereavement: Studies of Grief in Adult Life,* 2d ed. (Madison, Conn.: International Universities Press, 1987); T. A. Rando, *Grief, Dying, and Death: Clinical Interventions for Caregivers* (Champaign, Ill.: Research Press, 1984); B. Raphael, *The Anatomy of Bereavement* (New York: Basic Books, 1983); and C. M. Sanders, *Grief: The Mourning After* (New York: John Wiley and Sons, 1989).

2. S. S. Fox, *Good Grief: Helping Groups of Children When a Friend Dies* (Boston: The New England Association for the Education of Young Children, 1988); S. S. Fox, "Helping Child Deal with Death Teaches Valuable Skills," *The Psychiatric Times,* August 1988, 10–11; and J. W. Worden, *Grief Counseling and Grief Therapy: A Handbook for the Mental Health Practitioner,* 2d ed. (New York: Springer, 1991).

3. T. Attig, "The Importance of Conceiving of Grief as an Active Process," *Death Studies* 16 (1991): 385–93.

4. E. Kübler-Ross, *On Death and Dying* (New York: Macmillan, 1969).

5. A. M. Metzger, "A Q-Methodological Study of the Kübler-Ross Stage Theory," *Omega: Journal of Death and Dying* 10 (1979): 291–302; R. Schulz and D. Aderman, "Clinical Research and the Stages of Dying," *Omega: Journal of Death and Dying* 5 (1974): 137–44; L. Feigenberg, *Terminal Care: Friendship Contracts with Dying Cancer Patients* (New York: Brunner-Mazel, 1980); R. Kastenbaum, *Death, Society, and Human Experience,* 4th ed. (Columbus: Merrill, 1991); E. M. Pattison, *The Experience of Dying* (Englewood Cliffs, N.J.: Prentice-Hall, 1977); E. Shneidman, *Voices of Death* (New York: Harper and Row, 1980); and A. Weisman, "The Psychiatrist and the Inexorable," in *New Meanings of Death,* ed. H. Feifel (New York: McGraw-Hill, 1977), 107–22.

6. P. A. Potter and A. G. Perry, *Basic Nursing: Theory and Practice* (St. Louis: C. V. Mosby, 1987).

7. C. A. Corr and D. M. Corr, *Hospice Care: Principles and Practice* (New York: Springer, 1983); C. M. Saunders, ed., *The Management of Terminal Malignant Disease,* 2d ed. (London: Edward Arnold, 1984); and S. Stoddard, *The Hospice Movement: A Better Way of Caring for the Dying* (New York: Stein and Day, 1978).

8. B. Glaser and A. Straus, *Awareness of Dying* (Chicago: Aldine, 1965); B. Glaser and A. Strauss, *Time for Dying* (Chicago: Aldine, 1968); J. Hinton, *Dying* (New York: Penguin, 1967); D. Sudnow, *Passing On: The Social Organization of Dying* (Engle-wood Cliffs, N.J.: Prentice-Hall, 1967); A. Weisman, *On Dying and Denying: A Psychiatric Study of Terminality* (New York: Behavioral Publications, 1972).

9. R. S. Lazarus and S. Folkman, *Stress, Appraisal, and Coping* (New York: Springer, 1984); A. Monat and R. S. Lazarus, eds., *Stress and Coping: An Anthology,* 3d ed. (New York: Columbia University Press, 1991); and R. W. White, "Strategies of Adaptation: An Attempt at Systematic Description," in *Coping and Adaptation,* ed. G. V. Coelho, D. A. Hamburg, and J. E. Adams (New York: Basic Books, 1974), 47–68.

10. A. Stedeford, *Facing Death: Patients, Families and Professionals* (London: William Heinemann, 1984); and A. Weisman, *The Coping Capacity: On the Nature of Being Mortal* (New York: Human Sciences Press, 1984).

11. C. A. Corr, "Copying with Dying: Lessons That We Should and Should Not Learn from the Work of Elisabeth Kübler-Ross, *Death Studies* 17, no. 1 (1993): 69–83.

12. E. M. Brady, "Telling the Story: Ethics and Dying," *Hospital Progress* 60 (1979): 57–62.

13. R. Kastenbaum, "Hospice: Philosophy and Practice," in *Encyclopedia of Death,* ed. R. Kastenbaum and B. Kastenbaum (Phoenix: Oryx Press, 1989), 143–46.

14. C. A. Corr, "Some Impressions from a Hospice-Related Visit to Poland," *The Journal of Palliative Care* 7 (1991): 53–57.

15. S. du Boulay, *Cicely Saunders: The Founder of the Modern Hospice Movement* (London: Hodder and Stoughton, 1984); and A. J. J. Gilmore, "Hospice Development in the United Kingdom," in Kastenbaum and Kastenbaum, eds., *Encyclopedia of Death,* 149–52.

16. Saunders, *Management of Terminal Malignant Disease;* and National Hospice Organization, *Standards of a Hospice Program of Care* (Arlington, Va.: NHO, 1987.)

17. J. Hinton, "The Physical and Mental Distress of the Dying," *Quarterly Journal of Medicine* new series, 32 (1963): 1–21; and W. D. Rees, "The Distress of Dying," *British Medical Journal* 2 (1972): 105–7.

18. A. Maslow, *The Farther Reaches of Human Nature* (New York: Viking Penguin, 1971).

19. S. Lack, "I Want to Die While I'm Still Alive," *Death Education,* 1 (1977): 168.

20. C. M. Parkes, "Dying at Home: Home or Hospital? Terminal Care as Seen by Surviving Spouses," *Journal of the Royal College of General Practitioners* 28 (1978): 22.

21. Ibid., 26.

22. E. H. Erikson, *Childhood and Society,* 2d ed. (New York: W. W. Norton, 1963).

23. R. N. Butler, "The Life Review: An Interpretation of Reminiscence in the Aged," *Psychiatry* 26, no. 1 (1963): 65–76.

24. E. Kübler-Ross, *Death: The Final Stage of Growth* (Englewood Cliffs, N.J.: Prentice-Hall, 1975).

25. Lazarus and Folkman, *Stress, Appraisal, and Coping*, 141.

26. Weisman, *The Coping Capacity*, 36.

27. H. Selye, *The Stress of Life* (New York: McGraw-Hill, 1956).

28. V. Frankl, *Man's Search for Meaning*, rev. ed. (New York: Simon and Schuster, 1984), 86.

29. T. Rosenthal, *How Could I Not Be Among You?*, New York: George Braziller, 1973), 39.

Part IV: Death in Life

Death Education for Living

PATRICK VERNON DEAN, "Is Death Education a 'Nasty Little Secret'? A Call to Break the Alleged Silence." Published by permission of the author. Copyright © 1994 by Patrick Vernon Dean.

Notes

1. P. Schlafly, "Death Comes into the Open," *Brooklyn Spectator*, 13 April 1988.

2. R. G. Stevenson, "The Eye of the Beholder: The Media Look at Death Education," *Death Studies* 14, no. 2 (1990): 162.

3. Schlafly, "Death Comes into the Open."

4. F. M. Bordewich, "Mortal Fears: Courses in 'Death Education' Get Mixed Reviews," *The Atlantic*, February 1988, 30–34.

5. K. J. Doka, "The Crumbling Taboo: The Rise of Death Education," *New Directions for Student Services* 31 (September 1985): 85–95.

6. H. Wass, M. D. Miller, and G. Thornton, "Death Education and Grief/Suicide Intervention in the Public Schools," *Death Studies* 14, no. 3 (1990): 253–68.

7. Quoted in Bordewich, "Mortal Fears."

8. Ibid.

9. Wass, Miller, and Thornton, "Death Education."

10. International Work Group on Death, Dying, and Bereavement, "A Statement of Assumptions and Principles Concerning Education About Death, Dying, and Bereavement," *Death Studies* 16, no. 1 (1992): 59–65.

HANNELORE WASS, "Visions in Death Education," in *Death: Completion and Discovery*, ed. Charles A. Corr and Richard A. Pacholski (Hartford, Conn.: Association for Death Education and Counseling, 1987), 5–16. Originally presented as a keynote address at the Seventh Annual Meeting of the Forum for Death Education and Counseling, Philadelphia, April 1985. Adapted by permission of the author and the Association for Death Education and Counseling. Copyright © 1987.

Notes

1. I. Spiegel-Rosing and H. Petzold, eds., *Die Begleitung Sterbender—Theorie und Praxis der Thanatotherapie* (Paderborn: Junfermann Verlag, 1984).

2. V. R. Pine, "A Socio-Historical Portrait of Death Education," *Death Education* 1, no. 1 (1977): 57–84.

3. V. R. Pine, "The Age of Maturity for Death Education: A Socio-Historical Portrait of the Era 1976–1985," *Death Studies* 10, no. 3 (1986): 209–31.

4. J. Naisbitt, *Megatrends* (New York: Warner Books, 1982).

Acknowledging Our Mortality

ALLAN B. CHINEN, "The Mortal King," in *Once Upon a Midlife: Classic Stories and Mythic Tales to Illuminate the Middle Years* (Los Angeles: Jeremy P. Tarcher, 1992), 89–90. Reprinted by permission of the author. Copyright © 1992 by Allan B. Chinen.

THOMAS ATTIG, "Coping with Mortality: An Essay on Self-Mourning," *Death Studies* 13, no. 4 (1989): 361–70. Adapted by permission of the author and Taylor and Francis, Inc. Copyright © 1989.

Notes

1. E. Shneidman, *Voices of Death* (New York: Harper and Row, 1980), 143.
2. W. Worden, *Grief Counseling and Grief Therapy* (New York: Springer, 1982).
3. E. Becker, *The Denial of Death* (New York: Free Press, 1973).
4. R. Lifton, *The Broken Connection* (New York: Basic Books, 1983).
5. Worden, *Grief Counseling and Grief Therapy*; and C. M. Parkes and R. Weiss, *Recovery from Bereavement* (New York: Basic Books, 1983).

6. T. Attig, "Relearning the World: Toward a Phenomenology of Grieving," *British Journal for Phenomenology and Existential Philosophy* 21, no. 1 (1990): 53–66.
7. Exploration of the analogues to acute, delayed, chronic, normal, and abnormal grieving in the case of self-mourning must await another occasion, though I am confident that they exist.

ALFRED G. KILLILEA, *The Politics of Being Mortal* (Lexington: University Press of Kentucky, 1988). Excerpt, pages 148–58, reprinted by permission of the author and The University Press of Kentucky. Copyright © 1988.

Notes

1. Glenn Tinder, *Political Thinking* (Boston: Little, Brown, 1986), 6.
2. William Safire, "Ode to Greed," *New York Times*, 5 January 1986, E19.
3. Edmund Burke, "Reflections on the Revolution in France," in *The Great Political Theories,* vol. 2, ed. Michael Curtis (New York: Avon, 1981), 56.
4. Federal Emergency Management Agency, "Crisis Relocation Instructions for Washington County, Rhode Island," 14.

SANDRA L. BERTMAN, "Bearing the Unbearable: From Loss, the Gain," *Health Values: Achieving High Level Wellness* 7, no. 1 (1983): 24–32. Adapted by permission of the author and *Health Values: The Journal of Health Behavior, Education, and Promotion.* Copyright © 1983.

Notes

1. *Dying*, film (Boston: WGBH TV, 1976).
2. *How Could I Not Be Among You?*, film (Briarcliff Manor, NY: Benchmark Films, 1971).
3. For this insight, I am grateful to Richard Sewall's Amherst Convocation address, reprinted in *William Alumni Review* (Fall 1975), 2–4.
4. E. Dickinson, "By a Departing Light," in *The Poems of Emily Dickinson,* vol. 3, ed. T. Johnson (Cambridge, Mass.: Belknap Press of Harvard University Press, 1955), 1157.
5. K. Swenson, "Virginia," in *An Attic of Ideals—A Collection of Poetry* (Garden City, N.Y.: Doubleday, 1974), 5.
6. L. Tolstoy, *The Death of Ivan Ilych* (New York: Health Sciences Press, 1973).

7. W. C. Williams, "The Last Words of My English Grandmother," in *Selected Poems of William Carlos Williams* (New York: New Directions Books, 1968), 94–96.
8. M. Jury and D. Jury, *Gramp* (New York: Grossman Publishing, 1976).
9. J. B. S. Haldane, "Cancer's a Funny Thing," in *The Oxford Book of Twentieth Century Verse,* ed. C. Larkin (Oxford: Oxford University Press, 1973), 252.
10. J. Dickey, "The Cancer Match," in *The Eye-Beaters, Blood, the Victory, Madness, Buck-head and Mercy* (New York: Doubleday, 1970), 31–32.
11. N. Cousins, *Anatomy of an Illness as Perceived by the Patient* (New York: W. W. Norton, 1979).

12. Cousins cites Fry's "The Respiratory Components of Mirthful Laughter," *Journal of Biological Psychology* 19, no. 2 (1977): 35–50; and Paskind, "Effect of Laughter on Muscle Tone," *Archives of Neurology and Psychiatry* 28 (1932): 623–28. In rebuttal, see S. Kahn's critique, "The Anatomy of Norman Cousins' Illness," *Mount Sinai Journal of Medicine* 48, no. 4 (1981): 305–14.

13. K. Shapiro, "The Leg," in *V-Letter and Other Poems* (New York: Royal and Hitchcock, 1944), 38.

14. A. Lorde, *The Cancer Journals* (Argyle: Spinsters, 1980).

15. D. Linett, "Gifts," *Ms.*, March 1978, 67–71.

16. E. Spencer, "Faerie Queen," in *Edward Spencer's Poetry* (New York: W. W. Norton, 1968).

17. W. Shakespeare, *Titus Andronicus,* in *The Riverside Shakespeare,* ed. G. B. Evans (Boston: Houghton Mifflin, 1974), 1034.

18. W. Shakespeare, *Macbeth,* in *Shakespeare, The Complete Works,* ed. G. Harrison (New York: Harcourt Brace, 1948), 1212.

19. J. Donne, "Devotion," in *John Donne, Selected Prose,* ed. H. Gardner and T. Healy (London: Clarendon Press, 1967), 100.

20. M. Eckart, quoted in L. Buscaglia, *Personhood* (Thorofare, N.J.: Charles B. Slack, 1978), 138.